FOOD ENGINEERING AND PROCESS APPLICATIONS

Volume 1

TRANSPORT PHENOMENA

Proceedings of the Fourth International Congress on Engineering and Food held between 7 and 10 July 1985 at Edmonton, Alberta, Canada

ADVISORY EDITORIAL BOARD

FOOD ENGINEERING AND PROCESS APPLICATIONS

Volume 1

TRANSPORT PHENOMENA

Edited by

M. LE MAGUER and P. JELEN

Department of Food Science, University of Alberta, Edmonton, Alberta, Canada

ELSEVIER APPLIED SCIENCE PUBLISHERS
LONDON and NEW YORK

ELSEVIER APPLIED SCIENCE PUBLISHERS LTD
Crown House, Linton Road, Barking, Essex IG11 8JU, England

Sole Distributor in the USA and Canada
ELSEVIER SCIENCE PUBLISHING CO., INC.
52 Vanderbilt Avenue, New York, NY 10017, USA

WITH 93 TABLES AND 206 ILLUSTRATIONS

© ELSEVIER APPLIED SCIENCE PUBLISHERS LTD 1986
(except Chapter 6)

British Library Cataloguing in Publication Data

Food engineering and process applications.
1. Food industry and trade
I. Le Maguer, M. II. Jelen, P.
664 TP370

Library of Congress Cataloging-in-Publication Data

Food engineering and process applications.

"Proceedings of the Fourth International Congress
on Engineering and Food held between 7th and 10th July
1985 at Edmonton, Alberta, Canada"—V. 1, p.
Organized under the auspices of the faculties of agriculture
and engineering of the University of Alberta.
Includes bibliographies and index.
Contents: v. 1. Transport phenomena—v. 2 Unit
operations.
1. Food industry and trade—Congresses.
I. Le Maguer, M. II. Jelen, P. (Pavel) III. International Congress on Engineering and Food (4th: 1985:
Edmonton, Alta.) IV. University of Alberta. Faculty of
Agriculture and Forestry. V. University of Alberta.

Faculty of Engineering.
TP368.F617 1986   664   86-11622
ISBN 1-85166-022-4 (v. 1)

The selection and presentation of material and the opinions expressed in this publication
are the sole responsibility of the authors concerned.

Printed in Great Britain by The Universities Press (Belfast) Ltd.

FOREWORD

It was an honour for Canada to serve as host for the 4th International Congress on Engineering and Food. Food engineering and the whole concept of food processing are matters of vital national and international interest. It is fitting that this Congress was held in Edmonton, a city that symbolizes the Canadian spirit and will to achieve.

Governments everywhere cannot ignore the agri-food sector when it comes to laying down national policies. In Canada, 40% of our economic activity is related in some way to our agri-food industry. The 4000 food and beverage processing companies make a significant contribution to this effort.

It has long been acknowledged that research has a crucial role to play in creating national prosperity, through growth and enhanced competitiveness of the industry. Any discussion of food processing research implies transfer of technology. The importance of technology transfer cannot be emphasized enough. It must be a primary concern of all food processors, researchers and engineers. A Canadian example of technology transfer is the development of our edible oil industry. Three decades ago there was no edible oil industry in Canada based on rapeseed. Now, our version of rapeseed, canola, is a major cash crop for domestic processing and export. Nowadays, Canadian canola is a commodity to be reckoned with on the world stage.

It is important for the future of many countries in the world that we move more vigorously than in the past to raise the productive capacity and competitive level of the food processing industry. If we succeed, the world will become less dependent upon raw material exports from producing countries such as Canada. Other countries must take the same approach by focusing on commodities important to them.

The food processing industry in various parts of the world is not an island to itself. It does have a social responsibility to the countries in which it operates. All of us in the food business have a responsibility to feed people who do not have enough to eat. There are no easy solutions to the problems of hunger, but if each country built a strong and dynamic food industry and thereby created jobs, wealth and economic strength, we could end the hunger on this planet. As professionals in the food industry we must not lose sight of our collective responsibility to provide a safe, abundant and wholesome food supply for all, and we must share our knowledge with others. This book is an excellent example of international cooperation and goodwill among the food scientists and engineers who can influence the progress in development of new food processing techniques for tomorrow.

Dr E. J. LeRoux
Assistant Deputy Minister, Research
Agriculture, Canada

PREFACE

The two volumes of *Food Engineering and Process Applications* were assembled from the papers presented at the Fourth International Congress on Engineering and Food held in Edmonton, Canada, in July 1985.

The Congress was organized under the auspices of the Faculties of Agriculture and Engineering of the University of Alberta and the sponsorship of national and international engineering and food science societies. It was supported with major grants from the Natural Sciences and Engineering Research Council of Canada, the Regional Industrial Expansion program of the government of Canada, the Alberta Agriculture Research Council, and the University of Alberta.

This is the third in a series of compilations which have now contributed significantly to the literature in Food Engineering. It presents a broad coverage of basic and applied research subjects dealing with the application of engineering principles to food processing operations. It shows again the evolution of Food Engineering towards a well defined and identifiable field of engineering in its own right and illustrates the vast potential of engineering scientists and industrial researchers to generate new and original information.

Because of the large number of contributions included, it was decided to organize the work in two volumes with distinctly different themes. Volume 1 deals more specifically with basic aspects of physical and transport properties of foods, kinetics and mathematical modeling, selected heat and mass transfer problems and thermal processing and irradiation. Volume 2 is concerned with various unit operations and industrial processes and includes most of the invited symposia papers supplemented with contributions in the areas of Food Freezing,

Extrusion Engineering, Membrane Processing, Genetic Engineering, Energy and Food Processing Operations, or Industrial Engineering and Process Control. Its final section contains a selection of papers addressing the ever present problem of Food Engineering in developing countries. While the selection of the contributions for the respective volumes may appear somewhat arbitrary, it is a result of our deliberate attempt to finish with two approximately equal volumes dealing with the two dominant themes of contemporary Food Engineering—transport phenomena and unit operations.

Although we as editors must assume full responsibility for the final product, we would be remiss not to express our thanks to many of our colleagues listed as the Editorial Board who assisted us with screening the contributions for their technical suitability. Sincere thanks are also due to Dr R. Biswal for helping at different stages of the preparation of the volumes, and finally to our wives, Ivy and Sylva, for constant encouragement and understanding which made our tasks much easier.

M. Le Maguer
P. Jelen

CONTENTS

III. Transport Properties

IV. Kinetics and Mathematical Modeling

V. Heat and Mass Transfer Operations

VI. Thermal Processing

VII. Irradiation Processing of Food

1

A FLOOD TIDE FOR BIO-ENGINEERS

JOSEPH H. HULSE

*Vice-President (Research Programs), International Development Research
Centre,* POB 8500, Ottawa, Ontario, Canada K1G 3H9*

ABSTRACT

*Most present day food technologies including milling, baking, brewing,
acid fermentations, dehydration and refrigeration are directly derived
from ancient domestic crafts. Though the chemist and the microbiologist
have significantly contributed to a greater understanding of the nature,
composition, protection and preservation of foods and their raw
materials, it is the engineer who progressively has replaced human
physical labour with machines powered successively by water, wind,
steam and electricity. Advances in mechanization have resulted more
from perceptive empiricism than from basic scientific principles.*

*The future calls for a new breed of bio-engineers: men and women
capable of developing industrial processes based upon a wide assortment of biological conversions. It requires also scientists of broad and
long-sighted vision whose perspective extends beyond the laboratory
walls; managers who can comprehend and control the complex
biotechnological systems upon which industries of the future will
depend.*

'There is a tide in the affairs of man
Which when taken at the flood
Leads on to fortune.
On such a full sea we are now afloat
And we must take the current where it serves
Or lose our ventures.'

* The views expressed in this paper are those of the author and not necessarily of the
International Development Research Centre.

1

A flood tide is fast overtaking the world's small community of biological engineers. Whether they float to fortune or sink in sorrow depends upon the philosophy, prescience, perception and persistence they bring to bear upon the opportunities that await them.

'La vie est une fonction chimique' wrote Antoine Lavoisier in 1780. Indeed chemistry has contributed much to the knowledge of food composition and analytical methods by which the consuming public is protected from naturally occurring, adventitious, or intentional adulteration, superfluous sophistication and unwanted contamination of its food. Following Pasteur, microbiologists have identified—and differentiated between—the beneficial and pathogenic microbial species. More recently, physics has helped us to a better understanding of the structure and rheology of food materials and provided the many elegant instruments which are the everyday tools of the analyst and quality control specialist.

Nonetheless, the history of food technology is dominated by engineering: by the replacement of human labour, first by animal and later by machine power. Food engineering can thus be regarded both as a progenitor and a progeny of the Industrial Revolution. Food technology has contributed greatly to the variety, wholesomeness and appeal of the foods available to the world's wealthy nations. But its most evident benefit has been to reduce the human effort needed in the factory, the restaurant and the home.

ORIGINS OF FOOD TECHNOLOGY

Almost all our modern food processing technologies are based upon domestic arts and crafts that have been in existence for a long time. Five thousand years ago Peking man (*Sinanthropus pekinensis*) ground grains, crushed berries and cooked his food. Grain mills, bakeries and breweries existed in the royal courts of Egypt more than 6000 years before Eduard Buchner and Emil Fischer laid the basis for our understanding of the enzymic conversion of carbohydrates in panary and alcoholic fermentation.

Stone Age Britons 3000 years ago oven dried their cereal grains to prevent sprouting during winter storage. Australia's ingenuity in storing cereals grains in 25 000 tonne gas-tight silos under an atmosphere of carbon dioxide generated from dry ice pellets was anticipated by Egyptians and inhabitants of what is now Saudi Arabia more than

5000 years ago. The Arabian farmers controlled post-harvest infestation by covering and sealing each grain filled amphora with an impervious goat skin. The carbon dioxide generated by respiration asphyxiated all of the insects present.

Seneca describes how the Republican Romans preserved prawns in snow carried from the Appenines packed in cereal straw and chaff. Termites used evaporative cooling to air condition their mound dwellings aeons before Joule and Kelvin identified and quantified the principles of refrigeration.

Northern and southern Amerindians and southern Africans solar dried their surplus meat to produce pemmican, charqui and biltong respectively. The northern tribes compensated for the loss of ascorbic acid from the fresh meat by mixing their dried pemmican with Saskatoon berries. The southern Amerindians, in what is now Peru, used atmospheric lyophilization to dehydrate potatoes and water elution to remove toxic cyanogenic glucosides from cassava and toxic saponins from potatoes, quinoa and other edible seeds.

Osmotic dehydration with salt was common in China during the Hia dynasty more than 4000 years ago. Between 2000 and 3000 years ago the people of northern India were importing sun dried fish from the Arabian Sea while the Greeks were importing a similar product from the Bosphorus, together with dried plums (prunes) from Damascus and dried grapes (raisins) from Bertytus. Apicius, the Roman gourmet, described how to make semi-moist foods by mixing chopped fresh meat with honey and salt before drying to a soft but stable composition.

Boil-in-the-bag and smoked-dried sausage had their origins in Ancient Rome. Apicius described how chopped spiced meats were sealed in a cleaned sow's womb or in the cleaned body cavity of a squid before boiling or smoking. In his book 'De re Coquinaria' (on cookery) written in the first century, Apicius gives recipes for a fascinating variety of finfish, shellfish, carcass and organ meat sausages.

Even Burger King and MacDonalds had their antecedents in the Thermopolia, the street food stands of Republican Rome which sold sausage and other hot meat sandwiches along with soups and spiced wine.

Almost all the ancient tribes of Asia and the Mediterranean practised preservation by acetic and lactic fermentations. Five thousand years ago the Sumerians and Egyptians converted all their animal

Joseph H. Hulse

milk to cheese rather than drinking it. The Sumerians had a saying: 'If God wished man to have clean milk to drink he would have placed the udder at the front end of the cow'.

The enhancement of color, flavor and texture by spices, vegetable extracts and other additives was well known to the ancient Greeks and Romans. Cato, in his Agri Cultur, the oldest surviving Latin prose work written about 200 B.C., describes how to separate starch from wheat and how to employ it as a thickener for custards and sauces. Enrichment with essential nutrients was in evidence in 1500 B.C. when the Chinese added burnt sponge to the food of people suffering from goiter. Sponge, being an aquatic plant, is a source of iodine.

Though the mechanical expression of oil from olives and other plant sources has been familiar for ages, the solvent extraction of oilseeds, the catalytic molecular rearrangement of fatty acids, and the hydrogenation of naturally occurring lipids are among the few modern food technologies directly attributable to modern chemistry and engineering rather than to an ancient domestic craft.

GRAIN MILLING—ANCIENT TO MODERN

A brief review of the development of grain milling, baking and brewing may bring the contribution made by engineering to food technology into historical perspective.

Unlike avian species, *Homo sapiens* cannot easily digest uncooked whole cereal grains. The earliest cereals eaten around the Mediterranean were probably the seeds of emmer and einkorn. The tough indigestible hulls of these wild grasses were firmly attached to the seeds and were removed by parching followed by pounding in a pestle and mortar, the mortar being a natural declivity in a rock, the pestle being a heavy cylindrical stone club. Sometime between 8000 and 10 000 years ago the first naked wheats, free of the outer hull, appeared probably as the progeny of a promiscuous outcross between emmer and some other wild grasses. These eventually became the cultivated grains of the Middle East.

Following the pestle and mortar come the first primitive saddle-stone mill: a lower stationary slab of stone with an upper concave surface and an upper stone with a lower flattened surface rubbed over the lower stone by a woman on her knees.

About 1000 B.C. in Greece the shearing action of the saddle-stone hand mill was improved by cutting grooves in a herring bone pattern on the interfaces of the upper and lower stones. Sometime later a wooden lever attached to a modified upper stone permitted a slave to move it backwards and forwards with one hand while feeding grain with the other hand through a hopper and an eye hole in the upper stone.

Thus around 500 B.C. we see the first rudimentary continuous process in food technology, the raw material being fed in and the end product issuing forth in more or less continuous flow. Later the Romans developed the rotary quern in which the upper stone rotated continually while the lower stone remained stationary. At first the lower stone (the *meta*) was conical or dome shaped and the upper stone (the *catillus*) was concave. Later both were flattened and in both the grain entered continually through a hopper and an eye hole, the milled product being carried to the outer circumference by the centrifugal force of rotation. Since, like the music, the millstone went round and around, it could be propelled by an animal blindfolded to walk in a perpetual circle.

Water, Wind, Steam and Electricity
The first mill driven by water power may have been inspired by the Egyptian shadoof which for thousands of years has employed animal power to raise water in a simple bucket elevator from the irrigation canals fed from the Nile, into the farmers' fields. In the Roman water mill, a paddled water wheel rotated around a horizontal axis with a wooden pinwheel which engaged in a slotted drum at the base of a vertical drive shaft. The vertical drive shaft rotated the upper millstone. The first windmills appeared in the 11th century; water and to a lesser extent wind provided the milling power until well into the 19th century.

In 1761 John Smeaton, an Englishman who spent most of his life designing improvements in water and windmills, coined the term 'civil engineer' to distinguish his profession from 'military engineers' who until that time were the only engineers recognized as such.

The first industrial use of the steam engine in 1784 was in the London Albion flour mills in a system invented by James Watt. The steam locomotive didn't make its first journey until 1825. The earliest steam powered mill in North America was built in Pittsburgh in 1808 and it is less than 100 years since flour mills driven by steam power equalled in number those driven by water. By this time, in 1887, the first mill driven by electric motors was built in Laramie, Wyoming.

Roller Mills
The first metal roller mill, in which the grain is torn open and progressively reduced in particle size between counter-rotating metal rolls, appeared in 1834 in Switzerland but it took another 50 years of engineering empiricism to iron the mechanical bugs out of the system. (Biological bugs still remain as the bane of every miller's existence.)

The modern flour mill is indeed a tribute to engineering skill. But its fundamental principle is the same as that of the Egyptian, Greek and Roman mills. The modern corrugated break rolls are direct descendants of the corrugated saddle stone. Successively, water, wind, steam and electricity have turned the millstones and vibrated the ever more efficient metal and textile screens which replaced the papyrus and linen hand sieves of the Egyptians and Romans. The ancient practice of hand-winnowing finds its modern equivalent in the middlings purifier, an enclosed vibrating gravity table of screens with progressively increasing coarse mesh from which the fine bran is removed by suction fans. When mill screens reached their limit of practical efficiency at a mesh size of between 60 and 80 μm, the engineer designed the air classifier capable of separating below a cut size of 10 μm by opposing a rotor-induced centrifugal force with a centrifugal air drag.

The engineer relieved the miller from the fatigue of heaving bags of grain and flour up and down by providing an assortment of bucket elevators, screw, worm and fluidized bed conveyors. The millers' comparatively recent invention of 'instant flour', produced by agglomerating flour particles with an aqueous film, is based on the principle used for generations in rural Africa to make couscous. Most of the industrial development was the engineering of twin-cone agglomerators and continuous fluid bed dryers.

Thanks to the engineer, the modern miller can produce and conveniently transport a much wider range and variety of fractions from a single shipment of wheat than could his Roman forebear. Nevertheless, the basic milling process remains the same. The engineer has simply mechanized and refined it.

BREAD AND BEER

The same may be said for baking and brewing. No technologies have exerted a more persistent and pervasive influence on human kind over so long a period as the conversion of carbohydrate to ethanol and carbon dioxide. Bread, beer and wine making were established more than 8000 years ago. Ethanol distillation was known to the Chinese before 1200 B.C. when the Chinese emperor issued an edict to discourage alcoholism.

The long standing debate about which came first, bread or beer, has little meaning since their origins, raw materials and end products are essentially the same. It is improbable that aerated loaves could be fashioned out of the coarse meal ground from the early wild emmer and einkorn. Until the Egyptians and Babylonians cultivated naked wheats and improved their milling technologies to produce fine flour, their cereals would be eaten largely as porridge or as flat cakes. At some point more than 6000 years ago, a wild yeast found its way into the porridge or the flat bread dough and the human race was on its way to the squeeze test and the six pack.

The first known commercial bakery integrated with a flour mill appeared in Rome about 200 B.C. though Babylonian and Egyptian slaves had been making wheat, barley and beer bread long before that. Bakeries were slower to be mechanized than were flour mills. Though the first travelling belt oven was invented in 1810 by Vice Admiral of the British Fleet Isaac Coffin, most ovens consisted of a static sole heated by wood or coke well into this century. Admiral Coffin's oven was not very fuel efficient since the belt travelled outside the oven from the point of exit to re-entry.

The widespread use of mechanical dough mixers was not evident until after World War I. Though several have been invented and sold, to my knowledge no continuous dough mixer has survived. Mixing remains essentially a batch operation: continuous operational flow starts at the point at which the dough is divided then moulded, baked, cooled and wrapped. In light of the extraordinary range of designs it would appear that mechanical batch dough mixers are derived more from empiricism than from fundamental principles. Only after Elton and his colleagues demonstrated at Chorleywood that bulk fermentation could be replaced by mechanical work exceeding 40 kJ/kg of dough within less than 5 min of mixing did empiricism appear to make way for systematic measurement. Also, since dough dividers are volumetric in principle, the weights delivered follow a normal distribution curve, a fact now employed in the design of automatic feedback mechanisms.

It was a maxim among Scottish bakers that 'there's mair in the

bakin' than the makin''. Certainly much engineering effort has gone
into the design of baking ovens, particularly to conserve energy
through the recycling of the oven gases. Nevertheless, until comparatively recently more has been accomplished by trial and error than
from basic principles.

A Canadian invention to accelerate the rate of bread cooling was
not very successful. Hot bread was moved on racks into a large metal
chamber which was closed and a partial vacuum drawn. The increased
rate of evaporation accelerated the cooling process. However, the
weight loss was also significantly increased and, since water is the food
technologists' cheapest ingredient, this was not considered particularly
satisfactory.

Meanwhile, the brewers were making faster progress than the
bakers in replacing men with machines. Galland's pneumatic malting
apparatus appeared in 1885, followed by the Saladin box with its
screws to turn the malt, leading to the more recent Wanderhaufen
moving malting couch in which steeped barley enters at one end and
by means of a turning and shifting mechanism is delivered ready for
the kiln floor at the exit end.

It would be misleading to leave the impression that all progress in
milling, baking and brewing is attributable solely to inventive engineering. Indeed, since many of the inventions came about empirically, engineers in flour mills needed the guidance of cereal chemists
and technologists to relate composition and quality of the milled
products. Fermentation industries owe much to the microbiologists'
development of more efficient yeast strains and control of unwanted
organisms, and to the biochemist's growing comprehension of enzyme
catalyzed reactions.

CANADIAN CONTRIBUTIONS

It is disappointing that Canadian enterprises appear to have contributed relatively little to the development and manufacture in the
mechanization of flour mills, bakeries, breweries and other similar
industries. It is indeed surprising considering that we probably know as
much about the structure and behavior of wheat and barley as any
nation on earth and that, not very long ago, the world's largest
brewing company, the largest baking company and the largest distilling
empire were each owned by Canadians.

Scientists at the Prairie Regional Laboratory in Saskatoon, with support from IDRC, employed rotating carborundum or resinoid discs inside a rubber-lined casing to remove the outer seed coats from sorghum, millets and other coarse grains. This stands as one of the few examples of Canadian engineering ingenuity applied to cereal processing technologies.

THE FUTURE FOR BIO-ENGINEERING

After taking a brief look at the history of engineering development in our most basic and traditional food industries, it is interesting to speculate upon what lies in the future for bio-engineering.

Most challenging are the promises of the nascent and newly emerging biotechnologies, among which the immobilization of enzymes and living cells present a bewildering array of tantalizing opportunities. Even a casual survey of the literature reveals the many hundreds of substances and structures being examined in laboratories studying reactions catalyzed by immobilized enzymes and cells.

The dominance of empiricism is evident even among the more advanced immobilization methods, with systems dependent upon adsorption, covalent attachments, entrapment, encapsulation, diffusion and ultrafiltration being compared in pursuit of biological conversion processes. Each possible immobilization system is made all the more complex by a mystifying assortment of alternative carriers and means of incorporating and stabilizing cells and enzymes while maintaining their biological efficiency.

Not all scientists are endowed with a gift of vision far beyond the laboratory door. Laboratory techniques of enzyme immobilization cannot progress to viable industrial biotechnologies without a clear longsighted downstream vision not readily apparent in all research institutions. Industrial success requires accurate anticipation of the probable impediments to efficient and economic scale-up beyond the laboratory and the pilot plant to full-scale manufacture. It demands a shrewd assessment of potential market demand and what cost each market can bear. Thus a process profitable for pharmaceutical and other high mark-up biologicals could quickly drive a food manufacturer to bankruptcy. The nature and desirable properties of the alternative carriers, together with the multifarious factors which influence the biological efficiency of immobilized enzymes themselves

Joseph H. Hulse

may well be unfamiliar to many processing engineers. In a recent thoughtful paper Dr Magnin* of the Connaught Laboratories has well identified the resources needed and difficulties encountered in scaling-up the production of vaccines and hormones.

Many of the heads in the food engineering research community have bumped against the obstacles encountered in progressing from a 100 ml flask in the laboratory to a 1000 litre fermentor in the factory. The problems of heat and mass transfer, of maintaining and monitoring biological activity and quality as scale-up progresses, are too many to mention. As we seek to replace batch with continuous fermentations and to expand these systems to new processes and new products, the difficulties will multiply and, at least in the short term, the demand for biological engineers will inevitably exceed the supply. Herein lies a stimulating challenge for our universities.

My often repeated comment that what the engineer has contributed to industrial food technology has resulted more from empiricism than from fundamental principles is not intended as a derogation of the engineers's integrity, intellect or imagination. Empiricism is abundantly evident among the biological components of technological innovation. The traditional technologies, born and nurtured in empiricism, long preceded even the remotest scientific cognizance of the complex biochemical and biophysical changes that take place during ethanolic, acetic and lactic food fermentations. It is therefore not surprising that much of what we presently lump together under the name 'biotechnology' results more from perceptive empiricism than from an understanding of basic principles.

While recognizing the need for more basic research in molecular biology and cell biochemistry, and the impossibility of drawing a sharp dividing line between basic and applied research, we should be concerned that all too often applied research intended to produce usable, economic and socially acceptable biotechnologies starts at the wrong end of the spectrum. All too many endeavours begin in the research laboratory when they should start in the market place.

If *The Economist* is to be believed, of the more than 400 biotechnology laboratories established in North America over the past decade, only about 25 have successfully survived. The successful ones appear to be those which have integrated themselves with commercial

---

* Biotechnologies: Opportunities and Constraints, International Development Research Centre, IDRC MR110e.

industrial organizations. Their research is thus guided by market research and intelligence and by the practical experience that emanates from the factory floor.

While fully accepting the need for and importance of highly trained specialists in biological engineering and all the other amalgam of disciplines that contribute to biotechnological development, we should recognize the urgent need for some new breeds of bioscientific people. The new generations of fermentation industries will need engineering physicists with a broad understanding of the nature and behaviour of living cells and reactive biological materials: scientists able to resolve the complexities of fluid flow, heat and mass transfer in packed columns and other vehicles designed to contain an astounding array of alternative permeable carriers for active cells and enzymes; people competent to design, construct and operate the various states of scale-up as they progress from the laboratory to manufacturing units.

Equally necessary are men and women who comprehend in broader and longer perspective the biological sciences and their potential applications; people who are as conscious of the demands of the market place as of the integration of resources needed for research, systematic development to full-scale manufacture, safe and effective delivery to the identified users.

One of the Biblical proverbs tells us that 'Where there is no vision the people will perish'.

Though biotechnology appears unlikely immediately to perish, it will require the guidance of biological engineers of remarkable vision and comprehension if it is to deliver all of the benefits it has the potential to offer.

Part I
Rheological Properties

2

DETERMINATION OF THE FLOW PARAMETERS OF FLUID FOODS USING A DIGITIZER AND A PERSONAL COMPUTER

G. KALETUNC GENCER, G. V. BARBOSA CANOVAS, M. D. NORMAND, J. R. ROSENAU and M. PELEG

Department of Food Engineering, University of Massachusetts, Amherst, Massachusetts 01003, U.S.A.

ABSTRACT

Experimental flow data of semi-liquid foods and gum solutions, obtained by a coaxial viscosimeter, were digitized and processed using a graphics tablet and a personal computer. The data files so created were used to estimate the yield stress from the apparent viscosity versus shear stress relationships and to calculate the constants of Herschel-Bulkley, Casson and a modified Casson model. The latter was done by an especially developed nonlinear regression program and by linear regression of the transforms of these models, incorporating an independently determined value of the yield stress. Comparison of the results with SPSS calculated values (on a mainframe computer) showed that the procedures developed for the personal computer yielded satisfactory results.

INTRODUCTION

Experimental viscosimetric data are frequently in the form of a curve on a recorder chart. Calculation of flow constants, therefore, requires a tedious process of data transfer before a computer can be used for this purpose. The ideal way to overcome this difficulty is to interface the rheometer directly with a computer so that calculations can be done simultaneously with the measurements. Modern rheometers are indeed equipped with such hardware which is usually offered as an option. Such hardware, however, is usually fairly expensive and often cannot be used for any other purpose or with other instruments. For this reason, it is sometimes advantageous to use hardware that does not require a specific and permanent connection with one instrument. The graphics tablet (or digitizer) is one such device. Its input is the recorded curve of any instrument. Consequently, its accuracy is limited to that of the particular instrument and its recording system. It is, however, a handy and inexpensive piece of equipment that can be connected to most personal computers, thus making its application even more attractive.

This communication describes the applicability of a digitizer–personal computer combination to the processing of viscosimetric data.

MATERIALS AND METHODS

Experimental torque versus rpm curves of semi-liquid foods and gum suspensions were recorded by a Rotovisco 3 coaxial viscosimeter (Haake, Inc., Saddle Brook, New Jersey) in a manner and under the conditions described by Barbosa-Canovas and Peleg.[1] The curves were digitized and processed (see Figs. 1 and 2) using an Apple II+ computer and a digitizer (HIPAD, Houston Instruments, Inc., Houston, Texas). As previously demonstrated,[2] the digitizing process, despite being done through tracing the curves by hand, did not introduce any appreciable error.

The calculation of the flow curves in terms of shear stress (τ) versus shear rate ($\dot{\gamma}$) relationships were based on the instrument and the particular sensor constants as well as a correction formula for the shear rate as described by Brodkey,[3] i.e.

$$\dot{\gamma}_{\text{cor}} = \frac{1 - (r_1/r_2)^2}{n[1 - (r_1/r_2)^{2/n}]} \dot{\gamma}_{\text{N}} \tag{1}$$

where $\dot{\gamma}_{\text{cor}}$ is the corrected shear rate, $\dot{\gamma}_{\text{N}}$ the Newtonian shear rate (calculated with the conversion formula provided by the instrument's manufacturer), r_1 and r_2 the internal and external radii of the sensor and n the slope of the log torque versus log rpm relationship. The data files of τ versus $\dot{\gamma}_{\text{cor}}$, were used to calculate the yield stress (τ_0) from the η_{AP} versus τ relationship as described by Kaletunc-Gencer and Peleg.[2] With and without these yield stress values the data were fitted

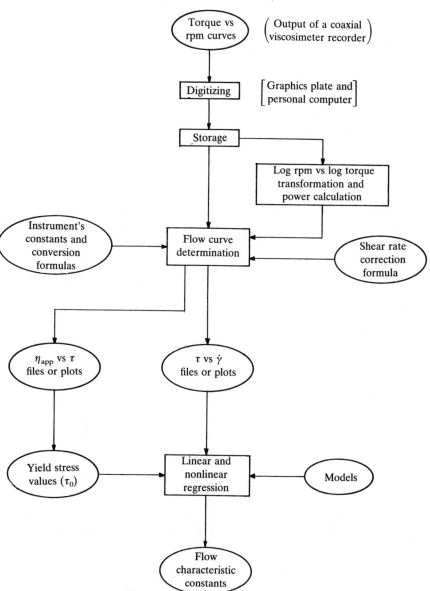

Fig. 1. The steps in the flow parameters determination.

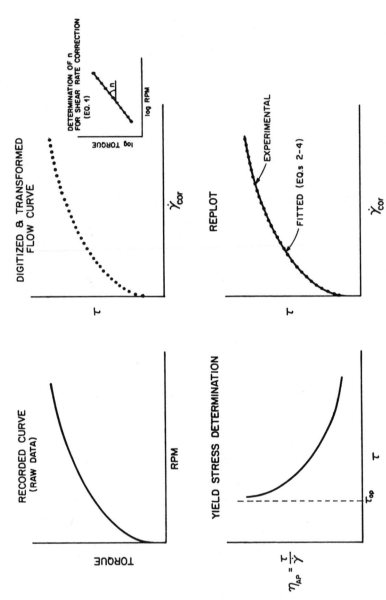

Fig. 2. Schematic view of the type of information processed and produced during the flow parameters determination (τ, $\dot{\gamma}$ and η_{AP} are the shear stress, shear rate and apparent viscosity, respectively).

with the following models:

$$\text{Herschel-Bulkley} \quad \tau = \tau_0 + K_1 \dot{\gamma}^n \tag{2}$$

$$\text{Casson} \quad \tau^{1/2} = \tau_0^{1/2} + K_2 \dot{\gamma}^{1/2} \tag{3}$$

$$\text{Modified Casson} \quad \tau^{1/2} = \tau_0^{1/2} + K_3 \dot{\gamma}^m \tag{4}$$

The fit was done through nonlinear regression or linear regression of the transformed relationships incorporating the predetermined value of the yield stress, i.e. (τ_{OP}):

$$\log(\tau - \tau_{OP}) \doteq \log K_1 + n \log \dot{\gamma} \tag{5}$$

$$\tau^{1/2} = K_2 \dot{\gamma}^{1/2} + \tau_0^{1/2} \tag{6}$$

$$\log(\tau^{1/2} - \tau_{OP}^{1/2}) = \log K_3 + m \log \dot{\gamma} \tag{7}$$

The results of the nonlinear regression procedure, especially adapted for the Apple II computer, were compared to those obtained by the SPSS package on a mainframe computer.

RESULTS AND DISCUSSION

Comparison of the rheological constants calculated for different models by the described methods is shown in Table I. The table illustrates that the constants were, for all practical purposes, the same irrespective of the method used, which demonstrates that a personal computer has sufficient power to handle such tasks. The constants calculated from the linear regression of the transforms (Eqs. 5–7) were slightly different from those calculated by nonlinear regression. This is a result of the different weight that is assigned to the different parts of the curves by the two calculation procedures.[4] The differences, however, were not of significant implication and the general character of the material was not lost through these transformations. As could be expected,[1,5] both the Herschel-Bulkley and the modified Casson equation had a similar fit as judged by the sum of squares or the mean square error. This is not so much a characteristic of the tested materials but merely a demonstration of the fact that flow curves' shapes can be fitted by more than one mathematical model provided they have three experimentally determined constants.

TABLE I

Comparison of flow constants of semi-liquid foods and gum solutions obtained by different calculation procedures

Material	τ_{OP_2} (N/m^2)	Method	Herschel-Bulkley (Eq. 2) τ_0	K_1	n	Casson (Eq. 3) τ_0	K_2	Modified Casson (Eq. 4) τ_0	K_3	m
Mustard (Gulden's)	50	Linear regression	(50)	12·77	0·354	70·58	0·223	(50)	0.90	0·305
		Nonlinear regression Apple	52·65	12·52	0·350	71·37	0·218	45·20	1·26	0·252
		Nonlinear regression SPSS	52·65	12·52	0·350	71·40	0·218	48·30	1·10	0·269
Baby Food Banana (Beech Nut)	15	Linear regression	(15)	7·18	0·583	23·89	0·589	(15)	0·99	0·425
		Nonlinear regression Apple	14·36	7·43	0·578	26·34	0·567	7·89	1·70	0·341
		Nonlinear regression SPSS	14·36	7·43	0·578	26·31	0·567	7·90	1·70	0·341
Apple Sauce (Stop and Shop)	0	Linear regression	(0)	58·29	0·113	73·84	0·121	(0)	7·63	0·056
		Nonlinear regression Apple	0·00	61·45	0·102	75·26	0·114	0·00	7·84	0·051
		Nonlinear regression SPSS	0·00	61·45	0·102	75·34	0·114	0·00	7·84	0·051
1% Guar	0	Linear regression	(0)	8·74	0·326	18·21	0·176	(0)	3·03	0·164
		Nonlinear regression Apple	0·00	11·62	0·273	21·03	0·156	0·00	3·41	0·137
		Nonlinear regression SPSS	0·00	11·62	0·273	21·07	0·156	0·00	3·41	0·137
0.5% Carra-geenan 0.5% Guar pH = 4.0	0	Linear regression	(0)	5·33	0·317	10·10	0·142	(0)	2·31	0·159
		Nonlinear regression Apple	0·00	5·87	0·298	11·21	0·131	0·00	2·42	0·149
		Nonlinear regression SPSS	0·00	5·87	0·298	11·22	0·131	0·00	2·42	0·149

ACKNOWLEDGEMENT

Contribution of the Massachusetts Agricultural Experiment Station at Amherst. The authors express their thanks to Mr Richard J. Grant for the graphical assistance.

REFERENCES

1. Barbosa-Canovas, G. V. and Peleg, M. Flow parameters of selected commercial semi-liquid food products. *J. Text. Stud.* **14:** 213, 1983.
2. Kaletunc-Gencer, G. and Peleg, M. Digitizer aided determination of yield stress in semi-liquid foods. *J. Food Sci.* **49:** 1620, 1984.
3. Brodkey, R. S. *The Phenomena of Fluid Motions.* Addison-Wesley, Reading, Mass., 1967.
4. Caceci, M. S. and Cacheris, W. D. Fitting curves to data. *BYTE* **19:** 340, 1984.
5. Kaletunc-Gencer, G. Interactions of selected gums in solution and the effects of pH and common food ingredients on these interactions. Ph.D. dissertation, University of Massachusetts, Amherst, Mass., 1985.

3

EFFECT OF TEMPERATURE ON VISCOSITY OF FLUID FOODS WITH HIGH SUGAR CONTENT

M. A. RAO, R. S. SHALLENBERGER, and H. J. COOLEY

Department of Food Science and Technology, New York State Agricultural Experiment Station, Cornell University, Geneva, New York 14456, U.S.A.

ABSTRACT

The effect of temperature on the viscosity of 65 °Brix sugar solutions, and apple and grape juice samples (55–68 °Brix) was better described by the Williams–Landel–Ferry (WLF) and the Fulcher (FR) models than the Arrhenius (AR) model. In the case of fruit juices, the magnitudes of the activation energy of the AR model, and the parameters T_0 and T_g of the FR and the WLF models decreased with dilution. Plots of $(T - T_g)$ versus $\log_{10}(\eta/\eta_g)$ showed that data for each class of foods can be represented on a single curve.

INTRODUCTION

Fluid foods (FF) with high concentrations of sugars, such as syrups and concentrated fruit juices are important items of commerce. Rheological properties of fluid foods are useful in the design of operations related to the processing of the foods, in sensory analysis, and in quality control.[1] Previous studies[2,3] have shown that the effect of temperature on viscosity (apparent viscosity of nonNewtonian fluids) of high sugar FF is more pronounced than for low sugar FF. In addition, the effect, as indicated by the Arrhenius activation energy, is more pronounced at low temperatures than at high temperatures.[3] Consequently, the Arrhenius model (AR) (Eq. 1) may not be adequate for describing the effect of temperature on high sugar FF at low temperatures.[3]

$$\eta_a = \eta_\infty \exp(E_a/RT) \tag{1}$$

In Eq. (1), η_a is the apparent viscosity (Pa.s), η_∞ is a parameter that is considered as the viscosity at infinite temperature (Pa.s), E_a is the activation energy (kcal/mole), and T is the temperature (K).

The objectives of the present study were to test the applicability of the AR, the Fulcher (FR) (Eq. 2), and the Williams–Landel–Ferry (WLF) (Eq. 3) models to describe the effect of temperature on high sugar foods.

$$\ln \eta = A + \frac{B}{T - T_0} \tag{2}$$

$$\ln (\eta/\eta_g) = -17 \cdot 44(T - T_g)/[51 \cdot 6 + (T - T_g)] \tag{3}$$

In the latter two equations A, B, T_0, η_g, and T_g are parameters to be determined from experimental data. T_g and η_g are a reference temperature (K) and a reference viscosity (Pa.s), respectively. They are commonly known as the glass transition temperature and the viscosity at the glass transition temperature, respectively.[4]

The AR relationship has been employed extensively for quantifying the effect of temperature on flow properties of fluid foods.[1,5] The FR model has been used to a limited extent on polymers, but the WLF equation has been applied extensively for describing the effect of temperature on zero shear viscosities of polymers and to a limited extent to viscosity of low molecular weight organic liquids and inorganic glasses.[4] Recently, it was also employed to describe the effect of temperature on the viscosity of aqueous solutions of a mixture of 87·5% sucrose and 12·5% fructose, 91·9% to 97·6% by weight.[6] The applicability of the FR and WLF equations to concentrated fruit juices will be of interest.

The WLF equation is an empirical equation that is based on a reference temperature (T_g) and the viscosity at the reference temperature (η_g). The reference temperature T_g, known as the glass transition temperature, is the point on the temperature scale where the thermal expansion coefficient undergoes a discontinuity. It also corresponds to a change in the slope of a plot of specific volume against temperature.[4] This phenomenon is characteristic of any liquid that can be super-cooled to a sufficiently low temperature without crystallization and it can be explained in terms of the concept of free volume. The numerical constants in the WLF relationship (Eq. 3) are those that have been found to be satisfactory for a large number of amorphous polymers and the applicability of the relationship to fruit juices is of special interest.

MATERIALS AND METHODS

Samples of Juice and Sugar Solutions

Depectinized apple and grape juices were prepared in our pilot plant and concentrated in a laboratory evaporator to the desired concentration (55–68 °Brix). Aqueous solutions of sucrose, glucose, and fructose of 65 °Brix were prepared by mixing the required quantities in distilled water. The pH of four solutions was about 5·4. In addition, one solution with pH of 3·44 was studied in order to determine if the studied models can indicate differences in pH.

Rheological Data of Samples

Viscosity data on the FF were obtained with a concentric cylinder viscometer (Haake RV2, System MV1). The temperature range for the sugar solutions was −20 to 40 °C. For the 50 °Brix concentrated fruit juices the lower temperature was −10 °C and for the other concentrations it was −15 °C; the higher temperature for the fruit juices was 40 °C. The temperature of each sample was measured with a copper–constantan thermocouple, made out of Teflon insulated wire 0·013 cm in diameter, placed in the gap between the concentric cylinders. Shear rate–shear stress data were obtained on a test sample after it had reached the desired temperature.

Depectinized and filtered apple and grape juices have been shown to be Newtonian fluids[2,3] due to the absence of either suspended matter or dissolved high molecular weight polymers such as pectins. Thus, one can employ the Newtonian viscosity function for determining the effect of temperature. The AR, FR and the WLF relationships (Eqs. 1–3) were tested for predicting the effect of temperature on the viscosity. A nonlinear regression analysis program (GENSTAT, Rothamsted Experiment Station, U.K.) was employed for determining the parameters in each equation.

RESULTS AND DISCUSSION

The results for the sugar solutions and the two fruit juices were similar in that all the studied models described well the effect of temperature. However, for the high sugar FF the WLF equation was better than the other models as indicated by the sum of the squares of the deviation between the data and the predicted values (ss). The magnitudes of the

TABLE I
Parameters of the Arrhenius, Fulcher, and the Williams–Landel–Ferry models for apple and grape concentrates

Product	Arrhenius		Fulcher			Williams–Landel–Ferry	
	η_{00} (Pa.s)	E_a (kcal/mole)	A	B	T_0 (K)	η_g (Pa.s)	T_g (K)
Apple 68·3 °Brix	$1·366 \times 10^{-15}$	18·86	$-16·72$	2 415·2	132·78	$5·91 \times 10^{10}$	193·98
	ss = 0·102 6	$R^2 = 0·999\ 5$	ss = 0·013 56		$R^2 = 0·999\ 9$	ss = 0·012 73	$R^2 = 0·999\ 9$
Apple 64·9 °Brix	$1·671 \times 10^{-15}$	18·12	$-17·41$	2 382·5	130·88	$2·57 \times 10^{10}$	191·36
	ss = 0·028 7	$R^2 = 0·998\ 5$	ss = 0·013 60		$R^2 = 0·999\ 3$	ss = 0·012 22	$R^2 = 0·999\ 4$
Apple 60·1 °Brix	$2·61 \times 10^{-13}$	14·78	$-15·83$	2 097·7	124·26	$4·03 \times 10^{10}$	176·74
	ss = 0·001 1	$R^2 = 0·997\ 0$	ss = 0·002 08		$R^2 = 0·998\ 1$	ss = 0·002 07	$R^2 = 0·998\ 1$
Apple 55·0 °Brix	$5·05 \times 10^{-11}$	11·46	$-13·97$	2 062·4	93·95	$21·81 \times 10^{10}$	145·79
	ss = 0·001 0	$R^2 = 0·991\ 2$	ss = 0·000 48		$R^2 = 0·995\ 8$	ss = 0·000 49	$R^2 = 0·995\ 8$
Grape 68·3 °Brix	$2·15 \times 10^{-14}$	17·44	$-15·54$	2 392·3	125·69	$16·3 \times 10^{10}$	186·80
	ss = 0·317 7	$R^2 = 0·999\ 0$	ss = 0·141 1		$R^2 = 0·999\ 5$	ss = 0·120 4	$R^2 = 0·999\ 6$
Grape 64·5 °Brix	$9·81 \times 10^{-13}$	14·93	$-15·31$	2 398·3	115·14	$18·88 \times 10^{10}$	177·40
	ss = 0·039 5	$R^2 = 0·998\ 6$	ss = 0·021 5		$R^2 = 0·999\ 2$	ss = 0·019 0	$R^2 = 0·999\ 3$
Grape 59·9 °Brix	$2·94 \times 10^{-12}$	13·77	$-15·68$	2 412·6	106·99	$12·98 \times 10^{10}$	170·23
	ss = 0·006 2	$R^2 = 0·997\ 8$	ss = 0·000 8		$R^2 = 0·998\ 6$	ss = 0·003 7	$R^2 = 0·998\ 7$
Grape 54·0 °Brix	$7·61 \times 10^{-11}$	11·60	$-15·11$	2 499·2	84·47	$24·18 \times 10^{10}$	153·18
	ss = 0·001 3	$R^2 = 0·996\ 9$	ss = 0·000 8		$R^2 = 0·998\ 1$	ss = 0·000 9	$R^2 = 0·998\ 0$

TABLE II

Parameters of the Arrhenius, Fulcher, and the Williams–Landel–Ferry models for sugar solutions

Product	Arrhenius		Fulcher			Williams–Landel–Ferry	
	η_{00} (Pa.s)	E_a (kcal/mole)	A	B	$T_0\ K$	η_g (Pa.s)	$T_g\ K$
Fructose 100%, pH = 5·42	$2\cdot53 \times 10^{-15}$ ss = 0·028 96	17·84 $R^2 = 0\cdot999\ 5$	$-17\cdot27$ ss = 0·005 87	2 415·5	126·98 $R^2 = 0\cdot999\ 9$	$3\cdot36 \times 10^{10}$ ss = 0·000 524	188·31 $R^2 = 0\cdot999\ 9$
Fructose 70% Glucose 30%, pH = 5·39	$2\cdot51 \times 10^{-15}$ ss = 0·032 21	17·84 $R^2 = 0\cdot999\ 4$	$-17\cdot18$ ss = 0·006 35	2 415·2	126·31 $R^2 = 0\cdot999\ 9$	$3\cdot64 \times 10^{10}$ ss = 0·004 57	187·68 $R^2 = 0\cdot999\ 9$
Fructose 70% Glucose 20% Sucrose 10%, pH = 5·54	$7\cdot74 \times 10^{-15}$ ss = 0·027 68	17·18 $R^2 = 0\cdot999\ 3$	$-16\cdot64$ ss = 0·012 49	2 368·1	123·73 $R^2 = 0\cdot999\ 7$	$5\cdot08 \times 10^{10}$ ss = 0·011 07	184·02 $R^2 = 0\cdot999\ 7$
Fructose 45% Glucose 46% Sucrose 8%, pH = 5·40	$2\cdot17 \times 10^{-15}$ ss = 0·071 01	17·84 $R^2 = 0\cdot998\ 4$	$-15\cdot77$ ss = 0·005 75	2 250·8	124·24 $R^2 = 0\cdot999\ 9$	$7\cdot62 \times 10^{10}$ ss = 0·005 17	181·34 $R^2 = 0\cdot999\ 9$
Fructose 70% Glucose 20% Sucrose 10%, pH = 3·45	$1\cdot06 \times 10^{-14}$ ss = 0·007 88	17·15 $R^2 = 0\cdot999\ 9$	$-16\cdot40$ ss = 0·008 08	2 384·2	122·90 $R^2 = 0\cdot999\ 9$	$6\cdot88 \times 10^{10}$ ss = 0·009 38	183·66 $R^2 = 0\cdot999\ 9$

parameters ss and R^2 of the three models are given in Tables I and II for apple and grape juices and for sugar solutions, respectively.

Applicability of AR and FR Models

The AR model is satisfactory for the FF of about 55 °Brix. However, for the high sugar FF it is not satisfactory over the entire temperature range.[3] The FR model (Eq. 2) is better than the AR model for the high sugar FF, but its chief drawback is that one needs to deal with three constants. The model's parameters have different values for the different FF indicating sensitivity to composition of the foods. In the case of fruit juices, the magnitude of T_0 increased with increase in sugar content.

Applicability of WLF Model

The WLF model has the advantage of only two constants. Further, the use of the numerical constants of polymers for the FF appears to be satisfactory for describing the effect of temperature on viscosity of high sugar foods.

In the case of the fruit juices, the magnitude of T_g decreased with decrease in sugar content. This result and the low magnitudes of T_g are consistent with the observation of Soesanto and Williams[6] for fructose/sucrose solutions and with the magnitude of T_g for water of 127 K. In contrast to T_g, η_g did not show a consistent trend with sugar content and there are not enough data to indicate its behavior with certainty. Further, magnitudes of η_g are highly sensitive to small deviations in T_g[4,6] and there are no η_g data for water to indicate whether it decreases or increases with sugar concentration. In this respect, Soesanto and Williams[6] speculate that γ_g decreases exponentially with dilution.

Figures 1, 2 and 3 are plots of $(T - T_g)$ versus $\log \eta/\eta_g$ for apple juice samples, grape juice samples, and sugar solutions, respectively. They indicate that generalized plots for the effect of temperature on viscosity of high sugar FF can be readily constructed.

It is emphasized that the magnitudes of T_g and η_g presented in this study are those obtained by curve fitting and that direct experimental confirmation of their magnitudes was not attempted. The WLF equation is not applicable at high temperatures far above the freezing points where the proportion of free volume is probably about 0·3 instead of 0·03. For polymers, the WLF equation has been found to be satisfactory for temperatures between T_g and $T_g + 100$ °C.[4] Figures 1–3

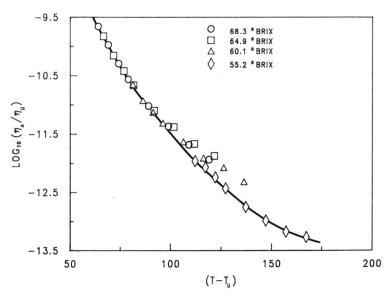

Fig. 1. Plot of $(T - T_g)$ against log (η/η_g) for apple juice samples.

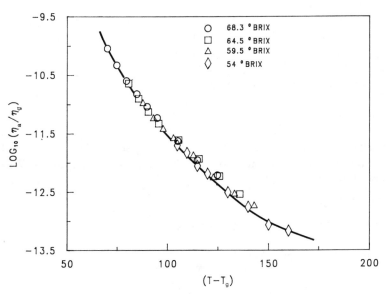

Fig. 2. Plot of $(T - T_g)$ against log (η/η_g) for grape juice samples.

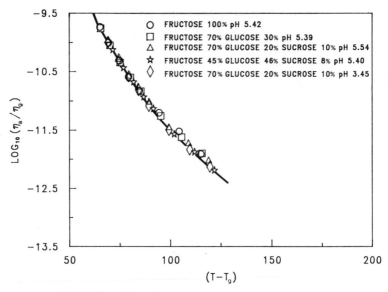

Fig. 3. Plot of $(T - T_g)$ against log (η/η_g) for sugar solutions.

show that the relationship appears to be valid up to 150 °C above T_g. Because T_g increases with increase in sugar content, its magnitudes will be higher than 0 °C for foods with very high sugar content.[6] In this respect, because the WLF relationship is approximately valid in the range 100–150 °C above T_g, it probably will not be applicable to very high sugar foods at low temperatures.

It appears that the WLF equation can describe well the effect of temperature on viscosity of high sugar foods such as concentrated fruit juices. It was employed for describing the effect of temperature on the apparent viscosity of concentrated orange juice.[7] There is a need, however, to document the magnitudes of the parameters of the WLF model for other foods.

REFERENCES

1. Rao, M. A. Rheology of liquid foods—A review. *J. Text. Stud.* **8:** 135, 1977.
2. Saravacos, G. D. Effect of temperature on viscosity of fruit juices and purees. *J. Food Sci.* **35:** 122, 1970.
3. Rao, M. A., Colley, H. J. and Vitali, A. A. Flow properties of concentrated juices at low temperatures. *Food Technol.* **38**(3): 113, 1984.

4. Ferry, J. D. *Viscoelastic Properties of Polymers,* 3rd edn. John Wiley, New York, 1980.
5. Holdsworth, S. D. Applicability of rheological models to the interpretation of flow and processing behaviour of fluid food products. *J. Text. Stud.* **2:** 393, 1971.
6. Soesanto, T. and Williams, M. C. Viscometric interpretation of viscosity for concentrated and dilute sugar solutions. *J. Phys. Chem.* **85:** 3338, 1981.
7. Rao, M. A., Vitali, A. A. and Brunello, G. Effect of temperature and pulp content on flow properties of low-pulp concentrated orange juice. *Lebensmittel Wissenschaft und Technologie* (submitted for publication).

4

RHEOLOGICAL BEHAVIOR OF COCONUT MILK

A. A. VITALI, M. P. SOLER, and M. A. RAO*

*Instituto de Tecnologia de Alimentos, Caixa Postal 139,
13.100 Campinas, S.P., Brazil*

* *Department of Food Science and Technology, New York State Agricultural
Experiment Station, Cornell University, Geneva, New York 14456, U.S.A.*

ABSTRACT

The flow properties of three coconut milk samples determined with a concentric cylinder viscometer were well described by the simple power law model over the temperature range 15–50 °C. The samples exhibited mild time dependent behavior and at steady state they were mildly shear-thining fluids. The magnitude of the flow behavior index was between 0·76 and 0·94; the lower values were those for a sample containing dissolved gums. The magnitude of the consistency index was high for samples containing either high sugar or dissolved gums. The Arrhenius model described well the effect of temperature on the apparent viscosity at $100 s^{-1}$ and the magnitudes of activation energy were high for samples containing high sugar content.

INTRODUCTION

Rheological properties are important in engineering applications related to the processing and handling of foods. They are also important in quality control and sensory analysis of foods.[1] Coconut milk is an important food item in Brazil that also has a great potential for export to a number of countries. It is made from the juice extracted from the endosperm of coconuts and it is an emulsion containing sugars, proteins, lipids, salts, and water with the major components being water and lipids. The coconut milk industry is in the process of introducing a single phase milky product in place of the two

33

phase product that had predominated the Brazilian markets. The present study was undertaken because data on the rheological behavior of coconut milk were not encountered in the literature.

MATERIALS AND METHODS

Materials

A commercial coconut milk sample ('Leite de Coco', Sococo, Brazil) (Sample A) from 200 ml bottles and a commercial high sugar coconut milk sample ('Crem Coco', Sococo, Brazil) (Sample B) in 400 ml cans, and a coconut milk sample prepared in our pilot plant (Sample C) were studied. Coconut milk for sample C was obtained by pressing in a screw press (FMC Corpn, model 35, with 0·51 mm diameter finisher holes) pieces of coconut that were obtained by cutting coconut meat in a hammer mill. The milk from the press was heated to 90 °C in a steam kettle and 0·06% by weight of a mixture of guar gum and sodium alginate (Ligomme 34, CELA-SATIA Produtos Quimicos S. A., São Paulo) and 0·20% by weight of sodium carboxymethylcellulose (CMC) were added. The mixture was homogenized (Creamery Package, Model 3DDL) in two stages at 50 kg/cm^2 and at 150 kg/cm^2, placed in 200 ml bottles, capped, and pasteurized ($F_0 = 3$) in still retorts at 121 °C.

Methods

RPM-torque data were obtained with a concentric cylinder viscometer (Systems MS-A, Epprecht Rheomat 15, Contraves, Zurich) over the temperature range 15–50 °C. The data were obtained first for increasing values of RPM followed by decreasing values. In preliminary experiments, it was found that a steady torque reading was attained in about 45 s. For this reason, each torque reading was noted 1 min after the motor was turned on at a specific RPM. The torque data were converted to shear stress, τ (N/m^2), and the RPM data were converted to nonNewtonian shear rates, $\dot{q}$ (s^{-1}) by correcting the Newtonian shear rates provided by the manufacturer using the method in Refs. 2 and 3. The temperature of each sample was controlled with a circulating water bath (Haake, Inc.).

The simple power law model was used to describe the shear

rate–shear stress data:

$$\tau = K\dot{\gamma}^n \tag{1}$$

Where K is the consistency index (N s^n/m^2) and n is the flow behavior index. The apparent viscosity of the samples at $100\,\text{s}^{-1}$ was calculated from:

$$\eta_{100} = K100^{n-1} \tag{2}$$

The effect of temperature on η_{100} was determined from the Arrhenius equation:

$$\eta_{100} = \eta_\infty \exp\left(E_a/RT\right) \tag{3}$$

Where η_∞ is viscosity at infinite shear rate, E_a is the activation energy of flow (kcal/mole), R is the gas constant (kcal/mole K), and T is temperature (K). The parameters K and n, and η_∞ and E_a were calculated by linear regression analysis.

The °Brix, pH, and the total solids were determined by standard procedures, while the fat content was determined by the method used for butter.[4]

RESULTS AND DISCUSSION

The °Brix, pH, total solids, and the fat content of the samples are given in Table I. It is seen that while Sample B was high in soluble and total solids, its fat content was lower than that of Samples A and C probably due to the addition of sugars to a coconut milk sample.

The power law model (Eq. 1) fit well the shear rate–shear stress data and Fig. 1 illustrates the data for Sample C at 15, 30 and 49·5 °C. The magnitudes of the power law parameters of the samples are given

TABLE I
Characteristics of coconut milk samples studied

Sample	pH	°Brix	Total solids (%)	Fat content (%)
Sample A	5·8	8·0	36·9	33·5
Sample B	5·6	58·4	60·5	7·5
Sample C	5·0	8·4	51·6	34·5

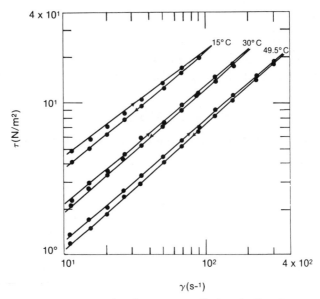

Fig. 1. Shear rate–shear stress data for coconut milk Sample C at three temperatures.

in Table II. At a given temperature, the magnitudes of K in descending RPM are lower than those in the ascending order indicating that the samples exhibited time-dependent rheological behavior.

The data obtained in descending order was considered to represent steady state rheological behavior and they can be used to compare the behavior of the samples at equal temperatures. Samples A and C were nearly equal in °Brix and fat content, but the total solids of the latter were higher due to added gums. The addition of gums to Sample C resulted in higher magnitudes of the consistency index. In comparison to Samples A and B, the lower magnitudes of the flow behavior index of Sample C are due to the higher fat content and the addition of gums. Sample B had the highest magnitudes of the consistency index mainly due to the high total solids content.

Effect of Temperature on Apparent Viscosity

The Arrhenius model (Eq. 3) fits well the effect of temperature on η_{100}. The magnitudes of η_∞ and E_a, and R^2 for the regression are given

TABLE II
Power law parameters of the coconut milk samples

Temperature (°C)	Ascending RPM		Descending RPM	
	$K(Ns^n/m^2)$	$n(-)$	$K(Ns^n/m^2)$	$n(-)$
	Sample A			
15·0	0·070	0·82	0·037	0·91
20·0	0·070	0·80	0·034	0·90
30·0	0·054	0·80	0·025	0·91
40·0	0·038	0·83	0·015	0·97
50·0	0·025	0·87	0·015	0·94
	Sample B			
15·0	1·189	0·75	0·405	0·84
20·0	0·903	0·75	0·299	0·83
29·8	0·544	0·78	0·196	0·83
39·9	0·313	0·81	0·127	0·84
49·5	0·226	0·81	0·090	0·84
	Sample C			
15·0	0·918	0·68	0·639	0·76
20·0	0·592	0·74	0·469	0·79
30·0	0·365	0·77	0·304	0·80
40·0	0·248	0·79	0·209	0·82
49·5	0·191	0·80	0·158	0·83

TABLE III
Parameters of the Arrhenius model for the effect of temperature
on steady state apparent viscosities at $100 \, s^{-1}$

Sample	$\eta_\infty(Pa.s)$	$E_a(kcal/mole)$	R^2
Sample A	$2·122 \times 10^{-5}$	4·02	0·992
Sample B	$3·442 \times 10^{-7}$	7·98	0·998
Sample C	$8·228 \times 10^{-6}$	5·81	0·997

in Table III. Sample B had the highest value of E_a due to the very high sugar content. This result is consistent with the earlier observation that fluid foods with high sugar content have relatively high magnitudes of E_a.[5,6]

ACKNOWLEDGEMENTS

This work was supported by the Conselho Nacional de Desenvolvimento Cientifico e Tecnologico, Brazil, in the form of a Visiting

Professorship (to MAR). B. Giovanetti promoted stimulating discussions of the study.

REFERENCES

1. Rao, M. A. Rheology of liquid foods—a review. *J. Text. Stud.* **8:** 135, 1977.
2. Brodkey, R. S. *The Phenomena of Fluid Motions.* Addison-Wesley, Reading, Massachusetts, 1967.
3. Rao, M. A. Measurement of flow properties of fluid foods—developments, limitations, and interpretation of phenomena. *J. Text. Stud.* **8:** 257, 1977.
4. Lara, A. D. W. H. Normas Analiticas do Instituto Adolfo Lutz, Vol. 1. Metodos Quimicos e Fisicos para Analise de Alimentos, Secretaria da Saude, São Paulo, 1976.
5. Saravacos, G. D. Effect of temperature on viscosity of fruit juices and purees. *J. Food Sci.* **35:** 122, 1970.
6. Rao, M. A., Cooley, H. J. and Vitali, A. A. Flow properties of concentrated juices at low temperatures. *Food Technol.* **38**(3): 113, 1984.

5

FLOW PROPERTIES OF 7s AND 11s SOY PROTEIN FRACTIONS

M. A. RAO, D. SRINIVASAN*, J. E. KINSELLA* and H. J. COOLEY

Department of Food Science and Technology, New York State Agricultural Experiment Station, Cornell University, Geneva, New York 14456, U.S.A.

*Institute of Food Science, Cornell University, Ithaca, New York 14853, U.S.A.

ABSTRACT

Dispersions of 7s and 11s soy protein fractions of pH 8·5 were found to be Newtonian fluids up to concentrations of 10%. The dispersions of 7s protein had higher viscosities and activation energies of flow than those of 11s protein up to 10% concentration due to the more open structure of 7s protein. Dispersions of the higher molecular weight 11s protein above 10% were shear-thinning fluids. Gels of 3–7% dispersions of 11s, formed by heating in boiling water, had higher activation energies of flow than the corresponding 7s dispersions. Dilute solution viscosity data on 7% 11s gel indicated significant expansion of the molecule due to heating and a high value of Huggins' interaction coefficient (k'); the latter suggesting densely packed spherical molecules. Kinetic data on gelling of a 7% 11s dispersion suggest two step zero order processes at each temperature with activation energies of the first step being much higher than those of the second step.

INTRODUCTION

Flow properties of fluid food systems are useful for understanding the role of chemical structure. In this respect, both concentrated and dilute solutions can be employed; the latter provide information regarding the size of the solute molecules and the solute–solvent interactions. In addition, flow properties are useful in the design of handling systems as well as sensory analysis of fluid foods.

Rheological properties of isolates and fractions of soy protein were studied by a number of workers.[1-4] The properties of rapeseed protein dispersions were studied by Gill and Tung.[5,6]

It has been shown[1] that when soy proteins are heated to high temperatures and cooled immediately, irreversible gels are formed. The objectives of the present study were to quantify the effect of temperature and concentration on sols and gels made from dispersions of 7s and 11s soy protein fractions that were subjected to different heat treatments and electrostatic forces.

MATERIALS AND METHODS

Dispersions of Protein Isolates
The soy protein fractions were prepared as described earlier.[4] Dispersions of the fractions were prepared by dispersing measured amounts in distilled water with a magnetic stirrer. The pH of the dispersions were adjusted with either 1 N HCl or NaOH.

Steady Shear Rheology Data
Steady shear rate–shear stress data were obtained with a Haake RV2 viscometer. System NV was used for low viscosity dispersions and system MV1 was used for high viscosity dispersions and gels. Temperature of the samples was controlled with a water bath (Lauda K2/R, Brinkman Instruments). NonNewtonian gels were characterized by the simple power law model:

$$\tau = K\gamma^n \tag{1}$$

where τ is shear stress (N/m^2), K is the consistency index, n is the flow behavior index ($-$), and γ is the shear rate (s^{-1}). This model is applicable because the dispersions and gels did not exhibit yield stresses.

Effect of Temperature on Viscosities
The effect of temperature on the viscosities of the dispersions was described by the Arrhenius relationship:

$$\eta = \eta_\infty \exp\left(E_a/RT\right) \tag{2}$$

In Eq. (2), η is the viscosity (Pa. s), η_∞(Pa. s) is the viscosity at infinite temperature, E_a is the activation energy of flow (kcal/mole), R is the gas constant (kcal/mole K), and T is the absolute temperature.

Intrinsic Viscosity

Dilute solution viscosity data were obtained with glass capillary viscometers (Cannon–Fenske, nos. 50 and 100). They were employed in plots of concentration (C) against (η_{sp}/C) for the determination of intrinsic viscosities, where $\eta_{sp} = \eta_{rel} - 1$, $\eta_{rel} = \eta_p/\eta_s$ is the relative viscosity, η_p is the viscosity of the sol or gel derived from the protein, and η_s is the viscosity of the solvent.

Shear rate–shear stress data on unheated sols (pH 8·5) were obtained over the concentration range 3–16% and temperature range 10–40 °C. Gels were prepared by heating sols (20 ml) of 3%, 5%, and 7% (pH 8·5) in a test tube (2 cm dia. × 17·5 cm long) for 5 min and cooling immediately in ice water. The rheological properties of the gels were also determined over the temperature range 10–40 °C. Kinetics of sol–gel transformation were studied on a 7% 11s pH 8·5 dispersion at 69·5 °C, 85 °C, and 100 °C, and at 85 °C on a pH 6·8 dispersion.

RESULTS AND DISCUSSION

Rheology of Sols

The viscosity (Pa.s), the consistency index at high concentrations, of the dispersions (pH 8.5) increased with increase in concentrations (Fig. 1). From Fig. 1, it appears that at low concentrations, even though the 7s molecules have a lower molecular weight their open structure contributes to the higher viscosity. This is also consistent with the observation that 7s protein fraction has a higher intrinsic viscosity than the 11s fraction.[7] However, at concentrations higher than about 13·6% the viscosity of 11s dispersions was higher than that of the 7s dispersions due to the higher molecular weight of about 360 000 for 11s versus about 170 000 for the 7s fraction.

Dispersions of both fractions changed from Newtonian to nonNewtonian shear-thinning fluids at concentrations above 10%. The magnitude of the flow behavior index of 7s dispersions above 10% ranged between 0·82 and 0·98, with the lower magnitudes being those at the low temperatures. The flow behavior index of the 11s

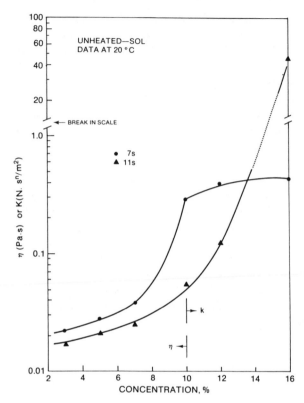

Fig. 1. Effect of concentration on viscosity (or consistency index) of 7s and 11s soy protein sols.

dispersions decreased drastically from about 0·90 at 12% concentration to 0·55 for the 16% concentration. This relatively severe shear-thinning behavior of the 11s dispersions is due to the higher molecular weight, viz. about 360 000 for 11s compared to about 170 000 for 7s, that resulted in a much more shear dependent structure. We note here that shear dependent structures are formed at low concentrations (>0·5%) in the case of very high molecular weight compounds such as carbohydrate polymers.

It has been shown that at high concentrations, dispersions of protein isolates such as promine-D exhibit yield stresses.[3] For this reason, yield stresses were estimated by extrapolation of the shear rate–shear stress data using the Casson equation

$$\tau^{0.5} - K_{0c} = K_c \gamma^{0.5} \tag{3}$$

In Eq. (3), K_c and K_{0c} are constants to be determined, and the yield stress $\tau_0 = K_{0c}$.[2] Magnitudes of the Casson yield stress were small for 7s protein fractions of all concentrations and up to dispersion concentration of 12% for the 11s. The 16% 11s dispersion exhibited magnitudes of yield stress of about 1·6 N/m². The 16% 11s dispersions also exhibited thixotropic flow behavior, with the consistency indexes of the samples in increasing order of shear rates being about half of those in the decreasing order. Ageing the 16% 11s dispersion overnight at 5 °C resulted in a dispersion with no time dependent behavior and consistency indexes about five to ten times less, depending on the temperature of measurement, than those of the freshly prepared dispersion.

Effect of Temperature on Sols and Gels

Magnitudes of Arrhenius activation energy (E_a) of sols and gels of the protein fractions were determined from viscosity data between 10 °C

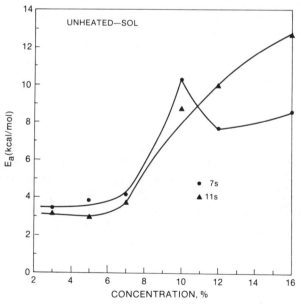

Fig. 2. Activation energy flow of sols of 7s and 11s soy proteins.

TABLE I
Effect of temperature on viscosity of 7s sols and gels, pH 8·5

Concentration (%)	Heating time[a] (min)	E_a (kcal/mol) (10–40 °C)
3	0	3·5
3	5	3·7
5	0	3·8
5	5	3·9
7	0	4·1
7	5	4·9

[a] In boiling water at 98 °C.

and 40 °C. For sols, E_a increased with concentration for both 7s and 11s fractions indicating that intermolecular interactions increased with concentration (Fig. 2).

At low concentrations (3–7%), there was not much difference in the effect of temperature on viscosity of sols of 7s protein fraction at pH 8·5 and gels formed by heating in boiling water for 5 min (Table I). As shown in Table I, the magnitudes of the activation energy of the gels were slightly higher than those of the corresponding sols indicating that there were greater intermolecular interactions in the case of gels. In contrast, the magnitudes of the activation energy of the gels of 11s protein fraction were much higher than those of the corresponding sols (Table II) indicating significant intermolecular interactions, a result confirmed by dilute solution viscosity data to be discussed later. The difference in the magnitudes of E_a of the sols and gels indicates the contribution of the sol–gel transformation to the flow processes. From

TABLE II
Effect of temperature on viscosity of 11s sols and gels, pH 8·5

Concentration (%)	Heating time[a] (min)	E_a (kcal/mol) (10–40 °C)
3	0	3·1
3	5	3·1
5	0	2·9
5	5	7·2
7	0	3·7
7	5	5·6

[a] In boiling water at 98 °C.

the data in Tables I and II, the contribution of the phase transition is relatively small and increases with concentration between 3% and 7%. It was between 0·1 and 0·8 kcal/mole for the 7s dispersions and between 0·0 and 4·3 kcal/mole for the 11s dispersions.

Intrinsic Viscosities of 11s Sols and Gels

Because the 7%, 11s gels showed significantly higher viscosities than the corresponding sols, their dilute solution viscosities were determined in order to gain more information on molecular size and solute–solvent interactions (Fig. 3). The linear portion of the dilute

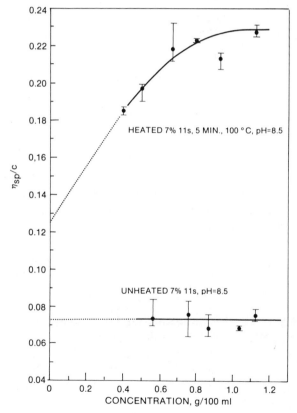

Fig. 3. Dilute solution viscosity data of 7% 11s sol and gel formed by heating for 5 min. in boiling water.

solution viscosity data can be described by Huggins' equation:

$$(\eta_{sp}/C) = [\eta] + k'[\eta]^2 C \qquad (4)$$

In Eq. (4) $[\eta]$ is the intrinsic viscosity, k' is the interaction coefficient, C is the concentration (g/100 ml), and η_p and η_s indicate the viscosities of the protein dispersion and the solvent, respectively. Figure 3 clearly contrasts the rheological behavior of the sols and gels at low concentrations. First, the slope of the line for the sol is very small suggesting that there is very little interaction between the protein fraction molecules. In this respect it is of interest to note that similar dilute solution behavior was reported for charged polymers in glucose syrup.[8] In contrast, the dilute solution viscosity data for the gel have a positive slope indicating hydrodynamic interaction between pairs of molecules and intermolecular attraction.

For the linear region of the gel data, k' is 9·06 and this high value of interaction coefficient suggests dense spherical and strongly interacting molecules.

The intrinsic viscosity of the 11s sol is about 0·073 and is higher but in reasonable agreement with the value of 0·057 reported[7] for a 11s dispersion at pH 7·6; it is also higher than the value 0·0638 reported for 7s fraction at pH 7·6.[9] It is emphasized that the data shown in Fig. 3 are based on 4–6 viscosity determinations at each concentration and that, as shown, one can expect scatter in the measured magnitudes of viscosity. In addition, the method of preparation of the protein influences its molecular size. For these reasons, it is suggested that the range of magnitudes of intrinsic viscosity reported by Diep *et al.*[7] and in the present study are in reasonable agreement.

The magnitude of the intrinsic viscosity of the gel is nearly twice that of the corresponding sol; the magnitude of the intrinsic viscosity for the gel is 0·125. This suggests that extensive expansion of the molecule had occurred due to the application of heat.

Kinetics of Sol–Gel Transformation for 11s Protein

One can expect the sol–gel transformation to depend both on the temperature and on the time of heating. Sols of 7% 11s fraction (pH 8·5) were heated at different temperatures (69·5–100 °C) for different lengths of time and their viscosities were determined at 25 °C. The viscosity data are plotted in Fig. 4.

At each temperature, one can fit two linear equations to the time–viscosity data suggesting that the sol–gel process can be de-

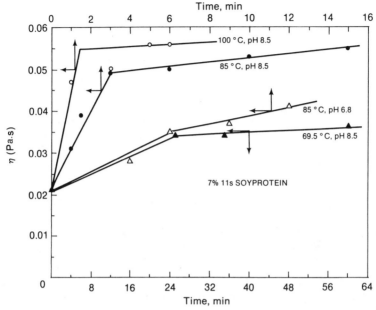

Fig. 4. Kinetic data on viscosities of sols and gels of 7% 11s soy protein.

scribed by two zero order processes. The data in Fig. 4 suggest that the first step is more intensive than the second step. For example, the zero order rate constant of the first stage is $0 \cdot 0243 \, min^{-1}$ at 100 °C and $9 \cdot 615 \times 10^{-4} \, min^{-1}$ at 85 °C. Indeed the first stage represents a plot of specific viscosity of gel with respect to that of the sol, i.e. the intercept at $t = 0$ is the viscosity of the sol. The intercept of the second stage is related to the substrate at the end of the first stage and its magnitude is also dependent on temperature. Further, it appears that the energy of activation of the first step is much higher than that of the second. Limited data do not permit accurate determination of the magnitudes of activation energy, but it is suggested that the magnitude of the former is about 16–20 kcal/mole while that of the latter is of the order of about 8 kcal/mole.

From Fig. 4, it can be seen that the slopes of the two stage process also indicate difference in the sol–gel transformation at different magnitudes of pH. At 85 °C, the zero order reaction rate constant of the first stage is $9 \cdot 5 \times 10^{-3} \, min^{-1}$ at pH 8·5 and it is $2 \cdot 25 \times 10^{-3} \, min^{-1}$ at pH 6·8. The reaction rate constants for the second step are

TABLE III
Effect of pH on sols and gels of 7s soyprotein fraction

Concentration (%)	pH	Heating time[a] (min)	η (Pa.s) or K (Ns^n/m^2) at 20 °C
7	8·5	0	0·038 (η)[b]
7	8·5	5	0·047 (η)
7	5·54	0	0·028 (η)
7	5·54	5	35·4 (K)[b]
			$n = 0·42$

[a] In boiling water at 98 °C.
[b] Values × 10^{-1}.

$4·839 \times 10^{-4}$ min^{-1} and $9·615 \times 10^{-4}$ min^{-1} for pH 8·5 and pH 6·8, respectively. Overall, lowering the pH of the 7% 11s dispersion resulted in a lowering of the gel viscosity. In contrast, drastic lowering of the pH of a 7% 7s dispersion from 8·5 to 5·54 resulted in a significant thickening accompanied by a change to shear-thinning behavior of the gel (Table III). This is due to the proximity to the isoelectric point and the formation of coagulum.

REFERENCES

1. Castimpoolas, N. and Meyer, E. W. Gelation phenomenon of soybean globulins. 1. Protein–protein interactions. *Cereal Chem.* **47:** 559–70, 1970.
2. Castimpoolas, N. and Meyer, E. W. Gelation phenomena of soybean globulins. II. Protein–water miscible solvent interactions. *Cereal Chem.* **48:** 150–167, 1971.
3. Hermansson, A. M. Functional properties of proteins for foods—flow properties. *J. Text. Stud.* **5:** 425–39, 1975.
4. Babajimopolous, M., Damodaran, S., Rizvi, S. S. H. and Kinsella, J. E. Effects of various anions on the rheological and gelling behavior of soy proteins: thermodynamic observations. *J. Agric. Food Chem.* **31:** 1270–5, 1983.
5. Gill, T. A. and Tung, M. A. Thermally induced gelation of the 12s rapeseed glycoprotein. *J. Food Sci.* **43:** 1481–5, 1978.
6. Gill, T. A. and Tung, M. A. Chemistry and ultrastructure of a major aleurone protein of rapeseed meal. *Cereal Chem.* **55:** 180–8, 1978.
7. Diep, O., Boulet, M. and Castaigne, F. Effect of extreme pH and salt concentration on intrinsic viscosity and Huggins' constant (k') of 7s and 11s soybean globulins. *Can. Inst. Food Sci. Technol. J.* **15:** 316–18, 1982.
8. Elfak, A. M., Pass, G. and Phillips, G. O. The viscosity of dilute solutions of κ-carrageenan and sodium carboxymethylcellulose. *J. Sci. Fd Agric.* **29:** 557–62, 1978.
9. Koshiyama, I. Chemical and physical properties of a 7s protein in soybean globulins. *Cereal Chem.* **45:** 394–404, 1968.

6

FACTORS AFFECTING THE RHEOLOGICAL PROPERTIES OF RESTRUCTURED BEEF STEAKS

B. W. BERRY

*Meat Science Laboratory, Agricultural Research Service,
U.S. Department of Agriculture, Beltsville, Maryland 20705, U.S.A.*

ABSTRACT

Numerous separate studies were conducted to assess the effects of various processing and cooking procedures on the rheological properties of restructured beef steaks. Classifying the effects of the processing and cooking procedures on restructured steak texture as major, some, minor or nonsignificant, particle size of meat for restructuring was the only variable classified as having a major effect. Fat and connective tissue levels had some effect on textural properties. Use of different muscles, blade tenderization, pre-rigor pressurization, meat temperature during flaking, use of weights on steaks during cooking and sample temperature during evaluation had minor effects on textural properties. Nonsignificant effects were found for blending times and salt levels. Steaks made from larger flake particles were possessive of more fibrousness, greater hardness but less uniformity of first bite, less complete shearing following two chews and greater amounts of detectable gristle. Increased levels of fat (10, 14, 18, 22%) in steaks resulted in increased detectable connective tissue with a slight reduction in Instron Newton values. Consumers appear capable of detecting planned differences in connective tissue in restructured steaks, but don't always consider steaks with low levels of connective tissue as acceptable.

INTRODUCTION

Steak meat has been and continues to be one of the most consumer desired and thus expensive items from the beef carcass. Unfortunately, only a certain volume of 'high quality' muscles for steaks exist on the carcass. The meat industry in an attempt to increase the volume of steak or steak-type products has utilized processing techniques to 'add value' to lower priced muscles and cuts by processing them into 'restructured' or 'intermediate-value' products. Intermediate value means in this situation that restructured products, because of texture and many other factors, have a value intermediate to other products; for example, between ground beef and intact muscle steak. Decisions have to be made as to whether the product is value-added or intermediate value before rheological (more appropriately, texture, for this product) characteristics of the product can be defined. In other words, is the restructured product to simulate, for example, an intact steak or be a product identified as being different from an intact steak, but with a lower value?

Complete knowledge of the effects of raw material composition, processing and cooking on textural properties of restructured meat products hasn't been available. The studies that are reported herein were conducted by the Meat Science Research Laboratory, U.S.D.A., in an effort to gain a broader understanding of the factors affecting texture in restructured beef steaks.

MATERIALS AND METHODS

Specific variations in product processing, cooking and evaluation will be given in conjunction with the appropriate results. The following are general procedures applicable to most of the studies in this project.

Processing

The boneless meat was reduced in temperature to $-1\,°C$ and flake cut with an Urschel Comitrol (Model 3600). The 2J03750 D head was used in studies where flake size was not being compared. The flaked meat was placed in a Keebler mixer and mixed under vacuum for 8 min with 0.5% NaCl and 0.25% $Na_5P_3O_{10}$. The mixed meat was stuffed into 1.5 ml polyethylene casings using a Vemag stuffer (Model Robot 100 S2). The logs, which weighed between 6.7 and 7.2 kg, were frozen to $-18.6\,°C$ and then tempered to $-3\,°C$ over an 18-h period. The meat logs were pressed in a Bettcher press (Model 70) at 3.4 MPa. Logs were 10.8 cm in diameter after pressing. Steaks (170 g, 1.70 cm thick) were sliced using a Bettcher cleaver (Model 39). Steaks were vacuum packaged and held at $-18.6\,°C$ for 2 weeks before being subjected to textural and other evaluations.

Cooking

Steaks were cooked from the frozen state on Faberware Open Hearth broilers to an internal temperature of $70\,°C$. Steaks were turned after 12 min, after which iron constantan thermocouples were inserted into the geometric center of each steak to monitor temperature. The steaks were then turned, with additional turning being employed to create uniform browning. The steaks were weighed before and after cooking to determine cooking losses. The cooking times to achieve $70\,°C$ were also recorded. Frozen and cooked steak thickness, lengths and widths were recorded. After cooking, steaks were cut and visually scored by two people for internal degree of doneness using photographic standards (8 = very rare, 1 = very well done).

Texture Profile Panel Evaluations

A total of eight panelists comprised the texture profile panel. The various textural properties, procedures and definitions used by the panel for this product are listed in Table I. Intact steaks were presented to the panel immediately after cooking for appraisal of visual characteristics. Where $2.54\,cm^2$ sections were required, they were placed in a foil pouch (with holes to allow steam to escape) and then placed in a covered roaster maintained at $51\,°C$. Panelists used 15-cm long, unstructured lines to mark their scores for the characteristics listed in Table I with a low level or degree of a characteristic marked on the left side of the line. Rulers were used to determine the numerical location of the mark in relation to the 15-cm scale.

Instron Measurements

Steaks were cooked as previously described and subjected to measurement of maximum shear force with an Instron Universal Testing Machine (Model 1122) and a straight edge shear blade. Steaks were sized to be $5.1\,cm$ wide and then each section was sheared six times. Steak thickness was determined before shearing at each of the six shearing sites in each steak so that Newton values could be calculated.

TABLE I
Texture profile panel characteristics, procedures and definitions for restructured beef
steaks

I. Visual
  A. Distortion—Steak is visually evaluated for the degree that the steak has warped
     or changes in configuration from its original raw-frozen shape. Macro distortion
     is degree overall steak has distorted. Micro distortion is the degree to which
     cooked surfaces look uneven or rough
  B. Fibrousness–Steak is cut in half and the cross section is visually evaluated for
     the degree that the sample resembles steak or has no disruption of components
II. Partial compression
  A. Springiness—Place a warm, 2·54 cm² piece in the mouth and, using the molars
     against the cooked surfaces, press lightly five times. Wait 2 s between each
     press. Springiness is the perceived degree and speed with which the sample
     returns to original height and thickness
III. First bite
  Take a warm, 2·54 cm² piece and place it in the mouth in the same manner as for
  partial compression and evaluate for:
  A. Hardness—Amount of force required to bite through sample
  B. Cohesiveness—The degree to which the sample deforms before shearing
  C. Moisture release—Amount of juiciness perceived during the first bite
  D. Uniformity—The degree to which the force needed to shear the sample is
     the same across the bite area
IV. Mastication
  Take a warm, 2·54 cm² sample, make the first incision as for first bite. Then turn the
  two pieces 90° and take a second bite. Evaluate for:
  A. Sample breakdown at two chews—Check the appropriate breakdown
     category(ies). These are identified in Table V
     Continue chewing and evaluate for:
  B. Juiciness—The amount of juice released after seven chews
  C. Size of chewed pieces—The perceived size of clearly separate pieces or pieces
     held together only by connective tissue web. Evaluated after 10 chews
  D. Gristle—The amount of rubbery particles present after 10 chews
  E. Cohesiveness of mass—The degree to which particles stick together. This is
     evaluated at its maximum degree between 10 and 35 chews
  F. Uniformity of mass—Degree to which components of the mass are the same.
     Evaluated after 25 chews
  G. Webbed connective tissue—Amount of connective tissue present just before
     swallowing
  H. Number of chews—Total number of chews to accurately determine the amount
     of webbed connective tissue
  I. Overall gristle—Overall impression of the amount of rubbery particles through-
     out mastication
  J. Overall webbed connective tissue—Amount of firm thread-like connective
     tissue present throughout mastication
V. After-swallow
  A. Tooth pack—Amount of sample remaining in between teeth after swallowing
  B. Mouth coating—Amount of film residue left on mouth surface after swallowing

RESULTS AND DISCUSSION

A summarization is given in Table II of the general effects of processing and cooking variations on textural properties of restructured steaks. Most of the results and discussion will deal with the variables that exerted 'major' or 'some' effect on textural properties.

TABLE II
Effects of processing and cooking variations on overall rheological properties of restructured steaks

Processing, cooking variations	General effects on rheological properties
Flake meat particle sizes	Major
Fat levels	Some
Connective tissue levels	Some
Different muscles	Minor
Blade tenderization of muscles	Minor
Pre-rigor pressurization of muscles	Minor
Meat temperature during flaking	Minor
Final internal cooked temperature	Minor
Use of weights on steaks during cooking to prevent distortion	Minor
Sample temperature during evaluations	Minor
Blending times	None, nonsignificant
Salt levels	None, nonsignificant

Meat Particle Sizes

Variations in meat flake size have been shown in our studies to produce the largest and most consistent differences in textural properties in restructured steaks. Selected data given in Table III illustrate these differences. Generally, steaks manufactured from larger flake sizes (larger Comitrol head size numbers) had more steak surface distortion (micro), greater fibrousness, greater first bite hardness, less first bite uniformity, less complete shearing after two chews, less uniformity of mass and greater amounts of detectable connective tissue than steaks processed from smaller flake sizes (smaller Comitrol head size numbers). To some degree, this was true for Instron data, however, Instron values in steaks processed from muscle flaked with the 1628 head were similar to those processed from the 060 head. The 1628 head produces flake sizes that are 40·6 mm thick in contrast to the 1·5 mm thick pieces derived from the 060 head.

TABLE III
Effects of Comitrol head sizes on selected textural properties of restructured beef steaks

Comitrol head size	1610	1614	1620	1628	750	510	390	270	180	060
Visual[h]										
Micro distortion	6·5[a]	5·5[ab]	4·9[bc]	4·6[bcd]	5·3[ab]	4·0[cde]	4·3[cde]	3·3[de]	3·5[de]	3·9[cde]
Fibrousness	8·5[a]	7·8[ab]	7·5[ab]	6·1[bc]	6·1[bc]	6·7[ab]	6·1[bc]	4·7[c]	4·6[c]	4·4[c]
First bite[h]										
Hardness	10·1[a]	9·4[ab]	9·5[ab]	7·1[ef]	9·0[bc]	8·6[bcd]	7·9[cde]	7·6[def]	7·6[def]	6·6[f]
Uniformity	7·0[e]	10·0[d]	9·7[d]	11·8[bc]	10·0[d]	11·2[c]	11·3[c]	12·6[ab]	12·8[ab]	13·5[a]
Breakdown category[i]										
Complete shearing	0·0	11·1	13·3	28·6	9·1	15·4	32·0	45·8	50·0	75·0
Incomplete chunky separation-threads	37·5	11·1	26·7	3·6	9·1	3·8	16·0	0·0	0·0	0·0
Mastication[h]										
Uniformity of chewed mass	7·6[f]	10·0[de]	9·6[e]	12·0[bc]	9·6[e]	11·1[de]	10·6[de]	12·1[bc]	12·9[ab]	13·8[a]
Overall gristle	5·5[a]	3·9[b]	3·3[bc]	1·1[def]	2·0[cde]	2·3[cd]	2·2[cd]	0·9[ef]	0·1[f]	0·1[f]
Instron values										
Maximum shear force, kg	53·4[a]	23·7[ef]	21·8[f]	18·1[g]	40·1[c]	44·5[b]	33·9[d]	26·8[e]	24·6[ef]	15·0[g]
N/cm²	61·8[a]	27·5[de]	24·2[de]	21·0[e]	43·7[c]	51·2[b]	37·9[c]	28·3[d]	27·2[d]	18·4[e]

[a,b,c,d,e,f,g] Means in the same row bearing different superscripts are significantly ($P < 0.05$) different.

[h] Refer to Table I for definitions of characteristics. All values based on 15-point scale.

[i] Values are percentage frequencies of sample evaluations within Comitrol head sizes that were classified into the breakdown categories.

54

However, the 1628 head has 28 vertical cutting posts which made the width of the flake pieces quite small. These results would indicate that both thickness and width of the flaked meat particles must be considered when determining the impact of meat particle size on texture of restructured meats. In many of the studies conducted at the USDA Meat Science Research Laboratory it was determined that considerable variability existed in restructured steak texture, but that flake meat particle size did influence texture in a consistent manner. One study was conducted to evaluate the effects of flake size using pork rather than beef muscle. Previous studies conducted by the U.S. Army Natick Research and Development Center had shown that salt was not needed to produce acceptable bind in restructured steaks or chops manufactured from pork. Thus the data in Table IV from our studies does not include salt in the manufacturing procedures. The range in flake size was the same as for the beef steaks (Table III) although not as many textural properties were affected by flake size. Fibrousness, first bite uniformity, and gristle values according to flake size were very similar between the beef and pork steaks. Instron values obtained for pork manufactured using 1610 flaked pieces were much lower than steaks manufactured from beef using this Comitrol head.

TABLE IV

Effects of Comitrol head sizes on selected textural properties of restructured pork steaks

Property	Comitrol head size				
	1610	*1620*	*750*	*510*	*060*
Texture profile panel values					
Fibrousness[e]	7·6[ab]	8·6[a]	6·5[b]	6·4[b]	3·7[c]
First bite uniformity[e]	6·9[a]	9·8[b]	11·7[cd]	10·9[bc]	13·1[d]
Cohesiveness of mass[e]	10·0[a]	9·3[ab]	7·4[bc]	6·6[c]	5·8[c]
Gristle[e]	5·4[a]	2·7[b]	2·3[c]	1·2[c]	0·1[d]
Instron values					
Shear force, kg	22·5[a]	19·6[b]	17·6[c]	19·0[b]	10·0[d]
Newtons	19·5[a]	27·0[a]	23·8[b]	23·4[b]	13·9[c]

[a,b,c,d] Means in the same row bearing different superscripts are significantly ($P < 0.06$) different.
[e] Refer to Table I for definitions of characteristics. All values based on a 15-point scale.

B. W. Berry

The effects of restructuring method on texture profile characteristics of restructured steaks made from pre-rigor pressurized beef are given in Table V. Chunking and forming produced more macro and micro distortion in cooked steaks than did flaking and forming. As expected, chunked and formed steaks were rated as more fibrous than flaked and formed steaks. During first bite with incisors, greater hardness and cohesiveness, but less uniformity, was found for samples from chunked and formed steaks than for flaked and formed steaks. Size of chewed pieces, number of chews, gristle and overall gristle were higher in the chunked and formed steaks compared to the flaked and formed steaks. One of the differences between the two products, was the high frequency that panelists classified chunked and formed steaks as having incomplete chunky separation with either threads or crust, compared to flaked and formed steaks. It might be expected that

TABLE V

Effects of restructuring method on texture profile characteristics of restructured steaks

	Restructuring method	
Characteristic	*Flaked and formed*	*Chunked and formed*
Visual		
Macro distortion	4·8[b]	5·7[c]
Micro distortion	4·8[b]	6·1[c]
Fibrousness	5·9[b]	8·3[c]
Partial compression[a]		
Springiness	8·1[b]	9·2[c]
First bite[a]		
Hardness	7·9[b]	9·2[c]
Cohesiveness	9·0[b]	10·1[c]
Uniformity	10·4[b]	9·8[c]
Mastication[a]		
Size of chewed pieces	9·0[b]	9·8[c]
Gristle	1·7[b]	2·7[c]
Cohesiveness of mass	9·4[b]	10·6[c]
Uniformity of mass	11·0[b]	10·3[c]
Number of chews	52·8[b]	63·1[c]
Overall gristle	2·0[b]	2·8[c]

[a] Refer to Table I for definitions of characteristics. All values based on a 15-point scale.
[b,c] Means in the same row bearing different superscripts are significantly ($P < 0.05$) different.

chunked and formed steaks would first weaken during minimal chewing at the binding sites between the chunks. Shear force and Newton values were affected by a significant ($P < 0.05$) interaction involving restructuring method and NaCl levels used in this study (0·0, 0·25, 0·50). The use of 0·50% NaCl resulted in lower shear force and Newton values for flaked and formed steaks, but higher shear force and Newton values for chunked and formed steaks compared to the other treatments (data not in tabular form). In the case of Newtons, the lower values for flaked and formed steaks containing 0·50% NaCl may be due to the increase in steak thickness following cooking, while the other formulations decreased in steak thickness as a result of cooking.

U.S.D.A. Choice, Yield Grade 2 and 3 square-cut chucks were used to process restructured beef steaks to contain either 10, 14, 18 or 22% fat (Table VI). Texture profile panel visual scores and actual physical measurements after cooking revealed greater distortion in steaks containing higher fat levels. Steaks processed to have 18 and 22% fat had higher juiciness, moisture release and mouth-coating values than steaks processed to have 10 and 14% fat. Restructured steaks manufactured to have 22% fat (highest level) were rated as having more gristle and webbed tissue; an indication that trimming to reduce fat may also reduce connective tissue. Texture profile panelists found higher levels of fat to produce a more chunky type of sample breakdown after two chews than was the case for lower levels of fat. Instron maximum shear force values did not differ among fat levels. However, shear force values expressed as Newtons (where steak thickness is considered) revealed less force for steaks from formulations with 18 and 22% fat. This illustrates the importance of considering cooked steak thickness (which was greater for steaks with 18 and 22% fat) as well as standardized width when making shear force determinations.

Using different intensities of trimming for tendons and heavy deposits of connective tissue, restructured beef steaks were manufactured to have either extra high, high or low levels of connective tissue. Steaks were subjected to consumer response studies involving 500 consumers in addition to texture profile, Instron and cooking evaluations. Relatively few of the texture profile characteristics were affected by connective tissue levels (Table VII). Gristle amount both at 10 chews and overall was rated higher for steaks with extra high levels of connective tissue compared to the other two formulations. Instron

TABLE VI

Effects of fat level on selected visual, first bite and mastication textural characteristics and cooking and Instron values of restructured beef steaks

Characteristic	10	14	18	22	Contrast[b]
Visual[a]					
Distortion	4·0	4·1	5·8	5·2	L ($P<0.002$)
Fibrousness	6·9	6·3	6·2	7·8	Q ($P<0.002$)
First Bite[a]					
Moisture release	6·0	5·5	7·1	7·5	L ($P<0.002$)
Uniformity	10·7	11·0	10·0	9·2	L ($P<0.004$)
Mastication[a]					
Juiciness	6·5	6·4	7·9	8·5	L ($P<0.0001$)
Gristle	3·6	3·2	2·7	5·4	Q ($P<0.001$)
Webbed tissue	3·6	4·7	3·8	6·5	L ($P<0.006$)
Number of chews	51·0	58·0	57·9	64·1	L ($P<0.001$)
Cooking, Instron values					
Degree of doneness score[c]	3·5	3·0	2·8	3·0	L ($P<0.01$)
Change (increase or decrease) in steak thickness from raw to cooked, %	1·18	−2·32	5·46	3·13	
Change (increase or decrease) in steak diameter from raw to cooked, %	−13·2	−13·8	−14·7	−19·8	L ($P<0.002$)
Instron maximum shear force, kg	18·6	18·5	16·1	17·3	
Instron, N/cm^2	21·5	22·6	17·1	19·5	L ($P<0.002$)

[a] Refer to Table I for definitions of characteristics. All values based on a 15-point scale.
[b] Significance level of orthogonal contrasts. L = linear, Q = quadratic.
[c] Degree of doneness based on an 8 point photographic scale where 1 = very well done and 8 = very rare.

TABLE VII

Effects of connective tissue levels in restructured beef steaks on selected texture profile panel evaluations, cooking properties, Instron values and collagen content

Characteristic	Connective tissue levels		
	Extra high	High	Low
Surface[a]			
Macro distortion	5·8[c]	8·2[b]	6·7[c]
First bite[a]			
Hardness	8·2[b]	6·1[c]	7·1[bc]
Uniformity	9·1[c]	9·9[c]	11·8[b]
Masticatory[c]			
Uniformity of mass	8·1[d]	9·5[cd]	11·9[b]
Number of chews	63·4[b]	43·4[c]	54·7[c]
Gristle—10 chews	5·5[b]	2·9[c]	1·3[c]
Overall gristle	5·8[b]	2·5[c]	1·2[c]
Cooking properties, Instron values			
Cooking loss, %	32·4[b]	27·4[c]	27·6[c]
Cooking time/g, min	0·169[b]	0·168[bc]	0·160[c]
Change in steak thickness from raw to cooked, %	0·81	1·05	−0·52
Change in steak length from raw to cooked, %	−22·3	−22·3	−20·3
Change in steak width from raw to cooked, narrowest section, %	16·8[b]	1·8[c]	−1·9[c]
Change in steak width from raw to cooked, middle section, %	5·5[b]	2·0[bc]	0·5[c]
Change in steak width from raw to cooked, widest section, %	−8·4[c]	−9·8[bc]	−10·5[b]
Instron maximum shear force, kg	22·1[b]	14·6[c]	15·0[b]
Instron, N/cm²	25·8[b]	15·9[c]	16·3[c]
Total collagen values, mg/g wet basis	16·4[b]	12·6[bc]	9·4[c]

[a] Refer to Table I for definitions of characteristics. All values based on a 15-point scale.
[b,c,d] Means in the same row bearing different superscripts are significantly ($P < 0.05$) different.

maximum shear and Newton values were greater for steaks with extra high connective tissue versus those with low levels of connective tissue. Total collagen values were higher in steaks with extra high connective tissue compared to steaks with low amounts of connective tissue, but the differences were not as large as anticipated.

The effects of sex and two age groups on detection of connective tissue in the steaks is presented in Table VIII. Males found more connective tissue than did females in steaks with extra high levels of

TABLE VIII
Effects of sex and age of consumers in detecting which samples had the most connective tissue[a]

Test comparison	Sex		Age, years	
	Males	Females	<40	40 and over
Extra-high	84·0	59·1	80·0	66·7
vs				
high	16·0	40·9	20·0	33·3
Chi-square, probability	3·6,	$P = <0.06$	1·0,	$P = <0.31$
High	36·0	52·0	45·8	42·3
vs				
low	64·0	48·0	54·2	57·7
Chi-square, probability	1·3,	$P = <0.25$	0·06,	$P = <0.80$
Extra-high	84·0	80·8	88·0	77·8
vs				
low	16·0	19·2	12·0	22·2
Chi-square, probability	0·09,	$P = <0.76$	0·95,	$P = <0.33$

[a] Values are percentages within either sex or age that indicate which test product was thought to have the greatest amount of gristle. Three different groups of 50 consumers made the three comparisons.

connective tissue compared to steaks with high levels of connective tissue. In comparing the high with the low connective tissue steaks, almost two-thirds of the males felt the steaks manufactured to have low connective tissue had higher detectable connective tissue than steaks processed to have high levels of connective tissue. Regardless of sex or age category, most of the consumers who were asked to compare extra high versus low levels of connective tissue, found the extra high connective tissue steaks possessive of more connective tissue.

In Table IX are responses given by consumers to questions concerning these restructured beef steaks. Over 50% of the consumers evaluating extra high connective tissue steaks found the amount of gristle excessive, while only 13·4% of the consumers felt the gristle amount was excessive in steaks manufactured to have low levels of connective tissue. This provides some indication that consumers can detect created differences in connective tissue in these types of products. Interestingly, 10·2, 20·2 and 30·9% of the consumer responses indicated that steaks with extra high, high and low levels of connective tissue, respectively, were not acceptable. Consumers identified high amounts of gristle as being undesirable in a logical manner

TABLE IX

Consumer response to questions concerning restructured beef steaks made to
have varying levels of connective tissue[a]

Question	Connective tissue level		
	Extra high	High	Low
For beef in this form, was the amount of gristle:			
Excessive?	57·1	38·5	13·4
About right?	40·8	56·2	84·9
Not enough?	2·1	5·3	1·6
Compared to beef you have previously consumed, was the amount of gristle:			
More?	56·4	41·0	14·4
The same?	24·0	26·9	50·6
Less?	19·6	32·0	35·0
In terms of overall acceptability, how would you classify this beef?			
Very acceptable	27·9	18·2	15·9
Just acceptable	61·9	62·5	53·2
Not acceptable	10·2	20·2	30·9
What undesirable characteristics did you find in this beef?			
High amount of gristle	20·7	13·1	9·2
Texture, tough	33·2	24·6	15·0
Dry	5·3	3·4	5·8
Flavor, aroma	21·4	35·4	30·9
Excess fat	11·0	12·7	12·7
Appearance	8·4	10·8	16·4

[a] Values are percentages of response frequencies within connective tissue levels.

and thus, the cause of this response would appear to be in the higher
frequency of undesirable flavor and appearance in steaks with low
levels of connective tissue versus those with extra high levels of
connective tissue. This does not imply that connective tissue plays a
role in flavor enhancement of restructured meats, however, this
flavor–connective tissue relationship may merit further investigation.

Briefly, this paragraph will summarize studies where processing and
cooking variables have exerted minor or nonsignificant effects on
properties of restructured steaks. The use of pre-rigor pressurization
of muscle produced similar textural properties in restructured steaks to
that achieved from post-rigor nonpressurized muscle from the same
carcasses. Thus, when one considers the possible muscle shortening of

the pre-rigor muscle, the pressurization might indeed be improving texture in these products. The use of chuck rather than round muscles from U.S. Choice carcasses has given higher sensory panel tenderness scores, less sensory panel detected connective tissue, with greater collagen solubility as determined by chemical means. The use of blade tenderization of muscle (up to 12 pass-throughs) prior to restructuring has reduced shear values, but not greatly altered other texture measurements. The use of long slow water bath cooking (sealed pouches) to various final cooked temperatures did reduce some variability in shear force values regardless of final temperature, perhaps due to the absence of crust formation. Variations in meat temperature during flaking, blending times, sample temperature during evaluations and methods to prevent steak distortion during cooking were generally ineffective in changing textural properties of restructured steaks.

ACKNOWLEDGEMENTS

The author wishes to acknowledge the financial support and product provided by Mr John Secrist and Mr Joe Smith of the U.S. Army Natick Research and Development Center. The author also wishes to gratefully acknowledge the technical assistance of Marilyn Stanfield and Sue Douglass. This project was a contributing project to Western Regional Research Project W-145. Reference to a brand or firm name does not constitute endorsement by the U.S.D.A.

7

THE RELATIONSHIP OF COMPOSITE CHARACTERISTICS TO RHEOLOGICAL PROPERTIES OF SURIMI SOL AND GEL

C. M. LEE and J. M. KIM

Department of Food Science and Nutrition, University of Rhode Island, Kingston, Rhode Island 02881–0809, U.S.A.

ABSTRACT

The ingredient-dependent flow behavior of sol and textural properties of gel were studied in relation to their composite characteristics. Composite characteristics were varied by dispersing a varying amount of potato starch and/or egg albumin in a surimi sol as well as by altering the physical state of the dispersed phase through heating. The pseudoplastic flow and consistency of composite surimi sols were surimi concentration-dependent. Changes in compression and tensile properties of surimi gels were a function of the level of starch and albumin. Textural properties of the surimi gels (SE) containing both starch and albumin became albumin-dependent as the albumin level increased. From image analysis, the increased gel strength by the addition of potato starch was attributed to increased density of the protein matrix and a formation of elastic starch globules. A maximum composite reinforcing effect of potato starch was achieved at a 6% level with an optimum particle density of starch globules. On the other hand, albumin simply filled in the matrix without exhibiting a composite reinforcing effect due to a lack of its compatibility with myofibrillar proteins of the surimi.

INTRODUCTION

Surimi is mechanically separated fish flesh that has been washed with water and mixed with cryoprotectants for a good frozen shelf-life. It is used as an intermediate product for a variety of fabricated seafoods.

63

Unlike soy protein, owing to its high concentration of myofibrillar protein, surimi produces an elastic and chewy texture which can be made to resemble that of shellfish meat. Surimi-based shellfish analogs are prepared by extruding a surimi paste into various shapes. Subsequent heat-setting produces a firm and elastic gel which can resemble shellfish meat in shape as well as in texture.

In preparation of surimi gels, various ingredients are added to surimi in order to improve texture and freeze–thaw stability, as well as to produce products economically. The textural properties of surimi gel are influenced by the composite characteristics which are determined by the type and level of ingredients as well as the dispersion and physical state of particulate ingredients. Thus the optimization of ingredient-dependent texture can be accomplished by selecting appropriate composite characteristics.

The objective of this study was to determine how composite characteristics influence the rheological properties of both sol and gel, specifically ingredient-dependent flow behavior of sol and textural properties of gel. Potato starch and egg albumin were chosen as main ingredient variables since they appear to be the most effective in modifying texture and freeze–thaw stability. For these reasons, they are being extensively used in the industry, while other ingredients such as lactalbumin and soy protein are being considered as substitutes for egg albumin.[1] Starch and egg albumin participate in gel formation while surimi protein serves as a continuous phase. Both starch and egg albumin are believed to improve the surimi gel texture by rounding off the rubberiness while imparting desirable gel strength and elasticity through a composite reinforcing effect and water binding.[2]

MATERIALS AND METHODS

Ingredients. Potato starch (15% moisture) was obtained from Colby starch (Caribou, Maine), while egg albumin in a spray-dried form (8% moisture) was obtained from Monark Egg Corp. (Kansas City, Missouri).

Preparation of surimi. Surimi was prepared from red hake (Urophycis chuss) caught off Galilee, Rhode Island. Following the procedure described by Lee,[3] preparation of surimi was carried out at the pilot plant equipped with a complete production line which consisted of meat-bone separator (Baader 694), washing tank (500-gallon capacity with a pedal mixer), rotary rinse, screw press (Bibum SR1000) and strainer (Bibum SUM420). Initially, the fish flesh was subjected to 3 washings at a ratio of 1 meat to 4 water (w/w). The strained and dewatered minced meat was mixed with cryoprotectants (4% sorbitol, 4% sugar and 0·2% sodium tripolyphosphate on a minced meat weight basis) in a 40-quart cutter mixer (Hobart VCM40) for 30 s at a low speed setting (1750 rpm), vacuum packed in and frozen stored at $-20\,°C$. The pH, moisture and gel strength of the finished surimi were 6·8, 78% and 937 g for penetration force and 40·6 kg for compressive force, respectively.

Preparation of surimi sol. Half-thawed surimi $(-2\,°C)$ was initially chopped for 30 s, followed by the addition of 2·5% salt and half the water with chopping continued for 2 min. At this point, starch and/or egg albumin and the remaining water were added at varying levels. Chopping was continued for 10 min. The final temperature of the paste was kept below $12\,°C$. Calculated amounts of water were added to adjust the final moisture level of all formulas at 78% in order for the results to consistently reflect the effect of ingredients.

Evaluation of Flow Behavior of Surimi Sol
For the measurement of viscosity, a small portion of the resulting paste was placed in a 150 ml plastic cup without leaving any large air pockets. In less than 2 min after completion of chopping, a measurement was made on a Brookfield digital rheometer at 1, 2·5, 5, 10, 20, 50 and 100 rpm using a spindle (number 7, 3 mm diameter rod) at 20 mm depth. Readings were made from a 1 min span rheogram (torque versus time) by picking a point from which a stable curve started. From the viscosity measurement, flow curve (shear stress versus shear rate), consistency index and flow behavior index were obtained.

Preparation of Surimi Gel for Texture Measurement
For the measurement of tensile force and extension, a portion of the paste was extruded into a thin sheet (1.5 mm thick, 20 mm wide and 70 mm long) and partially heat set at $50\,°C$ for 15 min in an oven. Tensile force was used as an index of elasticity which measures the resistance of an extrudate to breakage due to tensile stress. Tensile extension was used as an index of stretchability to measure the ability

to stretch without breaking. This test is useful for predicting the tensile properties of extrudate during a fabrication process which involves various strenuous stretching and folding steps.

For measurement of textural properties of surimi gels, the remaining paste was stuffed into casings (Nojax cellulose, 30 mm diameter) and cooked immediately in a water bath at 90 °C for 40 min. After cooling in running water, the gel was left overnight to fully equilibrate to room temperature prior to testing on an Instron Testing machine (model 1122). The specimens were prepared by cutting the gel (27 mm diameter) into an exact 25 mm length. The measurement of texture followed the procedures described in Lee.[1]

A compression test was performed at 90% deformation for measurement of both compressive force at failure and expressible fluid. Compressive force was used as an index of cohesiveness of the gel matrix. Penetration force was measured as a resistance of the gel matrix to penetrate using a 8 mm diameter rod at 90% deformation. This test was used as an index of rigidity which is equivalent to the Japanese jelly strength test.[4] Compressive energy was measured by a sum of energy expanded during the second and third compressions at 90% deformation and used as an index of chewiness.

Analysis of Composite Characteristics
Composite characteristics were assessed by examining the microstructure under a light microscope and the dispersion pattern of the particulate ingredients with an image analyzer. Specimens for microstructure analysis were prepared from both uncooked paste and cooked gel following the procedure described in Lee.[2] After being frozen in liquid N_2, 12 μm thick sections were stained in hematoxylin. Color photomicrographs were prepared at 60 and 150 magnifications and used for an image analysis. A Bioquant image analysis system (R & M Biometrics, Nashville, TN) set up on an IBM PC was employed to measure the particle density and mean size of starch granules before and after cooking. The morphological changes in starch granules in the surimi gel, with and without egg albumin, due to gelatinization were closely examined in terms of changes in shape and size. The dispersion of egg albumin could not be examined because the staining technique employed did not differentiate the egg albumin protein from the fish protein.

Analysis of Data

The data were analyzed for the statistical significance and correlation, employing the Statistical Analysis System (SAS Institute Inc., Cary, NC).

RESULTS AND DISCUSSION

Flow Behavior of Surimi Sol

Flow curves of the surimi sols containing potato starch and egg albumin at varying levels are shown in Fig. 1. As the levels of both starch and albumin increased, the surimi sols became less pseudoplastic. This is indicated by a moderation of the flow curve (Fig. 1) as well as by an increased flow behavior index (n) (Table 1). Conversely, the consistency index (K) decreased with increases in the levels of both starch and albumin. When compared at an equal level, starch resulted

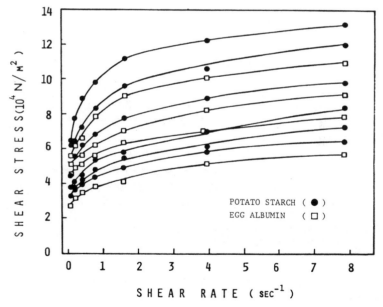

Fig. 1. *Flow curves of surimi sols containing either potato starch or egg albumin at varying levels.*

TABLE I

Behavior of surimi sols containing potato starch and/or egg albumin at varying levels

| S/E | Solid | | $K(10^4)$ | | | n | | |
(S–E)	Surimi	S/E (S–E)	S	E	(SE)	S	E	(SE)
0	22	0	13			0·112		
(2–8)	(16·3)	(1·3–5·5)			(6·6)			(0·12)
3	19·7	2·28/2·55	11·2	10·7		0·147	0·131	
(4–6)	(16·4)	(2·5–4·1)			(6·8)			(0·157)
6	17·8	4·14/4·6	9·2	8·5		0·149	0·149	
(5–5)	(16·4)	(3·2–3·4)			(7·0)			(0·168)
9	16·3	5·67/6·3	7·4	7·1		0·160	0·154	
(6–4)	(16·4)	(3·8–2·7)			(7·4)			(0·144)
12	15·0	6·96/7·7	6·4	5·2		0·175	0·178	
(8–2)	(16·5)	(5·1–1·14)			(7·6)			(0·155)
15	13·9	8·06/–	6·0			0·218		

Correlation between ingredients and rheological parameters.

S/E System:

Surimi Solid: $K = 0·98 X_1 - 7·16 \ (r = 0·99)$

$n = -0·01 X_1 + 0·35 \ (r = -0·93)$

where $X_1 =$ surimi solid.

Starch Solid: $K = -0·92 X_2 + 13·03 \ (r = -0·99)$

$n = 0·01 X_2 + 0·11 \ (r = 0·93)$

where $X_2 =$ starch solid.

Egg Albumin Solid: $K = -0·99 X_3 + 13·12 \ (r = -0·99)$

$Y = -0·008 X_3 + 0·11 \ (r = 0·98)$

where $X_3 =$ egg albumin solid.

S–E System:

Starch Solid: $K = 0·28 X_4 + 6·18 \ (r = 0·97)$

Egg Albumin Solid: $K = -0·26 X_5 + 7·98 \ (r = -0·97)$

where $X_4 =$ starch solid; $X_5 =$ egg albumin solid

* *S/E System*: Surimi sols were prepared with either potato starch or egg albumin.

S–E System: Surimi sols were prepared with both potato starch and egg albumin.

in a higher K than albumin. Overall, there were no significant differences in n between starch and albumin except for the 3% level where the starch-containing sol had a significantly greater n than the egg-albumin containing one ($P < 0·05$).

When both potato starch and egg albumin in varying combinations

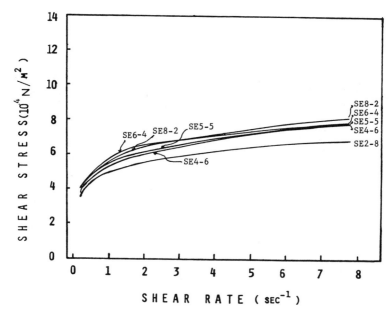

Fig. 2. Flow curves of surimi sols containing both potato starch and egg albumin in varying combinations. (The combined level for all combinations was 10%.)

were incorporated into surimi at a combined level of 10%, their flow curves cluttered together (Fig. 2). Variations in both K and n were nonsignificant ($P < 0.05$) among the different combinations of starch and albumin (SE) (Table I), except for SE5-5 which had the highest n value indicating the least pseudoplastic flow among the combinations studied. Nevertheless, there was a trend whereby K increased with an increase in the ratio of starch to albumin.

As shown in Table I, the flow behavior in terms of n was surimi-dependent. At a constant surimi concentration, as in the case of S–E, there was no discernible pattern of changes in flow behavior affected by starch and albumin. However, K increased with an increase in the level of starch and decreased with an increase in the level of albumin.

Textural Properties

As the level of potato starch increased, both compressive force (cohesiveness) and penetration force (rigidity) increased in a rather

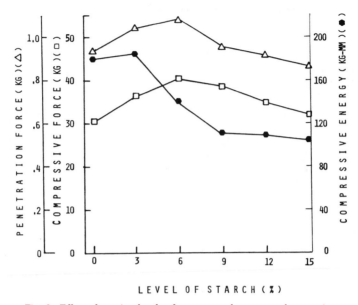

Fig. 3. Effect of varying levels of potato starch on textural properties.

linear fashion up to 6% and then started to decrease (Fig. 3). Up to a 15% level, compressive force of the gel containing starch was higher than one without starch. A similar trend was seen for the penetration force up to the 9% level. On the other hand, compressive energy (chewiness) decreased markedly after the level of starch reached 3%, indicating that the starch-containing gel became significantly less chewy beyond the 3% level ($P < 0.01$).

In contrast to potato starch, addition of egg albumin markedly reduced the values of all textural parameters in a linear fashion as seen in Fig. 4. This result clearly indicates that, unlike starch, albumin does not have a composite reinforcing effect by which gel is strengthened. It appears that albumin reduces gel strength by interfering with the formation of a rigid matrix made up with myofibrillar proteins. Such interference with gel formation by albumin was ascribed to retardation of cross-linking of actomyosin.[5,6]

Tensile force (elasticity) of partially heat-set extrudate decreased with increases in levels of both starch and albumin (Fig. 5). On the other hand, tensile extension (stretchability) changed little with levels of starch, but it increased with an increase in egg albumin up to 6%

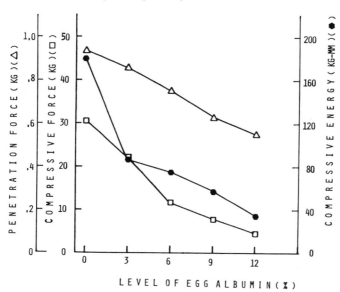

Fig. 4. *Effect of varying levels of egg albumin on textural properties.*

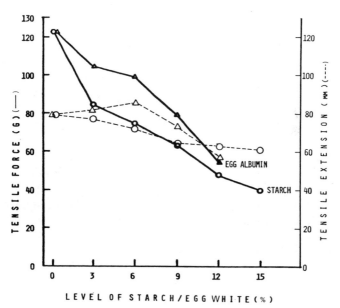

Fig. 5. *Effect of starch and egg albumin on tensile properties of partially heat-set extrudate.*

followed by a sharp drop afterwards. Overall, up to the 9% level of
albumin, both tensile force and extension of the extrudate containing
albumin remained higher than those of the extrudate containing
starch.

As shown in Fig. 6, when both starch and albumin were added
together in varying combinations, with a combined level of 10%, all
values of textural parameters except for chewiness, linearly decreased
with an increase in albumin. Since a constant level of surimi was used
in all formulas, such changes in the values of textural parameters were
clearly due to the effect of albumin. This suggests that (1) albumin
overrides the gel strengthening effect of starch; (2) textural properties
of SE containing surimi gels are albumin-dependent; and (3) no
synergism exists between starch and albumin in texture modification.
This finding was further supported by the results previously depicted in
Fig. 4. The pattern of the decreases in both rigidity and cohesiveness,
with n increase in the level of albumin, was strikingly similar between
the gels prepared with albumin alone and the gels with albumin and

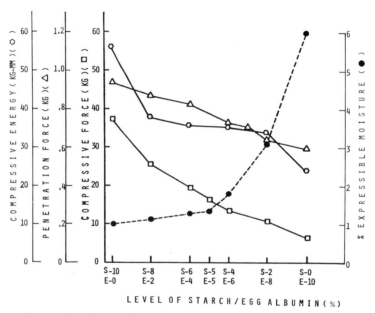

Fig. 6. The combined effect of potato starch and egg albumin on textural properties and
expressible moisture. (The combined level for all combinations was 10%.)

starch. To minimize the gel weakening effect of albumin which takes place at high levels, in current commercial practice it is recommended that egg albumin be added at a level less than 2% in a dry form or 17% in a raw egg white form (12% solid) on a surimi weight basis.

A decrease in gel strength with albumin was accompanied by an increase in the amount of expressible moisture. Figure 6 shows that the amount of expressible moisture increased with the addition of up to a 5% level of albumin in combination with starch. However, beyond the 5% level, there was a substantial increase in the amount of expressible moisture, indicating a marked decrease in the ability of the matrix to hold the water under the compression applied. Such a decrease in the water-binding ability of the matrix would make the gel less freeze–thaw stable.

When egg albumin was added with potato starch at a 10% combined level, the tensile force of the partially heat-set extrudate increased only up to the 5% level (Fig. 7). Tensile extension increased up to the

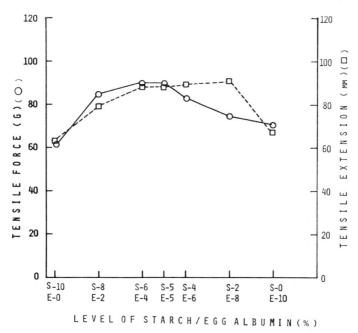

Fig. 7. The combined effect of potato starch and egg albumin on tensile properties of partially heat-set extrudate.

4% level and then leveled off. When the level reached 8%, there was a marked decrease. It is interesting to note that tensile force values of the S–E extrudates were approximately the mean of those of extrudates made with albumin and starch. Conversely, tensile extension did not follow the same pattern of tensile force. Instead, it followed the level of albumin, indicating that tensile extension was albumin-dependent.

Microstructure Analysis
According to the image analysis as shown in Fig. 8, before cooking, the distribution of starch granules was a function of the level of starch added while the size remained unchanged. After cooking, starch granules expanded 35 times as a result of swelling through gelatinization (Figs. 9, 10). A question may be raised as to how such swelling of starch makes the gel more cohesive and firmer as seen previously in Fig. 3. Two possible explanations can be given: one is an increased density of the protein matrix resulting from the transfer of moisture from the matrix to the swelling starch granules; the other one is a formation of a large number of elastic starch globules through

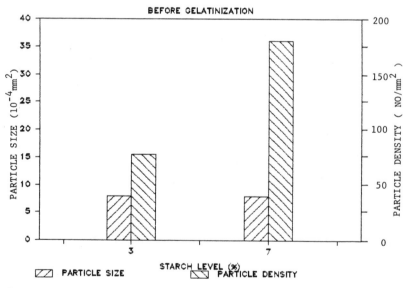

Fig. 8. Image analysis on changes in the distribution of starch granules before cooking as a function of the potato starch level.

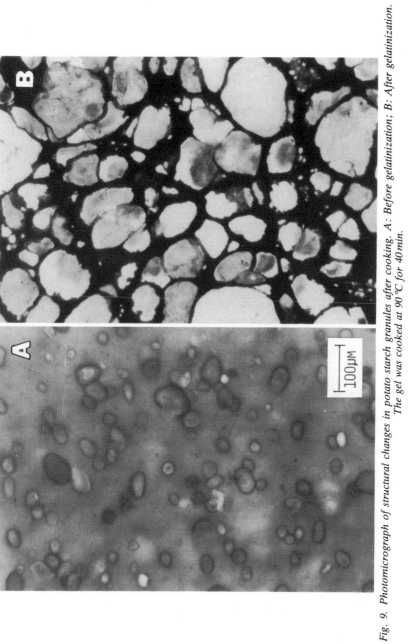

Fig. 9. Photomicrograph of structural changes in potato starch granules after cooking. A: Before gelatinization; B: After gelatinization. The gel was cooked at 90 °C for 40 min.

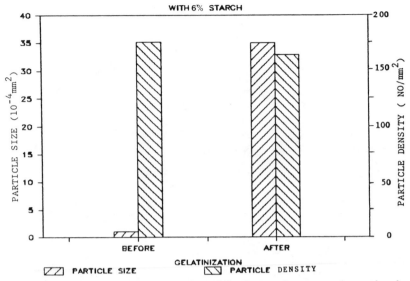

Fig. 10. *Image analysis on changes in size and distribution of potato starch granules after cooking at a 6% level.*

gelatinization. These explanations substantiate a previous report that the swelling of starch granules coincided with an increase in rigidity when starches having different swelling properties were incorporated into surimi gels.[7] In addition to firming of gel through increased density of protein matrix, gelatinized starch globules make the gel firm and elastic by acting as elastic masses within a protein matrix. However, a maximum composite reinforcing effect of starch can not be achieved if the protein matrix is filled with too many starch globules. As previously shown in Fig. 1, a level of starch greater than 9% caused a decrease in gel strength. It is believed that egg albumin simply fills in the matrix without exhibiting a composite effect. It reduces the matrix continuity due to its lack of compatibility with myofibrillar protein of surimi. In setting a gel, the surimi protein produces a highly cohesive and elastic gel, while egg albumin produces a gel lacking cohesiveness and elasticity.

Addition of starch together with egg albumin resulted in smaller size starch globules being present in significantly smaller numbers ($P <$ 0·05) (Fig. 11). The reduction in size and number could have resulted from competition for water between starch granules and egg albumin.

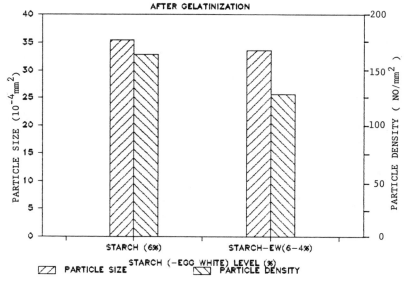

Fig. 11. *Image analysis on comparison in size and distribution of gelatinized potato globules in surimi gels between starch itself and starch–egg albumin combination.*

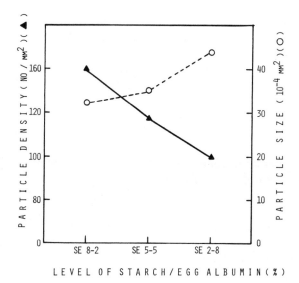

Fig. 12. *Image analysis on size and distribution of potato starch globules in varying combinations of starch and egg albumin.*

Such a competition may have made the water less available to starch. As a consequence, starch granules could not fully swell during gelatinization. Along with the gel weakening effect of egg albumin, such an incomplete swelling may have partly reflected the lower textural strength of the gel containing 6% starch and 4% egg albumin as compared to a gel containing only 6% starch (Figs. 3 and 6, respectively).

The changes in size of starch globules in the presence of egg albumin appeared to be a function of the level of starch (Fig. 12). The size of the starch granules became smaller as the level of starch increased, irrespective of the level of egg albumin. This suggests that the size of starch globules is determined by competition for water not only between starch and egg albumin but also between starch granules themselves.

CONCLUSIONS

1. In order to keep the extent of gel weakening by egg albumin moderate while rendering meaty texture,[2] the ratio of egg albumin to starch should be carefully manipulated.

2. The excessive addition of egg albumin will not only weaken the gel strength, but will also make the gel more prone to the freeze–thaw deterioration.

3. The independent rheological behavior of starch and albumin in the surimi gel supports the absence of synergism between starch and albumin in textural modification.

4. Addition of both starch and egg albumin does not significantly improve the elasticity and stretchability of the partially heat-set extrudate.

5. The composite reinforcing effect of starch varies with the type and level of starch incorporated.

ACKNOWLEDGEMENTS

This work was supported by the Office of Sea Grant, NOAA, U.S. Department of Commerce, under Grant No. NA81AA-D-00073. Rhode Island Agricultural Experiment Station Contribution Number: 2301.

REFERENCES

1. Lee, C. M. Surimi processing: surimi manufacturing and fabrication of surimi-based products. Presented during the symposium, *Structured seafood products* at the 45th IFT Annual Meeting, Atlanta, GA, June 9–12, 1985.
2. Lee, C. M. Microstructure of meat emulsions in relation to fat stabilization. *Food Microstruct.* **4:** 63, 1985.
3. Lee, C. M. Surimi process technology. *Food Technol.* **38**(11): 69, 1984.
4. Tokai Regional Fisheries Research Laboratory. Standard procedures for quality evaluation of frozen surimi. Tokyo, Japan. Jan. 31, 1980.
5. Okada, M. Effect of washing on the jelly forming ability of fish meat. *Bull. Jap. Soc. Sci. Fish* **30:** 25, 1964.
6. Shimizu, Y. and Nishioka, F. Interactions between horse mackerel actomyosin and sarcoplasmic proteins during heat coagulation. *Bull. Jap. Soc. Sci. Fish* **40:** 231, 1974.
7. Wu, M. C., Hamnn, D. D. and Lanier, T. C. Rheological and calorimetric investigations of starch–fish protein systems during thermal processing. *J. Text. Stud.* **16:** 53, 1985.

8

DYNAMIC RHEOLOGICAL BEHAVIOR OF MICROBIAL SUSPENSIONS

T. OOLMAN, E. WALITZA and H. CHMIEL

Fraunhoferinstitut für Grenzflächen und Bioverfahrenstechnik, Nobelstrasse 12, D-7000 Stuttgart, Federal Republic of Germany

ABSTRACT

The steady and dynamic rheological behaviors of Streptomyces broths has been measured and modelled. The rheological behavior is highly influenced by the inter- and intrastructuring of the individual microbial pellets, and is therefore strongly dependent on the cell concentration and the magnitude of the induced shear. The fermentation broths are shown to have a viscoelastic behavior very similar to that of aqueous polyacrylamide solutions. Direct correlations between the steady and dynamic rheological behavior have been developed. The influence of viscoelastic properties on transport phenomena in gas-sparged, stirred-tank reactors is discussed.

INTRODUCTION

The rheology of a microbial broth is determined primarily by the concentration and the morphology of the suspended microorganisms. This relationship was investigated for a pellet-morphology *Streptomyces* broth in both steady and transient shear flow. Two structural parameters appear to have a significant effect on the observed rheological behavior: the extent of interparticle structuring at low and intermediate shear rates; and the deformation of individual microbial pellets at high shear rates. These shear induced structural changes are responsible for the flow behavior observed under all conditions investigated in this study. For technical fermentations the rheological behavior is significant in as much as it influences momentum, heat, and mass transfer within the reactor, and thereby influences the productivity of the microbial suspension. The hydrodynamic conditions in a gas-sparged, stirred-tank bioreactor are inherently transient. Therefore the dynamic flow behavior has been given particular attention in this study.

MATERIALS AND METHODS

The microorganism used in this study is a *Streptomyces*. This bacteria produces the antifungal antibiotic Nikkomycin as a resting phase metabolic product and is therefore of great commercial interest. This organism grows in a filamentous morphology, which can be clearly seen in the electron micrograph shown in Fig. 1.

The primary morphological structure of *Streptomyces* is a highly branched filamentous network of bacterial cells with a filament

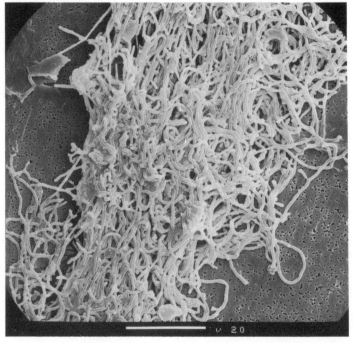

Fig. 1. Electron micrograph of the morphological structure of Streptomyces, *1100×.*

diameter of less than half a micrometre. This primary structure is incorporated into discrete pellets which vary in size from approximately 0·1 to 1·0 mm. This highly structured morphology is responsible for the complex rheological behavior of the cell suspensions, which will be discussed subsequently.

The rheometer chosen for measuring broth rheology is the Rheometrics Fluids Rheometer. A Couette geometry with an internal radius of 24 mm and a gap width of 3 mm was chosen. We reconstructed the outer cylinder of the Couette device out of transparent plexiglass in order to allow observation of large scale structural changes during rheological measurements.

The fermentation broths were grown in shake flasks on a complex medium. The concentration of suspended cells was varied by adding filtrate of previous samples.

RESULTS

The apparent viscosities are shown in Fig. 2 as a function of shear rate. The solid lines are the data for two *Streptomyces* suspensions of

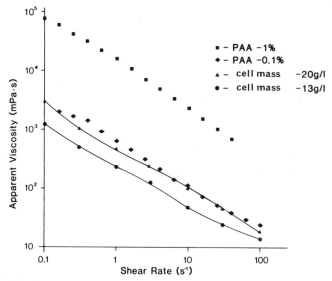

Fig. 2. Apparent viscosity of Streptomyces *suspensions and aqueous polyacrylamide solutions as a function of the steady shear rate.*

differing cell concentrations. The rheological behavior of these fermentation broths is seen to be very pseudoplastic, i.e. shear-thinning. The apparent viscosities of two aqueous solutions of polyacrylamide are also shown here. The data for the microbial suspension are quite similar to that of a 0·1% Polyacrylamide (PAA) solution.

Previous investigators of fermentation broth rheology have measured only this steady, apparent viscosity.[1,2,3] However, mass transfer in multiphase systems occurs under very complex hydrodynamic conditions. Our efforts are directed towards a better understanding of the dynamic rheological behavior, i.e. the complex viscosity, of such suspensions. The definition of the complex viscosity, η^*, is given below for small amplitude oscillations with frequency ω.

$$\tau^* = \eta^* \dot{\gamma}^* \qquad (1)$$

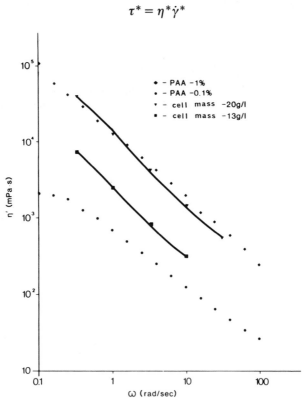

Fig. 3. Viscous component of the dynamic viscosity of Streptomyces suspensions and aqueous polyacrylamide solutions as a function of the dynamic frequency. Shear amplitude is 1%.

Here $\dot{\gamma}^*$ is the induced sinusoidal, oscillatory shear rate and τ^* the observed oscillatory shear stress, both of which could be represented as complex numbers.

$$\dot{\gamma}^* = \dot{\gamma}_0 \exp{(i\omega t)} \tag{2}$$

$$\tau^* = \tau_0 \exp{(i(\omega t + \zeta))} \tag{3}$$

Here $\dot{\gamma}^*$ has the amplitude $\dot{\gamma}_0$ and frequency ω, and τ^* has the amplitude τ_0, frequency ω and phase shift relative to $\dot{\gamma}^*$ of ζ. In the case of a Newtonian fluid the shear stress and shear rate will be in phase ($\zeta = 0$), and the viscosity will be a real number. However, when the fluid exhibits elastic character, the shear stress will be phase shifted with the shear rate, and the viscosity will be a complex number. η^* can be broken into its real and imaginary parts

$$\eta^* = \eta' - i\eta'' \tag{4}$$

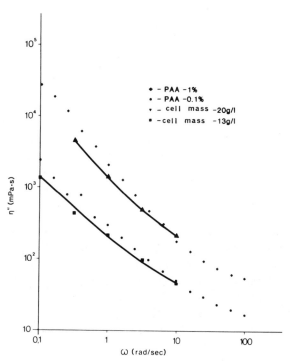

Fig. 4. *Elastic component of the dynamic viscosity of* Streptomyces *suspensions and aqueous polyacrylamide solutions as a function of the dynamic frequency. Shear amplitude is 1%.*

Here η' is the viscous component of the complex viscosity and is measured as the in-phase component of the shear stress. η'' is the elastic component of η^* and is measured as the out-of-phase component of the shear stress. Viscoelastic behavior has the mechanical analog of a dash-pot and spring in series.

In Figs. 3 and 4 the dynamic rheological measurements for the fermentation broths are compared directly with measurements for PAA solutions. The viscous parameter, η', shown in Fig. 3, is similar for a cell suspension with a concentration of 21 g/litre and a 1% PAA solution. Recall that the apparent viscosity of this broth compared more closely to the 0·1% PAA solution. For the elastic parameter, η'', the comparison shown in Fig. 4 is observed. It is seen that the viscoelastic behavior of these broths is quite similar to that of the PAA solutions.

DISCUSSION

In Fig. 5 the steady rheological behavior of the broths is compared with a semi-empirical rheological model. The development of this model will be discussed in a later publication. Two distinct regions of flow behavior can be observed. For low shear rates the rheological behavior is determined by the structuring of the small microbial pellets into large agglomerates. As the shear rate is increased this structuring is disrupted, resulting in a decreased resistance to shear and a decreased apparent viscosity of the fluid. At sufficiently high shear rates the intra-particle structuring will be totally disrupted and a constant apparent viscosity should be approached. However, in this high shear region a second effect must also be considered. Under high shear stresses the pellets will deform significantly from spherical, allowing for the formation of particle sheets which exhibit less resistance to flow and, therefore, a lower apparent viscosity. The shear rate at which this transition occurs is observed in Fig. 5 (for the higher cell concentrations) at a shear rate of approximately 3/s. This transition is adequately characterized in this model by the viscoelastic stress relaxation time, λ. The implications of this model are that even the steady rheological behavior is strongly dependent on the dynamic rheological parameters.

Momentum, heat and mass transfer in an air-sparged, stirred-tank reactor occurs predominantly under transient hydrodynamic condi-

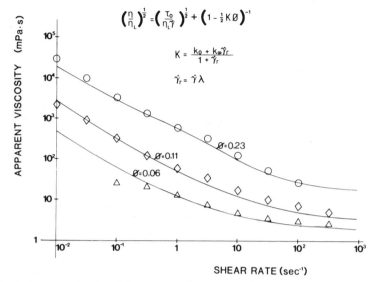

$$\left(\frac{\eta}{\eta_L}\right)^{\frac{1}{2}} = \left(\frac{\tau_0}{\eta_L\dot\gamma}\right)^{\frac{1}{2}} + \left(1 - \tfrac{1}{2}K\emptyset\right)^{-1}$$

$$K = \frac{k_0 + k_\infty\dot\gamma_r}{1 + \dot\gamma_r}$$

$$\dot\gamma_r = \dot\gamma\lambda$$

SHEAR RATE (sec^{-1})

Fig. 5. Apparent viscosity of Streptomyces *suspensions of varying cell concentration as a function of the steady shear rate.* ϕ *is the volumetric cell density. Solid lines represent the semi-empirical model.*

tions. Three phenomena which are particularly important for mass transfer in such a system are: transport in turbulent flow, interfacial mass transfer from sparged air bubbles, and mixing of the bulk liquid phase. All of these phenomema occur under transient hydrodynamic conditions, and therefore will be strongly influenced by the viscoelasticity of the fermentation broth. In the following the application of the observed viscoelastic behavior of a fermentation broth to the modeling of these transport phenomena is discussed.

In Figs. 3 and 4 the strong similarity between the rheological behavior of the *Streptomyces* broths and polyacrylamide solutions has been shown. Transport behavior in polymer solutions has been extensively studied by various investigators. For example, Fig. 6 (Ref. 4) shows the effect of polymer additives on energy dissipation in turbulent flow, the so-called drag reduction effect.

For the polymer solutions the transition to turbulent flow occurs at larger Reynolds numbers and the friction factor in turbulent flow is lower than for Newtonian fluids. The *Streptomyces* suspensions with which we worked should behave similarly to the PAA solutions shown here. By analogy we could predict the reduction of heat and mass

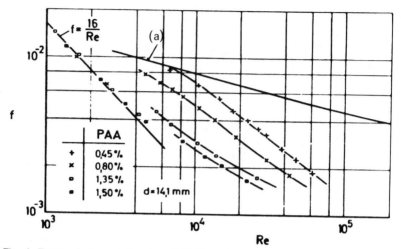

Fig. 6. Friction factor as a function of the Reynolds number for aqueous polyacrylamide solutions of varying concentrations (from Chmiel[4]). (a) Newtonian fluids according to Prandtl.

transfer coefficients in turbulent flow due to the viscoelasticity of the fermentation broth.

Equation (5) gives a typical approach for predicting the Sherwood number, and thus the interfacial mass transfer coefficient, for bubbles in creeping flow.[5,6]

$$\mathrm{Sh} = \frac{k_L d}{D_{AB}} = \sqrt{\frac{2}{\pi}} \left[\int_0^\pi U_\theta \sin^2 \theta \, d\theta \right]^{0.5} \mathrm{Pe}^{0.5} \tag{5}$$

For Newtonian fluids a coefficient of 0·65 is theoretically obtained from this integration. For non-Newtonian fluids an appropriate transient rheological model must be chosen. Our future work will include the development of such a model for viscoelastic fermentation fluids.

Figure 7 shows the effect of viscoelasticity on mixing in a gas-sparged, stirred-tank reactor.[7] Here we see the power number, i.e. the dimensionless energy dissipation rate, presented for three different aqueous polymer solutions: glycerin solutions, which are Newtonian; CMC solutions, which are mildly viscoelastic; and PAA solutions, which are strongly viscoelastic. The abscissa is the Galilei number, which decreases with increasing polymer concentrations. The vis-

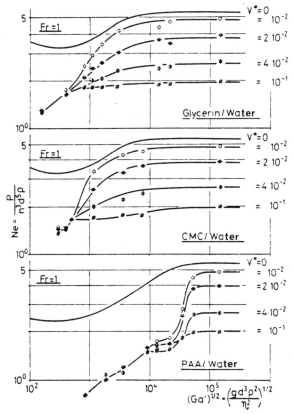

Fig. 7. Power number as a function of Galilei number and gas sparging rate for varying concentrations of three polymer solutions (from Höcker and Langer[7]).

coelasticities of our microbial suspensions are similar to those of the PAA solutions presented on the left hand side of this diagram. For these highly viscoelastic fluids very poor mixing within the gassed reactor is observed in comparison to less elastic fluids of equivalent viscosity. These results indicate that the viscoelasticity of the fermentation broth plays a key roll in determining the appropriate reactor geometry. The importance of selecting the proper model system is also seen here. Several investigators have previously used CMC solutions as model fluids for predicting mixing effects in fermentation broths. Here we can clearly see that such an approach would lead to false conclusions for *Streptomyces* fermentations.

The few examples which have been presented here are not a conclusive study of the effects of viscoelasticity on transport processes in bioreactors. However, it is clear that the viscoelasticity of the broth must be considered for the proper design and operation of biochemical reactors.

ACKNOWLEDGEMENTS

Dr Oolman gratefully acknowledges his receipt of an Alexander von Humboldt fellowship for his work on this project.

REFERENCES

1. Metz, B., Kossen, W. W. F. and van Suijdam, J. C. *Adv. Biochem. Eng.* **2,** Springer-Verlag, 1979.
2. Whittler, R., Matthes, R. and Schuegerl, K. *Eur. J. Appl. Microbiol. Biotechnol.* **18:** 17–23, 1983.
3. Roels, J. A., van den Berg, J. and Voncker, R. M. *Biotechnol. Bioeng.* **16:** 181, 1974.
4. Chmiel, H., Ph.D. Thesis, Rheinisch-Westfaelischen Technischen Hochschule Aachen, July 1971.
5. Baird, M. H. A. and Hamielec, A. E. *Can. J. Chem. Eng.* **50:** 128, 1962.
6. Moo-Young, M. and Hirose, T. *Can. J. Chem. Eng.* **50:** 128, 1972.
7. Höecker, H. and Langer, G. *Rheol. Acta* **16:** 400, 1977.

Part II
Physical and Thermodynamic Properties

9

EFFECTS OF TEMPERATURE AND COMPOSITION ON THE THERMAL PROPERTIES OF FOODS

YOUNGHEE CHOI and MARTIN R. OKOS*

Department of Food Science and Technology, Kyungpok National University, Taegu, Korea

* Agricultural Engineering Department, Purdue University, West Lafayette, Indiana 47907, U.S.A.

ABSTRACT

Thermal properties of pure component solids were determined by the proposed model, which was based on the weight fraction and the thermal properties of major pure components of food products, in a temperature range of -40 to $150\,°C$ from the experimental values of 0%, 10%, 30%, 60% and 95% solid content suspensions. For the frozen foods, the unfrozen water factors were predicted by the projected freezing point depression. The thermal property values predicted by the proposed models from pure major components in this study were within 3·9% error to the literature values of liquid foods and within 4·7% error to the experimental values determined for evaporated milk, orange juice and bratwurst sausage.

NOMENCLATURE

$a_1, a_2, a_3 =$ constants (Table I)
$b_1, b_2, b_3 =$ constants
$c_1, c_2 \quad =$ constants
$C_p \quad\quad =$ heat capacity (kJ/kg K, kJ/kg °C)
$K \quad\quad =$ thermal conductivity (W/m K, W/m °C)
$R \quad\quad =$ gas constant (J/K mol, J/K kg)
$T \quad\quad =$ temperature (K, °C)
$X \quad\quad =$ volume or mass fraction

Greek letters

α = thermal diffusivity (m^2/s)
λ = latent heat of freezing (J/kg or J/mol)
ρ = density (kg/m^3)

Subscripts

i   = component i
w   = water

Superscripts

v   = volume based
w   = mass based

INTRODUCTION

Many researchers have developed mathematical models, which can be used to predict the thermal properties of food products. However, they do not apply to a wide range of temperatures and compositions of food products. When thermal properties are needed for various process conditions the most efficient and practical way to obtain them is by models based on the process conditions. In general, composition, mass density and temperature are the main factors or process conditions affecting thermal properties. Thermal conductivity and thermal diffusivity are affected by composition, density and temperature, while specific heat is affected only by composition and temperature. It is relatively more difficult to determine thermal conductivity and thermal diffusivity than specific heat. General mathematical models to predict the thermal conductivity, thermal diffusivity, density and specific heat of food products based on temperature, composition and structure of food would be valuable for engineers and scientists.

The overall objective of this study is to develop general models to predict the thermal properties of food products based on the weight fractions and the thermal properties of major pure components. The thermal property values predicted by the proposed models will be compared to literature and experimental thermal property data of foods. In order to accomplish the overall objective, it will be necessary:

1. To measure the thermal properties, such as thermal conductivity,

thermal diffusivity, density and specific heat, of major components of food products and the same properties in food products.

2. To determine the effects of ice during freezing processes on the thermal properties of food products.

3. To develop general mathematical models to predict the thermal properties of food products based on the thermal properties of each major component for the temperature range of −40 to 150 °C.

METHODOLOGY

The major food components considered were protein (albumin, casein, whey protein, meat protein and gluten), lipids (milk fat, vegetable oil, lard and corn oil), carbohydrates (dextrose, lactose, sugar and starch), fiber (cellulose and pectin) and salts. A modified probe method was used to measure thermal conductivity and thermal diffusivity of pure component suspensions of each major component of food products for the solids content range of 10–60% in the temperature range of −40 to 150 °C. Density and specific heat of the samples were measured with a volumetric pycnometer and a differential scanning calorimeter, respectively. The experimental values obtained were used to develop general mathematical models with the weight fractions of major components of foods.

For frozen foods thermal conductivity and thermal diffusivity data were collected for the temperature range of −40 to 0 °C by the probe method. The sample was heated up from −40 °C in an ethylene glycol–water (50%/50%) bath at the heating rate of less than 1 °C/min.

In determining density values, since it was difficult to measure the volume of the sample below 0 °C, the density values were indirectly determined after measuring thermal conductivity for two samples with different water content.

In general, the methods or techniques used to measure thermal properties of frozen foods are not different from methods used for unfrozen foods. The uniqueness of frozen food property data is in the interpretation of the results and in assuming that data represent the true properties of the product. With known unfrozen water fraction based on molecular weight at a given temperature during food freezing, the thermal properties of the product can be determined using appropriate model equations and thermal properties of the product solids, ice and water. Therefore, the thermal properties of various frozen foods can be predicted as a function of temperature between $-40\,°C$ and the initial freezing point of the product. Several different approaches and models have been applied to predicting the thermal conductivity of foods as a function of temperature and composition expressed as weight fraction or volume fraction. The weight fraction of each major component of food materials is usually reported and also is an easily measurable factor compared to the volume fraction. In the thermal conductivity model, volume fractions can be estimated in terms of the weight fraction and density of the pure component as shown in Table I.

The thermal conductivity equation of the pure components was assumed to depend on temperature. Both first order and second order terms were considered when developing models. It was found that a linear model is not sufficient for the thermal conductivity of pure components, because the thermal conductivity–temperature data showed that they are not in a linear relationship. Therefore, a quadratic model was used to predict the thermal conductivity of each pure component in this study.

By definition, the density of a sample is determined by dividing the weight by the volume. Therefore, assuming no volume change on

TABLE I
Models used to predict thermal properties of foods

Thermal conductivity $K = \sum K_i X_i^v$

Density $\rho = \dfrac{1}{\sum X_i^w / \rho_i}$

Thermal diffusivity $\alpha = \sum \alpha_i X_i^v$

Specific heat $C_p = \sum C_{p_i} X_i^w$

Unfrozen water fraction $\dfrac{\lambda}{R} \left| \dfrac{1}{T_0} - \dfrac{1}{T_i} \right| = \ln \left| \dfrac{X_w^w / M_w}{X_w^w / M_w + \sum X_i^w / M_i} \right|$,

where $X_i^v = X_i^w / \rho_i / \sum X_i^w / \rho_i$ i = component (protein, lipids, etc.)

$K_i = a_1 + a_2 T + a_3 T^2$ $\rho_i = C_1 + C_2 T$

$\alpha_i = b_1 + b_2 T + b_3 T^2$ $C_{p_i} = d_1 + d_2 T + d_3 T^2$

and

X_i^w is the weight fraction of component i, p_i is the pure component density and X_i^v the estimated volume fraction mixing, the density for all the cases in this study can be represented by a function of weight fractions and densities of the major pure components in food products. After determining from all the models the thermal conductivity, density and specific heat, the thermal diffusivity can be calculated from them. The denominator which is a product of density and specific heat is a factor based on volume. Since both numerator and denominator are based on volume, the thermal diffusivity model was also assumed to be a function of the volume fraction. Thermal diffusivity models of pure components based upon weight fractions were also considered when developing models.

The density, specific heat and thermal diffusivity models of pure components were considered as both linear and quadratic functions of temperature in the range of −40 to 150 °C. It was found that a quadratic model was a better fit for the thermal diffusivity and specific heat data of each pure component. However, the density versus temperature data showed that it was linear.

RESULTS

The thermal property values for pure component suspensions of each major component of food products were measured for solid contents from 0% to 95% and in the temperature range −40 to 150 °C, and the same properties in food product samples. Then, the thermal properties of the pure component solids were determined in the above temperature range from the experimental values of three different solid content suspensions using the selected models.

A study of the effect of temperature on the thermal properties of pure component solids of food products was conducted in the above temperature range. Densities of pure component solids were found to decrease linearly with increase in temperature. For the other thermal properties, however, quadratic models were employed to predict the thermal properties of pure component solids in this study. The properties of pure water are given in Table II.

General mathematical models to predict the thermal properties of food products were developed on the basis of the thermal properties of each pure component and its weight fraction which is an easily measurable factor compared to the volume fraction. For the frozen foods, the unfrozen water fractions at the different temperatures below

TABLE II
Thermal properties for water and ice as a function of temperature

	Temperature functions	Standard error	Standard % error (%)
Water	$K_w = 5\cdot710\,9 \times 10^{-1} + 1\cdot762\,5 \times 10^{-3}T - 6\cdot703\,6 \times 10^{-6}T^2$	0·002 8	0·45
	$\alpha_w = 1\cdot316\,8 \times 10^{-1} + 6\cdot247\,7 \times 10^{-4}T - 2\cdot402\,2 \times 10^{-6}T^2$	$0\cdot002\,2 \times 10^{-6}$	1·44
	$\rho_w = 9\cdot971\,8 \times 10^2 + 3\cdot143\,9 \times 10^{-3}T - 3\cdot757\,4 \times 10^{-3}T^2$	2·104 4	0·22
	$C_{pw1}{}^* = 4\cdot081\,7 - 5\cdot306\,2 \times 10^{-3}T + 9\cdot951\,6 \times 10^{-4}T^2$	0·098 8	2·15
	$C_{pw2}{}^* = 4\cdot176\,2 - 9\cdot086\,4 \times 10^{-5}T + 5\cdot473\,1 \times 10^{-6}T^2$	0·015 9	0·38
Ice	$K_I = 2\cdot219\,6 - 6\cdot248\,9 \times 10^{-3}T + 1\cdot015\,4 \times 10^{-4}T^2$	0·007 9	0·79
	$\alpha_I = 1\cdot175\,6 - 6\cdot083\,3 \times 10^{-3}T + 9\cdot503\,7 \times 10^{-5}T^2$	$0\cdot004\,4 \times 10^{-6}$	0·33
	$\rho_I = 9\cdot168\,9 \times 10^2 - 1\cdot307\,1 \times 10^{-1}T$	0·538 2	0·06
	$C_{pI} = 2\cdot062\,3 + 6\cdot076\,9 \times 10^{-3}T$	0·001 4	0·07

* C_{pw1} = for the temperature range of −40–0 °C.
C_{pw2} = for the temperature range of 0–150 °C.

the initial freezing point were determined from the product freezing point depression using the average molecular weights given in Table III. The thermal property models of each pure component of foods were developed within 5·5% error. For practical use, group models given in Table IV for the thermal properties of major components, such as protein, fat, carbohydrate, fiber and ash, are more applicable than the models of each pure component in predicting the thermal properties of food products, because the weight fractions of these major components in food samples are more conveniently obtainable factors than the weight fractions of each pure component within each

TABLE III
Average molecular weights of pure components used to predict freezing point depression

Components	M.W.	Components	M.W.
Albumin	45 000	Dextrose	180
Whey protein	30 000	Lactose	342
Casein	1 000 000	Sugar	342
Meat protein	350 000	Starch	300 000
Gluten	60 000	Pectin	50 000
Milksalt	158	Cellulose	300 000

TABLE IV
Group models of major components of foods

Thermal property	Major component	Group models temperature function	Standard error	Standard % error (%)
K W/m°C	Protein	$K = 1.7881 \times 10^{-1} + 1.1958 \times 10^{-3}T - 2.7178 \times 10^{-6}T^2$	0.012	5.91
	Fat	$K = 1.8071 \times 10^{-1} - 2.7604 \times 10^{-3}T - 1.7749 \times 10^{-7}T^2$	0.0032	1.95
	Carbohydrate	$K = 2.0141 \times 10^{-1} + 1.3874 \times 10^{-3}T - 4.3312 \times 10^{-6}T^2$	0.0134	5.42
	Fiber	$K = 1.8331 \times 10^{-1} + 1.2497 \times 10^{-3}T - 3.1683 \times 10^{-6}T^2$	0.0127	5.55
	Ash	$K = 3.2962 \times 10^{-1} + 1.4011 \times 10^{-3}T - 2.9069 \times 10^{-6}T^2$	0.0083	2.15
α m²/s	Protein	$\alpha = 6.8714 \times 10^{-2} + 4.7578 \times 10^{-4}T - 1.4646 \times 10^{-6}T^2$	0.0038	4.50
	Fat	$\alpha = 9.8777 \times 10^{-2} - 1.2569 \times 10^{-4}T - 3.8286 \times 10^{-8}T^2$	0.0020	2.15
	Carbohydrate	$\alpha = 8.0842 \times 10^{-2} + 5.3052 \times 10^{-4}T - 2.3218 \times 10^{-6}T^2$	0.0058	5.84
	Fiber	$\alpha = 7.3976 \times 10^{-2} + 5.1902 \times 10^{-4}T - 2.2202 \times 10^{-6}T^2$	0.0026	3.14
	Ash	$\alpha = 1.2461 \times 10^{-1} + 3.7321 \times 10^{-4}T - 1.2244 \times 10^{-6}T^2$	0.0022	1.61
ρ kg/m³	Protein	$\rho = 1.3299 \times 10^3 - 5.1840 \times 10^{-1}T$	39.9501	3.07
	Fat	$\rho = 9.2559 \times 10^2 - 4.1757 \times 10^{-1}T$	4.2554	0.47
	Carbohydrate	$\rho = 1.5991 \times 10^3 - 3.1046 \times 10^{-1}T$	93.1249	5.98
	Fiber	$\rho = 1.3115 \times 10^3 - 3.6589 \times 10^{-1}T$	8.2687	0.64
	Ash	$\rho = 2.4238 \times 10^3 - 2.8063 \times 10^{-1}T$	2.2315	0.09
C_p kJ/kg°C	Protein	$C_p = 2.0082 + 1.2089 \times 10^{-3}T - 1.3129 \times 10^{-6}T^2$	0.1147	5.57
	Fat	$C_p = 1.9842 + 1.4733 \times 10^{-3}T - 4.8008 \times 10^{-6}T^2$	0.0236	1.16
	Carbohydrate	$C_p = 1.5488 + 1.9625 \times 10^{-3}T - 5.9399 \times 10^{-6}T^2$	0.0986	5.96
	Fiber	$C_p = 1.8459 + 1.8306 \times 10^{-3}T - 4.6509 \times 10^{-6}T^2$	0.0293	1.66
	Ash	$C_p = 1.0926 + 1.8896 \times 10^{-3}T - 3.6817 \times 10^{-6}T^2$	0.0296	2.47

TABLE V
Comparison between model and literature values of thermal properties
for liquid foods

Thermal property	No. of data	Standard error	Standard % error (%)
K	300	0·017 2	2·91 (0·31–5·86)
α	115	0·005 3 × 10⁻⁶	3·81 (0·85–6·94)
ρ	165	20·192 4	1·98 (0·18–6·59)
C_p	148	0·117 2	3·21 (0·37–6·72)

group. Therefore, the group models were also developed within 6% error. The thermal property values by the proposed group models of major components were predicted within 3·9% error of the literature values of liquid foods, as shown in Table V and within 4·7% error of the experimental values of the food product samples as shown in Table VI. A comparison of the measured value of thermal conductivity for three foods, with models using pure components is shown in Fig. 1. Similar results were obtained for thermal diffusivity, density and specific heat.

TABLE VI
Comparison between model and experimental values of thermal properties for food
products

Thermal property	Foods	Standard error	Standard % error (%)
K	Evaporated milk	0·028 9	3·52
	Concentrated orange juice	0·022 7	2·94
	Bratwurst sausage	0·029 1	4·54
α	Evaporated milk	0·012 1 × 10⁻⁶	3·59
	Concentrated orange juice	0·008 3 × 10⁻⁶	2·79
	Bratwurst sausage	0·012 3 × 10⁻⁶	4·64
ρ	Evaporated milk	15·172 7	1·45
	Concentrated orange juice	9·373 9	0·80
	Bratwurst sausage	10·684 1	1·06
C_p	Evaporated milk	0·045 6	1·31
	Concentrated orange juice	0·037 2	1·22
	Bratwurst sausage	0·071 8	2·56

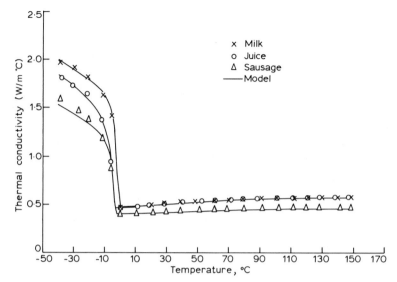

Fig. 1. Thermal conductivity of food product samples.

REFERENCES

1. Baghe-Khandan, M. S. Experimental and mathematical analysis of cooking effects on thermal conductivity of beef. Ph.D. Thesis, Purdue University, W. Lafayette, Indiana, 1978.
2. Choi, Y. Effects of water content and temperature on the thermal properties of tomato juice. M.S.E. Thesis, Purdue University, W. Lafayette, Indiana, 1981.
3. Choi, Y. and Okos, M. R. The thermal properties of tomato juice concentrates. *Trans ASAE* **26**(1): 305–11, 1983.
4. Watt, B. K. and Merrill, A. L. *Composition of Foods.* Agricultural Handbook No. 8. U.S. Depart. of Agriculture, 1975.

10

PULSE METHOD APPLIED TO FOODSTUFFS: THERMAL DIFFUSIVITY DETERMINATION

J. ANDRIEU, E. GONNET and M. LAURENT*

Laboratoire de Génie chimique et alimentaire, Université des Sciences et Techniques du Languedoc, 34060 Montpellier Cedex, France

* Laboratoire de Physique Industrielle, INSA Lyon, 69621 Villeurbanne Cedex, France

ABSTRACT

The pulse method has been applied to measure thermal diffusivity of model food systems (gels: sucrose + water and gelatine + water) and of some foodstuffs at 20 °C. To our knowledge, this method, largely known for inorganic material, has never been used for biological products.

Thermal diffusivity values were obtained from experimental thermograms by a new analysis technique using partial moments (zeroth moment and minus one moment) and an identification function calculated from a monodimensional heat transfer model.

The data agree well with the values given by an independent transient method, namely the hot wire method. As far as gels are concerned, data could be interpreted by the series model giving intrinsic conductivities in agreement with literature values. Repeatability and reproducibility of the method were about 3–4%.

This technique has the main advantage of reducing water migration due to small thermal perturbations in time and space (0·5 °C) and short experimental times (2–3 min).

NOMENCLATURE

a	= thermal diffusivity (m²/s)
$\bar{C}_p, C_{p,i}$	= sample and component i heat capacity respectively (J/kg/m³)

D_k	= constant defined by Eq. (9)
e	= sample thickness (m)
$f(Bi)$, $g(Bi)$	= functions of Biot number
h_1, h_2	= convective and radiative heat transfer coefficients on front face and back face respectively $(W/m^2/K)$
Bi	= Biot number
$F(m_{-1})$ or $F(m^*_{-1})$	= identification function
m_n	= nth order moment (s^{n+1})
m_0	= zeroth order experimental partial moment (s)
m^*_0	= zeroth order theoretical partial moment (no dimension)
m_{-1}	= minus one experimental partial moment (no dimension)
m^*_{-1}	= minus one theoretical partial moment (no dimension)
Q	= pulse energy by unit surface (J/m^2)
t	= time (s)
t^*	= reduced time $t^* = t/\tau_0$
t_α, t_β	= time corresponding to $T_n = \alpha$ and $T_n = \beta$ respectively (s)
t^*_α, t^*_β	= reduced time corresponding to $T^* = \alpha$ and $T^* = \beta$ respectively
T	= temperature change with respect to initial temperature (°C)
T_{max}	= maximum temperature change (°C)
T_n	= experimental reduced temperature $T_n = T/T_{max}$
T_a	= adiabatic temperature $T_a = Q/c_p\rho_g e$ (°C)
T_0	= initial temperature on front face $T_0 = Q/c_p\rho_g\delta$ (°C)
T_r	= theoretical reduced temperature $T_r = T/T_a$
$T_{r,max}$	= theoretical reduced maximum temperature
T^*	= theoretical normalized temperature
x	= abscissa along heat penetration direction (m)
x_i	= mass fraction of component i
X_k	= roots of transcendental Eqs. (7) and (10)

Greek letters

α, β	= partial moments integration boundary
δ	= penetration depth of pulse energy in front face at $t = 0^+$ (m)

ρ_g, ρ_i	= gel and component i density respectively (kg/m^3)
λ_g, λ_i	= gel and intrinsic component i conductivity (W/ m K)
ε_i	= component i volume fraction
τ_0	= time constant defined by $\tau_0 = e^2/a$ (s)

Subscripts

a	= adiabatic
g	= gel
0	= initial
p	= protein
r	= reduced
s	= sucrose
w	= water
1	= front face
2	= rear face

INTRODUCTION

Thermophysical data (heat capacity, transformation enthalpy, thermal conductivity and diffusivity) are basic data in designing and simulating heat treatment processes in food engineering (cooling, heating, drying, freeze drying, etc.). Due to the large diversity of foodstuffs (composition, texture, variety, etc.) accurate and fast techniques are necessary in order to measure those properties.

Consequently, it is not surprising that much work has been done to set up measurement techniques and, on the other hand, to obtain experimental data for different temperatures and compositions. Several literature reviews were published recently[1,2,3,4] and the various correlation formulae compiled and criticized.[5] Nevertheless, many values remain unknown outside the range 20–80 °C or do not agree with each other.

Concerning foodstuffs, in order to limit water migration and evaporation, it seems that transient techniques are most largely used. In these methods, a step thermal perturbation is applied to one face of the sample and the temperature variation is measured as a function of time inside or at the boundary of the material—for example by the hot wire technique experimented by Sweat.[7,8]

Nevertheless, the pulse method, well known for inorganic materials (metals, alloys, plastics, etc.), has never been used, to our knowledge, for foodstuffs or biological products.[9,10,11] Indeed, it has three main advantages:

—short experimental times,
—low thermal perturbation,
—large range of application (temperature, composition).

METHOD DESCRIPTION

Heat Transfer Model

The sample, shaped as a two parallel faced disk of uniform thickness e, is submitted on its front face to an energy pulse during a very short time. The temperature change recorded on the opposite side gives a thermogram from which thermal diffusivity a, can be calculated (Fig. 1).

If we suppose that transfer is unidirectional, the material homogeneous and that thermal properties are independent of temperature, the classical heat balance equation is:

$$\frac{\partial^2 T}{\partial x^2} = \frac{1}{a}\frac{\partial T}{\partial t} \tag{1}$$

where T is the temperature change with respect to initial temperature which is the ambient temperature.

If radiant and convective heat losses on the front and on the rear face are characterized respectively by the equivalent heat transfer coefficients h_1 and h_2, the initial and boundary conditions are written as:

Boundary condition

$$x = 0 \qquad t > 0 \qquad \lambda \frac{dT}{dx} = h_1 T \tag{2}$$

$$x = e \qquad t > 0 \qquad \lambda \frac{dT}{dx} = -h_2 T \tag{3}$$

If an opaque material is submitted to a uniform heat pulse, energy is absorbed on the front face inside a very thin layer of thickness (δ) so

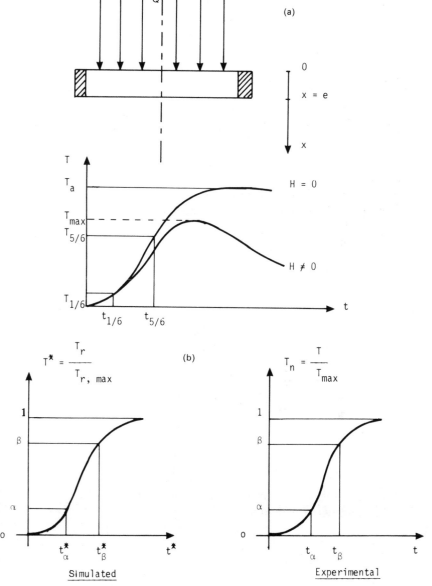

Fig. 1. Pulse method principle. (a) Schema of pulse method; (b) schema of reduced thermograms.

that the initial condition can be written as:

Initial condition

$$t = 0 \qquad 0 < x < \delta \qquad T = T_0 = \frac{Q}{C_p \rho_g \delta} \tag{4}$$

$$\delta < x < e \qquad T = 0$$

(initial temperature is taken as original temperature).

The general solutions of this type of equation system defined by relations (1)–(4) are given in Ozisik[12] and depend on the time constant $\tau_0 = e^2/a$ and on the values of Biot numbers, $Bi_1 = h_1 e/\lambda$ and $Bi_2 = h_2 e/\lambda$. Owing to particular values of these numbers, the analytical solutions are:

(a) $Bi_1 = Bi_2 = 0$ (i.e. no heat losses)

The temperature evolution on the back face ($x = e$), noted $T(e, t)$, is given by:[13]

$$T(e, t) = T_a \left[1 + \sum_{n=1}^{\infty} \cos(n\pi) \exp(-n^2 \pi^2 t^*) \right] \tag{5}$$

where $T_a = Q/C_p \rho_g e$, represents the adiabatic temperature and

$$t^* = t \mid \tau_0 \text{ the reduced time.}$$

(b) $Bi_1 = Bi_2 = Bi$ (i.e. equal losses on each face)

The solution is now given by the relation:

$$T(e, t) = 2T_a \left\{ \sum_{k=1}^{\infty} \frac{X_k \cos X_k + Bi \sin X_k}{X_k + (Bi + 2)\dfrac{Bi}{X_k}} \right\} \exp(-X_k^2 t^*) \tag{6}$$

where X_k are the roots of the transcendental equation:

$$2Bi - (X_k^2 - Bi^2) \frac{\operatorname{tg} X_k}{X_k} = 0 \tag{7}$$

(c) $Bi_1 \neq Bi_2$ (i.e. different losses on each face)

The thermogram equation is:

$$T(e, t) = 2T_a \left\{ \sum_{k=1}^{\infty} (X_k \cos X_k + Bi_1 \sin X_k) \right\} D_k \exp(-X_k^2 t)^* \tag{8}$$

with:

$$D_k = \frac{X_k}{(X_k^2 + Bi_1^2)\left(1 + \dfrac{Bi_2}{X_k^2 + Bi_2^2}\right) + Bi_1} \tag{9}$$

and where X_k are the roots of the transcendental equation:

$$(X_k^2 - Bi_1 Bi_2) \, \text{tg} \, X_k = X_k(Bi_1 + Bi_2) \tag{10}$$

The different methods for calculating thermal diffusivity were compiled and criticized.[9,10] The main difficulty lies in calculation or estimation of heat losses (Bi_1 or Bi_2), the thermogram being sensitive to these parameters (maximum, shape). One of the most general and satisfactory analyses was proposed by Degiovanni[9] in the case of a cylindrical sample (bidirectional transfer). This method is based on the use of experimental and theoretical normalized temperatures.

Theoretical reduced temperature T^* is defined by the relation:

$$T^* = \frac{T_r}{T_{r,max}} \quad \text{with} \quad T_r = \frac{T(e, t)}{T_a}$$

The experimental reduced temperature T_n is given by the relation:

$$T_n = \frac{T}{T_{max}}$$

where T_{max} is the maximum temperature (cf. Fig. 1).

After determination of the points (α, t_α) and (β, t_β) on experimental reduced thermograms (cf. Fig. 1), this author calculates the diffusivity with the relation:

$$a = \frac{e^2}{t_\beta} t_\beta^* \tag{11}$$

where the reduced time t_β^*, characteristic of heat losses, is calculated by the following empirical relation (for example, in the case of arbitrary values $\alpha = 1/2$ and $\beta = 5/6$):

$$t_{5/6}^* = 0{\cdot}954 - 1{\cdot}58\left(\frac{t_{1/2}}{t_{5/6}}\right) + 0{\cdot}558\left(\frac{t_{1/2}}{t_{5/6}}\right)^2 \tag{12}$$

t_α and t_β represent the elapsed time to obtain experimental temperatures respectively equal to αT_{max} and βT_{max}.

Thermogram analysis by method moments
Nevertheless, the main disadvantage of the previous method is that it uses few points to calculate thermal diffusivity.[12]

Furthermore, the moments theory is a general parameter identification method. It has been used by many authors, especially by Andrieu to obtain thermodynamic and kinetic adsorption constants[14,15] and by Degiovanni to calculate thermal diffusivity.[16]

nth order partial moments are defined by the relation:

$$m_n = \int_{t_\alpha}^{t_\beta} t^n T(e, t) \, dt \tag{13}$$

where t_α corresponds to $T_n = \alpha$ and t_β corresponds to $T_n = \beta$.

If $n = 0$, m_0 zeroth moment.

$n = -1$, m_{-1} minus one moment (independent of time scale).

Thermograms simulation shows that normalized curves $T_r = f(t^*)$ only depend on one parameter, that is to say Biot number Bi (cf. Fig. 2), the influence of thickness (e) and diffusivity (a) being included in the reduced time t^*; thus it is necessary to choose two moments in order to identify, from experimental thermograms $T = f(t)$, the values of parameters Bi and τ_0.

Partial moments m_0 and m_{-1} were adopted in order to give more

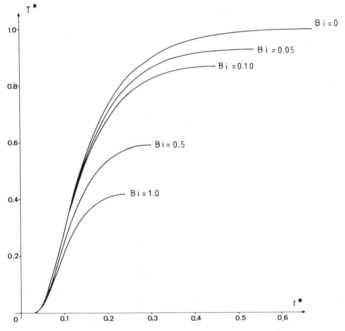

Fig. 2. Reduced thermograms simulation as a function of BIOT number Bi.

weight to short times during which diffusivity influence is preponderant with respect to the influence of heat losses; the following arbitrary values, $\alpha = 1/6$, $\beta = 5/6$, were chosen as boundary for partial moment calculations.

Besides, it must be emphasized that minus one moment which is independent from time unit (no dimension), is the same for experimental and theoretical thermograms.

Normalized theoretical partial moments m_0^* and m_{-1}^* (function of Biot number) are given by the following relations:

$$m_0^* = \int_{t^*_{1/6}}^{t^*_{5/6}} T^* \, dt^* = f(Bi) \tag{14}$$

and

$$m_{-1}^* = \int_{t^*_{1/6}}^{t^*_{5/6}} \frac{T^*}{t^*} \, dt^* = g(Bi) \tag{15}$$

Results obtained by the numerical integration of relations (6), (14) and (15) are gathered in Table I. The elimination of the parameter Bi between (14) and (15) leads to the identification function $m_0^* = F(m_{-1}^*)$ drawn on Fig. 3.

For calculation of theoretical moments m_0^* and m_{-1}^* by numerical analysis with a computer, we observed that it was necessary to have at least 12 terms in the series represented by relation (6) due to the influence of high order terms for short times. So, for each Bi value, the first 12 roots of Eq. (7) were calculated, each of them being located in intervals of amplitude $\pi/12$.

It is worth noting that for this heat transfer model, the use of relations (8) and (9) instead of relations (6) and (7) (unequal losses) does not change the identification function (Fig. 3), so that, for a set of integration boundary values (α, β), this function is unique. The least square fitting by a second order polynomial gives the following relation

TABLE I
Theoretical partial moments for boundary values $\alpha = 1/6$; $\beta = 5/6$

Bi	0	0·05	0·10	0·50	1
m_0^*	0·096	0·08	0·079	0·057	0·045
m_{-1}^*	0·573	0·536	0·525	0·455	0·409

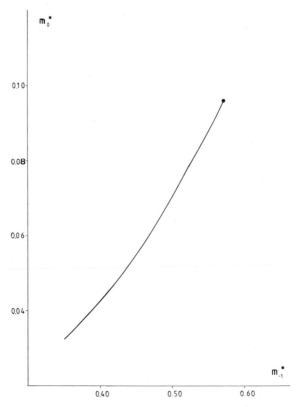

Fig. 3. *Identification function* $m_0^* = F(m_{-1}^*)$.

(equation of curve in Fig. 3):

$$m_0^* = -0\cdot0231 + 0\cdot0527 \cdot m_{-1}^* + 0\cdot270 m_{-1}^{*\,2} \tag{16}$$

with a correlation coefficient $r = 0\cdot9998$.

Reduced partial experimental moments are calculated by the general relation (13), that is to say:

$$m_0 = \int_{t_{1/6}}^{t_{5/6}} T_n \, dt \tag{17}$$

and

$$m_{-1} = \int_{t_{1/6}}^{t_{5/6}} \frac{T_n}{t} \, dt \tag{18}$$

Due to the general relation between moments:

$$m_n^* = \frac{m_n}{\tau_0^{n+1}} \tag{19}$$

we obtain:

$$m_{-1}^* = m_{-1} \tag{19'}$$

and

$$m_0^* = \frac{m_0}{\tau_0} \tag{19''}$$

Combination of (16) and (19″) gives:

$$\tau_0 = \frac{m_0}{m_0^*} = \frac{m_0}{F(m^* - 1)}$$

and finally, introducing (19′)

$$a = \frac{e^2 F(m_{-1}^*)}{m_0} \tag{20}$$

If the uniform thickness of the sample is measured with precision (micrometer), relation (20) gives the thermal diffusivity by calculating both experimental moments m_0 and m_{-1}.

APPARATUS

The apparatus, schematized in Fig. 4, it similar to that used by A. Degiovanni;[9] it is composed of:

—a pulse generator equipped with a flash lamp; this device delivers a radiant energy pulse of about 800 J during 10^{-2} s;
—a temperature detector, consisting of a semiconductor thermo-couple (bismuth telluride, Bi_2Te_3) with high thermoelectric power (360 μV/°C at 20 °C) and very short delay time ($<10^{-4}$ s);
—a potentiometric recorder (0·4 mV full scale).

The measurement cell, placed inside a thermoregulated chamber, has a cylindrical shape (diameter = 30 mm, height = 6 mm); its bottom, made with thin copper sheet ($e \approx 1/10$ mm) has to ensure good mechanical rigidity (uniform thickness) without introducing significant thermal resistance.

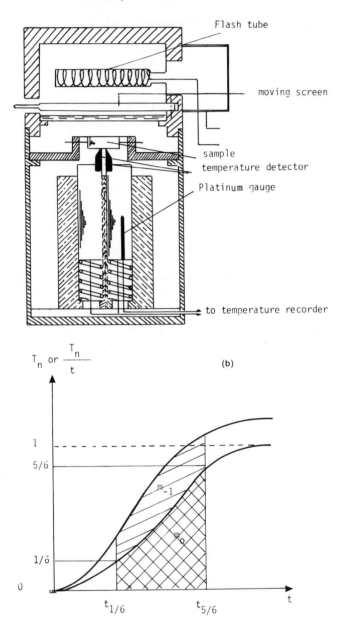

Fig. 4. Apparatus schema. (a) Schema of measurement chamber; (b) schema of partial experimental moments.

This device allows accurate measurements of small temperature changes; all the results given below correspond to temperature changes less than 0·5 °C. The total experimental time is about 2–3 min. Sucrose gels were prepared with distilled water, pure sucrose and agar-agar by heating during 20 min at 100 °C. Gelatine gels were prepared with distilled water and pure gelatine by heating at 60 °C during 1/2 h. For both kinds of gels, mass fraction of water varied between 100% and 60%, measurements being done at 20 °C. Some experiments were also performed at that temperature for a few commercial fruits and vegetables.

RESULTS

Calibration of the apparatus with pure highly viscous liquids (glycerine, polyethylene glycol, etc.) leads to literature values with a mean deviation of 4%. With the same sample (i.e. the same gel preparation in a given cell), the mean repeatability of thermal diffusivity values is about 3%.

This variation can be explained by the accuracy of the elements of the measuring chain (mainly temperature detector) and by errors in thermogram analysis, i.e. in calculation of experimental moments, and in determination of theoretical zeroth moment m_0^* with identification function. Reproducibility of thermal diffusivity values—different samples of the same composition prepared with the same protocol—is about 4%. In order to attenuate variations due to fluctuation in gel texture, data plotted on Figs. 6–9 correspond to mean values obtained from at least four samples of the same composition, two determinations being made for each sample.

The volume fraction ε_i of a component i is calculated from the mass fraction x_i and the densities ρ_i and ρ_g by the relation:

$$\varepsilon_i = \frac{x_i \rho_g}{\rho_i} \qquad (21)$$

Gel densities ρ_g were measured by picnometry. Linear relationships obtained (cf. Fig. 5)—plot $1/\rho_g = f(x_i)$—show that the volumes of the different components are additive and that the gel density is given by:

$$\frac{1}{\rho_g} = \sum_i \frac{x_i}{\rho_i} \qquad (22)$$

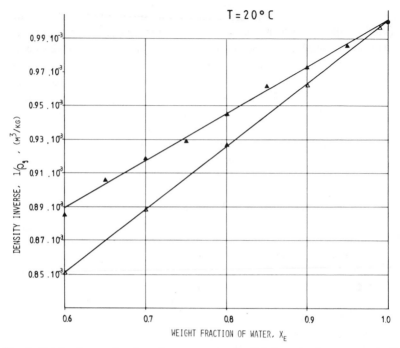

Fig. 5. Gel density as a function of water content. ▲, *Gelatine gels*; △, *sucrose gels*; ●,
pure water.

This relation leads to intrinsic densities for water, sucrose ($\rho_s =$
1600 kg/m^3) and gelatine ($\rho_p = 1380$ kg/m^3) in agreement with literature values, i.e. respectively ($\rho_s = 1550$ kg/m^3) and ($\rho_p = 1380$ kg/m^3).[1]

In order to establish the coherence of our results, thermal conductivities calculated by the relation:

$$\lambda_g = aC_p\rho_g \tag{23}$$

were compared with thermal conductivities experimentally obtained
for the same systems by an independent method which is also a
transient method previously used for foodstuffs, namely the hot wire
method.[7,20]

For application of relation (23) heat capacity was calculated by the
following relation:

$$\bar{C}_p = \sum_i C_{p,i}x_i \tag{24}$$

Gel conductivities were interpreted by the series model; this simple model, already used by Yano *et al.*[18,19] in the case of protein gels, leads to the following relation:

$$\frac{1}{\lambda_g} = \sum_i \frac{\varepsilon_i}{\lambda_i} \qquad (25)$$

and, for example, in the case of binary mixtures (water (w) + sucrose (s)), to

$$\frac{1}{\lambda_g} = \frac{\varepsilon_w}{\lambda_w} + \frac{1 - \varepsilon_w}{\lambda_s} \qquad (25')$$

λ_w and λ_s being respectively water and sucrose intrinsic thermal conductivities.

Sucrose + Water Systems

Thermal diffusivities and conductivities obtained by the pulse method at 20 °C are plotted in Fig. 6 as a function of water content; in Fig. 7,

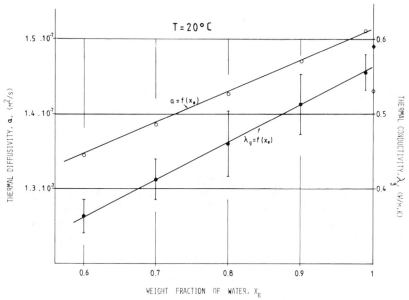

Fig. 6. *Thermal diffusivities and conductivities of sucrose gels as a function of water content by pulse method.* ◆, *Pure water conductivity*; ◇, *pure water diffusivity.*

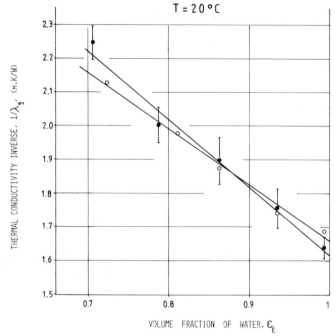

Fig. 7. *Comparison of thermal conductivity data obtained by two transient methods. Series model coordinates.* ●, *Pulse method*; ○, *hot wire probe method.*

these results are compared with thermal conductivities obtained by the hot wire method in the coordinate system indicated by relation (25'). These results can be correlated by the following equation:

$$\frac{1}{\lambda_g} = 3 \cdot 73 - 2 \cdot 11 \varepsilon_w; \quad \text{with} \quad r = 0 \cdot 995 \tag{26}$$

As can be seen, the two independent techniques give coherent results, and, on the other hand, these data can be interpreted by the series model. With the slope and the intercept of the straight line (Fig. 7), we obtain the following intrinsic conductivities $\lambda_w = 0 \cdot 61$ W/m K; $\lambda_s = 0 \cdot 27$ W/m K. These values are in agreement with literature values, i.e. $\lambda_w = 0 \cdot 60$ W/m K and $\lambda_s = 0 \cdot 25$ W/m K.

Gelatine + Water System

At the temperature of 20 °C, data obtained with the pulse method are given in Fig. 8 and comparison with the hot wire probe values is shown

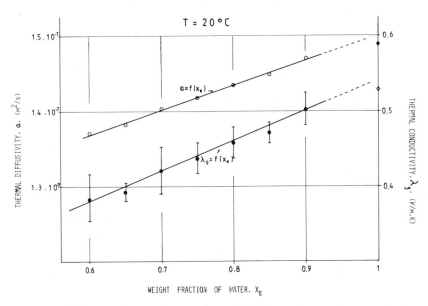

Fig. 8. Thermal diffusivities and conductivities of gelatine gels as a function of water content by pulse method. ◆, Pure water conductivity; ◇, pure water diffusivity.

on Fig. 9. It can be observed again that the inverse of the thermal conductivity increases linearly with water volume fraction and that the two techniques do not give significantly different conductivities. The straight line $1/\lambda_g = f(\varepsilon_w)$ (cf. Fig. 9) can be represented by the relation:

$$\frac{1}{\lambda_g} = 3 \cdot 18 - 1 \cdot 55 \varepsilon_w; \quad \text{with} \quad r = -0 \cdot 996 \tag{27}$$

from which intrinsic conductivities $\lambda_w = 0 \cdot 61$ W/m K and $\lambda_p = 0 \cdot 31$ W/ m K are derived. These values are in accordance with literature values, i.e. $\lambda_e = 0 \cdot 60$ W/m K and $\lambda_p = 0 \cdot 28$ W/m K.[19,21]

A few measurements were done for some commercial fruits and vegetables. The increase of the relative error (7%) in some cases is explained by the difficulty in preparing samples of uniform thickness and by the heterogeneity of the samples (variety, maturity, composition, porosity. . . .). Results are gathered and compared to literature data in Table II.

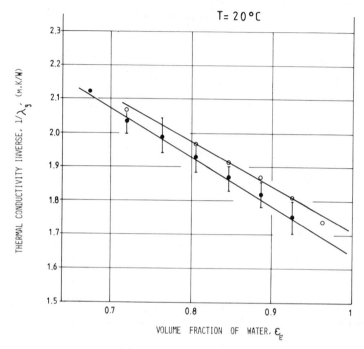

Fig. 9. Comparison of thermal conductivity data obtained by two transient methods. Series model coordinates. ●, Pulse method; ○, hot wire probe method.

This set of data shows that the pulse method is a convenient and accurate method to determine thermal diffusivity of aqueous gels and of some commercial fruits and vegetables. Obtained data are in good agreement with literature values and, also with the values given by the hot wire probe method for the same kind of gels and foodstuffs.

TABLE II
Thermal diffusivities of some fruits and vegetables at 20 °C (m² s)

Product	Banana	Avocado	Cucumber	Carrot	Potato
Literature value[2,7]	$1·42 \times 10^{-7}$	$1·21 \times 10^{-7}$	$1·54 \times 10^{-7}$	$1·55 \times 10^{-7}$	$1·42 \times 10^{-7}$
Hot wire probe	$1·46 \times 10^{-7}$	$1·27 \times 10^{-7}$	$1·39 \times 10^{-7}$	$1·40 \times 10^{-7}$	$1·48 \times 10^{-7}$
Pulse method	$1·37 \times 10^{-7}$	$1·32 \times 10^{-7}$	$1·41 \times 10^{-7}$	$1·55 \times 10^{-7}$	$1·53 \times 10^{-7}$

CONCLUSIONS

The pulse method or 'flash' method is convenient for measuring thermal diffusivity of model food systems (gels) and of fruits and vegetables which can be shaped as slabs of uniform thickness (about 4–10 mm). We applied this method to two types of gels, water + sucrose and gelatine + water and to some fruits and vegetables at 20 °C. Identification of thermal diffusivity by the partial moments method—calculated for the increasing part of the thermogram—proves to be very useful and accurate.

Besides, thermal diffusivity data are coherent with results given by an independent transient technique, namely the hot wire method. Gel thermal conductivities can be interpreted by the series model which gives intrinsic thermal conductivity values, in good agreement with literature values. The main advantages of this method are:

—rapidity and easiness of use (2–3 min);
—low thermal perturbation limited in time and space (maximum temperature change $\Delta T < 0.5\,°C$, which does not influence diffusivity value).

Due to those two advantages, it hinders water migration and evaporation, which is an important problem for biological materials.

—heat capacity $\rho \cdot C_p$ can be determined after calibration with a standard of same dimension and shape;
—application in a large temperature range even in the frozen state.

Nevertheless, samples must be obtained as a uniform thickness slab—so that sample preparation must be done with care—and reliable and sensitive temperature detectors must be employed.

For these reasons, we think that this method, still unknown in food engineering and technology laboratories, should be rapidly introduced for thermal properties determination of foodstuffs like pasta, syrups, gels, etc.

ACKNOWLEDGEMENTS

The authors are grateful to Mr J. P. Caron and Miss E. Michaud for the technical and experimental aid that they received during this work.

REFERENCES

1. Meffert, H. F. Th. *Physical Properties of Foods*, Part 3, *History, aims, results and future of thermophysical properties*. Applied Science, London, 1983, pp. 229–68.
2. Mohsenin, N. N. *Thermal Properties of Food and Agricultural Materials*, Part III, *Thermal conductivity, thermal diffusivity and unit surface conductance*. Gordon and Breach, New York, 1978, pp. 122–97 and 288–398.
3. Woodams, E. E. and Nowrey, J. E. Literature values of thermal conductivities of foods. *Food Technol.* **22:** 150–8, 1968.
4. Qashou, M. S., Vachon, R. I. and Touloukian, Y. S. Thermal conductivity of foods (1972). *ASHRAE Transactions*, 78, Research report n° 2224 RP 62.
5. Ohlsson, T. *Physical Properties of Foods*, Part 3, *The measurement of thermal properties*. Applied Science, London, 1983, pp. 313–30.
6. Mellor, J. D. *Physical Properties of Foods*, Part 3, *Critical evaluation of thermophysical properties of foodstuffs and outline of future developments*. Applied Science, London, 1983, pp. 351–4.
7. Sweat, V. E. Experimental values of thermal conductivity of selected fruits and vegetables. *J. Food Sci.* **39:** 1080–3, 1974.
8. Sweat V. E. and Parmelee, C. E. Measurement of thermal conductivity of dairy products and margarines. *J. Food Proc. Eng.* **2:** 187–97, 1978.
9. Degiovanni, A. Diffusivité et méthode flash. *Revue générale de thermique*, **185:** 417–42, 1977.
10. Degiovanni, A. and Gery, A. Etat actuel des techniques impulsionnelles appliquées à la détermination de la diffusivité thermique. Bulletin national de métrologie, 1975, pp. 5–15.
11. Taylor, R. E. and Maglic, K. D. *Compendium of Thermophysical Property Measurement Methods*, Part 8, *Pulse method for thermal diffusivity measurement*. Plenum Publishing Corporation, New York, 1984, pp. 305–36.
12. Ozisik, M. N. *Heat Conduction*. John Wiley, New York, 1980.
13. Parker, W. J., Jenkins, R. J., Buttler, C. P. and Abbot, J. L. Flash method of determining thermal diffusivity, heat capacity and thermal conductivity. *J. Appl. Phys.* **32:** 1679, 1961.
14. Andrieu, J. and Smith, J. M. Gas–liquid reactions in chromatographic columns. *Chem. Eng. J.* **20:** 211–18.
15. Andrieu, J. and Smith, J. M. Rate parameters for adsorption of CO_2 in beds of carbon particles. *A.I.Ch.E. J.* **26** (6): 944–7, 1980.
16. Degiovanni, A. Thermal diffusivity identification using partial time moment. *9th European Conference on Thermophysical Properties*, 17–21 Sept. 1984, Manchester, U. K.
17. Gonnet, E. Thèse de docteur-ingénieur. Contribution à l'etude des propriétés thermiques des produits alimentaires. Université des Sciences et Techniques du Languedoc, Montpellier, 1986.
18. Yano, T., Kong, Y., Miyawaki, O. and Nakamura, K. The intrinsic thermal conductivity of wet soy protein. *J. Food Sci.* **46:** 1357–61, 1981.
19. Kong, J., Miyawaki, O., Nakamura, K. and Yano, T. The intrinsic thermal conductivity of some wet proteins in relation to their hydrophobicity. *Agr. Biol. Chem.* **46**(3): 783–8, 1982.
20. Miles, C. A., Van Beek G. and Veerkama, C. H. *Physical Properties of Foods*, Part 3, *Calculation of thermal properties of foods*. Applied Science, London, 1983, pp. 269–312.

11

EFFECTIVE THERMAL CONDUCTIVITY PREDICTIONS USING THE PERCOLATION THEORY

M. MATTEA, M. J. URBICAIN and E. ROTSTEIN

Planta Piloto de Ingeniería Química, Úniversidad Nacional del Sur, 12 de Octubre 1842, Bahía Blanca, Argentina 8000

ABSTRACT

A dynamic model based on Voronoi tessellation is used to simulate a vegetable tissue as it undergoes dehydration in a two dimensional domain. This is done starting from a cell and intercellular space distribution which reproduces the structure at full turgor and allowing the pores to expand and the cells to shrink as moisture decreases, subject to the restriction of minimum cell perimeter. Finite element techniques associated with variational principles are then used to evaluate the upper and lower bounds of effective thermal conductivity as a function of moisture content. The predicted values for the case of apples when compared to experimental data, show reasonable agreement.

INTRODUCTION

Thermal conductivity of foodstuffs as a function of water content is a relevant parameter in dehydration analysis. Nevertheless, there is a scarcity of data and most of the published results refer to fresh foods. Rha[1] made an extensive review of data for fresh foods. Sweat[2] showed results for selected fruits and vegetables in a range of moisture contents between 60 and 100% on a wet basis, depending on the product. Lozano *et al.*[3] reported data for apples from full turgor to bone dry moisture content.

The practical need for these data and its scarcity make it valuable to develop predictive equations applicable to the full range of moisture contents. Very few predictive models are available and none takes into consideration the structural changes undergone by the material. In this work a vegetable tissue is considered from the standpoint of its cellular structure and a method to predict its effective thermal conductivity is developed. To do this the tissue is represented by a suitable geometrical pattern which represents the cells and the intercellular air spaces. The porosity increase and the shrinkage of the sample as moisture decreases, are taken into account to make the analysis more realistic.

MATERIALS AND METHODS

The Physical System
The cellular tissue is regarded as a composite chaotic medium, made up of cells and pores. In a simplified picture the cells may be regarded as pockets of aqueous solutions enveloped by a thin wall. The intercellular air spaces, pores, are randomly distributed, in amount and size which varies with the food product being considered.

As dehydration proceeds, the following significant phenomena take place simultaneously. Each cell loses water, decreasing in volume and increasing the concentration of the solutions it contains. The tissue as a whole deforms and shrinks. The voids increase in size and eventually, at low water contents, new pores appear.

Theory. Structural Changes as Dehydration Proceeds
The tissue is represented as a Voronoi tesselation performed on a two dimensional domain representing a transverse cut on a tissue sample. The Voronoi mosaic is obtained by dividing the plane into a finite number of irregular convex polygons. Through a random process some of the polygons are considered cells and the others voids, in such a way that the area fraction of voids equals the initial (full turgor) porosity of the product.

To represent the structural changes that take place as dehydration proceeds, the area of the ith cell $A_{c,i}$ and the bulk tissue area A_b are assumed to depart from the initial values $A_{c,i}^0$ and A_b^0 through the cellular and bulk volume shrinkage coefficients s_c and s_b,[4] which in turn depend on the water content:

$$A_{c,i} = s_c A_{c,i}^0 \tag{1}$$

$$A_b = s_b A_b^0 \tag{2}$$

From Eqs. (1) and (2) and designating as f^0 the cell volume fraction, it follows that the porosity of the sample ε is given by:

$$\varepsilon = 1 - \frac{s_c}{s_b} f^0 \tag{3}$$

The porosity has been related to water content, X, in a previous work:[4]

$$\varepsilon = 1 - \frac{0 \cdot 852 - 0 \cdot 462 \exp(-0 \cdot 66X)}{1 \cdot 54 \exp(-0 \cdot 051X)} \tag{4}$$

To tie this result to the geometrical representation outlined above, the equations above must be related to the coordinates of the polygon's vertices. To do this and to obtain a unique solution an additional condition is specified. This is that the solution for each X value must result in a minimum cellular perimeter S_c, defined as:

$$S_c = \sum_{i=1}^{n_c} S_{c,i} \tag{5}$$

where $S_{c,i}$ is the perimeter of the ith polygon representing the ith cell and n_c the total number of cells considered. The problem is then posed as a minimization one:

$$\text{Find coordinates } x^*, y^* \text{ which minimize } S_c \tag{6}$$

subject to:

$$A_{c,i} - s_c A_{c,i}^0 = 0 \quad \text{for} \quad i = 1, 2, \ldots, n_c \tag{7}$$

$$A_b - s_b A_b^0 = 0 \tag{8}$$

and it is solved using the Lagrange method to obtain x^* and y^* for different moisture contents.

Effective Thermal Conductivity

On the basis of the above model, the effective thermal conductivity, k, was found. For this purpose the definition of Hashin and Strickman[5] was used:

$$k_{\text{eff}} = \frac{\langle k\mathbf{E}^2 \rangle}{\langle \mathbf{E} \rangle^2} = \frac{\langle \mathbf{q} \rangle^2}{\langle \mathbf{q}/k \rangle} \tag{9}$$

where the operator $\langle \ \rangle$ is the area average:

$$\langle \psi \rangle = \frac{1}{A} \int_A \psi \, \mathrm{d}A \tag{10}$$

k is the local thermal conductivity value, $\mathbf{E}$ is the temperature gradient:

$$\mathbf{E} = \nabla T \tag{11}$$

and the energy flux $\mathbf{q}$ is the curl of the vector function $\mathbf{G}$:

$$\mathbf{q} = \nabla \times \mathbf{G} \tag{12}$$

In two dimensions $\mathbf{G}$ may be taken as:

$$\mathbf{G} = \mathbf{e}_3 G(x, y) \tag{13}$$

If T^t and G^t are approximation functions for T and G, it is possible to find upper and lower bounds for k_{eff} using the variational principle associated with Eqs. (11)–(13):

$$\frac{\langle \mathbf{q} \rangle^2}{\langle (\nabla \times \mathbf{G}^t)^2 / k \rangle} < k_{\text{eff}} < \frac{\langle k(\nabla T^t)^2 \rangle}{\langle \mathbf{E} \rangle^2} \tag{14}$$

Equation (14) was evaluated using the finite element method. To do this the domain was divided into triangles, connecting the centroids of each polygon with the polygon vertices. In each triangle a linear approximation to T^t and G^t was used:

$$T^e = N_i T_i + N_j T_j + N_k T_k \tag{15}$$

$$G^e = N_i G_i + N_j G_j + N_k G_k \tag{16}$$

where i, j, k are the nodes defining the eth element and N_i, N_j, N_k are the corresponding interpolation functions. The node values T_m, G_m for $m = i, j, k$ are the unknowns to be found and they must be such that the functions $I(T)$ and $I(G)$:

$$I(T) = \langle k(\nabla T^t)^2 \rangle \tag{17}$$

$$I(G) = \left\langle \frac{\nabla \times \mathbf{G}^t}{k} \right\rangle \tag{18}$$

are minimized.

The boundary conditions corresponding to G and T are sketched in Fig. 1.

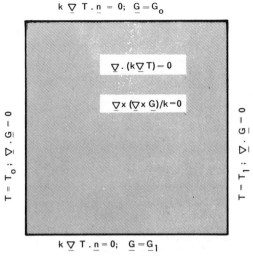

Fig. 1. Boundary conditions.

Food, Cell and Void Conductivities

To test the theory, the experimental effective thermal conductivity of apples reported earlier[3] was compared with values predicted with the above procedure. This requires, to make the method fully predictive, the specification of the local values of the thermal conductivities of cells k_c, and pores, k_p. For the former it was assumed that the thermal conductivity of a glucose solution, Eq. (19), was a reasonable approximation[6] and for the latter the value for air was used:

$$k_c = 0{\cdot}602 - \frac{0{\cdot}242}{0{\cdot}76 + X} \quad \text{W/mK} \tag{19}$$

$$k_p = 0{\cdot}026 \quad \text{W/mK} \tag{20}$$

A computer program was written to simulate and graph the behavior of the tissue and calculate the effective thermal conductivity, with the methods described above.

RESULTS

Figures 2–4 are computer graphics illustrating the simulated fruit tissue as dehydration proceeds. Figure 2 corresponds to the fresh

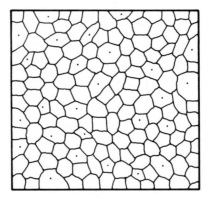

Fig. 2. Voronoi representation at full turgor ($X = 7\cdot3$).

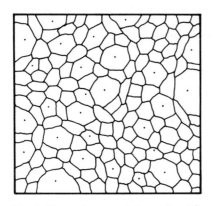

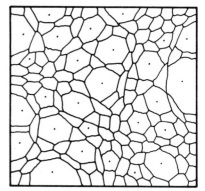

Fig. 3. Voronoi representation at $X = 4\cdot3$.   _Fig. 4. Voronoi representation at $X = 1\cdot5$._

tissue, $X = 7\cdot3$, where the crosses identify voids and the other polygons are cells. Figures 3 and 4 correspond to $X = 4\cdot3$ and $X = 1\cdot5$, respectively. Voids, or cells, can be followed as they change in size and position as X decreases. Notice that Fig. 2 shows the initial size of the sample. Figures 3 and 4 correspond to samples which have shrunk and then have been returned to the original scale to facilitate comparison.

Figure 5 gives $k_{\text{eff}}/k_{\text{w}}$ as a function of moisture content, k_{w} being the thermal conductivity of liquid water at 20 °C. Both predicted and experimental[3] results are shown.

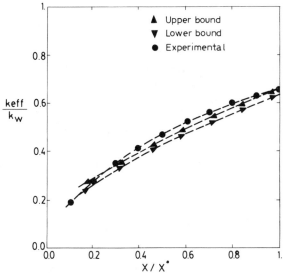

Fig. 5. Predicted and experimental effective thermal conductivity of Granny Smith apples.

DISCUSSION

The results presented are part of an effort to tie the modeling of physical properties and processes to what actually happens to the food tissue under consideration. Earlier attempts based on starting from full polygons representing cells from which the pores were formed by 'emptying' cells at random, resulted in poor simulations. A better approach is the process described above, where the cells and inter-cellular spaces are distributed at random simulating the porosity of the full turgor structure and then dynamically simulating the changes as X decreases, with the restriction of minimum cellular perimeter.[7] The physical picture thus obtained is more realistic, as illustrated in Figs. 2–4.

The idea of minimizing the perimeter results from the fact that each cell is subject to internal pressure and it should tend to aggregate into a shape that would minimize the surface area. In a two-dimensional domain, this is equivalent to a perimeter minimization.

The predicted values (Fig. 5), are reasonably close to the ex-perimental data. The underpredictions are at worst between 4 and 8%, a result usually within tolerance for practical purposes and improvable by using a more detailed description of the cell contents.

The method is admittedly heavy in its mathematic and computational content but, once it has been implemented, it presents a tool which should be useful for the application illustrated as well as in the general area of processing cellular tissues.

ACKNOWLEDGEMENTS

The financial aid of CONICET (Consejo Nacional de Investigaciones Científicas y Técnicas, Argentina) is gratefully acknowledged.

REFERENCES

1. Rha, C. K. Thermal properties of food materials. In *Theory, Determination and Control of Physical Properties of Food Materials*. D. Reidel, Dordrecht, Holland-Boston, 1975.
2. Sweat, V. E. Experimental values of thermal conductivity of selected fruits and vegetables. *J. Food Sci.* **39:** 1080, 1977.
3. Lozano, J. E., Urbicain, M. J. and Rotstein, E. Thermal conductivity of apples as a function of moisture content. *J. Food Sci.* **44:** 198, 1979.
4. Lozano, J. E., Rotstein, E. and Urbicain, M. J. Total porosity and open pore porosity in the drying of fruits. *J. Food Sci.* **45:** 1403, 1980.
5. Hashin, Z. and Strickman, J. A variational approach to the theory of the effective magnetic permeability of multiphase materials. *J. Appl. Phys.* **33:** 3125, 1962.
6. Riedel, L. Warmeleitfähigkeitsmessungen an Zuckerlösungen Fruchtsäften und Milch. *Chem. Ing. Tech.* **21:** 340, 1949.
7. Mattea, M. Prediction of thermal conductivity of foodstuffs. Ph.D. Thesis. Universidad del Sur, Argentina, 1984.

12

EFFECT OF SILICON DIOXIDE ON THE THERMAL CONDUCTIVITY OF LIQUID AND POWDERED FOODS

J. SALEK and R. VILLOTA

Department of Food Science, University of Illinois, Urbana, Illinois 61801, U.S.A.

ABSTRACT

An investigation was carried out to study the effects of silicon dioxide on the thermal conductivity of a variety of food products in their liquid and powder states. Silicon dioxide may be added to liquid systems prior to dehydration or to the final powder products to act as a conditioner (improving flowability), as an antiagglomerant and as an anti-caking agent. Flow and handling of fine powders present difficulties in most cases because of their tendency to bridge, clog ducts and plug machines. Operations that would highly benefit from the addition of silicon dioxide include for instance, spray drying, fluidization, transport within a processing plant and metering for packaging. Hence, this additive will facilitate continuous processing. The addition of silicon dioxide, however, may also contribute to the alteration of thermal properties of the materials to which it is incorporated resulting in process behavior modification. Taking into consideration all of these factors, representative powdered model systems such as corn starch, corn meal, granulated and powdered sugar and skim milk, all mixed with silicon dioxide at different levels ranging from 0 to 1·5% (dry basis), were analyzed for changes in thermal conductivity resulting from silica incorporation. Liquid systems corresponding to each powder mixture, each containing 0·3 kg dry solids/kg of solution, were also studied.

Thermal conductivity in powder systems was measured using a concentric cylinder device employing either the steady or the unsteady state method, while measurements in liquid systems were carried out using a thermal conductivity probe according to the design of Sweat.[1]

The presence of silicon dioxide in liquid systems was observed to

131

have a variable effect on thermal conductivity depending upon the medium to which it was added. In those cases where silicon dioxide decreased the thermal conductivity, the formation of a film occurred on the wall of the probe creating a fouling effect, thus limiting the heat transfer from the probe into the food sample. However, in cases where silicon dioxide exhibited a high degree of affinity for the food powder, little difference in thermal conductivity was observed when the powder was reconstituted in water.

On the other hand, the thermal conductivity of powdered food materials was highly improved when an optimum concentration of silicon dioxide was added. It is considered that the observed improvement in thermal conductivity resulting from silica addition is a result of an increase in the effective heat transfer area of the powdered food material and decreased voidage. Since silicon dioxide has a thermal conductivity higher than that of air, improved heat transfer would result when silica is present. Our findings clearly point out that a number of thermal processes can benefit from the addition of silicon dioxide, and that the efficiency of silicon dioxide in improving thermal conductivity is primarily seen when systems approach a nearly dried state.

INTRODUCTION

A large number of food products are currently available in the form of powders. Depending on their chemical composition, a series of problems may arise during their manufacturing and storage. Thermoplasticity, hygroscopicity, crystallization of sugar components, static charge buildup and colloidal aggregation are, for instance, characteristics that will affect the quality of these products and will demand more costly processes and operations. These factors in turn will highly affect the thermal conductivity of the food product and thus its performance during processing. The addition of compounds such as silicon dioxide has contributed to obtaining better and more stable products.

It has been reported that the presence of small solid particles such as silicon dioxide prevent the interlocking of bigger particles by reducing their minimum fluidization velocity, their slugging and channeling during fluidization, and their clumping and caking during storage. However, the presence of such conditioners also changes the physical and chemical properties of the food material.

Mohsenin[3] underlined the dependency of heat conductivity on cellular structure, density, and moisture of food material. These parameters would have a greater effect on thermal conductivity than the temperature. Therefore, the temperature at which the measurement of thermal properties is carried out must be such that it would not change the physical and chemical characteristics of the food sample.

It is expected that the presence of silicon dioxide will have a marked effect on the bulk properties of food powders including their compressibility and surface area properties, since the small silicon dioxide particles will fill the void space between large host particles.[4]

The behavior of glidants has been explained for the specific case of salt by Peleg and Hollenback.[5] Silicon dioxide in such a system may play three possible roles, namely: (1) interruption of liquid binding, (2) lubrication, and (3) competition for adsorbed water.

Since when weak liquid bridges exist, a severe caking problem results as in the case with granular salt, the interruption of such bridges caused by the presence of insoluble conditioner particles (SiO_2) at the host particle surface results in a significant improvement of the powder's flowability. Furthermore, SiO_2 particles can act as a lubricant by either creating a smoother surface or by acting as minirollers placed between salt particles. Finally, SiO_2 may compete with salt for the available water, thus reducing the salt hygroscopicity.

The effectiveness of glidants will highly depend upon the type of interaction between the components in the mixture. Usually there is an optimum proportion for each mixture. Gold *et al.*[6] found that smaller amounts of conditioner, finer than the host particle, were needed for maximum flow. Above this optimum concentration the glidant will have either no effect or a negative effect on the physical characteristics of the powder. Several studies on this effect have been reported in the literature.[7,8]

Silicon dioxide may form an 'ordered mixture' when there is a high degree of affinity for the surface of the food powder.[5] When SiO_2 is added in excess or it does not interact with the powdered food, this compound may be found randomly distributed in the bulk and a 'random mixture' is formed.

Silicon dioxide addition may also contribute to improvement in the thermal conductivity of food products, thus having a secondary role in addition to being a conditioning agent. Therefore, the goal of this investigation was to study the effect of SiO_2 incorporation on the thermal conductivity of food powders. This information would lead to the optimization of processes such as dehydration and to a better formulation of feed materials to be used in thermal operations.

The following equation was used to calculate thermal conductivity in a concentric cylinder apparatus during steady-state conditions:

$$k = Q(\ln (r_2/r_1))/2\pi L(T_2 - T_1) \tag{1}$$

where r_1 and r_2 are the radii at which the temperatures T_1 and T_2 were measured; Q is the amount of heat supplied to the system by the heater; L is the length of the cylinder, and k is the thermal conductivity of the sample.

The thermal conductivity probe developed by Sweat[1] is widely used to measure thermal conductivity of liquid systems in food products with high moisture content. The working equation is as follows:

$$\Delta T = (Q/4\pi k)\Delta \ln \theta \tag{2}$$

where ΔT is the change in temperature detected in the probe; Q is the amount of heat generated in the probe; k is the thermal conductivity of the sample, and θ is the time. The slope of Eq. (2) is related to the thermal conductivity of the sample. The advantages of using this method are the short time required and the negligible temperature change in the food sample.

EXPERIMENTAL DESIGN

In this particular investigation a concentric cylinder model was used, which differs from the one described by Ohja *et al.*[9] in that the heater has been placed in a 1/4″ I.D. copper pipe in such a way that it works also as a thermal conductivity probe similar to the one designed by Sweat.[1] Therefore, it was possible to measure the thermal conductivity of food powders using both methods in the same apparatus and during the same experiment.

Experiments were carried out under steady-state conditions, meaning that the same amount of heat was provided until the temperature of the sample did not change with time, usually occurring after 2–2·5 h. An assumption was made that the food materials tested were *isotropic* or, in other words, that their thermal conductivity was independent of the direction of the heat. Since the length (L) of the tube is large compared with its radius (r), the effect of end temperature was assumed negligible, and, thus, the mean profile temperature at the middle portion $(L/2)$ of the sample holder tube was determined by simply averaging the radial temperatures. Temperatures were monitored by means of copper constantan thermocouples placed at various locations of the apparatus. The positions of the thermocouples used to monitor temperature within the food powder, were selected in such a way that it was possible to measure temperature in the radial direction.

It was also possible to measure the thermal conductivity (k) of food powder systems during the unsteady state period. In both cases, values of k were in good agreement for the food powder systems used in this investigation. For liquid systems, the apparatus used was the thermal conductivity probe developed by Sweat.[1] It is based on a line heat source, the theory of which has been amply discussed in the literature.

Powder materials used as model systems were: corn starch, corn meal, granulated and powdered sugar, and skim milk. The moisture content was set at 0·06 kg of water/kg of dry solids. Each powder was mixed with silicon dioxide (Cab-O-Sil, Cabot Corporation) at different concentrations ranging from 0 to 1·5%. Liquid systems at 0·3 kg of dry solids/kg of solution were prepared from the powder, using the same levels of SiO_2 as above, since previous studies had shown that there is an optimum concentration of SiO_2 which may be added to obtain a maximum effect in controlling flowability of powders and it lay within the range studied.

RESULTS AND DISCUSSION

As previously stated, thermal conductivity measurements for powder systems were carried out by means of concentric cylinders, and Eq. (1) was used to calculate thermal conductivity (k). For liquid systems, Eq. (2) was used. It was not required to determine a time constant, since the probe was calibrated using 0·4% agar solutions with $k = 0·627$ W/m . K and with pure glycerol with $k = 0·284$ W/m . K. Therefore, it was possible to calculate the probe's constant which in turn enabled calculation of the unknown k for each sample.

Liquid Systems
Figure 1 shows the effect of silicon dioxide on different liquid food systems at 0·3 kg of solids/kg of solution. In general, it can be said that

J. Salek and R. Villota

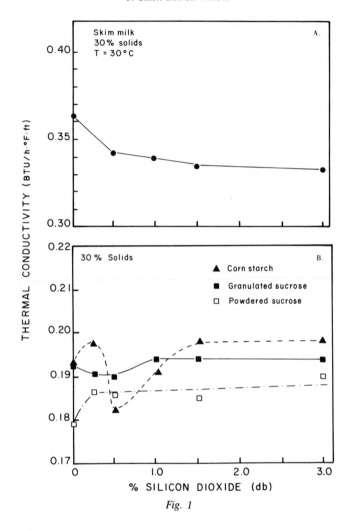

Fig. 1

this effect is highly dependent on the degree of interaction between SiO_2 and the food system. For example, in the specific case of skim milk, SiO_2 slightly decreased the thermal conductivity (Fig. 1A). This behavior may be attributed to silicon dioxide's coating ability; in fact, a film of SiO_2 formed at the surface of the probe, increasing the resistance to the heat flow, and therefore, higher temperatures were registered by the probe. Interestingly, there is a limiting concentration that would produce this effect. Beyond that point, SiO_2 did not show any effect on the thermal conductivity of the skim milk.

Corn starch solutions on the other hand showed a different behavior. The most ideal concentration of SiO_2 was determined to be at the 0·2% level; between 0·5% and 1·0%, thermal conductivity slightly decreased. It should be pointed out that the same phenomenon was observed in the flowability of the corn starch.

The presence of SiO_2 in granulated sugar solutions did not significantly affect the thermal conductivity, while for the commercial powdered sugar, SiO_2 slightly increased the thermal conductivity. This observed behavior may be influenced by the presence of 3% corn starch in the commercial grade powdered sugar (Fig. 1B).

Powder Systems

Values of k versus T are presented in Fig. 2 for a corn starch powder. This figure illustrates the effect of temperature as well as Cab-O-Sil concentration on the thermal conductivity of corn starch. It can be seen that the thermal conductivity of the pure starch decreases with increasing temperature most likely because of the formation of a dry caked layer with lower thermal conductivity—this situation being favored at increasing sample temperatures. Furthermore, observed trends may be explained by considering that at normal temperature and pressure, thermal conductivity is highly dependent on both temperature and voidage. The voidage may be taken as an indication of the degree of contact between particles; the lower the voidage, the higher the continuous heat transfer area among granules and the higher the thermal conductivity observed. On the other hand, a powder with high voidage would have low thermal conductivity. Hence, the effect of silicon dioxide on thermal conductivity would partially depend on its effect on the bulk density of the powder. In the specific case of SiO_2, part of the voidage in the food powder may be filled with the small silica particles, and since Cab-O-Sil has a higher thermal conductivity than air, the overall result is an increment in the bulk thermal conductivity of the powdered food material.

Another reason why silicon dioxide increases thermal conductivity is due to its ability to prevent caking and the formation of dry impermeable layers. Such layers exhibit a thermal conductivity lower than that of the original powder. In fact, this was observed in corn starch for which Cab-O-Sil has a high affinity. Therefore, higher concentrations of silica give higher thermal conductivity as illustrated

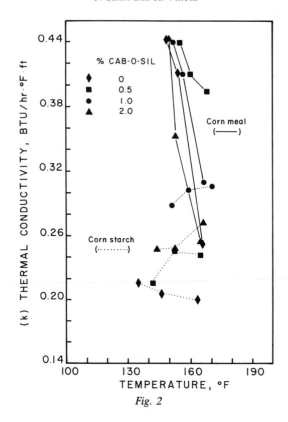

Fig. 2

in Fig. 3 which is a plot of thermal conductivity versus Cab-O-Sil concentration of corn starch. It was observed that the best improvement in thermal conductivity was at the 1% level of incorporation of silicon dioxide. Above this percentage, the thermal conductivity had the tendency to decline. Two reasons could be responsible for this phenomenon: (1) higher concentrations of Cab-O-Sil between starch granules may act as an insulating material; (2) since Cab-O-Sil has a higher hygroscopicity than corn starch, a decrease in the moisture content of the latter would result. It has been reported that the lower the moisture content, the lower the thermal conductivity of food materials. In Fig. 3, the same trend can be observed for skim milk powder as measured by the thermal conductivity probe.

It was observed that Cab-O-Sil does not improve the flowability of corn meal. A similar behavior was reported by Hollenbach *et al.*[2] when

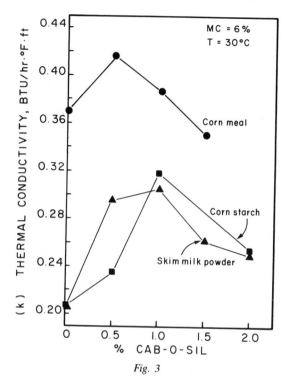

Fig. 3

measuring bulk density of soy protein. Results indicate that there are products which show high affinity for silicon dioxide while others may not exhibit any affinity at all, e.g. soy protein, corn meal, etc. This behavior may be responsible for the trends observed which show that Cab-O-Sil does not improve the thermal conductivity of corn meal (Fig. 2). The same trend can be observed in Fig. 3 which more clearly shows the effect of Cab-O-Sil concentration on the thermal conductivity of corn meal. In addition, it was noticed that the corn meal caking tendency was much more pronounced than that for corn starch, and therefore, lower thermal conductivities were observed at higher temperatures.

CONCLUSIONS

For liquid systems in the range of concentrations studied (0–1·5% dry basis), silicon dioxide has been shown to have no detrimental effect on the thermal conductivity of reconstituted powders with good affinity for silicon dioxide. The reason may be attributed to the fact that SiO_2 forms an 'ordered mixture', that is, it interacts with the reconstituted powder, and free SiO_2 cannot be found in the system. However, in the cases where SiO_2 forms a 'random mixture', because either it was added in excess or there is no affinity between the reconstituted powder and SiO_2, the thermal conductivity slightly decreases in the presence of SiO_2. This may be caused by the coating phenomenon due to the SiO_2 which forms a film on the wall of the thermal conductivity probe creating a resistance to the heat flow from the heat source into the food system surrounding the probe.

The incorporation of SiO_2 into the powder systems not only improves the flowability and bulk density, but also it increases the thermal conductivity of powdered food systems whenever an 'ordered mixture' is achieved. In most cases, there is an optimum percentage at which SiO_2 presented its maximum effect, usually between 0·5% and 1·0% dry basis. Two factors may be responsible for this behavior: (1) the small particles of Cab-O-Sil increase the effective continuous heat transfer area among particles, and (2) SiO_2 increases the bulk density, so that less voidage is present resulting in improved heat flow between particles.

REFERENCES

1. Sweat, V. E. Experimental values of thermal conductivity of selected fruit and vegetables. *J. Fd Sci.* **39:** 158, 1973.
2. Hollenbach, A. M., Peleg, M. and Rufner, R. Effect of four anticaking agents on the bulk characteristic of ground sugar. *J. Fd Sci.* **47:** 538, 1982.
3. Mohsenin, N. *Thermal Properties of Foods and Agricultural Materials.* Gordon and Breach Science Publishers, New York, 1980.
4. Peleg, M. and Mannheim, C. H. Effect of conditioners on the flow properties of powdered sucrose. *Powder Technol.* **7:** 45, 1973.
5. Peleg, M. and Hollenbach, A. M. Flow conditioners and anticaking agents. *Food Technol.* **38**(3), 1984.
6. Gold, G., Duvall, R. N., Palermo, B. T. and Slater, J. G. Effect of glidants on flowability of powdered materials. *J. Pharm. Sci.* **57:** 667, 1968.
7. Irani, R. R., Callis, G. F. and Liv, T. Flow conditioning and anticaking agents. *Ind. Eng. Chem.* **51:** 1285, 1959.
8. Irani, R. R. and Callis, C. F. The use of conditioning agents to improve the handling properties of cereal products. *Cereal Sci. Today* **5:** 1980, 1960.
9. Ojha, T. P., Farrall, A. W., Dhanak, A. M. and Stine, C. M. A Method of Determining Heat Transfer Through Powdered Food Products. Transactions of the ASAE paper No. 66-823, 1966.

13

THERMAL CONDUCTIVITY OF STARCH GELS

A. DRUSAS, M. TASSOPOULOS and G. D. SARAVACOS*

Department of Chemical Engineering, National Technical University, GR-10682, Athens, Greece
* Department of Food Science, Rutgers University, New Brunswick, New Jersey 08903, U.S.A.

ABSTRACT

The thermal conductivity (λ) of starch gels containing 6–20% solids was determined in the temperature range of 20–40 °C, using a modified guarded hot-plate apparatus. The thermal diffusivity (α) of the gels was estimated from transient heating measurements in a cylindrical container, applying a simplified solution of the unsteady-state conduction equation.

The experimental values of λ of starch gels at 30 °C decreased from 0·597 to 0·538 W/mK, as the solids concentration was increased from 6 to 20%. The thermal conductivity increased linearly with temperature at all solids concentrations. The rate of increase of λ with temperature was lower at starch concentrations higher than 10%. The thermal diffusivity at a mean temperature of 30 °C decreased from $1·461 \times 10^{-7}$ to $1·371 \times 10^{-7} m^2/s$, as the starch concentration of the gels was increased from 10 to 20%. Temperature had a slight positive effect at low solids concentrations. A break in the heating lines of semilog plots of temperature versus time was found in gels containing about 10% solids, indicating a change in gel structure at higher temperatures.

The thermal conductivity of starch gels, calculated from thermal diffusivity data at mean temperatures 20–30 °C was very close to the experimental values of λ, which were obtained by the guarded hot-plate method.

INTRODUCTION

The thermal conductivity and thermal diffusivity of foods are important physical properties needed in the engineering analysis and design of several food processes involving heat transfer. Limited data on the thermophysical properties of foods are available in the literature. Recently, an effort was undertaken within the European Economic Community (project COST 90) to standardize the methods of measurement and predict the thermophysical properties from compositional data of foods.[1,2]

There is a need for more accurate data on the thermophysical properties of foods and food components, using standardized measuring techniques. Gels of controlled composition and structure can be used to simulate foods in experimental investigations of physical and engineering properties. Carrageenan gels containing 2 and 30% solids were used as reference materials in the COST 90 project.[2]

The effect of solids content and temperature on the thermal conductivity of tomato paste was investigated recently, using two different measurement techniques.[3] The objective of this work was to measure the thermal conductivity and thermal diffusivity of starch gels at various concentrations and temperatures.

METHODS OF MEASUREMENT

Transient and steady-state methods can be used for the measurement of thermal conductivity and thermal diffusivity of foods.[1] The transient methods are simpler and quicker than the steady-state methods, but they involve more calculations. The steady-state methods are more accurate and the calculations are simpler, but they require a more rigorous experimental procedure.

In the steady-state (hot-plate) method the thermal conductivity (λ) of a sample of thickness Δx can be calculated from the measured heat flux $(\dot{q})$, if the temperature gradient $(\Delta T/\Delta x)$ is known:

$$\dot{q} = \lambda(\Delta T/\Delta x) \qquad (1)$$

The transient heating time (t) of a product in a cylindrical container is given by the following simplified solution of the unsteady-state equation for heat conduction:[4,5,6]

$$t = f \log\left(j\frac{T_a - T_0}{T_a - T}\right) \qquad (2)$$

where,

f = reciprocal of the slope of the heating line(s)
j = lag factor

T_a = external temperature (°C)

T_0, T = initial temperature and temperature after time t of the cylinder center (°C).

The inverse slope (f) and the lag factor (j) can be estimated graphically from a plot of log ($T_a - T$) versus time. For a long cylinder of internal radius r, the thermal diffusivity (α) can be estimated from the relationship,

$$\alpha = 0.398r^2/f \tag{3}$$

MATERIALS AND METHODS

Guarded Hot-plate Apparatus

A guarded hot-plate apparatus for measuring the thermal conductivity of liquids and pastes was constructed in our laboratory, based on the ASTM specifications.[3] The main unit was made from brass, and the upper (hot) plate was 98 mm diameter and 10 mm thick. An electrical resistance, made of manganin wire was embedded in the plate. The hot plate was surrounded by a guard ring of 149 mm diameter and 23 mm thickness, and a gap was formed between them by Teflon spacers, 2 mm at the top of the plate and 1 mm at the sides.

The lower (cold) plate had a diameter of 108 mm and a thickness of 23 mm. It was surrounded by a guard ring of 181 mm diameter and 23 mm thickness, from which it was separated by two 1 mm thick Teflon rings. Electrical heating of the upper plate was controlled by a power stabilizer and measured with an indicating digital ammeter, and voltmeter. The temperature of the plates was measured with insulated copper–constantan thermocouples, which were connected to a recording data logger. Two thermostatically controlled water baths were used to maintain the desired temperature constant to within ±0·1 °C.

Thermal Diffusivity Apparatus

The transient method of measuring thermal diffusivity, originally proposed by Dickerson, was used.[5,6] The basic part of the apparatus consisted of a brass tube of 48 mm inside diameter, 1 mm wall thickness and of 200 mm length, with Teflon caps at the ends.[3] The tube, filled with the sample, was placed in a water bath, maintained at a constant temperature (±0·1 °C). The temperature of the center of the sample was measured with a copper–constantan thermocouple, which was supported in an open glass tube of 1 mm inside diameter, and inserted along the axis of the cylinder. Another thermocouple was used to measure the bath temperature. The two temperatures were recorded at intervals of 2 min in a data logger.

Experimental Procedure

Starch gels of 6–20% solids content were prepared by dissolving corn starch powder in distilled water and heating to 80 °C with mild agitation. The hot colloid solution was poured into the measuring apparatus, forming a gel upon cooling. Most of the measurements in the hot-plate apparatus were made using gels of 2 mm thickness. The two plates were kept at the desired distance apart by Teflon spacers of the appropriate thickness (e.g. 2 mm). The upper plate was placed on the top of the hot solution, forcing to the sides the excess fluid and any trapped air. The cylindrical container of the transient method was filled with the hot starch solution, and the thermocouple glass tube was inserted at the appropriate position, before a gel was formed upon cooling.

In the steady-state method, the two plates were kept at a fixed temperature difference (2–5 °C) using the two water baths, maintained at selected temperatures. After a steady state was established, the temperature difference (ΔT) and the heat flux ($\dot{q}$) were recorded. Duplicate measurements were made and the average values are reported.

In the transient method, the tube containing the starch gel was first cooled in an ice-water bath for 2 h and then placed into the constant temperature water bath, where the temperature of the sample was recorded as a function of time. The density of the starch solutions was determined by weighing 50 ml of the sample at 20 °C. The specific heat of the starch gels was estimated as a function of the water content using the recommended formulae of the literature.[7]

RESULTS

Figure 1 shows the experimental values of thermal conductivity (λ) of starch gels at 4 concentrations and 3 temperatures, using the guarded hot-plate apparatus. The mean values of λ (two replicates) of the starch gels at 30 °C decreased from 0·597 to 0·538 W/mK as the solids concentration was increased from 6 to 20%. The precision of the

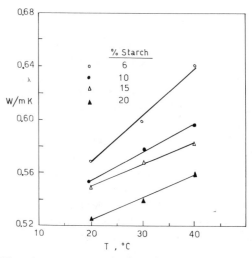

Fig. 1. Effect of temperature on the thermal conductivity (λ) of starch gels.

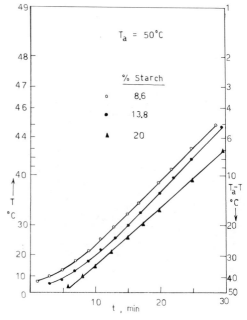

Fig. 2. Heating lines of starch gels in the cylindrical thermal diffusivity apparatus. Water-bath temperature $T_a = 50\,°C$.

measurements was satisfactory, the relative standard deviation ranging from 1·0 to 3·0%.

The thermal conductivity of the gels increased linearly with temperature in the range of 20–40 °C. The effect of temperature was stronger at low starch concentrations (6%), similar to the increase of λ with temperature of 2% carrageenan gels and of water.[2] A significant decrease in the slopes of the lines was found in gels containing more than 10% starch.

Figures 2 and 3 show the experimental plots of center temperature versus time of starch gels in the cylindrical apparatus of the transient method. Straight lines were obtained on the semilog plots in starch gels with low or high solids content. Broken straight lines were observed in gels containing about 10% starch at temperatures higher than 25 °C. Average values of the slopes of the broken lines were used in estimating the thermal diffusivity of the gels.

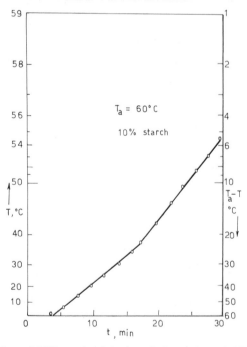

Fig. 3. Heating line of 10% starch gel in the cylindrical thermal diffusivity apparatus. Water-bath temperature $T_a = 60 °C$.

TABLE I
Experimental thermal diffusivities (α) of starch
gels

Starch %	$\alpha \times 10^7 (m^2/s)$		
	20 °C	*25 °C*	*30 °C*
10	1·387	1·398	1·461
15	1·359	1·341	1·441
20	1·388	1·345	1·371

Table I shows the estimated values of thermal diffusivity (α) of starch gels, using the transient method of heating the gel in the cylindrical apparatus.

The mean value of α (two replicates) at a mean temperature of 30 °C decreased from 1·461 × 10^{-7} to 1·371 × 10^{-7} m^2/s, as the concentration of the starch was increased from 10 to 20%. Temperature had a positive effect on α at low starch concentration (10%). However, at higher starch concentrations (15–20%) the effect of temperature was insignificant. Our results are in agreement with the values of α of food materials reported in the literature.[8]

The thermal conductivity can be calculated from the measured

TABLE II
Density (ρ) and specific heat (C_p) of starch gels

Starch %	ρ (kg/m^3)	C_p $(kJ/kg\,K)$		
		20 °C	*25 °C*	*30 °C*
10	1028	3·919	3·921	3·923
15	1050	3·785	3·788	3·791
20	1076	3·651	3·655	3·659

TABLE III
Calculated thermal conductivities (λ) from thermal diffusivity data of starch gels

Starch %	λ $(W/m\,K)$		
	20 °C	*25 °C*	*30 °C*
10	0·559	0·564	0·589
15	0·540	0·544	0·574
20	0·526	0·529	0·540

thermal diffusivity of the gels, if the density (ρ) and the specific heat (C_p) of the sample are known $(\alpha = \lambda/\rho C_p)$. Experimental values of the density and calculated values of the specific heat are given in Table II.

The calculated values of λ are given in Table III. It is shown that the steady-state and the transient methods yielded similar values of the thermal conductivity for the starch gels.

DISCUSSION

Starch gels were found to be convenient experimental materials, simulating foods, for investigating the thermophysical properties of foods. The results obtained in this work are in general agreement with the literature data. The thermal conductivity was found to increase with temperature more sharply in dilute than in high-solids gels. There appears to be an analogy between thermal conductivity and viscosity in this respect.[9]

The transient measurements yielded thermal diffusivities and thermal conductivities which were very close to the values obtained with the steady-state method. A break of the heating lines of $\log(T_a - T)$ versus time was observed in starch gels containing about 10% solids, while straight lines were obtained in dilute and concentrated gels. This change in slope (and thermal diffusivity) may be caused by structural and rheological changes of the gel as the temperature is raised. A similar effect was observed in the heating of tomato paste.[3]

There was no satisfactory agreement of our data with the correlations of thermal conductivity and thermal diffusivity as functions of water content and temperature, which have been suggested in the literature.[7] Development of more accurate models of prediction of the thermophysical properties of starch gels will require more experimental data over a wider range of concentration and temperature.

REFERENCES

1. Nesvadba, P. Methods for the measurement of thermal conductivity and diffusivity of foodstuffs. *J. Food Eng.* **1:** 95, 1982.
2. Kent, M., Christiansen, K., van Haneghem, I. A., Holtz, E., Morley, M. J., Nesvadba, P. and Poulsen, K. P. COST 90 collaborative measurements of thermal properties of foods. *J. Food Eng.* **3:** 117, 1984.
3. Drusas, A. E. and Saravacos, G. D. Thermal conductivity of tomato paste. *J. Food Eng.* **4:** 157, 1985.

4. Ball, C. O. and Olson, F. C. W. *Sterilization in Food Technology*. Academic Press, New York, 1957.
5. Dickerson, R. W. An apparatus for the measurement of thermal diffusivity of foods. *Food Technol.* **19:** 198, 1965.
6. Porsdal Poulsen, K. Thermal diffusivity of foods measured by simple equipment. *J. Food Eng.* **1:** 115, 1982.
7. Miles, C. A., van Beek, G. and Veerkamp, C. H. Calculation of thermophysical properties of foods. In *Physical Properties of Foods* (R. Jowitt *et al.* Eds). Elsevier Applied Science Publishers, London, 1983.
8. Kostaropoulos, A. E., Spiess, W. E. L. and Wolf, W. Anhaltswerte für Temperaturleitfähigkeit von Lebensmitteln. *Lebensm.-Wiss. u. Technol.* **8:** 108, 1975.
9. Saravacos, G. D. Effect of temperature on viscosity of fruit juices and purees. *J. Food Sci.* **35:** 122, 1970.

14

SOME ENGINEERING PROPERTIES OF AQUEOUS SOLUTIONS OF ETHANOL AND SODIUM CHLORIDE FOR A DEHYDROCOOLING PROCESS

M. LE MAGUER and R. N. BISWAL

Department of Food Science, The University of Alberta, Edmonton, Alberta, Canada, T6G 2P5

ABSTRACT

Correlations have been developed for estimating enthalpy and viscosity of the ternary mixtures of ethanol, NaCl and water. The models, which take into account the variation in the composition and temperature, are either semitheoretical or empirical in nature. Data used for estimating the parameters are on the pure components or on the binary mixtures of ethanol–water and NaCl–water. The aqueous solutions of ethanol and sodium chloride have applications in freezing and dehydrocooling of vegetables and other food materials.

INTRODUCTION

The use of aqueous solutions of ethanol and sodium chloride for direct contact freezing of food materials is a recent concept.[1,2] An optimum solution composition of AF 15–15 (aqueous freezant 15% wt ethanol and 15% wt NaCl) was suggested by Cipolletti and co-workers.[2] As freezing of food materials is an energy intensive process, Le Maguer and Biswal[3] suggested the use of AF 15–15 in a pre-freezing 'dehydrocooling' operation so as to reduce the energy requirements at the freezing step. 'Dehydrocooling' refers to a simultaneous dehydration and cooling of the product by direct contact with AF 15–15 in a temperature range above freezing so that ice formation does not take place in the product. The extent of cooling and dehydration depends on the requirements and the operational criteria of the system.

The design of a contactor and the computer simulation of the dehydrocooling operation requires data on the mass and heat transfer behaviour of the system. The use of AF solution for freezing and dehydrocooling being a novel concept, data on the physical and thermal properties of the ternary system (ethanol–NaCl–water) for engineering calculations are not available. The purpose of this paper is to present the models that were developed for the calculation of enthalpy and viscosity of the ternary system.

ENTHALPY CALCULATIONS

Modeling the enthalpy (H, kJ/kg mole) of a ternary system (1: ethanol, 2: water and 3: NaCl) can be done using enthalpy of the pure components H_i, and the integral heat of solution of the mixture (ΔH, kJ/kg mole):

$$H = \sum_{i=1}^{3} x_i H_i + \Delta H \tag{1}$$

where x_i is the mole fraction of the pure compound i ($i = 1, 2, 3$).

Enthalpy of Pure Components

The enthalpy of a pure component as a function of temperature is given by:

$$H_i = \int C_{pi}\, dT + H_{i0} \tag{2}$$

where C_{pi} is the heat capacity of component i (kJ/kg mole K), T is the temperature in K and H_{i0} is the enthalpy at a reference temperature T_0. Heat capacities of pure components at different temperatures were collected from literature: ethanol,[4] NaCl[5] and water,[6] and correlations on $C_{pi} = f_i(T)$ were developed using the standard least square best fit. These are presented in Table I.

TABLE I
Heat capacity of pure components as functions of temperature (T, K)

Component	Correlation (C_p: kJ/kg K)	Range (K)
Ethanol	$C_p = 4{\cdot}361\,6 - 0{\cdot}229\,6 \times 10^{-1}T + 0{\cdot}555 \times 10^{-4}T^2$	233–303
Water	$C_p = 1{\cdot}592\,6 \times 10^2 - 1{\cdot}599\,9T + 0{\cdot}550\,1 \times 10^{-2}T^2$ $- 0{\cdot}630\,2 \times 10^{-5}T^3$	233–313
NaCl	$C_p = 0{\cdot}735\,6 + 0{\cdot}182\,6 \times 10^{-2}T - 0{\cdot}205\,0 \times 10^{-5}T^2$	200–400

Integral Heat of Solution

Integral heat of solution, ΔH (kJ/kg mole) is the enthalpy change obtained upon mixing of the components of a solution. It is the contribution towards non-ideality of a mixture, and for a ternary system it can be obtained from:

$$\Delta H = \sum_{i=1}^{3} x_i \bar{H}_i - \sum_{i=1}^{3} x_i H_i \tag{3}$$

where $\bar{H}_i$ is the partial molar enthalpy of component i. Since the partial molar enthalpies are not easily estimated, we approached the problem from the consideration of a change in the standard free energy, ΔG. Starting from the definition of a total free energy (G) one can easily show that:[7]

$$\frac{\partial(\Delta G/T)}{\partial T} \bigg|_{P=\text{const.}} = -\frac{\Delta H}{T^2} \tag{4}$$

A comprehensive review on the use of Margules equation, Van Laar's equation and the 'q-equation' to obtain expressions for $(\Delta G/T)$ has been given by Wohl.[8] Each of these equations has been extended from binary to ternary systems. With reference to the 'ternary four suffice q-equation of Wohl' and assuming as a first approximation that there is no interaction between salt and ethanol, an expression for ΔH can be written as:

$$\frac{\Delta H}{RT^2(q_1 x_1 + q_2 x_2 + q_3 x_3)} = (A_1 + B_1 Z_1) Z_1 Z_2 + (A_2 + B_2 Z_2) Z_2 Z_3 \tag{5}$$

where q_i is an arbitrary factor replacing the molar volume of component i. It can be obtained through the van der Waals group volume contribution approach[9] and is given by:

$$q_i = \sum_{k=1}^{n} v_k^{(i)} R_k \tag{6}$$

where R_k is group volume constant of the group k $(k = 1, 2, \ldots, n)$ and v_k is the number of a particular group present in one molecule of the compound i. The generalized volume fraction Z_i is written as:

$$Z_i = \frac{x_i q_i}{\sum\limits_{i=1}^{3} x_i q_i} \tag{7}$$

The temperature dependency of ΔH is imbedded in the coefficients A_1, B_1, A_2 and B_2 which are assumed to vary linearly with temperature. The parameters of Eq. (5) are estimated from the data on the binary systems of water–ethanol and water–salt.

Ethanol–Water System

For a binary mixture of ethanol and water, Eq. (5) is rewritten as:

$$\frac{\Delta H}{RT^2(q_1x_1 + q_2x_2)Z_1Z_2} = A_1 + B_1Z_1 \tag{8}$$

where Z_1 and Z_2 are the volume fractions calculated on the binary basis. The constants q_1 and q_2 have been reported to be equal to 2·1055 and 0·92 respectively.[9] Data of Bosnjakovic and Grumbt[10] were used to evaluate the parameters A_1 and B_1. At each point in the temperature range 273–313 K, A_1 and B_1 were evaluated for the available concentration range of 0·0201–0·7785 mole fraction ethanol through a least square best fit. The temperature dependency of A_1 and B_1 as obtained with an r^2 of 0·997 for both are the following:

$$A_1 = -0·597 \times 10^{-1} + 0·174 \times 10^{-3}T \tag{8a}$$

$$B_1 = 0·674 \times 10^{-1} + 0·191 \times 10^{-3}T \tag{8b}$$

NaCl–Water System

For a binary mixture of NaCl and water (i.e. $x_1 = 0$) Eq. (5) is simplified to:

$$\frac{\Delta H}{RT^2(q_2x_2 + q_3x_3)Z_2Z_3} = A_2 + B_2Z_3 \tag{9}$$

Christensen and co-workers[11] have recently reported that q_3 is equal to 1·1287. The availability of experimental data on ΔH values for a wide range of temperature and composition is scanty. A good amount of data for a temperature range of 0–95 °C and concentrations near infinite dilution ($x_3 = 0·616 \times 10^{-4}$–0·3433 \times 10^{-3}$) is available.[12] Data, with few missing points, for a temperature range of 10–25 °C and a concentration range of $0·1802 \times 10^{-5}$–0·1449 \times 10^{-1}$ mole fraction NaCl, have been reported by Gulbransen and Robinson.[13] The availability of ΔH data for higher concentrations of NaCl is limited to room temperature, i.e. 25 °C.[14,15]

Using the available values of ΔH_s^{0},[12] $\bar{L}_2$ and $\bar{L}_3$ type of data[13] were transformed to ΔH as a function of temperature and composition through Eq. (10).[7]

$$\Delta H = x_2 \bar{L}_2 + x_3 \bar{L}_3 + x_3 \Delta H_s^0 \tag{10}$$

where $\bar{L}_2$ and $\bar{L}_3$ are the relative partial molar enthalpy of water and salt respectively, and ΔH_s^0 is the heat of solution at infinite dilution. For the available temperature range of 10–25 °C, the missing points in the concentration range of $x_3 = 0 \cdot 1798 \times 10^{-2} – 0 \cdot 1449 \times 10^{-1}$ were extrapolated. For each point in the temperature range, A_2 and B_2 were evaluated for the available concentration range through a least square best fit. It was found that linear approximation was adequate. The temperature dependency of A_2 and B_2 obtained through least square best fits with r^2 of $0 \cdot 977$ and $0 \cdot 976$ respectively are the following:

$$A_2 = 0 \cdot 766 \times 10^{-1} - 0 \cdot 247 \times 10^{-3} T \tag{9a}$$

$$B_2 = -0 \cdot 825 + 0 \cdot 270 \times 10^{-2} T \tag{9b}$$

VISCOSITY CALCULATIONS

Calculation of the viscosity of the ternary system is done using the viscosity of pure components and of binary mixtures of ethanol–water and NaCl–water. Viscosity of a pure liquid (μ_L, cP) can be estimated with very good accuracy by the equation of Makhija and Stairs as given below:[16]

$$\text{Log } \mu_L = A' + \frac{B'}{T - T'} \tag{11}$$

The parameters A', B' and T' for ethanol and water are given in Table II.

TABLE II
Constants in the viscosity correlation for pure compounds[16]

Liquid	A'	B'	T'	% Error	Range (°C)
Ethanol	$-2 \cdot 440\ 1$	$774 \cdot 414$	$-15 \cdot 249$	$2 \cdot 66$	-98 to $+70$
Water	$-1 \cdot 566\ 8$	$230 \cdot 298$	$146 \cdot 797$	$0 \cdot 51$	-10 to $+160$

Viscosity of Binary Systems

The effect of the interaction of ethanol and water towards the non-ideality of the solution has been taken into account through the consideration of excess free energy ΔG^*.[16] The ΔG^* for viscosity of a binary mixture can be expressed in the following form:

$$\Delta G^* = \ln \mu_{1-2} - (x_1 \ln \mu_1 + x_2 \ln \mu_2) \tag{12}$$

where μ_{1-2} is the viscosity of the binary mixture of water and ethanol. for a binary system, ΔG^* can also be expressed as a power series of x_i.[17]

$$\frac{\Delta G^*/RT}{x_1 x_2} = a + bx_1 + cx_1^2 + \ldots \quad \text{(Const. } T\text{)} \tag{13}$$

Combining Eqs. (12) and (13), one can write that:

$$\frac{\ln \mu_{1-2} - x_1 \ln \mu_1 - x_2 \ln \mu_2}{(x_1 x_2) T} = P_1 + P_2 x_1 + P_3 x_1^2 \tag{14}$$

For concentrations below 40% ethanol the contribution of $P_3 x_1^2$ is negligible. Upon simplification, Eq. (14) becomes Eq. (15).

$$\mu_{1-2} = \exp\left[x_1 x_2 T(P_1 + P_2 x_1) + x_1 \ln \mu_1 + x_2 \ln \mu_2\right] \tag{15}$$

Using data on the viscosity of ethanol–water mixtures[18] and the correlation for pure ethanol and water, the parameters P_1 and P_2 of Eq. (15) were obtained through a non-linear optimization program. The result is given below:

$$P_1 = 1 \cdot 1735 - \frac{0 \cdot 7266 \times 10^3}{T} + \frac{0 \cdot 1154 \times 10^6}{T^2} \tag{15a}$$

$$P_2 = 7 \cdot 6160 - \frac{0 \cdot 4514 \times 10^4}{T} + \frac{0 \cdot 6756 \times 10^6}{T^2} \tag{15b}$$

The validity of Eqs. (15a) and (15b) is for a temperature range of 0–40 °C and a concentration range of 0–0·2076 mole fraction ethanol.

The limitation of the application of Eq. (15) for the viscosity of NaCl–water system is that the pure NaCl is a solid. The empirical model that has been suggested for the viscosity of the binary mixture of NaCl and water is the following:

$$\ln \eta_R = \frac{x_3}{a' x_2 + b' x_3} \tag{16}$$

where η_R is the relative viscosity of NaCl–water with respect to water, and x_3 and x_2 are the mole fractions of salt and water respectively. Equation (16) can be rewritten as:

$$\ln \frac{\mu_{2-3}}{\mu_2} = \frac{C}{P_1' + P_2'C} \tag{17}$$

where $C = x_3/x_2$.

Available data on the binary mixtures of NaCl and water[19] were used to estimate the parameters P_1' and P_2' through a non-linear optimization package. Both P_1' and P_2' were found to be described adequately by the following expressions:

$$P_1' = 3\cdot0081 \times 10^3 - 20\cdot26T + 0\cdot342 \times 10^{-1}T^2 \tag{17a}$$

$$P_2' = -1\cdot2293 \times 10^3 + 8\cdot375T - 0\cdot143 \times 10^{-1}T^2 \tag{17b}$$

Equations (17a) and (17b) are valid for a temperature range of 273–373 K and a concentration range of $1\cdot8 \times 10^{-3}$–0·08 mole fraction of NaCl.

Estimating viscosity of a ternary system is more complex than the binary. One could extend the approach of estimating the non-ideality contribution through the excess free energy from binary to ternary system.[20,21]

DISCUSSION

The correlations developed on the enthalpy and viscosity of the ternary systems of ethanol, salt and water are good enough for practical use. The parameters of Eq. (5) for a ternary system have been estimated from the binary mixtures of NaCl–water and ethanol–water because of the unique nature of the equation. Upon estimation of these parameters for another binary system with water, this model can be extended for four components and so on. It should be mentioned that Eq. (5) ignores the three component interaction in the original equation of Wohl[8] (Eq. 60). The assumption that the impact of this term is negligible needs to be verified through experimental measurements. An attempt to develop a model for the viscosity of the ternary mixtures of ethanol, water and salt using the information at hand and limited experimental measurements is underway.

ACKNOWLEDGEMENTS

Funds for this research were provided by the Farming for the Future Program of the Government of Alberta. This support is gratefully acknowledged. The authors would like to thank Mr Bill Howe for his assistance during the course of this research.

REFERENCES

1. Robertson, G. H., Cipolletti, J. C., Farkas, D. F. and Secor, G. E. Methodology for direct contact freezing of vegetables in aqueous freezing media. *J. Food Sci.* **41**: 845–51, 1976.
2. Cipolletti, J. C., Robertson, G. H. and Farkas, D. F. Freezing of vegetables by direct contact with aqueous solutions of ethanol and sodium chloride. *J. Food Sci.* **42**(4): 911–16, 1977.
3. Le Maguer, M. and Biswal, R. N. Engineering Development and Economic Analysis of the Dehydrocooling Process. Report on the Farming for the Future Project No. 820050, Alberta Agriculture, Alberta, Canada, 1983.
4. Gallant, R. W. *The Physical Properties of Hydrocarbons, Vol. 2.* Gulf Publishing Co., Houston, Texas, 1970.
5. JANAF. *Thermodynamical Tables,* Catalog No. PB 168370, US Department of Commerce, NBS, Institute for Applied Technology, 1965.
6. Smithsonian Meteorological Tables. 6th Rev. edn, Publication No. 4014, p. 343, Smithsonian Miscellaneous Collection (114), Washington, 1949.
7. Klotz, I. M. and Rosenberg, R. M. *Chemical Thermodynamics: Basic Theory and Methods.* The Benjamin/Cummings Publishing Company, Menlo Park, California, 1974.
8. Wohl, K. Thermodynamic evaluation of binary and ternary liquid systems. *Trans. Am. Inst. Chem. Eng.* **42**: 215–49, 1946.
9. Fredenslund, A., Gmehling, J. and Rasmussen, P. *Vapor–Liquid Equilibria using UNIFAC: A Group-Contribution Method.* Elsevier Scientific Publishing Company, Amsterdam, 1977.
10. Bosnjakovic, F. and Grambt, I. A. Nurmeinhalt flüssiger älthylalkohl wasser-gemisch. *Forsch. Ing. Ves.* **2**: 12, 1931.
11. Christensen, C., Sander, B., Fredenslund, A. A. and Rasmussen, P. Towards the extension of UNIFAC to mixtures with electrolytes. *Fluid Phase Equilibria* **13**: 297–309, 1983.
12. Criss, C. M. and Cobble, J. W. The thermodynamic properties of high temperature aqueous solutions. I. Standard partial molal heat capacities of sodium chloride and barium chloride from 0 to 100°. *J. Am. Chem. Soc.* **83**: 3223–8, 1961.
13. Gulbransen, E. A. and Robinson, A. L. Thermodynamics of sodium chloride solution. *J. Am. Chem. Soc.* **56**: 2638–41, 1934.
14. Randall, M. and Bisson, C. S. The heat of solution and the partial molal heat content of the constituents in aqueous solutions of sodium chloride. *J. Am. Chem. Soc.* **42**: 347–67, 1919.
15. Robinson, A. L. The integral heats of dilution and the relative partial molal heat contents of aqueous sodium chloride solution at 25 °C. *J. Am. Chem. Soc.* **54**: 1311–8, 1932.
16. Reid, R. C., Prausnitz, J. M. and Sherwood, T. K. *The Properties of Gases and Liquids,* 3rd edn. McGraw-Hill, New York, 1977.

17. Smith, J. M. and Van Ness, H. C. *Introduction to Chemical Engineering Thermodynamics*, 3rd edn. McGraw-Hill, New York, 1975.
18. Rha, C. *Theory, Determination and Control of Physical Properties of Food Materials*. D. Reidel Publishing Company, Dordrecht-Holland, 1975.
19. International Critical Tables. No. 5, p. 15, 1929.
20. Chandramouli, V. V. and Laddha, G. S. Viscosity of ternary liquid mixtures. *Indian J. Technol.* **1:** 199–203, 1963.
21. Kalidas, R. and Laddha, G. S. Viscosity of ternary liquid mixtures. *J. Chem. Eng. Data* **9**(1): 142–5, 1964.

15

SOME ENGINEERING PROPERTIES OF WHEY

M. LE MAGUER, J. BOURGOIS and P. JELEN

*Department of Food Science, The University of Alberta, Edmonton, Alberta,
Canada T6G 2P5*

ABSTRACT

*Liquid whey concentrates were studied in the range 0–60% total solids
for their engineering properties. The density was expressed as a function
of the density of water at the same temperature and a polynomial in
percentage total solids. Whey solutions were found to behave as
Newtonian fluids below 20% solids. At higher concentrations, the
relationship between shear rates (γ) and shear stress (τ) was described
adequately by a power law. The heat capacity of dried whey (C_p) was
presented as a function of temperature. Determination of the freezing
point along with basic thermodynamic considerations allowed for the
development of equations for the freezing curve, the fraction of ice
formed and an adjusted value of the apparent molecular weight of the
solution.*

INTRODUCTION

The importance of cheese whey in industrial food processing has been
increasing steadily. Various advanced techniques, such as reverse
osmosis, ultrafiltration, gel filtration, or electrodialysis have been
applied in cheese whey processing. Reports concerning utilization of
whey in various food and nonfood products are numerous. Some
research has been devoted to the elucidation of the chemical composition and physical properties of whey proteins[1,3] and lactose.[1,2]

Because of its rather low solids content—a typical composition of
whey is 6·5% solids with 4·9% lactose, 0·9% proteins and 0·5%

161

ash[4]—the raw whey may be considered similar to water or a corresponding lactose solution for a rough estimate of some of the physical properties. Limited data on physical properties of pure lactose solutions are available,[1,2,5] while data for pure sucrose solutions are more complete;[6] these can sometimes be used for approximation of physical properties of more concentrated whey. Due to the presence of other whey solids (especially proteins and salts) and the relatively unknown contributions of these components to physical properties of liquid whey systems, the above mentioned approximations may be totally inadequate for process design, and certainly for more basic studies.

In a previous paper[7] we have reported preliminary results obtained on density and viscosity of cottage cheese whey solutions. As a continuation of this study the range of concentration was extended and the freezing curve was determined along with the heat capacity of dried whey (7% water). The more complete results are now presented for cottage cheese whey in the concentration ranges of 0–40% (viscosity) or 0–60% (freezing points).

MATERIAL AND METHODS

Liquid cottage cheese whey collected from an industrial plant in the Edmonton area was concentrated in a vacuum evaporator (69 mm Hg vacuum and 45 °C) until the concentration desired for the study was obtained. Some of the original product was also freeze-dried and the resulting powder was then packaged and stored at cold temperature for further reconstitution. Tests carried out on the whey powder obtained showed very little loss of solubility. Subsequent dilution to compare the results obtained with the concentrated liquid whey and the original whey showed virtually no difference. Consequently, the freeze-dried whey was used for convenience in delayed measurements. In this case solutions of approximate composition were prepared with distilled water, then stirred for approximately 1 h at 40 °C. Eventually a filtration step was added if undissolved solid remained in the solution. The solid content was then determined by drying in the oven at 80 °C and 67 mm Hg as was the case for the concentrated whey.

Density above and below room temperature was determined in a controlled temperature cabinet in which the whole measurement process was carried out in a pycnometer. Great accuracy can be achieved under these conditions due to the fact that all instruments necessary for the measurement are at the same temperature. A precalibration with water allowed for rigorous measurements; then the sample was introduced and measured at least three times. The mean square error expressed in percentage of the mean value was on the average 0·2%.

The viscosity was measured with a Cannon-Fenske viscosimeter (Model #50 and 100) modified to allow a variable pressure drop to be developed across the capillary tube. The set-up used allows variation of the shear rate by a factor of 500, usually sufficient to show any nonNewtonian behaviour. The pressure at the head of the capillary can be controlled to within 10 Pa when using water as the manometer fluid. The viscosimeter was placed in a temperature controlled bath with transparent walls to permit determination of flow-time by visual inspection. The variation in temperature was less than 0.5 °C for a run including at least 3 repeated measurements for each temperature and concentration. Thermal equilibration of the sample was carried in the glass tube of the viscosimeter for a period of no less than 10 min. The constant necessary to calculate the kinematic viscosity from the experiment was a function of temperature. It was determined by using water at the given temperature and then used for the whey measurement. The average mean square error expressed as previously indicated was 0·5%.

Freezing point and heat capacity determinations were carried out using the method of differential thermal analysis in a Dupont 900 DTA instrument suitably modified to allow for work at low temperatures. A typical run consisted of cooling the sample down to −100 °C using liquid nitrogen, followed by warming using natural convection, back to room temperature. An average rate of heating of about 1.5 °C/min was typical for this procedure.

RESULTS AND DISCUSSION

Correlations were based on the data reported in Ref. 7 and the newly measured values obtained in this study.

Density
All the measurements were fitted with an equation of the form:

$$\rho = \rho_w + f(W_s) \tag{1}$$

where ρ_w is the density of water (kg/m^3) at the corresponding temperature and W_s the % total solids for whey.

$$f(W_s) = AW_s + BW_s^2 \tag{2}$$

with $A = 4\cdot123$ and $B = 0\cdot00583$. The average error was $1\cdot1\%$ and the maximum error $2\cdot7\%$.

Viscosity for Concentrations less than 20%

An equation derived by Guth and Simha[8] was used to fit the data obtained for viscosity of whey in the range 0–20% for concentrations and 10–60 °C for temperatures.

$$\mu = \mu_w(A + BW_s + W_s^2) \tag{3}$$

where μ is the whey viscosity in Pa s, μ_w the water viscosity in the same units and W_s the % total solids. Although the original equation used a parameter ϕ related to the volume fraction of solids in the solution, we used the mass fraction W_s to make the equation readily usable. This is based on the fact that in the temperature interval considered the values of W_s and ϕ are proportional to each other and the results should vary only by about 2%. The numerical values for the constants,

$$A = 1\cdot004 \qquad B = 0\cdot0311 \qquad C = 0\cdot00147$$

were in excellent agreement with values proposed theoretically[8] as 1.0, 0·025, and 0·00141, respectively. The average departure from the experimental points was 2·6% with a maximum of 10% in the high concentration region.

Viscosity at Higher Concentration

Viscosity measurements were carried out on concentrated whey solutions in the range 25–40% solids and at a temperature of 40 °C. At lower temperatures problems occurred due to the crystallization of the lactose. Typical curves of shear stress versus shear rate, presented in Fig. 1, reveal the nonNewtonian nature of these solutions. A power law equation was adopted to describe the behavior of the solutions as follows:

$$\tau = b\gamma^s \tag{4}$$

where $\tau =$ shear stress $(N\,m^2)$, $\gamma =$ shear rate (s^{-1}), $b =$ consistency index $(N\,m^2\,s^s)$ and s flow behavior index (dimensionless).

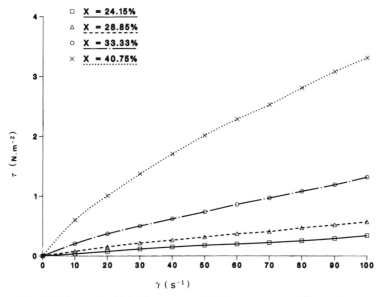

Fig. 1. *Shear stress versus shear rate at 40 °C for concentrated whey solutions.*

Table I gives the values of b and s for solutions of four different concentrations at 40 °C. As the concentration increased the solution became more and more nonNewtonian in nature as revealed by the flow behavior index. It has been shown that there exists, for food solutions such as starch paste and coagulated milk, a unique relationship between b and s at constant temperature.[9,10] This relationship is of the form:

$$\ln b = \ln \tau_0 - s \ln \gamma_0 \tag{5}$$

A plot of $\ln b$ versus s is presented in Fig. 2 and shows the expected

TABLE I
Values of b and s (Eq. 4) for $T = 40$ °C

$W_s(\%)$	$b(N\,m^2 \cdot s^s)$	s
24·15	$4·46 \times 10^{-3}$	0·942
28·85	$9·34 \times 10^{-3}$	0·897
33·33	$3·06 \times 10^{-2}$	0·813
40·75	$1·1 \times 10^{-1}$	0·740

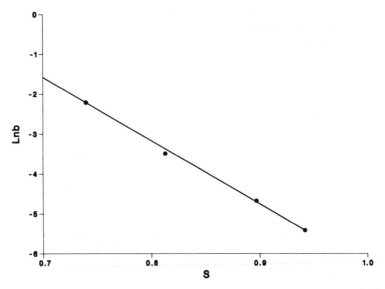

Fig. 2. Consistency index versus flow behaviour index at 40 °C in concentrated whey solutions.

relationship. Parameters τ_0 and γ_0 were calculated and found to be:

$$\tau_0 = 1.35 \times 10^4 \, \text{N m}^2 \quad \text{and} \quad \gamma_0 = 7.584 \times 10^6 \, \text{s}^{-1}$$

The ratio of τ_0 to γ_0, referred to[11] as the limiting viscosity at infinite shear rate, was shown to be theoretically equivalent to the viscosity of the Newtonian solution with the highest concentration at the same temperature. In our case, the concentration limit for the approximately Newtonian solution occurred at 20% solids with a viscosity of 1.8×10^{-3} Pa.s, while the ratio τ_0/γ_0 gives a limiting viscosity of 1.78×10^{-3} Pa.s, in very good agreement with the theory. The variation of s with concentration can be described by the empirical equation:

$$s = 1.27 - 1.36 \times 10^{-2} W_s \quad (W_s \geqslant 20\%) \tag{6}$$

where W_s is the percentage solids mass fraction.

This relationship shows that the value of $s = 1$, characteristic of a Newtonian fluid occurs at a concentration of 20% total solids. Furthermore assuming that the flow behavior index is not a function of temperature as shown for starch pastes,[12] it is possible to represent the apparent viscosity of the solution when W_s is greater than 20% by the following equation:

$$\mu = \mu(\text{Eq. 3}) \times (\gamma/\gamma_0)^{s-1} \tag{7}$$

where s is given by Eq. (6) and γ_0 has the value quoted above. For W_s less than 20% the viscosity is given by Eq. (3).

Heat Capacity

Following the technique described for the determination of the heat capacity of solids using differential thermal analysis, the sample of dried whey (7% residual moisture) was analyzed. Water content in the dry product was at such a low level that it was most likely very tightly bound to the surface of the solid and/or present as water of crystallization of lactose. Consequently, water interference did not appear at all in the DTA recordings obtained in the range -50 to $+60\,^{\circ}\text{C}$.

Correlating the data obtained with a polynomial in $t(^{\circ}\text{C})$ leads to the equation:

$$C_p = 1\cdot332 + 1\cdot05 \times 10^{-2}t + 1\cdot402 \times 10^{-4}t^2 \tag{8}$$

where t is in Celsius and C_p in kJ/kg K.

The adjusted values differed from the experimental ones by an average of $1\cdot36\%$ and a maximum of $2\cdot84\%$.

Freezing Curve

Experimental data points were obtained using the DTA in the range of 0–60% total solids concentration. From these original points a smoothing program was used to generate values at equal temperature intervals. From thermodynamic considerations a relationship between the water activity in the solution (a_w) and the temperature of freezing of the solution (T) can be derived.[13]

$$\log a_w = -4\cdot2091 \times 10^{-3}\theta - 0\cdot2152 \times 10^{-5}\theta^2 + 0\cdot359 \times 10^{-7}\theta^3$$
$$+ 0\cdot212 \times 10^{-9}\theta^4 + 0\cdot095 \times 10^{-12}\theta^5 \tag{9}$$

where θ is the freezing point lowering.

Assuming that Raoult's law applies to the whey solutions an estimate of the apparent molecular weight of the soluble solids was obtained as indicated by Heldman[14] and gave a value:

$$\bar{M}_s = 208 \text{ kg/kg mole} \tag{10}$$

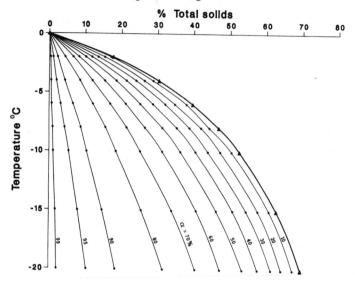

Fig. 3. Freezing curve and percentage of ice formed in whey solutions.

This compares with a value of 235 kg/kg mole reported by Bakshi and Johnson.[3] Using this average value of the molecular weight, values of x_w can be computed back using Eq. (11).

$$x_w = \frac{W_w/M_w}{W_w/M_w + (1 - W_w)/M_s} \tag{11}$$

Thus, through Eqs. (10) and (11), we have established a precise way to relate temperature and composition on the freezing curve. This knowledge can be used to generate important information such as the fraction of the total water frozen at a given temperature in a given solution. This parameter, usually referred to as α, was calculated as:

$$\alpha = (1 - W_s/W_s^*)/(1 - W_s), \tag{12}$$

(where W_s^* is the equilibrium concentration of a solution which freezes at the temperature t and W_s is the initial concentration of the solution to be frozen), and plotted in Fig. 3 using the previous results.

CONCLUSION

The data obtained experimentally by precise measurements provided working correlations for the basic physical properties necessary for design of equipment in whey processing. These correlations could be helpful also for basic engineering purposes and preliminary estimates of unit operations.

REFERENCES

1. Buma, T. J. Viscosity and density of concentrated lactose solutions and of concentrated cheese whey. *Neth. Milk Dairy J.* **34**(1): 65, 1980.
2. Miracco, J. L., Alzamora, S. M., Chirife, J. and Fontan, C. F. On the water activity of lactose solutions. *J. Food Sci.* **46**(5): 1612, 1981.
3. Bakshi, A. S. and Johnson, R. M. Calorimetric studies on whey freeze concentration. *J. Food Sci.* **48**: 1279, 1983.
4. Cerbulis, J., Woychick, J. H. and Wondolowski, V. Composition of commercial wheys. *J. Agr. Food Chem.* **20**: 5, 1057, 1972.
5. *Handbook of Chemistry and Physics* (1974–1975).
6. Honig, P. *Principle of Sugar Technology, Physical properties of sucrose*, Vol. 1, Elsevier Co., Amsterdam, London, New York, p. 18, 1953.
7. Le Maguer, M. and Jelen, P. Physical Properties of Whey. ASAE Winter Meeting. Paper No 74–6501, 1974.
8. Guth, E. and Simha, R. On the viscosity of suspensions of spherical particles (in German). *Kolloid Z.* **74**: 147, 1936.
9. Nedonchelle, Y. and Schutz, R. A. Cahiers du groupe Francais de rheologie. *Compt. Rend.* **265**, c-16, 1967.
10. Tuczyncki and Scott Blair, G. M. Dimensionless form of the double logarithmic equation relating shear stress to shear rate as applied to slowly coagulating milk. *Nature* **216**: 367, 1967.
11. Gruz, A., Russel, W. B. and Ollis, D. F. Shear viscosity of native and enzyme hydrolyzed amioca starch pastes. *AIChE Journal* **22**(5): 832–40, 1976.
12. Schutz, R. A. and Nedonchelle, Y. The Rheology of Concentrated Aqueous Carbohydrate Systems. *Proc. Ann. Conf. Br. Soc. Rheol.*, (R. E. Welton and R. W. Wharlow Eds.). Macmillan and Co Ltd, London, 1966.
13. Klotz. *Chemical Thermodynamics*. W. A. Benjamin Inc., New York, 1964.
14. Heldman, D. R. Predicting the relationship between unfrozen water fraction and temperature during food freezing using freezing point depression. *Trans. ASAE* 63–6, 1974.

16

PREDICTION OF WATER ACTIVITY IN GLUCOSE SOLUTIONS USING THE UNIFAC MODEL

G. S. CHOUDHURY and M. LE MAGUER

Department of Food Science, University of Alberta, Edmonton, Alberta T6G 2P5, Canada

ABSTRACT

Activity of water in glucose solutions is predicted using the UNIFAC model. Good agreement was observed between experimental and predicted values.

INTRODUCTION

The majority of foods are aqueous mixtures of which water is the most abundant component and its activity is therefore of crucial importance as a quality parameter. It plays a vital role in influencing microbial growth, kinetics of chemical and biochemical reactions, food rheology, packaging and drying of foods. The measurement of water activity above 0·95 presents several difficulties even using the most sensitive equipment.

The objective of this study was to test whether the UNIFAC model[1] could be used for the prediction of water activity in aqueous solutions. As a first test the model was used to estimate the activity of water in glucose solutions.

METHODOLOGY

The activity of a component is given by the equation:

$$a_i = x_i \gamma_i \tag{1}$$

where x_i is the mole fraction and γ_i the activity coefficient of component i. An estimation of γ of water in glucose solution will enable one to predict water activity in such solutions. The activity coefficient reflects the non-ideal behavior of a molecule in solution which, according to the UNIFAC model,[1] can be broken down into two independent parts: one associated with the differences in molecular sizes and the other associated with the interaction among functional groups. The activity coefficient of a component i is given by:

$$\ln \gamma_i = \quad \ln \gamma_i \quad + \quad \ln \gamma_i \tag{2}$$
$$\text{(combinatorial)} \quad \text{(residual)}$$

The combinatorial part of the activity is derived from the pure component properties such as group volume and area parameters and is given by:

$$\ln \gamma_i = \ln (\phi_i/x_i) + (Z/2)q_i \ln (\theta_i/\phi_i) + l_i - (\phi_i/x_i)\sum_j x_j l_j \tag{3}$$

where,

$\theta_i = q_i x_i / \sum_j q_j x_j =$ component area fraction
$\phi_i = r_i x_i / \sum_j r_j x_j =$ component volume fraction
$q_i = \sum_k v_k^{(i)} Q_k =$ component area parameter
$r_i = \sum_k v_k^{(i)} R_k =$ component volume parameter
$Q_k = A_k/2 \cdot 5 \times 10^9 =$ group area parameter
$R_k = V_k/15 \cdot 17 =$ group volume parameter
A_k and $V_k =$ Van der Waals area and volume of the group k^2.
$x_i =$ mole fraction of component i
$l_i = (Z/2)(r_i - q_i) - (r_i - 1)$
$Z =$ coordination number, set equal to 10.
$V_k^{(i)} =$ number of group k in component i

$15 \cdot 17$ and $2 \cdot 5 \times 10^9$ are normalization factors determined by volume and surface area of a CH_2 unit in polyethylene.[3]

The residual part of the activity coefficient is a function of group area fractions and their interactions in pure components and in mixtures. $\ln \gamma_i$ (residual) is given by:

$$\ln \gamma_i = \Sigma_k v_k^{(i)}(\ln \Gamma_k - \ln \Gamma_k^{(i)}) \tag{4}$$

The group activity coefficient is given by the following expression:

$$\ln \Gamma_k = Q_k \{1 - \ln (\Sigma_m \theta_m \psi_{mk}) - \Sigma_m(\theta_m \psi_{km}/\Sigma_n \theta_n \psi_{nm})\} \tag{5}$$

where,

$\theta_m = Q_m X_m / \Sigma_n Q_n X_n$ = area fraction of group m
$X_m = \Sigma_n x_n v_{mn} / \Sigma_n x_n \Sigma_m v_{mn}$ = group fraction
x_n = mole fraction of component n
$\psi_{mn} = \exp - \{(U_{mn} - U_{nn})/RT\} = \exp - (a_{mn}/T)$
    = group interaction parameter

APPLICATION

The glucose–water solution contains the functional groups CH_2, CH, OH, H_2O, CHO. The area and volume parameters of the constituent functional groups, used for the computation of the area and volume parameters of the components in order to obtain the combinatorial part of the activity coefficient, are shown in Table I.

The group-interaction parameters (a_{mn}) used in the computation of the residual part of the activity are shown in Table II. Upon comparing the experimental and predicted activities of water in glucose solutions, it was observed that the agreement is best when the value of a_{mn} for (H_2O, OH) is $-452 \cdot 6$ instead of $-229 \cdot 2$ as reported earlier.[4] This new a_{mn} for (H_2O, OH) was obtained by using a simplex optimization procedure.[5] Once these parameters are determined one simply varies the composition for a fixed temperature to obtain the predicted activity coefficients or activities.

TABLE I
Area and volume parameters of functional groups in a binary solution of glucose and water

Components	Functional groups	Number of groups (v_k)	Volume parameter (R_k)	Area parameter (Q_k)
Glucose	CH_2	1	0·674 4	0·540
	CH	4	0·446 9	0·228
	OH	5	1·000 0	1·200
	CHO	1	0·998 0	0·948
Water	H_2O	1	0·920 0	1·400

Source: Gmehling *et al.*[4]

TABLE II
Group-interaction parameters (a_{mn})

Groups	CH_2	CH	OH	H_2O	CHO
CH_2	0·0	0·0	986·5	1318·0	677·0
CH	0·0	0·0	986·5	1318·0	677·0
OH	156·4	156·4	0·0	353·5	441·8
H_2O	300·0	300·0	−452·6	0·0	−257·3
CHO	505·7	505·7	−404·8	232·7	0·0

Source: Gmehling et al.[4]

RESULTS AND DISCUSSION

The predicted values of water activity in glucose solutions at 25 °C compare well with the published experimental values[6–9] as shown in Fig. 1. The model, however, underestimates the activity of water in concentrated solutions. This behavior may be due to the free-volume effect in such solutions. Oishi and Prausnitz[10] have shown that the free-volume correction in polymer solutions provides a substantial improvement in the predicted activities of solvents using the UNIFAC

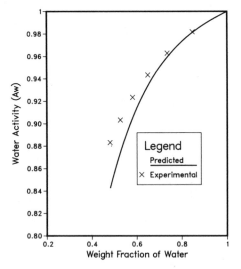

Fig. 1. Plot of water activity versus weight fraction of water at 25 °C.

model. According to Maurer and Prausnitz[11] the free-volume contribution cannot be neglected when dealing with polyatomic molecules. Work is in progress to implement this free-volume correction to improve the prediction of water activity in concentrated solutions.

CONCLUSION

The present study indicates that the UNIFAC model can be used to predict the activity of water in a complex aqueous solution. Further work is in progress to use this model to predict phase changes and partial equilibrium properties of components in an aqueous solution.

ACKNOWLEDGEMENTS

The authors would like to acknowledge the financial support of the National Sciences and Engineering Research Council of Canada provided for this project.

REFERENCES

1. Fredenslund, A., Gmehling, J. and Ramussen, P. *Vapour–liquid Equilibria Using UNIFAC*. Elsevier Scientific Company, New York, 1977.
2. Bondi, A. *Physical Properties of Molecular Crystals, Liquids and Glasses*. Wiley, New York, 1968.
3. Abrams, D. S. and Prausnitz, J. M. *AIChEJ* **21**: 116–28, 1975.
4. Gmehling, J., Rasmussen, P. and Fredenslund, A. *Ind. Eng. Chem. Process Des. Dev.* **21**: 118–27, 1982.
5. Toupin, C. J. Ph.D. Thesis, University of Alberta, Edmonton, Alberta T6G 2P5, Canada, 1985.
6. Audu, T. O. K., Loncin, M. and Weisser, H. *Lebensm. Wiss. u. Technol.* **11**: 31–4, 1978.
7. Ruegg, M. and Blanc, B. *Lebensm. Wiss. u. Technol.* **14**: 1–6, 1981.
8. Stokes, R. H. and Robinson, R. A. *J. Phys. Chem.* **70**(7): 2126–30, 1966.
9. *CRC Handbook of Chemistry and Physics*, 64th edn, (R. C. West, M. J. Astle and W. H. Beyer Eds) CRC Press Inc., Boca Raton, Florida, 1985.
10. Oishi, T. and Prausnitz, J. M. *Ind. Eng. Chem. Process Des. Dev.* **17**: 3, 333–9, 1978.
11. Maurer, G. and Prausnitz, J. M. *Fluid Phase Equilibria* **2**: 91–9, 1978.

17

DIFFUSIVITY AND ACTIVITY OF WATER IN AQUEOUS SOLUTIONS

ANDRÉE VOILLEY, JOHN R. ROSENAU* and HENRY G. SCHWARTZBERG*

Laboratoire de Biologie Physico-Chimique, ENSBANA, Université de Dijon, Dijon, France
* Department of Food Engineering University of Massachusetts, Amherst, Massachusetts 01003, U.S.A.

ABSTRACT

Losses of water from moist foods stored in environments containing a water vapor sink depend on the moisture content versus water activity characteristics of the food, the diffusivity of water in the food, and the moisture mass transfer coefficient for the environment. Methods for using extents and rates of water losses obtained from a series of simple drying tests to determine these factors and for modelling the moisture loss process are presented. Results obtained for aqueous solutions of polyethylene glycols and sugars are illustrated for PEG 20 000 (a polyethylene glycol) and MD63 (a maltodextrin).

INTRODUCTION

Moist foods lose water when stored in atmospheres containing a water vapor sink. It is often important to predict the extent and rate of exchange of moisture between the food and the sink. These processes depend on: (1) the moisture content versus activity of water (X versus a_w) of the food; (2) the diffusivity of water in the food; and (3) the mass transfer coefficient of the air (K_g).

In this work we use water loss data obtained at various conditions to develop and test methods for determining these properties and to establish predictive models for water transfer. Similar processes have been established by Fisch,[1] Gehrmann and Kast[2] and Furuta et al.;[3] but in these cases high air velocities rather than stagnant conditions, which usually occur during storage, were used. In many food systems, the diffusivity of water depends strongly on moisture content.[4-6] Further, foods usually shrink during drying. These factors cause computational difficulties with respect to predicting moisture loss rates. Methods of avoiding or minimizing these difficulties are developed and used in this work.

MATERIALS AND METHODS

Desorptions of water from solutions of sugars and polyethylene glycols (PEG) which initially contained 0·2–0·9 grams of dry matter and 50% (weight/weight) water were carried out at 25 °C. The tests were replicated three times for each material at each of ten relative humidities, which ranged between 11·15% and 90·2%. These humidities were maintained by using 150-mm diameter pans of saturated salt solutions recommended by COST 90.[7] The three samples in a set and the salt solutions were placed in thermostatted, one liter, shallow cylindrical chambers; and samples were periodically briefly withdrawn for weighing. While six sugars and four types of PEG were tested, we will only discuss results for PEG 20 000 and maltodextrin 63 (MD63). Their properties are listed in Table I. Similar moisture loss tests were carried out for 0·4 g loads of pure water. The samples were placed in 23-mm diameter, 24-mm deep glass pans; so the surface area of the water vapor sink greatly exceeded the sample surface area.

Ultimately, the sample weight reached a constant value. The moisture content at this weight, when plotted versus a_{we}, a_w for the

TABLE I
Characteristics of the substrates

Name	Origin	Molecular weight*	50% w/w solution	
			Density	A_w @ 25 °C
Polyethylene glycol PEG 20 000	Merck	22 000	1·091 @ 20 °C	0·920
Maltodextrin MD 63 † DE = 61·5	Roquettes	324	1·239 @ 25 °C	0·922

* Determined by cryometry (mean molecular weight).
† DE: Dextrose equivalent (g glucose per 100 g dry matter).

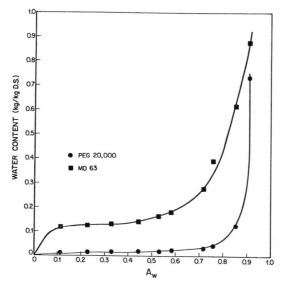

Fig. 1. Desorption isotherms for PEG 20 000 and MD63 at 25 °C.

salt solution used, provided the desorption isotherm for the samples
(Fig. 1).

THEORY

Drying is often initially controlled by mass transfer resistance in the
air, but subsequently may be controlled by diffusional resistance in the
material to be dried. If the Biot number (Bi) is less than 1, mass
transfer resistance in the air largely controls the rate of evaporation. If
Bi is greater than 5, internal diffusion mainly controls.

At stagnant conditions, Bi is initially low, but since the diffusivity of
water in food and the slope of the desorption isotherm decrease during
drying, Bi becomes large at the end of drying.

In this work, to avoid computational problems caused by shrinkage
during drying, we will use the moisture content, X, in kg water/kg dry
solids (DS), as the concentration unit for water, the incremental
nonvolatile load density, w, in kg DS/m^2 to describe the length of the
diffusion path and a diffusivity, D_w, which has the units (kg DS)^2/m^4 s
to describe the diffusivity of water. These differ from the concentration, C (kg water/m^3) infusion path length, r (m) and diffusivity, D_s

(m^2/s) frequently used in the diffusion partial differential equation (DPDE).

In terms of our units

$$\text{Bi} = K_g P^* W(M)/D_w \tag{1}$$

W is the total dry solids load per unit area; P^* is the vapor pressure of pure water (atm); $M = da_w/dX$ on the desorption isotherm at the surface moisture content, X_s; and K_g is the mass transfer coefficient for the air ($kg/m^2\,s\,atm$).

In these units, the DPDE for a slab is

$$\partial X/\partial t = \partial[D_w\,\partial X/\partial w]/\partial w \tag{2}$$

where t is time (s).

If D_w is constant and the sorption isotherm is straight, a solution for this equation is:

$$(\bar{X} - X_e)/(X_0 - X_e) = \sum_{n=0}^{\infty} F_n \exp{(-Q_n^2 D_w t/W^2)} \tag{3}$$

X_0 is the initial (uniform) moisture content of the food, X_e is the food moisture content in equilibrium with a_{we}, the a_w provided by the water vapor sink (saturated salt solution). In Eq. (3) the coefficients F_n and eigenvalues Q_n are functions of Bi. Similar equations with different F_n can be written to predict $(X_s - X_e)$ versus t; and $(X_s - X_e)/(\bar{X} - X_e)$ can be used to determine Bi or, in certain cases, merely to determine whether Bi is large or small.

Equation (3) can be truncated to provide Eq. (4), which is valid if t is large enough. If Bi is small, the range of validity extends to very small t.

$$(\bar{X} - X_e)/(X_0 - X_e) = F_1 \exp{(-Q_1^2 D_w t/W^2)} \tag{4}$$

If Eq. (4) is differentiated with respect to t and rearranged, we obtain

$$d(X - X_e)/dt = -(Q_1^2 D_w/W^2) \tag{5}$$

Therefore, when: D_w and Bi are constant; the a_w versus X isotherm for desorption is linear; Eq. (3) can be truncated; and Q_1 can be determined from $(X_s - X_e)/(X - X_e)$ or by other means, D_w can be determined from the slope of a plot of $d(X - X_e)/dt$ versus $(X - X_e)$, i.e. from Eq. (6).

Note: $d(X - X_e)/dt = dX/dt = (dm/dt)/AW$, where $-(dm/dt)$ is the weight loss rate and A is the sample surface area.

$$D_w = -[(dX/dt)/(X - X_e)](W/Q_1)^2 \tag{6}$$

However, D_w and Bi usually are not constant for foods, and numerical methods have to be used to solve Eq. (2). This is not difficult if the relationship between D_w and X is known; but great difficulty is encountered when drying tests are used to determine D_w versus X. Burdensome trial and error procedures have to be used; and even after good X versus t fits are obtained for particular cases, one cannot be sure that the solution is unique and general. Therefore, in this work to provide greater assurance with respect to generality, tests were carried out at different values of W and a_{we}. Though Eqs. (3) and (4) are not valid when the sorption isotherm is not straight and D_w is not constant, we used Eqs. (5) and (6) to provide guidance with respect to selecting initial trial values of D_w. Trial D_w versus X values from Eq. (6) were used in place of D_w versus local X to obtain numerical solutions of Eq. (2) and the following boundary condition:

$$-[D_w \, \partial X/\partial w] @ (w = W) = K_g P^*[M_s X_s + G - a_{we}] \tag{7}$$

G and M_s are respectively the $X = 0$ intercept and (da_w/dX) of the tangent line at the current X_s on the desorption isotherm (X versus a_w), and D_w is the diffusivity at $X = X_s$.

Values of X versus t were obtained from the numerical solution of the DPDE by averaging local X versus w values at particular values of t. These predicted X versus t were compared with the experimental X versus t; and the D_w versus local X function was progressively adjusted to improve the goodness of fit between the two sets of values. This was done until reasonably good consistent agreement between the experimental and predicted $\bar{X}$ were obtained for all tested values of W and a_{we}.

At low Bi, it can be shown by Taylor series expansion of the equation used to define Q_1 that

$$Q_1^2 \approx \text{Bi}/(1 + 0.34 \, \text{Bi}) \tag{8}$$

If Eqs. (8) and (1) are substituted in Eq. (5) we obtain:

$$-dm/dt = -W(dX/dt) = K_g P^*[X_s + G - a_{we}]/(1 + 0.34 \, \text{Bi}) \tag{9}$$

The only place where D_w appears in Eq. (9) is as part of Bi; but at stagnant conditions, Bi is small (e.g. between 0·05 and 0·3) when X_s is on the vertical portion of the sorption isotherm. Therefore, at the start of drying, i.e. when X is large, the effect of D_w is small; and it is difficult to determine D_w accurately in the high X range. By using experimental weight loss data, Eq. (9) can be solved for D_w, but D_w will not be very accurate. This occurs because K_g rather than D_w controls the initial stages of drying. For the same reason, D_w versus X values obtained from numerical solutions of the DPDE, Eq. (2), will also not be precise at high values of X. On the other hand, since K_g controls in the high X range, one can still predict $-d\bar{X}/dt$ accurately during the initial part of drying.

At high Bi, i.e. on the low-slope portion of the sorption isotherm, where X is small, D_w mainly controls the drying rate and hence can be determined accurately. At large Bi, it is reasonable to assume that $Q_1 = \pi Bi/(2 + 2Bi)$. We can substitute $Q_1 = \pi/2$ in Eq. (6) to obtain an initial estimate for D_w, with this value we can determine Bi and revised Q_1, which in turn can be used in Eq. (6) to obtain a revised D_w. This process was iterated until D_w convergence was obtained.

RESULTS

Trial values of K_g were determined from evaporation rates $(-dm/dt)$ for pure water by using Eq. (10).

$$K_g = -(dm/dt)/[AP^*(1 - a_{we})] \qquad (10)$$

where A, the pan surface area $= 4 \cdot 155 \times 10^{-4}\,\mathrm{m^2}$. To counterbalance the effect of vapor pressure reductions due to evaporative cooling on the apparent values of K_g, these K_g were plotted versus $(1 - a_{we})$ and the extrapolated value of K_g at $(1 - a_{we}) = 0$, i.e. $4 \cdot 95 \times 10^{-4}\,\mathrm{kg}$ water/$\mathrm{m^2}$ atm s was taken as the true K_g value. In other cases, abnormal or different values of K_g were encountered, and K_g was calculated using drying rates $-(dm/dt)_{init}$ obtained close to the start of drying for PEG and sugar solution samples; and Eq. (11) was used to calculate K_g.

$$K_g = (K_g)_{app}/[1 - (4/3)(K_g)_{app}P^*M(\sqrt{t/\pi D_w})] \qquad (11)$$

where

$$(K_g)_{app} = -(dm/dt)_{init}/[AP^*(a_{wo} - a_{we})] \qquad (12)$$

and a_{wo} is the a_w in equilibrium with X_0 and t is the elapsed time during which $-(dm/dt)_{init}$ is measured. Equation (11) is a rearranged, truncated form of short exposure time solutions for the DPDE for semi-infinite domains when surface mass transfer resistance is appreciable.

The K_g obtained from Eq. (10) or (11) were used to calculate a_{ws} (water activity at the sample surface) during the drying tests, i.e.

$$a_{ws} = -(dm/dt)/[AK_gP^*] + a_{we} \qquad (13)$$

a_{ws} was then used to determine X_s, the corresponding value of X on the desorption isotherm. $\bar{X}$ and $-(dX/dt)$ were determined from the weight loss versus time data.

In the low Bi range, values of $(X_s - X'_e)/(\bar{X} - X'_e) = R$, where $X'_e = (a_{we} - G)/M$, were used to estimate the Q_1 used in Eq. (6). X'_e rather than X_e is used in this formulation because of boundary condition invoked in Eq. (7). In conventional DPDE solutions, where linear sorption isotherms and constant D_w and Bi apply, $R = Q_1^2/\text{Bi}$ if

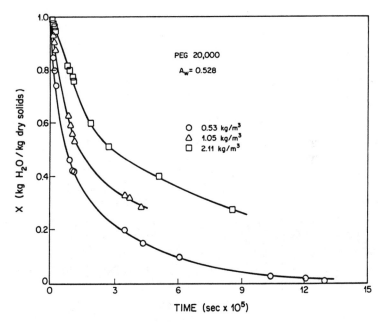

Fig. 2. Predicted and experimental kinetics of water desorption (X vs t) for PEG 20 000 at 25 °C for three different load densities with $a_{we} = 0.528$; experimental values for: $W = 0.53\,kg/m^2$ (□); $W = 1.05\,kg/m^2$ (△); $W = 2.11\,kg/m^2$ (○); solid lines are predicted values.

Eq. (4) is valid. Though these conditions do not apply in the present case, R was used to provide initial Q_1 and D_w estimates.

D_w values estimated from Eq. (6) were used in the initial numerical solutions of Eq. (2). The DGEAR routine for solving stiff partial differential equations, which is in the IMSL library of programs,[8] was used in solving Eq. (2).

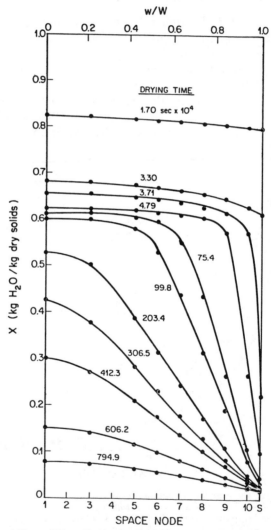

Fig. 3. Predicted X vs w/W profiles for water desorption from PEG 20 000 at $a_{wc} = 0.528$ and different drying times.

Repeated adjustment of the D_w versus X function ultimately provided good agreement between the experimental and predicted data. Typical predicted and experimental values of $\bar{X}$ versus t for PEG 20 000 are shown in Fig. 2. Typical local values of X versus w for PEG 20 000 at various times are shown in Fig. 3.

For PEG 20 000 the D_w versus X functions used to obtain the predicted X versus t and X versus w value are:

$$D_w = 5 \cdot 0 \times 10^{-5} (\text{kg DS})^2/\text{m}^4 \text{ s} \quad \text{for} \quad X > 0 \cdot 45$$

$$D_w = 5 \cdot 0 \times 10^{-6} (\text{kg DS})^2/\text{m}^4 \text{ s} \quad \text{for} \quad X < 0 \cdot 40$$

and $D_w = [5 \times 10^{-6} + (4 \cdot 5 \times 10^{-5})(X - 0 \cdot 40)/0 \cdot 45](\text{kg DS})^2/\text{m}^4 \text{ s}$

$$\text{for } 0 \cdot 40 < X < 0 \cdot 45.$$

The corresponding D_w versus X functions for MD 63 are:

$$D_w = 3 \cdot 6 \times 10^{-4} (\text{kg DS})^2/\text{m}^4 \text{ s} \quad \text{for} \quad X > 0 \cdot 6$$

and $D_w = 6 \cdot 0 \times 10^{-4} . X . (\text{kg DS})^2/\text{m}^4 \text{ s} \quad \text{for} \quad X < 0 \cdot 6.$

Predicted and experimental X versus t data for MD63 are plotted in Fig. 4 for W roughly equal to 1.2 kg DS/m^2 and four a_{we}: $0 \cdot 226$, $0 \cdot 528$, $0 \cdot 708$, and $0 \cdot 843$. Figures 2 and 4 indicate the relative goodness of fit obtained for predicted X versus t values.

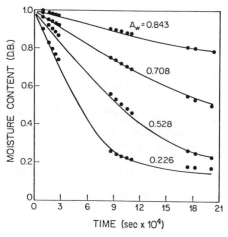

Fig. 4. *Predicted and experimental kinetics of water desorption (X vs t) for MD63 at 23 °C for four different water activity sink values: $a_{we} = 0 \cdot 226$; $a_{we} = 0 \cdot 528$; $a_{we} = 0 \cdot 708$; and $a_{we} = 0 \cdot 843$.*

DISCUSSION

A step change in D_w versus X may even occur in the $X = 0.40$–0.45 range for PEG 20 000; however, the DGEAR program used to numerically solve the DPDE cannot accommodate step changes. The sudden change in D_w for PEG 20 000 may be due to the formation of two liquid phases near $X = 0.40$. The PEG 20 000 solution becomes turbid during drying; and such turbidity is usually a sign that phase separation is occurring. Further, the steepness of the desorption isotherm for PEG 20 000 near $X = 0.40$ is also consistent with a sharp drop in X at a constant a_w, which would occur when two phases form.

For PEG 20 000; $-\,\mathrm{d}\bar{X}/\mathrm{d}t$ at constant $(\bar{X} - X_e)$ is inversely proportional to W. This is not surprising at the start of drying, when Bi is small. When Bi is small, Q_1^2 is roughly proportional to W and this cancels part of W^2 which appears in the exponential term in Eq. (4).

However, at large Bi, i.e. near the middle and end of drying, Q_1 is normally scarcely affected by W at all. The abnormal $-\mathrm{d}\bar{X}/\mathrm{d}t$ versus W behavior for PEG 20 000 in this range apparently is due to the nature of the D_w versus X function for PEG 20 000.

The ability of the procedures used to handle such unusual behavior and to provide consistent predictions for different values of a_{we} and W indicates that these procedures can probably be used effectively in a great many situations.

REFERENCES

1. Fisch, B. P. Diffusion and thermodynamics of water in potato starch gel. *Fundamental Aspects of the Dehydration of Foodstuffs.* Society of Chemical Industry, London, p. 143, 1958.
2. Gehrmann, D. and Kast, W. Drying of gels. *Proceedings of the First International Symposium on Drying.* Science Press, Princeton, pp. 239–46, 1978.
3. Furuta, T., Tsujimoto, S., Makino, H., Okazaki, M. and Tori, R. Measurement of the diffusion coefficient of water and ethanol in aqueous maltodextrin solution, *J. Food Eng.* **3:** 169, 1985.
4. King, C. J. Physical and chemical properties governing volatilization of flavor and aroma components. *Physical Properties of Foods,* (M. Peleg and E. Bagley Eds). AVI Publishing Co. Westport, Conn., 1983.
5. Menting, L. C., Hoogstad, B. and Thijssen, H. A. C. Diffusion coefficients of water and organic volatiles in carbohydrate–water systems. *J. Food Technol.* **5:** 111–26, 1970.
6. Thijssen, H. A. C. and Rulkens, W. H. Retention of aromas in drying food liquids. *De Ingenieur* **80**(47): 45–56, 1968.

7. Wolf, W., Spiess, W. E. L., Jung, G., Weisser, H., Bizot, H. and Duckworth, R. B. The water sorption isotherms of microcrystalline cellulose (MCC) and purified potato starch. Results of a collaborative study. *J. Food Eng.* **3:** 51–73, 1984.
8. Rice, J. R. *Numerical Methods, Software and Analysis, IMSL Reference Edition,* McGraw-Hill, New York, p. 292, 1983.

18

INFLUENCE OF TEMPERATURE ON SORPTION ISOTHERMS

H. WEISSER

Institut für Lebensmittelverfahrenstechnik der Universität Karlsruhe, Postfach 6380, Kaiserstraße 12, D-7500 Karlsruhe 1, Federal Republic of Germany

ABSTRACT

Sorption isotherms for ground, short-time roasted coffee were determined with four different sorption devices in the temperature range of 20–80 °C and also for conventionally roasted coffee at 20 °C. It was found that the three-parameter Guggenheim–Anderson–de Boer (GAB) equation fits the isotherms with great accuracy. The temperature dependent parameters for the GAB equation and the values of the relative percentage root mean square are given.

INTRODUCTION

For studies of the preservation processes of foods knowledge of water activity of the product is essential. In particular, knowledge of the isothermal equilibrium relationship between moisture content (w) and water activity (a_w) of the food represented by the moisture sorption isotherm is of great importance for the design and operation of various industrial processes like drying, conditioning, agglomerating, mixing, packaging and storage. In most cases water sorption isotherms have a sigmoid shaped curve which is described as a Type II isotherm as classified by Brunauer. As van den Berg[1] demonstrated the so called Guggenheim–Anderson–de Boer sorption equation (GAB) is a very useful tool for fitting data up to about $a_w = 0.9$. The GAB equation[2–4] was used for the standardized description and comparison of isotherms in laboratories in Europe[5] and in USA.[6] Weisser[7] showed that the GAB equation with temperature-dependent coefficients is suitable for describing the influence of temperature on sorption behaviour of several food components like apple-pectin, soy and whey protein, or sodium caseinate, in the range of 25–80 °C.

The present investigation was conducted to measure moisture sorption isotherms of commercially roasted ground coffee over a large temperature range, since similar data are missing from the published literature, e.g. Gane,[8] Ayerst,[9] Quast and Teixeira Neto,[10] Hayakawa et al.[11]

MATERIALS AND METHODS

Materials
Commercially available, either conventionally or short-time roasted ground coffee (Jacobs Krönung, Jacobs GmbH Bremen) was used.

Methods
The moisture content of the different samples was measured by means of a vacuum oven method (70 °C, 16 h, 130 mbar; DIN 10 764, p. 2) or by desiccating in a drying cabinet for at least 3 h at 105 °C and atmospheric pressure over molecular sieves as desiccant. Both methods gave the same results.

Samples taken for adsorption measurement were predried in a vacuum dryer for one day at a temperature of 50 °C and a pressure of about 1 mbar. Samples to be used for desorption measurement were conditioned for 1 month to a relative humidity of 0·85 (20 °C) or 0·82 (40 °C) by placing the weighing bottles in a desiccator with aqueous saturated KCl solution.

Three different types of sorbostats were used:

(i) In the range 20–40 °C most sorption isotherms were measured on the standardized COST sorbostat (COST = European Cooperation in the Field of Science and Technical Research), consisting of ten preserve jars (1 L Weck glass), which were kept at the desired temperature in an in-line thermostat.[12] Each COST sorbostat contained 5 or 6 weighing bottles (25 × 25 mm, DIN 12 605) with a sample mass of about 400 mg. Using ten aqueous saturated salt solutions the water activity was fairly evenly distributed over the range $0·1 < a_w < 0·9$. The relative humidity data of these salt solutions given in Greenspan's tables[13] were used since they are widely accepted by many researchers (Table I). The unknown values of four salts at 40 °C

TABLE I
Relative humidity of aqueous saturated salt solutions
at different temperatures

Salt	Relative humidity		
	20 °C	25 °C	40 °C
LiCl	0·113	0·112	0·112
CH_3COOK	0·231	0·226	0·201
$MgCl_2$	0·331	0·327	0·316
K_2CO_3	0·432	0·438	0·432
$Mg(NO_3)_2$	0·544	0·529	0·484
NaBr	0·591	0·577	0·530
$SrCl_2$	0·725	0·708	0·658
NaCl	0·755	0·753	0·747
KCl	0·851	0·843	0·821
$BaCl_2$	0·903	0·903	0·890

were determined by means of a dew-point hygrometer (General Eastern, Watertown, MA).

(ii) Additional measurements were carried out with a modification of the proximity equilibration cell originally developed by Lang *et al.*[14] The sorbostat called Miniex (Fig. 1) consists of a plastic weighing dish (diameter $d = 60$ mm, height $h = 35$ mm), containing a slurry of saturated salt solution in about 1/4 to 1/3 of its volume. A weighing

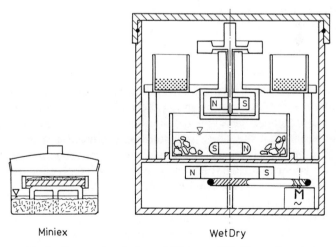

Miniex   WetDry

Fig. 1. Cross-sectional views of Miniex and WetDry sorbostats.

dish with a sintered glass base was placed on top of a trivet on which samples of about 1 g were equilibrated. Compared to the equilibration time of at least two weeks in the COST sorbostat the required conditioning time was reduced by more than half.

(iii) Commercially available sorbostats (WetDry, Büchi, Eislingen) with stirred headspace and stirred salt solutions to improve heat and mass transfer[15] were used in a constant temperature cabinet at 40 °C. As shown in Fig. 1 the sorbostat consists of a small desiccator ($d = 12$ cm, $h = 10$ cm) in which a perforated aluminium disk carrying up to eight weighing bottles is inserted together with a small magnetically operated ventilator. The electrolyte solution is placed in a Petri dish on the bottom of the sorbostat and can be stirred by means of a magnetic stirrer driven by a small 2 W motor running at a constant speed of about 150 rpm. Compared to the COST equipment, there was a reduction in time of about 1/3, but unfortunately, constant temperature could not be achieved within the WetDry sorbostat.

A two-temperature method was used to compare results obtained with the desiccator methods and to expand the temperature range up to 80 °C. Rotasorp, a sorption apparatus with rotatable sample plate which was built in our laboratory, was used to equilibrate up to 22 samples simultaneously.[7,16,17] After maintaining the samples of about 350 mg in sample dishes ($d = 14$ mm, $h = 9$ mm, stainless steel) at the desired equilibrium conditions for one day—which was found to be enough to approximate equilibrium—the moisture content was determined by drying.

RESULTS AND DISCUSSION

Influence of Roasting Process on Sorption Isotherm

A comparison of the sorption isotherms of conventionally and short-time roasted ground coffee determined at 20 °C in the COST sorbostat shows that the short-time roasting produced a slightly more hygroscopic product (Fig. 2). This might be explained by the increase in product volume during the high temperature, short-time roasting process which causes a larger inner surface.

Influence of Adsorption and Desorption

A remarkable hysteresis loop appears between adsorption and desorption. Figure 3 shows the isotherms measured in the COST sorbostat at

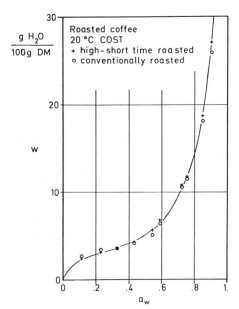

Fig. 2. Comparison of isotherm data for short-time and conventionally roasted ground coffee.

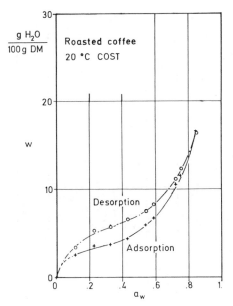

Fig. 3. Adsorption and desorption isotherm of short-time roasted coffee at 20 °C (COST sorbostat).

193

20 °C after an equilibration time of more than two weeks. Prior to use in the experiment, samples were conditioned for one month over a saturated LiCl or KCl solution to have a initial moisture content of about 2·5% for adsorption and 18% for desorption.

Having reached equilibrium, no time dependence of the hysteresis loop could be found at 20 °C. But measurements at 40 °C over a period of more than five months showed a continuous decrease of moisture content for the desorption samples. With increasing time a decrease of the hysteresis loop could be observed. This means that the desorption isotherm is not an equilibrium curve.

Measurements with Different Sorption Equipment

At 40 °C the adsorption isotherm of predried coffee was measured in three different sorbostats (COST, Miniex, WetDry) and in the Rotasorp sorption equipment. As shown in Fig. 4 there is very good agreement between the various sorption devices.

First experiments with the WetDry sorbostat showed a significant discrepancy compared to other results which was due to a temperature

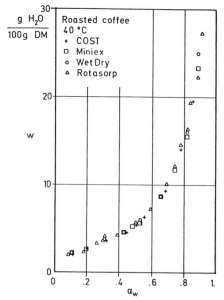

Fig. 4. Comparison of adsorption measurements on roasted ground coffee using four different devices at 40 °C.

gradient of 1·1 K between the stirred salt solution and the sample caused by a heat flux from the motor to the salt solution. The actual relative humidity around the sample was higher and had to be corrected by a factor which is the quotient of water vapour pressure at solution and sample temperature. To prevent undesired warming of the salt solution the bottom of the WetDry sorbostat had to be very carefully insulated or else the stirrer should be in operation for only a few minutes per hour.

Influence of Temperature

Figure 5 shows the influence of temperature on the adsorption isotherm. Measurements at 20, 25 (not shown in Fig. 5) and 40 °C were made in the COST sorbostat and at 40, 60 and 80 °C in the Rotasorp. The sigmoid shape of the curve decreases with increasing temperature. As usual, at constant moisture content an increase in temperature increases water activity considerably. This behaviour is common to solid foods, although sugars and sugar substitutes show the

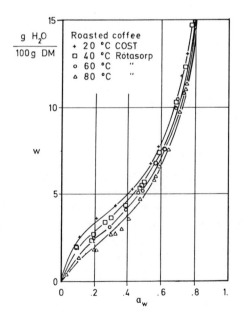

Fig. 5. *Influence of temperature on the adsorption isotherm of roasted ground coffee as determined using COST (20 °C) and Rotasorp equipment.*

opposite behaviour at higher temperatures and water activities because of solution of solids in water.[7]

Mathematical Description of Sorption Isotherm

Many investigators have reviewed published isotherm equations, e.g. van den Berg and Bruin,[2] Boquet et al.,[18] Iglesias and Chirife.[19] As van den Berg[1] pointed out, the Guggenheim–Anderson–de Boer (GAB) model, a three parameter equation, is very useful for precisely fitting sorption isotherms up to a_w values of 0.9.

$$\frac{w}{w_m} = \frac{CKa_w}{(1 - Ka_w)(1 - Ka_w + CKa_w)} \tag{1}$$

where

w_m = moisture content on dry basis at fully occupied active sorption sites with one molecule of water (called monolayer in BET theory);

w = moisture content at equilibrium a_w;

C = GAB sorption constant related to monolayer properties.

$C(T) = C' \exp (H_1 - H_m)/(RT)$

H_1 = total heat of sorption of the first layer on primary sites;

H_m = total heat of sorption of the multilayer which differs from the heat of condensation of pure liquid water;

C' = entropic accommodation factor;

T = temperature (K);

R = ideal gas constant.

K = GAB sorption constant related to multilayer properties

$K(T) = K' \exp (H_m - H_e)/(RT)$

H_e = heat of condensation of pure water vapour;

K' = entropic accommodation factor.

This GAB model can be considered as an extension of the well known and often used BET model of multimolecular localized homogeneous adsorption[20] taking into account the modified properties of the sorbed water molecules in the multilayer region. The three GAB constants depend on product characteristics and to some extent on temperature.[1,7] They may be determined from experimental results by using the least squares method for minimizing the absolute difference between measured and calculated water content[21] or by a nonlinear optimization program which estimates the parameters based on the steepest ascent method for optimization. As can be seen in Table II each method gives slightly different constants. Therefore the monolayer values w_m and the calculated heats of sorption are also different.

TABLE II

GAB and GAB(T) constants calculated from experimental results for short-time roasted and ground coffee

Fitted with least squares method

Temp (°C)	w_m ($g\,W/100\,g\,DM$)	$w_m(T)$	C	$C(T)$	K	$K(T)$	n	P (%)	$P(T)$ (%)
20	3·49	3·40	16·65	17·80	0·963	0·972	10	1·32	1·46
25	3·22	3·33	15·87	15·90	0·993	0·977	10	1·10	1·51
40	3·12	3·16	12·45	11·58	0·987	0·990	38	1·03	1·17
60	3·10	2·97	8·59	7·93	0·993	1·006	13	1·66	2·90
80	2·74	2·80	5·22	5·67	1·029	1·020	18	1·91	2·12

Fitted with nonlinear optimization method

Temp (°C)	w_m ($g\,W/100\,g\,DM$)	$w_m(T)$	C	$C(T)$	K	$K(T)$	n	P (%)	$P(T)$ (%)
20	3·42	3·43	19·73	16·08	0·966	0·972	10	1·40	1·54
25	3·36	3·44	12·27	13·61	0·985	0·972	10	1·13	1·53
40	3·57	3·47	7·15	8·51	0·961	0·969	38	1·37	1·22
60	3·60	3·50	4·82	4·86	0·966	0·967	13	2·40	2·36
80	3·43	3·53	3·21	2·96	0·967	0·965	18	2·32	2·52

n = number of observations.
P = mean relative deviation modulus. $P = 100/n \sum_{i=1}^{n} |w_{exp} - w_{cal}|/w_{exp}$

Parameters to determine GAB(T) constants according to Eq. (2)

Method	$w_m(T)$		$C(T)$		$K(T)$	
	w_m'	w_m''	C'	$H_1 - H_m$	K'	$H_m - H_e$
	($g/100\,g\,K$)			(kJ/mol)		(kJ/mol)
Least squares method	1·095	332	0·0213	16·40	1·292	−0·694
Nonlinear opt. method	4·027	−46·7	0·000756	24·29	0·927	0·116

The influence of temperature on all three GAB constants—in the original papers w_m is assumed to be constant—may be calculated with the following equations which are similar to the well known Arrhenius equation in reaction kinetics.

$$C(T) = C' \exp\left((H_1 - H_m)/(RT)\right)$$
$$K(T) = K' \exp\left((H_m - H_e)/(RT)\right) \qquad (2)$$
$$w_m(T) = w_m' \exp\left(w_m''/T\right)$$

where

w_m' = pre-exponential constant;
w_m'' = temperature coefficient.

Both regression methods show a strong temperature dependence of the sorption constant C. K and w_m appear to be virtually independent of temperature. While the regression analysis with the least squares method results in a decrease of K and an increase of w_m with increasing temperature, the nonlinear optimization method showed the opposite. Hence, calculations of the sorption isotherms of roasted and ground coffee could be made with temperature independent mean values of w_m and K. Table II summarizes the results of the isotherm analysis with the GAB equation (fit of the constants w_m, C, K for all five temperatures), and the GAB(T) equation (fit of the $w_m(T)$, $C(T)$, $K(T)$ constants for all five temperatures to Eq. (2)).

Figure 5 shows the experimental results as symbols and the calculated GAB(T) curves as continuous lines. A very good agreement is observed up to water activities of about 0.8.

CONCLUSIONS

(1) To achieve correct sorption results it is necessary to control the constancy of temperature in the whole sorption equipment, otherwise significant errors will be made, especially at higher water activities.

(2) Sorption isotherms determined using four different types of sorption equipment showed very good agreement within experimental error. The fastest devices were Rotasorp and Miniex with equilibrating times of one day and one week respectively.

(3) The GAB equation was found useful for describing the sorption isotherm of roasted and ground coffee. The three GAB constants depend to some extent on temperature. In particular the sorption constant C shows a great temperature dependence. In addition, these constants can provide information about the monolayer value w_m and the heat of sorption from the first and subsequent water layers.

ACKNOWLEDGEMENTS

The author expresses his thanks to Mr M. Schoch for his technical assistance and the students M. Benz, A. Hummel, J. Donat, H. Schuchmann (Institute of Food Process Engineering, University of Karlsruhe), for their valuable help.

REFERENCES

1. van den Berg, C. Vapour sorption equilibria and other water–starch interactions: A physico-chemical approach. Doctoral Thesis, Agricultural University Wageningen, Netherlands, 1981.
2. van den Berg, C. and Bruin, S. Water activity and its estimation in food systems: theoretical aspects. In *Water Activity: influence on Food Quality* (L. B. Rockland and G. F. Stewart Eds). Academic Press, New York, p. 1, 1981.
3. van den Berg, C. Description of water activity of foods for engineering purposes by means of the G.A.B. model of sorption. In *Engineering and Food: Engineering Sciences in the Food Industry* (B. McKenna Ed.), Vol. 1. Elsevier Applied Science Publishers, London, p. 311, 1984 (Proc. ICEF 3).
4. van den Berg, C. Development of B.E.T.-like models for sorption of water on foods, theory and relevance. In *Properties of Water in Foods in Relation to Quality and Stability* (D. Simatos and J. L. Multon Eds). Martinus Nijhoff Publishers, Dordrecht, p. 133, 1985 (Proc. ISOPOW III. Nato Asi Series, Series E, Applied Sciences, No. 90).
5. Wolf, W., Spiess, W. E. L., Jung, G., Weisser, H., Bizot, H. and Duckworth, R. B. The water-vapour sorption isotherms of microcrystalline cellulose (MCC) and of purified potato starch. Results of a Collaborative Study. *J. Food Eng.* **3:** 51, 1984.
6. Lomauro, C. J., Bakshi, A. S. and Labuza, T. P. Evaluation of food moisture sorption isotherm equations. Parts I and II. *Lebensm.-Wiss. u.-Technol.* **18:** 110 and 118, 1985.
7. Weisser, H. Influence of temperature on sorption equilibria. In *Properties of Water in Foods in Relation to Quality and Stability*. (D. Simatos and J. L. Multon Eds). Martinus Nijhoff Publishers, Dordrecht, p. 119, 1985 (Proc. ISOPOW III. Nato Asi Series, Series E, Applied Sciences, No. 90).
8. Gane, R. The water relations of some dried fruits, vegetables and plant products. *J. Sci. Food Agric.* **1:** 42, 1950.
9. Ayerst, G. Determination of water activity of some hygroscopic food materials by a dew-point method. *J. Sci. Food Agric.* **16:** 71, 1965.
10. Quast, D. G. and Teixeira Neto, R. O. Moisture problems of foods in tropical climates. *Food Technol.* **30**(5): 98, 1976.
11. Hayakawa, K.-I., Matas, J. and Hwang, M. P. Moisture sorption isotherms of coffee products. *J. Food Sci.* **43:** 1026, 1978.
12. Spiess, W. E. L. and Wolf, W. R. The results of the COST 90 Project on water activity. In *Physical Properties of Foods* (R. Jowitt *et al.* Eds). Elsevier Applied Science Publishers, London, p. 65, 1983 (Proc. COST 90 Final Seminar, Leuven).
13. Greenspan, L. Humidity fixed points of binary saturated aqueous solutions. *J. Res. NBS* **81A:** 89, 1976.
14. Lang, K. W., McCune, T. D. and Steinberg, M. P. A proximity equilibration cell for determination of sorption isotherm. *J. Food Sci.* **46:** 936, 1981.
15. Gal, S. Recent developments in techniques for obtaining complete sorption isotherms. In *Water Activity: Influence on Food Quality* (L. B. Rockland and G. F. Stewart Eds). Academic Press, New York, p. 89, 1981.
16. Bandyopadhyay, S., Weisser, H. and Loncin, M. Water adsorption isotherms of foods at high temperatures. *Lebensm.-Wiss. u.Technol.* **13:** 182, 1980.
17. Weisser, H., Weber, J. and Loncin, M. Water vapour sorption isotherms of sugar substitutes in the temperature range 25 to 80 °C. *ZFL, Int. Z. Lebensm. Technol. u. Verfahrenstechn.* **33:** 89, 1982.
18. Boquet, R., Chirife J. and Iglesias, H. A. Equations for fitting water sorption isotherms of foods: Part II. Evaluation of various two-parameter models. *J. Food Technol.* **13:** 319, 1978.

19. Iglesias, H. A. and Chirife, J. *Handbook of Food Isotherms. Parameters for Food and Food Components.* Academic Press, New York, 1982.
20. Brunauer, St., Emmett, P. H. and Teller, E. Adsorption of gases in multi-molecular layers. *J. Am. Chem. Soc.* **60:** 309, 1938.
21. Bizot, H. Using the 'G.A.B.' model to construct sorption isotherms. In *Physical Properties of Foods* (R. Jowitt *et al.* Eds). Elsevier Applied Science Publishers, London, p. 43, 1983 (Proc. COST 90 Final Seminar, Leuven).

19

EQUILIBRIUM MOISTURE CONTENT OF RICE

T. KAMEOKA,* D. S. JAYAS,† H. MORISHIMA‡ and
S. SOKHANSANJ

*Department of Agricultural Engineering, University of Saskatchewan,
Saskatoon, Saskatchewan, Canada S7N 0W0*
† *Department of Agricultural Engineering, University of Manitoba,
Winnipeg, Manitoba, Canada R3T 2N2*
‡ *Department of Agricultural Engineering, University of Tokyo, Japan*

ABSTRACT

*Desorption equilibrium moisture contents were determined using the
method of salt solutions (static method), for rough rice, brown rice and
rice hull at 20, 30 and 40 °C and eight different relative humidities in the
range 11·3–85·0%.*

*The Dubinin–Astakhov (D–A) equation[1] was used to smooth the
equilibrium moisture content data and then, using the correlated data
and the theoretical information, a modified D–A equation applicable to
grain was proposed. This modified equation uses the chemical potential
instead of the Polanyi adsorption potential.*

*The D–A equation was used to analyze the equilibrium moisture
content data of rough rice, brown rice and hull. Using the data
smoothed by this equation, the equilibrium moisture content difference
between rough rice, brown rice and hull was examined.*

INTRODUCTION

Paddy is a major crop in many Asian countries. Usually paddy is
dehulled to brown rice before storing. For a better understanding of
the drying and storage of cereals, their equilibrium moisture content is
the most important parameter. For most grains, however, equilibrium
moisture content data at high temperatures[2,3] are lacking. Especially,

* Present address: Department of Agricultural Machinery, Faculty of Agriculture, Mie
University, Tsu, Mie Pref. S14 Japan.

for brown rice and hull, no data on equilibrium moisture content could be found.

In a single kernel, the endosperm occupies the largest portion of hulled rice. The endosperm consists of starch granules and each granule contains many glucose units. This causes a great number of micropores ranging from $0 \cdot 1$ to $1 \cdot 0 \, \mu m$ in hulled rice. Water molecules in rice are bound with the $-OH-$ type of polar molecules in the structure of starch and protein, and then captured inside the micropores by the effect of intermolecular forces between water molecules and the surface of the absorbent. Furthermore, as the availability of water increases, the pore gets filled. Therefore, the sorption equation applicable to these three kinds of water states must be chosen when studying the water in rice.

There are many equations used to predict sorption isotherms.[1,4–7] The theories from which these equations were derived can be divided into four types: single layer adsorption; multilayer adsorption; capillary condensation; and adsorption potential theory. For biological materials, the adsorption potential theory can describe the full range of sorption phenomena. The equations of Halsey,[5] Chung and Pfost,[7] and Dubinin and Astakhov[1] were derived based on this adsorption potential theory and any of the three could be applied to analyze the experimental data. However, the D–A equation was used in this study of the effect of temperature on the equilibrium moisture content of rough rice, brown rice and hull mainly because this equation correlates best to Polanyi's potential theory.[8]

EXPERIMENTAL PROCEDURES

Saturated salt solutions with an excess of the salts were used to control the humidity at the constant temperatures. The relative humidity values for various salts and temperatures were taken from Refs. 9 and 10 and are given in Table I.

Eight humidity control chambers, for each desired relative humidity, were placed in temperature-controlled rooms at 20, 30 and 40 °C. The temperature of the room was controlled to an accuracy of $0 \cdot 5$ °C. About 10 g of rough rice, 10 g of brown rice and about 3 g of hull were put into separate petri glass dishes and then these three sample holders were put in the same humidity chamber. Figure 1 shows the schematic diagram of the humidity chamber with samples and sample holders.

The weight change was measured each day using an electric balance until the change in weight was less than 1 mg/day. The moisture

TABLE I

Equilibrium moisture content (MC) of rough rice, brown rice and hull (cv. Nipponbare, Desorption data)

Temp.			Salt used for humidity control							
			LiCl	CH$_3$COOK	MgCl$_2$	K$_2$CO$_3$	Mg(NO$_3$)$_2$	NaNO$_2$	NaCl	KCl
20 °C	Rough rice	RH (%)	11·3	22·8	33·0	43·3	54·6	66·0	75·5	85·0
		MC (% db)	6·12	8·79	10·67	12·4	14·01	16·09	18·73	20·95
	Brown rice	MC (% db)	6·37	9·29	11·2	13·29	15·33	17·25	19·62	22·12
	Hull	MC (% db)	4·48	6·83	8·39	10·1	11·71	13·82	16·29	18·12
30 °C	Rough rice	RH (%)	11·2	21·6	32·6	43·2	51·3	63·0	75·5	83·6
		MC (% db)	—	7·75	9·56	11·41	12·68	14·64	16·88	18·88
	Brown rice	MC (% db)	—	8·39	10·3	12·04	13·57	15·65	17·84	19·86
	Hull	MC (% db)	—	5·98	7·35	8·95	10·31	12·19	14·58	16·13
40 °C	Rough rice	RH (%)	11·2	20·4	31·6	43·1	48·3	60·0	75·5	82·0
		MC (% db)	5·05	7·08	8·73	10·52	11·41	13·25	15·86	17·77
	Brown rice	MC (% db)	5·37	7·59	9·24	11·31	12·31	14·21	17·06	18·93
	Hull	MC (% db)	3·67	5·28	6·55	8·15	9·04	10·45	13·23	14·7

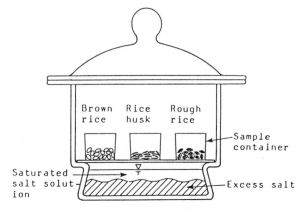

Fig. 1. A humidity control chamber.

content of the samples at this stage was considered to be the equilibrium moisture content.

The short grain rough rice (cv. Nipponbare) used in this study was harvested at an average kernel moisture content of 30% (d.b.). These samples were stored at 5 °C, in sealed plastic bags, prior to hulling. The hulls were removed using a laboratory model Satake huller.

RESULTS AND DISCUSSION

Figure 2 shows a sample of the experimental sorption data for rough rice at 30 °C. The sample took at least 55 days to attain equilibrium with the surrounding atmosphere. This time could be shortened if a small fan was installed to circulate the air. All curves except the one at 83·6% relative humidity showed the desorption process and decreased exponentially. However, the curve at 83·6% relative humidity showed the adsorption process increasing exponentially. In the case of rough rice, it has been reported that noticeable hysteresis between adsorption and desorption occurs over the relative humidity range of 30–70%.[11] All equilibrium data were regarded as desorption data because the difference between desorption and adsorption values at 83·6% relative humidity would be expected to be very small. The exact values of equilibrium moisture contents are shown in Table I.

Figure 3 shows a desorption plot at three temperatures. According to Polanyi's potential theory one would expect a single curve for all

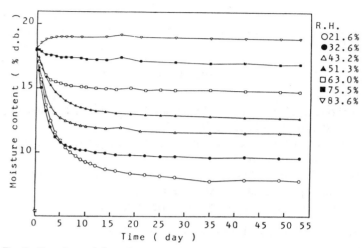

Fig. 2. *Experimental data of moisture content versus time for rough rice (30 °C).*

temperatures. The reason for this discrepancy in temperature dependence is that the binding energy for water on the site inside the grain changes with changing temperature. Each curve decreases in a similar fashion. This shows that the water inside the grain can be assumed to exist in various stages of interaction.

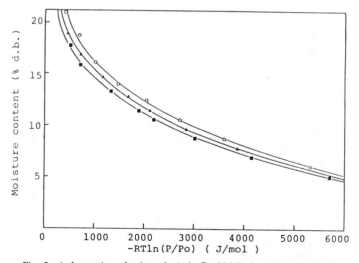

Fig. 3. *A desorption plot (rough rice).* ○, *20 °C;* ▲, *30 °C;* ■, *40 °C.*

In this work, the D–A equation was utilized because it is especially effective for material with many micropores. The D–A equation takes the form of:

$$M = Mo[\exp -(A/E)^n] \tag{1}$$

where:

> $n =$ positive real number less than 6 and shows the strength of adsorption, dimensionless,
>
> $Mo =$ limit of moisture content of the adsorption space represented by n, % dry basis,
>
> $M =$ equilibrium moisture content at temperature T, % dry basis,
>
> $E =$ adsorption characteristic energy (J/mol), and
>
> $A =$ differential molar work of adsorption (J/mol).

A can be calculated as a decrease in Gibb's free energy:

$$A = RT \ln (P_0/P) \tag{2}$$

where:

> $R =$ universal gas constant (J/mol K),
>
> $T =$ temperature (K),
>
> $P_0 =$ saturated vapor pressure at temperature T (Pa), and
>
> $P =$ equilibrium partial vapor pressure (Pa).

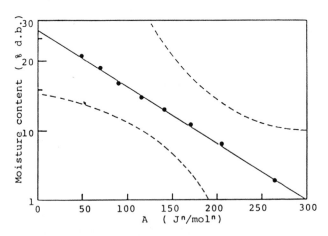

Fig. 4. Dubinin–Astakhov plot of water in rough rice. Convex downward dashed line represents a family of curves for $n > 0.65$ and convex upward represents curves for $n < 0.65$. $n = 0.65$ for straight line.

Taking the natural logarithm of both sides, Eq. (1) becomes:

$$\ln M = \ln Mo - (A/E)^n \tag{3}$$

The plot of $\ln M$ against (A/E) should be linear under the most suitable n. Figure 4 shows the D–A plot of water in rough rice.

When n is equal to 1, the curve is convex downwards and as n decreases, the curve first approaches a straight line and then convexes upwards gradually. Linear regression by using the least squares method was applied for different n values, and the n value giving the best correlation coefficient was adopted. As a result, almost identical values were obtained from each series of data of Table I. The n value was taken as 0·65 since the correlation coefficient with this n value for all series of data was above 0·999. The coefficients of the D–A equation at temperatures of 20, 30 and 40 °C are given in Table II.

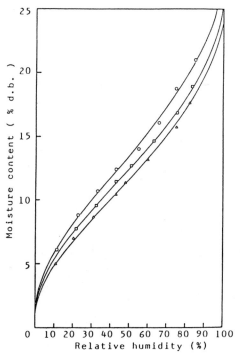

Fig. 5. *Equilibrium moisture content of rough rice.* ○, 20 °C; □, 30 °C; △, 40 °C; ——, *predicted.*

TABLE II
The coefficients of the D–A equation

	20 °C	30 °C	40 °C
Mo (% db)	27·36	25·16	24·20
n (dimensionless)	0·65	0·65	0·65

In order to combine the coefficients of the D–A equation shown in Table II into one expression, the results given in Table II and additional theoretical information were used[12] to derive a modified D–A equation applicable to grain. This equation, using the chemical potential difference $\Delta\mu$ instead of Polanyi's adsorption potential, is

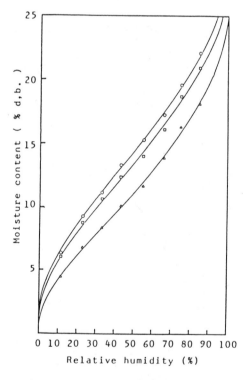

Fig. 6. Equilibrium moisture content of rough rice (□), brown rice (○), and hull (△) at 20 °C. ——, Predicted.

given as follows:

$$M = 27 \cdot 36 \left[\exp - \left(\frac{-\Delta\mu}{2891 \cdot 2} \right)^{0 \cdot 65} \right] \qquad (4)$$

$$\Delta\mu = -[29 \cdot 3 + (1 - \exp(0 \cdot 1254 Mo)](T - 293 \cdot 15) + RT \ln H \qquad (5)$$

This equation can be used to predict the equilibrium moisture content in all sorption regions (single layer adsorption, multilayer adsorption and capillary condensed water).

The equilibrium moisture content curves of water in rough rice at 20, 30 and 40 °C are shown in Fig. 5. Points show the observed data and the curves were calculated using the D–A equation. Similar plots were obtained for brown rice and hull. In all three kinds of materials, the isotherms are sigmoid in shape and equilibrium moisture content decreases, at the same relative humidity, as the temperature increases.

Figure 6 shows the comparison of the equilibrium moisture content among rough rice, brown rice and hull at 20 °C. Each curve has a similar sigmoid shape and this shows that each material is a similar sorption medium. The amount of water sorbed at constant relative humidity was the highest for brown rice and the lowest for hull. Rough rice had a value in between the two. Rough rice consists of brown rice and hull, and the calculated value by using the weight ratio of brown rice and hull in rough rice gives a close agreement with the value in Fig. 6.

REFERENCES

1. Dubinin, M. M. and Astakhov, V. A. Description of adsorption equilibrium of vapors on zeolites over wide ranges of temperature and pressure. *Adv. Chem. Ser.* **102:** 69, 1971.
2. Zuritz, C., Singh, R. P., Moini, S. M. and Henderson, S. M. Desorption isotherms of rough rice from 10 °C to 40 °C. *Trans. ASAE* **22:** 433, 1981.
3. Kato, K. Energy evaluation method of grain drier (I). Equilibrium moisture and enthalpy equations of rice in consideration of moisture concentration energy. *J. Soc. Agric. Mach., Japan* **43:** 443, 1981.
4. Brunauer, S., Emmett, P. H. and Teller, E. Adsorption of gases in multimolecular layers. *J. Am. Chem. Soc.* **60:** 309, 1938.
5. Halsey, G. Physical adsorption in non-uniform surfaces. *J. Chem. Phys.* **16:** 931, 1948.
6. Henderson, S. M. A basic concept of equilibrium moisture. *Agric. Eng.* **33:** 29, 1952.
7. Chung, D. S. and Pfost, H. B. Adsorption and desorption of water vapor by cereal grains and their products. *Trans. ASEA* **10:** 549, 1967.

8. Polanyi, M. Adsorption from the point of view of the third law of thermodynamics. *Verh. Deutsche Phys. Ges.* **16:** 1012, 1914.

9. Japanese Industrial Standards. JIS Z 8806–1981. Methods of humidity measurement. Tokyo, Japan, 1981.

10. Winston, P. W. and Bates, D. H. Saturated solutions for the control of humidity in biological research. *Ecology* **41:** 232–7, 1960.

11. Troller, J. A. and Christian, J. H. B. *Water activity and food.* Academic Press, New York, 1978.

12. Kameoka, T. Theoretical and experimental studies of rough rice drying. Ph.D. thesis, University of Tokyo, Japan, 1984.

20

ADSORPTION OF PROTEINS AND MICROORGANISMS AT STAINLESS STEEL SURFACES

JOSEF NASSAUER* and HEINZ-GERHARD KESSLER

Institute for Dairy Science and Food Process Engineering, Technical University of Munich, D-8050 Weihenstephan, Federal Republic of Germany

ABSTRACT

The objective of this research work was to determine the adsorption behavior of particles consisting of hydrophobic and hydrophilic groups in order to reduce fouling.

In the discussion of adsorption, electrostatic and van der Waals forces are of paramount importance. Van der Waals forces are often responsible for the adherence of hydrophobic groups. Electrical forces should be considered as stainless steel becomes electrically charged in contact with ionic liquids.

The electrical charge of pipes of stainless steel is described by the Galvani potential, measured by means of special electrodes.

The extent of adsorption of milk proteins and microorganisms is judged by the amount of material still adhering after a defined cleaning process.

It was found that globular proteins are mainly attracted by electrical forces.

Proteins, which can be distinguished in hydrophobic and hydrophilic regions are mostly adsorbed by their hydrophobic groups by means of van der Waals forces.

Microorganisms seem to be also adsorbed by electrical forces if they have sufficient electrophoretic mobility.

Practical application has shown that it is possible to reduce adsorption by varying the surface potential of stainless steel.

* Present address: Kraft Europe R & D Inc., D-8000 München 83, Unterbiberger Straße 15, Postfach 830550, Federal Republic of Germany.

INTRODUCTION

The adsorption of proteins and microorganisms is an important parameter in thermal processes such as pasteurization, UHT-treatment or evaporation. Due to this adsorption a fouling layer builds up which reduces the heat transfer, increases the pressure drop and limits the running time of a plant.[1]

At lower temperatures the adsorption of proteins may cause significant losses of product, for example in cheese manufacture. Further, adsorbed microorganisms can recontaminate the product, for example thermophilic microorganisms surviving pasteurization.

The objective of this paper is to study the adsorption behavior of particles consisting of hydrophobic and hydrophilic groups such as proteins and microorganisms. Therefore electrostatic and van der Waals forces should be mainly discussed.

Van der Waals forces are caused by interactions between induced dipoles[2-4] and are often responsible for the adherence of hydrophobic groups. Electrostatic forces should be considered in the adsorption of ions or charged particles at charged surfaces. As stainless steel becomes electrically charged in contact with ionic products, electrical forces are of main interest.

MATERIALS AND METHODS

Materials

The investigations were carried out in different pipes of stainless steel with a diameter of 10 mm. The Galvani potential was determined using a solution of calcium chloride. The pH of this solution was varied by adding muriatic acid or caustic soda. The mean value of the surface roughness was always smaller than 2 μm and had no significant effect on the extent of adsorption.[5]

For studying the adsorption behavior of different components, native and denatured whey proteins, caseins and microorganisms (*E. coli*) were chosen.

Methods

The electrical charge at the surface of stainless steel was estimated by the Galvani potential measured by means of special electrodes. The amount of adsorbed proteins was determined in the following manner: the product was circulated in a pipe system for a defined time.

Afterwards the pipe was rinsed with water. Then the still adherent material was removed by special detergents and measured by means of the Folin method.[6] The residues of microorganisms were only qualitatively determined at the surface.

RESULTS

Galvani Potential

If stainless steel is put into a solution, chrome ions and hydroxyl ions leave the surface, due to their solution pressure.[7] Consequently the material becomes electrically charged. Equilibrium is reached when the solution pressure is compensated by the potential difference between the stainless steel and the solution. In order to measure this potential difference a reference electrode is required, for example a platinum electrode, put into N acid solution and circulated by hydrogen. The measured value of the voltage corresponds to the Galvani potential and can be described by the following equation:

$$Cr + 3H_2O \rightarrow Cr(OH)_3 + 3H^+ + 3e^- \qquad (1)$$

By means of the correlation between chemical potential, free reaction enthalpy and voltage we obtain the following equation for the Galvani potential (Fig. 1):

$$U = U_0 - 2 \cdot 3 \frac{RT}{F} \, pH \qquad (2)$$

U = voltage (V);
T = temperature (K);
F = Faraday constant = 96 500 C;
R = universal gas constant = 8·314 J/mol K.

The relationship indicates that the potential difference is decreasing linearly with the value of pH, assuming a constant temperature.

Measurement of the Galvani potential

To measure the potential difference—equal to the Galvani potential—in a pipe system, the reference electrode is fixed near the axis of the pipe and connected with the negative pole of a voltmeter, and the wall of the pipe is connected with the positive pole (Fig. 2). Consequently a

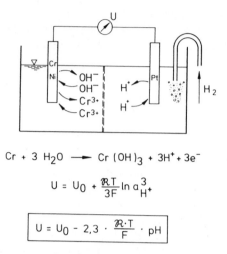

$$Cr + 3\,H_2O \longrightarrow Cr(OH)_3 + 3H^+ + 3e^-$$

$$U = U_0 + \frac{\mathcal{R}T}{3F}\ln a_{H^+}^3$$

$$\boxed{U = U_0 - 2{,}3 \cdot \frac{\mathcal{R}\cdot T}{F} \cdot pH}$$

Fig. 1. Galvani potential.

positive value corresponds to a positive electrical charge of the surface.

Galvani potential—time dependence

According to Eq. (2) the potential difference is strongly affected by the value of pH (Fig. 3).

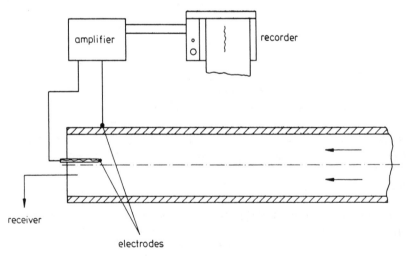

Fig. 2. Measurement of the Galvani potential in a pipe.

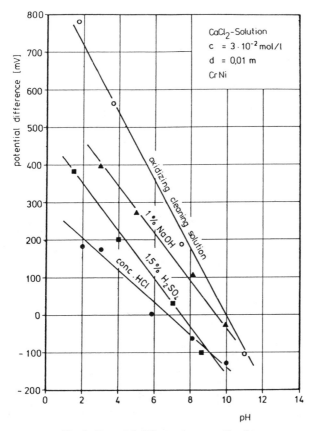

Fig. 3. Potential difference versus pH value.

In acid conditions there is a high positive potential up to 1000 mV. The voltage is decreasing nearly linear with the pH. The level of the potential is influenced by the pretreatment of the surface. The application of oxidizing cleaning solutions leads to a stronger passive layer of chrome hydroxide and consequently to a higher surface potential. It is easy to imagine that this positive charge strongly attracts negatively charged particles.

Correlation—Potential Difference—Residue of Protein

In Figs. 4–6, the residues as well as the potential difference are plotted versus time.

Considering native whey protein at a pH of 6·6 (Fig. 4) it is possible

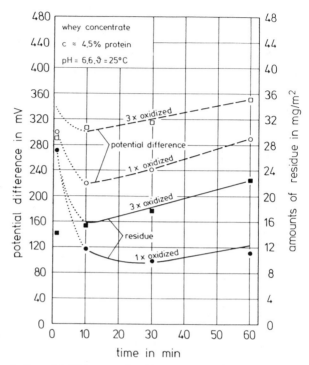

Fig. 4. Potential difference and residue versus time (native whey protein).

to notice that the adsorption of negative whey proteins is growing with increasing positive potential of the surface. This result indicates that the adsorption is due to electrical forces.[8,9]

Regarding the effect of time it can be stated that the potential difference increases with residues. This correlation will also prove the assumption of electrical adsorption. However, at pHs of 2·7 and 9·2 (Fig. 5) the potential difference is decreasing with increasing residues.

At both values of pH the whey proteins are more or less denatured. This means that the native globular whey protein is opened and the hidden hydrophobic groups are exposed. It can be assumed that denatured whey proteins do not now have a regular distribution of their electrical charge, but rather they can be distinguished in hydrophobic and hydrophilic regions. Taking into account these results it can be concluded that denatured whey proteins are mainly adsorbed due to their hydrophobic groups. Therefore in this case van der Waals forces are the most important phenomena.

Casein has a hydrophic-hydrophilic nature and exists normally in the

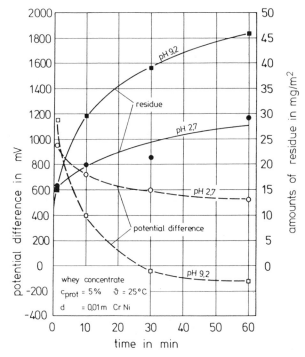

Fig. 5. Potential difference and residue versus time (denatured whey protein).

form of micelles. But by pumping a casein solution into a pipe system the micelles immediately near the wall are destroyed by the wall shear stress. For the adsorption at the surface of a pipe the casein can be considered as a detergent with hydrophilic–hydrophobic structure. So, for casein the potential difference decreases with increasing residues, analogous to denatured whey protein (Fig. 6).

Mechanisms of Protein Adsorption

From the results obtained it can be concluded that globular, native whey proteins are adsorbed at stainless steel by electrical forces. Hydrophilic groups, situated at the surface of the protein, have a great affinity for hydroxyl ions. Consequently their concentration is reduced immediately at the wall. Due to their solution pressure further hydroxyl ions leave the stainless steel and the positive charge of the surface increases. Denaturated whey proteins and casein adhere by their hydrophobic groups. These groups partly remove the water from the

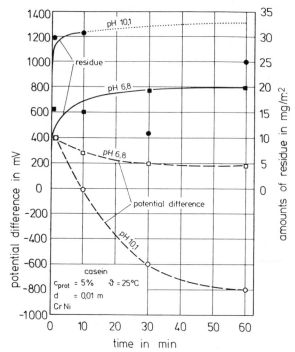

Fig. 6. Potential difference and residue versus time (casein).

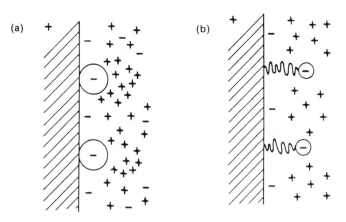

Fig. 7. Mechanisms of protein adsorption. (a) Native whey protein (electrostatic); (b) denatured whey protein, casein (van der Waals).

region immediately next to the wall. Therefore the outflow of hydroxyl ions is reduced and the potential decreases (Fig. 7).

Residues of Microorganisms

The investigations concerning the adsorption of microorganisms were carried out with different kinds of material, using *Escherichia coli* with a rather high electrophoretic mobility.

After the same cleaning process described for proteins, the residue of microorganisms was significant at hydrophilic surfaces such as stainless steel. However, on hydrophobic material—for example polyvinylchloride with plasticizer—residual microorganisms could not be detected. These results indicate that even microorganisms may be adsorbed by electrical forces if they have a sufficient electrical charge at the surface.

DISCUSSION

The electric adsorption of particles can be reduced if the surface has the same electrical charge or by the use of a hydrophic surface.

The adsorption of hydrophobic groups (van der Waals forces) can be decreased by a high positive charge of the surface.

Following these rules fouling can be significantly reduced. For example in cheese manufacture the cheese must be removed from the cheese mould. If the casein is positively charged it is of advantage to use a hydrophobic material. When using stainless steel it is necessary to pretreat the surface with oxidizing cleaning solutions in order to achieve a high positive charge.

In UHT-treatment of milk the whey proteins are denatured by a pre-holding phase at about 90 °C. So whey proteins and casein have the same kind of adsorption behavior. The adherence of hydrophobic groups is reduced by a high positive charge at the surface. In order to get these conditions the cleaning process must be finished with an oxidizing solution.

REFERENCES

1. Kessler, H. G. *Food Engineering and Dairy Technology.* Verlag A. Kessler, P.O. Box 1721, D-8050 Freising, 1981.
2. Hamaker, H. C. *Physica* **4:** 1058, 1937.

3. Landau, L. D. and Lifschitz, E. M. *Statistical Physics*. Pergamon Press, Oxford, 1959.
4. Krupp, H. *Adv. Coll. Interface Sci.* 111–239, 1967.
5. Nassauer, J. Wie frei von Rückständen lassen sich Oberflächen spülen? *Deutsche Molkerei-Zeitung* **44,** 1984.
6. Lowry, O. H. *et al.* Protein measurement with the Folin phenol reagent. *J. Biol. Chem.* **193:** 265–275, 1951.
7. Kaesche, H. *Die Korrosion der Metalle, 2. Auflage.* Springer-Verlag, Berlin-Heidelberg-New York, 1979.
8. Nassauer, J. Adsorption durch Oberflächenladung—Ein Problem der Lebensmittelverfahrenstechnik. Habilitationsschrift der Fakultät für Brauwesen, Lebensmitteltechnologie und Milchwissenschaft der Technischen Universität München, 1984.
9. Nassauer, J. Adsorption und Haftung an Oberflächen und Membranen. Eigenverlag, D-8051 Langenbach, 1985.

21

ISOLATION AND IDENTIFICATION OF VOLATILE COMPOUNDS OF HEAT TREATED SOYBEAN OILS

RAOUF M. A. EL SAADANY, F. M. H. ASHOUR, A. EL SHARKAWI and N. ABD EL AZIZ

Department of Food Science, Faculty of Agriculture, Zagazig University, 11 Fawzi el Mottii Street, Heliopolis, Cairo, Egypt

ABSTRACT

The volatile compounds which were isolated from the head-space of crude soybean oil as control sample, degummed soybean oil, soybean oils obtained from roasted seeds and seeds soaked in boiled water were identified using GLC technique. The volatile components of crude soybean oil consisted of four compounds which were: hexa-2-enal, octanol, heptanal and 2-octanol in descending percentages. Degummed oil fractionated into the components; hexanal, unknown, hex-2-enal and 2-octanol, in descending amounts. Roasted seed oil fractionated into three volatile compounds; pentanal, hexanal and hex-2-enal in descending amounts. Soaked seed oil contained: hex-2-enal, heptanal, pentanal and 2-octanol, also in descending amounts.

These results may be useful for studying the deterioration that may occur in soybean oil during storage to help in preventing flavor, deterioration, which presents a major problem with soybean oil.

INTRODUCTION

Flavor deterioration is a main characteristic of soybean oil and other linolenate-containing oils. Flavor deterioration starts as beany and grassy at the early stages and fishy or paint-like at the more advanced stages. Some investigators have suggested that the occurrence of flavor is an oxidative process.[3,9] Others have reported that it is not oxidative deterioration.[1,7] Mattck and Hand,[6] using GLC isolated and identified ethyl vinyl ketone as a volatile component which develops and contributes to the raw soybean oil odor and flavor. Moreover, Selke *et al.*[8] reported that the volatile compounds pentane and pentene were isolated from crude soybean oil. In addition, Mounts *et al.*[7] reported that pentanal and hexanal were isolated from soybean oil as volatile compounds. Jackson[5] identified the following soybean oil as volatile components in soybean oil using GC–MS: acetone, n-pentene, hexene, isopentanal, pentanal, 1-pentanol, hexanal, 1-hexanol, 2-heptanone, heptanal, 2-pentyl furan, benzaldehyde, dichlorobenzene, 2-nonanone, nonanal, 1-nonanol, 2-decanone and gamma-lactone.

This research aims to identify the volatile compounds present in soybean oil after some heat treatments, comparing it with that of crude soybean oil in order to try to solve the problem of flavor deterioration.

MATERIALS AND METHODS

Materials

Soybean seeds (Clark variety) were divided into four portions.

Treatment 1. The first portion was ground and soaked in n-hexane (40 °C) for 48 h, then the miccella was collected, filtered and the solvent was distilled off on a water bath and the last traces of the solvent were completely removed by distillation under vacuum. The oil was dried over anhydrous sodium sulphate, filtered and kept in brown glass bottles at −20 °C till analysis (control 1).

Treatment 2. Soybean oil which was obtained as previously described, was washed several times with hot water (90 °C). The oil was left in separating funnel till complete separation had occurred. The oily layer (upper layer) was collected, dried over anhydrous sodium sulphate, filtered and the oil was kept in brown bottles at −20 °C till analysis.

Treatment 3. Soybean seeds were roasted at 120 °C for 2 h in a drying oven, then the roasted seeds were ground and soaked in n-hexane. The oil was produced as mentioned before in treatment 1.

Treatment 4. Soybean seeds were soaked in boiling water for half an hour, then the seeds were air dried, ground and soaked in n-hexane and the oil was obtained as mentioned before in treatment 1.

Methods

Identification of the volatile compounds of soybean oil. For GLC
headspace analysis 4 g of soybean oils were placed in a vial, closed
tightly and heated in a 100 °C water bath for 30 min, and 0·5 ml vapor
were taken as samples using a micro-syringe and were injected into the
Gas Liquid Chromatograph apparatus (Klaus and Joseph, 1972).

A Pye Unicam GCV Gas Chromatograph was equipped with a dual
Flame Ionization Detector (FID). A coiled glass column (2·8 m ×
4 mm) was used, packed with washed acid–alkali and silanized
Diatomite C (100–120 mesh) and coated with 3% OV-17. The
operation was carried out isothermally, and the temperatures of
injector, column and detector were 200°, 85° and 300 °C respectively.
The gas flow rates were 30, 33 and 330 ml/min for nitrogen, hydrogen
and air, respectively. The chart speed was 1 cm/2 min and attenuation
was 16×10^4.

Hexanal, heptanal, octanal and nonanal were used as standard
aldehydes, hex-2-enal as alk-2-enal, 2-pentenone as ketones and
2-propanol, 2-octanol and nonanol as alcohols.

The retention times of the peaks of the pure samples were used in
the identification and characterization of the peaks of samples under
investigation.

The relative percentages of the volatile compounds were determined
by measuring the area under each peak, and the relative percentage of
each compound was calculated from the following equation:

$$\% \text{ of each component} = \frac{\text{Area under each peak}}{\text{Total area under all peaks}} \times 100$$

RESULTS AND DISCUSSION

**Separation and Identification of the Volatile Compounds of Soybean
Oils by GLC**

The results in Figs. 1–4 and Table I illustrate the head space volatile
components of soybean oil treatments 1–4. From these results it can
be noticed that crude soybean oil volatile components consisted of
four compounds arranged in the following descending order: hex-2-
enal, octanal, heptanal and 2-octanol. The relative percentages were
82·03%, 9·37%, 7·03% and 1·56% for the above mentioned com-

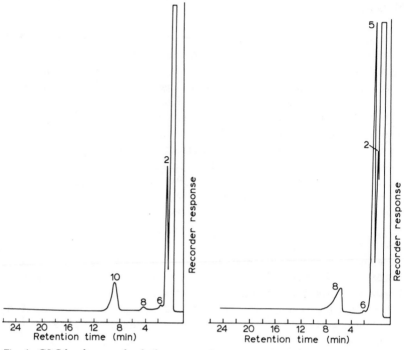

Fig. 1. GLC head space of volatile compounds in crude soybean oil.

Fig. 2. GLC head space of volatile compounds in degummed soybean oil.

pounds respectively. These results showed great differences to the
identified components reported by Mattck and Hand[6] who identified
ethyl vinyl ketone which contributes to the raw bean flavor. Dupuy *et
al.*[2] found pentanal and hexanal as volatile components in soybean oil.

From the same table, it can be noticed that using some technological
treatments either for soybean oil (degumming, treatment 2) or
soybean seeds (roasting and soaking in boiling water, treatments 3 and
4 respectively) showed another pattern in their volatile compounds.
Degumming or washing soybean oil with hot water induced some
changes in the components. The volatile components of degummed
soybean oil were also identified as four compounds but hexanal
represents the major compound which amounted to 73·74% and this
compound did not appear in the case of crude soybean oil. Also,
hex-2-enal was present at a lower percentage, 3·89%, than that in the

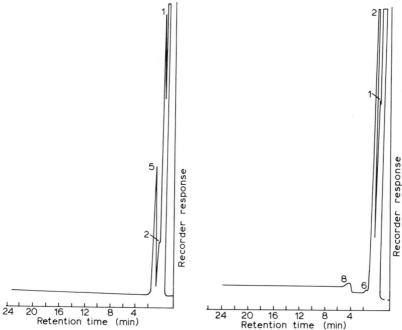

Fig. 3. GLC head space of volatile compounds in oil from roasted soybean seeds.

Fig. 4. GLC head space of volatile compounds in oil from soybean seeds after soaking in boiling water.

case of crude soybean oil. An unknown (1) (with RT 3·3) (Table I) was present at a moderate percentage of 22·26%. This compound was absolutely not detected in other soybean oil treatments.

From the same table it can be observed that the volatile compounds present in the oil of roasted soybean seeds only consisted of three compounds arranged in the following descending pattern; pentanal, hexanal and hex-2-enal with the following percentages, 80·91%, 18·27% and 0·80%, for the above mentioned compounds respectively.

Soaking of soybean seeds in boiling water showed that the volatile compounds of soybean oil consisted of four compounds and the major compound was hex-2-enal which represents 84·38% and the other compounds were found identical to the compounds present in the case of crude soybean oil, treatment 1, as shown from Table I except that pentanal was found at a moderate percentage of 7·52% and did not

TABLE I
The relative percentages of the volatile compounds of soybean oils

No.	Components	RT Cm.	Log RT	Treatments 1	2	3	4
1	Pentanal†	0·3	2·47	—	—	80·91	7·52
2	Hex-2-enal*	0·5	2·69	82·03	3·89	0·80	84·38
3	2-pentenone*	0·6	2·78	—	—	—	—
4	2-propanol*	0·6	2·78	—	—	—	—
5	Hexanal*	0·7	2·85	—	73·74	18·27	—
6	2-octanol*	1·0	3·00	1·56	0·14	—	0·22
7	Nonanol*	1·4	3·15	—	—	—	—
8	Heptanal*	2·3	3·36	7·03	—	—	7·86
9	Unknown (1)	3·3	3·52	—	22·26	—	—
10	Octanal*	5·2	3·71	9·37	—	—	—
11	Nonanal*	13·8	4·31	—	—	—	—

Treatment 1: Crude soybean oil.
Treatment 2: Degumming soybean oil.
Treatment 3: Roasting seeds oil.
Treatment 4: Soaking seeds oil in boiling water.
* Standard compounds injected.
† The compound was identified according to the method of Eisner *et al.* (1965) using log RT against number of carbon atoms.

appear in the case of the crude soybean oil. Also, octanal can not be detected in treatment 4, the oil from soaked seeds in boiling water.

Therefore, it could be concluded that technological heat treatments (degumming, roasting, and soaking soybean seeds in boiling water) induced noticeable changes in the volatile compounds present in the treated soybean oil samples due to these technological heat treatments.

These changes in the volatile components may be useful for increasing the progress in odor alteration and may help in some findings that may control or delay that phenomenon which is considered a main problem towards the consumption of soybean oil without any further treatments after extraction.

REFERENCES

1. Costa, H., del Duarte, M. P., Martins, R. M. and Samagaio, B. Stability and preservation of soybean oil. *Bol.-Inst. Azeite Prod. Oleaginosos* **4** (1): 75–86 1976; C. F. Chem. Abst. **83:** 103–106, 1978.

2. Dupuy, H. P., Rayner, E. T. and Wadsworth, J. I. Correlation of flavor score with volatiles of vegetables oils. *J. Am. Oil Chem. Soc.* **53:** 628–31, 1976.
3. Dutton, H. J., Schwab, A. W., Moser, J. C. and Cowan, J. C. The flavor problem of soybean oil. IV. Structure of compounds counteracting the effect of prooxidant metals. *J. Am. Oil Chem. Soc.* **25:** 385–8, 1948.
4. Eisner, J. and Firestone, D. Gas chromatography of unsaponifiable matter. II. Identification of vegetable oils by their sterols. *J. Assoc. Offic. Agric. Chemists* **46:** 542–50, 1963.
5. Jackson, H. W. Techniques for flavor and odor evaluation of soybean oil. *J. Am. Oil Chem. Soc.* **58:** 227–31, 1981.
6. Mattck, Leonard, R. and Hand, David B. Identification of a volatile component in soybeans that contributes to the raw bean flavor., *J. Agric. Food Chem.* **17:** 15–17, 1969.
7. Mounts, T. L., Warner, K. A., List, G. R. and Fredrich, J. P. Flavor and oxidative stability of hydrogenated and unhydrogenated soybean oils: effects of antioxidants. *J. Am. Oil Chem. Soc.* **55**(3): 345–9, 1978.
8. Selke, E. Helen, Moser, A. and Rohwedder, W. K. Tandem gas chromatography-mass spectrometry analysis of volatiles from soybean oil., *J. Am. Oil Chem. Soc.* **47:** 93–7 1970.
9. Uri, N. In *Autoxidant and Antioxidants,* Vol. 1, W. O. Lundberg (Ed.). John Wiley, New York, pp. 133–69, 1961.

Part III
Transport Properties

22

EFFECT OF PROCESSING ON PARTICLE SIZE DISTRIBUTION IN APPLESAUCE

R. C. ANANTHESWARAN,* M. R. McLELLAN and J. N. NOGUEIRA

Department of Food Science and Technology, New York State Agricultural Experiment Station, Cornell University, Geneva, New York 14456, U.S.A.

ABSTRACT

The effects of initial fruit firmness, finisher speed and finisher screen size on the particle size distribution of processed applesauce were studied for two cultivars, namely, R. I. Greening and Rome. The two cultivars behaved very differently in the particle size distribution at different initial firmness levels. Rome apples consistently produced a sauce with a smaller particle size as the initial firmness of the fruit decreased; whereas, applesauce made from R. I. Greening apples had a larger particle size as the fruit became softer. For both the cultivars, the particle size decreased with decreasing screen size. The effect of finisher speed on the resulting particle size distribution was very complex. With very firm apples, the particle size increased with finisher speed. With softer apples, the particle size initially increased with the finisher speed and then decreased at higher finisher speeds. An approach to kinematic modeling of the generation of particle size distribution is discussed.

INTRODUCTION

Apples are very widely processed in the United States and applesauce is a major product of commercial value.[1] It has been shown that sensory panelists use graininess, which is a manifestation of the particle size distribution, as a major attribute for discriminating

---

* Present address: Department of Food Science and Technology, 134 Filley Hall, University of Nebraska, Lincoln, Nebraska 68583-0919, U.S.A.

differences between applesauce. The particle size distribution also has a close relationship to lyophoresis and viscosity of the sauce.[2] Hence the proportion and size distribution of particles in applesauce is of significance from the point of view of quality assurance.

The particle size distribution in applesauce is influenced by several factors. Apple cultivar is the major factor.[3,4] The other factors that determine the particle size distribution are maturity of the fruit at harvest, storage and ripening regimes, handling of the fruit, the degree and extent of heat treatment before finishing, the type of finisher used, and the type of pump used to convey the final product.[4]

A complete study considering the effect of processing parameters on the particle size distribution has not been reported in the literature. The objective of this present study was to investigate the effect of fruit firmness, finisher speed, and finisher screen size on the particle size distribution in processed applesauce from two different cultivars.

MATERIALS AND METHODS

Processing

Two cultivars, namely R. I. Greening and Rome were used in this study. The apples were hand harvested according to optimum harvest dates as determined over a ten year period.[5] Immediately after harvest, the apples were stored at 0 °C and 80% RH until they were ready for processing.

The apples were processed as close as possible at an initial pressure test reading of 89·0, 66·7 and 44·5 N, as determined by Effeg Fruit Tester. The actual pressure test readings were made on 15 randomly selected apples with two measurements per apple. Then an average reading was computed. At the time of processing, the average readings were 92·5, 65·8 and 44·5 N for R. I. Greening, and 88·5, 67·2 and 57·8 N for Rome.

The apples were mechanically peeled and cored followed by hand trimming. They were then sliced and cooked at 100 °C for 2 min by direct steam injection in a continuous screw cooker. The cooked apples were then sent through a Langsenkamp finisher. Three different impeller speeds of the finisher (500, 700 and 900 rpm) and three different finisher screen sizes (0·16, 0·24 and 0·32 cm) were used in a factorial combination.

The product from the finisher was then adjusted to 16 °Brix ± 1° and to a consistency of 4·6 Bostwick reading (10 s at 65·6 °C). The sauce was then pumped through a shell and tube exchanger to preheat it to 90 °C and then filled directly into 303 size cans. The cans were promptly sealed under vacuum, rolled on a holding belt for 3 min, and cooled in a tank of cold water.

Particle Size Determination

The particle size distribution was measured by a sieve method as described by Kimball and Kertesz.[6] It consists of using a set of five US standard sieves with 20, 40, 60, 100 and 140 mesh openings. A 14 mesh sieve was added in this study. The nominal openings and the assumed average diameter of the particles of the fraction retained in each sieve is shown in Table I. The average effective particle size for the fraction retained on the top sieve was assumed to be 50% over the size of the openings. For the rest of the fractions, the effective particle size was assumed to be the average of the size of the opening of that particular sieve and of that of the one above it.

The actual procedure is briefly described below. 100 ml applesauce was mixed with 2000 ml distilled water in a beaker and then poured through the set of sieves very gently. The beaker was then rinsed thoroughly. The particles were then carefully washed through the sieves using a stream of water from a tube terminating in a tapered nozzle. Then each sieve was successively washed to transfer the particles onto a 250 ml graduated cylinder with the aid of a funnel. The solid fraction in each cylinder was then suction filtered onto a filter paper and dried. The amount of each sieve fraction was thus measured on a dry weight basis. The particle size distribution was then expressed

TABLE I
Sizes of standard sieves used and the assumed diameter of the average particle in the fraction retained in each sieve

Sieve number	Nominal sieve opening (mm)	Assumed average diameter of average particle (mm)
14	1·400	2·100
20	0·840	1·120
40	0·420	0·630
60	0·250	0·335
100	0·149	0·200
140	0·105	0·127

on a weighted average basis as shown below in terms of weighted average particle size (W-APS).

$$W\text{-}APS = \frac{\displaystyle\sum_{\substack{\text{All six}\\\text{cylinders}}} \left(\begin{array}{l}\text{Weight of fraction}\\\text{in cylinder}\end{array} \times \begin{array}{l}\text{Average diameter of particles}\\\text{in the fraction}\end{array}\right)}{\displaystyle\sum_{\substack{\text{All six}\\\text{cylinders}}} \left(\begin{array}{l}\text{Weight of fraction}\\\text{in cylinder}\end{array}\right)}$$

The processed applesauce was stored at 21 °C for 2 months prior to analysis of particle size distribution. All samples were analyzed in triplicate. Tukey's 'Honestly Significant Difference' (HSD) test was conducted on the means from the different treatment combinations. Minimum significant differences (MSD) were computed for $\alpha = 0.05$ or less.

RESULTS AND DISCUSSION

The three factors, namely, initial fruit firmness, finisher speed and finisher screen size, were found to significantly affect the W-APS. Figures 1 and 2 show the effect of these factors on W-APS for R. I. Greening and Rome, respectively. For both the cultivars, the W-APS decreased with decreasing screen size.

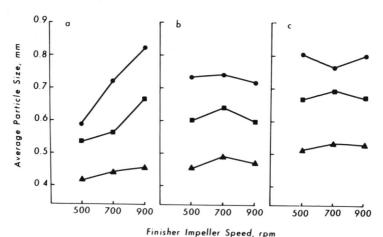

Fig. 1. *Effect of finisher speed, finisher screen size, and initial firmness on W-APS in R. I. Greening applesauce. a, 92·5 N; b, 65·8 N; c, 44·5 N. Screen size ●, 0·16 cm; ■, 0·24 cm; ▲, 0·32 cm.*

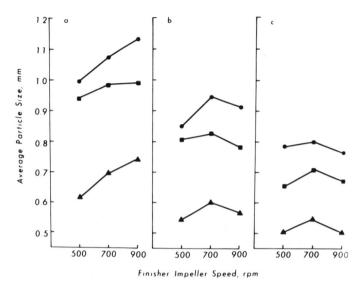

Fig. 2. *Effect of finisher speed, finisher screen size, and initial firmness on W-APS in Rome applesauce. a, 88·2 N; b, 67·2 N; c, 57·8 N. Screen size* ●, *0·16 cm;* ■, *0·24 cm;* ▲, *0·32 cm.*

The effect of finisher speed on the W-APS was found to be very complex. At high levels of firmness (89·0 N), the W-APS became larger with an increase in the finisher speed (Figs. 1a and 2a). As the finisher speed increases, the product gets extruded through the finisher screen at a faster rate. This reduces the mean residence time of the product in the finisher resulting in shorter exposure to the disintegration forces within the finisher. And this could be resulting in a larger particle size (Mechanism I).

At low to medium levels of firmness (44·5–66·7 N), the change of W-APS between 500 and 700 rpm was similar to that observed with hard fruit (89·0 N). In this case also, the cooked apple may have been firm enough to resist the disintegration forces in the finisher in the range of 500–700 rpm of finisher speed. And hence the residence time was the critical factor in determining the particle size, and so Mechanism I may be applicable here too.

But the trend was reversed when the finisher speed was increased beyond 700 rpm in the case of apples with low to medium levels of firmness. The W-APS was found to decrease with increase in finisher speed in this range (Figs. 1b, 1c, 2b and 2c). It could be that at these higher finisher speeds, the disintegration forces in the finisher were so high compared to the resistance offered by these soft fruits, that the residence time was no longer the critical factor in determining the W-APS (Mechanism II).

Based on intuition, it has been assumed in the past that the particle size will decrease with increased finished speed. This study shows that it is only true in a narrow range of settings.

From Fig. 3 it can also be seen that the general trend in the change of W-APS with decreasing firmness is different for the two cultivars. In the case of R. I. Greening, the W-APS tends to increase with a decrease in firmness, whereas it decreases in the case of Rome apples. This supports previous findings stressing the importance of cultivar in the quality of the applesauce.[7] This also highlights the difficulty encountered in initiating engineering studies to describe the processing behavior of different commodities.

The two kinematic events taking place in the finisher are: (1) disintegration of the apple tissue, and (2) 'extrusion' of the product through the screen. The average particle size in the final product is inversely proportional to the disintegration force and to the residence time of the product in the finisher. The residence time, in turn, is inversely proportional to the rate of 'extrusion' of the product through the finisher screen. Based on rheological principles, a semi-empirical model can then be constructed to predict the average particle size in the final product, knowing the initial firmness of the fruit, the finisher speed and the finisher screen size. The complete development and

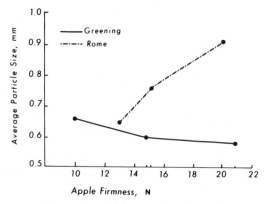

Fig. 3. Effect of initial firmness on the mean W-APS in R. I. Greening and Rome applesauce.

analysis of such a model and the fitting of the data will be reported in a further research paper.

REFERENCES

1. Anon. Annual Summary, New York State Crop Reporting Service. Albany, New York, 1984.
2. Toldby, V. and Wiley, R. C. Liquid–solids separation, a problem in processed applesauce. *J. Am. Soc. Hort. Sci.* **81:** 78, 1962.
3. Lee, Y. S., Salunkhe, D. K., Do, J. Y. and Olson, L. E. Physiological and biochemical factors influencing the quality of canned applesauce. *J. Am. Soc. Hort. Sci.* **88:** 116, 1965.
4. Mohr, W. P. Applesauce 'Grain'. *J. Text. Stud.* **4:** 263, 1973.
5. LaBelle, R. L. Mean date of harvest for apple cultivars as grown in Geneva, New York. Mimeo Circular, New York State Agricultural Experiment Station, Geneva, New York, 1973.
6. Kimball, L. B. and Kertesz, Z. I. Practical determination of size distribution of suspended particles in macerated tomato products. *Food Technol.* **6:** 68, 1952.
7. McLellan, M. R. and Massey, L. M. Jr. Effect of postharvest storage and ripening of apples on the sensory quality of processed applesauce. *J. Food Sci.* **49:** 1323, 1984.

23

EFFECT OF PEAT PARTICLE SIZE ON THE NUTRIENT CONTENT OF PEAT HYDROLYSATES

A. M. MARTIN and V. I. BAILEY

Food Science Program, Department of Biochemistry, Memorial University of Newfoundland, St. John's, Newfoundland, Canada A1B 3X9

ABSTRACT

Particle size fractions, varying from coarse to >60 mesh, were separated from samples of peat using a sieve. Other samples were ground and sifted. More than 50% (w/w) of the peat particles comprised the ≤18 mesh fraction; after grinding, more than 50% (w/w) of the peat is easily reduced to the ≥60 mesh fraction. The nitrogen content of peat and of peat acid hydrolysates made from each fraction decreased going from the coarse to the 18 mesh fraction, and substantially increased for the other fractions with smaller particle sizes. The total carbohydrate content in peat acid hydrolysates showed a similar pattern. The combined effect of the composition of the peat fractions and an enhanced hydrolysis process, as a consequence of increased surface area in the smaller particles, is discussed.

INTRODUCTION

Peat is a complex material consisting of a mixture of plant and microorganism remains at different stages of decay and physical disintegration. The organic residues found in peat are rich in carbohydrates, minerals and other substances which make peat a potential feedstock for the chemical and biochemical industries. Peat has been used as a substrate in fermentation processes.[1,2] The production of single cell protein has been the process most investigated when utilizing peat extracts or hydrolysates in submerged fermentation.[3-5] A product of interest to the food industry is the production of mushroom mycelium utilizing peat extract as the substrate source.[6,7]

239

Generally, autoclaved liquid acid hydrolysates, containing fermentable carbohydrates, are employed as the nutrient source in fermentations. The main objective of the acid treatment is to hydrolyse the cellulose present in peat. The study on the acid hydrolysis of peat and the extraction of carbohydrates is reported elsewhere.[8] In addition to carbohydrates, peat contains appreciable amounts of other nutrients, including nitrogen. As much as 5 ~ 6 t per ha, residing in the upper 300 mm of the peat profile, has been reported.[9]

Peat fragments range from easily identifiable coarse particles to smaller particles including dark coloured and amorphous humic materials.[10] The fibre content of peats is a taxonomic factor in differentiating types of peat such as fibre, mesic and humic, according to the Canadian System of Soil Classification.[11] It is assumed that the degree of decomposition of organic matter is reflected by the amount of fine particle-sized materials in the peats.[12] Several studies point to the relation between the physical and chemical characteristics of peat and to its particle size,[9] for the nitrogen content of amorphous colloidal material in peat is twice as high as that of the bulk peat.[13] The nitrogen content of the particle size fractions separated from peat and its rate of mineralization during incubation has been investigated.[9] In that work, peat particle fractions varying from 5 to 0·005 mm were utilized, and the results showed that nitrogen content increased as particle size decreased. About 50% of the nitrogen in the peat was contained in the fine fraction (0·15 ~ 0·005 mm).

The monosaccharide composition of peat fractions based on particle size has also been studied.[12] Contrary to the nitrogen content pattern it was found that, as a general trend, the total monosaccharide content decreased as particle size decreased.

In the acid hydrolysis processing of peat to extract soluble nutrients for use as a fermentation substrate, it is expected that the degree of peat–acid solution interaction during autoclaving will depend on peat particle size, because smaller particles have greater total surface area for a given weight. Two simple methods are available for obtaining small peat particles for hydrolysis. Peat can be ground to reduce the size of larger particles and then sieved to select small size particles; or peat can be just sieved to select the small size particles originally present in it. This paper studies and compares total carbohydrate and nitrogen contents of peat hydrolysates prepared from several ground peats and from sieved unground peat.

MATERIALS AND METHODS

Sphagnum peat moss (Sundew Peat Bog, Newfoundland, Canada) 50 ~ 70% moisture content, was dried in an oven (100 °C) to a constant weight. The dried peat was ground in a Waring blender for 2 min or in a laboratory mill (Cyclone Sample Mill, Tecator, Höganäs, Sweden) and then sieved in a Tyler Portable Sieve Shaker Model RX-24 (W. S. Tyler and Co. of Canada, Ltd). Other portions of the original peat were only dried and sieved. Peat hydrolysates were prepared by mixing 0·5 kg of the various particle size peat fractions (coarse, mesh no. 18, 35, 60, >60) and whole peat with 3 litres of 1·5% H_2SO_4 (v/v). The mixture was autoclaved at approximately 198·5 kPa (120 °C) for 2 h. Peat hydrolysates were obtained by vacuum filtration through Whatman No. 1 filter paper. Total carbohydrates (TCH) were obtained by the anthrone reagent method.[14] The nitrogen content of the peat and peat hydrolysates was calculated by the Kjeldahl method in a Kjeltec System (Tecator, Höganäs, Sweden).

RESULTS AND DISCUSSION

The peat particle size distribution (% weight) of the peat, before and after being ground, is shown in Table I. Although the particle size distribution in peat may differ from one bog to another and sometimes even in the same bog, as a function of several factors, our experience

TABLE I
Peat particle size distribution (% weight dry peat)

Mesh	Sifted peat	Blended and sifted	Milled and sifted
Coarse	56·4 ± 3·1	5·7 ± 0·5	—
18	8·7 ± 1·0	5·7 ± 0·6	—
25	8·9 ± 0·9	8·6 ± 1·1	0·06 ± 0·02
35	7·6 ± 0·9	12·9 ± 1·3	0·64 ± 0·13
45	4·4 ± 0·5	12·2 ± 0·9	3·5 ± 0·8
60	4·5 ± 0·7	34·8 ± 2·0	56·2 ± 4·0
>60	9·5 ± 1·1	20·1 ± 2·1	39·6 ± 2·5

Mean ± standard deviations.

reveals that more than 50% of the peat is in particles larger than 18 mesh. The fraction ⩾60 mesh accounts for approximately 5–15%, as was found in this work. Classification of particles smaller than 60 mesh was not conducted, for smaller particles would result in a difficult to handle dust. After ground in a blender or mill, the particle size distribution changed, as expected, with the ⩾60 mesh fraction accounting for 54·9% and 95·8%, respectively.

The nitrogen contents of the peat reported by different authors are given in Table II. The range of values for different bogs from the Atlantic Provinces of Canada[15] and for the Province of Newfoundland[16] compares well with those which apparently represent European bogs.[17] The values obtained in this work have a narrow range because the peat utilized is a slightly decomposed *Sphagnum* peat, with a degree of humification from H1 to H3 in the von Post scale.[18] From the point of view of nutrient extraction, this is the best peat, and its nitrogen value ranges from 5 to 10 mg/g dry peat,[17] which includes the range of values obtained in this work.

Table III reports the nitrogen content of the original peat fractions, together with the nitrogen content of the peat hydrolysates produced with these fractions. In both cases, the nitrogen content decreased as the particle size went from coarse to 18 or 35 mesh, and increased for particle sizes ⩾60 mesh. The latter agrees with previous findings[9] which reported that the nitrogen content of sifted peat increased as particle size decreased. However, the nitrogen content increase in peat hydrolysates as a function of the peat particle size is not only a function of the higher nitrogen content in smaller particles but is also a consequence of a better extraction process in the production of the hydrolysates due to the larger contact area for the reaction produced

TABLE II
Nitrogen content in peat

mg/g dry peat	Reference
whole peat	
4–20	Smith[15]
(Average: 9)	
6·7–20·4	Pollet[16]
5–19	Fuschman[17]
4·7–8·2	
(Average: 6·4)	This work

TABLE III
Nitrogen content in peat fractions and peat hydrolysates

Mesh	g/kg dry peat	g/litre peat hydrolysate
Coarse	7·61 ± 0·31	0·427 ± 0·020
18	6·91 ± 0·35	0·350 ± 0·025
35	5·93 ± 0·44	0·385 ± 0·029
60	8·01 ± 0·42[a]	0·504 ± 0·035
>60	8·21 ± 0·57[a]	0·460 ± 0·024
All fractions		
Original particle sizes		0·227 ± 0·021
Blended peat		0·275 ± 0·035
Milled peat		0·310 ± 0·029

Means within the same column followed by the same letters are not significantly ($P > 0.05$) different.

by smaller particles. This effect is shown by the enhanced values for the nitrogen content in peat hydrolysates prepared from all fractions, when peat is blended or milled (Table III). The nitrogen content in the peat hydrolysates obtained in this work were lower than the reported value of 1 g N/litre.[19] The hydrolysis conditions of our experiments were milder than those usually employed in the hydrolysation of peat because of our interest in producing fermentation substrates, where some biological active substances could be affected at higher temperatures. However, more research is needed to optimize the composition of the hydrolysates as a function of the process parameters.

TABLE IV
Total carbohydrate content in peat hydrolysates

Peat fraction (mesh)	Sifted peat (g/litre)	Blended and sifted peat (g/litre)	Milled and sifted peat (g/litre)
Coarse	32·0 ± 0·5[a,x]	31·8 ± 0·7[a,x]	
18	31·5 ± 0·6[b,x]	31·8 ± 0·9[a,x]	
35	33·1 ± 0·9[c,x]	34·0 ± 1·0[b,x]	
60	35·7 ± 1·4[d,z]	38·6 ± 1·3[c,y]	35·1 ± 1·3[a,z]
>60	35·3 ± 1·2[d,x]	58·0 ± 1·1[c,y]	36·9 ± 1·0[b,z]
All fractions	30·3 ± 0·8[e,x]	32·1 ± 0·9[a,y]	35·1 ± 1·1[a,z]

[a,b,c,d,e] Means within the same column followed by different letters are significantly ($P < 0.05$) different.
[x,y,z] Means within the same row followed by different letters are significantly ($P < 0.05$) different.

The carbohydrate content in peat could range between 46 and 57% of the dry peat.[15] In peat hydrolysates, values of 43 g monosaccharides/litre,[19] 6 ~ 13 g TCH/litre[20] and 34 g TCH/litre[3] have been reported. In our research, the TCH content of the peat hydrolysates has been between 25 and 40 g/litre, this variation is due basically to the variable carbohydrate content in the peat (if similar hydrolysis conditions are applied). In this work, a general trend to obtain higher TCH concentrations in peat hydrolysates made from small particle sizes was observed (Table IV). It has been reported[12] that the total monosaccharide content decreased as particle size decreased, although a reversed pattern was obtained in some peats, for the 40–200 mesh fractions. In our study, the enhanced extraction of carbohydrates in the hydrolysates at smaller particle sizes could be due to a better contact pattern in the reaction, as was stated before. Moreover, as seen in Table IV the values of TCH concentration for blended and sifted and milled and sifted peat, at the smaller particle sizes, are generally higher than those for sifted peat, which implies that peat fractions with high carbohydrate content are contributing to the carbohydrate value of the original smaller particles.

In general, it would be advisable to utilize smaller peat particles in the hydrolysation process. However, from the point of view of nutrient extraction (as for example, in the preparation of fermentation media), it is advisable to utilize the whole peat and not only the original small size particle fraction. It could be expected that besides carbohydrates, the concentration of other nutrient(s) depends upon the original peat particle size, smaller particles having lower nutrient concentrations. One hypothesis is to attribute to the wet environment of the peat bog an effect of leaching materials from the peat particles, with the smaller being the most leached. This fact could be true, in general, for soluble components, many of them having nutrient characteristics. Although this pattern was not observed for nitrogen, the complex organic composition of peat does not preclude it for other components.

ACKNOWLEDGEMENTS

This work was supported in part by a grant from the Natural Sciences and Engineering Research Council of Canada. The assistance of P. Mansfield, Department of Biochemistry, Memorial University of Newfoundland is appreciated.

REFERENCES

1. LeDuy, A. SCP from peat hydrolysates. *Process Biochem.* **15:** 5–7, 1979.
2. Martin, A. M. and Bailey, V. I. Production of fungal biomass in peat acid hydrolysates. *Proc. Int. Symposium on Peat Utilization*, Oct. 1, 1983. Bemidji State University, Bemidji, Minnesota, p. 301, 1984.
3. Quierzy, P., Therien, N. and LeDuy, A. Production of *Candida utilis* protein from peat extracts. *Biotechnol. Bioeng.* **21:** 1175, 1979.
4. Boa, J. M. and LeDuy, A. Acidophilic fungus SCP from peat hydrolysate. *Can. J. Chem. Eng.* **60:** 532, 1983.
5. Martin, A. M. and White, M. D. Growth of the acid-tolerant fungus *Scytalidium acidophilum* as a potential source of single-cell protein. *J. Food Sci.* **50:** 197, 1985.
6. Martin, A. M. Submerged production of *Agaricus campestris* mycelium in peat extracts. *J. Food Sci.* **48:** 206, 1983.
7. Martin, A. M. Submerged production of edible mushroom mycelium. *Can. Inst. Food Sci. Food Technol. J.* **16**(3): 215, 1983.
8. Martin, A. M. Extraction of fermentable carbohydrates from peat. *Proc. Third International Congress on Engineering and Food*, Dublin, Sept. 26–28, 1983 (B. M. McKenna Ed.). Elsevier Applied Science Publishers, London, Vol. 2, p. 863, 1984.
9. Wiliams, B. L. The nitrogen content of particle size fractions separated from peat and its rate of mineralization during incubation. *J. Soil Sci.* **34:** 113, 1983.
10. Farnham, R. S. and Finney, H. R. Classification and properties of organic soils. In *Advances in Agronomy* (A. G. Norman Ed.). Academic Press, New York, p. 115, 1965.
11. Canada Department of Agriculture. The system of soil classification for Canada. Publ. No. 1646, 83 pp., 1978.
12. Morita, H. and Levesque, M. Monosaccharide composition of peat fractions based on particle size. *Can. J. Soil Sci.* **60:** 285, 1980.
13. Powers, W. L. Characteristics of dispersable organic colloids in peat. *J. Agric. Res.* **44:** 97, 1932.
14. LeDuy, A., Kosaric, N. and Zajic, J. E. Correction factor for anthrone carbohydrate in coloured wastewater samples. *Proc. 10th Can. Water Poll. Res. Symp.*, p. 126, 1975.
15. Smith, D. G., Bryson, C., Thompson, E. M. and Young, E. G. Chemical composition of the peat bogs of the maritime provinces. *Can. J. Soil Sci.* **38:** 120, 1958.
16. Pollet, F. C. Nutrient contents of peat soils in Newfoundland. *Proc. 4th International Peat Congress*. Otaiemi, Finland, June 25–30, p. 461, 1972.
17. Fuchsman, Ch. H. *Peat, Industry Chemistry and Technology*. Academic Press, New York, 1980.
18. von Post, L. Arsb., *Sver. Geol. Unders* **19:** 4, 1925.
19. Zommers, Z., Trusle, E. and Iosifova, L. M. Chemical composition of a peat hydrolysate (in Russian). *Fermentatsiya* **96,** 1974.
20. Bogdanovskaya, Z. N., Evodkimova, G. A., Gurinovich, E. S., Raitsina, G. I. and Kostyukevich, L. I. Chemical composition of peat hydrolysates and the yeast yield under various peat-hydrolysates conditions (in Russian). *Mikroorganismy—Produtsenty Biol. Aktiv. Veshchetv*, **77,** 1973.

24

RESIDENCE TIME DISTRIBUTION IN A HORIZONTAL SSHE USED FOR UHT PROCESSING OF LIQUIDS CONTAINING SOLIDS

D. TAEYMANS, E. ROELANS and J. LENGES

CERIA—Station d'Essai d'Analy, Avenue Emile Gryzon 1, 1070 Brussels, Belgium

ABSTRACT

Evaluation of the effective thermal process in continuous flow UHT sterilization is complicated by the fact that all components of the medium may not spend the same time in the scraped-surface heat exchanger (SSHE). Unfortunately, idealized flow pattern such as piston flow is rarely achieved. Furthermore, when the liquid contains solid particles, the residence time distribution in both phases, liquid and solid, must be studied in order to determine the effectiveness of the thermal process on suspended solids.

Techniques of residence time distribution studies were applied to both phases. The solid phase was made of calcium alginate beads which were marked with a dye in order to study the hydrodynamics or with a microbiological tracer in order to follow the sterilization effect carried on the solid particles. Experimental work was carried out on a SSHE manufactured by CREPACO model 3HD620.

Study of hydrodynamics in the pilot SSHE was achieved by means of the evaluation of the residence time distribution of the disperse phase. Results indicated that the flow pattern diverged from the ideal piston flow. By measuring the dispersion, experiments showed the great influence of operating parameters such as rotational speed.

The mathematical model was applied to the kinetics of lethality of B. stearothermophilus *resulting from UHT processing.*

Comparison between experimental and predicted results is presented.

INTRODUCTION

Thermal treatments of food products can pertain to heating, or cooling, to pasteurization, sterilization, cooking, texturization, to the production of certain crystal structures, or else to freezing. Heat exchange may be significantly accelerated, if performed on a fluid food product, which is stirred and not wrapped.

Thus, heat treatments at high temperatures, for short times, e.g. HTST, carried out in a continuous manner, offer the advantage of optimizing the process and limiting dead times and thus guarantee the preservation of the nutritive and organoleptic properties of the substance.[1] Many types of equipment are available and also many applications, but technical and scientific data are scarce. In fact, the products to be processed are difficult to characterize, and experimental work only allows us to check the efficiency of a given treatment.[2]

Hence, there is a need to develop a research programme aiming to outline a model for processes of continuous thermal treatments in view of their optimization.

For such a vast field of applications, as mentioned above, it seemed necessary to develop some systematic approach, starting with a reference thermal treatment, which later on can be extrapolated to other industrial applications.

A choice has to be made for the investigation of heat transfer either for an homogeneous fluid product, with variable viscosity, or else for a product consisting of solid particles dispersed in a liquid, so as to obtain a product with a given resulting quality. Heat is transferred by means of a scraped surface heat exchanger, which offers the advantage of producing a good mixing of the mass and a high heat transfer coefficient, resulting from the scraping of the heated or cooled surfaces, by means of rotating scrapers.

This research programme aims to optimize continuous thermal treatments of viscous and particulate food products, in a scraped surface heat exchanger. The first step of the research programme pertains to the investigation of the dispersion of the residence times, and the evaluation of its effects on the thermal destruction of the microorganism entrapped in the solid particle.

THEORETICAL APPROACH

Microbiology

Heat sterilization aims towards the total destruction of all the microorganisms, including sporulated germs. Since the present investigation intends to quantify the sterilization effect, an adequate microbiological tracer is required. This would be spores, which are highly heat resistant, so as to allow numeration at the outlet of the equipment, and which are harmless, so as not to require special precautions during handling; *Bacillus stearothermophilus* was chosen.

Heat destruction of microorganisms and other food compounds can be characterized by the two parameters D_T and Z. D_T represents the period required to reduce the microbiological population, or any other occurring element, to one tenth of its former value at a given lethal temperature. Z represents the temperature which is required to reduce D_T to one tenth of its value. The numerical values found in the literature for these parameters vary for the same type of spores. These fluctuations are due to differences in evaluation methods, to the kind of spores, to the growth conditions and to the composition of the culture medium.[1,3]

To establish the heat destruction model, the values of the parameters Z and D_T have to be assessed with high accuracy.

Hydrodynamics[4]

For the treatment of bulk products, one has to make allowance for the different phenomena which characterize a continuous operation. The laminar or turbulent flow has a direct impact on the convective heat transfer. Furthermore, the type of flow monitors the residence time distribution in the equipment, and hence the quality distribution of the final product.

It should also be mentioned that the heat transfer inside a heterogeneous food product is limited also by its thermal conductivity and by the size of the suspended solid particles.

To obtain a product with adequate homogeneity, the ideal flow would be plug-flow. However, under such conditions the heat and mass transfer are slowed down, since the plug-flow has no radial or axial diffusion.

The perfectly mixed flow, which is another ideal model, presupposes an intense agitation which facilitates heat and mass transfer. But this intense agitation will also produce some heterogeneity of the final quality of the product.

Intermediary models are more often a good image of current practical conditions. The mathematical model of the residence time is attained thanks to the two ideal conditions of residence time, i.e.

—plug-flow
—perfectly mixed flow

Perfectly mixed flow:	$E(t) = \dfrac{1}{\bar{t}} \exp(-t/\bar{t})$
3 tanks in series:	$E(t) = \left(\dfrac{3}{\bar{t}}\right)^3 \dfrac{t^2}{2} \exp(-3t/\bar{t})$
5 tanks in series:	$E(t) = \left(\dfrac{5}{\bar{t}}\right)^5 \dfrac{t^4}{4!} \exp(-5t/\bar{t})$
Plug-flow:	No dispersion

Fig. 1. Residence time distributions.

as well as intermediary conditions:

—a series of 3 perfectly mixed tanks
—a series of 5 perfectly mixed tanks.

Figure 1 presents the equations of the flow residence time distribution we propose to use for studying this type of dispersion.

Heat Transfer

The sterilization period is related directly to the physical nature of the product.

High viscosity requires an increase of the sterilization time. Also, if products of high viscosity contain particles, the required time is even

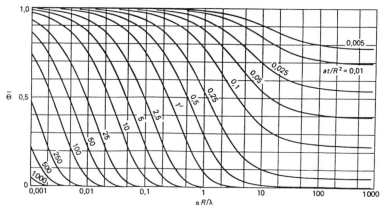

Fig. 2. Mean temperature of a sphere as a function of Fourier and Biot numbers (VDI-Wärmeatlas).

longer, because the heat transfer in this case takes place mainly by conduction instead of convection.[5,6]

Figure 2 illustrates the influence of the residence time of a particle in an installation, by means of the Fourier number; it also shows the influence of the heat transfer on the mean temperature of the particle by means of the Biot number.[7]

If the axial profile of temperature of the liquid phase is known, as well as the residence time of the particle in the equipment, it is then possible to calculate the sterilization effect.

Sterilizing Efficiency Prediction

To predict the sterilizing efficiency, this means estimating the value of $\log (N_0/N)$ where N_0 is the initial spore concentration and N the spore concentration after a definite time, it is necessary to know the residence time distribution and the longitudinal temperature profile.

MATERIALS AND METHODS

Pilot Equipment

The equipment is composed of:

— a heat exchanger with 3 independent heating tubes each having an exchange surface of $0.19\,m^2$ (manufactured by CREPACO model 3HD620);
— two volumetric pumps, with variable feed, fitted with rubber lobes, rotors, specially adapted for the pumping of suspensions (feeding and back pressure pumps);
— sample collector;
— feeding tanks fitted with agitation systems suitable for suspensions.

A general flow-sheet of the equipment is shown in Fig. 3. The three heat exchange tubes are made of stainless steel, with a diameter of 158 mm and a length of 508 mm. The first tube is especially designed for steam heating (232 °C) and the second one for heating or cooling with water, brine or glycol or other suitable liquid medium, the third one is part of a freezing system, where cooling is obtained by direct expansion refrigeration.

The rotors or dashers are also made of stainless steel and are fitted with four sizes of attached scraping blades, made of laminated plastic

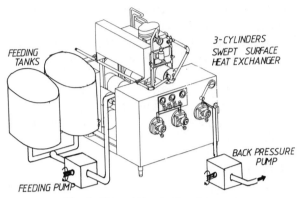

Fig. 3. General sketch of equipment.

food grade material, for thermal treatments above 0 °C, and also fitted
with four sizes of stainless steel blades, for cooling below 0 °C.

The ends of each tube are connected to the tanks into which run the
feeding and outlet lines for the products. The rotors are driven by
motors with adjustable speed.

The Tracers

The tracers used to study the influence of the residence time
distribution on the sterilizing efficiency are the following.

—physical tracer: Coomassi® Blue;
—microbiological tracer: spores of.*Bacillus stearothermophilus.*

The spores were prepared following the method described here:
preculture in the medium tryptone + glucose during 24 h at 55 °C,
sporulation in the medium peptone, tryptone, yeast extract, meat
extract, glucose during 96 h at 55 °C, centrifugation of the medium,
collection of spores maintained at 4 °C before using.

The Product

The product used for this study is made of calcium alginate beads in
suspension in water. For the purpose of the study, the alginate beads
were calibrated at diameter 6 mm, and the tracers were entrapped in
the beads. The sodium alginate solution was coloured with the dye in
order to produce blue beads for studying the residence time distribution of the solid phase only. The spores of *B. stearothermophilus* were
entrapped in the beads and the following experimental method was

used in order to measure the sterilizing efficiency of the beads in suspension.[8]

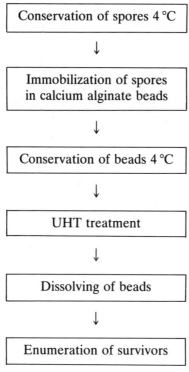

The following parameters can then be modified:

those which characterize the product

—particle size;
—granulometric distribution;
—concentration of the solid phase;
—density difference between solid and liquid;
—viscosity of the liquid phase;

and those which are characteristic of the process

—flowrate;
—rotational speed of the scrapers;
—plant configuration;
—temperature programme.

PRELIMINARY RESULTS

Residence Time Distribution

In order to study with good accuracy the residence time distribution and its influence on the sterilizing efficiency, the solid concentration at the outlet must be checked. This is done for each experiment and Fig. 4 shows the variations around a mean concentration.

A normal conclusion was that behavior of both phases were identical: that is when the suspension criterion, based on a minimum liquid mean velocity, was confirmed and the centrifugal forces were not too high, the collected samples were statistically identical. Under these conditions, the evaluation of the residence time distribution can be made on one phase only. However Fig. 5b shows that for a given rotational speed, the residence time distributions for the liquid phase and the solid phase are not identical. This figure shows that the measured mean residence time of the solid phase is greater than the calculated mean residence time, the ratio of the volume of the heat exchanger to the liquid flow rate. Figure 5a shows that the rotational

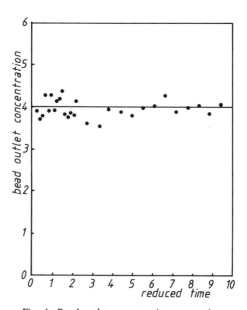

Fig. 4. Bead outlet concentration versus time.

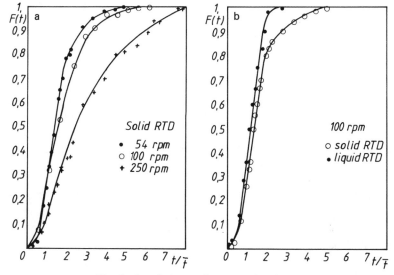

Fig. 5. *Cumulative residence time distribution.*

speed has a great influence on the measured mean residence time of the solid phase and that the flow pattern diverges from the ideal plug-flow when the rotational speed increases. A complete discussion and mathematical modelling appears in Brohet *et al.*[9]

Sterilizing Efficiency

The values given by the different mathematical models concerning the flow patterns and the temperature profiles (detailed in Refs. 10 and 11) are briefly summarized in Tables I and II using the following

TABLE I
Effect of modelized heat transfer on predicted N/N_0 (with $Bi = 18$)

	Outlet temperature		
$\bar{t}$ (s)	120 °C	130 °C	140 °C
240	0·99	0·96	0·61
480	0·93	0·37	$1·5 \times 10^{-2}$
720	0·36	$5·4 \times 10^{-5}$	$6·7 \times 10^{-40}$

TABLE II
Effect of modelized residence time distribution on predicted N/N_0 (with $k_{T\,(130\,°C)}$ = $0.066\,2\,\mathrm{s}^{-1}$)

	Model type			
$\bar{t}\,(s)$	Perfectly mixed flow	3 tanks in series	5 tanks in series	Plug-flow
240	5.9×10^{-2}	$4 \;\times 10^{-3}$	7.9×10^{-4}	1.3×10^{-7}
480	$3 \;\times 10^{-2}$	6.4×10^{-4}	4.6×10^{-4}	1.6×10^{-14}
720	$2 \;\times 10^{-2}$	2.1×10^{-4}	7.7×10^{-6}	$2 \;\times 10^{-21}$

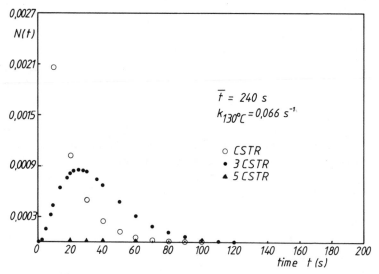

Fig. 6. Sterilizing efficiency as a function of flow pattern.

TABLE III
Experimental sterilizing efficiency (N/N_0)

Rotational speed (rpm)	Outlet temperature		
	120 °C	130 °C	140 °C
55	4.7×10^{-3}	6.8×10^{-3}*	5.5×10^{-4}
100	6.7×10^{-3}	4.5×10^{-3}*	1.1×10^{-3}
170	1.5×10^{-2}*	4.3×10^{-2}*	6.3×10^{-4}

* Non-significant results.

equation

$$\frac{N}{N_0} = \int_0^\infty \exp\left(-kt\right) E(t) \, dt$$

$$\log \frac{N_0}{N} = \int_0^t \frac{1}{D_T} \, dt$$

with also $D_T = 2{\cdot}303/k_T$.

CONCLUSIONS

Comparison between experimental and predicted results demonstrated that the influence of residence time distribution and heat transfer must be combined. It seems also that the influence of the rotational speed is not so important from the point of view of the sterilizing efficiency. When the rotational speed increases, the sterilizing efficiency does not vary very much.

It is possible to explain this fact as follows: when the rotational speed increases, the mean residence time of the solid particles increases also with a direct impact on the sterilizing efficiency. But at the same time, when the rotational speed increases, the residence time dispersion is more important.

At low rotational speeds, the flow pattern is almost plug-flow but at high rotational speeds, the flow pattern diverges greatly from plug-flow and is nearly perfectly mixed flow.

REFERENCES

1. Roelans, E. and Taeymans, D. Revue des Fermentations et Industries Alimentaires, T. 39 – No 5 – p. 115–122, I.I.F.-I.M.C.-C.E.R.I.A., B-1070 Bruxelles.
2. Shih, S. C., Cuevas, R., Porter, V. L. and Cheryan, M. Inactivation of *Bacillus stearothermophilus* spores in soybean water extracts at ultra-high temperatures in a scraped-surface heat exchanger. *J. Food Prot.* **45**(2): 145–9, February 1982.
3. Heiss, R. and Eichner, K. *Haltbarmachen von Lebensmitteln.* Springer, Berlin, 1984.
4. Wen, C. Y. and Fan, L. T. Models for flow systems and chemical reactors. *Chemical processing and engineering, An International Series.* Vol. 3 (L. F. Albright, R. N. Haddox and J. J. McKetta Eds). Marcel Dekker, New York, 1975.
5. Maingonnat, J.-F. Contribution à l'étude du comportement thermique d'un échangeur de chaleur à surface raclée. Thèse janvier 1982, ENSIA, Massy, France.
6. De Ruyter, Brunet. Estimation of process conditions for continuous sterilization of food containing particulates. *Food Technol.* **27**(7): 44, 1973.

258   D. Taeymans, E. Roelans and J. Lenges

7. Vdi-Wärmeatlas. Berechnumgsblätter für den Wärmeübergang. VDI-Verlag.
8. Dallyns, H., Falloon, W. C. and Bean, P. G. Method for the immobilization of bacterial spores in alginate gel. *Lab. Practice* **26:** 773, 1977.
9. Brohet, M., Roelans, E. and Taeymans, D. Sterilizing efficiency of solids in suspension in a scraped-surface heat exchanger. I. Residence time distribution. Paper accepted for *Belgian J. Food Chem. Biotechn.* **40,** 1985.
10. Ancion, A., Taïs, M., Roelans, E. and Taeymans, D. Sterilizing efficiency of solids in suspension in a scraped-surface heat exchanger. II. Hydrodynamics and heat transfer. Paper accepted for *Belgian J. Food Chem. Biotechn.* **40,** 1985.
11. Taeymans, D., Roelans, E. and Lenges, J. Influence of residence time distribution on the sterilization effect in a scraped-surface heat exchanger used for processing of liquids containing solid particles. IUFOST Symposium on Aseptic processing and packaging of foods, Tijlösand, Sweden, September 1985.

25

HEAT TRANSFER TO A POWER LAW FLUID IN TUBE FLOW: AN EXPERIMENTAL STUDY

I. FILKOVÁ, B. KOŽÍŠKOVÁ and P. FILKA*

Czech Technical University, Prague, Czechoslovakia

*Potravinoprojekt, Opletalova 4, Prague 11250, Czechoslovakia

ABSTRACT

An experimental study of heat transfer from power law fluids with variable rheology is presented. Experimental results of laminar flow in a cylindrical tube under uniform heat flux at the wall are compared with several established and popular correlations. The most suitable relationships were modified by exponents and constants. Hydraulic regions with both developing and fully developed velocity profiles were studied. Particular attention has been paid to forced convective heat transfer in flow with fully developed velocity and developing temperature profiles. Physical properties of test fluids were assumed to be temperature-dependent. The effect of natural convection was checked and considered negligible.

The procedure yielded two equations correlating local Nusselt number to tube geometry, flow condition and fluid properties.

According to our experimental results, the entry hydraulic length is significantly less important for heat transfer than had been expected.

NOMENCLATURE

c_p = specific heat capacity (J/kgK)
D = diameter (m)
k = thermal conductivity (W/mK)
K = coefficient of consistency (Pa s^n)
l_H, l_T = hydraulic, thermal length, resp. (m)
L = length of testing tube (m)

259

$\dot{m}$ = mass flow rate (kg/s)
n = flow index
$\dot{q}$ = heat flux (W/m^2)
T = temperature (°C)
v = velocity (m/s)
x = axial distance (m)
X^+ = axial coordinate = $(2x/\text{Pe}D)$
X^* = axial coordinate = $(x/\text{Pe}D)(4n/3n + 1)$
ρ = density (kg/m^3)

Subscripts

b = bulk
m = mean
x = local
w = wall
NN = non-Newtonian

INTRODUCTION

In the food processing industries the heat treatment of fluids is a very important operation. A commonly used equipment is typically a tube heat exchanger operating under forced convection. Since an ordinary tube heat exchanger used in the food industry is not long enough to achieve developed velocity and temperature profiles, the entrance thermal region with fully developed velocity profiles has been investigated. The food fluids are moderately to highly viscous, and many of them are classified as pseudoplastic, conforming with the power law rheological model. Thus attention has been paid to heat transfer from power law fluids flowing in a circular tube under conditions of constant wall heat flux. The problem was further restricted to laminar flow since the power law fluids seldom reached turbulent flow conditions.

Several attempts, both analytical and experimental, have been made in the past to develop a relationship which enabled one to calculate either overall or local Nusselt numbers for both Newtonian and non-Newtonian materials. There exist numerous analytical studies, but only a few works have employed an experimental approach. Our investigation is a contribution to this neglected field.

PROBLEM ANALYSIS AND CONDITIONS

Several aspects must be taken into consideration when convective heat transfer is being analysed, including natural convection, velocity and temperature profiles.

Natural Convection
Although the problem was restricted to forced convection only, the possibility that natural convection would also play a role had to be considered. According to Lykov *et al.*[7] the dimensionless product of Grashoff and Prandtl numbers (Gr Pr) indicates the importance of natural convection. If (Gr Pr) $< 8 \times 10^5$, heat transfer is governed by forced convection only, and the effect of natural convection can be neglected. This was our case since the (Gr Pr) never exceeded the critical value. During the experimental investigation the maximum value reached for power law fluids was 1867.

Velocity and Temperature Profiles
A circular tube in which a fluid flows under convective heat transfer condition can be divided into three axial regions; entrance, transient and fully developed region.

Entrance region. This region is situated near the tube entrance. Both velocity and temperature profiles are developing simultaneously. The so called hydraulic length, l_H, is necessary for the velocity profile to get fully developed. Consequently, the hydraulic length characterizes the entrance region, and depends on the tube diameter, flow velocity and fluid properties. For Newtonian fluids the following definition suggested in Petuchov[10] is widely used:

$$l_H = 0.064 \, \mathrm{Re} D \qquad (1)$$

A similar equation recommended in Ref. 4 has been employed for power law fluids:

$$l_H = 0.05 \, \mathrm{Re}_{NN} D \qquad (2)$$

The modified power law Reynolds number is given as follows:

$$\mathrm{Re}_{NN} = \frac{D^n v^{2-n} \rho}{K} \qquad (3)$$

where n, K are rheological properties of a fluid, v is the velocity, D the tube inner diameter, and ρ is the fluid density.

Transient region. In this region the velocity profile is fully developed while the temperature profile is still developing. The length of the transient region is called thermal length, l_T, and can be determined from the following relationship for Newtonian fluids presented in Petuchov:[10]

$$l_T = 0{\cdot}036 \, \text{Pe} D \tag{4}$$

where the Péclet number is given as

$$\text{Pe} = \frac{D v c_p \rho}{k} \tag{5}$$

Equation (5) contains the specific heat capacity, c_p, and the thermal conductivity, k, but no rheological parameters of the fluid; thus the equation can be used for non-Newtonian fluids, too.

Fully developed region. After passing the thermal entry length, l_T, both velocity and temperature profiles are fully developed. This occurs mainly in long tubes, usually 6 m or longer. In an ordinary heat exchanger the fully developed region is rarely achieved.

In our experimental conditions corresponding to the most common practical applications, attention has been paid to the entrance and transient regions only. The influence of the hydraulic length on the heat transfer coefficient has been considered.

Physical Properties of Test Fluids
Four power law fluids were selected for experimental investigation under different operating conditions, such as flowrate and heat flux at the tube wall. Three water solutions of CMC were selected as model fluids, while tomato juice was used as a typical representative of processed food liquids.

The thermo-physical properties of all the fluids in question were assumed to be temperature-dependent. The corresponding relationships were experimentally determined, and are summarized in Table I. The only exception was the temperature dependence of c_p and k for three CMC solutions which were supposed to be the same as for pure water. This procedure was adopted as recommended in several publications, e.g. Refs. 5, 9, 11 and 12.

TABLE I
Temperature dependent thermophysical properties of experimental fluids

Test fluid	Property	Temperature dependence
CMC 1 0·9%	$*\rho$	$\log = 2\cdot922 + 0\cdot097\,(1 - T/647\cdot35)^{2/7}$
	$\left.\begin{array}{c} c_p \\ k \end{array}\right\}$	same as water
	K	$0\cdot029 \exp\,(-0\cdot043T)$
	n	$0\cdot905 \exp\,(1\cdot91 \times 10^{-3}T)$, approx. $n = 0\cdot91$
CMC 2 1·2%	$*\rho$	$\log = 2\cdot922 + 0\cdot155\,(1 - T/647\cdot35)^{2/7}$
	$\left.\begin{array}{c} c_p \\ k \end{array}\right\}$	same as water
	K	$0\cdot091 \exp\,(-0\cdot041T)$
	n	$0\cdot808 \exp\,(1\cdot95 \times 10^{-3}T)$, approx. $n = 0\cdot84$
CMC 3 1·8%	$*\rho$	$\log = 2\cdot887 + 0\cdot155\,(1 - T/647\cdot35)^{2/7}$
	$\left.\begin{array}{c} c_p \\ k \end{array}\right\}$	same as water
	K	$0\cdot099 \exp\,(-0\cdot018T)$
	n	$0\cdot768 \exp\,(2\cdot37 \times 10^{-3}T)$, approx. $n = 0\cdot80$
tomato juice	ρ	$1036\cdot97 - 0\cdot451T$
	c_p	$3643\cdot92 + 2\cdot633T$
	k	$0\cdot570 - 4\cdot444 \times 10^{-3}T$
	K	$0\cdot728 \exp\,(-0\cdot058T)$
	n	$0\cdot453 \exp\,(7\cdot13 \times 10^{-3}T)$, approx. $n = 0\cdot54$

* Note T is in Kelvin.

Selection of Correlations

Numerous equations relating the dimensionless heat transfer coefficient, Nu, to operating conditions, tube geometry and fluid properties can be found in many references. Several widely established correlations for power law fluids were selected for prediction of local Nusselt numbers in the thermal entry region of a tube. Predicted data were compared with those obtained experimentally.

In the hydraulic entry region the relationship in Ref. 5 was selected and modified by the consistency factor suggested in Ref. 8.

$$\mathrm{Nu_x} = 1\cdot41\left[\frac{\pi}{2X^+}\frac{3n+1}{4n}\right]^{1/3}\left(\frac{K}{K_\mathrm{w}}\right)^{0\cdot1/n^{0\cdot7}} \tag{6}$$

valid for $X^+ = 2x/\mathrm{Pe}D < 0\cdot05$ or

$$\mathrm{Nu_x} = 4\cdot36\left(\frac{3n+1}{4n}\right)^{1/3}\left(\frac{K}{K_\mathrm{w}}\right)^{0\cdot1/n^{0\cdot7}} \tag{7}$$

valid for $X^+ \geqslant 0\cdot05$.

In the transition region, the following relationships suggested by Refs. 1, 5, 2 and 3 respectively were employed:

$$Nu_x = 1 \cdot 85 \left(\frac{\pi}{2X^+} \right)^{1/3 - 0 \cdot 03[1/(3n_w + 1/4n_w)]^{n_w}} \tag{8}$$

$$Nu_x = \left(\frac{3n + 1}{4n} \right)^{1/3} \left(\frac{K}{K_w} \right)^{0 \cdot 58 - 0 \cdot 44n} \times 4 \cdot 36 \{1 + [0 \cdot 376(X^+)^{-0 \cdot 33}]^6 \}^{1/6} \tag{9}$$

$$Nu_x = 1 \cdot 411 \left(\frac{3n + 1}{4n} \right)^{1/3} Gz_x^{1/3} \tag{10}$$

Equation (10) was rearranged as follows:

$$Nu_x = 1 \cdot 301 \left(\frac{4n}{3n + 1} \right)^{-1/3} \left(\frac{x}{PeD} \right)^{-1/3} = 1 \cdot 301(X^*)^{-1/3} \tag{11}$$

Equation (11) is valid for

$$\left(\frac{4}{\pi} \right) \left(\frac{3n + 1}{4n} \right) Gz_x > 100$$

$$Nu_x = 2Gz_x^{1/3} \left\{ \frac{K}{K_w} \left[\frac{3n + 1}{2(3n - 1)} \right] \right\}^{0 \cdot 14} \tag{12}$$

valid for $Gz_x > 100$.

The local Graetz number is given as

$$Gz = \frac{\dot{m}c_p}{kx}$$

When the experimental data were compared with those predicted, it became evident that the last two equations best accommodated our experimental data. Thus attention was restricted to Eqs. (11) and (12) only. A method of regression analysis was employed and the equations were altered by modified exponents and constants. According to the authors, Eq. (11) is applicable when the axial coordinate $X^* < 10^{-3}$, unlike Eq. (12) which may be used for $X^* < 10^{-2}$.

EXPERIMENTS

All experiments were carried out in the Food Engineering laboratory of the Czech Technical University in Prague, Czechoslovakia.

Apparatus

Experimental equipment is schematically depicted in Fig. 1. The working fluid was circulated through the closed-loop system by means of a screw pump, 2. The glass tube, 3, which was 25 mm in diameter and 4 m in height, opened to the atmosphere and served as both a calming and de-aerating section.

The test-section consisted of calming chamber, 4, testing tube, 5, and mixing chamber, 6, where the outlet mixing temperature was measured. Inside the calming chamber there was an impact baffle that helped to achieve a streamline flow at the entrance to the flow section.

The tube 5 was 3·02 m long made of stainless steel. Cross-sectional dimensions were 16 mm I.D. and 20 mm O.D. The condition of constant heat flux through the tube walls was achieved by Joulean heat. A low-tension current was passed through the walls, and by

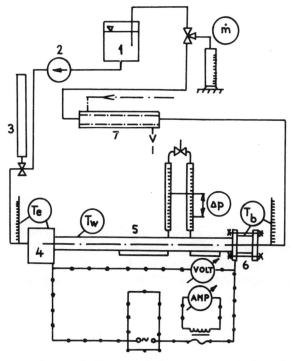

Fig. 1. Experimental set-up. 1, Storage tank; 2, screw pump; 3, glass tube; 4, calming chamber; 5, testing tube; 6, mixing chamber; 7, water cooler. ———, Test fluid; —·—·—, cooling water; —•—•—, electrical circuit; ○, measured variable.

regulating the input by means of a transformer, the maximum power of 2 kW could be attained.

In order to minimize heat conduction losses from the testing tube to the rest of the equipment, two flanges made of plastic materials were located at both ends of the tube. Moreover, the inlet flange provided a sharp-edge entrance. The energy supplied to the fluid was removed by the water-cooled heat exchanger, 7.

The tube wall temperatures were measured at nine axial locations along the tube length by copper–constantan thermocouples. The thermocouples were located at a distance $4D(i + 1)$, where $i = 0, 1, 2, \ldots, 8$. The entire test-section was insulated with polystyrene. The temperature measurements were continuously registered on a recorder which made it possible to visually determine when the system had thermally stabilized.

The flow rate was measured by a classical method using a weighing device and stopwatch. Two static pressure taps located far from the entrance, 1·76 m apart, enabled on-line determination of the rheological parameters of the test fluids.

Evaluation Procedure

Local heat transfer coefficients were determined from experimental results and Eq. (13).

$$h_x = h_{(i+1)} = \frac{\dot{q}}{T_{w(i+1)} - T_{b(i+1)}} \tag{13}$$

where wall temperature $T_{w(i+1)}$ and local bulk temperature $T_{b(i+1)}$ were measured in the location of the $(i + 1)$th thermocouple, along the tube.

The outside wall temperatures obtained experimentally had to be corrected for heat conduction through the wall in order to determine the temperature at the inside wall surface.

The bulk temperature was evaluated from the approximate energy balance

$$T_{b(i+1)} = \frac{16\dot{q}}{\rho c_p v} [0.5(i^2) + 1.5(i) + 1] + T_0 \tag{14}$$

where T_0 is the inlet fluid temperature, v is mean flow velocity, $\dot{q}$ is the wall heat flux, and ρ, c_p are fluid properties.

Finally the local Nusselt number was calculated from

$$\mathrm{Nu_x} = \frac{h_x D}{k} \tag{15}$$

Thermal conductivity k together with rheological and thermal properties were evaluated at the local mean temperature, T_m.

$$T_m = \frac{T_w + T_b}{2} \tag{16}$$

Local Nusselt numbers obtained from Eq. (15) were compared with those predicted from Eqs. (11) and (12).

Experimental Conditions
In all, 392 experimental runs encompassing eight different values of $\dot{q}$ for four power law fluids were included in the evaluations. Besides power law fluids, 232 runs were made for six Newtonian fluids, such as distilled water as a calibrating fluid, glycerol, dextran, and three aqueous solutions of sucrose. All results dealing with Newtonian fluids can be found in Ref. 6. The ranges of experimental conditions, i.e. flow and heat transfer parameters are provided in Table II.

TABLE II
Range of experimental conditions for flow and heat transfer parameters used

Parameter	Minimum value	Maximum value
$\dot{q}$	5 125	9 671
$\mathrm{Re_{NN}}$	31	1 228
Pe	13 158	90 476
Gz	55	376
X^*	10^{-5}	10^{-2}
(Gr Pr)		1 867
T_w	40	90

RESULTS AND DISCUSSION

Hydraulic Length
Theoretically predicted hydraulic length ranges from 0·025 to 0·98 m for different Reynolds numbers, according to Eq. (2). When the experimentally obtained local Nusselt numbers were plotted against

the dimensionless non-Newtonian axial coordinate X^*, it became evident that the prediction was not reliable. Both Newtonian and non-Newtonian fluids demonstrated similar heat transfer behaviour near the tube entrance, within the entrance region. A typical data distribution is shown in Fig. 3 for a power law fluid (CMC 3), and in Fig. 2 for a Newtonian fluid of similar consistencies (glycerol). Note that in Fig. 2 the group ($Nu_{exp} Pr^{-1/3}$) is plotted against the Newtonian axial coordinate (x/PeD).

Comparison of Fig. 3 and Fig. 2 reveals that except for the data of the first thermocouple, located 0·064 m from the tube entrance, all experimental points follow a single line. For glycerol the predicted entrance region should be 0·387 m long. Thus it was expected that the first three thermocouples would still lie within the entrance region. However, the data distribution in Fig. 2 indicates that the hydraulic length is no longer than 0·064 m. The experimental data of the second and third thermocouple clearly lie within the transition region with fully developed velocity profiles. Generally, in comparison with predicted hydraulic lengths ranging from 0·025 to 0·98 m, the actual length is restricted to the short region near the tube entrance falling within 0·064 and 0·192 m.

Based on these results it may be concluded that the entrance region is shorter than expected, and consequently less important for the heat

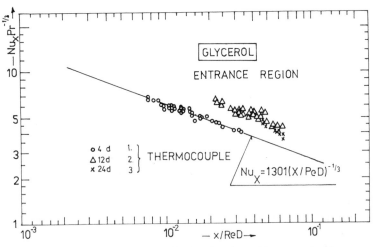

Fig. 2. *Experimental heat transfer data for glycerol in entrance region.*

transfer process. Thus, more data could be used for evaluation of heat transfer coefficients since more data conformed with the condition of fully developed velocity profiles. Thus a total of 392 experimental points were evaluated instead of 188 points originally selected.

Heat Transfer

Regressional analysis was employed in order to obtain appropriate constants and exponents to be introduced into the selected equations (11) and (12). This procedure yielded two modified correlations that best accommodated the experimental results.

$$\mathrm{Nu}_x = = 1 \cdot 229 (X)^{-0.36} \tag{17}$$

as a modification of Eq. (11), and

$$\mathrm{Nu}_x = 1 \cdot 972 \, \mathrm{Gz}_x^{0.274} \left[\frac{K}{K_w} \frac{3n+1}{2(3n-1)} \right]^{0.14} \tag{18}$$

as a modification of Eq. (12). Unlike Eq. (17), Eq. (18) also expresses the influence of temperature dependent consistency coefficient K on heat transfer process.

Both equations are valid for $X^* < 10^{-2}$. It should be pointed out that the difference between an original exponent (-0.33) in Eq. (11)

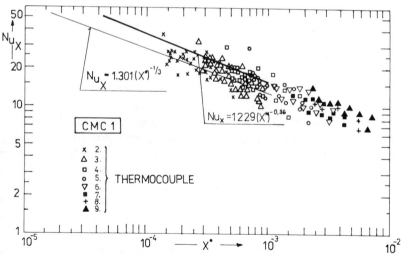

Fig. 3. Comparison of experimental heat transfer data for CMC 1—Eq. (11) versus (17).

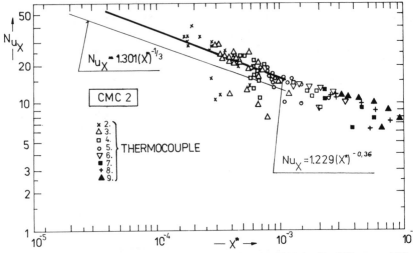

Fig. 4. Comparison of experimental heat transfer data for CMC 2—Eq. (11) versus (17).

and a new exponent (-0.36) in Eq. (17) was investigated and found statistically significant.

In Figs. 3, 4 and 5, the experimental local Nusselt number for three CMC solutions is plotted against the axial coordinate X^*. In Fig. 6 the results for tomato juice are shown. Also shown on these figures for the purpose of comparison are predictions obtained from the original correlation (11) and the modification (17). A similar procedure was adopted in order to modify Eq. (12).

In general the experimental Nu_x is higher, more so near the entrance to the testing tube. A possible explanation for the discrepancy may be related to the difficulty of accurately determining the outlet bulk temperature. Even though a mixer was located inside the chamber, 6, it could presumably be inadequate for perfect mixing. After examination of Figs. 3–6 it is evident that the best agreement for predicted and experimental data is achieved for tomato juice rather than for CMC solutions. Regarding the three CMC solutions, the discrepancy increases with the CMC concentration. The results of water-like CMC 1 are much better than those of CMC 3. This may be due in part to the fact that unlike tomato juice the thermophysical properties of CMC solutions were assumed to be those of pure water. This may explain both the generally less satisfactory agreement of

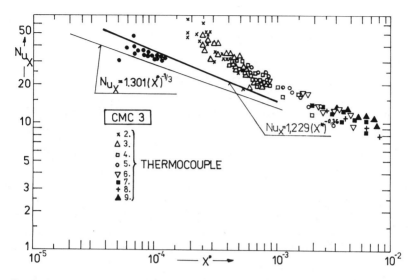

Fig. 5. Comparison of experimental heat transfer data for CMC 3—Eq. (11) versus (17).

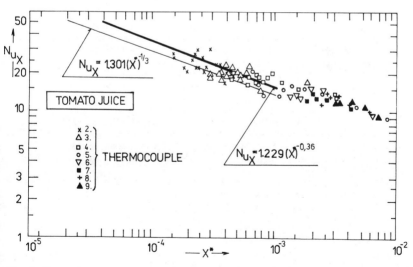

Fig. 6. Comparison of experimental heat transfer data for tomato juice—Eq. (11) versus (17).

CMC data in comparison with tomato juice, and the discrepancy between different CMC solutions.

CONCLUSIONS

Based on our 392 experimental data the following conclusions may be drawn:

— The hydraulic length in laminar flow at constant wall heat flux is shorter and less important than expected and predicted.

— Except for the short part of a tube near the entrance, the heat transfer coefficient can be correlated using Eqs. (17) and (18), both valid for $X^* < 10^{-2}$. Equation (18) better expresses the temperature variation of the consistency coefficient. Both correlations are capable of predicting heat transfer rates within reasonable engineering accuracy.

— More experimental work needs to be done especially with real food materials.

REFERENCES

1. Basett, C. E. and Welty, J. R. Non-Newtonian heat transfer in the thermal entrance region of uniformly heated horizontal pipes. *AIChE J.* **21:** 699, 1975.
2. Bird, R. B. Zur theorie des wärmeübergangs an nicht-Newtonesche flüssigkeiten bei laminarer röhrströmung. *Chemie-Ing.-Tecknik* **31:** 566–72, 1959.
3. Charm, S. E. and Merrill, E. W. Heat transfer coefficients in straight tubes for pseudoplastic food materials in streamline flow. *Food Res.* **24:** 319–31, 1959.
4. Christiansen, E. B. and Craig, S. E. Heat transfer to pseudoplastic fluids in laminar flow. *AIChE J.* **8:** 154–60, 1962.
5. Joshi, S. D. and Bergles, A. E. Experimental study of laminar heat transfer to in-tube flow of non-Newtonian fluids. *J. Heat Transfer* **102:** 397, 1980.
6. Kožíšková, B. Heat transfer in a flow of consistent food materials (Czech). Ph.D. Thesis, Czech Technical University, Prague, Czechoslovakia, 1983.
7. Lykov, A. V. *et al.* Aggregated problems of convective heat transfer (Russian), Minsk, USSR, 1971.
8. Mizushina, T. *et al.* Laminar heat transfer to non-Newtonian fluids in a circular tube (constant heat flux). *Kagaku Kogaku* **31:** 250–5, 1967.
9. Oliver, D. R. and Jensen, V. G. Heat transfer to pseudoplastic fluids in laminar flow in horizontal tubes. *Chem. Eng. Sci.* **9:** 115, 1964.
10. Petuchov, B. S. Heat transfer and pressure drop in laminar tube flow (Russian). *Energia*, Moskva, USSR, 1967.
11. Šesták, J. Flow and heat transfer to non-Newtonian fluids (Czech). Ph.D. Thesis, Czech Technical University, Prague, Czechoslovakia, 1965.
12. Yoo, S. Heat transfer and friction factors for non-Newtonian fluids in turbulent pipe flow. Ph.D. Thesis, University of Illinois at Chicago Circle, 1975.

26

COEFFICIENTS FOR AIR-TO-SOLID HEAT TRANSFER FOR UNIFORMLY SPACED ARRAYS OF RECTANGULAR FOODS

AMELIA RUBIOLO DE REINICK* and HENRY G. SCHWARTZBERG

Department of Food Engineering, University of Massachusetts, Amherst, Massachusetts 01003, U.S.A.

* Consejo Nacional de Investigaciones Científicas y Tecnicas, Argentina

ABSTRACT

Unsteady state heating and cooling of aluminum inserts were used to measure side, front and back surface heat-transfer coefficients (h) for single blocks and in the first and second rows of arrays of blocks.

Values of h were calculated using measured temperature versus time histories for the inserts, at various position and flow arrangements.

Marked discrepancies occurred when the experimental h values were compared with h values calculated using available Reynolds number (Re) versus Nusselt number (Nu) correlations in which Re and Nu were both based on either the hydraulic diameter or on the flow path lengths.

The experimental h values were then empirically correlated by the equation $Nu = C.Re^n$ in which the characteristic length in Nu and Re was either a local average axial distance L_{av}, a combination of differential and integral flow path lengths, or the hydraulic diameter D' and the C and n corresponding to these choices and the various positions tested were determined. The best correlation was obtained when the combined lengths were used, but the expressions involved are complicated. Equally acceptable correlation was obtained when L_{av} was used, in which case, $C = 0.21$ and $n = 0.69$ for cooling and $C = 0.37$ and $n = 0.63$ for heating. The equation and these values of C and n correlated with the experimental data to within $\pm 10-15\%$.

INTRODUCTION

Methods for predicting average temperature versus time behavior during freezing and thawing can be used for arrays of objects placed in an air stream if the heat transfer coefficients, h, for the surfaces of the objects are known.[1]

Little information concerning h for the various surfaces of rectangular blocks[2] appears to be available for gas-to-solid heat transfer. That is, the values of h associated with different package geometries, package surfaces and package spacing arrangements do not appear to have been determined.

For well-defined geometries[3] at specified flow conditions, h is frequently correlated by expressions of the form:

$$\text{Nu} = \frac{hL}{k} = C' \, \text{Re}^n \, \text{Pr}^m \tag{1}$$

$$J_\text{h} = St \, \text{Pr}^{2/3} = C'' \, \text{Re}^p \tag{2}$$

The constants C' and C'' are defined for different solid shape geometries; in the present case, it should also be a function of the geometric arrangement of the array of solids.

There is an interaction between the spacing between objects and the rate of air flow around the objects. Consequently, the value of h at the object's surfaces will depend on both the size and relative proportions of the object, and the space between adjacent objects. Relationships between these geometric factors, h and the air flow are not adequately known. When correlating h, surfaces of slab-like or rectangular objects which lie parallel to the air flow, might be considered as isolated flat plates or as part of the boundary surfaces of a rectangular duct. Available flat-plate-based correlations[3] utilize Nusselt numbers and Reynolds numbers based on the downstream length of the surface; and the correlations for ducts[4] use Nusselt numbers and Reynolds numbers based on the hydraulic diameter of the duct.

MATERIALS AND METHODS

Method for Measuring Surface Heat Transfer Coefficient for Solid Objects

The Biot number Bi equals ha/k, where a is a characteristic dimension of an object and k is the thermal conductivity. If Bi is sufficiently small, the temperature of an object undergoing unsteady state heat transfer will be nearly uniform.[5]

Small values of Bi can be obtained by using an object which is relatively small, and/or by using an object with large k. To measure h, 12·7-mm and 25·4-mm thick aluminum slabs, having a large k value, were embedded in 0·15-m square, 25 and 50-mm thick dummy packages made of styrofoam, a good insulator with a small heat capacity. The exposed surface of the slab, at which h was measured, was flush with the surface of the dummy package (see Fig. 1). The rate of temperature change of the slab was used to determine heat transfer rates and the h for the exposed surface. Air flow was parallel to the side surface of the slab along its length and perpendicular to its front and back surfaces.

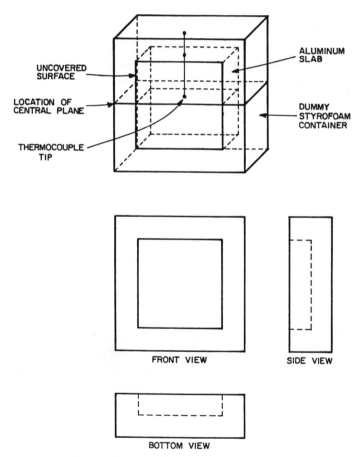

Fig. 1. Aluminum block insulated with Styrofoam.

Since heat transfer through the insulated surfaces is negligibly small, the average temperature $\bar{t}$ versus time, θ, for the aluminum block is described by Eq. (3).

$$\ln\left[\frac{\bar{t} - t_a}{t_1 - t_a}\right] = \frac{-hA\theta}{(1 + f\,\mathrm{Bi})V\rho_s c_{ps}} \tag{3}$$

where A is the surface area, V is the volume, ρ_s the density, c_{ps} the heat capacity and t_1 the initial temperature of the slab; t_a is the air temperature.

Because of the high degree of uniformity of the aluminum block temperature, t, $\bar{t}$ can be replaced by the temperature t_c, measured by a thermocouple whose tip is positioned in the center of the block.[6] Alternatively, thermocouples could be embedded at uniformly-spaced intervals in the block and $\bar{t}$ based on the temperatures indicated by these thermocouples could be used. The latter technique provides a more valid value for $\bar{t}$, and simultaneously demonstrates the degree to which a uniform temperature has been obtained.

Equation (3) can be rearranged to calculate h. Alternatively, one can use a semilog plot of $(\bar{t} - t_a)/(t_1 - t_a)$ versus θ to determine h (see Fig. 2). Regression routines provided by SPSS[7] were used to determine the slopes of such plots and hence h. The values of V, A and ρ_s for the aluminum can be readily measured; values of c_{ps} can be determined by simple calorimetric measurement. By using these values and initially assuming that Bi is negligibly small, one can obtain an initial estimate for h. Once this is known, a revised estimate for Bi can be obtained. This can be used to obtain a revised estimate of h. The process can be iterated until convergence to any desired degree of accuracy is achieved. In this work, even the first Bi correction did not change the value of h by a significant amount.

Surface heat transfer coefficients for block-like objects depend on the velocity of the air stream in contact with the object. The array was placed on a flat surface in a wind tunnel which provided uniform velocities ranging between 0·5 and 7·6 m/s at air temperatures ranging from 15 to 20 °C for cooling and between 25 and 30 °C for heating. The long side of the blocks were usually placed parallel to the air flow, but in some cases they were placed perpendicular. Mid-channel air velocities were measured, roughly 1 cm before the first row of blocks, and mid-way between the first and second row and the second and third row of blocks of the array shown in Fig. 3, for different spacings

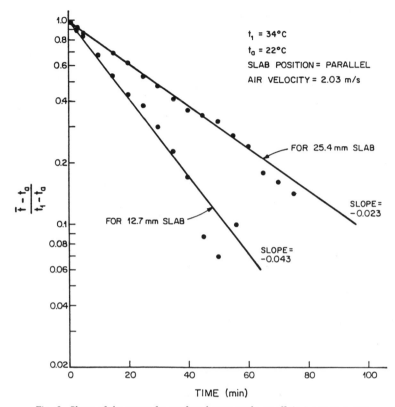

Fig. 2. Slope of the curve for surface heat transfer coefficient measurement.

between the parallel blocks. The velocities were measured using a portable hot-wire anemometer (Kurz Instruments Series 400) with an accuracy of ±2% of full-scale range. This instrument has a reproducibility of ±0·25% of full scale between −20 °C and +55 °C. The anemometer sensor was placed in the middle of the channel halfway between the top of the block and its base.

Heating tests were carried out using an initial block temperature of −10 °C and air temperatures of 25–30 °C. Cooling tests were carried out using an initial block temperature of 37 °C and air temperatures of 15–20 °C.

Predicted values (h_2) were calculated using the following correlations in which the Reynolds number (Re_2) and Nusselt number (Nu_2)

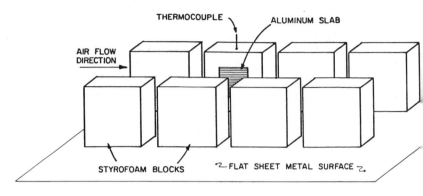

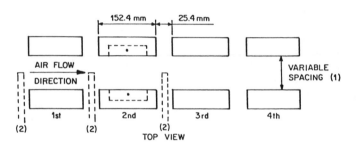

(1) 25.4 mm, 63.5 mm, 127.0 mm, 254.0 mm

(2) ANEMOMETER TIP: INSERTED AT THESE POSITIONS
TO MEASURE AIR VELOCITY

Fig. 3. Block arrangement for surface-heat transfer determination.

were based on the hydraulic diameter (D'):[4]

$$\text{For } 2\,000 < \text{Re}_2 < 10\,000$$

$$\text{Nu}_2 = 0\cdot116[(\text{Re}_2)^{2/3} - 125]\,\text{Pr}^{1/3}[1 + (D'/L')^{2/3}] \qquad (4)$$

$$\text{For } \text{Re}_2 \geq 10\,000$$

$$\text{Nu}_2 = 0\cdot023(\text{Re}_2)^{0\cdot8}\,\text{Pr}^{1/3} \qquad (5)$$

When $L'/D' \leq 60$, $h_2 = h_{2(\text{eq})}[1 + 1\cdot4(D'/L')]$, where $h_{2(\text{eq})}$ is the value obtained from either Eqs. (4) or (5) and L' is the duct length.

Alternative, predicted values of h (h_3) were calculated, using Reynolds numbers (Re_3) based on flow path length L' and Nusselt numbers (Nu_3) from:

$$Nu_3 = 0 \cdot 648(Re_3)^{1/2} Pr^{1/3} \qquad (6)$$

which is frequently used for flat plates.[3]

The L' values used in determining Nu_3 and Re_3 for Eq. (6) were the length of the first block alone, when determining h_3 for the first block, and the combined length of both the blocks and the intervening space when determining h_3 for the second block. This choice of lengths is not precisely correct, but is conservative and leads to higher predicted Nu_3 values. Nevertheless, the Nu_3 values calculated this way were significantly smaller than the experimental Nu values.

For Eqs. (4) and (5) the air properties used were those corresponding to the bulk fluid temperature; in Eq. (6) the air properties were taken at the average of the plate and air temperatures.

Heat Transfer Coefficient Correlation

Measured values of h at the first and second position in the arrangement shown in Fig. 3, for each geometric arrangement used in this work, were used to evaluate the validity of Eqs. (4), (5) and (6) and determine coefficients and exponents for alternative correlations.

The dimensionless groups used to correlate forced convection are Re, Nu and Pr. Since Pr for air is insensitive to change of temperature, we did not attempt to determine its effect.[8] Air velocities and/or the clearance between objects were changed to obtain different Re values which were used in the following simplified correlation equation:

$$Nu = C\,Re^n \qquad (7)$$

Nu and Re at selected conditions were correlated with a SPSS non-linear-regression routine[7] to determine C and n. Three different characteristic lengths (D', L_{av} or L_{di}) were used in Nu and Re to evaluate alternative bases for correlation; furthermore,

$$\bar{h} = \frac{1}{L^*} \int_s^r h_x \, dx \qquad (8)$$

Where s is axial distance of the leading edge of the block, L^* is the length of the block, $r = s + L^*$, and

$$h_x = Ck\left(\frac{\rho_v}{\mu}\right)^n x^{(n-1)} \qquad (9)$$

Finally:

$$\text{Nu} = \frac{\bar{h}L^*}{k} = \frac{C}{n}[(\text{Re}_r)^n - (\text{Re}_s)^n] \tag{10}$$

$\text{Re}_r = (\rho v r)/\mu$ and $\text{Re}_s = (\rho v s)/\mu$, and ρ, v and μ are the density, velocity and viscosity of the air.

RESULTS

The air velocity in the center of the channel was constant around the first block, but decreased after the second one. The difference between

TABLE I
Typical h values at various experimental conditions

Air velocity (m/s)	Surface	Spacing (cm)	$h_{(1)}^*$ (W/m²K)	$h_{(2)}^*$ (W/m²K)	Heat transfer mode
0·5	Front	∞	13·3	—	Cooling
0·5	Back	∞	10·7	—	Cooling
0·5	Side	6·35	18·3	16·0	Cooling
2·5	Side	6·35	35·5	34·2	Cooling
4·0	Side	6·35	51·9	49·9	Cooling
5·1	Side	6·35	61·0	50·7	Cooling
5·1	Side	2·54	62·8	43·7	Cooling
7·6	Side	6·35	86·9	59·2	Cooling
7·6	Side	12·70	86·3	58·8	Cooling
7·6	Side	25·40	76·8	59·3	Cooling
7·6	Side	∞	86·3	76·2	Cooling
7·6	Front	∞	53·2	—	Cooling
7·6	Back	∞	48·2	—	Cooling
0·5	Front	∞	18·2	—	Heating
0·5	Back	∞	17·3	—	Heating
0·5	Side	6·35	18·9	18·2	Heating
2·5	Side	6·35	39·9	31·0	Heating
4·0	Side	6·35	53·1	51·1	Heating
5·1	Side	6·35	68·1	55·9	Heating
5·1	Side	2·54	64·8	57·3	Heating
7·6	Side	6·35	86·6	67·2	Heating
7·6	Side	12·70	80·3	60·1	Heating
7·6	Side	25·40	77·1	67·3	Heating
7·6	Side	∞	73·3	58·3	Heating
7·6	Front	∞	53·8	—	Heating
7·6	Back	∞	49·4	—	Heating

* $h_{(1)}$ and $h_{(2)}$ are respectively the heat transfer coefficients for blocks in the first and second row.

the initial velocity and the discharge velocity was larger for smaller spacing.

The mid-channel velocity 10–20 mm above the bottom of the blocks was roughly 20% of the velocity near the middle of block, and 1 cm below the top of the block the velocity was 10–15% higher than the velocity near the middle of the block. Mid-channel, mid-block velocities are used in our subsequent tabulations and correlations.[9]

Typical results for various heat-transfer tests are listed in Table I. It can be seen that h increased markedly as the air velocity increased, was smaller for the second block than for the first block, and did not change very much when the spacing between parallel blocks changed. During heating, h was slightly larger than during cooling. The h for the front and back surfaces of the block were about 25–45% lower than h for the side surfaces.

Typical log–log plots of Nu versus Re are shown in Figs. 4 and 5. It can be seen that the available flat plate and duct correlations of Nu versus Re, (Eqs. (6) and (5) respectively), predict Nu values which are much smaller than the experimental values. Moreover, the log–log

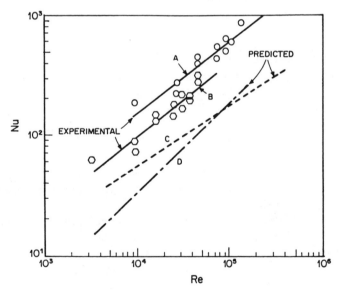

Fig. 4. Nusselt versus Reynolds correlation for cooling block in 2nd row and 63·5 mm spacing. A, empirical-best-fit Nu versus Re plot for Nu and Re based on L_{av}; B, empirical-best-fit Nu versus Re plot for Nu and Re based on D'; C, Nu versus Re, flat plate correlation, Eq. (6); D, Nu versus Re, duct correlation, Eq. (5).

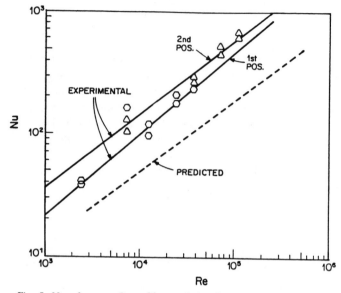

Fig. 5. Nusselt versus Reynolds correlation for single row of objects.

slope for the duct-based correlation is greater than the log Nu versus log Re slope for the experimental data. It is difficult to distinguish the relative goodness of fit for log Nu versus log Re plots for D'- and L_{av}-based regressions of Eq. (7). The same difficulty was encountered when Eqs. (8)–(10) were used. When all the results were compared, Eqs. (8)–(10) provided correlations which exhibited least scatter. However, the results obtained with L_{av}-based Nu and Re were only slightly poorer than the results using these equations. Since L_{av} are much easier to calculate and convenient to apply, they were used in our subsequent work.

Different values of c and n were obtained[10] for each set of conditions, such as spacing, block size, etc., but C and n are highly interdependent; when n decreases C increases. Further, only two C and n pairs, one for heating and one for cooling could be used to correlate all the side surface heat transfer data. For cooling, C and n were respectively 0·21 and 0·69 and for heating the corresponding values were 0·37 and 0·63.

CONCLUSIONS

Heat transfer coefficients predicted by currently available correlations for ducts and flat plates are significantly smaller than experimental values for the side surfaces of rectangular blocks placed in arrays of equidistant similar blocks. The experimental h values can be reasonably well correlated by Eq. (7), when the characteristic length in Nu and Re is L_{av}, the distance from the beginning of the array to the middle of the side surface of the object. Somewhat better correlation is provided when Nu and Re are based on the approach used in Eqs. (8)–(10), but these equations are less convenient to use.

ACKNOWLEDGEMENT

Thanks are expressed to Mr Richard J. Grant for the graphical assistance.

REFERENCES

1. Schwartzberg, H. G., Rosenau, J. R. and Haight, J. R. The Prediction of Freezing and Thawing Temperature versus Time Behavior Through the Use of Effective Heat Capacity Equations. Int. Inst. Ref. Commissions C1, C2. Karlsruhe, **1**: 311, 1977.
2. Chavarria, V. M. and Heldman, D. R. Measurement of convective heat transfer coefficients during food freezing processes. *J. Food Sci.* **49**(3): 810, 1984.
3. Holman, J. P. *Heat Transfer.* McGraw-Hill, New York, 1981.
4. Perry, R. H. and Chilton, C. H. *Chemical Engineers Handbook,* 5th edn. McGraw-Hill, New York, 1973.
5. Schwartzberg, H. G. Mathematical Analysis of the Freezing and Thawing of Foods. Paper Presented at the AICHE Summer National Meeting, Detroit, Michigan, 1981.
6. Footrakul, P. Freezing and thawing effects on the quality and heat transfer characteristic of ground beef. Ph.D. Dissertation, University of Massachusetts, 1976.
7. Robinson, B. SPSS Document No 4574, Linear and Non Linear Regression. Northwestern University, Chicago, 1981.
8. Knudsen, J. and Katz, D. L. *Fluid Dynamics and Heat Transfer.* McGraw-Hill, New York, 1958.
9. Lind, I. and Skjoldebrand, C. Surface heat and mass transfer during thawing. In: *Engineering and Food,* Volume 1, *Engineering Sciences in the Food Industry* (B. McKenna, ed.) Elsevier Applied Science Publishers, London, 1984.
10. Reinick, A. C. Rubiolo de. Mathematical model on freezing and thawing. Ph.D. Dissertation, University of Massachusetts, 1985.

27

HEAT TRANSFER COEFFICIENTS IN FLAME STERILIZATION OF SIMULATED CANNED LIQUID FOODS

R. D. PERALTA RODRIGUEZ* and R. L. MERSON

Department of Food Science and Technology, University of California, Davis, California 95616, U.S.A.

ABSTRACT

Internal, external and overall heat transfer coefficients were calculated from experimental heat penetration data, external can surface temperatures, and combustion gas temperature data using silicone fluids in rotating cans. Crossflow Reynolds number and can-burner separation were varied and existing correlations gave order-of-magnitude agreement. In all cases, the external heat transfer coefficient was the controlling rate parameter, with values ranging from 16·3 to 22·2 W/m^2K.

NOMENCLATURE

A_c = external area of can, taken in calculations to be the cylindrical area (m^2)
A_i = inside cylindrical area of can (m^2)
C_l = specific heat capacity of liquid food (kJ/kg K)
C_{pg} = average specific heat capacity of combustion gases (kJ/kg K)
D = can diameter (m)
D_r = diameter of rollers in single can simulator (m)
E = can headspace (m)
F_{cf} = view factor from can to flame, dimensionless
Gr = Grashof number, Gr = $\beta_g \Delta T D^3 \rho_g^2 / \mu_g^2$, dimensionless
H = can height (m)

* Present address: *Centro de Investigacion en Quimica Aplicada, Apdo. postal 379, C. P. 25000, Saltillo, Coahuila, Mexico.*

h_c = external heat transfer coefficient (W/m^{2}K)

h_i = internal heat transfer coefficient (W/m^{2}K)

K_g = thermal conductivity of combustion gases (W/mK)

K_l = thermal conductivity of liquid food (W/mK)

M_l = mass of liquid food in can (kg)

Nu$_c$ = external Nusselt number, Nu$_c = h_c D/K_g$, dimensionless

Nu$_i$ = internal Nusselt number, Nu$_i = h_i D/K_l$, dimensionless

Nu$_m$ = modified Nusselt number, Nu$_m = UD/K_l$, dimensionless

Pr$_i$ = internal Prandtl number, Pr$_i = \mu_l C_l/K_l$, dimensionless

Pr$_s$ = crossflow Prandtl number, Pr$_s = \mu_g C_{pg}/K_g$, dimensionless

$\dot{Q}_a$ = rate of heat accumulation in liquid (W)

$\dot{Q}$ = rate of heat transfer to can (W)

Re = rotating Reynolds number, Re $= Dv_p\rho_g/\mu_g$, dimensionless

Re$_i$ = internal Reynolds number, Re$_i = D_r(\pi D\omega)\rho_l/\mu_l$, dimensionless

Re$_s$ = crossflow Reynolds number, Re$_s = Dv_s\rho_g/\mu_g$, dimensionless

T_f = theoretical flame temperature assuming dissociation and ionization (K)

T_g = temperature of combustion gases leaving flame (K)

$T_{g\theta}$ = experimental arithmetic average temperature of combustion gases surrounding can (K)

T_l = temperature of liquid food (K)

T_0 = initial temperature of liquid food (K)

T_{si} = inside temperature of can surface (K)

T_{so} = temperature of external can surface (K)

ΔT = temperature difference, $\Delta T = T_g - T_{so}$ (K)

t = time (s)

U = overall heat transfer coefficient (W/m^{2}K)

v_p = cylinder surface peripheral velocity (m/s)

v_s = crossflow gas velocity (m/s)

α_c = absorptivity of can, dimensionless

β_g = coefficient of thermal expansion, $1/T$ for an ideal gas (K^{-1})

ε_f = emissivity of flame, dimensionless

μ_b = viscosity of liquid evaluated at average bulk temperature between start and end of process (Pa s)

μ_g = viscosity of combustion gases (Pa s)

μ_l = viscosity of liquid food (Pa s)

μ_0 = viscosity of liquid evaluated at average temperature of can wall between start and end of process (Pa s)

π = constant, 3·141 59...

ρ_g = density of combustion gases (kg/m^3)

ρ_l = density of liquid food (g/m^3)
σ = Boltzmann constant, 5·667 892 4 × 10^{-6} W/m^{2}K^4
ω = Rotational speed of can (rev/s)
θ = angular position (radians)

INTRODUCTION

Direct flame ('Steriflamme') sterilization of convection-heating foods consists of four steps: steam preheating, direct flame heating of rapidly rotating cans, temperature holding, and water spray cooling.[1–6] Of critical importance is the direct flame heating section which must produce the required sterilization temperature without under- or overheating. This work concerns heat transfer coefficients for this section.

To date, design of flame sterilization systems has been primarily empirical, with only a few attempts at theoretical evaluation.[7–11] Furthermore, heat transfer coefficients are scarce.[8,12–15] Correlations for the internal heat transfer coefficient in liquid canned foods have been developed by Quast and Siozawa,[16] see Ref. 8

$$\mathrm{Nu_i} = 0·17(\mathrm{Re_i})^{0·52}(\mathrm{Pr_i})^{1/3}(H/E)^{1/3} \tag{1}$$

and by Soulé:[17]

$$\mathrm{Nu_i} = 0·434(\mathrm{Re_i})^{0·571}(\mathrm{Pr_i})^{0·278}(H/D)^{0·356}(\mu_b/\mu_0)^{0·154} \tag{2}$$

A correlation for the average overall coefficient for flame heating of CMC solutions under conditions simulating commercial flame sterilization is:[18]

$$\mathrm{Nu_m} = 0·433(\mathrm{Re_i})^{0·56}(\mathrm{Pr_i})^{0·60}(\mathrm{Re})^{-0·68} \tag{3}$$

External heat transfer to a rotating cylinder in heated air, with and without crossflow can be correlated[19] by:

$$\mathrm{Nu_c} = 0·135[(0·5\,\mathrm{Re}^2 + \mathrm{Re_s^2} + \mathrm{Gr})\mathrm{Pr_s}]^{1·3} \tag{4}$$

where Re is a rotational Reynolds number based on cylinder rotational speed and Re$_s$ is a crossflow Reynolds number based on linear gas velocity.

The current study reports a method of estimating internal, external and overall heat transfer coefficients during flame heating of simulated liquid foods under conditions in which theoretical, idealized models describe the heat transfer phenomena. The method was applied to data obtained in heating experiments of silicone fluids in 303×406 cans, and the results were compared with values calculated from existing correlations.

Derivation of Equations Used to Estimate Heat Transfer Coefficients

The heat transfer coefficients of concern are: (1) the external convective film coefficient, h_c, defined by

$$\dot{Q} = h_c A_c (T_g - T_{so}) + \alpha_c A_c \sigma (\varepsilon_f F_{cf} T_f^4 - T_{so}^4) \tag{5}$$

which expresses the rate of heat transfer to the external surface of the can by convection from the hot combustion gases and by radiation from the flame;[9] (2) the internal convective film coefficient, h_i, from the inside can surface to the liquid, defined by

$$\dot{Q} = h_i A_i (T_{si} - T_l) \tag{6}$$

and (3) the overall coefficient, U, defined by

$$\dot{Q} = U A_c (T_g - T_l) + \frac{U A_c \alpha_c \sigma}{h_c} (\varepsilon_f F_{cf} T_f^4 - T_{so}^4) \tag{7}$$

Since the can wall has a high thermal conductivity and is only $0.25\,mm$ thick, $T_{si} \approx T_{so}$, $A_i \approx A_c$ and the overall resistance to heat transfer from the combustion gases to the liquid is accurately approximated by

$$\frac{1}{U} = \frac{1}{h_c} + \frac{1}{h_i} \tag{8}$$

Furthermore, h_i can be obtained experimentally by measuring the rate that energy is accumulated in the liquid

$$\dot{Q}_a = M_l C_l \frac{dT_l}{dt} \tag{9}$$

and comparing with Eq. (6) to give

$$h_i = \frac{M_l C_l \dfrac{dT_l}{dt}}{A_c (T_{so} - T_l)} \tag{10}$$

Solving Eqs. (7) and (9) simultaneously gives an approximate expression for the liquid temperature[9]

$$\frac{T_l - T_g}{T_0 - T_g} = \exp\left(-\frac{UA_c}{M_l C_l}t\right) - \frac{\alpha_c \sigma (\varepsilon_f F_{cf} T_f^4 - T_{so}^4)}{h_c(T_g - T_0)}\left[1 - \exp\left(-\frac{A_c}{M_l C_l}t\right)\right]$$

(11)

Experimentally, the temperature of the combustion gases surrounding the can is a function of angular position, i.e. $T_g = T_g(\theta)$. Since the heat transfer coefficients being estimated are average coefficients over the cylindrical surface of the can, the gas temperature was averaged from experimental data by

$$T_{g\theta} = \frac{\int_0^{2\pi} T_g(\theta)\,d\theta}{\int_0^{2\pi} d\theta}$$

(12)

Substituting $T_{g\theta}$ for T_g and h_c from (8) into (11) gives

$$f(U) = \exp\left(-\frac{UA_c}{M_l C_l}t\right) - \frac{\alpha_c \sigma (\varepsilon_f F_{cf} T_f^4 - T_{so}^4)}{\left(\dfrac{1}{U} - \dfrac{1}{h_i}\right)^{-1}(T_{g\theta} - T_0)}$$

$$\times \left[1 - \exp\left(-\frac{A_c}{M_l C_l}t\right)\right] - \frac{T_l - T_{g\theta}}{T_0 - T_{g\theta}} = 0$$

(13)

which can be solved for U by trial and error using experimental values of the other parameters.

MATERIALS AND METHODS

Experimental

Determination of h_i from Eq. (10) requires experimental values of T_l, T_{so} and liquid heating rate dT_l/dt. In addition, values for T_f and $T_{g\theta}$ are needed to find U from Eq. (13).

The single-can process simulator used in the experiments has been described in detail elsewhere.[10,11] The simulator consisted of a $11 \cdot 1 \times 11 \cdot 1$ cm propane–air burner, over which a liquid-filled 303×406 can was heated while rotating at 30 rpm. To measure liquid heating rates, a bakelite insulated copper–constantan thermocouple was placed in the silicone fluid at the can center. Surface temperature was measured inside the can with a surface thermocouple cemented to the axial midpoint of the can wall and insulated to protect it from the liquid. This surface temperature was assumed to equal T_{so} and was also assumed uniform longitudinally since the burner covered the entire can length. Time–temperature data were obtained for five stoichiometric propane–air flow rates and five separation distances between can and burner.

To determine $T_{g\theta}$, two empty nonrotating 303×406 cans without ends were used to support thermocouples in the gases. One can, designed to measure gas temperature as a function of radial position, had a chromel–alumel thermocouple positioned at the midplane of the can and held at various distances from the wall by a thermocouple receptacle (Model C-5, O. F. Ecklund, Inc., Lakeland, FL) cemented on the inside wall. Lead wires were protected by a 0·64 cm o.d., 6·0 cm long stainless steel tube containing a two-hole ceramic insulator. The exposed junction was positioned 1·0, 0·5 or 0·3 cm from the can wall. Thermocouple output was recorded on a digital data logger (Model PD-2064, Esterline Angus Instrument Corp., Indianapolis, IN).

The second can, used to measure gas temperature as a function of axial position, was fitted with three brass stuffing boxes (designed for plastic pouches, O. F. Ecklund, Inc.) soldered in a straight line on the inside can wall at 0·00, 2·10, and 4·20 cm from the midplane. Thermocouple probes (Omega Engineering, Inc.) were prepared by inserting 0·076 mm diameter platinum–platinum/13% rhodium leads into two-hole ceramic insulators encased in 0·16 cm o.d. Inconel 600 protection tubes. The measuring junctions were positioned 1·00 cm from the can surface. Outputs were registered in an HP3054DL digital data logger (Hewlett Packard Co.).

These can-thermocouple assemblies did not rotate continuously, but were positioned manually to measure combustion gas temperature at $45°$ intervals from $\theta = 0$ (shortest distance from can to burner) to $\theta = 2\pi$. The temperature field was mapped for each flow condition to determine the effects of crossflow velocity and can-burner separation.

Numerical computations

Heating rate data were calculated from linear regression equations reported by Peralta Rodriguez[11] obtained in heating experiments with silicone oils. Can surface temperature as a function of time was obtained by digitizing analog graphs of the surface temperature.[11] The FORTRAN calculational procedure consisted of evaluating the internal film coefficient from Eq. (10), the overall heat transfer coefficient from Eq. (13) (using a Newton–Raphson method), and the external film coefficient from Eq. (8). The initial estimate for U was obtained by neglecting radiation in Eq. (11). U and h_c were arbitrarily set equal to zero if $T_{so} \leqslant T_1$ or if $T_1 \leqslant T_0$.

The radiation parameters needed in Eq. (13) were calculated as in Refs. 9–11. T_f was 2240 K,[20] can metal absorbtivity α_c for the tin-free steel was 0·6,[21] ε_f was 0·0248,[22] and view factors F_{cf} in Table III were calculated by the method of Sparrow and Cess.[23]

RESULTS AND DISCUSSION

Temperature of the Gases Surrounding the Can

As expected, the radial temperature gradient data (Table I) indicate a lower gas temperature near the can surface compared to the bulk of the hot gases for the bottom half of the can (near the flame). For a rotating can containing a liquid food this gradient would probably be more pronounced since heat would be taken into the liquid more efficiently than for the empty experimental can. Nevertheless, it was assumed that the external temperature measured 1·0 cm from the can truly represented the combustion gas temperature for driving force calculations.

TABLE I

Temperature distribution around axial midplane of a 303×406 nonrotating can. Air flow rate, 29·0 standard litres/min; propane flow rate, 1·00 standard litres/min; can–burner separation, 3·5 cm

Position of thermocouple (degrees)	Temperature (°C) Distance from can surface (cm)		
	(1·0)	(0·5)	(0·3)
0	435·1 ± 4·3*	393·3 ± 3·2	382·7 ± 2·6
45	407·4 ± 12·9	383·6 ± 4·0	374·4 ± 4·6
90	335·5 ± 7·2	327·4 ± 8·5	288·0 ± 3·6
135	214·2 ± 2·7	227·4 ± 4·2	222·0 ± 5·9
180	146·9 ± 1·6	150·1 ± 1·1	153·9 ± 1·3
225	215·4 ± 7·4	217·4 ± 2·1	202·9 ± 1·8
270	320·3 ± 3·9	307·4 ± 4·6	303·3 ± 3·4
315	417·2 ± 8·6	379·8 ± 6·4	374·8 ± 3·4

* Mean ± standard deviation for five replications at 15 s intervals.

A total of 33 experiments were conducted to obtain the temperature distribution of gases surrounding the can 1·0 cm from the surface (Fig. 1). For the burner used here, the gas temperature was reasonably uniform from one end of the can to the other[11] but showed typical variation[14,24] with angular position. The minimum gas temperature was located above the top of the can and varied with crossflow velocity and can–burner separation distance. Under certain operating conditions there was a region at the top of the can which transferred heat away from the can, causing periodic cooling of the can surface. This

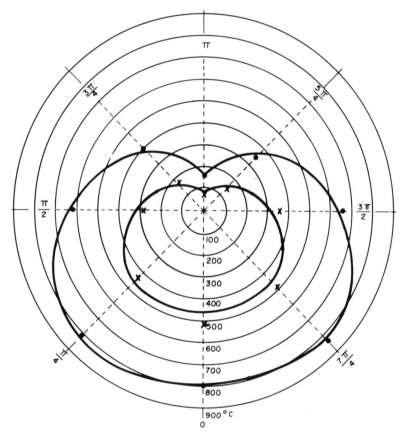

Fig. 1. *Temperature profiles around can at the midplane, 1·0 cm from surface. Can–burner separation 3·5 cm. Each data point is the average of 15 determinations (3 independent experiments with at least 5 temperature readings each at 10 or 20 s intervals).* × *Low gas flow rate* ($Re_s = 150$). ● *High gas flow rate* ($Re_s = 350$).

situation could complicate measuring can surface temperatures for process control; it also presents an opportunity for optimizing energy use by adjusting gas flow rate and can–burner separation to minimize heat loss.

Paulus and Ojo[24] reported temperature profiles 0·3 cm from the can surface for a rotating can. Their profile was asymmetrical, distorted in the direction of rotation, perhaps because they used a narrow burner placed parallel to the can axis.

Can Wall Temperature
A typical profile of the surface temperature (Fig. 2) is a complex function of time, depending on can rotational speed, liquid viscosity, combustion gas crossflow velocity, and can–burner separation.[11,18] The periodic variations evident at the surface are damped out within the liquid.

Heat Transfer Coefficients
Experimental coefficients varied with time,[11] asymptotically approaching constant values after 0·5–1 min heating. Values in Tables II and III are for 121·1 °C liquid temperature.

The internal heat transfer coefficient should be only slightly dependent on burner gas flow rate; experimental values showed random variation with crossflow Reynolds number (Table II). Analysis of variance (3 replicates) showed that differences between values at different Re_s values were significant at the 5% level. Experimental difficulties may account for the fluctuations: (1) surface and liquid temperatures were difficult to synchronize since the former were obtained on a strip chart while the latter were recorded in a data logger. (2) Choice of the instantaneous surface temperature during digitization could have introduced random error since the surface temperature varied periodically, whereas liquid temperature variations were damped by agitation and further smoothed by linear regression equations.

The crossflow Reynolds number has a more important effect on the external and overall heat transfer coefficients (Table II). As expected, both coefficients increased with increasing crossflow Reynolds number, the differences being statistically significant at the 5% level. Thus, the improvement in liquid heating rates caused by increasing burner rates (higher crossflow Reynolds numbers) is the result of two factors: increased driving force (as indicated by higher combustion gas

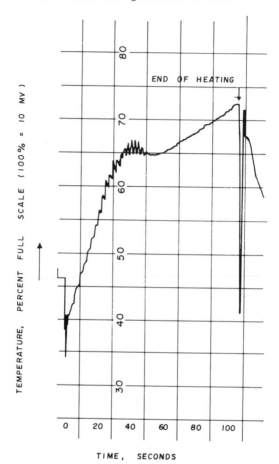

Fig. 2. Typical can surface temperature profile during flame heating.

temperatures) and decreased resistance to heat transfer (as demonstrated by the heat transfer coefficients presented here).

With respect to can–burner separation (Table III), the internal film coefficient varied randomly (although differences between h_i values at different distances were statistically significant at the 5% level) for 0·0013 Pa s silicone fluid. However, data for 0·0479 Pa s fluid[11] remained statistically constant for the five can–burner distances tested. The observations about experimental difficulties described for internal heat transfer coefficients are also valid for these experiments.

TABLE II
Effect of crossflow Reynolds number on heat transfer coefficients. Silicone fluid
$(1\cdot3 \times 10^{-3}$ Pa s) in 303×406 can rotating at 30 rpm. $Re_i = 15\,000$; $Pr_i = 6$; can–burner
separation $= 3\cdot5$ cm

	Heat transfer coefficients (W/m^2K)					
	Internal		External		Overall	
Re_s	Expt'l*	Predicted[1]	Expt'l*	Predicted[2]	Expt'l*	Predicted[3]
150	286	261	16·4	8·0	15·6	13·6
220	272	263	17·7	8·0	16·6	15·1
285	334	267	18·2	8·2	17·3	16·0
310	408	265	21·6	8·3	20·5	16·5
350	322	269	22·2	8·4	20·8	17·0

* Average of triplicate experiments.
[1] Soulé.[17]
[2] Kays and Bjorklund.[19]
[3] Teixeira Neto.[18]

Contrary to expectations, experimental values of h_c and U increased
slightly as the can–burner distance was increased. Based on 3–4
replications, the increases were significant at the 5% level. Since the
convective heat transfer coefficient depends principally upon fluid
dynamics that should not change with can–burner configuration, one
would expect h_c to remain constant (Table III). A possible explanation

TABLE III
Effect of can–burner separation on heat transfer coefficients. Silicone fluid $(1\cdot3 \times 10^{-3}$ Pa s) in 303×406 can rotating at 30 rpm. $Re_i = 15\,000$; $Pr_i = 6$; $Re_s = 285$; $Re = 90$

		Heat transfer coefficients (W/m^2K)					
		Internal		External		Overall	
Distance (cm)	View factor[1]	Expt'l*	Predicted[2]	Expt'l*	Predicted[3]	Expt'l*	Predicted[4]
1·2	0·16	318	269	16·3	8·2	15·4	16·0
1·5	0·15	486	263	17·7	8·2	17·1	16·0
2·5	0·12	437	267	18·3	8·2	17·6	16·0
3·5	0·11	334	267	18·2	8·2	17·3	16·0
5·0	0·08	347	258	19·8	8·2	18·8	16·0

* Average of triplicate experiments.
[1] Peralta Rodriguez.[11]
[2] Soulé.[17]
[3] Kays and Bjorklund.[19]
[4] Teixeira Neto.[18]

is that errors in the values of α_c, ε, T_f or F_{cf} exaggerated the importance of the view factor in the radiation term in Eq. (5), and this error is in turn reflected in U calculated from Eq. (13).

Heat transfer coefficients predicted by correlations in the literature give order-of-magnitude agreement with experimental coefficients (Tables II and III). For all cases considered, the external film coefficient is the controlling resistance in flame heating of canned liquids.

Quast and Siozawa's correlation (Eq. 1) predicted a film coefficient which gave differences (with respect to experimental values) of -47% to -75%. In general, Soulé's correlation gave reasonable agreement, underpredicting experimental values from 3% to 26%, except for $Re_s = 310$ (35%) (Table II) and can–burner separations 1·5 cm and 2·5 cm (46% and 39%, respectively) in Table III. Both correlations were used within their range of applicability.

The Kays and Bjorklund correlation (Eq. 4) for the external film coefficient predicted values which differed -43% to -62% from experimental values. This discrepancy indicates that their correlation is not applicable to the flame system, in which the crossflow, generated by a flame close to the cylinder, may not have been uniform.

The Teixeira Neto correlation (Eq. 3) indicates excellent agreement with experimental values in Tables II and III, with deviations from $+4\%$ to -20%. However, for other data, the correlation overestimated the overall heat transfer coefficient by $+30\%$ to $+65\%$. A possible reason is that his system used a ribbon burner at right angles to the axis of rotation in contrast to the square burner used here. Additionally, the correlation was used for $Re = 90$, which is outside its limits of applicability. Furthermore, in contrast to other research, the Teixeira Neto correlation is based on data suggesting that the internal resistance controls the rate of heat transfer; for example, for 1·5% CMC solutions in cans rotating at 100 rpm, values for internal, external, and overall coefficients were reported as 7·3, 36·4 and 15·3 W/m^2K, respectively. The correlation uses a Nusselt number based on the thermal conductivity of the can contents. In the experimental results presented here, the magnitude of the overall film coefficient is controlled by the external resistance (i.e. $U \approx h_c$); therefore, the overall coefficient would be expected to be a function of the physical properties of the external fluid rather than of the can contents.

CONCLUSIONS

Even though it is not easily implemented because of the complexity of the system, the method presented here permits order-of-magnitude estimation of internal, external and overall heat transfer coefficients from experimental time–temperature data for liquid foods during heating by a gas flame. Soulé's correlation[17] underestimates the internal film coefficient for liquid foods in axially rotating cans by 30% compared to experimental values. Kays and Bjorklund's correlation[19] for the external film coefficient gives order-of-magnitude estimates only. It is possible that by modifying this correlation to take into account the heat source, a better estimate of the external film coefficient can be obtained. Teixeira Neto's equation for estimating overall heat transfer coefficients in flame processing also gives only order-of-magnitude agreement with data in the present research which utilized an unusual square burner configuration. Work is needed to closely simulate commercial machines, so that research results can be applied directly to the industrial situation.

ACKNOWLEDGEMENTS

The work was supported by USDA Marketing Hatch funds, by a grant from the Continental Can Co., and by a fellowship to the senior author from CONACYT.

REFERENCES

1. Beauvais, M., Thomas, G. and Cheftel, H. A new method for heat processing canned foods. *Food Technol.* **15**(4): 5, 1961.
2. AIFST–CSIRO. Flame sterilization. Specialist courses for the food industry. No. 2. Austr. Inst. of Food Sci. and Technol. and CSIRO, North Ryde, New South Wales, Australia, 1972.
3. Casimir, D. J. Flame sterilization. *CSIRO Food Research Quarterly* **35**(2): 34–9, 1975.
4. Leonard, S. J., Merson, R. L., Marsh, G. L., York, G. K., Heil, J. R. and Wolcott, T. Flame sterilization of canned foods: An overview. *J. Food Sci.* **40**: 246–9, 1975.
5. Leonard, S. J., Marsh, G. L., Merson, R. L., York, G. K., Heil, J. R., Fryer, S., Wolcott, T. and Ansar, A. Comparative procedures for calculating Steriflamme thermal processes. *J. Food Sci.* **40**: 250–3, 1975.

6. Leonard, S. J., Marsh, G. L., Merson, R. L., York, G. K., Buhlert, J. E., Heil, J. R. and Wolcott, T. Chemical, physical and biological aspects of canned whole peeled tomatoes when thermally processed by Steriflamme. *J. Food Sci.* **40:** 254–6, 1975.
7. Ojo, A. Wärmeübertragungsverhältnisse bei der Flammen Sterilization. Ing. thesis University of Karlsruhe, 1972.
8. Merson, R. L., Leonard, S. J., Mejia, E. and Heil, J. R. Temperature distribution and liquid-side heat transfer coefficients in model liquid foods in cans undergoing flame sterilization heating. *J. Food Proc. Eng.* **4:** 85–98, 1980.
9. Peralta Rodriguez, R. D. and Merson, R. L. Heat transfer and chemical kinetics during flame sterilization. *AIChE Symposium Series* **78**(218): 58–67, 1982.
10. Peralta Rodriguez, R. D. and Merson, R. L. Experimental verification of a heat transfer model for simulated liquid foods undergoing flame sterilization. *J. Food Sci.* **48**(3): 726–33, 1983.
11. Peralta Rodriguez, E. D. Heat transfer to simulated canned liquid foods undergoing flame sterilization. Ph.D. Dissertation, University of California, Davis, 1982.
12. Wu, B. K. Aspects of heat transfer in flame sterilization of canned milk. M.S Thesis, University of New South Wales, Australia, 1971.
13. Casimir, D. J., Hunting, J. N. and Rutledge, R. J. Control of the thermal process in flame sterilization. *CSIRO Food Research Quarterly* **35**(2): 63–7, 1975.
14. Fujiwara, M. External heat transfer coefficient during canning by flame sterilization M.S. Thesis, University of California, Davis, 1975.
15. Fujiwara, M. and Merson, R. L. External heat transfer during canning by flame sterilization. Paper No. 25e. AIChE 51st Nat'l. Mtg., Kansas City, MO, 1976.
16. Quast, D. G. and Siozawa, Y. Y. Heat transfer rates during heating of axially rotated cans. *Proc. IV Int. Congress Food Sci. and Technol.*, Vol. IV, pp. 458–68 1974.
17. Soulé, C. Internal heat transfer coefficients in liquid canned foods. M.S. Thesis University of California, Davis, 1981.
18. Teixeira Neto, R. O. Heat transfer rates to liquid foods during flame sterilization. *J. Food Sci.* **47**(2): 476–81, 1982.
19. Kays, W. M. and Bjorklund, I. S. Heat transfer from a rotating cylinder with and without crossflow. *Trans. ASME, Series C* **80:** 70–8, 1958.
20. Siegel, R. and Howell, J. R. *Thermal Radiation Heat Transfer.* McGraw-Hill, New York, 1972.
21. Gubareff, G. G., Jamisen, J. E. and Torberg, R. H. *Thermal Radiation Properties Survey,* 2nd edn. Honeywell Research Center, Minneapolis, MN, 1960.
22. Hottel, H. C. Radiant heat transmission. In *Heat Transmission,* 3rd edn (W. H. McAdams Ed.), Chapt. 4. McGraw-Hill, New York, 1954.
23. Sparrow, E. M. and Cess, R. D. *Radiation Heat Transfer.* McGraw-Hill, New York, 1978.
24. Paulus, K. and Ojo, A. Heat transfer during flame sterilization. *Proc. IV Int. Congress Food Sci. and Technol.,* Vol. IV, pp. 443–8, 1974.

Part IV
Kinetics and Mathematical Modeling

28

REACTION RATES USING DIFFERENTIAL SCANNING CALORIMETRY

CONSTANTINE SANDU and DARYL LUND

Department of Food Science, University of Wisconsin-Madison, 1605 Linden Drive, Madison, Wisconsin 53706, U.S.A.

ABSTRACT

With increased use of computers in data acquisition and analysis, differential scanning calorimetry can utilize and benefit from more powerful models to estimate apparent kinetic parameters of reactions. Such models are the subject of this contribution to the analysis of (1) systems of single reactions, and (2) systems of multiple reactions.

A DSC curve acts as a 'fingerprint' of the transformation occurring in the reacting system. A set of general equations can be derived from the features of the DSC curve, when two process parameters are used as independent variables: the initial concentration of reactant and the heating rate.

For a system that involves single reactions, the equations derived from the peak, shape, first inflection point, and area under the DSC curve allow estimation of order of reaction, activation energy, heat of reaction and pre-exponential factor. For zero- and first-order reactions, these relations require Linear Regression Analysis, whereas for a general order of reaction Nonlinear Regression Analysis must be applied.

Two systems involving multiple reactions have been analyzed: (a) irreversible first-order parallel reactions and (b) irreversible first-order consecutive reactions. Two different relations have been derived based on the feature of the DSC curve at its maxima/minima. In case (a), the relation encompasses the area under the curve up to the maximum/ minimum. In case (b), the deflection of the DSC curve at maximum/ minimum is utilized. In both cases, Nonlinear Regression Analysis is required to estimate activation energy, heat of reaction and pre-exponential factor of each reaction.

301

A model for corrections to the DSC record was developed for the transition baseline. The equation applies equally to systems involving single or multiple reactions (with some assumptions for the latter) and describes the conditions under which the transition baseline can be considered an extension of the pretransition baseline.

NOMENCLATURE

A = apparent pre-exponential factor $(\text{kg-mol}/(\text{m}^3\,\text{s}))/(\text{kg-mol } \text{m}^3)^n$

b = deflection of the DSC curve when a single reaction occurs (W)

B = deflection of the DSC curve when multiple reactions occur (W)

C = chemical species (reactant)

C^* = intermediate chemical species

C_r = mass of reference material multiplied by its heat capacity (J/K)

E = apparent activation energy (J/kg-mol)

f = fraction conversion of the reactant (dimensionless)

k = apparent constant of reaction $(\text{kg-mol}/(\text{m}^3\,\text{s}))/(\text{kg-mol}/\text{m}^3)$

m = amount of reactant (kg-mol)

n = apparent order of reaction (dimensionless)

R = 8314 J/(kg-mol K), gas constant

R_0 = heat transfer resistance (K/W)

s = integral value of DSC curve when a single reaction occurs (W K); when s^* the dimension is (W s)

S = integral value of DSC curve when multiple reactions occur (W K)

t = time (s)

T = temperature (K)

V = volume of reacting system (m^3)

y_1 = signal of DSC record during pretransition (pretransition baseline) (W)

y_2 = signal of DSC record during transition (W)

$(y_2 \pm b)$ = transition baseline (W)

y_3 = signal of DSC record during post-transition (post-transition baseline) (W)

α = heating rate (K/s)

$$\beta_1 = A_1 E_1 / R$$
$$\beta_2 = A_2 E_2 / R$$
$$\beta_3 = E_1 / R$$
$$\beta_4 = E_2 / R$$
$$\beta_5 = m_0 (\Delta H_{R1})$$
$$\beta_6 = m_0 (\Delta H_{R2})$$
$$\beta_7 = (\beta_1 / \beta_3)^2$$
$$\beta_8 = (\beta_2 / \beta_4)^2$$
$$\beta_9 = \beta_3 - \beta_4$$
$$\beta_{10} = \beta_4 - \beta_3$$
$$\beta_{11} = \beta_1 \beta_2 / (\beta_3 \beta_4)$$
$$\beta_{12} = m_{01}^{-1} ((\Delta H_{R1}) - (\Delta H_{R2}))^{-1}$$
$$\beta_{13} = \beta_{11} (\Delta H_{R2}) / ((\Delta H_{R1}) - (\Delta H_{R2}))$$
$$\beta_{14} = \beta_1 / \beta_3$$
$$\beta_{15} = \beta_2 / \beta_4$$
$$\beta_{16} = \beta_{14} / \beta_3$$
$$\beta_{17} = \beta_3 + \beta_4$$

(ΔH_R) = apparent heat of reaction (J/kg-mol)
v = generalized stoichiometric coefficient (dimensionless)
ξ = extent of reaction (kg-mol)

Subscripts

1 = pertaining to reaction 1
2 = pertaining to reaction 2
i = pertaining to a given maximum/minimum
m = maximum/minimum
0 = initial
s = pertaining to the sample
t = total

INTRODUCTION

The DSC technique is designed to monitor the difference in energy flow into a sample (that is, reacting system) and a reference material as a function of temperature or time, when both materials are subject to a controlled temperature program. The *DSC record* shows the difference in energy flow (W) plotted on the ordinate for a conventional representation of the endothermic/exothermic effects versus temperature (K) or time (s) on the abscissa.

To assess the real signal produced by the chemical/physical transformation in the reacting system, the DSC record must be corrected. Typical corrections of a DSC record include: nonlinearity, heating rate, thermal lag, and baseline. Whereas the first two corrections are technical problems, the last two are analytical and can be incorporated into every model used to evaluate DSC data. The term *DSC curve* will refer to the corrected record.

The DSC curve is the fingerprint of the chemical/physical transformation occurring in the reacting system. Consequently, in analyzing the DSC curve, a set of equations can be derived to estimate the *apparent reaction-kinetic parameters*.

The heat capacity of the sample material (that is, reacting system) changes from that given by the mixture of the reactants, before the chemical/physical transformation, to that given by the mixture of the products of reaction, after the transformation. During the transformation, the heat capacity is that of a mixture of reactants and products of reaction corresponding to the instantaneous progress of the reaction. At the same time, the transformation energy signal can be practically neglected before and after the transformation. As a result, the DSC record/curve reveals three distinct states: *pretransition, transition, and post-transition*.

At any time, the signal on the ordinate of the DSC record is the result of three effects: an instrumental signal; a signal due to the sensible heat difference between sample and reference materials; and a signal due to the chemical/physical transformation in the sample material (provided the reference material is inert). The sum of the first two effects represents the *baseline of the DSC record*. Practically, only during the transition state is the baseline not identical with the signal on the ordinate of the DSC record.

SYSTEMS INVOLVING SINGLE REACTIONS

A set of equations was derived from the DSC curve by Sandu *et al.*[1] to calculate the apparent kinetic parameters including order of reaction, activation energy, heat of reaction, and pre-exponential factor. The model assumes a homogeneous chemical reaction in a liquid system characterized by one single extent of reaction:

$$n C \rightarrow \text{Products of reaction} \qquad (1)$$

where n is the apparent order of reaction (dimensionless); and C designates a chemical species.

The mathematics of the model is based on the features of the DSC curve (that is, peak, shape, first inflection point and area under the curve) as functions of two main process parameters: heating rate and initial concentration of the reactant. Linear/nonlinear regression analysis has to be applied to the experimental data to obtain the kinetic parameters.[1]

Equation (34) in Ref. 1, based on the well-known model of Borchardt and Daniels,[2] was previously given without any mathematical proof. Here we consider its derivation since it is critical to our analysis.

The deflection of the DSC curve from baseline can be written as (see also Ref. 3):

$$b = (\Delta H_R) m_0 \frac{df}{dt} \qquad (2)$$

where b is the pure transformation signal (W); (ΔH_R) is the apparent heat of reaction (J/kg mol), assumed constant; m_0 is the initial amount of reactant (kg-mol); f is the fraction conversion (dimensionless); and t is time (s). Necessarily, the total area under the DSC curve is $s_t^* = (\Delta H_R) m_0$. With this condition in Eq. (2), it can be easily shown that:

$$-\frac{dm}{dt} = \frac{m_0}{s_t^*} b \qquad (3)$$

where m is the instantaneous amount of reactant (kg-mol); and s_t^* is the total area under the DSC curve (Ws). Equation (3) gives the rate of reaction. As a result, the instantaneous amount of reactant at a given time is given as:

$$m = m_0 - \frac{m_0}{s_t^*} \int_0^t b \, dt \qquad (4)$$

where the integral is the partial area under the DSC curve s* (W s), up to the time t. Using Eqs. (3) and (4) in the relation for the definition of the constant of reaction, the result is:

$$k = \left(\frac{s_t^* V}{m_0}\right)^{n-1} b / (s_t^* - s^*) \qquad (5)$$

where k is the apparent constant of reaction $(kg\text{-}mol/(m^3 s))/(kg\text{-}mol/m^3)^n$; V is the volume of the reacting sample (m^3), assumed constant. Equation (5) is the classical result of Borchardt and Daniels (see Eq. (19) in Ref. 2). Finally, using temperature as the abscissa of the DSC curve, substituting the Arrhenius equation, and taking the logarithm, Eq. (5) becomes:

$$\ln b = \ln \left(\frac{A}{\alpha} (s_t/C_0)^{1-n} \right) + n \ln (s_t - s) - \frac{E}{RT} \tag{6}$$

where A is the apparent preexponential factor $(kg\text{-}mol/(m^3 s))/(kg\text{-}mol/m^3)^n$; α is the heating rate (K/s); s_t is the total area under the DSC curve $(W\,K)$; C_0 is the initial concentration of the reactant $(kg\text{-}mol/m^3)$; s is the partial area under the DSC curve $(W\,K)$; E is the apparent activation energy $(J/kg\text{-}mol)$; $R = 8314\,J/(kg\text{-}mol\,K)$; and T is temperature (K).

Consider Eq. (6) for the conditions at the peak of a zero-order reaction:

$$\ln b_m \simeq \ln \left(\frac{A\,s_m}{\alpha\,C_0} \right) - \frac{E}{RT_m} \tag{7}$$

where m stands for the curve peak (maximum or minimum). The assumption was made that for a zero order reaction the relation $s_t \simeq s_m$ holds. Further, introducing Eqs. (32) and (17) from Ref. 1 into Eq. (7) above the result is:

$$b_m \simeq \frac{E(\Delta H_R)m_0}{R} \frac{\alpha}{T_m^2} \tag{8}$$

For a zero-order reaction the deflection at the peak of the DSC curve is directly proportional to α/T_m^2, when $m_0 = \text{const}$.

SYSTEMS INVOLVING MULTIPLE REACTIONS

The DSC curve of a system involving multiple reactions is the resultant of chemical/physical transformations occurring simultaneously at different reaction rates and with different apparent heats of reaction. Modeling systems of this type results in mathematics which does not always end in simple close relations. In this section we attempt to derive the apparent reaction-kinetic parameters from the DSC curve generated by a system involving either (a) two irreversible, first-order, parallel reactions or (b) two irreversible, first-order, consecutive reactions. The model assumes homogeneous chemical reactions in a liquid system characterized by two extents of reaction.

Depending on the ratio between the reaction rates as well as on the exothermic/endothermic effects, the DSC curve (of a system involving two extents of reactions) can display a series of patterns: two distinct maxima/minima (with one minimum/maximum); one distinct maximum and one distinct minimum; only one distinct maximum/minimum, preceded or followed by a less distinct one. The immediate result is that the DSC curve can have one to three places where the first derivative $dB/dT = 0$. This feature of the DSC curve is used extensively in the subsequent modeling.

The pure transformation signal of a system involving two extents of reaction $B(W)$ is:

$$B = b_1 + b_2 \tag{9}$$

where b_1 is the signal pertaining to reaction 1 (W); and b_2 is the signal pertaining to reaction 2 (W).

For multiple reaction systems it is convenient to work in terms of the extent of reaction (Hill,[4] pp. 2–3):

$$\xi = (m - m_0)/v \tag{10}$$

where ξ is the extent of a given reaction (kg-mol); and v is the generalized stoichiometric coefficient (dimensionless), defined as positive for a product species and negative for a reactant species. Consequently, Eq. (2) can be rewritten as:

$$b = -v(\Delta H_R) \frac{d\xi}{dt} \tag{11}$$

When only two first-order reactions are involved in the system, the total signal in Eq. (9) becomes:

$$B = (\Delta H_{R1}) \frac{d\xi_1}{dt} + (\Delta H_{R2}) \frac{d\xi_2}{dt} \tag{12}$$

where subscripts 1 and 2 indicate reaction 1 and reaction 2, respectively. If the abscissa of the DSC curve is temperature, the substitution $dt = dT/\alpha$ is used in this result.

First-order Parallel Reactions

Consider that species C undergoes two first-order parallel reactions:

$$C \rightarrow \text{products of reaction 1}$$
$$C \rightarrow \text{products of reaction 2} \tag{13}$$

The progress of reaction can be described by the following system of differential equations:

$$\frac{d\xi_1}{dt} = k_1(m_0 - \xi_1 - \xi_2)$$
$$\frac{d\xi_2}{dt} = k_2(m_0 - \xi_1 - \xi_2) \tag{14}$$

To uncouple these equations, divide the first by the second, integrate and use the result back into the system of Eq. (14). Then changing the independent variable from t to T, and substituting Arrhenius correlations for the constants of reaction, the system of equations becomes:

$$\frac{d\xi_1}{dT} = \frac{A_1}{\alpha} m_0 \exp\left(-\frac{E_1}{RT}\right) - \left(\frac{A_1}{\alpha}\exp\left(-\frac{E_1}{RT}\right) + \frac{A_2}{\alpha}\exp\left(-\frac{E_2}{RT}\right)\right)\xi_1$$
$$\frac{d\xi_2}{dT} = \frac{A_2}{\alpha} m_0 \exp\left(-\frac{E_2}{RT}\right) - \left(\frac{A_1}{\alpha}\exp\left(-\frac{E_1}{RT}\right) + \frac{A_2}{\alpha}\exp\left(-\frac{E_2}{RT}\right)\right)\xi_2 \tag{15}$$

These two equations are substituted into Eq. (12), and from the condition $dB/dT = 0$ it can be shown, after tedious mathematical manipulations, that the following relation is valid:

$$\frac{-\dfrac{\beta_2}{T_{mi}^2}\exp(\beta_3/T_{mi}) + \dfrac{\beta_8}{\alpha}\exp(\beta_9/T_{mi}) + \dfrac{\beta_{11}}{\alpha}}{\dfrac{\beta_1}{T_{mi}^2}\exp(\beta_4/T_{mi}) - \dfrac{\beta_7}{\alpha}\exp(\beta_{10}/T_{mi}) - \dfrac{\beta_{11}}{\alpha}} = \frac{\beta_5 - S_{mi}/\alpha}{\beta_6 - S_{mi}/\alpha} \tag{16}$$

where T_{mi} is the temperature at a given maximum/minimum (K); S_{mi} is the area under the DSC curve up to a given maximum/minimum (W K); and β_1–β_6 are constants which embody the kinetic parameters of the two reactions (see Nomenclature). The other constants β_7–β_{11} are directly related to the first group (see Nomenclature).

Using Nonlinear Regression Analysis on a set of experimental data α, T_{mi}, S_{mi}, at $m_0 = \text{const.}$, six kinetic parameters can be estimated from the values of β_1–β_6; these parameters are: A_1, E_1, (ΔH_{R1}), A_2, E_2, (ΔH_{R2}). Attention has to be given to the real sign of the integral values S_{mi} in Eq. (16).

First-order Consecutive Reactions

Consider a species C which undergoes two first-order consecutive reactions:

$$C \rightarrow C^*$$
$$C^* \rightarrow \text{products of reaction} \tag{17}$$

The following system of differential equations describes the progress of reaction:

$$\frac{d\xi_1}{dt} = k_1(m_{01} - \xi_1)$$
$$\frac{d\xi_2}{dt} = k_2(m_{02} - \xi_2) - k_1(m_{01} - \xi_1) \tag{18}$$

First, change the independent variable from t to T, and substitute Arrhenius correlations for the constants of reactions. Then introduce the results into Eq. (12) and find the relation $dB/dT = 0$.

The intermediate relation obtained so far will include the ratio $(m_{01} - \xi_1)/[(\Delta H_{R2})(m_{02} - \xi_2)]$ which needs an explicit correlation with the data measurable on the DSC curve. First it can be shown that:

$$(\Delta H_{R2})(m_{02} - \xi_2) = \frac{1}{k_2}(B - k_1((\Delta H_{R1}) - (\Delta H_{R2}))(m_{01} - \xi_1)) \tag{19}$$

where k_1 and k_2 are constants of reaction, replaceable through Arrhenius correlations, and B is the total signal of the transformation (W). Next, assuming that the extent of reaction 1 does not depend on the subsequent reaction, the differential equation of reaction 1 is easily solved to give:

$$(m_{01} - \xi_1) \simeq m_{01} \exp\left(-\frac{A_1}{\alpha} \frac{RT^2}{E_1} \exp\left(-\frac{E_1}{RT}\right)\right) \tag{20}$$

where the approximation means Eq. (12) in Ref. 1 was used to obtain this result.

After these manipulations, this final result is valid:

$$
\frac{-\dfrac{\beta_4}{T_{mi}^2}\exp\left(\beta_{17}/T_{mi}\right)+\dfrac{\beta_{15}}{\alpha}\exp\left(\beta_3/T_{mi}\right)}{\dfrac{\beta_1}{T_{mi}^2}\exp\left(\beta_4/T_{mi}\right)-\dfrac{\beta_7}{\alpha}\exp\left(\beta_{10}/T_{mi}\right)+\dfrac{\beta_{13}}{\alpha}}
$$

$$
=\frac{\exp\left(-\beta_{16}\dfrac{T_{mi}^2}{\alpha}\exp\left(-\beta_3/T_{mi}\right)\right)}{\beta_{12}B_{mi}-\beta_{14}\exp\left(-\left(\dfrac{\beta_3}{T_{mi}}+\beta_{16}\dfrac{T_{mi}^2}{\alpha}\exp\left(-\beta_3/T_{mi}\right)\right)\right)}\tag{21}
$$

where B_{mi} is the deflection of DSC curve at a given maximum
minimum (W); and the constants (β's) embody the kinetic parameter
of the two reactions (see Nomenclature).

Using Nonlinear Regression Analysis on a set of experimental dat
α, T_{mi}, B_{mi}, at $m_{01}=$ const., the kinetic parameters of both reaction
can be determined from the values of regression coefficients. Particu
larly, Eq. (21) does not encompass the value m_{02}; the equation is no
valid for $(\Delta H_{R1})=(\Delta H_{R2})$. Attention has to be given to the real sig
of the deflection B_{mi}.

CORRECTIONS TO THE DSC RECORD

A DSC record requires a series of corrections to obtain the real signa
of the chemical/physical transformation (that is, the DSC curve
Sandu and Lund[5] recently suggested a model for these corrections i
connection with systems that involve single reactions. The major resu
of their analysis was the equation of the transition baseline:

$$
(y_2 \pm b) = y_1 + f\left((y_3 - y_1) + \alpha_s C_r R_0 \frac{d(y_3 - y_1)}{dT_s}\right) - \alpha_s C_r R_0 \frac{d(y_2 - y_1)}{dT_s}\tag{22}
$$

where y_1 and y_2 are the equations describing the pretransition an
post-transitions baselines; f is the fraction conversion; C_r is the mass c
reference material multiplied by its heat capacity (J/K); R_0 is the hea
transfer resistance (K/W); and s refers to the sample material.

If there is no change in heat capacities and either the heating rate o
the heat transfer resistance is very small, then from Eq. (22) th

ransition baseline is merely an extension of the pretransition baseline. Any departure from these conditions makes the calculation of the ransition baseline necessary. The way to accomplish this calculation is outlined in Ref. 5.

It is interesting to note that Eq. (22) holds equally for systems nvolving two extents of reaction (analyzed in the previous section), if ertain assumptions are fulfilled. For parallel reactions, the heat apacities of products 1 and products 2 need to be almost equal, whereas for a system with series reactions, the heat capacities of the ntermediate product and the final products need to be close. Also, if he reaction constants are sufficiently different, it can be assumed that he onset temperature (see Eq. (16) in Ref. 5 is entirely dependent on he earlier reaction, and similarly the final temperature (see Eq. (17) n Ref. 5) depends completely on the latter reaction.

CONCLUSIONS

n connection with two previous publications,[1,5] the mathematical modeling presented by the authors on reaction rates using DSC is an attempt to develop a complete computational basis around DSC. The DSC offers the advantages of a fast and precise technique, if the physics and mathematics describing its operation are well understood.

To have tenable mathematical formulations for data analysis, a eries of boundary conditions and assumptions have been embedded nto the final results. It is a matter of testing these results against some standard transformations before their usefulness can be accepted.

Most of the results have been expressed in such a way that Linear/Nonlinear Regression Analysis has to be applied to the experimental data. Nevertheless, the relations that have to be re-gressed are fairly involved. At this moment the authors cannot assess he problems raised by the convergence ability of these relations or by he minimum experimental data required to assure a successful egression analysis. These aspects are the subject of ongoing research.

ACKNOWLEDGEMENTS

This paper is a contribution from the College of Agricultural and Life Sciences, University of Wisconsin-Madison and was made possible by a grant from the National Dairy Promotion and Research Board, an Dairy Research Foundation.

REFERENCES

1. Sandu, C., Lund, D. and Park, K.-H. Reaction kinetic parameters obtained fro differential scanning calorimetric data. In *Mathematical Modelling in Science an Technology*, (X. J. R. Avula, R. E. Kalman, A. I. Liapis, and E. Y. Rodin, Eds pp. 489–94. Pergamon Press, New York, 1984.
2. Borchardt, H. J. and Daniels, F. The application of differential thermal analysis t the study of reaction kinetics. *J. Am. Chem. Soc.* **79**(1): 41–6, 1957.
3. Rogers, R. N. and Smith, L. C. Application of scanning calorimetry to the study c chemical kinetics. *Thermochimica Acta* **1**: 1–9, 1970.
4. Hill, C. G. *An Introduction to Chemical Engineering Kinetics and Reactor Desig* John Wiley, New York, 1977.
5. Sandu, C. and Lund, D. Differential scanning calorimetric model for corrections t the DSC record. *Thermochimica Acta* **88**(2): 453–9, 1985.

29

KINETICS OF ASCORBIC ACID DEGRADATION IN STORED INTERMEDIATE MOISTURE APPLES

RAKESH K. SINGH and DARYL B. LUND

epartment of Food Science, University of Wisconsin, Madison, Wisconsin 53706, U.S.A.

ABSTRACT

scorbic acid degradation in stored intermediate moisture apples (IMA) as studied as a function of storage temperature and product water ctivity (a_w). Analysis of kinetic data suggested first order reaction inetics, and the value of the rate constant increased with increasing ither temperature or a_w or both. A mathematical model was developed ased on this study. The model uses the Arrhenius relationship for mperature dependence and an empirical model for a_w dependence of he rate constant.

INTRODUCTION

*enerally, intermediate moisture foods can be consumed without ehydration, and are shelf-stable without refrigeration or thermal rocessing. Therefore, these foods have potential application in eveloping countries, military and space-flight rations or other situaions where refrigeration or thermal processing facilities are adequate.[1-3]

Ascorbic acid (vitamin C) is usually selected as an index of the utrient quality because of its labile nature as compared to the other utrients in foods. Degradation of ascorbic acid depends on several actors which include; oxygen, pH, metal ion catalysis, light, temperaure and moisture content or water activity (a_w). However, in ackaged stored foods, the major factors which could affect the egradative reactions are storage temperature and the product a_w.

Therefore, the specific objectives of this study were: (1) to obtain kinetic data on ascorbic acid (AA) degradation as a function of temperature and a_w of intermediate moisture apples (IMA), and (2) to develop mathematical model(s) to describe the effect of storage temperature and a_w on the rate of AA degradation in IMA.

MATERIALS AND METHODS

Preparation of Intermediate Moisture Apples
IMA were prepared by drying peeled, sliced and sulfited (i.e. dipped in 2% $NaHSO_3$ solution for 5–6 min) red delicious apples to various moisture contents. Drying was carried out in a batch type air dehydrator at 70 °C dry bulb temperature and 20% relative humidity.

Determination of Moisture Content
Moisture contents of IMA were measured according to AOAC procedures using a vacuum oven.[4] All the measurements were conducted in duplicate.

Water Activity Measurement
The vapor pressure manometric (VPM) technique as described by Labuza[5] was used to measure a_w.

Measurement of Ascorbic Acid (AA)
Concentration of ascorbic acid was measured using high performance liquid chromatography (HPLC). An HPLC (model ALC-202) equipped with a pump (Model 6000A), injector (Model U6K, Water Assoc., Milford, MA), and an Ultraviolet detector (Gilson Model 111 Middleton, WI) set at 254 nm wavelength were used. The detector signal was recorded on a Varian (Model 9176) recorder. The chromatographic column was a 30 cm × 3·9 mm i.d. μBondapak C_{18} (Water Assoc.). A 0·3% metaphosphoric acid solution was used as mobile phase.

Ascorbic acid standard solutions were prepared and diluted to 20 mg/100 ml in 6% HPO_3 for storage. Standard curves were prepared from data obtained on the standard solution by plotting ascorbic acid concentrations against corresponding peak heights.

Sample Preparation for HPLC Analysis'

The procedure of AVC[6] was used for extracting ascorbic acid from stored and freshly prepared apple slices. All determinations were made in triplicate.

RESULTS AND DISCUSSION

The concentration of ascorbic acid in stored IMA was measured as described previously. A recovery test of added ascorbic acid was also carried out in order to test the accuracy of extraction and determination of ascorbic acid by the method of AVC.[6]

Recovery of Added Ascorbic Acid

Extraction of ascorbic acid (AA) from apple samples was performed by using 10 μg/ml standard AA solution and 6% HPO_3. Peak heights of HPLC chromatograms for standard AA solution, apple samples fortified with AA, and nonfortified apple samples were measured. These peak heights were converted into corresponding AA concentrations using a standard curve. Eventually, the percentage recovery of added AA was calculated by Eq. (1).

$$\% \text{ recovery} = \frac{C_{af} - C_{anf}}{C_a} \times 100 \tag{1}$$

TABLE I
Recovery of added ascorbic acid from apples

	Moisture content $\left(\dfrac{g\ water}{g\ d.s.}\right)$	Concentration of ascorbic acid ($\mu g/g\ d.s.$)	% Recovery of added AA
Fresh apples	5·67	121·6(0·101)[a]	101·66(0·92)
IMA	0·701	118·5(0·34)	99·20(0·85)
(no storage)	0·535	117·3(0·16)	98·89(0·89)
	0·393	116·0(0·21)	97·95(0·77)
	0·209	114·8(0·11)	97·73(0·72)

[a] Percentage deviation, number of replicates = 8.

316   *Rakesh K. Singh and Daryl B. Lund*

where:

C_{af} = AA concentration in fortified apples (μg/ml)
C_{anf} = AA concentration in nonfortified apples (μg/ml)
C_a = AA concentration in standard solution (μg/ml)

Concentrations of ascorbic acid in apples at various moisture contents and corresponding percentage recoveries as calculated by Eq (1) are shown in Table I. The results indicated that the recovery of added AA was in the range of 97·7–101·7% depending on the moisture content of the samples. As the moisture content decreased the recovery of added AA from the samples also decreased. This might have been caused by the rehydration characteristics of dehydrated samples.

Ascorbic Acid Stability in Isothermally Stored IMA

The degradation of L-ascorbic acid in intermediate moisture apple (IMA) stored in sealed screw cap jars was determined as a function of moisture content and storage temperature. Intermediate moisture

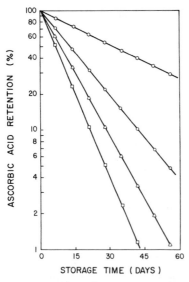 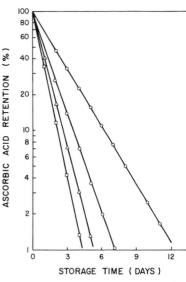

Fig. 1. Ascorbic acid retention as a function of storage time and a_w at 25 °C: ◯ (a_w = 0·62); ◯ (a_w = 0·77); △ (a_w = 0·83); □ (a_w = 0·88).

Fig. 2. Ascorbic acid retention as a function of storage time and a_w at 55 °C: ◯ (a_w = 0·62); ◯ (a_w = 0·77); △ (a_w = 0·83); □ (a_w = 0·88).

TABLE II
Rate constants and half-lives for AA loss as a function of water activity and
storage temperatures in stored IMA

Temperature (°C)	a_w	Rate constant k_c (day^{-1})	Percentage mean deviation in k_c	Half-life (days)
25	0·623	0·022 0	0·17	31·5
	0·765	0·055 1	0·41	12·6
	0·828	0·081 8	0·67	8·5
	0·875	0·112	1·48	6·2
55	0·666	0·385	1·70	1·8
	0·797	0·660	0·023	1·1
	0·852	1·084	8·54	0·6
	0·894	1·175	3·53	0·6

pples were adjusted to 0·209, 0·393, 0·535 and 0·701 g water/g d.s.
moisture contents and then stored at temperatures of 25, 35, 45 and
55 °C. The results conformed to the first-order kinetic function at all
moisture contents and storage temperatures. Nonetheless, the moisture content levels were converted to corresponding water activity
levels using the sorption isotherm model as it is presented by Singh.[7]
Examples of such results are shown in Figs. 1 and 2 at two
temperatures (25 and 55 °C) and four water activities. Coefficients of
determination (R^2) associated with these plots were greater than 96%.
The first-order rate constants and half-lives for AA degradation in
stored IMA are presented in Table II. These data show an increase in
the rate of AA loss with increasing water activity at a constant
temperature.

The temperature dependence of AA loss could be described by the
Arrhenius equation. However, the following section describes the
development of a mathematical model as a function of temperature
and a_w of the reaction rate constant for AA degradation.

Development of Kinetic Model for AA Loss

The results in this study indicated first-order reaction kinetics for AA
loss in stored IMA. The first-order reaction kinetics is expressed as:

$$\frac{dc}{d\Theta} = -k_c c \qquad (2)$$

where:

  c = ascorbic acid concentration (μg/g d.s.)
  Θ = time (day)
  k_c = rate constant (day^{-1})

Integration of Eq. (2) resulted in:

$$\ln \frac{c}{c_0} = -k_c \Theta \tag{3}$$

where c_0 = AA concentration at zero storage time (μg/g d.s.).

A term percentage retention ($c\%$) of AA was defined as:

$$c\% = \frac{c}{c_0} \times 100 \tag{4}$$

Combining Eqs. (3) and (4), the percentage retention can be expressed as:

$$c\% = \exp (6 \cdot 6051 - k_c \Theta) \tag{5}$$

Equation (5) can be used to describe retention of AA as a function of time at constant temperature and water activity. Values of k_c at various temperatures and water activities are shown in Table II.

The dependence of rate constant (k_c) on the water activity was modeled by a logarithmic model as given in Eq. (6):

$$\ln (k_c) = \ln (k_R) + p_1(a_w - a_{w,R}) \tag{6}$$

where:

  k_R = reference rate constant (day^{-1}); p_1 = parameter,
  $a_{w,R}$ = reference water activity.

Values of $\ln (k_R)$ and p_1 can be estimated by the least squares analysis of the data at each temperature, whereas the best estimate for $a_{w,R}$ should be the mean value of a_w.[8]

Since the variance of k_c was not constant, a weighted linear regression analysis was used to determine the parameters $\ln (k_R)$ and p_1.[9] The variance in $\ln (k_c)$ can be related to the variance in k_c by Eq. (7):

$$\text{Var} (\ln k_c) = \frac{S_k^2}{k_c^2} \tag{7}$$

where S_k^2 = estimated variance in k_c.

The results also indicated that the model could be modified to include the effect of temperature on reaction constant rate using the Arrhenius equation for the temperature dependence and a reference temperature of 313 K (the mean temperature in the experiment); Eq. (1) was modified as follows:

$$\ln(k_c) = p_0 + p_1(a_w - 0.8) - p_2\left(\frac{1}{T} - \frac{1}{313}\right)$$
$$+ p_3(a_w - 0.8)\left(\frac{1}{T} - \frac{1}{313}\right) \tag{8}$$

The data of Table II were subjected to regression analysis to determine the values of the parameters. The regression analysis was performed using the appropriate weights in $\ln(k_c)$. The coefficient of determination (R^2) was 100% indicating an excellent fit of the rate constant data with Eq. (8). Standard errors in p_0, p_1, and p_2 were less than 1% whereas that in p_3 was approximately 15%.

Substituting the values of the parameters into Eq. (8) and transforming to the antilogarithm yields:

$$k_c = 0.22 \exp\left[5.7(a_w - 0.8) - (7500 - 4100(a_w - 0.8))\left(\frac{1}{T} - \frac{1}{313}\right)\right] \tag{9}$$

The activation energy (E_c) for ascorbic acid destruction as a function of a_w can be estimated from Eq. (10):

$$\frac{E_c}{R} = 7500 - 4100(a_w - 0.8) \tag{10}$$

Values of E_c and its 95% confidence intervals are shown in Table III. As a_w increases in the range 0·6–0·9, there is an apparent decrease

TABLE III
Activation energy for AA destruction and its 95%
C.I. at various a_w

a_w	$E_c(kJ/g\,mol)$	95% C.I. $(kJ/g\,mol)$
0·62	68	±2
0·70	66	±1
0·80	62	±0·5
0·89	59	±1

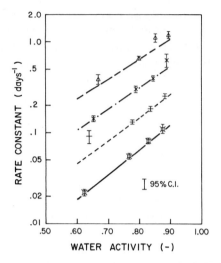

Fig. 3. Rate constant for ascorbic acid degradation as a function of a_w and temperature: □ 25 °C; + 35 °C; × 45 °C; △ 55 °C.

in the activation energy. A similar effect of a_w on E_c was noted by Riemer and Karel.[10] However, Reimer and Karel used an exponential model to describe the dependence of activation energy on a_w. Nonetheless, values of E_c for AA destruction found in this study were in close agreement with those reported in the literature[10–12] despite differences in composition and experimental techniques.

The rate constant data in Table II and lines calculated by Eq. (9) are plotted in Fig. 3. From this, it appears that a first order kinetic model adequately describes the data for degradation of ascorbic acid in stored IMA.

CONCLUSIONS

Kinetic data on degradation of ascorbic acid in stored IMA as a function of temperature and water activity were generated. Analysis of this data suggested first order reaction kinetics. Values of rate constant increased with increasing either temperature or a_w or both. A mathematical model to describe the effect of temperature and a_w on the rate constant was developed.

REFERENCES

1. Brockman, M. C. Development of intermediate moisture foods for military use. *Food Technol.* **24:** 896, 1970.
2. Kaplow, M. Commercial development of intermediate moisture foods. *Food Technol.* **24:** 899, 1970.
3. Smith, M. C. and Ashby, W. T. Intermediate moisture foods for manned space-flights. Presented at the 29th Annual Meeting of the Institute of Food Technol., Chicago, IL, 1969.
4. AOAC. *Official Methods of Analysis,* 13th edn. Association of Official Analytical Chemists, Washington, DC, 1980.
5. Labuza, T. P. Storage stability and improvement of intermediate moisture foods. Final Report, NASA, Food and Nutrition Office, Houston, TX, Contract No. NAS9-10658, 1976.
6. AVC. *Methods of Vitamin Assay.* The Association of Vitamin Chemists., Inc., Interscience, New York, 1966.
7. Singh, R. K. Kinetics and computer simulation of storage stability in intermediate moisture foods. Ph.D. thesis, University of Wisconsin, Madison, WI, 1983.
8. Box, G. E. P., Hunter, W. G. and Hunter, J. S. *Statistics for Experimenters. An Introduction to Design, Data Analysis, and Model Building.* John Wiley, New York, 1978.
9. Draper, N. and Smith, H. *Applied Regression Analysis,* 2nd edn. John Wiley, New York, 1981.
10. Riemer, J. and Karel, M. 1978. Shelf-life studies of vitamin C during food storage: Prediction of L-ascorbic acid retention in dehydrated tomato juice. *J. Food Process & Preserv.* **1:** 293, 1978.
11. Dennison, D. B. Degradation of ascorbic acid in dehydrated model food system during storage. Ph.D. thesis, Michigan State University, East Lansing, MI.
12. Kirk, J. Influence of water activity on stability of vitamins in dehydrated foods. In *Water Activity: Influences on Food Quality.* Academic Press, New York, p. 531, 1981.

30

KINETICS OF FOLATE DEGRADATION DURING FOOD PROCESSING

J. G. HAWKES and R. VILLOTA

Department of Food Science, University of Illinois, 1304 W. Pennsylvania Avenue, Urbana, Illinois 60801, U.S.A.

ABSTRACT

Folacin stability is highly dependent on a large variety of factors such as sample composition, moisture content, pH and temperature. Some of these parameters were isolated to determine their effects on the reaction kinetics of folate degradation utilizing folic acid (FA) and derivatives such as tetrahydrofolic acid (THF) and 5-methyltetrahydrofolic acid (5-CH$_3$THF) as measured by HPLC. A series of isothermal conditions were chosen to simulate processing conditions in terms of temperature, moisture content and residence time. As expected, results showed that stability of FA was much greater than either THF or 5-CH$_3$THF with respect to the parameters studied, and that all folates studied appeared to follow first-order degradation kinetics over narrow temperature ranges. Increased rates of degradation were observed with decreasing pH (7·0–2·0), and with increasing moisture content in a range from 5 to 40 g water/100 g solids increased rate constants were obtained for all three folates.

An attempt was made to monitor nutrient retention as a function of moisture content and temperature during spray dehydration. With mixed current flow and constant residence time and feed rate, it was observed that the lower the inlet temperature (160–210 °C), the higher the rate of folate degradation for both cellulose and protein samples; however, concurrent moisture changes are occurring with a higher moisture content associated with lower inlet temperatures. In the case with cocurrent flow on the other hand, although decreasing inlet temperature from 300 to 210 °C showed similar overall trends, increasing feed rate and simultaneously decreasing outlet temperature showed

*increased folate retention. Our results indicate that complete moisture/
temperature profiles and information on residence time are required in
order to optimize folate retention during dehydration.*

INTRODUCTION

Increasing concerns over world nutrition, with particular regard to
folate deficiencies found in various segments of the population[1-8] have
initiated studies on folacin stability and fortification of natural and
engineered food products.[9-15] Folates comprise a large heterogeneous
group of water-soluble vitamin derivatives with a common basic
structure but variable biological activity. The complexity of
differentiation of the various derivatives and the lack of well established procedures for their analysis in conjunction with their physiological and biochemical importance in the metabolism of man have
created a great deal of interest in their investigation.

In order to ensure reasonable shelf-life, certain food products must
be subjected to different types of processes and processing conditions.
This investigation has attempted to simulate processing conditions in
terms of temperature and residence times and isolate the effects of
parameters such as sample composition, moisture content and pH on
the reaction kinetics of folate degradation utilizing folic acid (FA), and
its derivatives, 5-methyltetrahydrofolic acid ($5-CH_3THF$) and tetrahydrofolic acid (THF). Relating these various kinetic data to actual
food processes will allow for optimization of processing conditions for
a given nutrient.

To date, most of the literature concerning folic acid deals with its
chemical or nutritional aspects rather than the more applied topic of
food processing and its effects on vitamin content. Investigations
concerning the stability of folates to processing operations have
considered the heating and cooking of foods mostly by conventional
methods. Effects of other processes such as freezing, dehydration,
irradiation and microwave heating have not been adequately
investigated.[16]

Of particular importance to food processing is the determination of
any nutritional and organoleptic changes that may occur as a result of
processing conditions encountered in operations such as evaporation,
sterilization, dehydration, etc. It is not only important to establish the

extent of these undesirable changes, but it is also critical to know the rate at which such changes occur.[31] By collecting kinetic data as a function of various parameters, it may be possible to design and optimize a given process for the highest quality product. However, information regarding kinetics of thermal destruction of specific folacin derivatives is limited. General studies have shown that losses of folates may occur as a result of: (1) heat treatment,[16] (2) temperature and oxygen,[17] (3) source of heat,[18] (4) light,[19] (5) chemical environment,[20] (6) pH[21-23] (7) leaching losses,[16] and (8) effect of metal ion contamination to catalyze oxidation reactions.[24]

More kinetic information is needed regarding the degradation of various folates in order to better understand their mechanisms of interaction as a function of a variety of variables. An important factor in many food processes such as dehydration or evaporation is moisture content; therefore, one of the goals of this paper was to isolate moisture content as one of the factors affecting reaction rates of folate degradation and to relate work carried out at isothermal conditions to actual food processes.

METHODOLOGY

Various model systems containing either microcrystalline cellulose (Avicel PH101, FMC Corp.) with or without carboxymethyl cellulose (CMC-7HF, Hercules, Inc.) and/or glycerol or soy protein concentrate (Arcon F, ADM) were prepared simulating various food types (liquid or solid) undergoing different types of processes. Variables such as moisture content, pH and temperature were monitored and their effect was measured in terms of kinetic rates of folate degradation under isothermal conditions. In addition, actual food processes such as spray dehydration were performed.

Initial studies were carried out with three types of folates: folic acid, 5-methyltetrahydrofolic acid and tetrahydrofolic acid (Sigma Chemical Co.) in aqueous solutions. Effect of pH on rate of degradation of folates with temperature was determined by adjusting the pH with either 0.1 N NaOH or HCl instead of buffer solutions since folate degradation may be altered by the presence of different buffer ions at a similar pH.[20] Subsequent analysis of samples was carried out by HPLC.

The effect of moisture content of folate degradation was determined in a semi-solid microcrystalline cellulose–glycerol matrix containing folate. Most information to date on kinetics of folate degradation has been obtained in aqueous systems.[17,18,20,25-28] However, it is also important to study the stability of folates as a function of moisture and temperature since a great deal of processed foods, whether with low moisture or intermediate moisture levels, contribute to our daily supply of this vitamin. Glycerol: Avicel mixtures (4:6) containing 20 μg folate/g solids at various moisture contents, 5–40 g water/100 g solids (0·3–0·8 water activity at 20 °C), were used to simulate the effect of moisture on rates of folate degradation. Incorporation of glycerol facilitated mixing and distribution of ingredients throughout the matrix by maintaining a greater degree of plasticity in the samples, especially those at very low moisture levels.[30]

All samples were treated similarly by placing the material in small tubes (6 mm diameter × 50 mm) to minimize come-up time, and held in a constant temperature bath at temperatures from 40 to 100 °C. Aqueous samples were analyzed directly after filtering. Solid samples were extracted with pH 7·0 buffer, centrifuged and filtered through a 0·45 μm filter immediately prior to analysis. Analysis of folates was performed by two different HPLC methods. The first method accomplished a separation of several derivatives, namely THF, para-amino benzoyl glutamic acid and 5-CH$_3$THF or folic acid using a Waters μ-Bondapak C$_{18}$ column with a mobile phase of 30–35% methanol–water and 0·05 M tetrabutyl ammonium phosphate buffer. This method provided reasonable separation of standards and relatively pure systems. The second HPLC method, however, established a good separation of mixtures of folic acid and 5-methyl THF, which otherwise would coelute. This second system utilized a Supelcosil LC-18 5 μm column with a mobile phase of 14–25% ethanol–water and 0·0025 M tetrabutyl ammonium phosphate buffer.

In the case with the spray drying processing systems, both a Niro model mixed-current drier and a cocurrent Anhydro Compact Spray Drier both equipped with centrifugal atomizers were utilized. Solutions containing up to 20% solids (Avicel or Arcon F) with 100 μg/ml of folic acid were spray dried followed by analysis of samples for retention of the nutrient as a function of inlet temperature (ranging from 160–210 °C for the Niro to 210–300 °C for the Anhydro compact spray drier) as well as moisture content of the final product after recovery from the cyclone and inner walls of the drier.

RESULTS AND DISCUSSION

As pointed out by several authors, pH is an important parameter to consider in folate degradation.[18,20,26-28] Studies were conducted using three different folates at different pH levels to determine their sensitivity. Results showed that, as expected, stability of folic acid is much higher than that of the more labile derivatives, THF and 5-methyl THF, under all conditions tested. Even at low temperatures of 40 and 50 °C in aqueous solution at pH 7·0, there is relatively low retention of 5-methyl THF after 5 h of heating as compared with folic acid (Fig. 1). In fact, as seen in Fig. 2, folic acid shows high stability up to 16 h at 80 °C at both pH 7·0 and 4·0. By contrast, THF shows a high degree of instability at 80 °C which is emphasized with decreasing

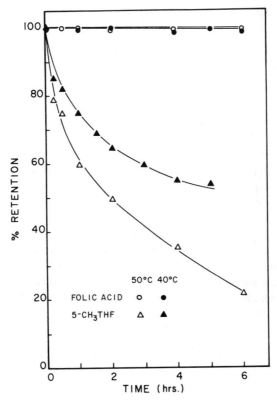

Fig. 1. Relative stability of 5-methyltetrahydrofolic acid and folic acid at pH 7·0.

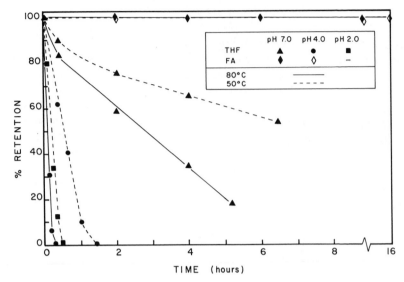

Fig. 2. *Relative stability of tetrahydrofolic acid and folic acid at different pH and temperature.*

pH, probably due to the high level of substitution on the pterin ring system as compared with folic acid. The same trend is observed at 50 °C with lower rate constants. Due to this dependency of folate stability on pH, it was decided to work in all cases at pH 7·0, where folates appear to be more stable.

With regard to the effect of moisture content on folate degradation (Table I), relatively low rate constants for folic acid were also observed as compared with those of the two derivatives, THF and 5-CH$_3$THF, confirming its greater stability in the range of moisture contents studied (5–40 g water/100 g solids). In all cases increasing reaction rates were attained with increasing moisture contents. Using 5-CH$_3$THF as an example, the reaction rate constant for this vitamer appears to gradually increase between 5–11 g water/100 g solids followed by a sharp increase up to 40 g water/100 g solids (Fig. 3). The point at which this exponential increase occurs may be due to a change in the physical state of the mixture; the higher the content of water, the more dough-like consistency that the material possesses and the greater its ability to conduct heat.

In the case of spray drying, it is difficult to characterize the influence

TABLE I
Effect of moisture content (MC) on rate constants for folate degradation

	$\dfrac{MC}{g\,H_2O}$ $\dfrac{}{100\,g\,solids}$	K (min^{-1})	R	R^2	$T_{1/2}$ (min)
THF	5·0	0·008 97	0·900	0·809	77·3
50 °C	11·0	0·011 63	0·895	0·801	59·6
	27·0	0·019 78	0·989	0·978	35·0
5-CH₃-THF	5·0	0·007 075	0·987	0·974	98·0
80 °C	6·8	0·007 098	0·993	0·986	97·7
	11·0	0·007 249	0·997	0·994	95·6
	18·0	0·009 377	0·985	0·970	73·9
	27·0	0·011 59	0·989	0·980	59·8
	40·0	0·014 78	0·994	0·987	46·9
FA	5·0	0·000 501 4	0·957	0·916	1382
80 °C	6·8	0·000 518 2	0·949	0·901	1338
	11·0	0·000 521 9	0·945	0·893	1328
	18·0	0·000 649 1	0·950	0·903	1068
	27·0	0·000 726 3	0·932	0·869	954

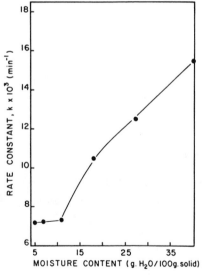

Fig. 3. Rate constant for 5-methyltetrahydrofolic acid degradation versus moisture content at 80 °C.

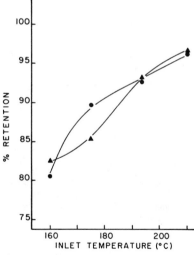

Fig. 4. Folic acid retention in different model systems after spray drying at different temperatures using a Niro mixed current drier. ▲, Microcrystalline cellulose; ●, soy protein concentrate.

of processing parameters on folate retention since several factors are changing simultaneously such as temperature, moisture content and physical state of the drying droplets. At constant residence time and feed rate using the mixed current Niro spray drier, it was observed that the lower the inlet temperature, the higher the rate of folate degradation; however, simultaneous moisture changes occur and results show that the lower the inlet temperature, the higher the final moisture content. The final moisture contents of the collected samples from the cyclone all fell within the range of 2–3·5% (g H_2O/100 g solids) and may not totally explain the observed phenomena. Most likely the overall air flow pattern in combination with the temperature and moisture profiles within the chamber as well as residence time contributed to the final results. Within the range of inlet and outlet temperatures studied for this particular system (160–210 °C and 82–100 °C, respectively), similar results were found in both the cellulose and protein systems (Fig. 4). In each case, samples collected from the surface of the walls showed slightly lower folate retention than those obtained as a final product from the cyclone (~5% less). This emphasizes the importance of improving the flowability of a product to prevent sticking to the walls of the chamber, thus minimizing residence time and minimizing exposure of the material to deleterious conditions.

Due to more versatility in terms of parameter control, it was decided to use the Anhydro compact spray drier with cocurrent flow to monitor temperature and moisture profiles within the chamber. Results from this system show a slightly different trend. Although the

TABLE II

Effect of spray drying temperature on folate retention and final moisture content

Inlet temperature	T_{out} (°C)	Feed rate (g/min)	Product temp. (°C)	Folate retention (μg/g)	Moisture content (g · H_2O/100 g solids)
300 °C	130	220	68·9	0·819	2·56
	125	330	73·9	1·048	1·99
	100	518	61·1	1·084	5·15
210 °C	120	21	70·0	0·169	2·33
	110	110	63·3	0·824	2·09
	94	172	57·2	0·873	3·02

rate of degradation appears to increase when dropping the inlet temperature from 300 to 210 °C as with the Niro mixed flow drier, additional information indicated that decreasing the outlet temperature, resulting from an increased feed rate, showed higher nutrient retention. Final moisture contents again were higher in those samples with lower outlet temperature (Table II).

It is necessary to consider what is actually happening to the droplets within the spray drier. The following are a number of parameters that may play an influential role in the degradation of a nutrient within a small particle: (1) the droplet size which may be affected by atomizer speed and feed rate, (2) the type of material in terms of density, viscosity, solids concentration (dissolved or suspended solids), (3) moisture content within the droplet as well as distribution within the drier, (4) temperature of the air, (5) air flow patterns within the drier, (6) residence times, and (7) chamber dimensions and design.

It is difficult to characterize the predominating parameters influencing retention of nutrients during dehydration. However, by estimating the average particle temperature in the drying chamber for a given set of conditions, it should be possible to relate studies under isothermal conditions to an actual dynamic process.

Overall, a tremendous number of parameters need to be carefully considered when generating predictions of nutrient retention. Spray-drier operating variables along with moisture content, temperature, available oxygen and residence times will all need to be considered in the optimization of folate retention during spray drying.

CONCLUSIONS

Folic acid was found by far to be more stable than either of the two derivatives, tetrahydrofolic acid or 5-methyltetrahydrofolic acid with respect to pH, temperature and moisture content. Greater stability occurred at neutral pH for these folates studied in addition to higher solubility. These are important factors not only for determining stability in different types of food systems but also in extraction procedures to determine folate content. Increasing moisture contents at low and intermediate moisture levels showed increased rates of degradation of folate for each of the derivatives tested. There remains, however, a great deal of work to calculate rate constants as affected by moisture in different temperature ranges and to determine if the degradation of various folates follows first-order kinetics as affected by different variables.

With regard to the application of kinetic data as a function of moisture content and temperature to an actual spray dehydration process, additional studies need to be conducted on establishing folate retention as affected by moisture content, temperature, particle size distribution, and residence time within the drying chamber. By relating these variables and obtaining sufficient kinetic data, it should be possible to predict retention and optimize a process for a given set of conditions. Our results, although preliminary, indicate that with complete moisture and temperature profiles, optimization of nutrient retention during spray dehydration may be obtained. A presentation of moisture and temperature profiles within the spray drier as related to nutrient retention will be discussed in further detail in a subsequent paper.

REFERENCES

1. Colman, N. Folate deficiency in humans. *Adv. Nutr. Res.* **1:** 77, 1977.
2. Thenen, S. W. Folacin content of supplemental foods for pregnancy. *J. Am. Dietetic Assoc.* **80**(3): 237, 1982.
3. Tamura, T. and Stokstad, E. L. R. Folate intake provided by average U.S. diet. (Diet consumption calculated from average per capita consumption of principal U.S. foods.) Unpublished data presented at ad hoc Review Group Meeting, Federation of American Societies for Experimental Biology, Bethesda, MD, March 23–24, 1981.
4. Tamura, T., Yoshimura, Y. and Arakawa, T. Human milk folate and folate status in lactating mothers and their infants. *Am. J. Clin. Nutr.* **33:** 193, 1980.
5. Bailey, L. B., Mahan, C. S. and Dimperio, D. Folacin and iron status in low-income pregnant adolescents and mature women. *Am. J. Clin. Nutr.* **33:** 1997, 1980.
6. Bailey, L. B., Wagner, P. A., Christakis, G. J., Araujo, P. E., Appledorf, H., Davis, C. G., Masteryanni, J. and Dinning, J. S. Folacin and iron status and hematological findings in predominately black elderly persons from urban low-income households. *Am. J. Clin. Nutr.* **32:** 2346, 1979.
7. Herbert, V., Colman, N., Spivak, M., Ocasio, E., Ghanta, V., Kimmel, K., Brenner, L., Freundlich, J. and Scott, J. Folic acid deficiency in the United States: folate assays in a prenatal clinic. *Am. J. Obstet. Gynecol.* **123:** 175, 1975.
8. Herbert, V. Folate metabolism and folate deficiency in developing countries. *Proceedings of 14th International Congress on Haematology,* Sao Paulo, Brazil, p. 6, 1972.
9. Colman, N. Addition of folic acid to staple foods as a selective nutrition intervention strategy. *Nutrition Reviews* **40**(8): 225, 1982.
10. Colman, N., Green, R. and Metz, J. Prevention of folate deficiency by food fortification. II. Absorption of folic acid from fortified staple foods. *Am. J. Clin. Nutr.* **28:** 459, 1975.

11. Colman, N., Larsen, J. V., Barker, M., Barker, E. A., Green, R. and Metz, J. Prevention of folate deficiency by food fortification. III. Effect in pregnant subjects of varying amounts of added folic acid. *Am. J. Clin. Nutr.* **28:** 465, 1975.
12. Colman, N., Barker, M., Green, R. and Metz, J. Prevention of folate deficiency in pregnancy by food fortification. *Am. J. Clin. Nutr.* **27:** 339, 1974.
13. Colman, N., Green, R., Stevens, K. and Metz, J. Prevention of folate deficiency by food fortification. VI. The antimegaloblastic effect of folic acid-fortified maize meal. *S. Afr. Med. J.* **48:** 1795, 1974.
14. Colman, N., Larsen, J. V., Barker, M., Barker, E. A., Green, R. and Metz, J. Prevention of folate deficiency by food fortification. V. A pilot field trial of folic acid-fortified maize meal. *S. Afr. Med. J.* **48:** 1763, 1974.
15. Kaunitz, J. D. and Lindenbaum, J. The bioavailability of folic acid added to wine. *Ann. Intern. Med.* **87:** 542, 1977.
16. Malin, J. D. Folic acid. *World Review of Nutrition and Dietetics* **21:** 198, 1975.
17. Chen, T.-S. and Cooper, R. G. Thermal destruction of folacin: effect of ascorbic acid, oxygen, and temperature. *J. Food Sci.* **44:** 713, 1979.
18. Cooper, R. G., Chen, T.-S. and King, M. A. Thermal destruction of folacin in microwave and conventional baking. *J. Am. Dietetic Assoc.* **73:** 406, 1978.
19. Stokstad, E. L. R. and Koch, J. Folic acid metabolism. *Physiol. Rev.* **47:** 83, 1967.
20. O'Broin, J. D., Temperley, I. J., Brown, J. P. and Scott, J. M. Nutritional stability of various naturally occurring monoglutamate derivatives of folic acid. *Am. J. Clin. Nutr.* **28:** 438, 1975.
21. Blakley, R. L. *The Biochemistry of Folic Acid and Related Pteridines.* Amsterdam, North Holland, 1969.
22. Rabinowitz, J. C. Preparation and properties of 5,10-methenyltetrahydrofolic acid and 10-formyltetrahydrofolic acid. In *Methods in Enzymology VI* (S. P. Colowick and N. O. Kaplan Eds). Academic Press, New York, 1963.
23. Stokstad, E. L. R. Some properties of a growth factor for *Lactobacillus casei. J. Biol. Chem.* **149:** 573, 1943.
24. Vonderschmitt, D. J. and Scrimgeour, K. G. Reaction of Cu^{2+} and Fe^{3+} with tetrahydropteridines. *Biochem. Biophys. Res. Commun.* **28**(3): 302, 1967.
25. Day, B. P. F. and Gregory, J. F. Thermal stability of folic acid and 5-methyltetrahydrofolic acid in liquid model food systems. *J. Food Sci.* **48**(2): 581, 1983.
26. Paine-Wilson, B. and Chen, T.-S. Thermal destruction of folacin: effect of pH and buffer ions. *J. Food Sci.* **44**(3): 719, 1979.
27. Mnkeni, A. P. and Beveridge, T. Thermal destruction of pteroyl-glutamic acid in buffer and model food systems. *J. Food Sci.* **47**(6): 2038, 1982.
28. Mnkeni, A. P. and Beveridge, T. Thermal destruction of 5-methyltetrahydrofolic acid in buffer and model systems. *J. Food Sci.* **48**(2): 595, 1983.
29. Ruddick, J. E., Vanderstoep, J. and Richards, J. F. Kinetics of thermal degradation of 5-CH$_3$THF. *J. Food Sci.* **45:** 1019, 1980.
30. Heidelbaugh, N. D. Effect of water-binding agents on the catalyzed oxidation of methyl linoleate. Ph.D. Thesis, M.I.T., 1969.
31. Villota, R. and Hawkes, J. G. Kinetics of nutrients and organoleptic changes in foods during processing, Winter Meeting of the American Society of Agricultural Engineers, Dec., 1983.
32. Masters, K. *Spray Drying Handbook,* 3rd edn. Halsted Press, Div. of John Wiley, New York, 1979.

31

REACTION KINETICS OF THE DENATURATION
OF WHEY PROTEINS

F. DANNENBERG and H. G. KESSLER

Institute for Dairy Science and Food Process Engineering, Technical University of Munich, D-8050 Weihenstephan, Federal Republic of Germany

ABSTRACT

The concentrations of the native β-lactoglobulins A and B (β-lg A, β-lg B) as well as of α-lactalbumin (α-la) remaining in skim milk after heat treatments under strictly controlled conditions (70–150 °C, 2–5400 s), were determined by means of ultrathin-layer isoelectric focusing. A study of the reaction kinetics revealed that the denaturation of β-lg A and B in skim milk can be described as a reaction of the 1·5 order. The denaturation of α-lactalbumin was a reaction of the first order. It was found that all the whey protein fractions had two different denaturation behaviors dependent on the temperature range as manifested by the energies of activation. These energies could be determined separately for both the low and the high temperature ranges (< or > 90 °C for β-lg A and B and < or > 80 °C for α–la). By this means it is possible to calculate the expected degree of denaturation after any heat treatment.

INTRODUCTION

A large number of dairy processes are affected by the denaturation of whey proteins. Thus, undesirable effects may be produced such as cooked flavour but there may also be desirable ones such as an improved capacity for water binding and a more rigid gel structure in yogurt or a reduction in the amount of product deposit formed on heating. Denaturation is an extremely complex process not directly accessible to the usual analytical methods. Indeed, consecutive reactions are determined. The kinetics of the denaturation of isolated

335

whey proteins in buffer solutions have been studied by Briggs and Hull,[1] Larson and Jennes,[2] Dupont,[3] Sawyer et al.,[4] Rueg et al.[5] and Park and Lund.[11] There is no agreement amongst the authors about the order of the reaction. Lyster[6] and Hillier and Lyster[7] carried out reaction kinetic studies over a wide temperature range on individual whey protein fractions in almost unchanged products such as milk and whey.

In the work described here the content of denatured β-lactoglobulin A and B (β-lg A, β-lg B) and of α-lactalbumin (α-la) remaining in skim milk after a precisely laid down heat treatment was determined using the effective technique of ultrathin-layer isoelectric focusing (UThLIEF) according to Radola.[8] A knowledge of the reaction kinetics of the processes should make it possible to gain more insight into the complex denaturation behaviour of the three main whey protein fractions so that dairy processes may be better understood and their outcome pre-determined.

MATERIAL AND METHODS

Fresh skim milk was heated in a plant developed especially for the study of reaction kinetics (Fig. 1). Temperatures ranged from 70 to 150 °C and holding time from 2 to 5400 s. It was possible to achieve extremely short heating-up and cooling-down times by using tubular heat exchangers with internal diameters of only 1·3 mm and wall thickness of 0·14 mm. Heating was carried out with water from a thermostatically controlled water bath or with saturated steam whose temperature was also controlled. After a heating-up period of only about 0·3 s the product passed to an equally thermostatically controlled holding tube in which it was kept for the desired time at the desired temperature by means of controlled magnetic valves. The product was then rapidly cooled in a heat exchanger (of the same dimensions as the heating system) with ice water. All materials in contact with the product were made of stainless steel. This miniature plant was cleaned by the CIP system and sterilized with steam.

Analyses
Casein and denatured whey proteins were precipitated at pH 4·6 from the heated samples and the untreated raw controls. They were then subjected without further pretreatment to UThLIEF on a 50 μm thick

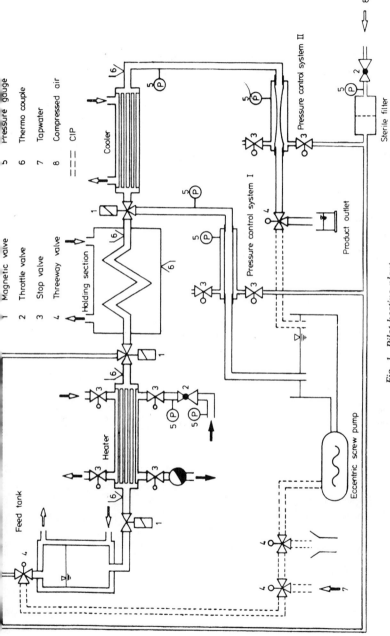

Fig. 1. Pilot heating plant.

polyacrylamide gel. The method of Radola[8] was used with some modifications (necessary because of special separation problems) for the preparation of the gels and the electrode solutions, the application of the samples and for making the separated fractions visible. A method of obtaining quantitative results was developed using a densitometer (Ultroscan LKB), an integrator (3390, Hewlett Packard) and a personal computer. By this means the rates of denaturation of the three main fractions of the whey proteins could be determined. The size of the areas, determined by the integrator and corrected by means of an internal standard, was taken as a measure of the protein concentrations. The standard deviations of the values of these areas were as low as about 3% for β-lg and about 6% for α-la.

Reaction Kinetics

For a decomposition reaction of the nth order of reaction the following equation is suitable:

$$-\frac{dC}{dt} = k_n C^n \tag{1}$$

The rate constant k_n of the reaction is influenced by temperature. If the initial concentration C_0 falls to C_t after a time t then the ratio of C_t to C_0 can be obtained from Eq. (1) and is given by Eq. (2):

$$\frac{C_t}{C_0} = [1 + (n-1)kt]^{1/1-n} \quad \text{for} \quad n \neq 1 \tag{2}$$

Equation (3) applies in the special case of a reaction of the first order ($n = 1$).

$$\frac{C_t}{C_0} = \exp(-kt) \tag{3}$$

In (2) and (3) the rate constant is:

$$k = K_n C_0^{n-1} \tag{4}$$

To evaluate the experimental results $(C_t/C_0)^{1-n}$ should be plotted against time using Eq. (2a).

$$(C_t/C_0)^{1-n} = 1 + (n-1)kt \tag{2a}$$

The term n, which represents the order of the reaction, should be adjusted to a value that makes it possible to plot Eq. (2a) as a straight line. After having obtained a value for n by this means the rate constant can then be found from the slope $(n-1)k$ of the straight line.

The temperature dependence of the rate constant is given by the integrated form of the Arrhenius equation:

$$k = k_0 \exp\left(-\frac{E_a}{RT}\right) \qquad (5)$$

where

k_0 = the rate constant when $1/T = 0$,
E_a = the energy of activation in J/mol,
R = the universal gas constant = $8\cdot314$ J/(mol K) and
T = the absolute temperature in K.

RESULTS

The effect of the time and temperature of heat treatment on the rates of denaturation of β-lg B and α-la are shown in Figs. 4 and 5, which also give the degree of denaturation in percentage.

The Order of Reaction

The mechanism of the denaturation of the whey proteins is extremely complex, being governed by several different, mutually interacting reactions taking place at the same time and forming intermediate products. In this respect it differs from other decomposition reactions important in food processing. Complex mechanisms of this sort can produce reaction kinetics of a higher order as well as kinetics of a fractional order. Indeed, an examination of the reaction kinetics of the denaturation of two variants of β-lg showed marked deviations from a first order reaction. Nor could the reactions be described as second order ones. However, when the measurements were plotted, using Eq. (2), for a reaction of 1·5 order

$$(C_t/C_0)^{-0\cdot5} = 1 + 0\cdot5kt \qquad (6)$$

straight lines similar to those in Fig. 2 were obtained. This shows that it is possible to obtain a good description of the denaturation of β-lg B over the whole range of times and temperatures of heat treatment examined. The same results were obtained for the A variant when a value of $n = 1\cdot5$ was used.

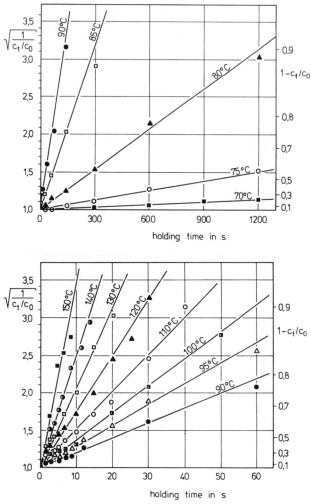

Fig. 2. Denaturation of β-lactoglobulin B, reaction order n = 1·5.

The denaturation of α-la was found to be a first order reaction. This agrees with the findings of Lyster[6] and Hillier and Lyster.[7]

The Arrhenius Plot
The slopes of the straight lines in Fig. 2 give the rate constants of a reaction for any given temperature (see also Eq. 6). When the natural

logarithms of k (obtained from Eq. 5) are plotted against the reciprocal of the absolute temperature each protein fraction yields two straight lines. The energies of activation E_a can be obtained from the slopes of the straight lines $(-E_a/R)$. When E_a is known k_0 can be found from Eq. (5) (Fig. 3).

Time/Temperature Graphs

The property of the reactions which lends itself best for a comparison of results is the rate of denaturation expressed as a percentage: $(D\% = 100(1 - C_t/C_0))$. Using the appropriate values for E_a and k_0

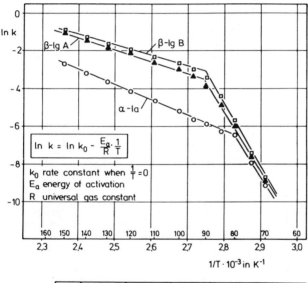

$$\ln k = \ln k_0 - \frac{E_a}{R} \cdot \frac{1}{T}$$

k_0 rate constant when $\frac{1}{T} = 0$
E_a energy of activation
R universal gas constant

	n	Temp.[°C]	E_a[kJ/mol]	$\ln k_0$	r	Δx[%]
β - lg A	1,5	70 - 90	265	84,1	0,996	2
		90 -150	54	14,4	0,997	2
β - lg B	1,5	70 - 90	280	89,4	0,995	3
		90 -150	48	12,7	0,999	3
α - la	1	70 - 80	268	84,9	0,997	3
		80 -150	68	16,7	0,999	2

Fig. 3. Arrhenius-plot and reaction kinetic data for denaturation of whey proteins (n = reaction order, r = correlation factor, Δx = mean relative difference between measured and calculated values).

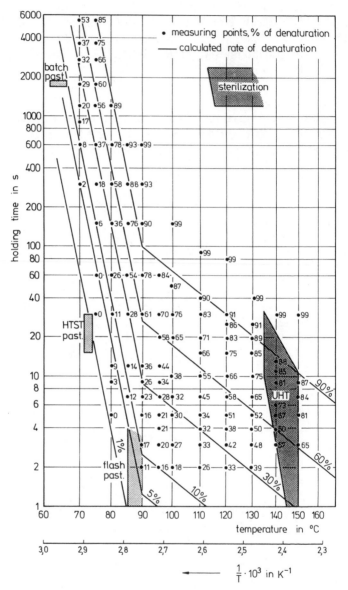

Fig. 4. Denaturation of β-lactoglobulin B in milk; calculated and measured (figures a measuring point stated in percentage of denaturation).

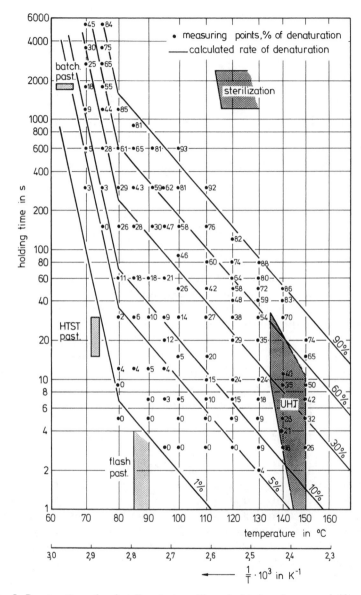

Fig. 5. Denaturation of α-lactalbumin in milk; calculated and measured (figures at measuring points stated in percentage of denaturation).

(Fig. 3) percentage denaturation rates for every temperature/time combination can be calculated.

$$n = 1: D\% = 100\left(1 - \exp\left[-k_0 t \exp\left(-\frac{E_a}{R} \cdot \frac{1}{T}\right)\right]\right) \quad (7)$$

$$n = 1\cdot 5: D\% = 100\left(1 - \left[1 + 0\cdot 5 k_0 t \exp\left(-\frac{E_a}{R} \cdot \frac{1}{T}\right)\right]^{-2}\right) \quad (8)$$

Equations (7) and (8) were used to calculate the rates of denaturation (in %) of α-la and β-lg B. Straight lines were obtained when log time was plotted against the reciprocal of the absolute temperature (Figs. 4 and 5).

DISCUSSION

The results of the work described above show that it is possible to describe the denaturation of individual protein fractions by reaction kinetic equations despite the fact that the kinetics of these reactions are very complex. The reactions are of a fractional order and have different activation energies in a low and high temperature range. Figures 4 and 5 show that there is good agreement between calculated and measured values. This is demonstrated by the small value of the error $\Delta x\%$ (Fig. 3) which represents the mean relative difference between measured and calculated denaturation rates. Activation energies were determined based on the assumption that the denaturation of β-lg was a reaction of $n = 1\cdot 5$ order and that of α-la was a first order reaction. The correlation was good in all cases ($r > 0\cdot 99$) (Fig. 3).

The findings of Larson and Jennes[2] and of Gough and Jennes[9] are different from ours. They have found the denaturation of β-lg to be a first order reaction. Larson *et al.* used a model solution and determined the concentration of SH-groups liberated during denaturation. They found an activition energy of 365 kJ/mol, while Gough *et al.* report values of 275 kJ/mol for the denaturation of β-lg A and 323 kJ/mol for that of β-lg B. The latter authors monitored denaturation by determining the residual protein in heated buffer solutions by means of the microKjeldahl method. However, they did their experiments over a relatively narrow temperature range, namely 60–75 °C, and this might make their reaction kinetic data somewhat uncertain.

Hillier and Lyster[7] determined the content of undenatured β-lg A and B in heated milk samples by means of electrophoresis. They could not obtain a straight line plot of the Arrhenius equation for heat treatment below 95 °C. It was therefore not possible to assign a constant value to the activation energy in this temperature range. At temperatures ranging from 95 to 150 °C they found activation energies of 36 kJ/mol for the denaturation of β-lg A and of 31 kJ/mol for that of β-lg B. These results compare well with our own. These authors reported that the heat sensitivities of the two genetic variants of β-lactoglobulin in the temperature range below 95 °C were the reverse of those above that temperature, a phenomenon which we were unable to confirm. We agree with Gough and Jennes[9] and with Dupont[3] and Sawyer[10] that the B variant is distinctly more heat sensitive than the A one at all temperatures. Both Hillier *et al.* and Lyster regard the denaturation of β-lg as a reaction of the second order. It seems that in both cases the degrees of denaturation measured was never more than about 60–70%. The difference between the 1·5 order found by us and the order of 2 found by the above authors is probably due to the fact that a much higher degree of denaturation, namely of at least 90%, is necessary to obtain a precise value for the order of the reaction (Fig. 2).

All results show clearly that every whey protein fraction studied had different denaturation behavior, expressed in terms of the energy of activation, in each of two temperature ranges. For α-la the limit of the lower temperature range is at about 80 °C and for β-lg A and B at about 90 °C. The reason for the changes in activation energy (changes in the slopes of the straight lines in Figs. 3–5) is probably the existence of at least two completely different reaction mechanisms in the two temperature ranges. The numerical values of the activation energies found in the low temperature range (about 250–300 kJ/mol) suggest that denaturation involves an unfolding and refolding of the protein molecule. This view is supported by the findings of Rueg *et al.*[5] who found by microcalorimetry for β-lg an endothermal heat effect only up to about 90 °C and for α-la only up to 80 °C. This means that the unfolding of the molecules (which is still reversible at this stage) and which is accompanied by the adsorption of energy, is completed at these temperatures.

The mechanisms of the reactions taking place at the higher temperatures are completely different. The reactions consist of quite different interactions of parts of the protein structure with each other and with the surrounding medium. This manifests itself in a considerable reduced activation energy.

Although a number of different reactions take place between the molecules in the course of denaturation the experimentally determined kinetic parameters make it possible to calculate in advance the likely degree of denaturation of individual protein fractions during heat treatment over a wide time/temperature range. Using the data obtained from experiments it should be possible to evaluate the influence of a well defined protein denaturation on processes in the dairy industry.

REFERENCES

1. Briggs, D. R. and Hull, R. Studies on protein denaturation. I. Electrophoretic study kinetics at neutrality of heat denaturation of β-lactoglobulin. *J. Am. Chem. Soc.* **64:** 2007, 1945.
2. Larson, B. L. and Jennes, R. Characterization of the sulfhydryl groups and the kinetics of the heat denaturation of crystalline β-lactoglobulin. *J. Am. Chem. Soc.* **74:** 3090, 1952.
3. Dupont, M. Comparison de la thermodénaturation des β-lactoglobulines A et B à pH 6·85. *Biochim. Biophys. Acta* **94:** 573, 1965.
4. Sawyer, W. H., Norton, R. S., Nichol, L. W. and McKenzie, G. H. Thermodenaturation of bovine β-lactoglobulin kinetics and the introduction of β-structure. *Biochim. Biophys. Acta* **243:** 19, 1971.
5. Rueg, M., Morr, U. and Blanc, B. A calorimetric study of the thermal denaturation of whey proteins in simulated milk ultrafiltrate. *J. Dairy Res.* **44:** 509, 1977.
6. Lyster, R. L. J. The denaturation of α-lactalbumin and β-lactoglobulin in heated milk. *J. Dairy Res.* **37:** 233, 1970.
7. Hillier, R. M. and Lyster, R. L. Whey protein denaturation in heated milk and cheese whey. *J. Dairy Res.* **43:** 259, 1979.
8. Radola, B. J. Ultrathin-layer isoelectric focusing in 50–100 μm polyacrylamide gels on silanized glass plates or polyester films. *Electrophoresis* **I:** 43, 1980.
9. Gough, P. and Jennes, R. Heat denaturation of β-lactoglobulins A and B. *J. Dairy Sci.* **45:** 1023, 1962.
10. Sawyer, W. H. Heat denaturation of bovine β-lactoglobulins and relevance of disulfide aggregation. *J. Dairy Sci.* **51:** 232, 1968.
11. Park, K. M. and Lund, D. B. Calorimetric study of thermal denaturation of β-lactoglobulin. *J. Dairy Sci.* **67**(8): 1699, 1984.

32

MATHEMATICAL MODELING OF RICE KERNEL EXPANSION AS A FUNCTION OF HYDRATION

D. G. MERCER, R. R. SIRETT, and T. J. MAURICE

General Foods Research Department, 520 William Street, Cobourg, Ontario, Canada K9A 4L4

ABSTRACT

Rice kernel expansion during cooking is a key factor in rice processing and is a function of water content. As the rice takes up moisture, the starch matrix begins to swell, and continues to do so until the cooking reaction is quenched or all available water is consumed. Samples of uncooked milled rice were hydrated in hot water (ca. 93 °C). The samples were quenched by cold water after various cooking times to obtain a range of moisture levels. These kernels were then tested for their moisture content and for volume by means of a water displacement technique. A mathematical model of the rice kernel volume expansion as a function of moisture content was developed based on a series of experimental cooking trials. This model was tested over a range of moistures from 28% to 76% (wet basis) and accurately predicted the degree of kernel expansion for 753 experimental samples.

INTRODUCTION

A key factor in the processing of rice is obtaining the proper degree of hydration. As the rice kernel takes up moisture during cooking, the starch matrix begins to swell and continues to do so until the cooking reaction is quenched, or until all available water has been consumed. The degree of swelling is a significant quality parameter and is closely related to moisture content as will be shown. The amount of swelling can be expressed in terms of a volume expansion factor (VEF) which is the ratio of the swollen kernel volume to its non-swollen volume.

The purpose of this paper is to describe the development of a mathematical model to predict the volume expansion factor (VEF) of rice as a function of its moisture content. The utility of the model lies in the fact that determination of VEF values from basic principles is a time-consuming process involving density and moisture determinations of both cooked and uncooked rice. A knowledge of the relationship between moisture and volume expansion would prove valuable especially with the implementation of on-line moisture measurement techniques. This would allow for rapid and reliable information on quality attributes of the processed rice to be obtained on a frequent or continuous basis.

The volume expansion factor (VEF) of rice can be defined by the following equation:

$$VEF = \frac{\text{(milled rice density)} \times (1 \cdot 0 - (\%\ \text{moisture}/100))}{\text{(cooked rice density)} \times (1 \cdot 0 - (\%\ \text{moisture}/100))} \quad (1)$$

where:

% moisture in the numerator is of milled rice
% moisture in the denominator is of cooked rice.

The second term in both the numerator and denominator of Eq. (1) reduces to the solids content of the milled and cooked rice, respectively. These values are expressed in weight of solids per weight of hydrated rice. Multiplying each of the terms by the appropriate density factor in Eq. (1) gives the weight of solids per volume of milled or cooked rice. If units of grams and millilitres are used, Eq. (1) becomes:

$$VEF = \frac{\text{(g solids/ml milled rice)}}{\text{(g solids/ml cooked rice)}} \quad (2)$$

which can be reduced further to:

$$VEF = \frac{\text{ml cooked rice}}{\text{ml milled rice}} \quad (3)$$

By definition, the VEF of milled rice has a value of unity. A VEF of 2·5 would indicate that the volume of a unit weight of rice had expanded to two and a half times its initial volume after cooking.

METHODOLOGY

Samples of uncooked milled rice were hydrated in hot water (ca. 93 °C). At regular intervals over the course of a 30–40 min cook, samples were withdrawn and quenched in cool water (25 °C). This gave a range of moisture levels from 28% to 76% on a wet basis. Each sample was tested for its moisture content using an oven moisture method. In addition, the density of the hydrated rice was determined using a water displacement technique. Typically, 10–20 g of hydrated rice were added to a pre-weighed graduated cylinder containing 50 ml water at room temperature. From the change in volume taken immediately after adding the hydrated rice to the water and the corresponding weight of the added rice kernels, it is possible to calculate the density of the hydrated kernels in units of grams per millilitre. Comparing these values to the density and moisture content of uncooked rice by inclusion in Eq. (1) gives the degree of volume expansion due to cooking.

RESULTS AND DISCUSSION

Initial results showed that a linear relationship existed between the volume expansion factor of the hydrated rice kernels and their moisture content expressed on a dry weight basis (i.e. grams of water per gram of dry solids). A plot of VEF versus the absolute water loading on a dry weight basis gave the following relationship:

$$VEF = 1 \cdot 174 \times \frac{\text{(grams of water)}}{\text{(grams dry solids)}} + 0 \cdot 973 \tag{4}$$

Equation (4) has been plotted in Fig. 1. Data points used to derive this curve have been omitted for clarity.

It is a more common practice, however, to express water content on a 'percent wet basis'. Equation (4) can be modified to conform to this convention:

$$VEF = 1 \cdot 174 \times \left\{ \frac{1}{(1 - (m/100))} - 1 \right\} + 0 \cdot 973 \tag{5}$$

where m = wet basis moisture in percent.

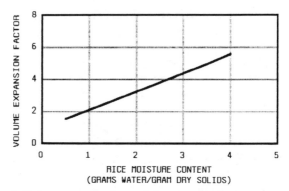

Fig. 1. Volume expansion factor of rice versus dry basis rice moisture.

Equation (5) can then be used to predict volume expansion factors for various wet basis moistures as shown in Fig. 2. VEF's have been plotted over the moisture range from 20% to 80%.

A total of 753 samples of hydrated rice were tested for their volume expansion and were compared to the curve defined by Eq. (4). Equation (4) was selected to linearize the response between VEF and the rice moisture content. Samples ranging from 28% moisture (0·39 g water/g solids) to 76% moisture (3·17 g water/g solids) were examined. Agreement between the sample population and the prediction curve was excellent. The overall standard deviation was 0·10 VEF units. The 'R-squared' value, determined by linear regression analysis, was 0·969, and the coefficient of variation was less than 3·0%. The

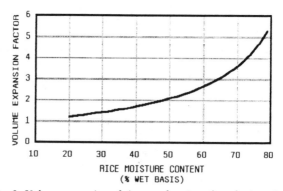

Fig. 2. Volume expansion of rice as a function of wet basis moisture.

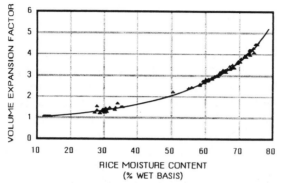

Fig. 3. Comparison of experimentally determined volume expansion factors to mathematically predicted values.

95% confidence interval for the slope of the curve defined by Eq. (4) was $1\cdot174 \pm 0\cdot015$. The 95% confidence interval for the intercept was $0\cdot973 \pm 0\cdot048$. Figure 3 shows the results of 75 randomly selected test results plotted against wet basis moistures. Inclusion of all data points was not feasible on such a small scale as presented here. The curve shown in Fig. 3 represents the mathematically predicted values from Eq. (5). Results from ten uncooked milled rice samples with moisture contents from $12\cdot96\%$ to $14\cdot18\%$ have also been included in Fig. 3. These samples have volume expansion factors of $1\cdot00$ by definition. As can be seen, all observations agree closely with predicted values.

Application of the Model

Having established the high degree of correlation between the VEF values predicted by the model and those obtained experimentally, it is now possible to explore the potential applications of such a model. Up to this time, moisture levels were the sole means of determining whether or not the rice processing had gone to its desired completion. While moisture is intimately linked to the volume expansion of a rice kernel, it does not convey the full magnitude of the physical and chemical changes that are occurring within the starch matrix. Consider the example of two batches of rice processed to 66% and 68% moisture. These two examples appear to differ by only 2% moisture on a wet basis, but their absolute water contents and VEF's reflect a truer picture of what has happened during processing. At 66%

moisture, the rice kernels would contain 1·94 g of water per gram of dry solids and would have a volume expansion factor of 3·18 as calculated from Eq. (4). At 68% moisture, the water loading would be 2·13 g of water per gram of dry solids, and the resultant VEF would be 3·40. If we consider a similar 2% increase in wet basis moisture from 73% to 75%, the absolute water content changes from 2·70 g of water per gram of dry solids to 3·00 g per gram of dry solids. The volume expansion factor would increase from 4·06 at 73% moisture to 4·40 at 75% moisture. Thus, a 2% increase in the wet basis moisture from 66% to 68% gives a 0·19 g increase in the water content of a gram of dry solids and a 0·22 VEF unit change in the volume expansion factor. A similar 2% change in moisture from 73% to 75% would give a water loading increase of 0·30 g per gram of dry solids and a VEF increase of 0·34 units. During processing, the process operator sees only that there is a 2% moisture change but this does not reflect the increase of 0·22 VEF units at the moisture levels in the lower moisture example or the 0·34 VEF unit change over the same wet basis moisture increase at the higher example moisture levels. The impact of the same moisture change varies significantly depending on the starting moisture level.

Future Applications

Recent developments in the field of image analysis have brought about the potential for direct measurement of particle sizes, thereby affording the opportunity to calculate volumes based on actual physical dimensions of a particle. Knowing the diameter, or width, of a hydrated rice kernel and its length would allow for the calculation of a volume expansion factor when compared to the dimensions of uncooked milled rice. If a rice kernel were treated as a cylinder, the volume of that kernel could be expressed as:

$$v = \frac{\pi d^2 L}{4} \tag{6}$$

where:

    v = volume of the cylinder
    d = diameter
    L = length.

Using the subscript 1 to denote milled rice prior to hydration and subscript 2 to designate cooked or hydrated kernels, the following equations can be written:

$$v_1 = \frac{\pi}{4} d_1^2 L_1 \tag{7}$$

and:

$$v_2 = \frac{\pi}{4} d_2^2 L_2 \tag{8}$$

where v_1 and v_2 are the volumes of uncooked rice kernels, respectively.

Combining Eq. (7) and (8) gives the fractional volume change due to hydration, which is the volume expansion factor, or VEF.

$$\text{VEF} = v_2/v_1 = (d_2^2 L_2)/(d_1^2 L_1) = (d_2/d_1)^2 \times L_2/L_1 \tag{9}$$

Values of the lengths and diameters can be determined from image analysis and can be used to calculate the VEF's. Using the VEF value and the curve shown in Fig. 2, it is a simple matter to determine the rice kernel moisture. This would then eliminate the need for actual moisture determination and the associated problems of slowness in oven moisture testing and of surface water retention in continuous instrumental analysis. However the precision and accuracy of the method are still to be determined.

SUMMARY

Through development of a mathematical model to predict kernel volume expansion from moisture measurements, information pertaining to the structural properties of the kernels may be easily and reliably obtained. Low moistures indicate a low level of volume expansion and an undercooked or hard, partially-swollen kernel. Selection of a degree of volume expansion to give the desired quality attributes indicates the corresponding finished product moisture. Such structural information gives a higher level of understanding to the overall processing sequence than working with moisture content alone, and can be a vital aid in future process control work.

33

MATHEMATICAL MODELS FOR MOISTURE LOSSES FROM RESPIRING FOOD PRODUCTS

SUDHIR K. SASTRY

Department of Food Science, Pennsylvania State University, 111 Borland Laboratory, University Park, Pennsylvania 16802, U.S.A.

ABSTRACT

Quality degradation of high moisture foods is frequently associated with losses of moisture. This loss is twofold in nature; a loss in salable weight, and a loss in acceptability which causes the consumer to reject the entire product. The latter is more serious, since it results in a greater net loss. The design of suitable refrigerated facilities to minimize moisture loss and quality degradation is a considerable challenge to engineers. Minimization of moisture loss in a refrigerated facility requires the use of evaporator temperatures that are very close to the desired dry bulb temperature of the facility. Under conditions of high load, this involves removal of large amounts of latent heat with minimum temperature differences. Proper design of storage facilities requires knowledge of the transport properties of foods and their packaging materials. In addition, mathematical models are necessary for optimization of design and operation of the facility.

The phenomenon of moisture loss from stored high-moisture foods is relatively well characterized for products that are nonrespiring. However, respiring food products such as fruits and vegetables exhibit complex moisture loss behaviour due to internal heat generation. Further, the transport properties, particularly the permeability of the epidermis to water vapor transport, may vary with time, as the product matures. Mathematical modeling of this phenomenon is a relatively recent endeavor. This paper reviews and discusses the models that have been developed in this area.

NOMENCLATURE

A = surface area of commodity
a_w = water activity
C_p = specific heat of water vapor
d = skin thickness
D = diffusion coefficient of water vapor through air
f = fraction of product surface area covered by pores
h_d = convective mass transfer coefficient
k_s = thermal conductivity of pore material
k_{ta} = transpiration coefficient of product (area basis)
L = latent heat of vaporization of water
m = transpiration rate (flux) of product
m_p = rate of moisture loss per unit pore area
p_s = water vapor pressure at evaporating surface
p_{sat} = saturation water vapor pressure
p_{00} = ambient water vapor pressure
R = radius of product
R_d = universal gas constant
T = temperature
T_b = ambient dry-bulb temperature
T_s = temperature of evaporating surface
u = resistance factor = vapor flow through air/vapor flow through porous membrane
u' = heat generation rate per unit volume
x_1 = fraction of product surface behaving as an open water zone
x_2 = fraction of product surface behaving as a porous membrane

MATHEMATICAL MODELS

A literature review[1] identified a number of factors to be considered in the modeling of the transpiration process. These include vapor pressure difference, air velocity, heat of respiration, product dimensions and geometry, epidermal permeability, maturity and water activity. Many of the mathematical models discussed consider certain of these factors as important, and others to be of little consequence. Models will be discussed in light of these assumptions. Mathematical models which do not account for all these factors may still be adequate for many applications. However, in many other situations, such as discussed by Gaffney *et al.*,[2] these models may be in considerable error. Thus the choice of model may be dictated by the situation under consideration. In the case of several models of comparable accuracy in a given situation, mathematical simplicity may be used as a criterion for selection.

The available mathematical models may be classed into the following groups:

1. linear model,
2. nonlinear model,
3. analytical model, and
4. numerical model.

The models discussed in this paper relate primarily to moisture losses from individual fruits or vegetables in refrigerated storage. Bulk storage modeling has also been attempted, using the basic models for single particle losses. However, this is of considerably greater complexity due to the wide variation in the possible storage configurations in bulk, and is not the major thrust of this paper.

Linear Model

The simplest model for moisture loss is the linear model, which considers the transpiration rate (rate of moisture loss per unit product surface area) to be linearly related to the water vapor pressure difference between the product and the environment. Thus:

$$m = k_{ta}(p_s - p_{00}) \tag{1}$$

This model has been used by Lentz and Rooke,[3] Gentry,[4] Dypolt[5] and Talbot.[6] The key assumptions of the model are that the evaporating surface is at the temperature T_b of the environment, and that the vapor pressure p_s is the saturation water vapor pressure at that temperature. The model thereby neglects evaporative cooling, respiratory heat generation and water activity effects. Further, the model lumps the mass transfer coefficients associated with the skin and boundary layer resistances. Under conditions of moderate water vapor differences, the linear model provides reasonably accurate predictions of moisture losses. However, under conditions of low and high water vapor pressure differences, the model may deviate considerably from experimental data. The errors are primarily due to the estimate of the vapor pressure p_s of the evaporating surface. The exact value of p_s depends on the energy balance at the evaporating surface. Under steady-state conditions, the energy loss due to evaporative cooling is balanced by the energy gains from respiratory heat generation and the environment. At moderate and high water vapor pressure differences, evaporative cooling is the dominant influence, and respiratory heat generation effects may be considered negligible. However, under storage conditions approaching saturation, respiratory heat generation becomes an increasingly important factor influencing the surface temperature, T_s. The water vapor pressure at the evaporating surface is determined as:

$$P_s = a_w p_{sat}(T_s) \qquad (2)$$

Under storage conditions approaching saturation, the evaporative cooling effect is small and the value of p_s depends on the relative influences of two factors: (1) respiratory heat generation, which tends to raise the surface temperature, and consequently the vapor pressure, and (2) water activity, which tends to lower the water vapor pressure. If the respiratory effect is the greater, the product will lose moisture even under saturated storage conditions, as noted by Lentz and Rooke[3] and Gac.[7,8] If the water activity effect is dominant, the product will be in equilibrium with the environment at a relative humidity less than 100%, and will gain moisture when stored under saturated conditions. This effect has been noted by Ghani.[9]

Since the linear model assumes that

$$p_s = p_{sat}(T_b) \qquad (3)$$

it tends to overpredict the moisture loss under low humidity conditions, when evaporative cooling effects become significant. Under high humidity storage conditions it may either under- or overpredict moisture losses depending on respiratory heat generation and water activity effects. Since the mass transfer coefficient k_{ta} includes the combined resistances of epidermal and boundary layers, the value may vary with changing air velocities. This is particularly likely in the case of products such as lettuce, cabbage and mushrooms, which do not possess epidermal layers and consequently present an open water surface to the environment. In such situations, the boundary layer and product resistances are of comparable magnitude, and changing air velocities could greatly affect the value of k_{ta}, necessitating the inconvenient concept of a transpiration coefficient which varies with air velocity.

The deviations of linear model predictions with water vapor

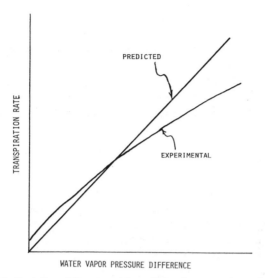

Fig. 1. *Deviation of linear model prediction from experimental results.*

pressure difference are illustrated in Fig. 1. This model is useful in situations of moderate water vapor pressure difference, and for products with low epidermal permeabilities (where air velocity changes have minor effects).

Nonlinear Model

The overprediction of the linear model under high water vapor pressure differences has led to development of the nonlinear model. The first of this kind has been developed by Fockens and Meffert.[10] Villa[11] has used a similar approach. This model assumes that skin cells are rounded and turgid at low vapor pressure gradients, but flatten out and cause high diffusional resistance under high gradients. Thus, the transpiration ceofficient (overall mass transfer coefficient) becomes a function of water vapor pressure difference.

$$k_{ta} = k_{ta}(p_s, p_{00}) \qquad (4)$$

The nonlinear model also considers the product epidermis to consist of three parts: the first being impervious to water vapor movement, the second behaving as a porous membrane permitting diffusion, and the third approximating an open water surface, with no diffusional resistance. The surfaces of individual products are modeled as a combination of the three parts. In addition, the model considers the boundary layer resistance to water vapor diffusion separately from the epidermal resistance. Thus, the model is more advantageous than the linear model in the sense that it can be applied to a wider range of product types, regardless of the air velocity.

The nonlinear model is generally represented by an equation of the form:

$$m = [x_1 h_d / R_d T + x_2 / (1/h_d + ud/D)](p_s - p_{00}) \tag{5}$$

The principal shortcoming of the nonlinear model is the assumption that the evaporating surface is at the ambient temperature. The vapor pressure is calculated according to Eq. (3). Thus the model neglects the effects of evaporative cooling, respiratory heat generation and water activity. Under environmental conditions approaching saturation, the model predictions may be erroneous for the same reasons as the linear model. Since the transpiration coefficient is determined as a function by fitting the model to experimental data, the prediction at high water vapor pressure differences could well be adequate provided that conditions are similar to those under which the data were collected.

The nonlinear model addresses a question of considerable importance; whether or not the transpiration coefficient is a function of the water vapor pressure difference. There is considerable merit to the concept of a variable transpiration coefficient, since biological materials would be expected to react to their environment. However, the overpredictions of the linear model at high vapor gradients may be due in part to the effects of evaporative cooling (neglected in the present case) and the force-fitting of a nonlinear model may be unnecessary to account for some of these effects. This point is discussed further in later sections.

The nonlinear model is useful for a wider range of conditions than the linear model. Its limitations are situations involving relative humidities close to saturation, and conditions outside the range over which data were collected. Modeling of the epidermal structure would make it applicable to a wide range of product types.

Analytical Model
The analytical model has been developed to account for the discrepancies between linear model predictions and experiment. The

model is applicable to commodities of approximately spherical shape, possessing uniform and largely impervious skins. The governing equations are:[12]

$$m = (p_s - p_{00})/[d/Df + 1/h_d] \qquad (6)$$

where p_s is determined using the relationship of Eq. (2), and

$$T_s = T_b - [Lm_p - u'R/3]\{\exp(C_p m_p d/k_s) - 1\}/c_p m_p \qquad (7)$$

where:

$$m_p = m/f \qquad (8)$$

The model takes into account the effects of respiratory heat generation, evaporative cooling and water activity, and predicts a surface temperature rise under saturated environmental conditions. Since surface water vapor pressures are calculated based on the energy balance at the evaporating surface, the model provides accurate prediction under high water vapor pressure differences. It has been shown[12] that for tomatoes, under the range of conditions tested, evaporative cooling can account for the deviations of linear model and experiment. Thus, for the range of conditions studied, the assumption of a variable transpiration coefficient is unnecessary. This does not mean that the concept of variable transpiration coefficient is invalid; indeed such a concept would be most useful over large ranges of vapor gradients. The study does emphasize that other factors must be considered before modeling the transpiration coefficient as a variable entity. The importance of the evaporative cooling component has since been verified by Gaffney *et al.*[2] Figure 2(a, b) illustrates the linearizing effect that occurs when the surface vapor pressure is calculated from Eq. (2) instead of Eq. (3).

The analytical model is applicable to commodities of spherical shape, with an epidermis of uniform thickness which is impervious over a large fraction of its surface area (e.g. apples, plums and tomatoes). The evaporation is considered to be localized at the porous regions of the product epidermis; thus the model is not intended for use with commodities that approximate open water surfaces. The temperature gradient between the evaporating surface and the environment is considered to occur primarily across the porous section of the epidermal layer.

The three models discussed up to this point possess the advantage of simplicity. However, for modeling of moisture losses from irregular shaped food products, numerical models are necessary.

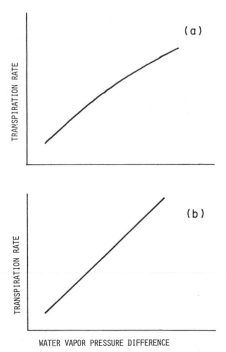

Fig. 2. Plot of transpiration rate versus water vapour pressure difference when surface vapour pressure is (a) calculated from Eq. (3), and (b) calculated from Eq. (2).

Numerical Models

Numerical models are necessary for simulation of heat and mass transfer in many situations where analytical solutions cannot be obtained. Most numerical models simulating moisture losses have been developed primarily to simulate the precooling process. These models have been developed for solution of transient heat transfer equations, but can, at least in principle, be applied to storage situations. Most of these models involve the solution of heat transfer equations with mass transfer and other boundary conditions, using finite difference or finite element analyses. A number of such models exist, and an extensive discussion of them is beyond the scope of this paper. A brief description of some representative models is provided, but the major part of this discussion will focus on two recent models; those of Hayakawa and Succar[13] and of Chau et al.[14]

Fockens and Meffert[10] developed a model for simultaneous heat and mass transfer during cooling; however, they neglected the effect of evaporative cooling. Baird and Gaffney[15] developed a numerical model for predicting heat transfer in bulk loads. This model was later revised to include moisture loss calculation. Srinivasa Murthy *et al.*[16] determined moisture losses during cooling but neglected respiratory effects in their model. Hayakawa[17] developed a model for slab shaped products that included respiratory effects. Abdul-Majeed *et al.*[18] considered the coupled effects of heat and mass transfer at the surface of food products, but neglected the heat of respiration.

Hayakawa and Succar[13] solved the one-dimensional heat conduction equation with temperature-dependent thermal properties and respiratory heat generation in spherical coordinates, using the finite element method. They used a boundary condition which included convective heat transfer and moisture loss terms. The model also considered cases when condensation may occur on the product surface, and its effect on the transpiration coefficient. They reported good agreement between model and experiment.

Chau *et al.*[14] developed a model for heat transfer and moisture loss in spherical fresh produce, by solving the heat conduction equation in spherical coordinates with internal heat generation, and using surface moisture transfer, convection and radiation in the boundary conditions. They determined the surface water vapor pressure from an energy balance on the product surface, and used a water activity value of 0·97–0·99 in their computations. They reported good agreement with known analytical solutions.

For most situations requiring accurate calculation of moisture losses, and for complex product geometries, the use of numerical models is important. The presently available models provide a good starting point. Most models at the present time consider the transpiration process as time-independent due to lack of data on transpiration coefficients as functions of maturity. Data in this area would be most useful. Further, most numerical models (except that of Fockens and Meffert[10]) consider the evaporation to be spread throughout the product surface. For products which approximate a largely impervious layer with small, localized avenues of moisture transfer, further modeling is necessary.

SUMMARY

A review is presented of some mathematical models for prediction of moisture losses from respiring food products. Further effort is needed to model maturity-related changes in storage and to model the transport phenomena for products of irregular geometries. Much basic data are needed relating to transpiration coefficients as functions of vapor pressure difference and maturity. Reliable data in this area requires carefully controlled experiments and suitable mathematical models. Gaffney *et al.*[2] present an extensive discussion of the errors in transpiration rate prediction due to errors in mathematical modeling. Finally, models are needed to determine moisture losses in bulk storage.

REFERENCES

1. Sastry, S. K., Baird, C. D. and Buffington, D. E. Transpiration rates of certain fruits and vegetables. *ASHRAE Transactions* **84:** 237, 1978.
2. Gaffney, J. J., Baird, C. D. and Chau, K. V. Influences of airflow rate, respiration, evaporative cooling and other factors affecting weight loss calculations for fruits and vegetables. *ASHRAE Transactions* **91**, (in press), 1985.
3. Lentz, C. P. and Rooke, E. A. Rates of moisture loss of apples under refrigerated storage conditions. *Food Technol.* **18:** 119, 1964.
4. Gentry, J. P. A procedure for rapidly determining the transpiration rates and epidermal permeabilities of fruits. Ph.D. Dissertation, Michigan State University, East Lansing, MI, 1970.
5. Dypolt, D. J. Determination of transpiration rates of green peppers. M.S. Thesis, University of Florida, Gainesville, FL, 1972.
6. Talbot, M. T. Transpiration rates of snap green beans. M.S. Thesis, University of Florida, Gainesville, FL, 1973.
7. Gac, A. Influence of the relative humidity of air on the loss of weight of harvested fruits during storage and ripening. Proc. 9th. Intl. Cong. Refgn., pp 4012–18, 4042–45, 1955.
8. Gac, A. Weight losses in cold storage products. *Comptes Rendus Hebdomadaires des Seances de L'Academie d'Agriculture de France* **57**(11): 907–14, 1971.
9. Ghani, A. I. The effect of different relative humidities on the change in weight of table grapes. M.S. Thesis, University of California, Davis, CA, 1953.
10. Fockens, F. H. and Meffert, H. F. Th. Biophysical properties of horticultural products related to loss of moisture during cooling down. *J. Sci. Food Agric.* **23:** 285, 1972.
11. Villa, L. G. Single particle convective moisture loss from horticultural products in storage. Ph.D. Dissertation, Michigan State University, East Lansing, MI, 1973.
12. Sastry, S. K. and Buffington, D. E. Transpiration rates of stored perishable commodities: a mathematical model and experiments on tomatoes. *ASHRAE Transactions* **88:** 159, 1982.
13. Hayakawa, K-I. and Succar, J. Heat transfer and moisture loss of spherical fresh produce. *J. Food Sci.* **47:** 596, 1982.
14. Chau, K. V., Gaffney, J. J. and Bellagha, S. Simulation of heat and mass transfer in products with internal heat generation and transpiration. ASAE paper no. 84–6513. American Society of Agricultural Engineers, St. Joseph, MI, 1984.
15. Baird, C. D. and Gaffney, J. J. A numerical procedure for calculating heat transfer in bulk loads of fruits and vegetables. *ASHRAE Transactions* **82:** 525, 1976.

16. Srinivasa Murthy, S., Krishna Murthy, M. V. and Ramachandran, A. Heat transfer during aircooling and storage of moist food products—II. Spherical and cylindrical shapes. *Trans. ASAE* **19:** 249, 1976.
17. Hayakawa, K-I. Computerized simulation for heat transfer and moisture loss from an idealized fresh produce. *Trans. ASAE* **21:** 1015, 1978.
18. Abdul-Majeed, P. M., Srinivasa Murthy, S. and Krishna Murthy, M. V. Prediction of air cooling characteristics of moist food products. *Trans. ASAE* **23:** 788, 1980.

34

MATHEMATICAL MODELING AND ANALYSIS OF
YOGHURT FERMENTATIONS

M. D. ONER, L. E. ERICKSON and S. S. YANG

Departments of Chemical Engineering and Statistics, Durland Hall, Kansas State University, Manhattan, Kansas 66506, U.S.A.

ABSTRACT

Two different strains of the yoghurt cultures Lactobacillus bulgaricus *and* Streptococcus thermophilus *were grown anaerobically on 3% nonfat dry milk in pure and mixed culture using batch followed by fed-batch culture methods. Samples were analyzed for biomass, lactose, galactose, glucose, lactic acid, and other acid products. S. thermophilus* (Microlife) *utilized much more of the galactose than the other three cultures. The exponential growth region of the data was analyzed to estimate maximum specific growth rate and growth and product yields. Covariate adjustment methods were used together with biomass, substrate, and product data. Spline functions were used to smooth the data and to estimate specific rates. The true growth yield and maintenance parameters and the product formation kinetic parameters were estimated using covariate adjustment methods, the results of the exponential growth region analysis, and the results of data smoothing.*

INTRODUCTION

Yoghurt production is of considerable interest because it is produced in many parts of the world and there is interest in improving the manufacturing process. The purpose of this work is to illustrate the application of some new methods of analysis and report the results of experiments with two different mixed cultures of *Lactobacillus bulgaricus* and *Streptococcus thermophilus*. A full account of the work is presented elsewhere.[1]

MATERIALS AND METHODS

Fermentor

A bench scale fermentor (Model 19 manufactured by New Brunswick Scientific Co.) was used. A 7 liter stirred container with four vertical baffles was agitated at 600 RPM with a flat blade impeller. Pure nitrogen gas was passed through the fermentor at 250 ml/min to provide anaerobic conditions.

The temperature was maintained at 37 °C for *S. thermophilus* cultures and at 42 °C for *L. bulgaricus* and mixed cultures. The pH of the medium was controlled using a New Brunswick Scientific Co. Model pH-22 controller. The pH was not allowed to go below 6·5 for *S. thermophilus* in pure culture and 5·6 for *L. bulgaricus* in pure and mixed culture. Foaming was controlled using an antifoam spray produced by Arthur H. Thomas Co. Sigmamotor peristaltic pumps were used for feeding and sampling. The feed reservoir was placed on a Circuit and Systems Model CMP-25 digital balance and a continuous readout of the weight was monitored.

Organisms

The following organisms were used as pure and mixed cultures: *Lactobacillus bulgaricus* ATCC-11842, *Streptococcus thermophilus* ATCC-19258, *Lactobacillus bulgaricus* (Microlife), and *Streptococcus thermophilus* (Microlife).

Media

The media used for the experimental work was 3% nonfat dry milk in distilled water. Food Club instant nonfat dry milk, which has the following compositional information in weight per cent, was used: protein 35·2%, carbohydrate 52·9%, fat 0%, sodium 0·55%, and potassium 1·72%. A 3% solution of dry milk in water contains about 15 g/liter of lactose.

Fermentation

Inoculum preparation is described in detail elsewhere.[1] In the case of mixed cultures, the concentration of biomass in each of the pure cultures was measured and the inoculum was adjusted to give 1:1 ratio of the two organisms in the inoculum.

A total of six runs were made; each strain was cultured individually and the two ATCC organisms were cultured as a mixed culture and the two Microlife organisms were cultured together.

Approximately five liters of medium containing 3% dry milk were autoclaved in the fermentor vessel at 138 kPa for 15 min. After the temperature had returned to 30 °C, the media was inoculated and the connections were made to start the fermentation. A period of 1·5–3 h was allowed for adaptation of the culture before regular sampling was started. During the fermentation process samples were collected every 30 min using a peristaltic pump. The sample volume, discarded volume, volume added through fed batch operation, and volume of base added for pH control were measured and recorded. The pH of the culture broth was also recorded at this time. The biomass measurement and the rate of base addition were used to decide on the time to start the fed batch culture operation. When the growth rate appeared to be slowing, the feeding of sterile 3% dry milk broth was started using a peristaltic pump; the flow rate was generally between 100 and 150 g/h. The purpose of the fed batch operation was to collect data at lower specific growth rates.

Analytical Methods

Cell dry weight analysis: For biomass measurement, the method of Kanasaki *et al.*[2] was modified and used as described elsewhere.[1]

Cell count procedure: A direct cell count method[3] was performed on samples collected during mixed culture runs.[1]

Lactose, glucose, galactose, and lactic acid concentrations: Ten ml samples were treated with a drop of $2 N$ H_2SO_4 and centrifuged at 2000 RPM for 10 min. The decantate was filtered through 0·45 μm filter paper and the concentration was measured using high performance liquid chromatography (HPLC) using a Varian 520 (Column: HPLC column for organic acid analysis, Aminex Ion Exclusion HPX-87H 300X7·8 mm; detector: Refractive index detector; Oven temperature: 45 °C; solvent flow rate: 0·9 ml/min; 2% propionic acid was used as internal standard).

Volume of culture: The culture volume at each point in time was calculated by starting with a known culture volume and subtracting the measured values of samples removed from the vessel, and adding the amount fed and the amount of base added. No corrections were made for changes due to evaporation of water, nutrient consumption and product formation.

DATA ANALYSIS

The methods of data analysis are described in detail elsewhere.[1] They include a method to select the exponential region of batch growth, a method to estimate growth yield and product yield under exponential growth conditions, and a covariate adjustment method[4] to estimate the maximum specific growth rate based on biomass, substrate, and product measurements from the exponential growth region.

A response surface method of smoothing data using spline functions is applied to estimate the specific growth rate, the specific rate of lactose consumption, the specific rate of galactose production, and the specific rate of lactic acid production. Glucose was consumed as soon as it was produced; thus, glucose concentration was assumed to be zero in this work. The values of the spline function smoothing parameters were selected such that the response surface criterion function was minimized; the closure of the available electron balance was used as the response surface criterion function.

The true growth yield and maintenance parameters and the product formation kinetic parameters are estimated using the covariate adjustment method[4] and Pirt's model.[5] All of the measurements are used simultaneously. The relationship among the product formation kinetic parameters and the bioenergetic parameters has been presented previously.[6] The bioenergetic parameters are estimated and then the values of the product formation kinetic parameters are calculated. The estimates obtained from analysis of the exponential growth region are used in place of the smoothed data for that region to obtain some of the bioenergetic parameter estimates. When only the smoothed data set is used, this corresponds to data set A; data set B involves using the exponential region estimates as one data point in place of the data used to analyze the exponential region; and data set C involves using the exponential region estimates as many times as the number of data points replaced.

RESULTS AND DISCUSSION

Figures 1 and 2 show the growth curves and product concentrations, respectively, for the six experimental runs. *L. bulgaricus,* ATCC-11842, was grown in batch culture in Run 1; fed-batch culture was not attempted because of curd formation in batch culture. Runs 2–6 are

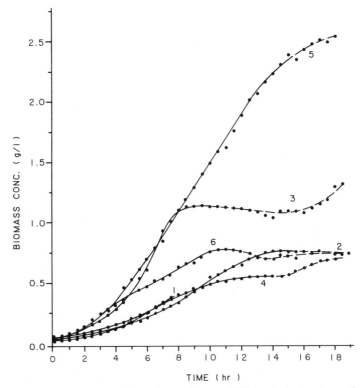

Fig. 1. Biomass growth curves for yoghurt cultures; solid lines are for batch growth while dashed lines refer to fed-batch culture. Run numbers are indicated on the graph.

batch culture followed by fed-batch culture; *S. thermophilus*, ATCC-9258 was used in Run 2; the two ATCC cultures were grown as a mixed culture in Run 2; the two ATCC cultures were grown as a mixed culture in Run 3; *L. bulgaricus*, Microlife, was grown in Run 4; *S. thermophilus*, Microlife, was cultured in Run 5; and the two Microlife cultures were grown in mixed culture in Run 6.

In Figs. 1 and 2, a solid line is used to represent the batch culture results while a dashed line is used for the fed-batch results. These results are presented in tabular form, elsewhere.[1]

Figure 1 shows much greater biomass production in Run 5 compared to the other results. *S. thermophilus*, Microlife, consumed galactose to a much greater extent than the other cultures.[1] Table I shows that *S. thermophilus*, Microlife, has the largest estimated value of true growth

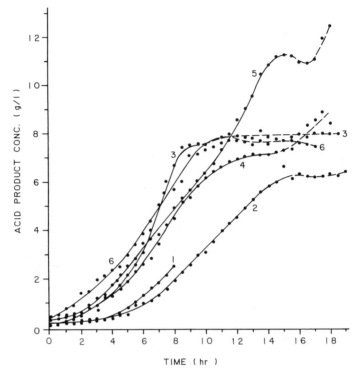

Fig. 2. Total acid product concentration for each of the experiments; solid lines are for batch operation while dashed lines are for fed-batch operation. Run numbers are indicated on the graph.

yield, η_{max}. The high production of acid products in Fig. 2, for Run 5, is due to the additional substrate consumption which results because of galactose consumption.

For each of the runs, the specific growth rate, specific substrate consumption rate, and specific product formation rate decreased as the concentration of lactic acid increased. Figure 3 shows the variation of the specific rates as a function of lactic acid concentration for Run 6. The horizontal lines represent specific rates as estimated from analysis of the exponential growth region data. The large specific rate values at low lactic acid concentrations, which exceed the exponential region estimates, are due to the inability of the spline functions to provide good derivative estimates at the start of the batch curve.[1] The reason for this is discussed elsewhere.[1]

TABLE I

Point and 95% confidence interval estimates* of true growth yield, η_{max}, maintenance coefficient, m_e, and exponential region yield parameters, η_1 and ξ_{p1}

Run No.	$m_e (h^{-1})$		η_{max}		η_1		ξ_{p1}	
	Point	Interval	Point	Interval	Point	Interval	Point	Interval
1	0·361	−0·092, 0·813	0·198	0·149, 0·296	0·169	0·127, 0·210	0·832	0·640, 1·023
2	0·419	0·359, 0·531	0·206	0·186, 0·231	0·144	0·132, 0·156	0·804	0·731, 0·877
3	0·298	0·172, 0·424	0·208	0·185, 0·236	0·173	0·151, 0·195	0·760	0·657, 0·867
4	0·064	−0·189, 0·317	0·106	0·088, 0·132	0·114	0·071, 0·156	0·840	0·625, 1·057
5	0·106	0·051, 0·162	0·254	0·236, 0·276	0·237	0·225, 0·248	0·823	0·778, 0·867
6	0·381	0·306, 0·455	0·175	0·159, 0·194	0·152	0·128, 0·175	0·854	0·716, 0·973

* Estimates of η_{max} and m_e are for data set B and Form II.[1] Estimates of available electron growth yield, η_1, and product yield, ξ_{p1}, are obtained using linear regression for data in the exponential growth region.[1]

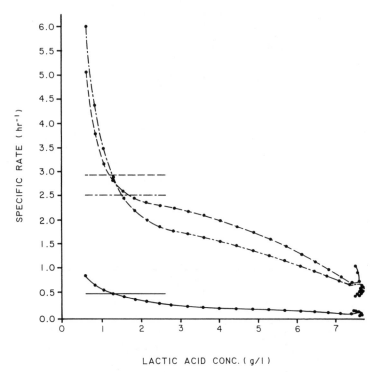

Fig. 3. Variation of specific growth rate (solid line), specific substrate consumption ra (dashed line), and specific product formation rate (dot-dash line) with lactic ac concentration for Run 6; horizontal lines show the corresponding estimates based analysis of the exponential region. Units are g carbon/g carbon (h) for the specific rate

Table I presents estimates for the bioenergetic parameters. The tru growth yield, η_{max}, and the maintenance coefficient, m_e, are presente in available electron units.[1,6] The parameter estimates of η_{max} and m are for Form II[6] and data set B in which the parameter estimates fro exponential analysis are used as one data point in place of the da used to analyze the exponential region.[1] The growth yield, η_1, an product yield, ξ_{p1}, for the exponential region are also presented available electron units.[1] The value of η_1 should be less than the tru growth yield, η_{max}.

The results in Table I are reasonable results. All values of η_{max} a less than the theoretical maximum value of 0·305 estimated using moles of ATP/mole glucose and 31·9 g cells/mole ATP.[6] The estin

TABLE II

Point and 95% confidence interval estimates* of maximum specific growth rate, μ_{max}, and product formation kinetic parameters, α_e and β

| Run No. | $\mu_{max}(h^{-1})$ | | α_e | | $\beta_e(h^{-1})$ | |
	Point	Interval	Point	Interval	Point	Interval
1	0·394	0·350, 0·438	3·958	3·423, 4·491	0·382	0·194, 0·570
2	0·281	0·267, 0·294	4·107	3·810, 4·405	0·373	0·295, 0·451
3	0·413	0·395, 0·431	3·815	3·500, 4·131	0·298	0·219, 0·378
4	0·319	0·298, 0·340	6·468	4·995, 7·230	0·215	0·024, 0·406
5	0·467	0·434, 0·500	3·139	2·984, 3·294	0·079	0·037, 0·121
6	0·411	0·376, 0·446	4·747	4·528, 4·967	0·379	0·323, 0·436

* Estimates of α_e and β_e are for data set C and Form II.

ated values in Table I may be compared to the values reported previously.[6] The results for Run 1 with *L. bulgaricus*, ATCC-11842 suggest that two moles of ATP/mole glucose are produced while the results of Samuel *et al.*[6,7] suggest that only one mole of ATP may be produced per mole of glucose. The results for Run 4 with *L. bulgaricus*, Microlife, are in reasonable agreement with the results of Samuel *et al.*[6,7]

The product yield, ξ_p, depends on the specific growth rate, μ, according to the expression[6]

$$\xi_p = 1 - \frac{\mu}{\dfrac{\mu}{\eta_{max}} + m_e} \tag{1}$$

The product yields associated with exponential growth, ξ_{p1}, should be smaller than those obtained at lower specific growth rates.[6] In this work, the integrated product available electron yield[1] for each of the runs exceeded the product yield for the exponential region. The average integrated product yield is 0·93 while the average exponential region product yield is 0·82.

The parameter estimation results in Table II include estimated values of maximum specific growth rate, μ_{max}, from the analysis of the exponential growth region and estimated values of the product formation kinetic parameters α_e and β_e in the expression[6]

$$\frac{\mu}{\eta}\xi_p = \alpha_e\mu + \beta_e \tag{2}$$

where

$$\alpha_e = \frac{1}{\eta_{max}} - 1 \tag{3}$$

and $\beta_e = m_e$. The estimated values of α_e and β_e in Table II are those for Form II and data set C.[1,6] The results for data set B and those for data set C are in reasonably good agreement;[1] however, the results for data set A, for Run 2, are not in good agreement with the results using data sets B and C. Since the estimates for η_{max} exceed the theoretical maximum value for data set A, for Run 2, it is clear that the estimates for data sets B and C are better.

One of the contributions of this work is the methodology of data analysis. This is described in detail elsewhere.[1]

ACKNOWLEDGEMENT

This work was supported in part by the National Science Foundation.

1. Oner, M. D. Estimation of yield and kinetic parameters in lactic acid fermentations for yoghurt cultures. Ph.D. Dissertation, Kansas State University, Manhattan, KS, 1985.
2. Kanasaki, M., Brehany, S., Hillier, A. J. and Jago, G. R. Effect of temperature on the growth and acid production of lactic acid bacteria, 1. A rapid method for the estimation of bacterial populations in milk. *Austr. J. Dairy Technol.* **30:** 142, 1975.
3. Marth, E. H. (Ed.) *Standard Methods for the Examination of Dairy Products,* 14th edn. American Public Health Association, Inc., Washington, D.C., 1978.
4. Solomon, B. O., Oner, M. D., Erickson, L. E. and Yang, S. S. Estimation of parameters where dependent observations are related by equality constraints. *AIChE Journal* **30:** 747, 1984.
5. Pirt, S. J. *Principles of Microbe and Cell Cultivation.* Blackwell, Oxford, 1975.
6. Oner, M. D., Erickson, L. E. and Yang, S. S. Estimation of yield, maintenance, and product formation kinetic parameters in anaerobic fermentations. *Biotechnol. Bioeng.* **26:** 1436, 1984.
7. Samuel, W. A., Lee, Y. Y. and Anthony, W. B. Lactic acid fermentation of crude sorghum extract. *Biotechnol. Bioeng.* **22:** 757, 1980.

35

PREDICTING CHANGES IN MICROBIAL POPULATIONS IN MEAT: GROWTH OF *CLOSTRIDIUM PERFRINGENS*

D. R. THOMPSON*, F. F. BUSTA and R. W. SCHMIDT

Agricultural Engineering Department, University of Minnesota, St. Paul, Minnesota 55108, U.S.A.

ABSTRACT

The purpose for this study was to evolve a model for predicting the growth and inactivation of Clostridium perfringens *in beef during roasting in an air oven. This required development of an effective heat transfer model and the linking of the predicted temperatures with a mathematical model of* C. perfringens *growth and inactivation.*

The heat transfer model was based on data from the roasting of forty beef muscles (beef knuckle (sirloin tip), inside round and outside round) in five ovens; each set at four separate temperatures. The beef muscles ranged in weight from 2·3 to 3·8 kg. Temperatures were monitored at several locations in each muscle by thermocouples connected with a multi-point recorder.

The log of the temperature difference between an effective driving temperature and the temperature at the coldest point in the roast decreases linearly with time during cooking. The effective driving temperature is substantially less than the oven temperature. For oven temperatures between 90 and 205 °C, the effective driving temperature was between 70 and 95 °C. The parameters for the heat transfer model were estimated from the experimental data.

The predicted Clostridium perfringens *population based on the heat transfer model and the* C. perfringens *population dynamics model agree well with experimental population data.*

* Present address: Department of Agricultural Engineering, Oklahoma State University, Stillwater, Oklahoma 74078, U.S.A.

INTRODUCTION

Clostridium perfringens has been frequently found and implicated in outbreaks of food-borne illness associated with meat and meat products.[1] Extensive growth and inactivation data for *C. perfringens* recorded during isothermal and linearly rising temperature conditions have been reported[2] and modeled.[3] The model has subsequently been improved to correspond with more recent inactivation data.[4] This model which is based on kinetic principles but requires 14 parameters explains over 90% of the variation in the reported growth and inactivation data. An evaluation of the mechanisms implied by the model[5] clearly illustrated that isothermal kinetic models and other simplications could not represent characteristics in the data.

This model requires a time–temperature profile for the slowest heating point in a roast as input data. In an existing process this temperature profile could be measured experimentally. However, when proposing a new process, it is desirable to estimate the population dynamics for the proposed process before constructing the production or pilot plant facility.

Various cooking models have been proposed previously. For this work, the heat transfer model is only one component in the simulation system and the time–temperature profile is only needed in the region of the roast that heats most slowly. For these reasons a simple, preferably an analytical, model was preferred. More sophisticated numerical procedures are frequently restricted to medium or large size computers with specific software systems. That would decrease the portability and increase the application costs for the model.

Analytical solutions for one dimensional heat transfer have been derived for a variety of surface heat transfer conditions.[6] The solutions derived in cartesian, cylindrical and spherical coordinates are generally infinite series. For easier application, some of these solutions have been reduced to graphical charts such as those given by Boelter *et al.*[7] Most of these charts assume convection heat transfer at the surface and one dimensional heat transfer. When two or three dimensional transfer must be modeled, the product of the component one-dimensional problem results represents the actual multi-dimensional result.[8]

The heat transfer into a beef muscle located in an air oven is frequently a two or three dimensional problem—depending on the size and shape of the muscle and the coordinate system selected. The significant heat transfer at the surface includes convection and the loss of heat due to evaporation. Radiation and conduction may also play minor roles. Furthermore, the thermal properties of the muscle tissue are both anisotropic and nonhomogeneous. Clearly a detailed mathematical representation of the heat transfer would be complex. The first term from the analytical solution to the one dimensional heat transfer problem can be represented by Eq. (1).[9]

$$\log_{10}(T_d - T) = -t/f + \log_{10}[j(T_d - T_i)]\qquad(1)$$

where:

T is the temperature at some location in an object at any time (°C);

T_d is the effective driving temperature (°C);

T_i is the initial temperature of the object at the start of the heating cycle (°C);

t is time from the start of heating cycle (min);

f is a parameter combining numerous heat transfer characteristics and is physically the time required to reduce the temperature difference by 90% or one log cycle;

j is defined to be:

$$\frac{T_d - T_p}{T_d - T_i}$$

in which T_p is a pseudo initial object temperature (°C); mathematically j corrects for the use of a single term instead of an infinite series to represent the solution.

This equation is widely used in the thermal processing industry to model temperatures during heating and cooling of canned food. In that application, the driving temperature is either the retort or cooling water temperature. No similar assumption can be made when roasting beef because the evaporation of moisture from the surface of the muscle will effectively reduce the driving temperature. Thus, the driving temperature becomes an additional parameter to be estimated.

The objective of this study was to develop a set of mathematical models to predict the population dynamics of *Clostridium perfringens* during roasting of beef muscles. Specifically, this effort attempted to model the heat transfer using Eq. (1), to determine the appropriate parameters for application of that model and to verify the application of that model and the population dynamics model[3] by comparing the predicted population profile with an experimentally measured profile.

MATERIALS AND METHODS

Data for verifying the applicability of the heat transfer model and estimating the necessary parameters was collected by roasting of 40 beef muscles. These muscles ranged in weight from 2·3 to 3·8 kg. The muscles used included beef knuckle (sirloin tip), inside round and outside round.

Five ovens were used to roast the beef muscles. Three were electric home ovens (Frigidaire model custom deluxe, Jenn-Air model 88370 and General Electric model JHP97G01WH). One gas oven was designed for home usage (Roper model 1399) and one was a commercial electric oven (General Electric model CN50) were also used. Each oven was operated at four temperatures (*set according to the indicator dial on the oven*). These temperatures were 93 °C, 107 °C 121 °C and 135 °C. Each treatment in one oven at one temperature was replicated. The roasts were assigned to treatments randomly.

The beef muscles were stored frozen until approximately one day before cooking. A muscle was thawed either wrapped in paper at room temperature overnight or in a refrigerator at 3 °C for 48 h. Each muscle was equilibrated to a uniform temperature near 0 °C prior to starting the cooking cycle.

Final preparation of each muscle included weighing; measuring the major, minor and intermediate axis dimensions; and instrumenting the muscle with thermocouples. Thermocouples were placed approximately in the center and at the one-fourth distance on each of the axes. Three thermocouples were placed under the surface, but as close to the surface as possible on the top, bottom and side of each roast. An additional thermocouple was used to monitor the oven temperature. All thermocouples in the roast were connected to a Leeds and Northrup Speedomax strip chart recorder (model 250), and the oven thermocouple was connected to a digital thermometer (Omega model 2176 AT). Each thermocouple was calibrated against a standard mercury-in-glass thermometer prior to usage.

The ovens were preheated until they had completed an on-off-on cycle prior to starting cooking. Individual beef muscles were placed in aluminum trays with the muscle fiber running parallel to the plane of the tray and then the tray with the instrumented muscle was placed on the lowest rack in the oven.

The experimental verification of the microorganism population dynamics utilized strain NCTC 8238 of *C. perfringens* from the

University of Minnesota culture collection. Since the initial *C. perfringens* population in a muscle is variable and multiple sampling is not feasible in a single unit, the raw beef strip method[10] was utilized. For this method the temperature recorded at the slowest heating point of a muscle is simulated in a water bath. The cooking cycle simulated was for cooking in water. This required different heat transfer parameters from those found in this study. Prepared beef samples pre-inoculated to known levels were placed randomly in a rack and incubated in the water bath programmed to follow the recorded temperature profile. The microorganism population was enumerated as described by Smith *et al.*[10]

RESULTS AND DISCUSSION

Actual mean oven temperatures varied from the set temperature as shown in Table I. The mean temperature for three ovens was close (within six degrees centigrade) to the set temperature, but the Jenn air oven averaged 13 °C below the set point and the Roger oven averaged 14 °C above the set point. No effort was made to readjust oven controls to bring the mean oven temperature closer to the set point temperature because another objective in the study was to determine the potential risk associated with roasting meat at low oven temperature settings. All of the oven controls cycled on and off, generating a temperature curve of approximately sinusoidal shape. The peak-to-peak temperature range for all of the home ovens was

TABLE I
Actual oven temperatures (°C)

Oven	Set point temperature (°C)			
	93	*107*	*121*	*135*
Frigidaire	99	109	125	ND
Jenn-Air	80	94	108	123
General Electric (home)	90	102	124	138
Roper (gas)	110	123	130	148
General Electric (commercial)	94	105	125	140

ND: no data due to thermocouple failure.

between 30 and 40 °C. The commercial oven peak-to-peak variation
was approximately 15 °C.

The temperature data from each roast was plotted consistent with
Eq. (1) as shown in Fig. 1. For each plot the driving temperature was
selected that gave a straight line (and maximum coefficient of

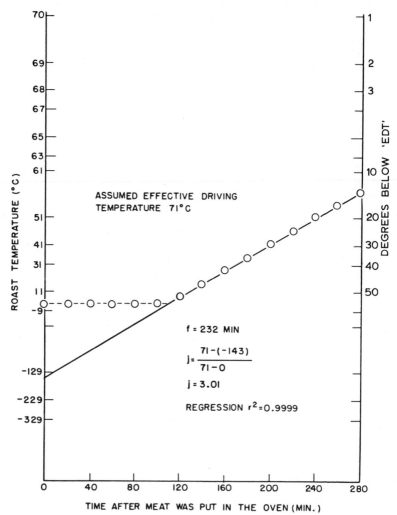

*Fig. 1. Heating a 2·6 kg beef knuckle in a General Electric commercial oven set at 93 °C
(91 °C actual mean oven temperature) with the thermocouple located at the geometric
center of the roast.*

etermination, r^2) for the plotted data points. Assumed driving emperatures that were either too high or too low generated nonlinear lots and lower r^2 values (Fig. 2). The early data points, as expected, lemonstrated a lag consistent with dropping the additional terms in he infinite series solution. The plot in Fig. 1 is typical of the good fit

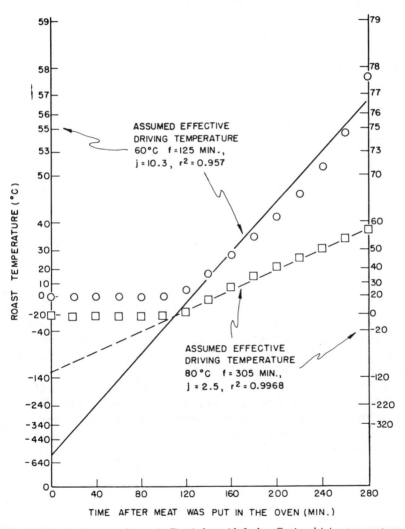

Fig. 2. Plotting the same data as in Fig. 1, but with faulty effective driving temperatures.

between the data and Eq. (1). The driving temperature which gave the best fit and the parameters *f* and *j* were recorded for each roast.

Correlation coefficients between *f, j*, driving temperature, major, minor and intermediate axis lengths, roast weight, oven temperature, roast type, and oven type were determined. The most significant correlation was between the oven temperature and the effective driving temperature. This correlation (0·85) was further verified by roasting three additional muscles with an oven set at 205 °C. A regression equation between actual oven temperature and effective driving temperature generated Eq. (2) which has an r^2 (coefficient of determination) value of 0.72.

$$T_d = 0·21T_0 + 50·5(°C) \tag{2}$$

where:

T_d is the effective driving temperature (°C);
T_0 is the mean actual oven temperature (°C).

As expected *f* and *j* have a high negative correlation. The reason for this is that a minor variation in one or more data points can adjust the slope of the heating curve. This has the effect of increasing or decreasing *j* and correspondingly decreasing or increasing *f* such that the line goes through the same region on the graph. This correlation simply represents the mathematical interrelationship between these parameters.

There was a mild correlation between the *f* and *j* factors and the roast dimensions. In particular the *j* parameter had a 0·51 correlation with the minor axis dimension of the roast. This positive correlation was expected because transferring heat a greater distance should cause a greater lag time before the onset of the logarithmic temperature rise. Likewise the *f* parameter had positive correlations of 0·44 and 0·39 with the intermediate and major axis dimensions. Larger roasts heat more slowly causing the slope to decrease (*f* becomes larger). Because of the narrow range of roast sizes utilized in this study, none of these correlations were sufficiently high to provide a good mathematical relationship between roast dimensions and the *f* and *j* parameters.

We had anticipated that the convection oven (Jenn-Air) might have a significantly lower *f* value than the conventional ovens. This did not occur. Apparently other sources of variation were greater than the effect of the convection oven.

Since the correlations between either *f* or *j* and other measured characteristics were not significant, these two values can be represented by their mean values from all of the data. The mean j value is 3·1 with a 95% confidence interval of 0·5. The mean f value was 240 min with a 95% confidence interval of 18 min.

Based on the mean values for f and j and the prediction of the effective driving temperature from the mean actual oven temperature by Eq. (2), the slowest heating region temperature in the roast can be predicted by Eq. (1). The temperatures during the lag period can be adequately described by assuming that the temperature at the slowest heating point remains constant (at the value of the initial temperature) until the temperatures predicted by Eq. (1) exceed the initial temperature. The measured temperatures typically exceed this approximation for a short time interval, but this is all occurring at temperatures well below the region in which significant cooking or microbial growth occurs.

The ultimate goal for this study was to generate a system of mathematical models to predict the *C. perfringens* population during

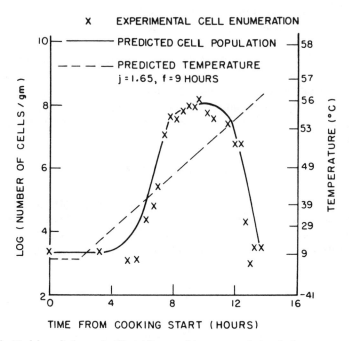

TIME FROM COOKING START (HOURS)

Fig. 3. Model predictions of a Clostridium perfringens *population during meat cooking.*

cooking of a roast. This capability was tested by predicting the temperature profile at the slowest heating point of a beef muscle of given dimensions. From the predicted temperature profile the population dynamics were estimated by the model previously published by Thompson and coworkers.[3] After measuring the characteristics of the beef muscle and instrumenting it with thermocouples, it was cooked in water. Water cooking was selected for this test because greater population changes occurred. This provided a more rigorous test for the models. Inoculated beef strips were subjected to the same temperature profile and enumerated. A comparison of the experimental and predicted values is shown in Fig. 3.

This was repeated on a second roast with similar results. As can be seen in Fig. 3, the system of models provides a good estimate of the population dynamics.

CONCLUSIONS

Equation (1) provides a good representation of the time–temperature profile at the cold point in a beef muscle during air oven roasting. For small beef muscles (2·3–3·8 kg), the f and j parameters can be represented by their means (240 min and 3·1, respectively), and the effective driving temperature can be predicted from the mean oven temperature and Eq. (2). After the initial temperature lag period, this equation effectively represents the internal roast temperature. When combined with a population dynamics model, the combination model can predict *C. perfringens* population dynamics during air oven roasting.

ACKNOWLEDGEMENTS

Published as Paper No. 14546 of the scientific journal series of the Minnesota Agricultural Experiment Station on research conducted under Minnesota Agricultural Experiment Station Project No. 12–030.

Mention of specific brands and models is not intended to be an endorsement.

REFERENCES

1. Walker, H. W. Food-borne illness from *Clostridium perfringens* in *Critical Reviews of Food Science and Nutrition* **7**(1): 71, CRC Press, Cleveland, Ohio, 1975.

2. Willardsen, R. R., Busta, F. F., Allen, C. E. and Smith, L. B. Growth and survival of *Clostridium perfringens* during constantly rising temperatures. *J. Food Sci.* **43:** 470–75, 1978.
3. Thompson, D. R., Willardsen, R. R., Busta, F. F. and Allen, C. E. *Clostridium perfringens* population dynamics during constant and rising temperatures in beef. *J. Food Sci.* **44:** 646–51, 1979.
4. Roy, R. J., Busta, F. F. and Thompson, D. R. Thermal inactivation of *Clostridium perfringens* after growth at several constant and linear rising temperatures. *J. Food Sci.* **46:** 1586–91, 1981.
5. Thompson, D. R. and Busta, F. F. Modeling microbial populations during meat cooking and cooling. *Trans. ASAE* **24**(6): 1664–70, 1981.
6. Carslaw, H. S. and Jaeger, J. C. *Conduction of Heat in Solids,* 2nd edn. Oxford University Press, Fair Lawn, New Jersey, 1959.
7. Boelter, L. M. K., Cherry, V. H. and Johnson, H. A. *Heat Transfer Notes.* University of California Press, Los Angeles, California, 1942.
8. Rohsenow, W. M. and Choi, H. *Heat, Mass and Momentum Transfer.* Prentice Hall, Englewood Cliffs, New Jersey, 1961.
9. Ball, C. O. and Olson, F. C. W. *Sterilization in Food Technology.* McGraw-Hill, New York, 1957.
10. Smith, L. B., Busta, F. F. and Allen, C. E. Effect of rising temperatures on growth and survival of *Clostridium perfringens* indigenous to raw beef. *J. Food Prot.* **43:** 520–4, 1980.

36

MODELING OF A BIOLOGICAL PROCESS FOR MERCURY DETOXIFICATION

A. D. CHRISTY, V. I. GEORGE, M. A. BURSTEIN, and C. L. HANSEN

Department of Agricultural Engineering, Ohio State University, Columbus, Ohio 43210, U.S.A.

ABSTRACT

A model for the biological removal of mercury from a contaminated nutrient solution is presented. The model predicts bacteria, glucose, and mercury concentrations on a dynamic basis. Experimental mixed culture studies were conducted to define and verify the numerical model coefficients.

INTRODUCTION

Toxic and potentially hazardous heavy metals are found in wastewater from many industrial sources. Among these substances, mercury is one of the most toxic and best understood examples of heavy metal pollution. Mining and industrial activities add approximately 12 500 metric tons of mercury to the environment each year.[1] Most of this is in the more toxic, mercuric(II) form. It is therefore important to develop effective processes for removing mercury from the environment. Industry is currently using either chemical. precipitation or reduction and filtration. In both cases, disposal of the precipitate creates a new problem.[2]

The proposed solution is to use mercury resistant strains of bacteria to reduce the more toxic mercuric(II) ion to volatile, elemental mercury which could then be condensed or recycled.[2,3] The objective of this research is to develop a dynamic model which can continuously predict the response of a biological mercury reduction process. Such a model could be used to gain better insight into the process, to aid the design of suitable process control mechanisms, and to facilitate future scale-up.

MATERIALS AND METHODS

Model Development

The model was based on previously developed relationships between bacterial growth and substrate utilization.[4,5] These relations, however, were determined without the presence of an inhibitor and in pure culture. The addition of a toxic substance such as mercury could be expected to alter the system behavior, as could the addition of competing strains of bacteria. Experimental studies were then performed to establish coefficient values in a mercury contaminated environment. The following equations constitute the proposed model:

$$\frac{dX}{dt} = Y\frac{dF}{dt} - K_d X \qquad (1)$$

$$\frac{dHg}{dt} = \frac{K_{cat}XHg}{K_a + Hg} \qquad (2)$$

$$\frac{dF}{dt} = D_r(F_r - F) \qquad (3)$$

where:

D_r = dilution coefficient (1/h)
F = glucose concentration in culture vessel (g/litre)
F_r = glucose concentration in reservoir (g/litre)
Hg = mercury concentration in culture vessel (mg/litre)
K_a = apparent binding constant for mercury (mg/litre)
K_{cat} = catalytic rate of mercury removal (mg/litre h)
K_d = microorganism decay coefficient (1/h)
t = time (h)
X = microorganism absorbance in culture vessel (no units)
Y = growth-yield coefficient (litre/g)

The block diagram of this model is shown in Fig. 1. Computer simulation was performed using the IBM CSMP III (Continuous System Modeling Program III). This is a comprehensive digital simulation language which allows the user to employ analog programming logic on large problems but requires no time or magnitude scaling.

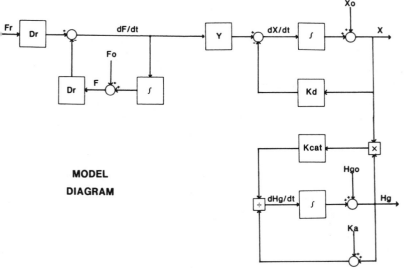

Fig. 1. *Block diagram of mercury removal model.*

Experimental Procedure

The three variables essential for obtaining numerical values for the model were bacterial concentration, glucose concentration, and mercury concentration. These three quantities were monitored under both steady state and dynamic conditions.[6]

The mixed culture included mercury resistant strains of three species of gram-negative bacteria: *Escherichia, Pseudomonas* and *Enterobacter*. The experimental equipment included a two litre continuous culture fermentor (New Brunswick Scientific Company's 'BioFlo' model C32), two influent vessels, and one effluent carboy. The influent substrate media was kept separate from the influent mercuric chloride solution. The two pumps were adjusted in order to provide a net 0·15/h dilution coefficient. The dilution coefficient is the reciprocal of the time required to fill the working volume (i.e. the reciprocal of the hydraulic retention time). The substrate media contained glucose and minimal nutrient salts. Bacteria were inoculated into the culture vessel and allowed to grow up in a batch environment before switching to continuous culturing. Fermentor instrumentation provided temperature control and monitoring, pH monitoring, agitation, aeration, and vapor release. Temperature was maintained at

37 °C. Sterile sampling techniques were employed to remove samples without contaminating the established culture.

Bacterial concentration was determined by optical density measured by absorbance at 490 nm on a Turner spectrophotometer. Glucose concentration was determined by a coupled chemical assay using glucose oxidase and peroxidase catalysts. Mercury concentration was determined by dithizone assay.

The steady state experiments were run by maintaining the influent glucose concentration at 2 g/litre and the influent mercury concentration at about 16 mg/litre. Samples were taken daily. The dynamic step tests were run by maintaining influent mercury concentration at 20 mg/litre, changing the glucose concentration from 0·5 to 2 g/litre. Samples were taken hourly for the first 6 h after the change, then at intervals of 2–3 h for a total of 15–20 h.

RESULTS

The results of two tests under steady state operating conditions are shown in Figs. 2a and 2b. These data were used to establish a qualitative understanding of the system. In both tests, initial bacterial absorbances were low (0·100 and 0·115 respectively) and initial glucose concentrations were high (1·91 g/litre and 1·68 g/litre). As each test progressed, it became apparent that an inverse relationship existed between these two variables; as bacterial levels increased, glucose levels in the culture vessel decreased, and vice versa. Final bacterial absorbances were high (0·55 and 0·52) and final glucose concentrations were low (0·038 g/litre and 0·623 g/litre). In addition, there was appreciable sensitivity in this relationship and no time lag.

In Fig. 2a, the mercury level in the culture vessel was initially 8·33 mg/litre, but fell to 0·398 mg/litre within 72 h. The mercury level had dropped to 1·06 mg/litre before the bacterial absorbance could increase from its low initial value of 0·1. Mercury levels stayed low throughout the remainder of the test, indicating that most of the inflowing 16 mg/litre of mercury was being volatilized and removed. At low bacterial concentrations, the mercury acted as a growth inhibitor; at higher bacterial concentrations, the mercury's effect was negligible. In Fig. 2b, the mercury level had already fallen during the batch phase and continued to stay between 0·0 and 0·195 mg/litre.

a)

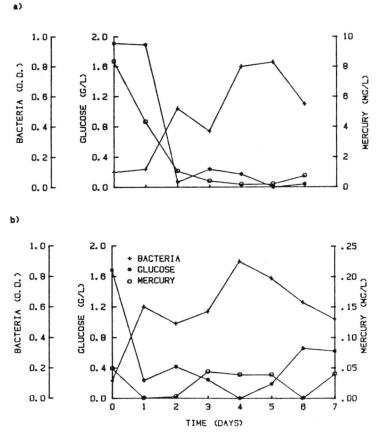

b)

Fig. 2. Chemostat response under steady state operating conditions: $F_r = 2\,g/litre$, $Hg_{in} = 16\,mg/litre$.

There was an inverse relationship between bacteria and glucose concentrations in both figures.

The results of two step tests (Figs. 3a and 3b) were used to determine numerical values for the model coefficients. In both tests, the influent glucose concentration underwent a step change from 0·5 to 2·0 g/litre at time zero. In response, the bacterial level in both cases experienced exponential growth. However, in Fig. 3a, there was a 4·5 h time lag before the exponential phase began. In Fig. 3b, there

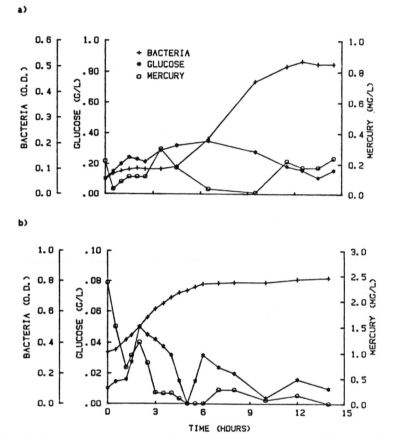

Fig. 3. Chemostat step response to changing glucose concentration: $F_r(step\ change) = 0.5-2\ g/litre,\ Hg_{in} = 20\ mg/litre.$

was no apparent time lag. The explanation for this behavior seems to be the different initial bacterial concentrations for the two tests, and their associated mercury concentrations. During the lag phase in Fig. 3a, bacterial absorbances fluctuated between 0·057 and 0·110; in Fig. 3b, the initial bacterial level was 0·339 and no lag phase occurred. The first order, exponential phases of both tests were remarkably similar. Logarithmic regression of the results shown in Figs. 3a and 3b yielded time constants of 3·56 h and 3·49 h respectively, with steady state gains of 0·453 and 0·476 respectively. The coefficients of determination (r^2) were 0·926 for Fig. 3a and 0·954 for Fig. 3b.

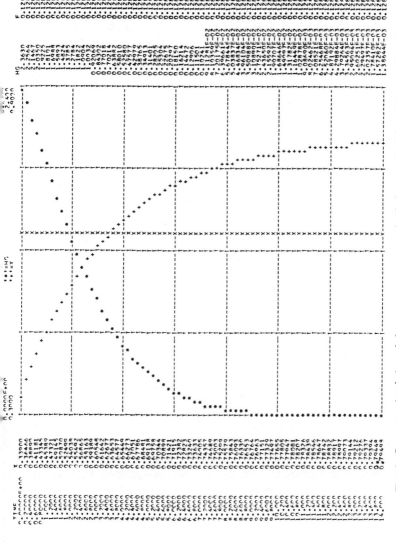

Fig. 4. Computer simulation of chemostat step response (with the same initial conditions as Fig. 3b).

Culture vessel glucose levels remained fairly constant in Fig. 3b, with all values less than 0·1 g/litre. Thus, the microorganisms were continuously consuming over 1·9 g/litre, or 95% of the influent glucose. In Fig. 3a, glucose levels rose during the bacterial lag phase, but steadily fell after bacterial growth commenced. Mercury levels in Fig. 3a remained low, with all values less than 0·297 mg/litre. In Fig. 3b, initial mercury concentration was 2·36 mg/litre. After 3 h, mercury levels had fallen to 0·216 mg/litre and remained below 0·277 mg/litre throughout the rest of the test. Therefore, in both tests, mercury volatilization and removal accounted for over 19·7 mg/litre, or 98·5%.

Experimental modeling by step testing[7] proved completely adequate in obtaining the coefficients for Eqs. (1) and (3). For the step tests, dF/dt was held constant. Glucose levels were averaged for both runs to give a value for F. Equation (2) contained two unknown parameters, K_{cat} and K_a, for which the step test procedure was unable to give a unique solution. For modeling purposes, values were chosen which gave the best percentage error (4·2%) relative to experimental data. The model coefficient values were as follows:

$$D_r = 0\text{·}15 \ 1/h$$
$$F = 0\text{·}128 \ g/litre$$
$$F_r = 2\text{·}0 \ g/litre$$
$$K_a = 11\text{·}0 \ mg/litre$$
$$K_{cat} = -8\text{·}73 \ mg/litre/h$$
$$K_d = 0\text{·}284 \ 1/h$$
$$Y = 0\text{·}470 \ litre/g$$

Figure 4 shows the model's step response using the same initial values as were observed in Fig. 3b. This computer simulation of the model was run using the IBM CSMP III.

DISCUSSION

The model compares favorably with the real system. The predictions of bacterial growth versus glucose levels were especially accurate, although further work is needed to refine the dynamic predictions of mercury and glucose. The model was run using the same initial values as observed experimentally and the results were statistically compared. The total standard error of estimate (including data from both runs) was 0·0329 for bacterial absorbance, 0·1446 for glucose concentration, and 0·1612 for mercury concentration. Such agreement indicates that the assumptions made during the model development were reasonable.

Both the experimental and model data attest to the suitability of biological removal as a treatment process for mercury contaminated wastewater.

ACKNOWLEDGEMENTS

Development of this model has been supported by The Ohio State University Department of Agricultural Engineering and the Ohio Agricultural Research and Development Center. The authors wish to thank Dr J. W. Williams and Dr O. Tuovinen for their assistance in microbiology, as well as C. Peterman, our laboratory technician.

REFERENCES

1. Silver, S. and Kinscherf, T. G. Genetic and biochemical basis for microbial transformations and detoxification of mercury and mercurial compounds. In *Biodegradation and Detoxification of Environmental Pollutants,* CRC Press Inc., Boca Raton, Fla., pp. 85–103, 1982.
2. Hansen, C. L., Zwolinski, G., Martin, D. and Williams, J. W. Bacterial removal of mercury from sewage. *Biotech. Bioeng. J.* **26:** 1330–4, 1984.
3. Summers, A. O. and Silver, S. Microbial transformations of metals. *Ann. Rev. Microbiol.* **32:** 637–72, 1978.
4. Metcalf and Eddy, Inc., *Wastewater Engineering.* McGraw-Hill, New York, pp. 373–421, 1972.
5. Bazin, M. (Ed.) *Mathematics in Microbiology.* Academic Press, London, 1983.
6. Christy, A. D. M.S. thesis, The Ohio State University, 1985 (in progress).
7. Doebelin, Ernest O. *System Dynamics.* Charles E. Merrill Publishing Co., Columbus, Ohio, pp. 273–306, 1972.

37

PERFORMANCE MODEL FOR MULTISTAGE COUNTERCURRENT CYCLONE SYSTEMS FOR SEPARATING FOOD COMPONENTS*

DOUGLAS S. McGINNIS

Engineering and Statistical Research Institute, Research Branch, Agriculture Canada, Ottawa, Ontario, Canada K1A OC6

ABSTRACT

Multistage countercurrent liquid cyclone systems are used by the food industry in a variety of separation processes to classify finely divided solids, clarify liquids, wash or extract substances from solids, or separate solids and/or liquids one from another. A computer algorithm was developed to calculate the flow rate distribution of each substance circulating in such a system, based upon their inlet feed rates, physical characteristics, solution chemistry, and upon the performance characteristics of each cyclone in the system. This paper describes the algorithm, and provides examples of how this can be used to predict the performances of systems designed for the leaching and recovery of soluble substances, or for the classification of solid particulates. The algorithm is adaptable to composite multistage systems for which the relationships between the feed and underflow stream flow rates of each component are known.

NOMENCLATURE

d = Stokes particle diameter (μm)
$fu(d)$ = fraction of particles under size d
$F(i, j)$ = underflow to throughput ratio for ith cyclone and jth flow component

* Contribution No. I-739, from Engineering & Statistical Research Institute, Research Branch, Agriculture Canada, Ottawa, Ontario, K1A OC6.

$G(j)$ = mass flow rate of the jth forwardflow feed substance (kg/min)

$g(i, j)$ = mass flow rate of the jth forwardflow feed substance flowing into the ith cyclone (kg/min)

n = number of stages or cyclones

$Q(k)$ = mass flow rate of the kth counterflow feed substance (kg/min)

$q(i, k)$ = mass flow rate of the kth counterflow feed substance flowing into the ith cyclone (kg/min)

R_c, R_0 = ratio of overflow to underflow for a single component for a single cyclone and multistage system respectively

R_f = ratio of counterflow to forwardflow feed flow rates

$T(i, j)$ = cyclone recirculation parameter for jth component fed into system at the first cyclone inlet

$U(i, k)$ = cyclone recirculation parameter for kth component fed into system at the last cyclone inlet

X = ratio of solution retained in solids to inert solids (kg/kg)

Y = concentration of solute in solution (total basis) (kg/kg)

$\alpha_1, \alpha_2, \beta$ = experimental constants for solute equilibrium concentration relationship

σ_1, σ_2 = experimental constants for particle size distribution relationship

Subscripts

a = solute
b = total inert solids
l = liquid
s = solvent

INTRODUCTION

The cyclone is ideal for many food processing applications in which the separation of components from food mixtures is a requirement. The liquid cyclone, or hydrocyclone, is used for separating suspended solids from liquid mixtures, or for separating suspended solids from one another. Also, the cyclone is used to separate two or more immiscible liquids and, by utilizing the solvent properties of the liquid, is employed in continuous extraction processes.

Despite the mechanical simplicity of cyclones, their design is not straightforward owing to the complex flow patterns which result from a particular selection of flow rate and set of cyclone dimensions (Fig. 1). Cyclone design has therefore depended greatly upon trial and error experimentation and less upon theory despite extensive research in this field. Nevertheless, numerous references[1,2,3,8] discuss cyclone design both from a practical and theoretical viewpoint.

The food industry has applied cyclones to increasingly more sophisticated systems involving multiple units in flow networks. Cyclones which have been connected to form a serial countercurrent flow network can be used in continuous washing and separation processes, such as in the production of starches and protein isolates from legume seeds[4] or potato starch.[5] The use of hydrocyclones in potato starch manufacture has resulted in a significant reduction in the amount of water required for starch washing.[6] Cyclones have also been applied to the processing of oil seeds, such as in the removal of gossypol from cottonseed and the separation of residual marc from miscella in conventional solvent extraction plants.[7] Cyclones are used most extensively in the starch industries, especially in the corn starch industry. In corn processing, cyclones are used in three distinct operations, namely germ separation, grit removal, and starch washing.

The generalized multistage countercurrent system is shown in Fig. 1. Each of the two feed streams may consist of a mixture of liquid(s), solute(s), and/or solid particulate(s). Typically, one stream will contain the components to be separated, while the other will consist of a pure liquid used for washing, extraction or dilution. Partial mixing of all components takes place throughout the network, while fractions of the input component streams exit from the overflow and underflow ports of the system.

Given the physical properties and solution chemistry of the various components to be processed, in addition to the processing objective(s), the specifications of the system are sought in terms of the number of cyclones, their arrangement, and their individual geometries. Optimization of the system involves seeking the most effective overall design subject to the greatest return on investment, or more simply in some cases, to maximize recovery or removal of one or more food components. The capability of predicting the distribution of component flows throughout the countercurrent flow network is fundamental to the optimization process. Calculation methods to

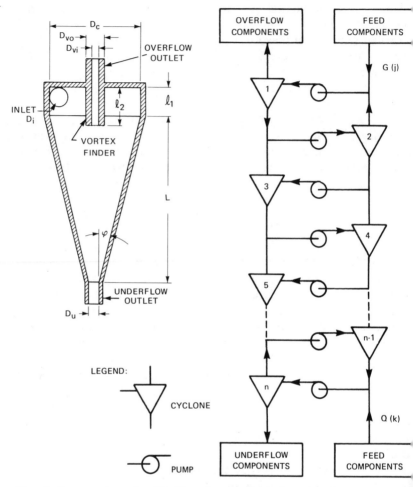

Fig. 1. Cross section of a liquid cyclone and schematic layout of a multistage countercurrent cyclone system having n stages.

accomplish this for cyclone systems, or other countercurrent system involving recirculation and variable underflow, were not found in th literature. The purpose of the work presented here, therefore, was to develop such a procedure for the design of systems used for solid-liquid extraction (leaching), washing, solids classification, and liquid-liquid or liquid–solid separation.

CALCULATION METHODS

Material Flow Distributions

Variable underflow. In the following analysis, $G(j)$ represents the mass flow rate of the jth component of the forwardflow feed stream entering the system upstream from the first cyclone (Fig. 1). Similarily, $Q(k)$ represents the mass flow rate of the kth component of the counterflow feed stream. Typically, $Q(k)$ is the flow rate of a solitary liquid ($k = 1$) used for washing, extraction or dilution, whereas $G(j)$ is the flow rate of either a liquid, solid or dissolved substance. The flow rate of each component, arising from the two feed streams, at the inlet to each cyclone is designated $g(i, j)$ or $q(i, k)$, each of which includes the recirculating portions. The sum of all such flow rates is the total mass flow rate entering each cyclone. For each cyclone, and for each component and flow condition therein, there exists an underflow to throughput value $F(i, j)$ or $F(i, k)$, where $0 \leqslant F \leqslant 1$. An algorithm for the calculation of the individual cyclone component flow rates was found in terms of these values, which proceeds as follows. First, the flow rate of the jth component entering the first cyclone is calculated:

$$g(1, j) = G(j)/T(n, j) \tag{1}$$

where:

$$T(1, j) = 1$$
$$\vdots$$
$$T(i, j) = 1 - \frac{F(n - i + 1, j)(1 - F(n - i + 2, j))}{T(i - 1, j)}$$
$$\vdots$$
$$T(n, j) = 1 - \frac{F(1, j)(1 - F(2, j))}{T(n - 1, j)}$$

Next, the flow rate of that component into each successive cyclone may be calculated from the flow rate of the component entering the preceding cyclone, as follows:

$$g(i, j) = \frac{F(i - 1, j)g(i - 1, j)}{T(n - i + 1, j)} \tag{2}$$

In a similar manner, the flow rate distribution of the countercurrent flow material may be calculated as follows:

$$q(n, k) = Q(k)/U(n, k) \tag{3}$$

$$q(i, k) = \frac{(1 - F(i + 1, k))q(i + 1, k)}{U(i, k)} \tag{4}$$

where:

$$U(1, k) = 1$$
$$\vdots$$
$$U(i, k) = 1 - \frac{F(i - 1, k)(1 - F(i, k))}{U(i - 1, k)}$$
$$\vdots$$
$$U(n, k) = 1 - \frac{F(n - 1, k)(1 - F(n, k))}{U(n - 1, k)}$$

The underflow to throughput ratio values used above are highly dependent upon the particular cyclone geometry, flux rate, and set of physical properties associated with the fluid mixture in each cyclone (e.g. density, concentration, viscosity, etc.). Determination of their values may be accomplished using mathematical models developed either from experimental data, working experience, or from a tested theoretical model. Because mutual interaction is bound to exist between one component and another, an accurate overall design solution or performance prediction will normally require iteration. There will be more discussion below on the calculation of F values for particle separation and leaching.

Constant underflow. In the simplest case, the underflow to throughput ratio for a given component may be constant over all cyclones as, for example, by design. The separation performance of this simple system depends upon the overflow/underflow ratio for the cyclones, R_c, and upon the ratio of the two inlet feed streams, R_f (feed ratio) which are calculated by:

$$R_c = \frac{1 - F}{F} \tag{5}$$

and

$$R_f = \frac{Q}{G} \tag{6}$$

where Q, G = flow rates of forwardflow and counterflow feed streams of one component.

The system overflow to underflow discharge ratio in this case may be calculated by:

$$R_0 = R_c \frac{(1 + R_c + R_c^2 + \cdots + R_c^{n-2}) + R_c^{n-1}(1 + R_f)}{1 + R_f[1 + R_c(1 + R_c + R_c^2 + \cdots + R_c^{n-2})]} \quad (7)$$

In the general case of variable underflow, R_0 may be calculated after solving for all of the component flow rate distributions using Eqs. 1)–(4). The equation is:

$$R_0 = \frac{\sum [g(1, j)(1 - F(1, j))] + \sum [q(1, k)(1 - F(1, k))]}{\sum [g(n, j)F(n, j)] + \sum [q(n, k)F(n, k)]} \quad (8)$$

Separation and Classification of Particulate Materials

The underflow to throughput ratio for solid particulate material is commonly referred to as the efficiency, and is highly dependent upon the particle size and shape, the fluid and particle densities, and the characteristics of the flow field of the liquid as determined by cyclone geometry, orifice sizes, fluid flow rate, and pressure gradient(s) between the cyclone cavity and its two outlets. The classification into two or more constituent solid materials from a multicomponent liquid mixture is accomplished on the basis of differences between their respective efficiencies, as determined by the above parameters, particularly particle size and density. When using Eqs. (1)–(4) to calculate the distribution of solids in the cyclone network, the dependence of efficiency on particle size necessitates that each particle size be considered as a unique subcomponent. Since the sizes of particulates of a given food material are continuously distributed over a particular size range, it is necessary that the particle size distribution of each material type be approximated as a histogram to permit the necessary subdivision into size subunits. The accuracy of this approximation improves with increasing numbers of size increments, which presents no practical limitation for the high speed computer.

To generate the efficiency values for each particle type and size (grade efficiency curve) requires a mathematical model. To be truly useful, this model must resolve the effects of the many parameters besides particle size which affect efficiency. Such a model may be obtained experimentally over a range of flow conditions, using a single cyclone identical to that which is planned for the countercurrent system. The advantage of this approach over the use of theoretical models for efficiency is the assurance provided; the disadvantage is it inflexibility as an optimization tool. The most promising theoretical model found was that developed by Bloor and Ingham.[8,9] Using the method, grade efficiency curves are predicted based upon calculation of critical particle trajectories in the flow field of the cyclone. The model resolves the effects of flow and cyclone geometry on particle movement, and provides a good theoretical basis for design optimization. Reasonable agreement between predictions using their model and experimental results was found. However, leakage to the overflow via the vortex finder was not accounted for in their model, and th model therefore predicts efficiencies which are higher than can b expected. Also, the effects of particle interference in concentrate mixtures was not taken into account. Nevertheless, as a design tool the theoretical model is considered extremely useful for initia investigations.

Leaching

In the leaching process, a mixture of finely divided solids and solvent fed into the system at one feed inlet, while pure solvent is fed into th other. In this arrangement, the flow rate of slurry entering the first c last cyclone must be established at a level which affects a full discharg of the inert solids fraction from the system underflow or overflow depending upon the direction of solids flow. Partial recirculation of th solids may be used to increase the solids retention time, but would n be necessary in most cases, since equilibrium will be attained rapidl owing to the low solids concentration (upper limit about 15%) an small particle sizes.

Since the solute resides in solution in both the inert solids and th free liquid, it is necessary to calculate the proportions in each at ever stage of the system. In doing this, it is convenient and reasonable t assume that equilibrium is achieved at each stage. The case fc non-equilibrium conditions at each stage is far more complex, and beyond the scope of this work.

Experimental equilibrium data is needed, therefore, to generate th underflow to throughput ratios for the solute component. These dat must provide the relationship between solution retained in the solid and the concentration of solute in the equilibrium solution. Th underflow to throughput ratios for the liquid and solid fractions wi vary from cyclone to cyclone, as determined theoretically or experimentally. The underflow to throughput value for the total solute is calculated as follows:

$$\bar{F}_a(1) = Y(1)X(1)(\bar{F}_b(i) - \bar{F}_1(i)) \cdot \frac{\bar{g}_b(i)}{\bar{g}_a(i)} + \bar{F}_1(1) \tag{9}$$

in which:

$$Y(i) = \frac{g_a(i)}{(g_a(i) + g_s(i) + q_s(i))} \tag{9a}$$

and

$$X(i) = \alpha_1 + \alpha_2 Y(i)^\beta \quad (\alpha_1, \alpha_2, \beta \text{ from experiment}) \tag{9b}$$

Because of the interdependence of the elements of $\bar{F}_a$, and of $\overline{F_a}$ with $\overline{g_a}$, the solution is found implicitly, in which Eq. (9) and the solution derived from Eqs. (1)–(4) are mutually satisfied.

EXAMPLES

Leaching of Oil from Meal Using Benzene

Equilibrium data supplied by Prabhudesai[10] was used in conjunction with hypothetical design data to demonstrate the utility of the model for predicting the performance of a multicyclone system for the extraction of oil from meal using benzene. Values for the constants used in Eq. (9b) were found by regression analysis to be $\alpha_1 = 0.5000$, $\alpha_2 = 0.2219$, $\beta = 1.6300$. In this example, each of six countercurrent cyclones was assumed to provide uniform liquid underflow and all of the solids were assumed to flow to the underflow stream of each cyclone. The total benzene flow rate into the system was held constant at a value of 10 kg/min, while the solvent feed ratio (R_f) and cyclone overflow/underflow ratio (R_c) were varied from 0.25 to 7.75 and from 0.5 to 4.0 respectively. Meal with an oil/inert solids ratio of 0.40 (w/w) was assumed to enter the system at a rate of 3.0 kg/min. Predicted oil recovery and overflow oil concentration were plotted against R_c and R_f (Fig. 2). These relationships suggest optimum paired values of the solvent feed ratio and cyclone overflow/underflow ratio at which the net economic return from recovered oil is maximized considering the cost of distillation. In general, the integration of an economic model with the performance model could be implemented to investigate the

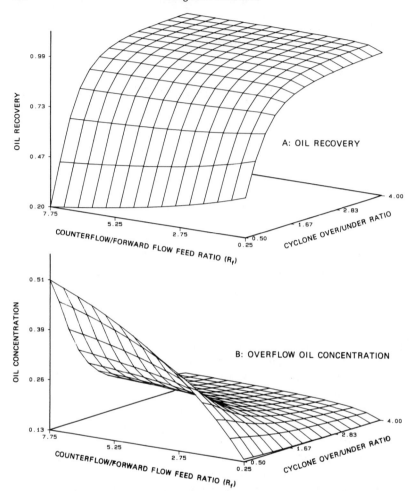

Fig. 2. Fraction of oil extracted from meal and recovered in the overflow stream of a six stage multicyclone system (A) and concentration of that oil (B) as functions of the benzene feed ratio (R_f) and cyclone overflow/underflow ratio (R_c) for a constant total benzene flow rate input of 10 kg/min.

economic effects of changes to all process variables, including for example, the number of cyclones, pumping rates and cyclone design.

Continuous Yeast Recovery from Fermentation Process

A hypothetical continuous process for the production of yeast involves growing yeast in a waste stream of aqueous carbohydrate media

TABLE I
Input and output data for yeast–starch separation example

	Program inputs	
(1) *Particles*	*Yeast*	*Starch*
Stokes density (g/ml)	1·03	1·55
Concentration (g/ml)	0·04	0·04
Maximum Stokes dia. (μm)	7·0	35·0
Minimum Stokes dia. (μm)	4·0	10·0
σ_1	2·0	1·61
σ_2	3·0	5·75
(2) *Fluid*		*Water*
Viscosity (g/(cm s))		$0·821 \cdot 10^{-2}$
Density (g/ml)		0·996
(3) *Operational*		
Counterflow liquid feed flow rate (ml/s)		45·0
Forwardflow liquid feed flow rate (ml/s)		45·0
Cyclone design flow rate (ml/s)		$77 \rightarrow 103$
(4) *Cyclone design*		
Feed inlet area (cm^2)		0·35
Vortex finder radius (cm)		1·52
Cyclone radius (cm)		2·18
Apex-vortex finder length (cm)		31·15
Semi-angle of cone (radians)		0·07
Underflow/throughput ratio (liquid)		0·40

Program output

) *Flow rate distribution*

Cyclone No.	Yeast Mass flow rate (g/s) Feed	Over	Under	Starch Mass flow rate (g/s) Feed	Over	Under	Total slurry Mass flow rate (g/s) Feed
1	2·038 7	1·800 0	0·238 7	1·824 5	0·020 3	1·804 3	102·790 3
2	0·269 1	0·238 7	0·030 4	1·832 4	0·024 5	1·807 9	92·203 6
3	0·034 2	0·030 4	0·003 8	1·838 8	0·028 1	1·810 7	86·091 8
4	0·004 2	0·003 8	0·000 5	1·844 0	0·030 9	1·813 0	82·144 8
5	0·000 5	0·000 5	0·000 1	1·847 2	0·033 3	1·813 9	79·529 4
6	0·000 1	0·000 1	0·000 0	1·813 9	0·034 1	1·779 7	77·752 5

) *Performance summary*	*Yeast*	*Starch*
System underflow/throughput ratio	0·000 0	0·988 7
Average cyclone underflow/throughput	0·111 5	0·984 4
System overflow/throughput ratio	1·000 0	0·011 3
Average cyclone overflow/throughput	0·888 5	0·015 6

containing suspended insoluble starch particles (amylopectin granules) within a reactor which is maintained at optimum growth conditions, as partly determined by nutrient concentration and cell population. The optimum cell population would be maintained by continuous removal of the yeast at a rate equal to its population growth rate. The yeast and starch would be separated using countercurrent cyclones, and the starch stream would undergo a heat treatment followed by hydrolysis to produce a glucose stream for recycling to the fermentor. The yeast stream would be centrifuged, washed and dried, and the aqueous phase returned to the fermentor.

The physical properties of yeast and starch were estimated in order to demonstrate the utility of the model for predicting the ability of a proposed cyclone system to provide the necessary separation. The separation efficiencies for each particle size and type were calculated using the method of Bloor and Ingham.[9] Yeast is known to exist as ovoid cells ranging in size from 4 to 7 μm. The starch was assumed to consist of finely divided, roughly spheroid particles in the size range of 10–35 μm. The particle size distributions were modelled as uni-modal distributions using a four parameter equation similar to Harris' three parameter equation, cited by Svarovsky:[3]

$$fu(d) = 1 - \left(1 - \left(\frac{d - d_{min}}{d_{max} - d_{min}}\right)^{\sigma_1}\right)^{\sigma_2} \tag{10}$$

in which σ_1, σ_2 are experimental parameters.

Table I presents a summary of the data used in this example, and the results for one particular choice of liquid flow rate, liquid feed ratio, and number of cyclones. With this system, 96% of the yeast exits in the overflow, while 98% of the starch exits in the underflow.

DISCUSSION

The algorithm presented in this paper provides an exact algebraic solution for the calculation of the flow rate distribution of any substance entering a multistage cyclone system consisting of any number of cyclones of varying design and performance. When used in conjunction with accurate submodels for the performance of each cyclone, the algorithm may be used as a tool for the design and optimization of systems used for leaching and/or separation processes such as found in the food industry, and elsewhere.

The basic algorithm may be used to calculate the performances of more complex systems involving composite arrangements of multistage countercurrent cyclone networks. Numerous design alternatives for each separation problem could therefore be explored fully, to ascertain their potential advantages and disadvantages in terms of separation and cost efficiencies.

REFERENCES

1. Bradley, D. *The Hydrocyclone*. Pergamon Press, London, 1965.
2. Kelsall, D. F. The theory and applications of the hydrocyclones. In *Solid Liquid Separation* (Pool and Doyle Eds.). Her Majesty's Stationery Office, London, 1966.
3. Svarovsky, L. *Solid–Liquid Separation*. Chemical Engineering Series, Butterworths, London-Boston, 1977.
4. Vose, J. R. Production and functionality of starches and protein isolates from legume seeds (field peas and horsebeans). *Cereal Chem.* **57**(6): 406–10, 1980.
5. Verberne, P. A new hydrocyclone process for the production of potato starch with lowest fresh water consumption. *Die Starke,* **9**: 303–7, 1977.
6. Bier, T. H. and Greene, M. R. Hydrocyclones as a process tool: simple . . . reliable . . . low cost. *Food Engineering,* March: 167/170, 1980.
7. Stavenger, P. L. and Van Note, R. H. Principles and theory of liquid cyclone oil seed processing. Tech. reprint 4225, Dorr-Oliver Inc., paper presented at 17th cottonseed processing clinic, sponsored by the U.S. Dept. Agriculture, New Orleans, Feb. 12, 1968.
8. Bloor, M. I. G. and Ingham, D. B. Investigation of the flow in a conical hydrocyclone. *Trans. Inst. Chem. Engrs* **51**: 36–41, 1973.
9. Bloor, M. I. G. and Ingham, D. B. On the efficiency of the industrial cyclone. *Trans. Inst. Chem. Engrs* **51**: 173–6, 1973.
10. Prabhudesai, R. K. Leaching. section 5.1 In *Handbook of Separation Techniques for Chemical Engineers* (P. A. Schweitzer, Ed.) Section 5.1, McGraw-Hill, New York, 1979.

38

MODELING OF COUNTERCURRENT, CROSSFLOW, SOLID–LIQUID EXTRACTORS AND EXPERIMENTAL VERIFICATION

S. I. FLORES DE HOYOS and HENRY G. SCHWARTZBERG*

Seccion Ingenieria en Alimentos, Depto. Ingenieria FES-UNAM, National University of Mexico
* Department of Food Engineering, University of Massachusetts, Amherst, MA 01003, U.S.A.

ABSTRACT

Superposition methods for predicting extraction yields and extract concentrations for belt extractors were developed and successfully tested for three stage extraction. Outlet concentrations, $y(t)$, versus time, t, for fixed beds extracted at a constant inlet extract concentration, Y_{in}, were used to generate simultaneous equations, which provided stage outlet concentrations and extraction yields. $y(t)$ versus t were successfully correlated by equations based on a solute material balance for a bed and on mass transfer at the leading edge of the extract entering the bed for downflow extractions, but not for upflow extractions, where nonuniform displacement occurred.

INTRODUCTION

Belt extractors' are widely used to extract food solutes. In these systems, extracts percolate through a horizontal moving bed of solids supported on a perforated moving belt or rotating annular or circular screen. Fresh solids are added at one end of the bed and spent solids discharge at the other. Extracts flow through the bed, are collected in sumps and resprayed on the bed to provide multistage, countercurrent, solid–liquid contacting. Stages are numbered from 1 to N starting with the solid's feed stage. R is the volume-flow rate of solids down the bed, E is the net, countercurrent, volume-flow rate of extract from stage to stage, X is the w/v concentration of solute in the solid, X_0 the

413

initial, uniform value of X and $y_n(t)$ is the (w/v) extract concentration out of stage n, at time t after extract is applied to the top of stage 1.

The solids travel across each sump in equal times, t_c. Sometimes extract is recirculated to make sure the bed is fully saturated; but herein it is assumed that the drainage resistance is adjusted so extract passes through the bed only once per stage. Then, the extract concentration sprayed on the bed in stage $(n-1)$ is Y_n, the average value of $y_n(t)$. If recirculation is used, this will not be true; but methods for specifying Y_{in} with recirculation have been developed;[1,2] and, if the Y_{in} are correctly specified, the general approach used herein can still be used.

Y_1 is the product extract concentration discharged from stage 1, and Y_{N+1} the solute concentration of the solvent entering stage N. It is assumed that: at equilibrium $y = MX$, M is independent of X and E/R remains constant, and the bed is initially deposited with its pores full of liquid whose concentration is MX_0. If $A = ME/R$, is large, extraction is faster for a given yield, P, or more complete for a given extraction time; but Y_1 is low.

Y_n is obtained by integrating $y_n(t)$ with respect to t between $(n-1)t_c$ and nt_c and dividing by t_c. It can be shown[1,2] that $y_n(t)$ versus t for a bed passing over a sump should be equal to that of a fixed bed of equal height, L, for same inlet X and Y, same extract velocity, V, A and t_c. Thus, belt extractors can be analyzed by analyzing the behavior of fixed-bed extractors subjected to sequences of extract flows similar to those occurring in a belt extractor. In these fixed beds, the solid volume divided by t_c equals R and the volume of extract discharged per cycle divided by t_c equals E.

In such analyses, we predict the extract discharge characteristics of fixed beds of solids initially at X_0 when Y_{in} progressively changes from Y_2 to Y_3, to . . . , to Y_N, and finally to Y_{N+1} every time t increases by t_c. If certain conditions are satisfied, superposition can be used to predict the $y_n(t)$ corresponding to inlet Y_2 through Y_{N+1}. These predictions are based on $y(t)$ versus t for the bed when extracted at constant Y_{in}. For linear extraction in such cases:

$$y(t) = MX_0[1 - S(t)] + Y_{in}S(t) \tag{1}$$

where $S(t)$ is the solution to the diffusion partial differential equation (DPDE) and associated boundary conditions (BC), initial conditions (IC) and auxiliary constraints (AC) for solid–liquid extraction in a fixed bed which provides $y(t)$ when $X_0 = 0$ and $Y_{in} = 1.0$. $MX_0[1 - S(t)]$

provides $y(t)$ when $Y_{in} = 0$ and $MX_0 = 1.0$. We will test whether experimentally determined $S(t)$ can be used in place of DPDE solutions in superposition-based analyses of belt extraction.

When superposition is applicable:

$$y_n(t) = MX_0[1 - S(t)] + Y_2[S(t)] + \sum_{i=2}^{i=n} [Y_{i+1} - Y_i]S[t - (i - 1)t_c] \quad (2)$$

and

$$Y_n = MX_0[1 - U_n] + Y_2 U_n + \sum_{i=2}^{i=n} [Y_{i+1} - Y_i]U_{i-1} \quad (3)$$

The summation terms in Eqs. (2) and (3) are not used when $n = 1$, and

$$U_i = (1/t_c) \int_{(n-1)t_c}^{nt_c} S(t)\, dt \quad (4)$$

Equation (3) is a part of a set of N simultaneous equations which can be conveniently rearranged and solved in matrix form if $S(t)$ and consequently U_i are available. Once Y_n are known experimentally or by solving the equation set (3), equation set (2) can be used to determine $y_n(t)$ versus t between $(n - 1)t_c$ and nt_c.

To use superposition as described above, the diffusion process, BC and AC must be linear, and $y(t)$ must be correctly specified by an $S(t)$ which effectively solves the DPDE for the particles in the bed and appropriate BC, IC and AC. The AC involve material balances for both solute transfer between the solid and the extract, and convective and diffusive axial transfer of solute in the extract. Because extract displacement in beds is sometimes unstable, it may not always be possible to specify the AC in ways that permit use of superposition.

Theoretical and numerical solutions for $S(t)$ have been published, but these solutions are not obeyed experimentally.[1,2] Discrepancies occur because of axial dispersion and nonuniform displacement for the extract and possibly because inappropriate BC or AC were used in solving the DPDE. Nevertheless, the $y(t)$ behavior of fixed beds is often quite regular, particularly when extract displacement is stable. In such cases, Flores[3] found that when t is less than the displacement time, t_f, a reasonable approximation is:

$$[1 - S(t)] = G(t) = 0.5\{\operatorname{erf}[(L - Vt)/\sqrt{4D_a t}] + \operatorname{erf}[(L + Vt)/\sqrt{4D_a t}]\}$$
$$(5)$$

D_a is the axial dispersion coefficient. When $t > t_f$:

$$[1 - S(t)] = G(t) + J_f \exp\left[-J_f B(t - t_f)/t_f\right] \tag{6}$$

where $B = Me/(1 - e)$, e is the bed porosity and J_f is $y(t)/MX_0$ at $t = t_f$, when the bed is initially filled with extract of concentration MX_0, $Y_{in} = 0$ and displacement during $t < t_f$ is pluglike. The J_f dependent term in Eq. (6) satisfies the solute material balance for the bed, when $y(t)$ (as observed) decays exponentially as t increases.

OBJECTIVE

The objective of this work was to test the ability of Eq. (1)–(6) to predict $y_n(t)$ versus t and Y_n versus n for belt extraction by means of tests carried out in a simulated three stage belt extractor.

EXPERIMENTAL

Figure 1 shows the arrangement used to test extraction behavior for fixed beds of alumina spheres and coarse, uniform, spent coffee grounds which contained infused solutions of sucrose or NaCl when Y_{in} was manipulated to simulate belt extraction. When determining $y(t)$

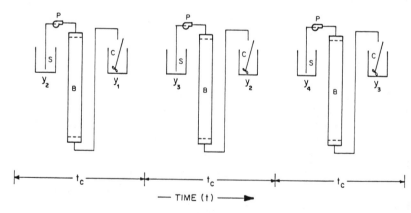

SIMULATED CROSS FLOW LEACHING SYSTEM

Fig. 1. Experimental setup for simulating three-stage, countercurrent, crossflow belt extraction: B, the bed; S extract feed tank; C, extract discharge tank; P, peristaltic pump.

versus t to check Eqs. (5) and (6), Y_{in} versus t was constant, but different L, V, Y_{in} and MX_0 (including $MX_0 = 0$) were tested. In all cases, the bed was filled with solid particles having a uniform X_0 and the interparticle pores were saturated with extract of concentration MX_0.

When belt extraction was simulated Y_{in}, was initially set at trial concentration Y_2 for t_c and extract with trial concentration Y_1 was collected. When $t = t_c$, Y_{in} was switched to a trial Y_3 and extract with a new Y_2 was collected between $t = t_c$ and $t = 2t_c$. At $t = 2t_c$, Y_{in} was switched to Y_4, which equalled 0 in these tests, and extraction was continued until $t = 3t_c$ during which extract with a new Y_3 was collected. The process was continued using the new Y_n to provide the Y_{in} for the next extraction sequence. When the Y_{in} became constant for several sequences, steady state was assumed and the run was terminated. When judiciously chosen initial Y_{in} were used, steady state was reached in four or five cycles and the run was terminated after eight or nine sequences.

In some cases, beds whose interstitial liquid initially contained Dextran Blue were tested to verify the applicability of Eq. (5); or pulses of Dextran Blue were added to feed extract to determine flow uniformity and measure D_a during displacement and extraction. Because of its molecular weight (2 000 000) Dextran Blue diffused in the solids very slowly and thus spread mainly because of dispersion in the extract.

RESULTS AND DISCUSSION

Curve I in Fig. 2 is a typical $[1 - S(t)]$ versus t curve for downflow extraction when $Y_{in} = 0$. The remaining curves in Fig. 2 will be discussed later. Curve I and similar curves obtained at other test conditions obeyed Eqs. (5) and (6) reasonably accurately over large ranges of t. As V decreased and L and t_f increased, J_f increased, but never reached $1 \cdot 0$ at $t = t_f$ as predicted in published DPDE solutions for extractions in fixed beds. For the particles tested it was found[3] that J_f could be predicted reasonably well by Eq. (7), which is based on analyzing mass transfer in a well-mixed zone at the leading edge of the entering extract.

$$J_f = 1 - \exp\{-[3k_{eff}L/(aBV)]/[1 + 3D_a k_{eff}/(aBV^2)]\} \qquad (7)$$

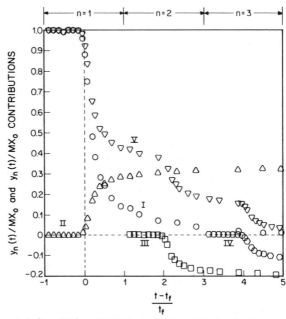

Fig. 2. Plots of: I, $[1-S(t)] = y(t)/MX_0$ versus $(t-t_f)/t_f$ for single stage extraction; II, III and IV, superposition contributions to $y_n(t)$ versus $(t-t_f)/t_f$ for three stage countercurrent crossflow extraction; and V, superposition-based, predicted y_n versus $(t-t_f)/t_f$ curve.

k_{eff} is the overall mass transfer coefficient in the well-mixed zone and a is the particle radius. $k_{eff} = \sqrt{4D_s/\pi t_e}$ times a correction term, where D_s is the diffusivity in the solid and t_e, the effective contact time in the well-mixed zone, is proportional to $\sqrt{4D_a t_f(\ln 2)/V}$. The correction term is a complex function of D_s, t_e, B, a^2, D_a and k_y, the liquid film mass transfer coefficient. Available M and D_s data,[4] published k_y correlations for fixed beds[5] and D_a values determined by the spreading of Dextran Blue pulses were used when testing the applicability of Eq. (7), which will be discussed in a separate paper. For stable displacement (i.e. for downflow extraction and for transfers of solute into the solid), Eqs. (5), (6) and (7) were reasonably accurate; but they did not work well for upflow extraction, where displacement was unstable and D_a was very large.

Figure 3 shows $y(t)/MX_0$ versus $(t-t_f)/t_f$ curves for simulated belt extraction at $L = 0.61$ m using sucrose at $MX_0 = 0.238$–0.240 as a solute contained in alumina spheres for which $a = 4.5$–4.9 mm, $e =$

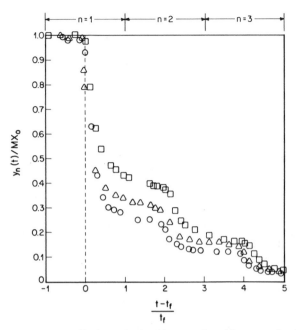

Fig. 3. *Plots of experimentally determined* $y_n(t)$ *versus* $(t - t_f)/t_f$ *curves for three different flow rates:* ($\square$) $E = 2 \cdot 0 \times 10^{-7} m^3/s$; ($\triangle$) $E = 5 \cdot 2 \times 10^{-7} m^3/s$; ($\bigcirc$) $E = 12 \cdot 0 \times 10^{-7} m^3/s$.

$0 \cdot 39 – 0 \cdot 40$, $M = 2 \cdot 76$ and $D_s = 0 \cdot 96 \times 10^{-10} \, \text{m}^2/\text{s}$. The runs were carried out at $A = 3 \cdot 91$, $B = 2 \cdot 17$ and $t_c = 1 \cdot 8 t_f$ for three $E - t_f$ pairs: ($\square$) $2 \cdot 0 \times 10^{-7} \, \text{m}^3/\text{s}$—2340 s; ($\triangle$) $5 \cdot 2 \times 10^{-7} \, \text{m}^3/\text{s}$—960 s; and ($\bigcirc$) $12 \cdot 0 \times 10^{-7} \, \text{m}^3/\text{s}$—408 s. The portions of the curves between $(t - t_f)/t_f = -1$ to 1, 1 to 3 and 3 to 5 respectively correspond to $y(t)/MX_0$ for the first, second and third stages of the simulated extractor. As previously noted, I in Fig. 2 is $[1 - S(t)]$. II is $(Y_2/MX_0)S(t)$; III, $[(Y_3 - Y_2)/MX_0][1 - S(t - t_c)]$; IV, $[(Y_4 - Y_3)/MX_0][1 - S(t - 2t_c)]$; and curve V, the sum of I, II, III and IV, is a composite dimensionless equivalent of Eq. (3) for $n = 1$, 2 and 3 and $E = 2 \cdot 0 \times 10^{-7} \, \text{m}^3/\text{s}$.

In Fig. 4 curve V from Fig. 2 is superimposed on the $E = 2 \cdot 0 \times 10^{-7} \, \text{m}^3/\text{s}$ curve from Fig. 3. The computed curve from Fig. 2 is almost identical to the experimental curve from Fig. 3. Similar good agreement was obtained at the other conditions tested. Therefore superposition as provided by Eq. (3) is a valid procedure for the conditions tested and experimental $S(t)$ versus t curves, rather than formal DPDE solutions, can be used at these conditions.

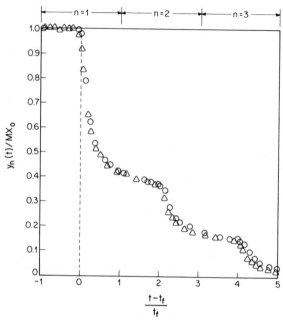

Fig. 4. *Comparison of calculated superposition-based* $y_n(t)$ *versus* $(t - t_f)/t_f$ (○) *and experimental* $y_n(t)$ *versus* $(t - t_f)/t_f$ (△) *curves for simulated three-stage, countercurrent, crossflow belt extraction.*

Table I lists extraction yields, P, experimental and predicted Y_n' (w/w extract concentrations) for the simulated three-stage (downflow) belt extractions and for two similar extractions using upflow. The predicted $Y_n' = Y_n/\rho$, where ρ is the extract density, and were calculated from Y_n obtained using $[1 - S(t)]$ based on Eqs. (5), (6) and (7) and independently measured or calculated D_a, D_s, M, and k_y data. $P = A(Y_1/MX_0) - B$, and excludes solute recirculated in the extract in the pores of the freshly filled bed.

The predicted and experimental Y_n' do not agree as well as the $y_n(t)$. Most likely this does not represent lack of applicability of superposition, but probably occurs because inaccurate independent data were used in Eqs. (5), (6) and (7); and, to a lesser extent, because Eqs. (5), (6) and (7) are imperfect. Because of the extract which is recirculated when providing an initially saturated bed, the P calculations are highly sensitive to small changes in Y_1. Therefore, the predicted and experimental P are much farther out of line than corresponding Y_1'.

TABLE I
Y'_n and P for simulated three stage belt extractions

E $(m^3/s \times 10^7)$	Flow direction	Type of Y'	$Y'(kg/kg)$				
			Y'_1	Y'_2	Y'_3	Y'_4	P
2·0	Down	Exp.	0·188	0·078	0·030	0	0·92
2·0	Down	Pred.	0·179	0·066	0·025	0	0·77
2·0	Up	Exp.	0·166	0·088	0·038	0	0·56
5·2	Down	Exp.	0·172	0·060	0·025	0	0·71
5·2	Down	Pred.	0·150	0·078	0·032	0	0·33
5·2	Up	Exp.	0·156	0·076	0·032	0	0·44
12·0	Down	Exp.	0·168	0·049	0·025	0	0·59

Table I shows that upflow caused marked decreases in Y'_1 and P. This, no doubt, is caused by the nonuniform displacement which occurred during upflow extraction. Nonuniformity of displacement and large axial dispersion during upflow extraction was clearly observed in the Dextran Blue pulse spreading tests used to measure D_a, which was 15–50 times larger for upflow than for downflow.

CONCLUSIONS

(1) Superposition based on experimentally determined $y(t)$ versus t curves for extractions in single fixed beds can be used to predict single-pass, belt-extraction behavior when displacement is stable. (2) Equations (5), (6) and (7) correlate $y(t)$ versus t reasonably well for stable downflow in fixed beds, but it may be better to use Eqs. (5) and (6) alone with regression-based values of J_f and D_a obtained directly from fixed bed extraction tests rather than use Eq. (7). (3) Unstable displacement will occur and reduce extraction efficiency when upflow extraction is used.

REFERENCES

1. Schwartzberg, H. G. Progress and problems in solid–liquid extraction. *Lat. Am. J. Heat Mass Transfer* **7**: 317–44, 1983.
2. Schwartzberg, H. G., Flores, S. I. and Zaman S. Analysis of multistage belt extractors, paper AIChE National Meeting, Denver, Colorado, August 28–31, 1983.

3. Flores, S. I. Analysis and simulation of countercurrent, crossflow belt extractors. Ph.D. thesis, University of Massachusetts, Amherst, Mass., 1985.
4. Chao, R. The performance of solid–liquid extraction in a binary batch system. Ph.D thesis, University of Massachusetts, Amherst, Mass., 1984.
5. Wilson, E. S. and Geankoplis, C. J. Mass transfer at very low Reynolds numbers in fixed beds. *IEC Fundam.* **5:** 9–14, 1956.

Part V

Heat and Mass Transfer Operations

39

THE INFLUENCE OF DRYING CONDITIONS
UPON REACTIVATION OF BAKER'S YEAST

K. ZIMMERMANN and W. BAUER

Technical University of Hamburg-Harburg, Eissendorfer Str. 38, 2100 Hamburg 90, Federal Republic of Germany

ABSTRACT

For the production of dried starter cultures the thermal drying conditions have to be controlled exactly to obtain maximum viability and enzyme activity after rehydration. In the drying process several parameters, including gas bulk temperature and moisture content of the microorganisms influence significantly the viability of the cells. A mathematical model using shrinking core analogy was developed to describe the drying process of microorganism pellets in a fluidized-bed drier. This model was combined with the deactivation kinetics of enzymes. Drying experiments were carried out in laboratory and technical scale fluid driers using baker's yeast. Enzyme deactivation kinetics were determined in separate experiments for alcohol dehydrogenase (ADH), glucose-6-phosphate dehydrogenase (G-6-PDH) and 6-phosphogluconate dehydrogenase (6-PGDH). Viability was measured as CO_2-production in anaerobic fermentation and O_2-demand in aerobic conditions. The experimental results of the drying process and enzyme deactivation were compared to the proposed drying model calculations with very good agreement.

NOMENCLATURE

a = specific particle surface area (1/m)
A = total particle surface area (m^2)
A_t = fluid bed cross-section area
A_E = active enzyme content (kg active enzyme/kg d.s.)

$A_{E,0}$ = initial active enzyme content (kg active enzyme/kg d.s.)
Bi   = Biot number of heat transfer
Bi′   = Biot number of mass transfer
$c_{p,w}$ = specific heat capacity of water (kJ/kg K)
d_p = particle diameter (m)
D = molecular diffusion coefficient water/air (m²/s)
D_{dry} = diffusion coefficient in dry yeast (m²/s)
E_d = deactivation energy (J/mol)
h_g = specific gas enthalpy (kJ/kg)
h_w = specific water enthalpy (kJ/kg)
Δh_v = specific evaporation enthalpy (kJ/kg)
k_d = rate constant of deactivation (1/s)
k_∞ = frequency factor (1/s)
m_g = gas mass (kg)
M_w = molecular weight of water (kg/kmol)
$\dot{m}_g$ = mass flow rate of gas (kg/s)
$\dot{n}_w$ = water flux (kg/m²s)
p = total pressure (Pa)
$\dot{q}$ = heat flux (W/m²)
r = wet core radius (m)
R = particle radius (m)
R = gas constant (J/kmol K)
r_d = deactivation rate (1/s)
t = time (s)
T = gas bulk temperature (K)
T_m = medium temperature (K)
T_s = surface temperature (K)
$\bar{X}$ = medium moisture content (kg water/kg d.s.)
X_{crit} = critical moisture content (kg water/kg d.s.)
X_{hygr} = hygroscopic moisture content (kg water/kg d.s.)
Y_w = gas water content (kg water/kg dry gas)
Y_w^* = gas water content at saturation (kg water/kg dry gas)
z = coordinate (m)

Greek symbols

α = heat transfer coefficient (W/m²K)
β = mass transfer coefficient (m/s)
ε = voidage
λ_{dry} = thermal conductivity of dry yeast (W/mK)
μ = diffusion resistance factor
φ = moisture content (kg water/kg yeast)

INTRODUCTION

A wide variety of microorganisms are being used as starter cultures in food processing: lactic acid bacteria in dairy industry, pediococci and micrococci in meat production and yeasts for the production of bakery products and wines.[1] Starter cultures are usually handled in liquid, frozen or dried form. Due to increased shelf-life and free flowability, storage and handling of dried starter cultures is easy compared to liquid or frozen starters.[2,3] As no free water is present the risk of bacterial infections is minimized.[4]

Various drying methods including lyophilization and vacuum drying are available for thermally sensitive materials like proteins. Usually only small volumes can be handled by these methods and production costs are high compared to spray drying or fluidized-bed drying.[5,6] Thermal drying methods are suitable for the production of dried bulk cultures such as lactic acid bacteria or active dry yeast at relatively low costs. However, thermal methods involve the risk of cell damage and protein denaturation due to temperature effects as shown by the loss of cell content at rehydration caused by cell membrane destruction.[7] Additionally cell components especially enzymes, may be significantly denatured causing loss of activity when high temperatures are applied at still high water content of the microorganisms.[8] Membrane destruction and enzyme denaturation lead to decreased viability of the microorganisms. In this investigation the yeast *S. cerevisiae*—which was dried in a fluidized-bed drier—was used as an example for the thermal drying of thermosensitive bulk products.

MODELLING CONCEPT

Viability and residual enzyme activity are influenced by the drying history and the drying parameters, i.e. drying time, gas and particle temperatures, maximum temperatures and moisture content of the microorganisms. Enzyme deactivation in the course of the drying process can be calculated knowing the relation between drying history and denaturation kinetics.

Mathematical Description of Enzyme Deactivation

For most enzymes thermal deactivation kinetics have been examined in pure solutions. However, thermal deactivation at 'in vivo' conditions may lead to results different to those obtained for pure solutions.

The moisture content of the thermally treated microorganisms plays an important role for the protection of the enzymes.[8,9]

To describe the influence of moisture content and protection mechanism of whole cells on the kinetic parameters of enzyme deactivation, thermal denaturation studies were carried out using whole microorganism pellets instead of dissolved pure enzymes.

The thermal deactivation of enzymes was described to follow first-order reaction kinetics.[10,11] The deactivation rate r_d of the enzymes, i.e. the loss of active enzyme per time is given by:

$$r_d = \frac{dA_E}{dt} = -k_d A_E \qquad (1)$$

with A_E being the concentration of active enzyme and k_d the rate constant for the deactivation.

Using the Arrhenius equation for temperature dependence of the rate constant k_d, the relative activity after a given time at temperature T is:

$$\ln \frac{A_E(t)}{A_{E,0}} = k_\infty \exp\left[-E_d/RT\right]t \qquad (2)$$

The dependence of enzyme deactivation on moisture content is expressed according to Luyben and coworkers[12] with the frequency factor k_∞ and the deactivation energy E_d being functions of the microorganism moisture content.

Mathematical Modelling of the Drying Process

The drying behaviour of the yeast pellet is described with means of a shrinking core model.[13] During the constant drying period the water evaporates from the surface of the pellet. The temperature T_s of the particle stays constant and can be calculated according to Krischer,[14] depending on the inlet drying gas temperature only. In the course of the drying process the particle diameter decreases with decreasing water content $\bar{X}$. The particle diameter d_p is calculated as a function of moisture content $\bar{X}$ by mass balance.[3]

When the moisture content of the yeast particle has reached the critical value X_{crit}, the drying behaviour changes. A drying front recedes into the pellet, delivering a shell of dry yeast cells with the hygroscopic moisture content X_{hygr} and a core of wet material with the critical moisture content X_{crit} (Fig. 1).

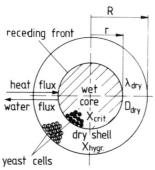

Fig. 1. Shrinking core model for a microorganism pellet; X_{crit}: critical moisture content of the yeast (kg water/kg d.s.); X_{hygr}: hygroscopic moisture content of the yeast (kg water/kg d.s.).

While water evaporates from the surface of the receding front, the dry shell becomes an additional vapour diffusion barrier. The diffusion coefficient and the thermal conductivity of the dry shell are D_{dry} and λ_{dry} respectively.

According to Schlünder[15] and Zabeschek[16] the water flux from the particle into the gas is given by

$$\dot{n}_w = \frac{\beta}{1 + B_i'\left(\dfrac{R}{r} - 1\right)} \frac{pM_w}{RT_m} \ln\left[\frac{Y_W^* + 0\cdot622}{Y_W + 0\cdot622}\right] \tag{3}$$

where β is the mass transfer coefficient according to Martin.[17]

The diffusion coefficient D_{dry} is a fraction of the molecular diffusion coefficient of water in air D:

$$D_{\text{dry}} = \frac{D}{\mu} \tag{4}$$

where μ, the diffusion resistance factor, is a function of the moisture content of the material, as vapour diffusion is assumed to be the only transport mechanism. This is confirmed by the experimental results presented in this paper as well as by other authors.[18,19] The heat flux from bulk gas to particle can be calculated by:

$$\dot{q} = \frac{\alpha}{1 + Bi\left(\dfrac{R}{r} - 1\right)} \frac{\Delta hv}{c_{p,w}} \ln\left[1 + \frac{c_{p,w}}{\Delta hv}(T - T_s)\right] \tag{5}$$

The heat transfer coefficient α is calculated similarly to the mass transfer coefficient β as given by Martin.[17] The thermal conductivity λ_{dry} for yeasts at hygroscopic moisture content was taken from Josic.[2] The evaporation enthalpy Δh_v was evaluated for the particles at surface temperature T_s of the core surface.

Equations (3) and (5) describe the local mass and heat flux for the single particle. For the fluidized-bed drying the following assumptions were made:

(i) ideal mixing of particles, i.e. identical particle temperature and moisture content in the whole bed;
(ii) plug flow of fluidizing gas;
(iii) adiabatic conditions for heat and mass transfer between solids and gas phase.

For a volume element $A_t \, dz$ with A_t being the cross-section area of the fluidized bed, mass and enthalpy balances (Eqs. (6) and (7)) for water in the fluidizing gas yield:[16]

$$\dot{n}_w(z) \, dA - \frac{d(\dot{m}_g Y_w)}{dz} \, dz = \frac{d(\Delta m_g Y_w)}{dt} \tag{6}$$

$$\dot{n}_w(z) \, dA h_w - \dot{q}(z) \, dA - \frac{d(\dot{m}_g h_g)}{dz} \, dz = \frac{d(\Delta m_g h_g)}{dt} \tag{7}$$

where A is the total surface area of the particles, $\dot{m}_g$ the mass flow rate of gas, h_w and h_g are the enthalpies for water and the fluidizing gas respectively, Δm_g is mass of the fluidizing gas in the volume element $A_t \, dz$.

The change of the total surface area of the particles is described by

$$dA = a A_t (1 - \varepsilon) \, dz \tag{8}$$

with ε the voidage of the fluidized bed. With Eqs. (3) and (5) of the shrinking core model the coupled unsteady state differential equation system was solved by means of a computer (PRIME 9950) using Runge–Kutta–Merson method.[21]

Combination of Enzyme Deactivation Kinetics and Drying Process

Using the shrinking core model for the description of the drying process in a fluidized-bed drier, the total enzyme deactivation is the combined effect of deactivation in the shell with hydroscopic moisture content X_{hygr} and temperature T_m and the deactivation of enzymes in the wet core with critical moisture content X_{crit} and temperature T_s. Equation (1) then yields:

$$\frac{dA_E}{dt} = -\left[k_d(X_{crit}, T_s)A_E \frac{r^2}{R^2} + k_d(X_{hygr}, T_m)A_E\left(1 - \frac{r^2}{R^2}\right)\right] \quad (9)$$

Thus combining Eq. (9) with the Arrhenius equation for the enzyme deactivation rate constant k_d and the mathematical model for fluidized-bed drying, the enzyme deactivation for any state in the course of the drying process can be calculated.

EXPERIMENTAL MATERIALS AND METHODS

Baker's yeast (*S. cerevisiae*) was obtained from Deutsche Hefewerke (DHW, type DZ). The yeast pellets were either produced by means of an edge mill delivering pellets of about 0·8 mm diameter or by extrusion with mean diameters of about 0·5 mm. The drying experiments were performed in a laboratory fluidized-bed drier (UNIGLATT) with 0·15 m diameter or a technical scale fluid bed of 1 m diameter (Glatt WSG 60). The bed mass was about 1 kg and 40 kg respectively. Yeast samples with different drying history, temperature, moisture content as function of time were rehydrated and analyzed for moisture content and enzyme activity of different enzymes (alcohol dehydrogenase [E.C. 1.1.1.1], glucose-6-phosphate dehydrogenase [E.C. 1.1.1.49], 6-phosphogluconate dehydrogenase [E.C. 1.1.1.44]). The enzyme activity was determined using standard assays[22] measuring the adsorbance in a spectral photometer (Shimadzu UV 240) at 340 nm and 30 °C. The activity is expressed in IU/mg Protein (μmol substrate/min × mg Protein).

The total amount of protein was determined by Biuret reaction[23] with serum albumin as reference material (spectral photometer, 548 nm). Rehydration of the yeast pellets was performed in a KH_2PO_4-buffer (pH = 7·2) at $T = 37$ °C, the dry yeast concentration being 7 mg/ml buffer. The buffer contained 1 mmol EDTA and 1 mmol dithiothreitol. After rehydration, the yeast cells were disrupted by an ultrasonic disintegrator (Fritsch, Laborette 19) with an output power of 150 W for 1 min. The disintegration was carried out in a cooled device keeping the temperature of the yeast suspension below 35 °C. For the spectrophotometric measurement the suspensions were centrifuged at 2000 g for 10 min.

The enzyme deactivation was carried out using whole yeast pellets with varying moisture content from initial value $\varphi = 0.67$ to $\varphi = 0.10$. To decrease the moisture content the pellets were slowly dried in a vacuum drier (CHRIST). Subsequently, the pellets were enclosed in plastic bags and kept in a water bath for varying time intervals. After heat treatment the yeast pellets were rehydrated and the enzymatic activity (ADH, 6-PGDH) was determined as described above.

The viability of the yeast cells was measured with a Warburg apparatus to determine CO_2-production and with an oxygen-probe (WTW, OXI 91) for the O_2-demand after rehydration. For the viability measurements yeast was rehydrated in KH_2PO_4-solution with pH = 4.5 and 0.030 mmol glucose solution was added. The concentration of dry yeast was 0.7 mg/ml solution.

RESULTS AND DISCUSSION

Enzymes in microorganism cells show a higher thermal stability than pure isolated enzymes. In Fig. 2 this effect is shown for the two enzymes ADH and 6-PGDH deactivated in whole yeast cells and in a solution. Pure enzymes as well as the whole yeast pellets were treated

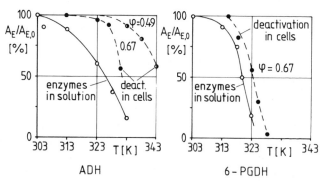

ADH   6-PGDH

Fig. 2. Relative activity $A_E/A_{E,0}$ for the enzymes ADH and 6-PGDH as a function of temperature T and moisture content φ. Enzymes (○) with concentrations of ADH 2×10^{-3} mg/ml and of 6-PGDH 0.1 mg/ml were incubated at various temperatures for 20 min in 0.1 M phosphate buffer, pH 7.2, containing 1 mmol EDTA and 1 mmol dithiothreitol. Yeast pellets with various moisture contents $\varphi = 0.67$ (●) or $\varphi = 0.49$ (◑) were heated at various temperatures for 20 min and after heating rehydrated in the buffer as described above. The data for isolated 6-PGDH were taken from Veronese and coworkers.[24] Enzyme activity after heating was determined using standard assay conditions.[22]

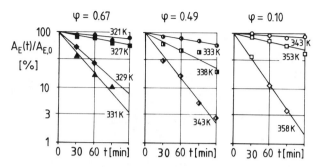

ig. 3. Residual activity $A_E(t)/A_{E,0}$ of ADH in yeast for varying moisture contents ($\varphi = 0.67; 0.49; 0.10$) and temperatures as a function of heating time t.

t different temperatures ranging from 303 K to 343 K for 20 min. After heat treatment the enzymes were extracted from the cells and ctivity was measured as described above. The data for isolated pure -PGDH were taken from Veronese and coworkers.[24] The enzymes of he yeast cell extracts show a significantly higher heat stability than the ure enzymes in the buffer solution. With decreasing moisture content ? the enzymes become more stable. For that reason the experiments ɔ evaluate the thermal deactivation kinetics of the enzymes had to be erformed using intact yeast cells.

The deactivation for endogenous ADH of yeast at different moisture ontents as a function of temperature and time is shown in Fig. 3. ɩctivity is expressed as a fraction of initial enzyme activity which is erived for untreated yeast. Increased heating time and increased emperature lead to lower enzyme activities. At high yeast moisture ontents ($\varphi_0 = 0.67$ kg water/kg yeast) the enzymes are more sensitive ɔ temperature than at low moisture content. To demonstrate this able I shows the temperatures for 50% ADH deactivation at a eating time of 30 min.

TABLE I
Alcohol dehydrogenase deactivation as a function of moisture content

Moisture content (kg water/kg yeast)	Temperature at which 50% deactivation occurs (K)
0·67	329
0·49	342
0·10	356

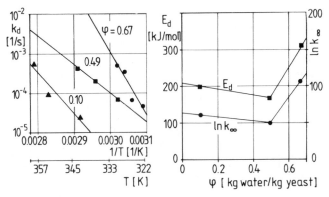

Fig. 4. *Arrhenius plot of enzyme deactivation rate (left) and deactivation energy E_d and frequency factor k_∞ as a function of moisture content φ (right).*

The dependence of deactivation energy E_d and frequency factor k_∞ on moisture content is shown in Fig. 4: both parameters show a minimum at a moisture content of about $\varphi = 0.49$. This effect has been described as well for the enzyme ribonuclease from wheat by Multon and Guilbot.[10] This might be due to the fact that water at the moisture content corresponding to the minimum value of activation energy has a maximum catalytic efficiency.

Enzyme deactivation can now be calculated combining these experimentally derived deactivation parameters with the parameters of

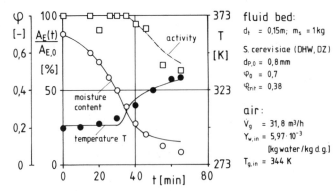

Fig. 5. *Comparison of calculated (lines) and experimental results for laboratory scale fluid bed drying of yeast; (□) ADH activity $A_E(t)/A_{E,0}$; (○) moisture content φ; (●) particle temperature.*

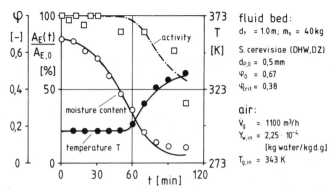

Fig. 6. Comparison of calculated (lines) and experimental results for technical scale fluid bed drying of yeast; (□) G-6PDH/6-PGDH activity $A_E(t)/A_{E,0}$; (○) moisture content φ; (●) particle temperature.

the drying process. Figures 5 and 6 show experimental and calculated data for fluidized-bed drying processes in laboratory and technical scale respectively, and for the activity loss in ADH, with respect to G-6-PDH/6-PGDH. The model for the fluidized-bed drier shows good agreement with the experimental data. Water content and bed temperature for the falling rate drying period are calculated using the diffusion resistance factor $\mu = 15$, which was evaluated by separate drying experiments.

The critical moisture content at the end of the constant drying period is $X_{crit} = 0.6$ (kg water/kg d.s.). The calculated combined data for these drying processes and the deactivation kinetics of the enzymes fit the experimentally activity retention in the course of the drying process very well. For viability measurements (CO_2-production, O_2-demand) no direct relation with enzymatic activity could be found. Viability data for the microorganism cells show lower values than enzyme activity for the same time and temperature of heat treatment. This effect may be due to membrane destruction of the cells.

ACKNOWLEDGEMENT

The authors wish to thank Dr Kirk from Deutsche Hefewerke Wandsbek/Hamburg for his helpful advice in microbiology as well as for material and technical support and Professor Dr Kasche, Department of Biology, University of Bremen, for advice in enzymatic analysis. The laboratory scale fluid bed drier (UNIGLATT) was loaned from the GLATT company. Appreciation is expressed to Miss A. Fuß, S. S. Uong and H.-J. Höwener for experimental assistance.

REFERENCES

1. Liepe, H. U. Starter cultures in meat production. In H. J. Rehm: *Biotechnology*, Vol. 3, (H. J. Rehm, Ed.) Verlag Chemie, pp. 400–23, 1982.
2. Robinson, R. K. Starter cultures for milk and meat processing. In *Biotechnology*, Vol. 5 (H. J. Rehm, Ed.) Verlag Chemie, pp. 192–208, 1982.
3. Zimmermann, K., Egerer, B. and Bauer, W. Flow and fluidization behaviour of yeasts in gas/solid fermentation and drying. *J. Chem. Engng Symp.* Ser. No. 91, pp. 257–69, 1985.
4. Philipp, S. Starterkulturen in der milchverarbeitenden Industrie. *Lebensmitteltechnik* **10:** 518–21, 1984.
5. Simon, E. J. Die Trocknung aktiver Backhefe in der Wirbelschicht. *Chemische Technik* **10:** 7, 703–7, 1981.
6. Külling, W. and Simon, E. J. Trocknung von Lebensmitteln im Wirbelbett. *Zeitschrift für Lebensmitteltechnologie und Verfahrenstechnik*, **29:** 1, 1–4, 1978.
7. Beker, M. J. *et al.* Characteristics of cellular membranes at rehydration of dehydrated yeast, *S. cerevisiae*. *Eur. J. Appl. Microbiol. Biotechnol.* **19:** 347–52, 1984.
8. Rothe, M. Thermoresistenz von Weizenenzymen in Abhängigkeit von der Feuchte des Mediums. *Ernährungsforschung* **10:** 29–36, 1965.
9. Daemen, A. L. H. The destruction of enzymes and bacteria during the spray-drying of milk and whey. *Neth. Milk Diary J.* **35:** 133–44, 1981.
10. Multon, J. L. and Guilbot, A. Water activity in relation to the thermal inactivation of enzymic proteins. In *Water Activity: Influences on Food Quality* (L. B. Rockland, and G. F. Stewart, Eds.) Academic Press, New York, 1981.
11. Labuza, T. P. Nutrient losses during drying and storage of dehydrated foods. *CRC Critical Reviews in Food Technology* **9:** 217–40, 1972.
12. Luyben, K. Ch. A. M. *et al.* Enzyme degradation during drying. *Biotech. Bioeng.* **24:** 533–52, 1982.
13. Hallström, A. and Wimmerstedt, R. Drying of porous granular materials. *Chem. Eng. Sci.* **38:** 9, 1507–16, 1983.
14. Krischer, O. and Kast, W., *Die wissenschaftlichen Grundlagen der Trocknungstechnik.* Springer Verlag, Berlin-Heidelberg-New York, 1978.
15. Schlünder, E. U. Fortschritte und Entwicklungstendenzen bei der Auslegung von Trocknern für vorgeformte Trocknungsgüter. *Chem.-Ing.-Tech.* **48:** 3, 190–9, 1976.
16. Zabeschek, G. Experimentelle Bestimmung und analytische Beschreibung der Trocknungsgeschwindigkeit rieselfähiger, kapillarporöser Güter in der Wirbelschicht. Thesis, Karlsruhe, 1977.
17. Martin, H. Wärme- und Stoffübertragung in der Wirbelschicht. *Chem.-Ing.-Tech.* **52:** 3, 199–209, 1980.
18. Haertling, M. Vorausberechnung von Trocknungsverlaufkurvne. VT *Verfahrenstechnik* **13:** 12, 923–7, 1979.
19. Görling, P. Trocknung von Kartoffelstücken. Thesis, TH Darmstadt, 1954.

20. Josic, D. Optimization of Process Conditions for the Production of Active Dry Yeast, *Lebensm. u. Technol.* 15 (1982) 1, 5/14.
21. Numerical Algorithms Group, FORTRAN Library Manual, Mark II, Vol. 2, Mayfield House, 256 Banbury Road, Oxford, 1984.
22. Bergmeier, H. U. *Methods of Enzymatic Analysis, Vol. 2,* 3rd edn. Verlag Chemie, Weinheim, Deerfield Beach, Florida, Basel, 1983.
23. Hill, F. Laboratory Manual: Biuret reaction, Deutsche Hefewerke, Hamburg/ Wandsbek.
24. Veronese, F. M. *et al.* General stability of thermophilic enzymes. Studies on 6-phosphogluconate dehydrogenase from *Bacillus stearothermophilus* and yeast. *J. Appl. Biochem.* **6:** 39–47, 1984.

40

COMPARISON OF DIFFERENT DRYING TECHNIQUES FOR PROCESSING ACTIVE DRY YEAST FOR USE IN FERMENTORS WITH IMMOBILIZED CELLS

D. TAEYMANS, E. ROELANS and J. LENGES

CERIA—Station d'Essai d'Analy, Avenue Emile Cryzon 1
1070 Brussels, Belgium

ABSTRACT

Single cell material can be dried to produce special physical forms which enable their use as biocatalysts. Biomass normally has a limit of time and temperature to which it can be exposed without creating unacceptable changes. The optimal drying conditions required to obtain active dry yeast (ADY) must be determined. Choice lies between long drying times at low temperatures or brief exposure to more severe conditions.

Brewers' yeast (a strain of Saccharomyces cerevisiae) *was chosen as whole cell material. The yeast was dried on a pilot plant scale in a batch fluid-bed drier or in a spray drier. Conditions (initial dry matter concentration, temperature and addition of thermoprotective agents) were varied in order to improve the relation between water activity, cell viability, fermentative power and glutathione release. Brewers' yeasts were also immobilized in calcium alginate beads before drying on the fluid-bed drier. Water activity appeared to have a great effect on the thermal resistance and the preservation of dried biomass and depended on the operating air temperature and addition of thermoprotective agent. The yeasts immobilized in calcium alginate beads were dried at the most favourable temperature (30 °C). Cell viability was more than 80% after rehydration with wort.*

INTRODUCTION

Drying of whole cell material is being utilized to produce special physical forms which enable their use as biocatalysts. It is known that

the basic quantitative component of the cell is water, which performs
number of functions.

Free water is a medium and substrate for biochemical reactions
while bound water determines the structure of biological macro
molecules and the interaction of various molecules. Cell dehydration
under certain conditions may cause transition of living organisms into
an anabiotic state. Cytological studies of the anabiotic state of yeast
organisms have demonstrated that dehydration causes an intensive
folding of the cytoplasmic membrane. The same conditions also cause
damage to the nuclear membrane rigidity. Structural damage to
intracellular membranes upon dehydration–rehydration is accom
panied by functional transformations as well.

During drying, the state of the *Saccharomyces cervisiae* cells may be
characterized by one of the four regions relative to the state of water
a solution region, a gel region, a mobile adsorbed water region and
localized water region. The most important differences of the physico
logical properties of the cells are observed when the cell passes from
the first region to the second region. In the gel region, the molecules
of water may no more serve as continuous solvent for biochemical

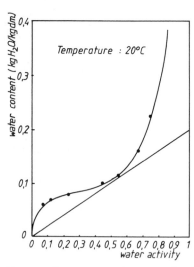

Fig. 1. Sorption isotherms of S.
cerevisiale.

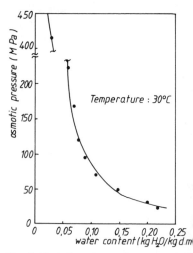

Fig. 2. Variation of osmotic pressure in the
cell of S. cerevisial as a function of the
water content.

eactions and this implies modifications of conformation of the high
olymers of the cell.[1]

The water activity may serve as a parameter to predict the retention
f several important properties by the microorganism. The sorption
sotherms represent the relation between the water content in the cell
nd its water activity (see Fig. 1).

The cell disruption following the cell wall rupture is combined with
he formation of protoplasts sensitive to the variations of osmotic
ressure. It has been shown[2] that the pressure increases in the cell
hen the water content in the cell decreases as shown in Fig. 2.

During rehydration, the dried yeasts absorb water until an equi-
brium is obtained. At the same time, the cell loses low molecular
eight compounds, which indicates a considerably increased per-
eability of the cytoplasmic membrane. Among substances leaking
rom the cell are amino acids, vitamins, nucleotides, inorganic
ompounds and others.

MATERIAL AND METHODS

n industrial strain of *Saccharomyces cerevisiae* (brewers' yeast) was
sed for the different drying experiments. Estimations of survivors
fter dehydration–rehydration were made on Petri plates, fermenta-
ive power was measured with a Warburg respirometer, and
pectrophotometry was used to measure the leakage of low molecular
eight compounds, such as glutathione. The yeasts were dried in a
pray drier or a fluid-bed dryer where it was also possible to dry
nmobilized yeasts in calcium alginate beads. Rehydration was
chieved in water wort or another rich medium at different tempera-
ures in order to improve the resulting survival of yeasts.

RESULTS

able I shows the results obtained for the spray drier (air inlet
emperature: 190 °C, air outlet temperature: 60 °C) with a mean drying
ate estimated at 2 kg water/h. The best survival obtained after
ehydration was 0·02%.

For the fluid-bed dryer, the mean drying rate was estimated at
·2 kg water evaporated per hour with the best final survival of 30%

TABLE I
Spray drying of yeasts (inlet air 190 °C, outlet air 60 °C)

	Water activity	Survival (N/N_0) (%)	Fermentative power	Glutathione release (%)
Without thermo-protection	0·335	0	0	78
With glycerol	0·345	0·02	0	25·5
With sodium alginate	0·305	0·005	0	29·0

(see Table II). Survival of yeast is markedly influenced by the water contents of the yeast as shown in Fig. 3.

The use of fermentors with immobilized yeasts in calcium alginate beads (common at the Unité de Biotechnologie, C.E.R.I.A.-I.I.F.-I.M.C.) has prompted the attempts at stabilization of immobilized yeasts by drying. It seemed that the environment of the cell was favourable for preserving the viability of the cells.

Different experiments were carried out on a batch fluid-bed dryer and results are shown in Fig. 4 where the influence of the bed height on the drying rate is shown and in Fig. 5 where the influence of the air flow rate on the yeast survival is shown.

The final yeast survival was better when the air flow rate decreased enough to cause an aggregative fluidization state with good heat transfer even though the final water activities for the two curves are similar. This important phenomenon may indicate that the carbohy-

TABLE II
Fluid-bed drying of yeasts

	Water activity	Survival (N_1/N_0)(%)	Fermentative power	Glutathione release (%)
Air inlet temperature 30 °C				
Without thermo-protection	0·820	26·0	40%	82·6
Air outlet temperature 35 °C				
Without thermo-protection	0·700	14·0	26%	83·5
With sorbitol	—	20·0	—	—
With sodium alginate	—	30·5	—	—
Yeast immobilized in Ca alginate	—	66	—	—

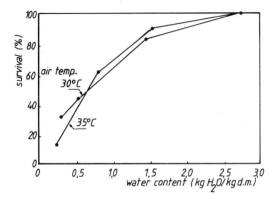

Fig. 3. Influence of the water content on the survival of yeast.

drates of the cells are consumed by respiration when the air flow rate is too high.

To prevent the deterioration of the cytoplasmic membrane and to preserve the rigidity of the cell wall, thermoprotective agents were used and mixed before gelification of the alginate beads. Table III shows the results obtained. These results showed that the final survival obtainable is very high but that the rehydration medium is very important.

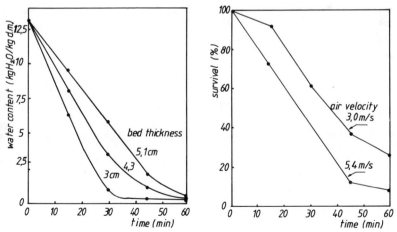

Fig. 4. Influence of bed height on drying rate.

Fig. 5. Influence of air flow rate on yeast survival.

TABLE III
Fluid-bed drying of immobilized yeasts: resulting survival after rehydration

Thermoprotective agent		Water (22 °C)		Wort (22 °C)	
		Rehydration medium			
Sorbitol	Water content (kg H_2O/kg d.m.)	0·29	0·17	0·29	0·17
	Water activity	0·72	0·68	0·72	0·68
	Survival (%)	63	54	78	57
Glycerol	Water content (kg H_2O/kg d.m.)	0·28	0·20	0·28	0·20
	Water activity	0·70	0·63	0·70	0·63
	Survival (%)	61	55	83	79

CONCLUSIONS

The use of immobilized yeast cells in continuous fermenters increase
the need for significant and stable quantities of these types of yeast
Drying may be considered as a suitable stabilization procedure.

The experimental results showed that the fluid-bed drying o
immobilized yeasts allows the preservation of high residual viabilit
(around 80%) which, together with a reduced volume and a
improved mechanical resistance, suggests possibilities for furthe
development of this process. Studies are currently in progress t
obtain a better knowledge of the behaviour and the physiology of th
yeast during the dehydration–rehydration steps.

REFERENCES

1. Koga, S. *et al.* Physical properties of cell water in partially dried *Saccharomyce
   cerevisiae. Biophys. J.* **6:** 665–74, 1966.
2. Josic, D. Optimization of process conditions for the production of active dry yeast
   Lebensm.-Wiss.-Technol. **15:** (1), 5–14, 1982.

41

EFFECT OF FREEZING CONDITIONS ON FREEZE DRYING RATE OF CONCENTRATED LIQUID FOODS

KOZO NAKAMURA, HITOSHI KUMAGAI and TOSHIMASA YANO

Department of Agricultural Chemistry, The University of Tokyo, Bunkyo-ku, Tokyo 113, Japan

ABSTRACT

The rate of freeze-drying was measured using a coffee extract in a well-instrumented experimental apparatus. The drying rate decreased gradually in the sample frozen slowly at a cooling rate of $-0.1\,°C/min$, whereas in the sample frozen rapidly the drying rate started to decrease significantly before the water content reached the level of unfreezable water. Cracks were observed in the rapidly frozen sample after drying, probably resulting in decreased contact between the sample and the plate heater and/or the slightly heat-conductive wall of the sample vessel. On the other hand, the vapor permeability was affected by the freezing temperature in our previous study. Therefore accumulation and analysis of more data are needed to elucidate whether the effect of freezing conditions is due to vapor permeation or heat transfer.

INTRODUCTION

Freeze-dried liquid foods such as tea and coffee exhibit better taste and aroma retention, less chemical degradation, and faster dissolution rates than the products of alternative evaporative drying processes. On the other hand the slow drying rate and the high cost of drying equipment are the main drawbacks of freeze-drying, and it is very important to be able to predict the drying rate and the temperature distribution in the materials in order to optimize the design of freeze-drying equipment and to select the conditions of drying.

The rate of freeze-drying is determined by a combination of two

445

transport phenomena, heat and mass transfers. The uniform retreating ice-front (URIF) model[1] has been used to analyze the experimental results of freeze-drying in consideration of the sample-surface resistance to vapor permeation.[2] The physical properties and the rate constants are involved in the equations of the URIF model. They are influenced to different degrees by the state of water in the frozen sample. For example, the volume fraction of ice or voidage should be calculated with respect to water bound and/or unfrozen in the concentrated amorphous solution. In the theoretical analysis of freeze-drying, however, the water in a sample is often assumed to be frozen completely. This assumption is not correct particularly in the case of concentrated samples.[2]

The almost constant rate of drying appearing in the early stage was analyzed with the modified URIF model incorporating voidage data measured by the DSC technique. The influence of initial water content on the vapor permeability, k, and on the surface resistance, R_s, was elucidated,[2] however, the vapor permeability depended not only on the initial water content but also on the temperature of the freezing process.

The influence of the freezing conditions before drying upon the transport properties during drying have been discussed[1] and an equation has been presented to relate the permeability k to certain parameters describing the porous structure of the dried material, that is, its voidage, pore size and tortuosity.[3] The relationship between the formation of the porous structure and the freezing conditions has not been well elucidated. Our study of freeze-drying was continued with the aim of measuring the drying rate using a sample frozen under controlled conditions. The main objective of this work was to optimize the freezing conditions and elucidate the ice morphology in frozen liquid foods.

MATERIALS AND METHODS

Experimental Material and its Characteristics

The concentrated coffee extract was obtained from an industrial manufacturer. A part of the frozen extract was melted one or two days before each experiment, and diluted with water to the desired solids concentration. The solution was degassed at a reduced pressure and stored in a refrigerator.

The amount of unfreezable water was measured by differential scanning calorimetry (DSC) at a heating rate of 5 °C/min after prior cooling down to at least −75 °C at the rate of 10 °C/min using the low temperature type of DSC (Rigaku Denki Kogyo Co., Ltd., L-DSC). 28·6% of the water contained in the original concentrated extract (solid matter 39·3%) was found to be unfreezable, while 13·5% was unfreezable in the solution containing 19·7% of solid matter. The amount of unfreezable water, based on the dry matter was 0·442 g/g for the original extract and 0·550 g/g for the diluted solution.

Experimental Apparatus

The sample vessel and the experimental freeze-drying apparatus are shown in Fig. 1.

The inner diameter and depth of the cylindrical sample vessel were 0·057 m and 0·030 m respectively. The bottom plate was of aluminum

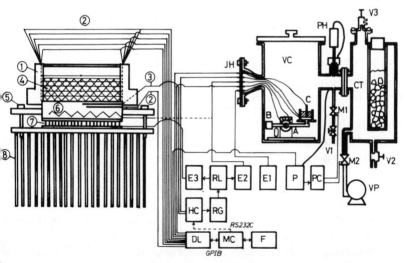

Fig. 1. *Experimental apparatus for cooling and freeze-drying. 1, sample vessel; 2, thermo-couple (C-C); 3, thermo-couple (Pt); 4, sample solution; 5, bolts; 6, heater (aluminum plate with micro-heater); 7, thermo module; 8, cooling fins. A, angular displacement detector; B, counter-balance; CT, cold-trap; C, sample vessel; E1, E2 and E3, electric power for element A, heater and thermo module; HC, controller of heater temperature; JH, hermetic connector; M1 and M2, solenoid valve; PC, pressure controller; P, Pirani gauge; PH, Pirani gauge head; VC, vacuum chamber (0·25 m I.D. × 0·3 m); VP, vacuum pump; V1, V2 and V3, valves; RL, relay contact; RG, regulator; DL, data logger; MC, micro computer; F, floppy disk unit.*

and functioned as heater or cooler. The wall was of hard porous plastic treated to prevent the liquid from permeating. The wall was covered with flexible porous plastic for improved thermal insulation. The five copper–constantan (C-C) thermocouple wires were spaced 0·003 m apart by means of a frame which could be slid vertically along grooves in the wall of the sample vessel.

A device shown as 'thermo module' (Fig. 1) was used for heat removal in controlled freezing of the sample solution. The sample vessel and the thermo module were mounted on the cooling fins and the fins were immersed in a low-temperature bath.

The freeze-drying vacuum chamber was of 0·25 m inside diameter and 0·3 m height. The device measuring the change in weight of the sample was placed in the vacuum chamber. The chamber was cooled by immersion of its base in the coolant and by circulation of the coolant through the flexible metallic tube wound around the upper part of the chamber.

The electrical signals for sample and chamber temperatures as well as sample weight and chamber pressure were all put through a data logger (Takeda Rikken Industry Co., Ltd., TR2723) to a personal computer (Fujitsu Ltd., FM-8), and the data were stored on a floppy disk. The heating or cooling temperature was controlled by a controller (Chino, SG-1000) to which a Pt thermocouple was connected from the aluminum plate.

Method

24 ml of the sample solution containing 19·7% solid matter was poured into the sample vessel. The sample vessel and the cooling unit were transferred to the cooling bath. The temperature of the aluminum plate was decreased to −30 °C at each chosen cooling rate after the temperature of the sample reached 0 °C. The sample vessel was left overnight at −30 °C, and the next day was transferred into the vacuum chamber and the freeze-drying operation was started.

The cooling of the vacuum chamber was started after the vacuum pump had been switched on to prevent drops of water and ice from attaching to the vessel wall before the start of freeze-drying.

RESULTS AND DISCUSSION

Figure 2 shows the freezing curves of the coffee extract as obtained by the five thermocouples. Supercooling was observed to a greater extent

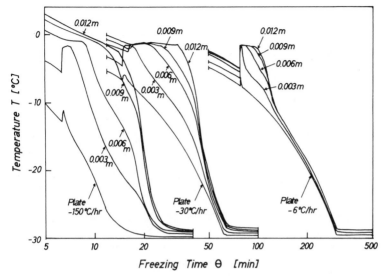

Fig. 2. Freezing curves for coffee extract (solid content 19·7%), obtained by 5 thermocouples at 3 different freezing temperatures.

at the slower freezing rates. The temperature of the samples cooled at rates of −6 °C/h (i.e. −0·1 °C/min) and −30 °C/h (i.e. −0·5 °C/min) rose to −1·5 °C soon after the supercooling, and this temperature was taken to be the freezing point of the sample solution. The freezing curve for the sample cooled rapidly (−150 °C/h or −2·5 °C/min) was irregular in comparison with those of the samples frozen more slowly. The phenomenon of supercooling did not appear in the upper part of the sample cooled rapidly.

The frozen samples were freeze-dried at the temperature of the aluminum plate, −10 °C, and at a pressure of 10 Pa (i.e. 0·1 mbar). The drying rates and the chamber temperature changed as shown in Fig. 3. The initial decrease in the drying rates may have been partly due to cooling of the vacuum chamber. The chamber temperature changed similarly in the three experiments, so that it can be assumed that the three samples were freeze-dried under the same conditions.

The drying rate for the slowly-frozen sample did not decrease at the later stages of drying as rapidly as that of the sample frozen at the cooling rate of −150 °C/h which started to decrease before the water content reached the level of unfreezable water. Cracks were observed

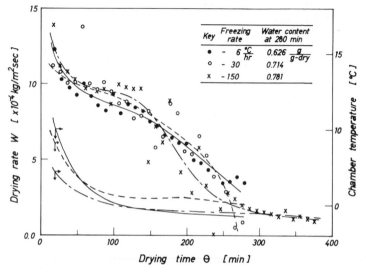

Fig. 3. Drying rate curves for 19·7% coffee extract frozen at different freezing rates.

in the dried product obtained from the rapidly frozen sample. The cracks were presumably generated during drying and probably reduced the contact between the sample and the heater plate or the wall. The generation of cracks might have decreased the rate of heat transfer and partly contributed to the reduction of the drying rate.

The rate of freeze-drying was influenced by the freezing conditions. The slower freezing rate was more preferable to keep the drying rate from falling significantly in the later stages of drying. Whether the effect of freezing rate was affected by vapor permeation or heat transfer could not be determined. More data need to be accumulated and analyzed.

REFERENCES

1. King, C. J. *Freeze-Drying of Foods,* CRC Press, 1971.
2. Kumagai, H., Nakamura, K. and Yano, T. Freeze-drying of concentrated liquid foods by back-face heating. *Proc. Fourth Int. Drying Symposium,* Vol. 2, Kyoto, p. 458, 1984.
3. Mellor, J. D. *Fundamentals of Freeze-Drying.* Academic Press New York, 1978.

42

SOLAR DRYING CHARACTERISTICS OF SULTANA RAISINS

G. S. RAOUZEOS and G. D. SARAVACOS*

Department of Chemical Engineering, National Technical University, GR-10682, Athens, Greece

* Department of Food Science, Rutgers University, New Brunswick, New Jersey 08903, U.S.A.

ABSTRACT

The drying characteristics of Sultana seedless grapes were investigated in a laboratory solar installation, consisting of a plate solar collector, a cabinet dryer, a thermal storage bed, and an auxiliary heater. The effect of various pretreatments on the drying rate of the grapes at constant temperature was studied in a laboratory tunnel dryer. Dipping of the grapes in a hot alkali solution increased the drying rate substantially. Addition of 2% ethyl oleate to the dipping solution improved further the drying rate. Increasing the air velocity in the dryer from 0·2 to 2·5 m/s accelerated the drying of the pretreated grapes.

Solar drying of the grapes was studied in two modes of operation of the installation: (1) Intermittent operation, involving heating of the process air in the solar collector and direct utilization of the hot air in the dryer during day-time. (2) Continuous operation, involving air heating in the collector, direct drying during day-time, and utilization of the thermal storage bed and the auxiliary heater during the night. Intermittent drying required 30–66·5 h, depending on the pretreatment of the grapes and the air velocity. Shorter times (19–60 h) and a higher quality dried product were obtained in the continuous operation of the solar system.

INTRODUCTION

Dried raisins are a commercially important fruit product in Mediterranean countries, Australia and the USA. Nearly 100 000 tons of

Sultana seedless raisins are produced yearly in Greece and most of the product is exported.

Raisins are produced by the traditional sun-drying process, i.e. exposing the ripe grapes to the solar radiation in the field for several days. This method utilizes a free energy source, but it has several disadvantages, such as long drying time, contamination of the product, and product losses due to adverse weather conditions. Application of fuel-consuming mechanical dryers could improve the drying operation, but the high cost of fuel makes the method less economical. Solar energy could replace conventional fuel in mechanical drying. Solar drying appears to have a potential for raisins and other fruits in regions of high solar radiation, such as Southern Greece.

Experimental data on the drying time and the quality of sun dried Sultana raisins were published in 1965.[1] The effects of pretreatments on the drying time and the quality of grapes and other waxy fruits have been reported.[2–4] Dipping of these fruits in solutions of ethyl oleate was found to accelerate drying and improve the quality of the dried product. A similar effect was observed in the drying of corn.[5]

The rising cost of fuels has created an interest in the application of solar energy to agricultural and industrial processes, especially drying, which requires large amounts of energy. A commercial solar dryer has been developed in California for drying raisins.[6] The development of solar dryers for Sultana grapes in the island of Crete was investigated recently in a joint project of the University of Hohenheim (W. Germany) and the Greek Ministry of Agriculture.[7] The experimental solar drying of Corinth currants in a cabinet solar dryer was described recently.[8]

Most of the work on solar drying has been concerned with the development of pilot scale or commercial dryers for a specific product. More systematic work is needed on the influence of the various products and operating parameters on the kinetics of drying.

The application of solar energy to air-heating and to drying of agricultural products was investigated during the last few years at the Technical University of Athens.[9] Sultana grapes were used as an experimental material. In another study the moisture sorption isotherms of the dried raisins were measured at various temperatures.[10] The objective of the present work was to investigate the drying rates of Sultana raisins, as affected by the pretreatment of the grapes and the drying conditions in a laboratory solar drying system.

MATERIALS AND METHODS

The Solar Drying Installation

The solar drying experiments were performed in a laboratory dryer, installed at the Athens campus of the National Technical University. The installation consisted of a flat plate solar collector for heating the drying air, a thermal storage bed, a cabinet dryer, and an auxiliary heater (Fig. 1).

The flat plate collector was designed and constructed on the basis of a detailed analysis of the various factors involved.[11,12] The collector had an effective absorbing surface of 3 m², and it was black-painted. A glass cover 3 mm thick was placed at a distance of 40 mm above the absorbing plate. The air stream was heated as it was flowing through a duct of rectangular cross section (1·50 m × 0·02 m) beneath the absorbing plate. The air duct and the absorbing plate were made of aluminum plate 0·5 mm thick. An insulation layer covered the edges and the rear side of the collector.

The thermal storage consisted of a bed of spheres 4 cm in diameter made of concrete, packed in a cylindrical vessel 0·50 m in diameter and 1·00 m high with an effective volume of 0·20 m³. The cabinet dryer of iron sheet construction was 1·20 m high with a cross section of 0·50 m × 0·50 m. The grapes were placed in single layers on screen trays and the air was passed in upflow through the product. Two centrifugal fans 1·2 and 0·5 kW circulated the air through the heating, thermal storage, and drying sections. An electrical resistance of maximum capacity 4 kW was used as an auxiliary heater. The drying installation could be operated as a one-pass or as a recirculation system.

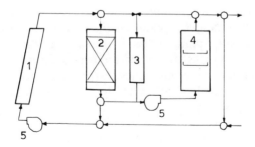

Fig. 1. Solar drying installation. 1, Flat plate solar collector; 2, thermal storage bed; 3, auxiliary heater; 4, cabinet dryer; 5, centrifugal fans.

Measuring and recording instruments were used for monitoring and recording the solar radiation, and the temperature, humidity, and velocity of the air. Drying experiments at a constant temperature were performed in a laboratory tunnel dryer, equiped with an electric heater and the necessary instruments.[13]

Materials and Experimental Procedure
Ripe Sultana seedless grapes from the Corinth area of Southern Greece were used in all experiments. The grape berries were separated from the stems and they were dipped in one of the following solutions: (1) 0·5% NaOH, (2) 0·5% NaOH + 2·0% ethyl oleate, and (3) 2·5% K_2CO_3 + 2·0% ethyl oleate. In order to determine the optimum conditions, dipping experiments were performed at room temperature, 80 or 100 °C for 10, 30, 60, or 300 s. The pretreated grapes were rinsed with cold water and they were dried as a single layer, approximately 1000 g of fresh product per tray. The drying rate was determined by weighing periodically the trays on a laboratory balance and calculating the moisture loss. Moisture content was expressed on dry basis, X (kg water/kg dry solids). The dry solids of each sample were determined by the vacuum oven method at 50 torr absolute pressure and 70 °C for 6 h. The initial moisture content was also estimated by measuring the °Brix with a refractometer.

The quality of the dried raisins was judged by the appearance of the product. A good quality product should have a light-yellow color, a soft texture and no crystallized sugars.

RESULTS

Conventional Drying Experiments
The optimum pretreatment conditions for short drying time and good quality raisins were: dipping solution temperature 80 °C, dipping time 30 s. Dipping the grapes at higher temperature resulted in a poor quality dried product. Pretreatment at ambient temperature required longer time, which had an adverse effect on the quality. Untreated grapes dried very slowly, due to the high resistance of the grape skins to the transfer of moisture.

Figure 2 shows the drying rates (dX/dt, kg water/kg solids h) versus the moisture (X, kg water/kg solids) of 3 samples of Sultana grapes processed in the laboratory tunnel dryer, which gave good quality

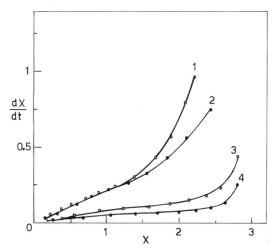

Fig. 2. Effect of pretreatment (dipping in alkali solutions for 30 s) on the drying rate (dX/dt, kg water/kg dry solids h) of Sultana grapes. Air temperature 60 °C, velocity 2·0 m/s. X, moisture content, dry basis. (1) 0·5% NaOH + 2·0% ethyl oleate, 80 °C, (2) 2·5% K_2CO_3 + 2·0% ethyl oleate, 80 °C, (3) 0·5% NaOH, 80 °C, (4) 0·5% NaOH, ambient temperature.

dried raisins. Drying was performed at 60 °C and air velocity of 2·0 m/s. The relative humidity of the drying air at 60 °C was approximately constant at 5%. The shortest drying time (14 h) was obtained with a dipping solution of 0·5% NaOH + 2·0% ethyl oleate. Dipping in a solution of 2·5% K_2CO_3 + 2·0% ethyl oleate required 19 h of drying, while the longest time (50 h) was obtained with a 0·5% NaOH dipping solution.

All the grape samples dried in the falling rate period, with no indication of a constant rate period. The grape berries were found to shrink continuously during drying, resulting in the characteristic wrinkles of the dried raisins.

Solar Drying Experiments
In the intermittent operation of the solar installation the air was first heated in the solar collector to 40–50 °C, then passed through the cabinet dryer and finally discharged into the atmosphere. There was no improvement of the intermittent operation when the air was passed through the thermal storage bed and then through the cabinet dryer.

In the continuous operation, most of the air was recirculated

TABLE I
Experimental solar drying of Sultana raisins

Sample[a]	Air velocity (m/s)	Temperature (°C)	Moisture X_0	content[b] X_f	Drying time (h)
I. Intermittent operation					
Untreated	0·2	39·3	3·60	1·14	66·5
	0·4	46·5	3·53	1·73	44·0
Treated	0·2	39·3	3·60	0·71	66·5
(0·5% NaOH)	2·5	39·1	3·60	0·28	30·5
II. Continuous operation					
Treated	0·8	48	3·18	0·16	60·0
(0·5% NaOH)					
Treated	2·0	42	3·18	0·16	19·0
(0·5% NaOH +					
2·0% ethyl oleate)					
Treated	0·8	48	3·18	0·16	54·0
(2·5% K_2CO_3 +					
2·0% ethyl oleate)	2·0	48	3·18	0·16	24·0

[a] All treatments in dipping solutions at 80 °C for 30 s.
[b] Moisture contents: X_0 (initial), X_f (final) on dry basis.

through the storage bed and the cabinet dryer, maintaining a rather uniform temperature of 42–48 °C. During the night it was necessary to use the auxiliary electrical heater.

Table I summarizes the experimental drying data of Sultana grapes in the intermittent and continuous operation of the solar installation. Figures 3 and 4 show typical drying curves of the grapes (moisture content, X versus time, t) at various pretreatments and drying conditions.

As in the preliminary experiments in the tunnel dryer, dipping of the grapes in pretreatment solutions accelerated the drying rates. Similar results were obtained in both intermittent and continuous operation.

Variation of the air velocity in the drying chamber from 0·2 to 2·5 m/s increased substantially the drying rates of the Sultana grapes. The effect of air velocity was more pronounced in the treated than the

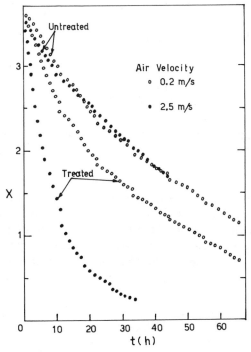

Fig. 3. *Intermittent solar drying curves of Sultana grapes (air temperature 39·1–46·5 °C, Table I). (X, moisture content, dry basis.)*

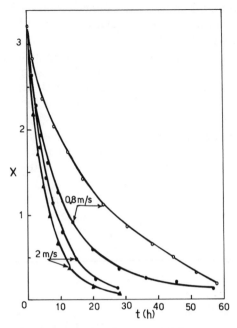

Fig. 4. Continuous solar drying curves of pretreated Sultana grapes (air temperatures 41·3–48 °C, Table I). (X, moisture content, dry basis.) ○, 0·5% NaOH; ●, 2·5% K_2CO_3 + 2·0% ethyl oleate; ▲, 0·5% NaOH + 2·0% ethyl oleate.

untreated samples, confirming the importance of the skin resistance to moisture transfer.

Intermittent solar drying required more time than continuous operation. The shortest drying time (19 h) was obtained by continuous operation of the solar system, with grapes pretreated in a solution of 0·5% NaOH + 2·0% ethyl oleate, at an air velocity of 2·0 m/s. The final moisture content of the raisins obtained in the continuous operation (16%, dry basis) is close to the moisture content of the commercial product. The drying time more than doubled when the cabinet dryer was operated at low air velocity (0·2 m/s).

DISCUSSION

Solar drying of grapes and other fruits appears to be a potential application of solar energy. Drying temperatures of 40–50 °C can be achieved with flat plate solar collectors. Drying of agricultural products is needed during the summer and early fall, when sufficient solar radiation is available.

Our experiments have shown that drying of Sultana grapes can be accomplished within 4–5 days of intermittent (day-time) operation of a simple solar installation, consisting of a flat plate collector connected to a cabinet dryer. A fan is needed to move the air at a relatively high velocity. Continuous operation reduces the drying time to 1–2 days, but additional equipment and energy is needed (thermal storage, auxiliary heating, and air-recirculation fan). A technical analysis of the solar system has shown that thermal storage has a definite potential in the drying of agricultural products.[14]

Pretreatment of the grapes in alkali solutions reduced the drying time considerably. Sodium hydroxide was more effective than potassium carbonate, but in farm application the latter may be preferred because it can be handled more safely. Our results confirmed the substantial increase of the drying rate of grapes by the addition of 2% ethyl oleate to the dipping solution. Ethyl oleate is a surface active agent which evidently acts on the skin of the grapes, facilitating the transfer of moisture from the berries to the air stream during drying.[15]

The operating conditions of the drying system are important in determining the drying time and the quality of the dried product. The temperature of the air stream depends mainly on the intensity of solar radiation and the type of solar collector. Air velocity affects strongly the drying rate, suggesting the need for forced circulation systems. Natural circulation dryers which have been suggested for the solar drying of farm crops are not suitable for fruit drying, because of the high portion of moisture which has to be removed from the fruit in a relatively short time. Other factors of dryer operation, such as tray loading and type of air flow (cross-flow or parallel), may be important and they should be considered.

ACKNOWLEDGEMENTS

The authors wish to acknowledge the support of the European Economic Community through the Cooperative Solar Project H, No. ESH-023-HE.

REFERENCES

1. Exachos, K. and Moisides, A. Investigation on the influence of various parameters on the drying time of Sultana grapes, and the quality of the final product. Institute of Technology of Plant Products Bulletin, No. 3, Athens, 1965.

2. Radler, F. The prevention of browning during the cold dipping treatment of Sultana grapes. *J. Sci. Food Agric.* **15:** 864, 1964.
3. Ponting, J. D. and McBean, D. M. Temperature and dipping treatment effects on drying times of grapes, prunes and other waxy fruits. *Food Technol.* **24:** 1403, 1970.
4. Bolin, H. R., Petrucci, V. and Fuller, G. Characteristics of mechanically harvested raisins produced by dehydration and by field drying. *J. Food Sci.* **40:** 1036, 1975.
5. Suarez, J. A., Loncin, M. and Chirife, J. A preliminary study on the effect of ethyl oleate dipping treatment on drying rate of grain corn. *J. Food Sci.* **49:** 236, 1984.
6. Carnegie, E. J., Niles, P. W. and Stine, W. B. Operation of an industrial solar drying system. Intl. Solar Energy Society Meeting. Atlanta, Georgia, 1979.
7. Eissen, W. and Muhlbauer, W. Development of low-cost solar grape dryers. UNESCO Working Group Meeting on Solar Drying. Perpignan, France, June 27–30, 1984.
8. Marousis, M., Tsambarlis, M. and Raouzeos G. Drying of grapes in a cabinet solar dryer. Preliminary results. First European Community Conference on Solar Heating, Amsterdam, Holland, 1984.
9. Saravacos, G. D. Solar drying of agricultural products. Final Report to E.E.C., Project H., No. ESH-023-HE, Brussels, 1983.
10. Saravacos, G. D., Tsiourvas, D. and Tsami, E. Effect of temperature on the adsorption isotherms of Sultana raisins. Presented at the 45th Annual I.F.T. Meeting, Atlanta, Georgia, June 9–11, 1985.
11. Yallouros, I. E., Raouzeos, G. S. and Saravacos, G. D. A parametric analysis of a flat plate solar air heater. *Technica Chronica (Athens)* **C1:** 65, 1981.
12. Duffie, J. A. and Beckman, W. A. *Solar Engineering of Thermal Processes.* Wiley-Interscience, New York, 1980.
13. Raouzeos, G. S. and Saravacos, G. D. Air-drying characteristics of starch gels. *Proc. 3rd Int. Drying Symposium* (J. C. Ashworth Ed.), Birmingham, Vol. 1, p. 91, 1982.
14. Maroulis, Z. B. Storage of solar energy in a bed of concrete (cement) balls. Doctoral dissertation, Department of Chemical Engineering, Technical University, Athens, Greece, 1984.
15. Saravacos, G. D. and Charm, S. E. Effect of surface-active agents on the dehydration of fruits and vegetables. *Food Technol.* **14:** 91, 1962.

43

EFFECTS OF PRETREATMENTS ON KINETICS
OF GRAPES DRYING

MARCO RIVA, CLAUDIO PERI and RAFFAELLA LOVINO*

Istituto di Tecnologie Alimentari, Università di Milano, Via Cebria 2, Milano 20133, Italy

* *Centro Ricerche Bonomo, Casteldelmonte, Bari, Italy*

ABSTRACT

The paper reports on kinetic data on dehydration of a white grape variety (Italia) obtained in experimental pilot-scale sun drying, air drying (at 50 °C and 70 °C air temperatures) and osmodehydration in a glycerol solution.

The results show that ethyl oleate dipping is the most effective in improving the drying process, resulting in a two-fold (in sun drying) to a six-fold (in air drying at 50 °C) increase of the rate-constant value.

Moreover, ethyl oleate dipping makes it possible to obtain better-quality products, lighter in color and with a brilliant surface appearance.

INTRODUCTION

Sun drying of grapes has been carried out for centuries in several Mediterranean countries. The process, which simply consists in exposing the grapes to direct sunlight, has been greatly improved with the selection of seedless grape varieties, having high sugar-to-acid ratio and with the application of pretreatment procedures based on dipping the grapes in a suspension of wood ashes in olive oil.

The scientific foundation of this practice recently has been demonstrated:[1,2] surfactants, resulting from the reaction of olive-oil fatty acids and the alkaline components of ashes, determine the removal of the grape's waxy coating, thus resulting in an increase of skin permeability to water transport.

Experiments with pure esters of C_{14}, C_{16} and C_{18} saturated and unsaturated fatty acids have shown that ethyl oleate is the most effective in improving drying kinetics.[2]

Recently, in systematic research into grape drying by forced air-convection, we have found that ethyl oleate has not only a simple solubilization effect on the waxy layer, but it also diffuses into the berry, considerably improving the internal water diffusion.[3]

The increasing consumer demand for natural safe and light foods is steadily expanding the use of dried grapes as such or in mixtures with other dried fruits and cereal snacks.[4] This fact has motivated our interest in the study of grape-drying processes, extending it to a number of varieties,[5] and to the comparison of dehydration techniques, including osmodehydration, which has generally been considered unsuitable for this application.[6]

This paper reports data obtained in experiments on sun and air drying and osmodehydration of a white grape variety under various operating conditions. The findings permit the comparison of the effects of the ethyl oleate pretreatment and of air temperature differences on the process kinetics and quality of dried grapes.

MATERIALS AND METHODS

A table-grape variety (Italia) was used after harvesting at full maturity followed by a few days of storage in a cold room. Samples were prepared for the drying tests by hand-removing the stems and subsequent sulphuring in a confined atmosphere under SO_2 vapours for 6 h. The average SO_2 content of the grapes was 900 ppm on fresh weight.

Table I reports the composition of sulphured fresh grapes. The data show the range of composition variations of the different batches employed in the different drying tests.

Pretreatments were carried out as follows:

(a) Dipping for 3 min at 40 °C in 3% ethyl oleate in a 2·5% K_2CO_3 solution. Grapes were then free-drained and left to rest for a few hours before drying.

(b) Dipping for 10 s at 90 °C in a 0·3% NaOH solution. Grapes were then rinsed in cold water and left to rest.

(c) Blanching in live steam (3 min at about 100 °C) followed by cooling with a cold-water rinse and subsequent resting.

TABLE I
Composition of fresh grapes (after sulphuring)

Dry matter	(g/100 g)	15–18
Absolute humidity	(kg H$_2$O/kg DM)	4·6–5·7
Reducing sugars	(g/100 gDM)	82–87
Titrable acidity	(g tart.ac./100 g DM)	2·5–2·9
Total SO$_2$	(mg SO$_2$/100 g DM)	270–350
Free SO$_2$	(mg SO$_2$/100 gDM)	150–180
Total phenolics	(mg gall.ac./100 g DM)	900–1300
Color: L hunter	(%)	30·5–32
Hue (A/B)		0·10–0·50
Average volume of berries	(cm^3)	6·5–7·2

(d) For comparison batches of grapes were also dried without any pretreatment.

(e) In one case (i.e. air drying at 50 °C), grapes were dried after manual peeling.

Drying Experiments

Air drying was carried out under forced-convection tangent flow conditions, in a cabinet equipped with trays in parallel. 1 kg of berries was spread over each tray in a single layer. Drying was carried out at two air temperatures: 50 °C at 15% relative humidity and 70 °C at 10% relative humidity. An exceedingly high flow rate of air was maintained, so that air conditions could be considered constant throughout the experiment and in every part of the drying cabinet.

At 30-min intervals trays were weighed and their position in the cabinet changed in order to obtain completely comparable experimental conditions. The experiments were stopped when the weight loss during the last hour was less than 1 per thousand by weight.

Sun drying tests were carried out by exposing a single layer of berries in wooden trays in the sun during the day and sheltering them at night. The air conditions varied during the day from about 22 °C and 70% relative humidity in the morning and evening to about 35 °C and 40% relative humidity in mid-day hours. During the night the temperature and relative humidity were maintained roughly constant at 20 °C and 65%, respectively. As a consequence of these variations, the drying cycle showed a typical fluctuating pattern: consequently the weight loss curves were drawn by actual-values interpolation. Sun-drying experiments were stopped after 10 days.

Osmodehydration was carried out in 5 kg batches of grapes with a pure solution of glycerol as the osmotic medium, in a 1 to 5 grape-to-solution weight ratio, at 20 °C, with continuous slow stirring by recirculation. Weight controls were carried out three times a day by removing the berries from the bath with a plastic wire basket, draining to remove excess solution, rinsing with water and surface drying with filter paper. Osmodehydration tests were stopped after 5 days.

After all drying tests the grapes were washed with water for 5 min at 40 °C and then gently dried with air at 50 °C. This treatment, which allows the removal of alkaline ethyl oleate residues from the surface of the grapes, failed to change the water content achieved in the previous drying tests.

Drying Kinetics
A simplified form of Fick's law was adopted for the computation of kinetic data:

$$\frac{n - n_\infty}{n_0 - n_\infty} = e^{-kt}$$

where n_0, n_∞, n are the absolute humidities of the initial sample, at equilibrium and at time t, respectively, and k is the rate constant value, related to the geometry of the sample and diffusivity of water.

The best fit of the experimental points to the above exponential regression curve obtained by computer, allowed the evaluation of n_∞, the equilibrium humidity value, and of k, the rate constant.

Analyses
Dry weight, total acidity, reducing sugars, total and free SO_2, and total phenolics were determined according to the Italian Official Methods of Analysis for Must and Wine.[7] The average volume of berries was evaluated by a toluene displacement method.

Color. The values of lightness (L), redness (a) and yellowness (b) of fresh and dried grapes were determined by direct reading with a Hunterlab colorimeter. Data were transformed in C.I.E. parameters.

RESULTS AND DISCUSSION

Figures 1, 2, 3 and 4 report the drying curves (drying rate versus absolute humidity) obtained in the various drying conditions. From

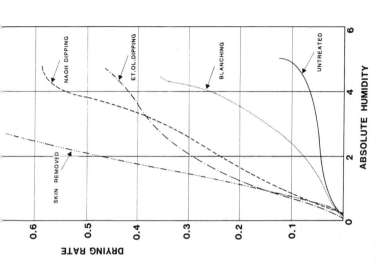

Fig. 2. *Drying curve obtained by air drying (50 °C). Drying rate, kg H₂O/kg DM/h; absolute humidity, kg H₂O/kg DM.*

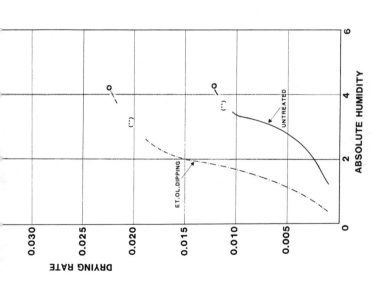

Fig. 1. *Drying curve obtained by sun drying. Drying rate, kg H₂O/kg DM/h; absolute humidity, kg H₂O/kg DM. (**), Reduced drying rate due to high moisture in atmosphere.*

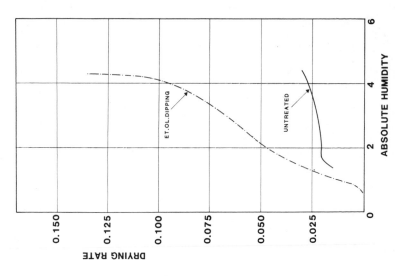

Fig. 4. *Drying curve obtained by osmodrying. Drying rate, kg H_2O/kg DM/h; absolute humidity, kg H_2O/kg DM.*

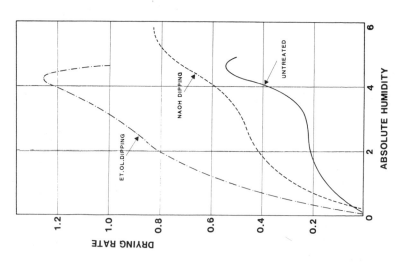

Fig. 3. *Drying curve obtained by air drying (70 °C). Drying rate, kg H_2O/kg DM; absolute humidity, kg H_2O/kg DM.*

these curves n_∞ and k were evaluated according to the procedure described in the Materials and Methods section, obtaining the values reported in Table II. Comparison of the data in Table II and curves 1–4, leads to the following conclusions.

(a) Among the various pretreatments, ethyl oleate dipping appears to be the most effective in increasing the drying rate. The constant-rate values for grapes predipped in ethyl oleate are from twice to six times higher than for untreated grapes. Comparing data of the air-drying tests it is clear that the effect of ethyl oleate dipping is much greater at 50 °C than at 70 °C.

As observed elsewhere,[8] increasing the air temperature activates the diffusion process, thus making the effect of pretreatments less evident. Comparing the shape of the drying curves it can be observed that the ethyl oleate pretreated grapes have higher drying rates especially in the lower humidity ranges; this may suggest that this pretreatment is effective not only in reducing skin resistance, but also in maintaining higher internal diffusivities during the process.

Ethyl oleate dipping may contribute to the diffusion of drying technologies in which the air is heated to relatively low temperatures (40–50 °C) with low-enthalpy sources (solar, geothermal, waste water). Also, it facilitates the drying of varieties with large berries such as that used in our experiments. Such varieties are more attractive than traditional raisins as snack products.

TABLE II
Rate-constant values (K) and Equilibrium Humidities (n_∞) of grapes dried with different processes and pretreatments

Drying process	Pretreatment	K-value ($h^{-1} \times 10^{-2}$)	n_∞ ($kg\,H_2O/kg\,DM$)
Sun drying	Untreated	0·22	0·16
Sun drying	Eth. Ol dipped	0·57	0·15
Osmodehydration	Untreated	1·06	0·75
Osmodehydration	Eth. Ol dipped	4·11	0·72
Air drying 50 °C	Untreated	3·47	0·12
Air drying 50 °C	Blanching	4·62	0·15
Air drying 50 °C	NaOH dipped	13·65	0·20
Air drying 50 °C	Eth. Ol dipped	17·66	0·14
Air drying 50 °C	Peeling	22·19	0·25
Air drying 70 °C	Untreated	15·03	0·12
Air drying 70 °C	NaOH dipp.	21·82	0·20
Air drying 70 °C	Eth. Ol dipped	30·48	0·08

(b) The steam blanching of grapes has very little effect on drying kinetics.

(c) Pretreatment with an alkaline solution is also effective in increasing the drying rate. However it can be noted that this pretreatment is more effective in increasing the drying rate during the early period.

(d) Experiments have shown that osmodehydration can be success-fully applied to grapes. In this process, the berry skin acts as a permselective membrane which allows the water to escape while hindering the migration of the osmotic medium inside the berry. In this case, the dipping pretreatment with ethyl oleate appears to be even more important than in other cases. It not only reduces the skin resistance to water diffusion, but, unlike alkaline dipping or blanching, it preserves the integrity of the skin, allowing it to act as a barrier against back-diffusion of the osmotic solutes.

Data reported in this paper are part of research in which we have extensively studied the osmodehydration of grapes in different operat-ing conditions.[9] Although we carried out experiments with various osmotic media (glucose, sucrose and inverted sugar syrups, polyal-cohols), we have chosen to present data obtained with glycerol, which gave the highest drying rates, due to the higher osmotic pressure and lower water activity attainable with glycerol than with mono- or disaccharide solutions.

The only disadvantage is that, being a small and hydrophilic molecule, glycerol diffuses more easily than sugar from the osmotic medium to the inside of the berries, reaching however a concentration of only a few percent at the end of the process. As an example, Fig. 5 reports mass-balance data of typical osmodehydration experiments.

Finally we should observe from Table II that the equilibrium humidity value of the osmodehydration process is higher than for air and sun drying. This is an obvious consequence of the fact that water diffusing out of the berries dilutes the glycerol, progressively reducing the driving force of the process.

However, at the end of the experiments, we reached relative humidities of about 80% which guarantee shelf-stability for months at room temperature.

(e) A final point concerning the equilibrium humidity of sun- and air-dried grapes is worth considering: in all cases, the equilibrium humidities correspond to relative humidities of 50–60%, which are higher than the true equilibrium humidities (i.e. the relative humidity

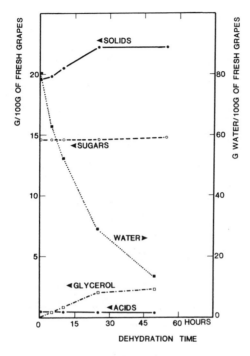

Fig. 5. Mass-balance of grape osmodehydration in pure glycerol.

of air). This means that the system evolves toward a condition of infinite resistance to the water diffusion, which is probably due to surface and/or internal impermeabilization phenomena.

It is interesting to note that these phenomena are minimized by the ethyl oleate pretreatments, leading to lower residual moisture.

Quality of Dried Grapes

Among the various determinations carried out on dried grapes, which are reported in detail elsewhere,[9] we have chosen to present the color parameters. In fact, color and appearance, more than other composition parameters, are affected by the drying conditions and determine the acceptability of the finished products. More intense browning of the grapes results from higher temperatures and longer residence time exposures as well as from greater losses of SO_2 during drying.

On the other hand, mechanical damage of the skin which may result from pretreatment or improper drying conditions determines an

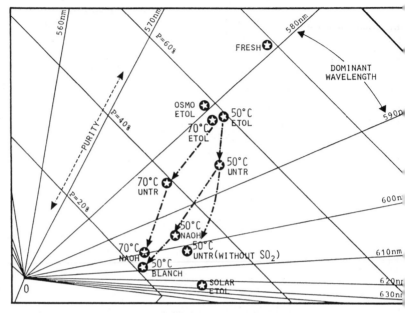

Fig. 6. C.I.E. chromaticity chart showing color values of fresh and dried grapes.

outflow of juice resulting in an unpleasant sticky appearance of th
berries.

Figure 6 shows a portion of the C.I.E. chromaticity diagrar
including wavelengths from 580 to 630 nm and ranging from 0 to 100%
purity.

The color characteristics of samples are approximately arrange
along a line of increasing browning (decreasing purity and increasin
dominant wavelength) from the ethyl oleate-pretreated to untreatec
NaOH-dipped and blanched grapes, in this order. Osmodehydrate
grapes have color characteristics close to those of fresh grapes, whil
sun-dried have suffered intense browning effects. This last case is th
combined result of long drying times, relatively high temperatures an
greater SO_2 losses (94% of initial content).

CONCLUSIONS

Ethyl oleate dipping, more than any other pretreatment, accelerate
drying kinetics and improves the quality and appearance of drie

grapes. To compare the effects of ethyl oleate pretreatment on drying kinetics, we report in Fig. 7 the percentage increase in the rate constant values, calculated on the basis of the k values of untreated samples.

It can be said that the ethyl oleate dipping pretreatment is the most useful when drying is carried out at 'intermediate' conditions. Its effect on drying velocity is comparatively smaller at 70 °C than at 50 °C, since the temperature plays an active role on water diffusion.

Even in the absence of comparable experimental data, we may presume that at temperatures higher than 70 °C the effect of ethyl oleate dipping on drying rate may become small or even negligible, however maintaining its positive effect on color and quality.

On the other hand, the ethyl oleate dipping also showed a relatively small effect in the sun-drying experiments. In this case, water evaporation at the berries' surface is so slow that little is gained by increasing skin permeability. However, even in this case, the ethyl oleate dipping pretreatment more than doubled the rate constant value, with evident benefit for the economy of the process and the quality of the product.

Its ability in reducing the skin resistance to water transfer without damaging the mechanical structure of the skin proves particularly useful in osmodehydration in which the skin should act as a selective

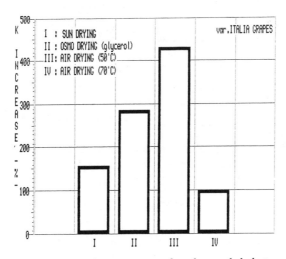

Fig. 7. Percentage increase of rate constant values due to ethyl oleate pretreatment.

barrier, allowing water to permeate from the inside of the berry outwards while hindering the diffusion of osmotic solutes from the outside.

ACKNOWLEDGEMENT

This research work was supported by CNR, Italy, special grant IPRA—sub-project 3, Paper No. 472.

REFERENCES

1. Grncarevic, M. Effect of various dipping treatments on the drying rate of grapes for raisins. *Am. J. Enol. Vitic.* **14:** 230–4, 1963.
2. Pointing, J. D. and McBean, D. M. Temperature and dipping treatment effects on drying rates and dipping times of grapes, prunes and other waxy fruits. *Food Technol.* **24:** 1403–6, 1970.
3. Riva, M. and Peri, C. Etude du séchage des raisins. 1-Effet de traitements de modification de la surface sur la cinétique du séchage. *Sciences des Alim.* **3:** 527–50, 1983.
4. Cullen, R. W. Raisins in light foods. *Cer. Food World* **30:** 233–5, 1985.
5. Riva, M. and Peri, C. Kinetics of sun and air drying of different varieties of seedless grapes. *J. Food Technol.* 1985 (in press).
6. Pointing, J. D. Osmotic dehydration of fruits. Recent modifications and applications. *Proc. Biochem.* **8:** 18–21, 1973.
7. Ministero Agricoltura E Foreste *Metodi ufficiali di analisi per vini, mosti ed aceti.* MAF, Roma, Italy, 1964.
8. Riva, M. and Peri, C. Osmotic dehydration of grapes. *Proc. 6th Int. Cong. Food Science and Technology,* Vol. I, Dublin, Eire, pp. 179, 1983.
9. Peri, C. and Riva, M. Etude du séchage des raisins. 2- Effet de traitements de modification de la surface sur la qualité du produit. *Sciences des Alim.* **4:** 273–86, 1984.

44

EFFECTS OF DRYING AND TEMPERING ON QUALITY OF PARBOILED RICE

L. VELUPILLAI and L. R. VERMA

Agricultural Engineering Department, Louisiana Agricultural Experiment Station, Louisiana State University Agricultural Center, Baton Rouge, Louisiana 70803, U.S.A.

ABSTRACT

A study of high temperature drying and tempering of parboiled rice was undertaken to evaluate the effects on grain quality. Thirty-six treatments, with three levels of air temperature, three levels of residual moisture content, and four levels of tempering, were performed on the Saturn variety, medium grain rice, parboiled under fixed conditions. The dried and tempered rice samples were then moisture equilibrated under room conditions and subjected to standard milling procedures. Analyses were performed to evaluate color and strength characteristics of the milled rice. Studies of changes of kernel hardness and strength properties with time were also performed during 93 hours after drying, on separate samples for a selected treatment combination.

The intermediate air temperature of 93·3 °C, for any single tempering treatment, produced the highest head yield in the rice samples. This trend, together with the increase of color and strength properties of the rice kernels was attributed to the extended parboiling effect at this temperature.

The tempering treatment TM2, realized the highest head rice yield especially at the 93·3 °C air temperature drying treatment. Tempering treatments, in general, other than treatment TM1, were beneficial in improving the head yield by nearly 8%.

INTRODUCTION

Rice is an important food crop in the world. Although it is generally utilized as a staple, this cereal is processed in the United States into several different products.[1,2]

Rice parboiling is a hydrothermic process applied as a treatment prior to the normal milling state. This process, believed to be of ancient origin, was probably invented to facilitate the easy removal of husk. Today, the most important advantage of the process is the increase of whole kernel yield. The essential steps involved in the process are: (a) soaking of rough rice, (b) steam heat treatment, (c) drying to levels of moisture suitable for subsequent processing. At the end of the steam heat treatment stage, the moisture content of the parboiled rice is usually approximately 35% wet basis (w.b.). The drying stage, though assuming different forms based on the practices in a particular country, is a very important step in the parboiling process. If the drying stage is not accomplished properly, the economic advantage of reduced breakage of rice due to parboiling will not be realized. Several studies[3,4] have indicated that to obtain good yields, drying of parboiled rice must be temporarily stopped at a moisture level of approximately 16% (w.b.). At this point, it is believed, the moisture distribution becomes more uniform. This temporary stoppage is often referred to as 'tempering'.

Previous studies in this area have shown that if drying was continued beyond a moisture level of 16% (w.b.) without any tempering, very low yields of whole kernels would result.[3,4] This indicates that changes in some properties of the grains occur after the initial drying stage. Breakage of nonparboiled rice during processing is caused by several factors. These are related to the physical properties of the rice grains and to the conditions under which the grain is milled.[5] When rice is properly parboiled many previous shortcomings such as cracks in the grains are eliminated.[6] Thus the most appropriate drying and tempering treatments would be the key to obtaining high whole kernel yields in parboiled rice.

The objectives of this study were to evaluate the grain quality changes brought about by selected drying and post-drying treatment combinations.

EXPERIMENTAL PROCEDURE

All treatments were performed on medium grain, Saturn variety rice. The soaking and steaming stages of the experiment were maintained constant for all treatments. Based on previous work,[7] and pilot investigations, a soak water temperature of 60 °C under atmospheric pressure for a period of 4 h was allowed for all samples prior to the steaming stage. The rice samples were steamed at 103·5 kPa for 10 min.

Upon completion of the steaming stage, the rice samples were immediately transferred to an experimental dryer. The dryer was preconditioned to the specific air flow and temperature. The air flow rate was maintained constant (4·955 m³/min) for all treatments. Three air temperatures of 65·6 °C, 93·3 °C and 140 °C were utilized. The rice samples were dried to approximately 18%, 16% and 14% moisture content (w.b.) respectively at each air temperature. Resident times to reach the above mentioned moisture levels were first determined and used throughout the study for the drying stage.

Four different post-drying treatments were selected and applied immediately after the drying stage was completed. These (designated as TM1–TM4) were:

TM1—The samples were spread on mesh trays and placed in an airing cupboard in the laboratory.

TM2—The samples were sealed in metal canisters and immediately transferred to an air oven preconditioned at 93·3 °C for the 93·3 °C and 140 °C drying air temperature treatments, and at 65·6 °C for the 65·6 °C drying air temperature treatments. The duration in the oven was 2 h, after which the samples were transferred to insulated containers, sealed and placed in the laboratory for 24 h. The samples were finally spread on mesh trays and placed in the airing cupboard.

TM3—On completion of the drying stage, the samples were quickly transferred to aluminum foil sachets and sealed. These sachets were then kept in the laboratory for 24 h, before being opened and the rice spread on mesh trays to be placed in the airing cupboard.

TM4—Immediately after drying, the samples of rice were transferred into insulated containers and sealed for 24 h, at the end of this period, the samples were spread on mesh trays and placed in the laboratory airing cupboard.

On completion of the parboiling, drying and tempering treatments, the samples were kept in the airing cupboard for approximately 10 days under room conditions. These samples were then sealed in plastic canisters. Approximately 3 weeks later, these samples were shelled, milled, and hand graded for separation of broken kernels. The

equipment and settings were based on standard laboratory procedures
Color analysis of the samples was performed on a Digital Tristimulu
Colorimeter. Six sound kernels from each replicate were tested in a
Instron Universal Testing machine to determine the ultimate tensil
stress.

At the 93·3 °C drying air temperature, a sample, after the parboilin
process, was dried to the 14% moisture (w.b.) level, and one half o
the sample was sealed in an insulated container while the other wa
spread on a mesh tray and kept in the laboratory. Bending tests (t
determine the ultimate tensile stress), and hardness tests wer
performed every 6 h for 33 h and then at the 45th, 69th and 93rd hour

A total of 36 treatments were included in the study. Thre
replications of each treatment were carried out in random order.

RESULTS AND DISCUSSION

Head Rice Yield

The variation of the drying air temperature resulted in a peak for th
head rice yield at the 93·3 °C air temperature (Table I). This trend wa
observed for all moisture levels and all tempering treatments. At th
93·3 °C temperature, tempering treatments TM2 and TM4 showed th
highest head yield. This trend was seen at all moisture levels. At al
three air temperatures, the head rice yield showed an almost linea
increase from the 14% to the 18% moisture levels, and the pattern wa
sustained over all the tempering treatments. This increase was steepe
at the 65·6 °C drying than at the other temperatures.

In the conventional usage, the term 'tempering' refers to a period o
time between drying stages when the grains are allowed to equilibrat
in terms of moisture. This allows the moisture within the rice kernel t
travel outwards to the surface of the grains, thus enabling faster dryin
in the next stage. Within the scope of this study, 'tempering' i
referred to in a broader sense to also include the fact that this provide
a suitable environment for relieving stresses developed in the grain
during the drying stage. It is not known, however, as to what th
actual form of the tempering treatment should be, and for how lon
this must be sustained to enable the realization of high head rice yield
The time based study, discussed later, provides some information i
this regard. In this context, it is also important to know what types o
stresses usually exist in grains after drying. It has been well docu
mented in the literature that the exposure to a typical dryin

TABLE I
Summary of treatments and results

Drying air np. (°C)	Final moisture level	Tempering treatment	Treatment number	Head rice yield (%)	Peak force in bending (kg)	Ultimate tensile stress (kg/cm²)	Total color diff.
65·6	18%	1	1	82·55	7·14	749·14	41·98
		2	2	90·56	4·98	503·35	41·76
		3	3	86·23	4·06	440·08	40·29
		4	4	88·12	6·00	748·86	40·92
	16%	1	5	79·88	8·20	883·60	40·69
		2	6	88·02	7·18	789·44	41·57
		3	7	87·65	5·98	627·39	41·21
		4	8	82·23	8·22	944·45	40·75
	14%	1	9	69·28	7·91	978·90	41·13
		2	10	83·44	7·24	765·96	41·07
		3	11	66·10	6·05	670·09	40·87
		4	12	74·09	4·68	600·15	40·23
93·3	18%	1	13	91·20	7·88	871·33	42·90
		2	14	95·35	9·23	1111·76	43·73
		3	15	92·57	9·06	981·31	41·79
		4	16	94·32	8·61	950·43	41·78
	16%	1	17	82·92	8·74	1055·25	41·98
		2	18	94·50	9·57	1060·59	43·64
		3	19	92·46	9·17	1022·82	41·22
		4	20	94·90	7·86	1033·30	42·49
	14%	1	21	80·83	8·42	923·93	40·84
		2	22	91·25	9·48	1128·86	43·48
		3	23	88·94	8·66	977·01	41·51
		4	24	91·36	8·17	902·06	41·57
140	18%	1	25	69·78	8·47	1026·66	36·89
		2	26	78·18	8·11	895·81	43·84
		3	27	76·81	7·66	836·74	41·32
		4	28	77·70	8·20	960·28	40·03
	16%	1	29	64·83	8·22	1051·84	37·72
		2	30	7·86	9·06	993·99	42·46
		3	31	76·13	8·33	980·73	39·87
		4	32	70·61	7·98	938·44	39·03
	14%	1	33	59·88	8·13	1111·09	38·54
		2	34	62·95	8·45	1010·88	38·75
		3	35	70·08	8·19	1036·36	39·93
		4	36	70·62	8·16	1053·18	38·69

environment causes thermal and moisture stresses in grains. Several workers have concluded that moisture stresses are more detrimental than thermal stresses with regard to breakage of rice in the milling process.

The highest head rice yield was recorded at the 93·3 °C temperature for TM2. Recalling the TM2 tempering procedure, it could be seen that among the four tempering treatments, TM2 provides the best environment for relieving stresses in the rice kernels. This effect has been reflected in the high head rice yields obtained from this treatment combination.

Addressing the change in head rice yield due to the varying moisture levels, it could be seen that the grains dried to 14% have had the longest exposure to the drying environment in all the air temperature groups. For the grains under this longer exposure, the moisture gradients and hence the moisture stresses would be higher than the 18% moisture level group at any air temperature treatment. Thus under any tempering treatment, rice grains at the 14% moisture level would tend to be less suitable, provided that all the residual stresses are not removed at the time of milling. It was seen that tempering treatments TM2, TM3 and TM4 as a group showed a significant improvement in head rice yield when compared to TM1. Differences in head yield still persisted for the 14, 16 and 18% moisture level treatments. In general, it appears that the 14% treatment grains enter the tempering stage under a higher state of stress than the 18% treatment groups, and that even after the tempering treatments, followed by an equilibration at room conditions prior to the milling stage, the stresses remained. The fact that the stresses were not completely relieved at the time of milling appears to be supported by the comparison of the strength data for TM1 and TM4 at the 14% level at 93·3 °C air temperature (Table I), with those recorded for the time-based study under similar treatments (Table II). At 93 h after completion of drying, the peak force required to cause failure of kernels under TM1 and TM4 were 5·85 and 5·74 kg respectively, whereas the samples that underwent the same treatment showed 8·42 and 8·17 kg respectively after several weeks. This trend was also seen for the ultimate tensile stress which increased from 661·08 and 504·39 kg/cm^2 to 923·93 and 902·06 kg/cm^2 respectively.

At the 93·3 °C drying air treatment, the results in terms of head rice yield due to TM2 and TM4 were similar at all moisture level treatments. This indicates that on an industrial scale, to achieve these

TABLE II

Results of time-based post-drying investigation

	Peak force in bending (kg)		Ultimate tensile stress (kg/cm²)		Hardness value (kg)	
Time (h)	TM1	TM4	TM1	TM4	TM1	TM4
0·0	0·909	*	*	*	0·757	0·757
9·0	5·252	2·673	630·63	*	5·379	4·347
15·0	5·369	3·712	504·81	360·83	7·660	4·648
21·0	5·698	2·029	600·22	193·29	8·030	4·280
27·0	5·773	3·051	674·39	281·37	8·485	4·545
33·0	5·898	4·222	686·20	521·69	8·324	5·284
45·0	5·737	4·566	452·76	468·67	7·893	5·773
69·0	6·335	5·595	721·39	529·91	9·063	7·841
93·0	5·852	5·739	661·08	504·39	10·625	8·818

TM 1 to 4 refer to the tempering treatments 1 to 4.
Data could not be obtained at these times due to the soft nature of the rice kernels.

head yield improvements (TM2 or TM4 over TM1), transferring the dried rice to an insulated bin would be more economical than maintaining the rice at a temperature approaching that of the drying air.

Keeping in mind that moisture and heat must be simultaneously present to bring about good parboiling results, the peak effect of the head rice yield at 93·3 °C has most likely been caused by the fact that exposure to the drying air at 93·3 °C has in effect extended the steam heat treatment stage. This temperature was the closest of the three used in the experiment to the typical steaming temperature. This appears to serve as an extension of the parboiling stage, bringing about the improvement in the head rice yield (increased steaming time in general produces an increase in head yield, the upper limit to this being darker color and deformity of the grains). At the 65·6 °C treatment the grains may have been insufficiently heated to cause the above mentioned effect. At the highest temperature of 140 °C, the rate of loss of moisture was more rapid. Hence the extended heat treatment was not as long as for the 93·3 °C treatment resulting in head yields lower than those at 93·3 °C.

The importance of tempering can be clearly seen when the improvements in head rice yields were reviewed with respect to the tempering treatments, as shown in Table III. The increase in % head yield due to any form of tempering other than mere exposure to the

TABLE III
Increase in head rice yield due to tempering

Drying air temperature (°C)	Moisture level at end of drying (%)	Average head yield from TM 2, 3 and 4 less head yield from TM 1(%)
140	18	7·77
	16	8·04
	14	8·00
93·3	18	2·88
	16	11·03
	14	9·69
65·6	18	5·75
	16	6·09
	14	5·26

TM 1 to 4 refer to the tempering treatments 1 to 4.

room conditions (as in TM1) is 7·94% at the 140 °C treatment, 7·87% at the 93·3 °C treatment and 5·7% at the 65·6 °C treatment (these are figures averaged over the moisture level treatments). These benefits are higher at the higher drying temperatures. The improvements in head rice yield at the highest temperature treatment are similar at all the moisture levels (Table III). This trend indicates that it is possible to effect improvements in head rice yield while still drying the parboiled rice down to near storage levels of moisture if a suitable form of tempering is utilized.

Color
The total color difference of the samples was shown to be significantly associated ($p < 0.01$) with the drying air temperature, level of moisture, and tempering treatments.

The color data showed high values at the 93·3 °C treatment, and the lowest values for the 140 °C treatment. The most plausible explanation here is the enhancement of the parboiling treatment as discussed earlier. The increase of the steaming treatment has been found to cause an increase of color difference data in parboiled rice.[1,8] For any increase of total color difference, it has been reported that effects of moisture and heat must both be present at the same time. Once these two requirements are satisfied, time would be an additional factor in increasing the color difference of parboiled rice. The rapid rate of moisture removal at the 140 °C air temperature appears to prevent any excess increase of color difference. Insufficient heating at 65·6 °C in comparison to that 93·3 °C appears to be the cause of the color values being, in general, lower than those at the 93·3 °C air temperature treatment.

Strength Characteristics

The strength characteristics that were considered were the peak force and the ultimate tensile stress in the bending mode for simply supported rice kernels loaded at the center in an Instron Universal Testing Machine. These were considered indicative of the ability of a particular batch of parboiled rice to resist the shelling and milling forces. The peak force and the ultimate tensile stress have both been significantly associated ($p < 0.01$) with the drying air temperature. These two characteristics were also significantly affected ($p < 0.05$) by the moisture level. An observation of the means in Table IV shows that the highest peak force and the highest ultimate tensile stress values were recorded at the 93·3 °C air temperature and tempering treatment TM2. This lends support to the concept of an enhancement of the parboiling treatment resulting in the increase of strength properties of the grains.

TABLE IV

Table of means for peak force and ultimate tensile stress (means are averaged over moisture levels)

Air temperature (°C)	Tempering treatment	Peak force in bending (kg)	Average	Ultimate tensile stress (kg/cm^2)	Average
65·6	1	7·74		870·90	
	2	6·29		572·50	
	3	4·98		544·42	
	4	6·30	6·33	764·48	688·07
93·3	1	8·34		950·16	
	2	9·42		1100·40	
	3	8·96		993·71	
	4	8·21	8·73	961·93	1001·55
140·0	1	7·92		1001·23	
	2	8·53		966·89	
	3	8·06		951·27	
	4	8·11	8·15	983·96	975·84

The variation of the peak force and ultimate tensile stress in bending with respect to the three moisture levels indicates that these values were the highest at the 16% moisture level with the exception of the ultimate tensile stress under the 140 °C treatment. It is possible that at the 16% moisture level, a transition of the starch characteristics may be taking place. Further investigations may be needed in this area.

The data for hardness, the compressive deformation of a rice kernel to yield point, were computed as the average of the yield point values obtained from the load deformation curves for several grains from a sample. It was seen that for TM4, there was a steady linear increase in the hardness after a period of 50 h. Comparison of data for the peak force and the ultimate tensile stress in bending (Tables I and II) showed that these two characteristics continued to steadily increase even after several weeks. This indicates a need to delay the milling of parboiled rice for at least 3–4 weeks.

REFERENCES

1. Rao, M. R. R. Rice processing effects on milling yields, protein content and cooking qualities. Louisiana State University, Agricultural Experimental Station Bulletin No 663, 1971.
2. Luh, B. S. Breakfast rice cereals and baby foods. In *Rice: Production and Utilization* (B. S. Luh ed.). AVI Publishing Company, Westport, Connecticut, 1980.
3. Bhattacharya, K. R. and Zakiuddin Ali, S. Improvement in commercial sun drying of parboiled paddy for milling quality. *Rice J.* **17:** 9, 1970.
4. Stipe, D. R., Wratten, F. T. and Miller, M. F. Drying steam treated naturally moist rough rice. Louisiana State University Rice Experiment Station, Crowley, Louisiana 68th annual progress report, 1976.
5. Spadaro, J. J., Matthews, J. and Wadsworth, J. I. Milling. In *Rice: Production and Utilization* (B. S. Luh Ed.). AVI Publishing Company, Westport, Connecticut, 1980.
6. Bhattacharya, K. R. Breakage of rice during milling and effect of parboiling. *Cereal Chemistry* **46:** 478, 1969.
7. Velupillai, L. The effect of level and distribution of moisture on parboiled rice quality. M.S. thesis, Louisiana State University, Baton Rouge, Louisiana, 1981.
8. Roberts, R. L. *et al.* Effect of processing conditions on the expanded volume, color and soluble starch of parboiled rice. *Cereal Chemistry* **31:** 121, 1954.

45

CAKING PHENOMENA IN TROPICAL FRUIT POWDERS

J. CAL-VIDAL, R. F. DE CARVALHO and S. C. S. SANTOS

Department of Food Science, ESAL, 37.200 Lavras, Brazil

ABSTRACT

Some food powders are very susceptible to physical changes responsible for the reduction of free flow during handling, mixing and storage operations, and the tendency to form rigid aggregates, as a direct consequence of a high hygroscopicity in this type of product. In the specific case of sugar-rich foods, such as dehydrated fruits and vegetables in powdered form, this type of problem is particularly serious. When the water is removed during spray-drying and freeze-drying, a high incidence of amorphous sugars results, which through the absorption of small amounts of water change to the crystalline state with the release of moisture. This released moisture may favor the formation of liquid bridges to promote the intensification of the caking phenomenon. In the present study, several tropical fruit powders obtained by freeze-drying and spray-drying were 'conditioned' under different temperature and relative humidity environments and the corresponding time and degree of caking were determined.

The studies of hygroscopicity and caking were conducted using an automatic controlled temperature and relative humidity chamber and desiccators with saturated salt solutions. The time and degree of caking was determined.

The degree and time of caking of tropical fruit powders were significantly dependent on the environment relative humidity (RH) or product water activity, at a given constant temperature. In addition, there are critical values for RH or temperature at which any one of the considered factors exerts a higher influence on the caking phenomenon.

INTRODUCTION

For proper handling in manufacturing operations and a high accept-ance at the consumer level, food powders must have good flow characteristics. As previously described[1-5] a high water sorption potential is a dominant factor for caking to occur. Thus, for a given type of food powder, an environment with a high relative humidity may favor a high rate of water adsorption and a caking condition afterwards. In the specific case of fruit powders containing soluble components such as sugars, the adsorbed water may provoke their dissolution and the formation of liquid bridges; after a subsequent dehydration, this results in caking. Among others, the relative humidity was the main factor responsible for caking in powders of freeze dried papaya,[5] dried onions,[2] garlic,[6] corn, wheat or potato starch, and sugars.[7]

The effect of environment temperature is also very significant because it can enhance the influence of the humidity factor by increasing the powder solubility and the humidity distribution.[2,8-10] In addition, high temperatures may favor the plasticity of sugar and fatty components with the formation of solid bridges following cooling.[1] This was observed in apple powder[11] which reached a state of high aggregation at temperatures above 38 °C, even with the low moisture content of 1%. The same authors found a similar behavior for orange powder and defined a 'stick point', which represents the temperature, at a given moisture content, under which a given powder starts agglomerating.[12,13]

The use of anti-caking agents has been investigated in several foods.[14-16] These substances, effective at concentrations of 2% or lower, have several modes of action to prevent the loss of flowability or caking of powders. In general, if the conditioner is to be effective, its particles must adhere to the host powder particles, thus affecting their surface properties. A review dealing with food-grade commercial flow conditioners and anti-caking agents appeared recently. Besides these, the use of other substances, such as lactose, starch, sucrose and cellulose has been suggested.[18-22]

In this work, investigations of the caking behaviour of several tropical fruit powders included the influence of processing conditions, the addition of anti-caking agents before and after freeze dehydration, and addition of sodium carboxymethyl cellulose (CMC) before spray-drying.

MATERIALS AND METHODS

Materials

Ripe yellow passion fruit (*Passiflora edulis,* f. *flavicarpa*), red guava (*Psidium guajava* L.) and avocado (*Persea americana,* Mill) from a commercial source were utilized in this study. The fruits were kept under refrigeration ($\cong 5\,°C$) until juice or pulp extraction. The soluble solids content (°Brix) of the fruits was monitored to assure a constant degree of ripening.

The anti-caking agents used were tricalcium phosphate (TCP) (Monsanto Company, St. Louis, MO., U.S.A.), Syloids 63FP and 244FP, consisting of 99·6% of SiO_2 (Grace-Davision Chemical, Baltimore, MA, U.S.A.) and 28AB (Rhodia, S.A., Paulinia, SP, Brazil). (28AB, approximate composition: SiO_2, 69·0%; Al_2O_3, 11·5%; Na_2O, 8·3%; H_2O, 8%; Na_2SO_4, 3·0%; CaO, 0·1%.) These substances were added to the juice or pulp at the 0·5, 1·0, 1·5 and 2·0% levels on the basis of total solids content of the fruit extract, either before freezing for freeze-drying or directly to the dried powder. In addition, sodium carboxymethyl cellulose (CMC) was tested with spray-drying of avocado to evaluate its anti-caking possibilities.

Freezing and Drying Procedures

Slow-frozen passion fruit samples were prepared in a Harris freezer (Harris MFG Co. Inc., Cambridge, MA, U.S.A.) at an average temperature of $-45\,°C$, and the fast frozen samples were prepared by a 'dropping technique'[23] which consisted of spraying the material directly into liquid nitrogen ($\cong -195\cdot8\,°C$). The guava samples were frozen by an immersion procedure[26] in a solution of CO_2 solid + ethyl alcohol ($\cong -72\,°C$). Before sublimation, the frozen samples were granulated mechanically.

Freeze-dried samples of passion fruit juice and guava pulp were obtained using a 12F Pilot Stokes Freeze Drier (Pennwalt Co., Philadelphia, PA, U.S.A.) and a Pilot Virtis 10–145MR-BA Freeze Drier (The Virtis Company Inc., Gardiner, NY, U.S.A.), respectively. Plate temperatures at the drying chamber ranged from 50 to 60 °C. At the end of dehydration, the material was milled in a Thomas–Willey Jr. mill (Arthur H. Thomas Co., Philadelphia, PA, U.S.A.) using 20 mesh screens (opening = 0·84 mm). The milled samples were kept in hermetic flasks for the caking conditioning and caking determinations.

The spray dried avocado powder was prepared in a Pilot Spray Drier Unit (Niro Atomizer Industria e Comercio Ltda., Diadema, SP, Brazil). Immediately before drying, CMC was added to the concentrate at the 0·5, 1·0 and 1·2% levels on the basis of the fruit total solids content. Spray-drying conditions were: inlet air temperature ≅200 °C; outlet air temperature ≅100 °C; feeding rate ≅900 g/h; total solids concentration of feeding solution ≅25–26·2%.

Environment Conditioning and Caking Determinations

To estimate the time for caking of freeze-dried passion fruit powder, the samples were exposed to several levels of relative humidity at 25 °C in a humidity and temperature controlled chamber model FR–381C-1 (Blue M, Blue Island, IL, U.S.A.). At certain time intervals the samples were examined for caking condition, and their water content was determined.[23]

In the case of the freeze-dried guava and spray dried avocado powders, the samples were conditioned under different relative humidity environments using saturated salt solutions inside hermetically

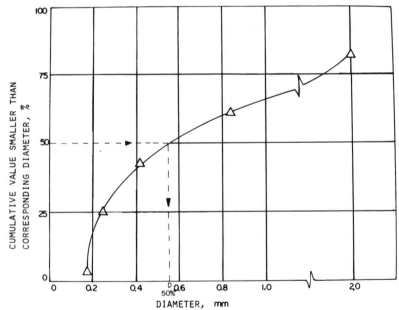

Fig. 1. Typical cumulative granulometric analysis for freeze dried guava powder.

sealed desiccators, placed in temperature controlled cabinets. The caking degree of the guava samples was determined following techniques described[24,25] using a vibrating system of screens (Produtest, São Paulo, SP, Brazil).[26] Figure 1 illustrates the procedure used to estimate the $D_{50\%}$ value taken as a caking index in this study. For the avocado samples the degree of caking was determined by the granulometric retention, expressed as the amount of powder held on screens with an opening of 2 mm.[27]

RESULTS AND DISCUSSION

Effect of Processing Conditions and Type of Anti-caking

Figures 2–4 show the time for caking of freeze-dried passion fruit powders. Three different anti-caking agents (TCP, 63FP and 244FP) were added to the passion fruit juice before slow or fast freezing and these samples were subsequently freeze-dried under a constant plate temperature of 50 and 60 °C. The histograms show the effect of the added anti-caking agents and processing conditions on the time for caking. Numbers above the bars indicate the water content (g/100 g solids) at the time when the caking condition was detected. These results were obtained in the powdered samples exposed to an environment at 25 °C with a relative humidity of 78%. In Fig. 2 (TCP) it is observed that the rate of freezing and the freeze-drying temperature did not exert a noticeable effect on the time for caking. The same behavior was observed for the samples with the anti-caking agent 63FP (Fig. 3), although this agent seemed to be less effective than TCP. Finally, the samples containing 244FT (Fig. 4) showed an effect of the freezing rate, with those frozen slowly exhibiting a significant reduction in the time for caking as compared with the fast frozen ones. This is probably due to structural effects, the ability of this anti-caking agent to adhere to the host particle surface, or to their surface compatibility.[17] From this result it can be concluded that anti-caking agent 244FP is the most effective when applied to fast frozen samples.

The effect of the anti-caking agent concentration, confirmed previous reports[28–30] that there is an effective concentration beyond which no further improvement of flowability can be observed. The actual concentrations at which maximal effectiveness is reached are affected by specific characteristics of the conditioner–host powder system and the achieved moisture content. The problem of poor crystal coverage

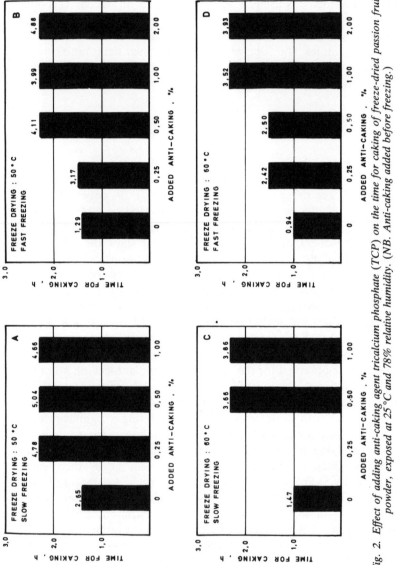

Fig. 2. Effect of adding anti-caking agent tricalcium phosphate (TCP) on the time for caking of freeze-dried passion fruit powder, exposed at 25°C and 78% relative humidity. (NB. Anti-caking added before freezing.)

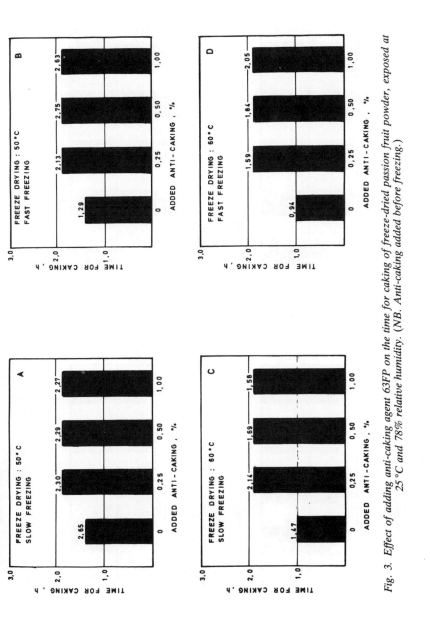

Fig. 3. *Effect of adding anti-caking agent 63FP on the time for caking of freeze-dried passion fruit powder, exposed at 25 °C and 78% relative humidity. (NB. Anti-caking added before freezing.)*

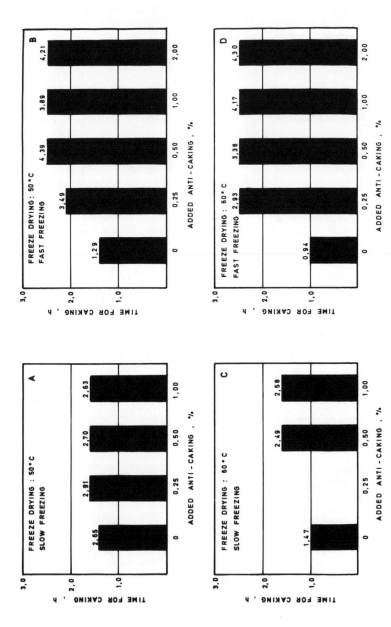

Fig. 4. Effect of adding anti-caking agent 244FP on the time for caking of freeze-dried passion fruit powder, exposed at 25 °C and 78% relative humidity. (NB. Anti-caking added before freezing.)

of the anti-caking agent affecting the hygroscopic behavior of freeze-dried passion fruit powder, was reported previously.[23,31]

Caking and Hygroscopic Equilibrium

The influence of the relative humidity (RH) on the degree of caking of freeze-dried guava powders containing anti-caking agents, added before or after the freeze dehydration process is shown in Figs. 5–7. It is observed that in the case of TCP (Fig. 5) there are critical values of RH beyond which the caking behavior changes drastically. In addition, it can be noticed that when the anti-caking agents were added after the freeze dehydration they were more effective in reducing caking than when added before freezing; this was also observed with the addition of 244FP and 28AB (Figs. 6 and 7). Again, the effect of anti-caking agent concentration appears superimposed for the reasons discussed above. In some instances this may contribute to the segregation problem as shown in some cases here (TCP and 28AB) and previously.[17,32,33]

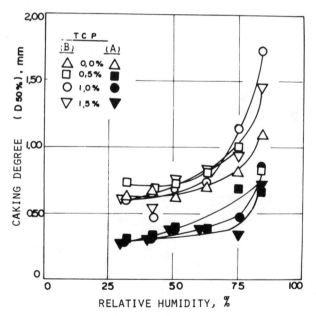

Fig. 5. *Effect of adding anti-caking agent tricalcium phosphate (TCP) before (B) and after (A) freeze dehydration of guava on the caking degree of the corresponding powder, exposed to several relative humidity conditions, at 34 °C.*

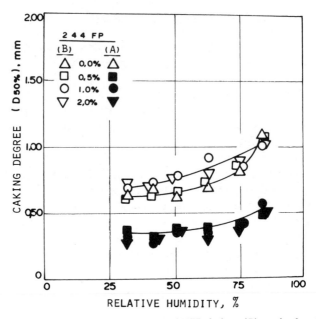

Fig. 6. Effect of adding anti-caking agent 244FP before (B) and after (A) freeze dehydration of guava on the caking degree of the corresponding powder, exposed to several relative humidity conditions, at 34 °C.

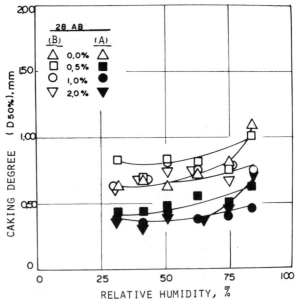

Fig. 7. Effect of adding anti-caking agent 28AB before (B) and after (A) freeze dehydration of guava on the caking degree of the corresponding powder, exposed to several relative humidity conditions, at 34 °C.

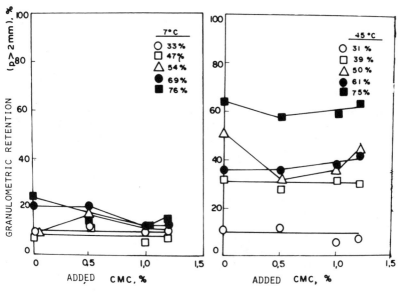

Fig. 8. Effect of adding CMC (sodium carboxymethyl cellulose) on the granulometric retention of spray-dried avocado, exposed to several levels of relative humidity, at 7 °C (left) and 25 °C (right).

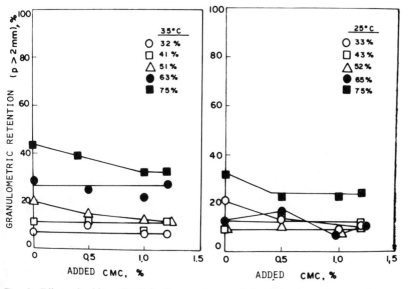

Fig. 9. Effect of adding CMC (sodium carboxymethyl cellulose) on the granulometric retention of spray-dried avocado powder, exposed to several levels of relative humidity, at 35 °C (left) and 45 °C (right).

Influence of Temperature and Other Factors
Figures 8 and 9 show the effect of adding sodium carboxymethyl cellulose (CMC) on the granulometric retention of spray-dried avocado exposed to environments of several relative humidities and temperatures. A significant increase of the granulometric retention occurred with the increase of relative humidity and temperature. The

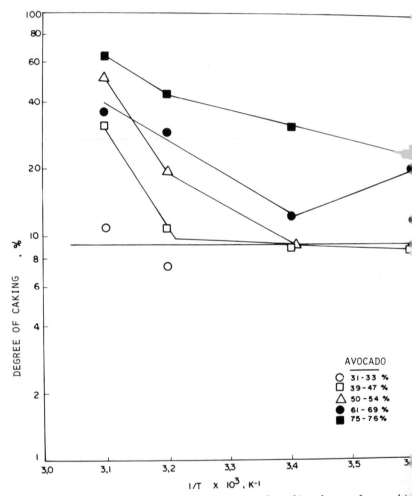

Fig. 10. *Effect of the environment temperature on the caking degree of spray-dried avocado powder, exposed to several levels of relative humidity.*

effect of CMC concentration seemed of little significance, with the granulometric retention practically independent of the amount added. Figure 10 shows the effect of the absolute environment temperature on powdered avocado. It can be observed that increasing the relative humidity to which the powder is exposed, the effect of temperature becomes more and more evident. These results are in agreement with those of others.[30,34–38]

ACKNOWLEDGEMENTS

Thanks are due to CNPq, Brasilia, Brazil, for awarding research fellowships to the second and third authors to carry out this investigation. Sincere thanks are also due the Food Engineering Laboratory, Universidade de São Paulo, and to Niro Atomizer, São Paulo, Brazil, for the use of some instruments.

REFERENCES

1. Moreyra, R. and Peleg, M. Propiedades físicas relacionadas con el flujo de alimentos en polvo. *Rev. Agroquím. Tecnol. Alim.* **21**(3): 322, 1981.
2. Peleg, M. and Mannheim, C. H. Caking of onion powders. *J. Food Technol.* **4**: 157, 1969.
3. Neumann, B. S. Powders. In *Flow Properties of Disperse Systems* (J. J. Hermans, Ed.), North-Holland, Amsterdam, Chap. 10, p. 382, 1953.
4. Lima, A. W. O. and Cal-Vidal, J. Hygroscopic behaviour of freeze dried bananas. *J. Food Technol.* **18**: 687, 1983.
5. De Gois, V.A. Comportamento higroscopico do mamão liofilizado com vistas ao estabelecimento de seu potencial de caking. M.Sc. thesis, ESAL, Lavras, Brazil, 1981.
6. Pruthi, J. S., Singh, L. J. and Lal, G. The equilibrium relative humidity of garlic powder. *J. Sci. Food Agric.* **10**(10): 359, 1959.
7. Shotton, E. and Harb, N. The effect of humidity and temperature on the cohesion of powders. *J. Pharm. Pharmacol.* **18**: 175, 1966.
8. Mannheim, C. H. Determination of the chemical and physical factors which regulate hygroscopicity in dehydrated foods as a basis for preventing water uptake, prolonging their storage life. Research Report 080–037. Technion-Israel Institute of Technology, Haifa, Israel, 1974.
9. Notter, G. K., Taylor, D. H. and Brekke, J. R. Pineapple juice powder. *Food Technol.* **12**(6): 363, 1958.
10. Notter, G. K., Taylor, D. H. and Downes, N. J. Orange juice powder. *Food Technol.* **13**(2): 113, 1959.
11. Lazar, M. E. and Morgan, A. I. Instant apple sauce. *Food Technol.* **20**(4): 179, 1966.
12. Lazar, M. E., Brown, A. H., Smith, G. S., Wong, F. F. and Lindquist, F. E.

Experimental production of tomato powder by spray drying. *Food Technol.* **10**(3): 129, 1956.

13. Pisecky, J. and Sorensen, I. H. Some aspects of whey drying. *Danish Dairy Ind.* (special issue), 1, 1976.

14. Irani, R. R., Vandersall, H. L. and Morgenthaler, W. W. Water vapor sorption in flow conditioning and cake inhibition. *Ind. Eng. Chem.* **53**(2): 141, 1961.

15. Moy, J. H., Oh, H. I. and Gavino, V. The effects of sucrose and calcium salts on the hygroscopicity of vacuum-puff freeze dried mango and guava nectars. *Proc. IVth. Int. Congress Fd Sci. Technol.* Vol. 2, 36, 1974.

16. Peleg, M. and Mannheim, C. H. Effect of conditioners on the flow properties of powdered sucrose. *Powder Technol.* **7:** 45, 1973.

17. Peleg, M. and Hollenbach, A. M. Flow conditioners and anticaking agents. *Food Technol.* **38**(3): 93, 1984.

18. Audu, T. O. K., Loncin, M. and Weisser, H. Sorption isotherms of sugars. *Lebensm. Wiss. Technol.* **11**(1): 31, 1978.

19. Nickerson, T. A. Lactose. In *Fundamentals of Dairy Chemistry* (Webb, B. H. and Johnson, K. R. Eds), Chap. 6. AVI, Westport, Conn., p. 273, 1972.

20. Vilder, J. Influence de la cristallisation du lactose dans le concentré de sérum sur l'hygroscopicité et l'agglomeration de la poudre de sérum. *Rev. l'Agric.* **28**(4): 963, 1975.

21. Brennan, J. G., Herrera, J. and Jowitt, R. A study of some of the factors affecting the spray drying of concentrated orange juice, on a laboratory scale. *J. Food Technol.* **6:** 295, 1971.

22. Hamano, M., Aoyama, Y and Sugimoto, H. Effect of sugars on water sorption of powdered soy sauce. *J. Agric. Chem. Soc.* **50**(7): 311, 1976.

23. Cal-Vidal, J. Comportamento higroscópico e poder autoaglomerante (caking) de suco de maracujá (*Passiflora edulis, f. flavicarpa*) liofilizado. Dr. Eng. Thesis, Universidade de São Paulo, São Paulo, Brazil, 1982.

24. Niro Atomizer, ed. Analytical methods for dried milk products, A/S Niro Atomizer, Copenhagen, 1978.

25. Rhodia. Agentes de condicionamento de pós e líquidos. *Bol.* (São Paulo), p. 1, 1981.

26. De Carvalho, R. F. Higroscopicidade e autoaglomeração (caking) de pós liofilizados de goiaba (*Psidium guajava* L.) contendo agentes anti-caking. M. Sc. thesis, ESAL, Lavras, Brazil, 1983.

27. Santos, S. C. S. Grau de caking de pós de abacate (*Persea americana*, Mill) obtidos por spray-drying. M. Sc. thesis, ESAL, Lavras, Brazil, 1983.

28. Irani, R. R., Callis, C. F. and Lin, T. Flow conditioning and anticaking agents. *Ind. Eng. Chem.* **51**(10): 1285, 1959.

29. Irani, R. R. and Callis, C. F. The handling properties of cereal products. *Cereal Sci. Today* **5**(7): 198, 1960.

30. Craik, D. J. and Miller, B. F. The flow properties of powders under humid conditions. *J. Pharm. Pharmacol.* **10:** 136T, 1958.

31. Cal-Vidal, J. and Falcone, M. Sorption kinetics of freeze-dried passion fruit juice. In *Engineering and Food* (McKenna, B. M. Ed.). Elsevier Applied Science Publishers Ltd., London, Chap. 50, 509, 1984.

32. Danish, F. O. and Parrot, E. L. Effect of concentration and size of lubricant on flow rate of granules. *J. Pharm. Sci.* **60:** 572, 1971.

33. Gjelstrup Kristensen, H. Studies on flow properties of powders. 4. Flow properties of tablet granulations and uniformity of tablet content. *Dansk. Tidsskr. Farm.* **43:** 213, 1969.

34. Peleg, M. and Mannheim, C. H. The mechanism of caking of powdered onion. *J. Food Process. Preserv.* **1:** 3, 1977.

35. Peleg, M., Mannheim, C. H. and Passy, N. Flow properties of some food powders. *J. Food Sci.* **38**(6): 959, 1973.
36. Pilpel, N. and Britten, J. R. Effects of temperature on the flow and tensile strength of powders. *Powder Technol.* **22:** 33, 1979.
37. Whynes, A. L. and Dee, T. P. The caking of granular fertilizers: an investigation on a laboratory scale. *J. Sci. Food Agric.* **8**(10): 577, 1957.
38. Hamano, M. and Sugimoto, H. Water sorption, reduction of caking and improvement of free flowingness of powdered soy sauce and miso. *J. Food Process. Preserv.* **2:** 185, 1978.

Part VI
Thermal Processing

46

RECENT DEVELOPMENTS IN THERMAL PROCESS DESIGN

R. LARRY MERSON and T. K. WOLCOTT

Department of Food Science and Technology, University of California, Davis, California 95616, U.S.A.

ABSTRACT

Equipment, packaging, and process innovations in the heat sterilization of foods are briefly reviewed. Topics include aseptic processing, flame sterilization, acidification, microwave sterilization, retort improvements, process control, and developments in plastic, paper and metal containers. Implications for research are discussed in the areas of heat transfer, mass transfer, thermobacteriology, and process design.

NOMENCLATURE

a = initial concentration of heat-labile constituent
A = area of can (m^2)
b = final concentration of heat-labile constituent
C_p = heat capacity of can contents (kJ/kg K)
D = can diameter (m)
D_A = diameter of end-over-end rotation (m)
D_r = diameter of rolling rotating can (m)
D_{Tref}^z = decimal reduction time; heating time required at temperature T_{ref} for 90% reduction of constituent with given z value (min)
F_{Tref}^z = lethal effect of a process; equivalent time at temperature T_{ref} for constituent with given z value (min)
g = acceleration due to gravity (m/s^2)
Gr = Grashof number, Gr = $gD^3\rho^2\beta\,\Delta T/\mu^2$ (dimensionless)
h = internal heat transfer coefficient (W/m^2K)
H = height of headspace (m)

501

k	= thermal conductivity of liquid (W/m K)
L	= height of can (m)
m	= mass of can contents (kg)
Nu	= Nusselt number, $\mathrm{Nu} = hD/k$ (dimensionless)
$\mathrm{Nu_A}$	= Nusselt number, $\mathrm{Nu_A} = hD_A/k$ (dimensionless)
$\mathrm{Nu_E}$	= end-over-end Nusselt number, $\mathrm{Nu_E} = hD/2k$ (dimensionless)
$\mathrm{Nu_R}$	= reel Nusselt number, $\mathrm{Nu_R} = hS/k$ (dimensionless)
Pr	= Prandtl number, $\mathrm{Pr} = \mu C_p/k$ (dimensionless)
Re	= Reynolds number, $\mathrm{Re} = D_r(\pi D\omega)\rho/\mu$ (dimensionless)
$\mathrm{Re_A}$	= Reynolds number, $\mathrm{Re_A} = D_A^2\omega_R\rho/60\mu$ (dimensionless)
$\mathrm{Re_E}$	= end-over-end Reynolds number, $\mathrm{Re_E} = \dfrac{\omega_E D^2 L\rho}{\mu(D+L)}$ (dimensionle
$\mathrm{Re_R}$	= reel Reynolds number, $\mathrm{Re_R} = S^2\omega_R\rho/\mu$ (dimensionless)
$\mathrm{Re_D}$	= Reynolds number, $\mathrm{Re_D} = D^2\omega_R\rho/60\mu$ (dimensionless)
S	= radius of Steritort reel (m)
t	= time (s)
t_1	= time at beginning of thermal process (s)
t_2	= time at end of thermal process (s)
T	= product temperature (K)
T_{ref}	= reference temperature (K)
T_{RT}	= retort temperature (K)
T_1	= temperature at beginning of heating (K)
T_2	= temperature at end of heating (K)
ΔT	= temperature difference in fluid (K)
U	= heat transfer coefficient (W/m^{2}K)
V_c	= volume of can (m^3)
V_p	= volume of liquid in can (m^3)
We	= Weber number, $\mathrm{We} = \pi\omega_E^2 L^2 D/4\sigma$ (dimensionless)
z	= temperature difference which causes ten-fold change in rate o bacterial destruction (K)
β	= coefficient of volumetric expansion (K^{-1})
μ	= fluid viscosity (Pa s)
μ_b	= fluid viscosity evaluated at average bulk temperature betwee the start and end of the process (Pa s)
μ_w	= fluid viscosity evaluated at average temperature of the can wal between the start and end of the process (Pa s)
ρ	= fluid density (kg/m^3)
σ	= liquid surface tension (N/m)
ω	= can rotational speed (revolutions/s)
ω_E	= end-over-end rotational speed (radians/s)
ω_R	= reel rotational speed (revolutions/min)

INTRODUCTION

Thermal process design comprises both the design and delivery of the time/temperature cycle that provides commercial sterility in foods. It encompasses both scientific analysis and physical design, that is, the design of both the process and the equipment. Since process innovation and invention often precede engineering analysis in food technology, this review combines recent technological advances in process development, equipment design and packaging related to heat processing of foods, with some of the implications of these developments for research in thermobacteriology, heat transfer, mass transfer, and process design calculation methodology.

PROCESSING INNOVATIONS

Aseptic Processing

In recent years, aseptic processing has created intense industrial interest. Used successfully with liquids for a number of years in Europe and Japan, aseptic filling rapidly gained attention in the U.S. beginning in 1981 when hydrogen peroxide was approved for sterilizing packaging materials. Typically, a feed pump continuously meters the liquid food through a heat exchanger (to bring the food to sterilizing temperature), then through a holding tube where sterilization is completed, a back pressure regulator valve, and a cooling heat exchanger to a sterile holding tank which feeds the aseptic filler. Presterilized containers are filled with cold product in a chamber that prevents recontamination and sealed with presterilized closures before leaving the aseptic environment. The process is successful because (1) it rapidly, uniformly, and continuously heats and cools the liquid, (2) high temperature, short time (HTST), or even ultrahigh temperature (UHT), sterilization may be used to minimize heat damage to the product, (3) energy is conserved and energy recovery (regeneration) schemes are possible, and (4) a wide variety of packaging options are available.

When the liquid food contains particles, achieving sterility while maintaining product integrity is more difficult. As one example of a successful process, Fig. 1 describes a typical pilot-scale line currently in research and development use by several companies.[1,2] Key features are the feed pump (a continuous, twin-piston, hydraulically-powered

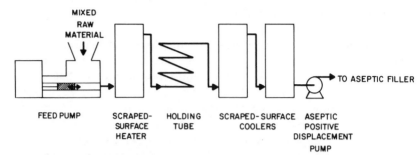

Fig. 1. Schematic diagram of aseptic processing of liquid food with particulates.

pump developed by Marlen Research Corp., Overland Park, KS) set to control line pressure, the scraped surface heat exchangers, and an aseptic positive displacement pump which provides back pressure and meters the food out of the system at a steady rate. The Marlen pump is important in preserving particulate identity; during operation, a cylindrical six-inch sleeve moves through the food and seals against an outlet port, trapping a quantity of liquid and particles. A tight-fitting piston then pushes the product through a check valve into the four-inch outlet line. Development of an aseptic filling machine for use with particulate foods has been announced recently.[3]

An alternative approach with some foods containing particulates is to sterilize the sauce and the particles separately. The Jupiter system, introduced in 1981,[4] uses a tumbling cone reactor to sterilize the particles in steam, while the liquid is processed optimally by a separate aseptic line; after cooling, the two fractions are recombined in the reactor prior to aseptic packaging. A recent study[5,6] proposes a water-fluidized bed to sterilize particles.

Flame Processing

Flame sterilization (Steriflamme) continues to be used on a small scale in North America for mushrooms and acid products; it is much more extensively employed in Europe and there are about 70 installations world wide. According to Paulson *et al.*,[7] without heat recovery procedures, flame sterilizers typically convert 26–29% of the fuel energy to heating cans and contents compared to nearly 40% for a vertical steam batch retort. However, energy savings could be instituted with the flame unit, and it was anticipated that with appropriate energy recovery devices the two processes would have comparable energy requirements.[8]

New low-liquid products packed in cans under high vacuum produced by flame or mechanical deaeration (Fig. 2) are expected on the market by the 1985 or 1986 packing season.[9] Typically, in this process, the food is first softened by blanching to aid filling. A lid is clinched on (but not sealed, in order that steam and air may escape) and the rotating can is carried across a flame to generate steam in the can to displace air. Further time over a burner dispels air from food tissue. The can is then double seamed without cooling and, for low acid foods, put through a flame sterilization process. For most fruits and other acid foods, the sterilization step is not necessary; enough heat treatment is provided in the blanching and deaeration to inactivate enzymes and harmful microorganisms. Alternatively, the deaeration

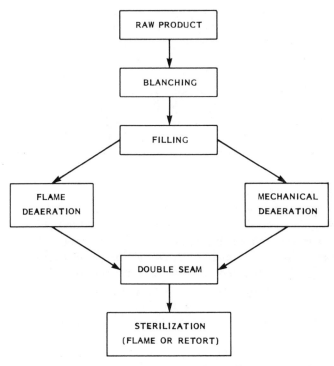

Fig. 2. *Schematic diagram of high vacuum sterilization processing.*

step can be carried out in a specially designed vacuum closing machine that provides adequate residence time (e.g. 7 s at 60 °C for green beans). The flame sterilization step is especially effective with the high vacuum products (compared to conventional liquid/particulate packs) because heat transfer rates in pure steam inside the can are very rapid and because the cans withstand higher temperature HTST processing with the noncondensable gases removed. If a conventional steam retort is used for the sterilization step, care must be exercised to bring the retort temperature up slowly to prevent can collapse under high steam pressure. More technical information has been reported on products[10–13] and container performance.[14]

Acidification
To reduce the severity of heat treatments required to achieve commercial sterility, foods may be acidified. Two ideas are of continuing interest: (1) converting low acid foods (pH > 4·6) to acid foods (pH < 4·6), and (2) lowering the pH of acid foods even further to shorten the process and significantly minimize product damage. Typical acidulants are food grade inorganic acids (e.g. hydrochloric or phosphoric) or organic acids (malic, citric, acetic). Addition is often limited by objectionable taste at high concentrations. American Can Company has recently announced[15,16] a process using a unique food grade acidulant which alters pH to useful levels without imparting a taste of its own. The process is most successful with yellow vegetables, shrimp, meat, rice, etc., but is not as effective with green vegetables whose chlorophyll is sensitive to acidic conditions.

Microwave Sterilization
Research on the use of microwaves for commercial or home blanching[17,18] and sterilization[18–21] continues, but the field has moved slowly in recent years compared to aseptic processing. There is still controversy as to whether microwaves are selectively lethal for microorganisms compared to usual heating processes.[18,22,23] Innovations include a device for pressure canning in a home microwave oven,[24] a laboratory microwave sterilizer,[25] a process for sterilizing pumpable foodstuffs in a pipe of low dielectric loss material[26] and microwave sterilization of agar media.[27] Direct measurement of temperatures during microwave sterilization using shielded thermocouples has been reported.[25,28]

EQUIPMENT INNOVATIONS

Improvements have been made in sterilizers to meet needs for modern containers or to effect process efficiencies. Batch retorts have been introduced which rotate the crates axially to give end-over-end rotation to the cans. Giving improved heat penetration for any container, these retorts are especially valuable in water cooks with overriding air pressure for plastic cans. A continuous retort, which can process virtually any container regardless of size, shape, or material has recently been introduced by FMC Corp.;[29] nonagitating crates are moved in and out of the pressurized-water sterilizing chamber through pressure locks.

Crateless retorts, introduced in 1964, have been installed in some 70–80 locations around the world to facilitate automated loading. Filled by dropping cans through water in the retort, this equipment introduces random orientation of the cans as another variable in the theoretical analysis of natural convection heating.

Hydrostatic cookers, while continuous in operation, are usually nonagitating as far as heat penetration is concerned. A modification enhances forced convection by allowing cans to roll on inclined ramps as they descend through the steam dome.

Commercial flame sterilizers have traditionally been linear machines with cans rolling on a track from one end of the machine to the other and then dropping to a lower level to travel in the reverse direction. The top level is an atmospheric steam preheater, the second is a heating ('rising') flame, a third is a 'holding' flame, and the last is water spray cooling. In a new prototype machine,[30] cans roll on a helical track through steam, flame, and cooling sections; this compact machine saves considerable floor space. Another improvement in flame sterilizers was accomplished by replacing the rod-shaped push bars by flat ones that created a controlled flow path for combustion gases around each can. This minimizes the effect of adjacent cans (or empty slots when the machine is not full), allowing use of a very small distance between cans and thus more efficient energy utilization.[30]

Control of retort operation using computer-based process control units is becoming a reality. Valves and timing schedules for loading, retorting, cooling, and unloading can be routinely operated under computer control. A goal is to have retorts, either batch or continuous, so closely monitored that a process deviation can be detected and compensated for during the cook, before cooling takes place. For example, a time–temperature sensor connected to a computer could continuously calculate accumulated lethality at the critical point in the food; if a process deviation occurs, for example, a drop in retort temperature, the program could predict the additional process time needed to complete processing of the batch safely and continue the cook for that time.[31]

Process control is particularly important in flame sterilizers, since it is not possible to monitor heating medium temperature as in a retort and, therefore, assume that all cans heat identically. Several methods have been reported recently for monitoring can temperatures in flame sterilizers. One method is a contact thermocouple;[32,33] another utilizes remote infrared sensors to 'read' the surface temperature of each can at critical points in the process, for example, at the beginning and end of the holding section.[33–35]

PACKAGING INNOVATIONS

A wide variety of packaging options are being offered for use with thermally processed foods. These include plastic and composite containers, retortable pouches, and a variety of innovations in metal cans.

Plastic Containers
This category includes rigid or semi-rigid thermoformed containers for use with aseptic or hot-fill-and-hold operations and also rigid plastic cans capable of withstanding retort temperatures. The needed combination of barrier properties (against microorganisms, oxygen, water vapor, oils, etc.), structural strength, sealability, product compatibility, and heat tolerance is obtained by using multi-layered plastics which are heated and thermoformed to make the containers. The key to current success is the availability of coextruded laminated sheets made by a process developed by Dow Chemical Corp. in the early 1970s. Individual resins are melted and coextruded together from a common feedblock to form the multilayered sheets. A typical laminate for low temperature use consists of polyethylene in contact with the food, an adhesive or 'tie' layer (typically ethyl-vinyl acetate, EVA), an oxygen barrier such as polyvinylidene chloride (PVDC, tradenamed Saran) or ethylene vinyl alcohol copolymer (EVAL or EVOH), another tie layer, and a layer of polystyrene or

polypropylene for rigidity. Polyethylene is used as the food contact surface because it is heat sealable, food compatible, and originally the only plastic approved by the U.S. Food and Drug Administration for hydrogen peroxide sterilization (this approval has recently been extended to all polyolefins). Lid stock often consists of coextruded polyethylene and barrier plastics or aluminium foil which has both barrier and printing qualities.

Some systems use preformed cups, sterilized either by hydrogen peroxide spray or vapor, or occasionally by steam, prior to filling.[36] If the containers are formed on site, coextruded sheet is fed into a sterile chamber, sterilized with a hydrogen peroxide solution (25–35% H_2O_2), dried with hot sterile air, heated to thermoforming temperature, drawn into containers, filled, and heat sealed with peroxide-sterilized lidding material before leaving the sterile environment. One company avoids the use of hydrogen peroxide by protecting the polyethylene food contact surface with a coextruded layer of polypropylene (or polybutylene on the lid stock) which is stripped off in the sterile thermoforming chamber; the exposed polyethylene is still sterile from the heat of the coextrusion process and thus ready for use without further treatment.[36,37] At least two companies (Rampart Packaging, Inc. and Dow Chemical) supply the coextruded plastics as single container 'blanks' rather than as large rolls of sheeting.[38]

For retortable cans, the coextruded material typically consists of a layer of polypropylene as a moisture barrier, a layer of Saran or EVOH oxygen barrier, and another layer of polypropylene for strength (with EVA tie layers). Polypropylene is used as the food contact surface because it is more heat stable than polyethylene; such a composite will reportedly withstand retorting at 121·1 °C for 45 min.[39] Since polypropylene softens at 126·7–132·2 °C, some companies use other plastics as the structural strength layer in laminated plastic cans, for example recrystallized polyethylene terephthalate (PET) or a modified polycarbonate. To minimize heat stresses which may cause container warping during retorting, Hercules, Inc. has developed a system to form containers from the molten polymers directly from the coextrusion feedblock rather than first forming composite sheets which are subsequently reheated and thermoformed at the container-making plant.[40] Lid stock for retortable plastic cans is made of similar heat sealable plastic laminates; one company uses a polyester to seal to a polypropylene body.[39] Another approach is to use a metal lid with a conventional double seam.[40]

Paper-based Containers

Brick-style containers which consist of paper/foil/polyethylene laminates are still the standard for aseptic packing of liquids.[41] They are sterilized by hydrogen peroxide, formed, filled, and sealed, all in an aseptic chamber.

Paper-based rigid composite cans are being developed for aseptic filling of acid products.[36,42,43] The most common, spiral wound body construction consists of a food contact layer (e.g. polyethylene/aluminium foil/polyethylene/kraft paper), two layers of glued kraft board stock and a label layer which may also contain aluminum foil. This construction will not withstand peroxide sterilization and must be sterilized by hot air, UV light, or superheated steam prior to filling. Lids are most commonly metal, double seamed to the paper-based bodies, but may also be roll stock (e.g. polyethylene/aluminium/PVC) heat sealed to the body.

Flexible Pouches and Bag-in-box Containers

Flexible retortable pouches have been reasonably successful in the military, camping, and specialty markets, and may still have a place in food service applications, but have been disappointing in most retail ventures.[44] The main problems are the slow filling/sealing machines and the labor intensiveness of the batch retorting operation.

On the other hand, large scale flexible bags aseptically filled and supported in collapsible wooden boxes are rapidly replacing 50 gallon drums for tomato paste and other products for remanufacture.[45,46] The large, 300 gallon bags effect economies in packaging materials and transportation costs. Smaller polyethylene/barrier-plastic pouches are marketed for aseptic filling of milk.[36] In another development for remanufacture, yogurt fruit is aseptically filled into stainless steel 'tote bins' for transport to dairy plants.[47]

Metal Cans

With all of the current excitement over aseptic packaging, it is easy to overlook the significant technological developments in metal cans, which are still the principal package for the vast majority of heat sterilized products. Soldered side seams can be replaced by thinner, stronger, welded side seams or 'cemented' side seams.[48] The side seam can be eliminated altogether with two piece extruded (drawn/redrawn or drawn-and-wall-ironed) cans. With organic coatings, tin-free steel cans may be used with most foods and even with light colored fruits if a high vacuum pack is employed.[14] Tapered two piece cans have replaced flattened/reformed cylindrical cans in Alaskan salmon packing operations;[49,50] the tapered cans nest to conserve shipping volume. finally, cans with special liners incorporating magnesium salts have been developed[51] for use in conjunction with special blanching techniques to preserve the color of canned green vegetables.

IMPLICATIONS FOR SCIENTIFIC AND ENGINEERING ANALYSIS

Many of the new developments discussed above have generated new design information or have pointed to the need for studies to obtain such information. Design parameters needed include kinetic data for destruction of bacteria, enzymes, nutrients or other quality factors, heat transfer rates during sterilization cycles, and even mass transfer rates connected with the process itself or with constituent loss during storage. More specifically, to use the fundamental thermal process design equation

$$F^z_{T_{ref}} = D^z_{T_{ref}}(\log a - \log b) = \int_{t_1}^{t_2} 10^{[T(t) - T_{ref}]/z} dt \qquad (1)$$

to determine the destruction of bacterial spores (or other heat labile constituents) from original concentration a (at time t_1) to final concentration b (at the end of the process t_2), one needs to know values for the heat resistance parameter D and its dependence z on temperature. One also needs to know the critical point temperature (or temperature distribution) T as a function of time; and in some cases, for example in continuous processing, the distribution of (residence) times involved. Examples of some recent developments are surveyed in the next paragraphs. The various methods of solving Eq. (1) for F or processing time t_2 have recently been reviewed by Cleland and Robertson.[52]

Thermobacteriology
High temperature, short time processing, either continuous (as in UHT sterilization or aseptic processing) or in containers (as in flame processing and especially high vacuum flame processing), has highlighted the need for heat resistance data at temperatures in the range of 120–160 °C. These data are difficult to acquire by classical methods,

for example, capillary tubes in an oil bath,[53,54] because the heating times must be extremely short, of the order of $0 \cdot 1$–$1 \cdot 0$ s, in order to have countable survivors even with initial counts of 10^9 spores/ml. A computer-controlled reactor to acquire such data has been reported[55,56] with precisely controlled residence times and sample temperatures monitored at 60 points/s. The reactor can be used for spores,[56] enzymes[57] or other heat labile factors. An alternative approach is to use a flow reactor, which achieves a step-wise increase in temperature by mixing two streams.[58]

In closely engineered systems, such as aseptic processing, where the entire thermal treatment may be only a few seconds, it is important to account properly for nonidealities in heat resistance data. For example, in process calculations, bacterial death is treated with first order kinetics; a plot of time versus the logarithm of survivor concentration is assumed to be linear. However, experimental survivor curves are routinely nonlinear. The curved region at very short heating times (which, incidentally, can be studied without significant heat transfer lag in the reactors discussed above) has been attributed by various authors to activation of super-dormant spores that will not grow with only ordinary heat activation, or to induced heat resistance during the first few seconds of heating.[59] Hayakawa et al.[60] have suggested an iterative method of determining D values by successively dropping points in the short-time curved region to maximize the correlation coefficient in a linear regression curve fit. Pflug and Bearman[61] have proposed an intercept ratio (defined as the ratio of the extrapolated initial count to true initial count) to describe the initial curvature; this procedure is not widely used in process calculations, however.

Another deviation from idealized first order kinetics for destruction of spores is the commonly observed tailing of survivor curves at longer heating times,[54,59,62] i.e. apparently the last survivors are more heat resistant than would be predicted from first order kinetics. This behaviour has been ascribed to mixed populations;[63] however, it is often observed even with pure cultures and may represent a non-normal distribution of heat resistances or heat-induced resistance. Tailing is routinely ignored in thermal process design calculations and may not be important with good manufacturing practice where initial spore counts are low, e.g. if one spore/million has exceptional heat resistance, the spoilage rate may still be acceptably low if the can contains only 100 spores.

There are also indications that the z value in Eq. (1) is not constant over a wide temperature range. For example, a plot of $\log D$ versus temperature (a phantom thermal death time curve) used to determine z is not straight into the ultrahigh temperature (UHT) range (130–160 °C), nor does an Arrhenius plot appear to correlate such data better.[56] Accounting for nonconstant z is seldom considered in process calculations.

Increased interest in acidification of foods has intensified the need for more precise methods and data for design of processes at low temperatures. Heat resistance data for enzymes, yeasts, and molds at low pH are scarce. Furthermore, acidification practices and plant breeding changes in raw material pH in some traditionally acid foods have raised the question that *Clostridium botulinum* may possibly be able to grow and produce toxin below the traditional value of pH 4·6. There is some evidence of such growth,[64,65] especially in protein-fortified media.

One approach to determining process safety is to use the left hand side of Eq. (1) to determine the level of bacterial destruction directly. For this purpose, Pflug[66] advocates the use of bioindicator units which contain known quantities of spores of known heat resistance; the units are placed in the food at the critical point and recovered at the end of the process for counting survivors. Teixeira *et al.*[67] have compared the heat transfer characteristics of plastic and aluminum bioindicator units.

Alternatively, one could use the right hand side of Eq. (1) to determine the process F value. David and Shoemaker[68] have described a transducer which simultaneously measures critical point product temperature and retort temperature and makes use of a logarithmic amplifier to give a signal proportional to the integral in Eq. (1) for a given z value (usually 10 °C); such a unit could be used directly for process control.

Heat Transfer

Modelling of natural convection heat transfer to liquids in vertical containers in a still retort has been innovatively attempted by Seiler *et al.*[69] by dividing the fluid into four regions. An annular region near the wall receives heat from the side and rises in plug flow. Across the top of the jar is a layer assumed to be completely mixed. Fluid from this layer travels in plug flow down the center cylindrical core of the container to a bottom layer which is also assumed to be completely mixed and without temperature gradients. Mass and energy balances on these zones yield a simple model that correctly predicts many features of natural convection heating, including a cold spot near the axis toward the bottom of the can; however, at present there is no convenient method of predicting the thickness of the layers involved, and these parameters are needed in the heat transfer analysis.

A spoilage problem in crateless retorts was solved by heat transfer analysis using finite element mathematics.[70] Cans of conduction heating food resting on the floor of the retort were insulated from the heating steam by the retort itself.

Modelling of heat transfer to conduction heating foods in hydrostatic cookers has been reported;[71] the work allows for inclusion of the considerable lethality achieved during the nonisothermal cooling leg of the cooker.

Most work on heat transfer to liquids in agitated retorts has taken the form of developing correlations for the time-averaged overall heat transfer coefficient U in the energy balance on the can:

$$UA(T_{RT} - T) = mC_p \frac{dT}{dt} \tag{2}$$

or

$$U = \frac{mC_p}{A(t_2 - t_1)} \int_{T_1}^{T_2} \frac{dT}{T_{RT} - T} \tag{3}$$

T_{RT} is the retort or heating medium temperature and subscripts 1 and 2 refer to the beginning and end of the batch heating process. Usual assumptions are that the can contents are completely mixed and the area for heat transfer is the entire surface area of the can. Often, the resistances of the steam and container wall are ignored, although these may amount to 7–10% of the total resistance.[72,73]

Recently reported correlations for steam heating are recorded in Table I. Typically, the overall or internal heat transfer coefficient is incorporated into a Nusselt number, which is correlated as a function of a Reynolds number to quantify rotational speed, a Prandtl number to account for most fluid properties, and frequently a geometrical factor to account for variation in can shape or headspace. The characteristic length in the Nusselt number and the Reynolds number is usually taken as the diameter or radius of rotation, which in the case of axially rotating cans is the can diameter and for a rotary cooker is the radius of the reel.

The correlations have been extended to nonNewtonian fluids by Rao and coworkers[74,75] and similar work has been attempted for flame

TABLE I

Correlations for coefficients of heat transfer to liquids in cans undergoing steam heating

Axial rotation, continuous	Reference
$Nu = 0.17\,Re^{0.52}\,Pr^{0.33}(L/H)^{0.33}$	76
$Nu = 0.434\,Re^{0.571}\,Pr^{0.278}(L/D)^{0.356}(\mu_b/\mu_w)^{0.154}$	72
Axial rotation, steritort	
$Nu_R = 115 + 15\,Re_R^{0.3}\,Pr^{0.08}$	77
$Nu_D = 0.135(Gr\,Pr)^{0.323} + 0.003\,91(Re_D\,Pr\,D/L)^{1.369}$	74
End-over-end rotation, continuous	
$Nu_E = 0.000\,017\,Re_E^{1.449}Pr^{1.19}\,We^{-0.551}(D/2L)^{0.932}(V_p/V_c)^{0.628}$	78
$Nu_A = 2.9\,Re_A^{0.436}\,Pr^{0.287}$	79

sterilization.[80,81] Current work includes extending the heat transfer analysis to include solid food particles in the can.

Although many authors usually put error limits on heat transfer coefficients calculated with such correlations, these are errors inherent in the experiments which determined the correlations with model foods. Errors and variations with real foods would be considerably higher and, with the present state of the art, no process designer would determine heat penetration data solely from the correlations. The value of the research at this point in our understanding is to provide a basis for rough predictions of processing times (for example in a preliminary estimate of the cooker size needed), to provide a check on experimental heating rates, to highlight unique situations where unexpected heating rates signal special conditions such as stratification, or overfilling, etc., and to gradually elucidate the mechanisms of heat transfer rates. In this last regard, much more work is needed in developing correlations using more realistic food models and real foods.

CURRENT RESEARCH NEEDS

Much more research is needed in general, on thermobacteriology and heat and mass transfer. The phenomenal interest in the rapidly advancing technology of aseptic processing of low acid foods has raised fears that some processors will move too quickly into the field without proper precautions for the dangers involved. Progress is required on heat transfer in holding tubes and heat exchangers and the safety of each product needs to be verified bacteriologically.

Mass transfer appears to be less important than heat transfer in thermal process design and has therefore received less attention. Nevertheless, development of vacuum packed products has signalled the need for analysis of gas transport in fresh food tissue. Acidification requires knowledge of acid diffusion in solid foods. Furthermore, heat transfer coefficients to fresh solid foods, as in blanching, canning or aseptic processing, are greatly affected by the evolution of gases from the food tissue. Food contamination by migration of adhesive components is one of the deterrents slowing progress in retortable pouch technology.

In summary, thermal process design takes the form of both theoretical engineering analysis and pragmatic developments based on marketing and the innovations of skilled and creative experts who understand mechanical design. From the food engineering point of view, until mathematical modelling reaches a much more sophisticated state, thermal process design must still be strongly supported by experimental evidence. In particular, expensive and time consuming inoculated pack experiments and careful monitoring of spoilage rates in commercial packs are still required to confirm our best theoretical designs.

REFERENCES

1. Wagner, J. N. Low acid foods. Breaking the low-acid barrier. *Food Eng.* **56**(10): 106, 107, 109, 110, 1984.
2. Swientek, R. J. Aseptic low-acid foods with particulates—soon a commercial reality. *Food Proc.* **46**(5): 136–139, 1985.
3. Mechura, F. *Barrier Plastics in Rigid Form-Fill-Seal Aseptic Plastic Packaging.* National Society of Plastics, Chicago, IL, June 18, 1985.
4. Hersom, A. C. and Shore, D. T. Aseptic processing of foods comprising sauce and solids. *Food Technol.* **35**(5): 53–62, 1981.
5. Sawada, H. Estimation of process conditions for bulk sterilization of particulate foods in water fluidized beds. M.S. thesis, University of California, Davis, 1984.
6. Sawada, H. and Merson, R. L. Estimation of process conditions for bulk sterilization of particulate foods in water fluidized beds. This volume, pp. 569–81.
7. Paulson, A. T., Tung, M. A., Lo, K. V. and Cumming, D. B. Energy use comparison between vertical still retorts and flame sterilizers for processing canned foods. Paper No. 216, 45th IFT Annual Meeting, Atlanta, GA, June 9–12, 1985.
8. Heil, J. R. High vacuum flame sterilization of particulate foods: Improved quality and economics. Proceedings of Future-Pak '83. First Int. Conf. on New Innovation in Packaging Technologies and Markets, Nov. 28–30, 1983, pp. 61–80, 1983.
9. Anon. Open flame sterilization. *Food Eng.* **56**(4): 110, 1984.
10. Seet, S. T., Heil, J. R., Leonard, S. J. and Brown, W. D. High vacuum flame sterilization of canned tuna: Preliminary process determination and quality evaluation. *J. Food Sci.* **48**(2): 364–9, 1983.

11. Heil, J. R., Carroad, P. A., Merson, R. L. and Leonard, S. Development of high vacuum flame processes for sliced peaches and pears. *J. Food Sci.* **48**(4): 1106–1112, 1983.
12. Leonard, S. J., Heil, J. R., Carroad, P. A., Merson, R. L. and Wolcott, T. K. High vacuum flame sterilized fruits: storage study on sliced clingstone peaches, sliced bartlett pears and diced fruit. *J. Food Sci.* **48**(5): 1484–91, 1983.
13. O'Mahony, M., Buteau, L., Klapman–Baker, K., Stavros, I., Alford, J., Leonard, S. J., Heil, J. R. and Wolcott, T. K. Sensory evaluation of high vacuum flame sterilized clingstone peaches, using ranking and signal detection measures with minimal cross-sensory interference. *J. Food Sci.* **48**(6): 1626–31, 1983.
14. Leonard, S. J., Heil, J. R., Carroad, P. A., Merson, R. L. and Wolcott, T. K. High vacuum flame sterilized fruits: Influence of can type on storage stability of vacuum packed peach and pear slices. *J. Food Sci.* **49**(1): 263–6, 1983.
15. Anon. Canning process improves quality. *Food. Eng.* **57**(4): 110, 1985.
16. Anon. IEFP exhibit report. New canning process doesn't destroy texture. *Prepared Foods* **154**(4): 84, 1985.
17. Glasscock, S. J., Axelson, J. M., Palmer, J. K., Phillips, J. A. and Taper, L. J. Microwave blanching of vegetables for frozen storage. *Home Economics Research J.* **11**(2): 149–58, 1982.
18. Thuery, J. Microwaves and their effects on materials. Industrial, agricultural/food and medical applications. Actualities Scientifiques et Techniques dans les Industries Agro-alimentaires, Centre de Documentation Internationale des Industries Utilisatrices de Produits Agricoles, No. 32, 1982.
19. Mudgett, R. E. and Schwartzberg, H. G. Microwave food processing: pasteurization and sterilization—a review. *AIChE Symposium Series* **78**(218): 1–11, 1982.
20. Tsuyuki, H. Sterilization and preservation of foods by microwave heating. *J. Jap. Soc. Food Sci. Technol.* **30**(1): 55–62, 1983.
21. International Microwave Power Institute. Proceedings of 17th Annual IMPI Symposium. *J. Microwave Power* **17**(4): 243–327, 1982.
22. Pedenko, A. I., Belitskii, B. I., Lerina, I. V., Maheev, Yu. V. and Kutashev, V. N. Effect of high frequency electromagnetic field on microorganisms. *Izvestiya Vysshikh Uchebnykh Zavedenii, Pishchevaya Tekhnologiya* **5**: 54–6, 1982.
23. Rosenberg, U. and Bogl, W. Influence of microwave heating on the bacterial count of food. *Fleischwirtschaft.* **62**(9): 1182–7, 1982.
24. Beauvais, M. P. and Camezon, R. E. Microwave canning apparatus. U.S. Patent Nos. 4,406,860; 4,406,861; and 4,409,454, 1983.
25. Loh, J. and Breene, W. M. A laboratory microwave sterilizer and its possible application toward improving texture of sterilized vegetables. *J. Food Proc. Preserv.* **7**(2): 77–92, 1983.
26. Enami, Y. and Ikeda, T. System for and method of sterilization of food material. UK Patent Application, 2,098,040 A, 1982.
27. Monk, P. R. and Stephenson, D. J. Microwave sterilization of media and membranes. *Food Technology in Australia* **37**(1): 14–15, 1985.
28. Peralta Rodriguez, R. D., Rodrigo, M. and Merson, R. L. Heat penetration measurement in glass jars undergoing microwave sterilization. Abstracts, Third Int. Cong. Eng. and Food. Dublin, Sept. 26–28, p. 433, 1983.
29. Anon. Retort for plastic cans ready for first installation. *Prepared Foods* **154**(4): 86, 1985.
30. Beauvais, M. Laboratoires St. George, St. Georges, France. Private communication, 1984.
31. Datta, A. K. and Teixeira, A. A. Computer-based retort control logic for precise on-line correction of process deviations Paper #212, Inst. of Food Technol. 45th Ann. Mtg., Atlanta, GA. June 9–12, 1985.

32. Cummings, D. B. and Wright, H. T. A thermocouple system for detecting centre temperature in cans processed by direct flame sterilizers. *Canad. Inst. Food Sci. Technol. J.* **17**(3): 152–6, 1984.

33. Leonard, S., Osaki, K. Heil, J. Monitoring flame sterilization processes. *Food Technol.* **38**(1): 47–50, 83, 1984.

34. Hannigan, K. J. Canning without retorts. *Food Eng.* **54**(12): 50–2, 1982.

35. Tamura, M. and Shoemaker, S. Real-time lethality evaluation during flame sterilization of canned foods. *J. Food Sci.* **5**(3): 808–11, 1985.

36. Bertrand, K. Aseptic—beyond brick-style packs. *Packaging* **29**(6): 65–70, 1984.

37. Anon. Another first for Real Fresh . . . aseptic plastic cups. *Food Eng.* **56**(4): 50, 1984.

38. Anon. Plastic barrier containers reshape food packaging. *Packaging* **30**(1): 25–9, 1985.

39. Morris, C. E. Retortable plastic cans. *Food Eng.* **56**(4): 58–9, 1984.

40. Hannigan, K. Thermoformed from molten plastic: retort cup. *Food Eng.* **56**(8): 66–7, 1984.

41. Mann, E. J. Aseptic/extended shelf life packaging. Part 2. *Dairy Industries International, U.K.* **49**(3): 11–12, 1984.

42. Giangiorgi, R. J. Cans, composite. *Packaging Encyclopedia and Yearbook,* Vol. **30**(4), 114–6, 1985.

43. Forcinio, H. HTST juice in 4-ply can costs less, tastes better. *Food & Drug Packaging* **47**(12): 5, 58, 1983.

44. Mans, J. Retort pouches: military, retail and food service. *Prepared Foods* **154**(5): 111, 112, 114, 116, 1985.

45. Nelson, P. E. Outlook for aseptic bag-in-box packaging of products for remanufacture. *Food Technol.* **38**(3): 72–3, 1984.

46. Anon. Automates savings aseptically. *Food Eng.* **56**(2): 86–7, 1984.

47. Drennan, B. Aseptic tote bins. *Food Eng.* **56**(6): 55–6, 1984.

48. Oki, Y. Advancement of cemented can manufacturing techniques in recent years. *Packaging Japan* **4**(18): 24–7, 1983.

49. Dilberakis, S. Tapered can evolves as standard. *Food & Drug Packaging* **48**(4): 5, 34–8, (1984).

50. Robe, K. Tapered cans replace 3-piece for salmon pack and eliminate collapse-reform operations. *Food Processing* **45**(4): 114–15, 1984.

51. Anon. Veri-green adds more users. *Food Eng.* **57**(4): 110, 1985.

52. Cleland, A. C. and Robertson, G. L. Determination of thermal processes to ensure commercial sterility of foods in cans. In *Developments in Food Preservation* (S. Thorne Ed.). Elsevier Applied Science Publishers, London, 1985.

53. David, J. R. D. Kinetics of inactivation of bacterial spores at high temperature in a computer-controlled reactor. Ph.D. thesis, University of California, Davis, 1985.

54. Davies, F. L., Underwood, H. M., Perkin, A. G. and Burton, H. Thermal death kinetics of *Bacillus stearothermophilus* spores at ultra high temperatures. I. Laboratory determination of temperature coefficients. *J. Food Technol.* **12**: 115–29, 1977.

55. David, J. R. D. and Merson, R. L. Reactor for measuring kinetic parameters for thermal processing at high temperatures: Heat transfer studies. Paper No. 214, 45th IFT Annual Meeting, Atlanta, GA. June 9–12, 1985.

56. David, J. R. D. and Merson, R. L. Kinetic parameters for thermal processing at high temperatures: heat resistance of *Bacillus stearothermophilus*. Engineering and Food 1985.

57. David, J. R. D. and Shoemaker, C. F. HTST inactivation of peroxidase in a computer controlled reactor. *J. Food Sci.* **50**: 674–7, 1985.

58. Swartzel, K. L. A continuous flow method for kinetic data generation. ASAE Paper No. 83–6501, 1983.
59. Komemushi, S. On the changes of death rate constant of bacterial spores in the course of heat sterilization. In *Heat Sterilization of Foods* (T. Motohiro and K. Hayakawa Eds.). Koseisha–Koseihaku Co., Tokyo, pp. 63–79, 1983.
60. Hayakawa, K., Matsuda, N., Kamaki, K. and Matsunawa, K. Computerized estimation of reaction kinetic parameters for thermal inactivation of microorganisms. *Lebensmittel–Wissenschaft u. Technologie* **14**(2): 70–8, 1980.
61. Pflug, I. J. and Bearman, W. B. Treatment of sterilization process microbial survival data. In *Laboratory Control and Statistical Analysis*. NASA Space Craft Sterilization Technology seminar, Cape Canaveral, FL, pp. 89–103, 1972.
62. Cerf, O. Tailing of survival curves of bacterial spores. *J. Appl. Microbiol.* **42**: 1–19, 1977.
63. Moats, W. Kinetics of thermal death of bacteria. *J. Bacteriol.* **105**: 165–71, 1971.
64. Smelt, J. P. P. M., Raatjes, G. J. M., Crowther, J. S. and Verrips, C. T. Growth and toxin formation by *Clostridium botulinum* at low pH values. *J. Appl. Bacteriol.* **52**(1): 75–82, 1982.
65. Tanaka, N. Toxin production by *Clostridium botulinum* in media at pH lower than 4·6. *J. Food Prot.* **45**(3): 234–7, 1982.
66. Pflug, I. J. Measuring the integrated time–temperature effect of a heat sterilization process using bacterial spores. *AIChE Symp. Ser. No. 218,* Vol. 78, pp. 68–75, 1982.
67. Teixeira, A. A., Rodriguez, A. C. and Manson, J. E. Comparison of heat transfer characteristics between plastic and aluminum bioindicator units. Paper No. 248, IFT 45th Annual Meeting, Atlanta, GA. June 9–12, 1985.
68. David, J. R. D. and Shoemaker, D. F. A transducer for the direct measurement of rates of lethality during thermal processing of foods. *J. Food Sci.* **50**(1): 223–5, 1985.
69. Seiler, L., Blaisdell, J. L., Naveh, D. and Pflug, I. J. A model for convection heating in food canning jars and metal cans. Unpublished manuscript, Ohio State University, University of Minnesota, 1982.
70. Naveh, D., Pflug, I. J. and Kopelman, I. J. Sterilization of food in containers with an end flat against a retort bottom: numerical analysis and experimental measurements. *J. Food Sci.* **49**(2): 461–7, 1984.
71. Young, K. E., Steffe, J. F. and Larkin, J. W. Product temperature prediction in hydrostatic retorts. *Trans. ASAE* **26**(1): 316–20, 1983.
72. Soule, C. L. and Merson, R. L. Heat transfer coefficients to liquids in axially rotated cans. *J. Food Process Eng.* **8**(1): 33–46, 1985.
73. Deniston, M. Heat transfer coefficients to liquids with food particles in axially rotating cans. M.S. thesis, University of California, Davis, 1984.
74. Rao, M. A., Cooley, H. J., Anantheswaran, R. C. and Ennis, R. W. Convective heat transfer to canned liquid foods in a Steritort. *J. Food Sci.* **50**(1): 150–4, 1985.
75. Anantheswaran, R. C. and Rao, M. A. Heat transfer to model non-Newtonian liquid foods in cans during end-over-end rotation. *J. Food Eng.* **4**: 21–35, 1985.
76. Quast, D. G. and Siozawa, Y. Y. Heat transfer rates during axially rotated cans. *Proc. 4th Int. Cong. Food Sci. Technol.,* Madrid, Spain, Vol. 4, pp. 458–468, 1974.
77. Lenz, M. K. and Lund, D. B. The lethality-Fourier number method, heating rate variations and lethality confidence intervals for forced-convection heated foods in containers. *J. Food Process Eng.* **2**(3): 227–71, 1978.
78. Duquenoy, A. Heat transfer to canned liquids. *Proc. 2nd Int. Congress Eng. and Food and 8th European Food Symp.* Vol. 1. Applied Science Publishers, London, pp. 483, 1980.

79. Anantheswaran, R. C. and Rao, M. A. Heat transfer to model Newtonian liquid foods in cans during end-over-end rotation. *J. Food. Eng.* **4:** 1–19, 1985.
80. Teixeira Neto, R. O. Heat transfer rate to liquid foods during flame sterilization. *J. Food Sci.* **47**(2): 476–81, 1982.
81. Peralta Rodriguez, R. D. and Merson, R. L. Heat transfer coefficients in flame sterilization of simulated canned liquid foods. This volume, pp. 285–300.

47

STEAM/AIR MEDIA FOR RETORT POUCH PROCESSING

MARVIN A. TUNG and HOSAHALLI S. RAMASWAMY

Department of Food Science, University of British Columbia, 2357 Main Mall, Suite 248, Vancouver, B.C., Canada V6T 2A2

ABSTRACT

This overview is concerned with studies on the application of steam/air heating media to thermal processing of foods in thin profile configurations. The research focused on evaluating heat transfer rates from steam/air mixtures, as influenced by temperature, steam content, flow rate and flow direction of the heat medium, as well as orientation and residual air content of test packages. Further, a methodology for temperature distribution and the concept of determining the minimum surface heat transfer requirement were developed. Steam content of the mixture was the dominant factor influencing the surface heat transfer coefficient with an exponential relationship between them. The effective heating rates of metal bricks used to simulate food packages were influenced only slightly by steam content and temperature of steam/air media. Large residual air contents in packages, up to 30 ml, did not effect the heating rate in a medium containing 65% steam at 115 or 120 °C, whereas even 10 ml residual air content was sufficient to cause major decrease in the heating rate while processing in steam/air media containing 85% steam.

INTRODUCTION

Thermally processed foods in thin profile flexible packages are becoming popular shelf stable products, and current predictions indicate they will be increasingly important in the future. The most common thin profile package is the retort pouch, a flexible laminated structure developed in the early 1950s. Currently, retort pouch foods are being marketed in many countries around the world.

Two methods are commonly used to commercially sterilize low-acid foods in flexible pouches: steam/air and water immersion/overpressure processes. The common feature of these methods is the ability to maintain retort pressure greater than the pressure within the pouch during processing. This is necessary in the heating period in order to overcome the tendency of gases within the pouch to expand and retard heat transfer, and during the cooling period to protect package integrity by increasing the supplementary external pressure to counteract internal vapor pressure which would otherwise tend to burst the pouch.

Water immersion processes have been used for many years to sterilize foods in glass containers; therefore much of the early work with retort pouches was carried out in water immersion retorts with overpressure processing. Modified systems were later developed specifically for retort pouch processing with special retort racks to support and separate individual pouches, and with provision for improved circulation of water as required for efficient heating of the products. The use of steam/air systems was a more recent innovation. There was some concern, particularly in North America, with the concept of combining air with steam because of the possibility of producing cold spots in the retort if the two gases were not efficiently mixed to produce a homogeneous environment. As with water immersion/overpressure processing, there is a potential for underprocessing in parts of the retort load if the heating media are not circulated effectively throughout the retort to provide sufficient heat transfer to all food packages. A great deal of fundamental information is needed to judge the efficacy of steam/air mixtures for thermal processing of foods.

When evaluating heating media for potential application to thermal processing operations, it is important to know the heat transfer characteristics achieved. Surface heat transfer coefficients associated with pure steam as a heating medium are known to be quite large.[1,2] Hence, when considering heat transfer from pure steam, the surface resistance is often neglected and the container surface is assumed to be at the retort temperature. However, in steam/air mixtures, the presence of air could cause interference with steam diffusivity to the package surface. This could reduce the rate of enthalpy release by condensation of steam, resulting in a lower surface heat transfer coefficient. Although steam/air processes for retortable pouches are widely utilized in Japan and are gaining popularity in Europe and North America,[3,4,5] very little attention has been focused on the most important property of the heating medium, the surface heat transfer coefficient.

Efficient application of a heating medium depends on a number of factors which promote the effective transfer of heat from the medium to the product. The heating rate at the center of the package can be limited by resistance at the package surface and/or by resistances within the package. A desirable medium would supply heat to the container surface at a rate sufficiently high so that the temperature rise at the product center is governed primarily by resistances within the package. In addition to the food product, significant resistances to heat transfer can arise from noncondensable gases that may be present within the package.

The effective heating rate index at the slowest heating point within a package of food was suggested by Ball[6] to be employed as a test of the overall efficacy of a heating medium. When heating in pure steam, the heating rate index is influenced by the properties of the container contents because of negligible surface resistance to heat transfer. For steam/air mixtures, which will have reduced surface heat transfer coefficients compared with pure steam, a lower limiting value of surface heat transfer coefficient may be identified beyond which the thermal process parameters would be essentially the same as for pure steam.

Temperature fluctuations and the presence of cold spots in retorts can be detrimental to sterilizing efficacy, especially for foods in thin profile packaging. Martens[7] reported that a deviation in retort temperature of $0.5\,°C$ can change the resulting process lethality by up to $F_0 = 3$ min depending on the temperature used for processing foods in flat containers. For a similar temperature deviation, Berry[8] reported differences in process lethalities up to 14% at $121\,°C$. Therefore, assurance of uniform temperature distribution during the retorting operation is vital for the success of steam/air processing.

This overview summarizes several studies carried out to evaluate the surface and effective rates of heat transfer from steam/air media in batch retorts. Further, in order to establish criteria for assessing the efficacy of steam/air mixtures, a method for studying temperature distribution in batch retorts and a concept for arriving at a minimal heat transfer requirement were developed.

A METHOD TO MEASURE SURFACE HEAT TRANSFER

Although it is important to know heat transfer characteristics of a heating medium before employing it for thermal processing, few studies have evaluated surface heat transfer coefficients (h) for steam/air mixtures. Previous reports[9-12] indicate that the steam content of a steam/air mixture was the major factor influencing surface heat transfer coefficients. The medium flow rate, nature of the test material and mode of steam condensation have also been identified as important factors.[1,2,13-16] Most of these studies employed steady state methods, with the surface temperature of the test material maintained at 5–20 °C below the temperature of the medium. Results obtained in this way may not be directly applicable to thermal processing of packaged foods in which the material surface is within a fraction of a degree of the temperature of the medium for a considerable part of the process time.

Materials and Methods

The initial challenge in this project was to develop an appropriate transient method for evaluation of surface heat transfer coefficients associated with steam/air mixtures. The method chosen involved heat conduction in a metal brick of uniform initial temperature when subjected to convective heat transfer at the surface by sudden exposure to a medium of constant temperature. The final equation relating the heating rate index (f_h) and surface heat transfer coefficient can be obtained as detailed in Ramaswamy *et al.*:[17]

$$f_h = \frac{2 \cdot 303}{\alpha\left(\dfrac{\beta^2(p1)}{a^2} + \dfrac{\beta^2(p2)}{b^2} + \dfrac{\beta^2(p3)}{c^2}\right)} \tag{1}$$

where α is the thermal diffusivity of the test brick of dimensions $2a \times 2b \times 2c$, and $\beta^2(p1)$, $\beta^2(p2)$ and $\beta^2(p3)$ are related to the Biot numbers (Bi), ha/k, hb/k and hc/k, respectively, involving the three dimensions given by

$$\beta(p) \tan [\beta(p)] = \text{Bi} \tag{2}$$

Quick release system. Essential requirements for the preceding mathematical analysis are a uniform initial temperature in the test brick and instantaneous exposure of the brick to the heating medium.

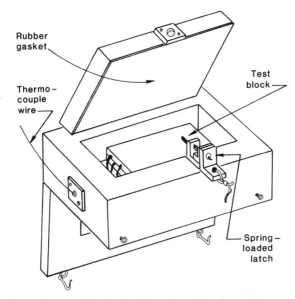

Fig. 1. An inverted view of the insulated box for quick release of the test brick into the heating medium.

A number of minutes would normally be required to achieve the desired steam/air condition (come-up time) in a batch-type retort and the temperature of a conductive test brick would follow the retort temperature rise during this period. In order to overcome this problem, a quick release system was developed. An inverted view of the quick release box is shown in Fig. 1. The system consisted of an insulated box to contain the test brick within the retort during the come-up period. When the desired steam/air condition was achieved, the box was opened by activating a latch on the spring-loaded door using a cable extending through a packing gland in the retort wall. Aluminum and stainless steel bricks of two different thicknesses with centrally located teflon-insulated 24 AWG copper/constantan thermocouples (Omega Engineering, Inc., Stamford, CT) were used in this study.

Testing procedure. For each test run, the environment temperature around the test brick was monitored using five copper/constantan thermocouples with a Kaye Ramp II Scanner/Processor data logger

(Kaye Instruments Inc., Bedford, MA). Time–temperature data at the center of the test brick after the instantaneous drop from the quick release system were recorded using a Digitec data logger (United Systems Corp., Dayton, OH), at 1 s intervals.

The fractional steam content of the mixture was calculated as the quotient of saturated steam pressure corresponding to the retort temperature, and the total retort pressure due to steam and air. Steam content of the mixture was expressed either as a decimal fraction or percentage.

The temperature difference between the medium and the center of the test brick was plotted on a logarithmic ordinate against time on a linear abscissa and the heating rate index, f_h, was evaluated from the slope of the least squares linear fit to the straight line portion of the curve. This f_h value was then used to determine the heat transfer coefficient by an iterative technique using Eqs. (1) and (2). Further details of the method are given in Ramaswamy *et al.*[17]

Results and Discussion

Some typical surface heat transfer coefficients evaluated by the procedure outlined are given in Table I. Results of this study are difficult to compare with published values, possibly because the majority of previous studies used steady state methods. The values for pure steam were in reasonable agreement with those reported in Refs. 1, 2 and 4. For steam/air mixtures, the coefficients reported in the literature[9,11,12,18] were considerably lower when compared with the results of this study. The lower values may be due to the use of low thermal conductivity test materials or noninstantaneous exposure of the test brick to the heating medium in these studies.[17]

TABLE I
Typical surface heat transfer coefficient results for steam/air mixtures in the positive flow retort[9]

Fractional steam content	f_h (s)	Surface heat transfer coefficient $(W/m^2\,°C)$
0·50	35·0	1 320
0·65	20·0	2 380
0·85	10·0	5 070
1·00	5·0	11 450

[a] Medium flow upward at 68 m³/h; aluminum brick.

SURFACE HEAT TRANSFER COEFFICIENTS FOR STEAM/AIR MIXTURES

An evaluation of the factors influencing surface heat transfer coefficients would be useful in understanding the critical factors involved in steam/air processing. The scarcity of such information is undoubtedly due to the difficulty in using test materials of high thermal conductivity because of unsteady temperatures during the come-up period of batch-type retorts. The methods and equipment described in the previous section overcame this problem and were used to gather more information in this area.

This project examined the effects of orientation of the test material and the medium composition (steam content), temperature, flow rate and flow direction on surface heat transfer coefficients of steam/air mixtures in two pilot scale retorts.

Materials and Methods

Positive flow retort. Experiments were carried out in a vertical positive flow steam/air retort similar in operation to the one employed by Pflug and Borrero.[19] Homogeneous steam/air mixtures were obtained in the retort by maintaining controlled setpoints of temperature and total pressure while a measured amount of air was constantly injected in the steam inlet line bypassing the controllers. To prevent pressure build-up caused by the added air, constant venting of the steam/air mixture occurred. Vented and condensed steam were replaced by steam to maintain the temperature setpoint and as a result, a homogeneous environment was maintained in the retort. The mixed steam and air were introduced either at the bottom or top of the retort with top or bottom venting, respectively, to provide a general flow direction of the medium either upward or downward. The medium flow rate was controlled by adjusting the air flow rate through a calibrated rotameter at a head pressure of 414 kPa. The flow rate was expressed in cubic meters per hour at standard conditions of temperature and pressure (25 °C, 101·3 kPa). This enabled a study of the heat transfer rates with different medium flow directions and rates.

Lagarde retort. Experiments were also carried out in a pilot scale single car Lagarde horizontal retort (Autoclaves J. Lagarde, Montelimar, France) located at the Research Station, Agriculture Canada,

Kentville, Nova Scotia. A turbo fan at the back end of the retort kept the heating medium in constant circulation throughout the retort to provide for uniform distribution of the heating medium during the come-up and cook cycles. The desired steam/air condition was established in the retort by controlling the medium temperature and total pressure. In this retort, the flow pattern was horizontal and flow rates were not changed. Steam/air composition and temperature were studied as process variables. Provisions were made in the quick release box to drop the test brick into the medium in either a vertical or horizontal orientation. In the vertical orientation, the brick was positioned with its larger face either parallel or perpendicular to the direction of medium flow.

Experimental design. A four level fractional factorial design, developed by Taguchi,[20] was employed initially to evaluate the factors influencing the heat transfer coefficients in the positive flow retort. Effects of fractional steam content (0·50, 0·65, 0·85 and 1·00), temperature (105, 110, 120 and 125 °C), medium flow rate (68 and 102 m^3/h) and flow direction (upward and downward) were studied. Steam/air composition (40–100% steam), temperature (105–130 °C) and brick orientation were the factors studied in the Lagarde retort.

In further experiments with the positive flow retort to characterize the effects of various factors on surface heat transfer, additional steam/air compositions were studied at different temperatures and flow rates for both upward and downward flow.

Relationships between the surface heat transfer coefficient and steam content were derived by least squares regression methods. In addition, the influence of different factors on these relationships were then examined by a covariance test.[21]

Results and Discussion

Positive flow retort. Analysis of variance of results from the initial fractional factorial experiment indicated that the effects of temperature and flow rate on the surface heat transfer coefficient were not significant ($p > 0·05$). The medium flow direction was found to be important ($p < 0·5$), while medium composition was found to be the major factor ($p < 0·01$) influencing surface heat transfer rates.

Relationship between h and S. Regression of surface heat transfer coefficients (h) from 258 test runs on the associated steam contents (S)

indicated strong hyperbolic, exponential and polynomial ($p < 0.05$ up to 3rd degree) relationships. The exponential function, which consistently resulted in large coefficients of determination (greater than 0.90 for all test conditions), was chosen to describe the heat transfer coefficient–steam content relationship as follows:

$$h = a \exp(bS) \qquad (3)$$

where a and b were parameters dependent on the characteristics of the heating medium.

Temperature effects. With the heating media flowing upward or downward, the exponential relationships between the heat transfer coefficient and steam content at 105 and 120 °C were not significantly different ($p > 0.05$). Other researchers[1,15,16,22] using steady state methods, have found that the surface heat transfer coefficient depends on the temperature of the medium or the temperature difference between the medium and the substrate. This apparent discrepancy may be due to differences in the nature of the testing methods.

Flow direction effects. Flow direction of the heating medium affected the surface heat transfer coefficient–steam content relationship ($p < 0.05$), with downward flowing steam/air providing higher values than those for upward flow (Fig. 2). The qualitative similarity of the relationships while using different test bricks indicated that the effect of medium flow direction was independent of the test brick employed. Equations for the curves fitted to the pooled data with steam/air flow upward was $h = 153 \exp(4.21\,S)$ ($n = 101$, $r^2 = 0.964$) and $h = 337 \exp(3.55\,S)$ ($n = 79$, $r^2 = 0.931$) for medium flow downward. The higher surface heat transfer coefficient associated with downward flow may be due to the forces of medium flow and gravity acting in the same direction, resulting in a more rapid removal of condensing steam from the surface of the test brick, thereby enhancing heat transfer. On the other hand, when the heating medium is flowing upward, the condensing film or droplets may be retarded from falling freely under gravity, resulting in a thicker layer of surface water with greater resistance to heat transfer.

Flow rate effects. The effect of medium flow rate (68 and 102 m³/h) was small and nonsignificant in the preliminary experiments. In further experiments using steam/air mixtures flowing upward, data were pooled from tests between 105 and 125 °C to obtain the heat transfer

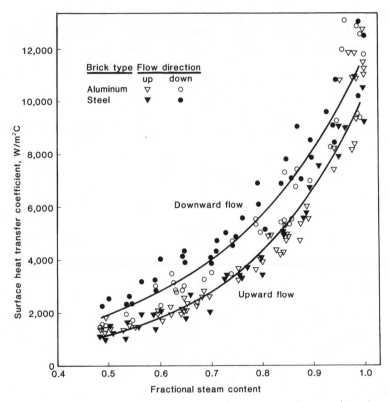

Fig. 2. *Surface heat transfer coefficient functions of steam content for steam/air mixtures in the positive flow retort.*

coefficient as a function of steam content at a flow rate of 68 m³/h, which was $h = 134 \exp(4.38\,S)$ ($n = 43$, $r^2 = 0.976$) as compared with $h = 158 \exp(4.30\,S)$ ($n = 15$, $r^2 = 0.972$) at 102 m²/h. These regression lines differed in level ($p < 0.05$) but not in slope. Increased turbulence of the heating medium at higher flow rates may explain the larger surface heat transfer coefficients. Further, at selected steam contents with upward and downward flow, linear relationships were observed between the surface heat transfer coefficient and flow rate in the 34–127 m³/h range.

Lagarde retort. In total, 182 test runs were carried out under varying conditions of steam content, temperature and test brick orientation. The exponential relationship between the surface heat transfer coefficient and steam content at 105–110 °C was not different ($p > 0.05$) from that at 120–125 °C, which indicated that the temperature effect was nonsignificant.

Brick orientation effects. The effect of the three test brick orientations on the h values was studied using aluminum test bricks. Surface heat transfer coefficients differed between horizontal and vertical orientation but not for parallel compared to perpendicular orientation (both vertical). The h values for horizontal orientations were generally lower than values for the vertical orientation with steam/air mixtures above 60% steam (Fig. 3). Lower values may be due to the presence

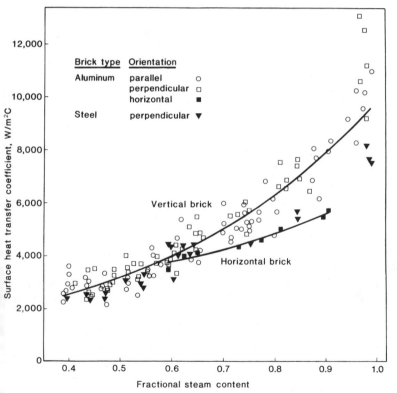

Fig. 3. *Surface heat transfer coefficient function of steam content for steam/air mixtures in the Lagarde retort.*

of a comparatively stagnant layer of water on the upper surface of the test brick resulting from steam condensation. In the vertical orientations there could be a more rapid removal of the film of condensing steam from the test surface due to gravity. Equations for the two curves drawn in Fig. 3 are $h = 1010 \exp (2 \cdot 26 \, S)$ $(n = 174, \ r^2 = 0 \cdot 904)$ for the vertical orientation and $h = 1670 \exp (1.32 \, S)$ $(n = 8, \ r^2 = 0 \cdot 940)$ for the horizontal brick orientation.

Summary of surface heat transfer results. These studies on surface heat transfer coefficients for steam/air mixtures in two pilot scale retorts indicated that medium composition and flow direction were factors of major importance. The h values increased linearly with the medium flow rate in the positive flow retort, but the effect of medium temperature was nonsignificant in both retort systems. When assessing the importance of these results for industrial applications, it should be recognized that these studies were carried out in relatively small pilot scale retorts with uninhibited medium flow. Retort type, design of the racking system and product loading patterns could substantially influence the flow behaviour of the medium and hence the associated surface heat transfer coefficients. Further results on surface heat transfer studies are detailed in Refs. 23–25.

EVALUATION OF TEMPERATURE DISTRIBUTION IN STEAM/AIR RETORTS

Temperature uniformity of the heating medium has been discussed earlier as a factor of major significance in steam/air processing of foods packed in flexible pouches. A steady temperature throughout the retort is important for delivery of the desired lethality to the packaged food.

Materials and Methods

Placement of thermocouples. Twenty to thirty precalibrated thermocouples were distributed throughout the retort to determine uniformity of the heating medium temperature with respect to thermocouple location and heating time. The thermocouple tips were secured at several probable cold spot locations within the racking systems, and in the surrounding volume of the retort. Two types of racks were employed to contain food-simulating test bricks in horizontal or vertical orientations for experiments carried out in the positive flow and Lagarde retorts.

Testing procedures. Temperature readings from all thermocouples were logged at 1-min intervals using Kaye Ramp II Scanner/Processor or Doric Digitrend 235 (Doric Scientific, San Diego, CA) data loggers and recorded on magnetic tape using a Columbia 300D Digital Cartridge Recorder (Columbia Data Products Inc., Columbia, MD). A computer-based method[26] was used to calculate the mean and standard deviation of temperature for each thermocouple location within the retort at each time interval. At the end of the heating period, the means and standard deviations of temperature during the cook period (excluding the come-up time) were computed for each thermocouple location, together with an overall mean temperature and standard deviation for the above time period including all thermocouple locations. These were plotted to facilitate study of the temperature uniformity with respect to location and time for a given processing condition.

Results and Discussion

Typical results for temperature distribution in a test run of the positive flow retort are represented in Figs. 4 and 5. The overall mean temperature of the retort during the cook period (excluding the come-up time of 5 min) was 120·05 °C and the overall standard deviation was 0·15 °C. Figure 4 is a plot of the means and standard deviations of temperature for all thermocouples at each recorded time during the cook period. This form of data display may be used to assess the ability of the control system to maintain the desired steam/air condition (a steady mean and a low standard deviation in temperature). Figure 5 is a plot of the mean temperature and its standard deviation at each thermocouple location over the entire cook period. This plot may be used to detect any cold spots among the thermocouple locations that had developed due to inadequate circulation of the heating medium. Repeated occurrence of cold spots at some locations might warrant design modifications of the racking system or distribution devices to alter the flow behavior of the media. Thus, considerable information on the uniformity of temperature distribution in a steam or steam/air retort for a given process condition

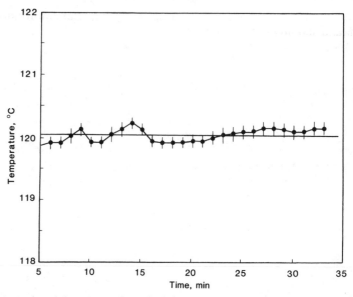

Fig. 4. A plot of the mean and standard deviation of temperature for all thermocouple locations at each minute during the cook period in a test run for the positive flow retort.

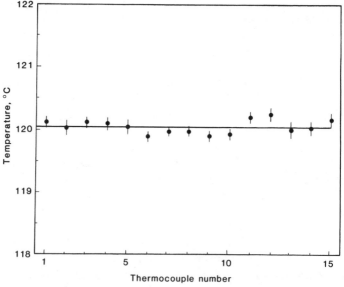

Fig. 5. A plot of the mean and standard deviation of temperature at each thermocouple location over the entire cook period in a test run for the positive flow retort.

could be obtained from this method of analyzing temperature distribution and stability data.

Temperature distribution is influenced greatly by retort design and operating procedures, and is therefore specific to the system under study. The retort size and shape, plumbing details, design and loading of the racking system, the method of achieving medium homogeneity, and other factors, could influence the temperature distribution achieved. In any case, the procedures described herein could be used to systematically evaluate the temperature distribution and stability in any retort.

HEAT PENETRATION STUDIES IN STEAM/AIR MIXTURES

In order to evaluate the overall effects of heat transfer within retorts, it is possible to make use of food-simulating test materials subjected to the process conditions under study. Suitable models for such tests would be materials with thermal properties similar to the foods of interest, in similar sizes and shapes, with tests carried out in a manner simulating production conditions. The major advantage of using food-simulating substances rather than foods is that the materials are more uniform from sample to sample and do not change with repeated use.

For heat penetration studies, the heating rate index (f_h) derived from the center temperature history during a thermal treatment may be taken as an indication of external process conditions, assuming that thermal properties within the test material remain constant from test to test. In this way, it should be possible to assess process variables with test devices that reflect the response expected of foods under similar circumstances.

Materials and Methods

Fabrication of test bricks. Test bricks were constructed from RTV 3110 silicone rubber (Dow Corning Corp., Midland, MI), rigid nylon and teflon, because these materials are known to have thermal properties similar to conduction-heating foods. All test bricks contained centrally located copper/constantan thermocouples. The reference heating rate indices for these test bricks were determined through heat penetration tests in a pure steam environment, assuming negligible surface resistance to heat transfer. These f_h values were used to compare the effects of various factors which may influence surface heat transfer and hence, the apparent f_h.

Experimental design. An L-27 three-level five-factor fractional factorial design[20] was used to study the effects of medium composition (fractional steam contents: 0·50, 0·65 and 0·85), temperature (105, 110 and 120 °C), flow rate (34 and 68 m^3/h) and flow direction (upward and downward), and rack type (horizontal and vertical) on heat transfer rates for the heating medium in the positive flow retort. The basis of comparison was the heating rate indices of the test bricks. A number of experiments was carried out beyond the factorial design to further investigate these effects. A full factorial design of experiments involving two processing temperatures (105 and 120 °C) and four fractional steam contents (0·50, 0·65, 0·85 and 1·00) was employed with two replications using the Lagarde retort.

In one series of tests, the bricks of nylon and silicone rubber were used without packaging in order to reduce experimental variability due to surface resistance while studying the effects of composition, temperature, flow rate and flow direction of the heating medium, and package orientation.

Further studies were also carried out to study the influence of residual air content in retort pouches on the heating rate indices. In these studies, teflon bricks were initially vacuum-packaged in retort pouches fitted with air-tight glands through which thermocouple wires were introduced to the geometric centers of the bricks. Known volumes of air (0–40 ml) and a selected volume (10 ml) of water, to provide the vapor pressure which exists in retort pouches containing moist foods, were injected into the pouches through a silicone rubber septum using a hypodermic syringe. A nondestructive method, based on weighing the package in water, was used to record volume changes in the packaged retort pouches. The method, as compared with water displacement destructive technique[27] following the weighing, was found to agree within 0·5 ml. Volume changes before and after a series of test runs were recorded by the nondestructive method and upon completion by the destructive test. The experiments were carried out in a 4-car commercial Lagarde retort located at Magic Pantry Foods in Hamilton, Ontario and in the positive flow retort at the University of British Columbia using operational variables of 65–85% steam at 115–120 °C.

Results and Discussion

The heating rate indices obtained for the several rectangular test bricks, while heating in 'pure' steam, were found to be $10 \cdot 26 \pm 0 \cdot 66$ min for the silicone rubber bricks, $13 \cdot 12 \pm 0 \cdot 59$ min for the thin nylon bricks, $21 \cdot 76 \pm 1 \cdot 1$ min for the thick nylon bricks and $17 \cdot 68 \pm 0 \cdot 70$ min for the teflon bricks. The coefficient of variation for f_h values due to different bricks and different test runs were in the $4 \cdot 0$–$6 \cdot 5\%$ range.

Heating rates in the positive flow retort. Analysis of variance of f_h values for nonpackaged nylon bricks, using the fractional factorial design, indicated that only package orientation was a significant ($p < 0 \cdot 05$) factor. The mean f_h value in the horizontal orientation was $3 \cdot 2\%$ higher than that in the vertical orientation.

TABLE II
Mean f_h values[a] for silicone rubber and nylon bricks[b] in the positive flow retort

| Steam content (%) | Temperature (°C) | Mean f_h value (min) | | | |
| | | Horizontal orientation | | Vertical orientation | |
		Rubber	Nylon	Rubber	Nylon
50	105	11·11	22·54	11·93	23·39
50	110	10·69	21·97	11·83	23·77
50	110	10·98	22·24	11·43	24·34
50	120	11·39	23·34	11·39	23·34
65	105	10·50	21·57	11·56	22·64
65	110	10·57	21·20	10·99	23·45
65	110	10·90	22·70	11·07	23·89
65	120	10·92	23·85	11·86	24·63
85	105	10·06	21·11	10·70	23·17
85	110	10·88	22·28	10·52	23·28
85	110	9·97	21·48	10·81	22·78
85	120	10·34	22·23	10·98	24·39
100	105	10·19	21·39	10·19	22·21
100	110	10·21	22·36	10·26	22·64
100	110	10·49	20·68	10·88	22·26
100	120	10·69	22·58	10·90	23·44

[a] Mean value from four silicone rubber and two nylon bricks.
[b] Silicone rubber bricks measured $1 \cdot 9 \times 12 \cdot 1 \times 17 \cdot 8$ cm, while nylon (thick) bricks measured $2 \cdot 4 \times 12 \cdot 1 \times 17 \cdot 8$ cm.

The results of a further study, employing a full factorial design with four levels of steam content and temperature and two package orientations, are shown as mean f_h values in Table II. All factors were found to influence f_h values ($p < 0.05$) for nylon bricks. The mean f_h values at steam contents of 50, 65, 85 and 100% were 23·12, 22·99, 22·59 and 22·20 min, respectively. These results appear to be consistent with the previously established association of higher rates of heat transfer with higher steam contents. The mean f_h value for bricks heated at 120 °C was 5·5% higher than the mean f_h for the bricks heated at 105 °C. Volume expansion at higher temperatures, resulting in an increased thickness of the test bricks, or reduced thermal diffusivity, could account for this finding. Orientation effects of the test bricks were reversed in this study, when compared with the earlier fractional factorial experiments. The mean f_h value in the vertical orientation was 5·7% higher than for the horizontal orientation.

Analysis of variance of f_h values for the nonpackaged siliconed rubber bricks indicated that steam content of the medium and orientation of the test bricks were significant ($p < 0.05$) factors. As found with the nylon bricks, lower f_h values were associated with higher steam contents (11·34, 11·05, 10·53 and 10·48 min at steam contents of 50, 65, 85 and 100%, respectively). The mean f_h value in the vertical orientation was about 4·3% higher than in the horizontal orientation. Medium temperature and all two-way interactions were found to be nonsignificant ($p > 0.05$).

Heating rates in the Lagarde retort. The mean f_h values for the full factorial analysis involving steam content (four levels), temperature (two levels), orientation (two levels) and replication (two levels) are given in Table III for the silicone rubber and nylon bricks.

An analysis of variance of the f_h values obtained for the silicone rubber bricks in vertical or horizontal orientation and the nylon bricks in horizontal orientation showed neither steam content nor temperature of the heating media to be significant ($p > 0.05$). Results also indicated that the f_h values were significantly influenced ($p < 0.05$) by brick orientation with values 5% higher in horizontal than in vertical orientation.

Influence of noncondensable gases on heating rates. The residual air content within the pouches at which the heating rate index of the packaged teflon bricks deviated from their vacuum-packed counter-

TABLE III
Mean f_h values[a] for silicone rubber and nylon bricks[b] in the Lagarde retort

| Steam content (%) | Temperature (°C) | Mean f_h value (min) | | |
| | | Horizontal orientation | | Vertical orientation |
		Rubber	Nylon	Rubber
50	105	10·32	13·62	10·34
50	105	10·54	12·53	9·82
50	120	10·58	12·42	10·16
50	120	10·68	12·24	10·08
65	105	10·16	12·94	10·90
65	105	10·39	12·82	9·80
65	120	10·72	12·20	10·37
65	120	10·68	12·92	9·59
85	105	9·98	12·49	10·06
85	105	10·51	12·81	10·05
85	120	10·35	12·81	9·48
85	120	10·91	12·24	9·69
100	105	10·21	12·74	9·81
100	105	10·66	13·37	10·36
100	120	10·88	13·82	10·22
100	120	10·36	12·54	9·63

[a] Mean value from two or three bricks of each type.
[b] Silicone rubber bricks measured $1·9 \times 12·1 \times 17·8$ cm, while nylon (thin) bricks measured $2·1 \times 12·1 \times 17·8$ cm.

parts, depended both on temperature and steam content of the heating medium (Table IV). The influencing factor was probably the overpressure in the retort which controlled expansion of the residual gases inside the pouch. Thus, the effect of residual air was much more significant at lower temperatures and higher steam contents. With steam content of 65% either at 115 or 120 °C, there was no appreciable decrease in heating rates even when up to 30 ml of residual air was present; presumably, the overpressure in the retort (90–110 kPa) must have prevented the entrapped air from expanding and thereby insulating the two larger surfaces of the brick. However, at 85% steam content, even 10 ml of residual air in pouches was sufficient to cause deterioration of the heat transfer rate. Hence, when higher processing overpressures are used, larger volumes of residual air could be permissible in the pouches without adversely affecting heat transfer rates. At a temperature of 115 °C when 65% steam was used, the air

TABLE IV
Mean f_h values[a] for packaged teflon bricks[b] in the Lagarde retort at different
residual air contents

Residual air content (ml)	Mean f_h value (min)					
	115°C			120°C		
	Steam content (%)			Steam content (%)		
	65	75	85	65	75	85
0–10	20·42	20·66	23·29	19·93	20·69	21·69
11–20	19·42	23·63	25·98	19·43	20·97	24·81
21–30	19·71	23·62	29·79	20·14	22·94	25·62
31–40	19·44	24·95	30·11	21·82	25·09	30·45

[a] Mean value from several packages.
[b] Teflon bricks measured $2 \cdot 1 \times 11 \times 15$ cm.

present in the pouch could expand up to 1·43 times its volume level at room temperature, whereas if 85% steam was used, it could expand to 4·36 times. A relationship for the expansion factor (E) can be obtained from the equation: $E = P_a T_s / T_a (P_t - P_s)$, where P_a is the atmospheric pressure, T_a is the air temperature at the time of filling, P_t is the total retort pressure, P_s is the steam pressure and T_s is the retort temperature (all in absolute measures). In order to make comparisons of steam/air processes at different steam contents and temperatures, the measured air content at room temperature were adjusted using the above equation and then compared with the respective heating rate indices. The results indicated that as the adjusted air content increased above 30–40 ml, heating rate indices increased and displayed greater variability, suggesting that these conditions would not provide assurance of efficient heat transfer.

In the positive flow retort, the influence of residual air on the rate of heat transfer was similar except that the heating rate indices showed a greater scatter and were slightly more sensitive to overpressure. Processing with 65% steam at 115 °C which was found to maintain acceptable heat penetration rates into pouch packs even at residual air contents of 30 ml (unadjusted) in the Lagarde retort, appeared to be effective only up to a residual air content of 15–20 ml. Furthermore, at adjusted air contents above 20–30 ml, the heating rates decreased and assurance of adequate heat transfer would not be provided. The reason for the differences in the effects of residual air content observed in the two retorts is not clear at this time, but could be due to differences in their heating media flow patterns or orientation of the packages relative to medium flow direction. Conclusions from these experiments and analyses are that higher processing overpressure provides a greater processing safety assurance with respect to effects of residual air and that such processing overpressure is a critical factor in processing of flexible containers.

Summary of heating rate results. In general, an increase in f_h values of up to 11% was observed as the steam content of the media in the positive flow retort decreased from 100% to 50%. Heating of test bricks at 120 °C also resulted in an increase in the f_h value (up to 5·5%) compared to heating at 105 °C. In the Lagarde retort, the effects of both steam content and temperature on the f_h values were nonsignificant ($p > 0.05$). No conclusion could be drawn with respect to package orientation effects; some results indicated a higher f_h value in the vertical orientation than in the horizontal while others showed the reverse trend. Entrapped air pouches (up to 30 ml) did not appear to influence the f_h values in the presence of large overpressures (65% steam content at 115 or 120 °C) while they resulted in large increases in f_h value in the unconstrained horizontal orientation when processed at 115–120 °C in media of steam contents above 65%.

HEATING RATE LIMITATIONS IMPOSED BY SURFACE HEAT TRANSFER

When foods packaged in a given size, shape and type of container are heated in a retort, the heating rate at the product center can be considered to be limited by one or both of the following: (1) surface heat transfer, and (2) conductivity or thermal diffusivity (conductivity/specific heat × density) of the foods. In other words, the limiting condition(s) in heat transfer may be the rate at which heat is delivered to the package surface and/or the rate at which heat is transmitted through the food to the center. For thermal processing, a desirable heating medium would supply heat to the container at a sufficiently high rate so that the thermal properties of the food, along with its size and shape, will control the rate of temperature rise at the product center. This is the usual situation for canned foods processed in steam, but it is possible, when using water immersion or steam/air mixtures, for the surface heat transfer to be a limiting factor in some cases.

Since the heating rate at the product center is commonly measured as the f_h value, a rate limiting surface heat transfer would be reflected in an f_h value larger than would be observed in an ideal heating medium. It must be noted that experimental variability is present in replicate measurements of the heating rate index for a given food and package, and this may be well over ±10% for foods in retort pouches. For example, variability was reported to be as high as ±21% by Tung and Garland,[28] while ±3·7 to 5·7% variations were found in the f_h values published by Pflug.[11] Thus, a variability of ±5% for the experimental evaluation of f_h values would be a conservative assumption, and a surface heat transfer coefficient value can be determined theoretically to give an f_h value no greater than 5% more than the f_h value obtainable with an infinite surface heat transfer coefficient. This h value can then be considered to be an estimate for a 'limiting surface heat transfer coefficient' beyond which f_h values could be predicted assuming infinite surface heat transfer, with less than 5% error involved.

Materials and Methods

A number of brick-shaped sizes was selected to represent a range of potential thin profile configurations. For each of these, a representative thermal conductivity (0·5 W/m °C) was selected, and for a range of thermal diffusivity, Eq. (1) was used initially to calculate an f_h value assuming an infinite surface heat transfer coefficient. This f_h value was increased by 5% to provide the upper limit that might be expected due to experimental variations, and the 'limiting' surface heat transfer coefficient which would provide this increased f_h was then back-calculated using Eq. (1). In order to test the acceptability of the above limiting heat transfer concept, heating rates for silicone rubber and nylon test bricks were calculated under selected conditions. Surface heat transfer coefficients required for these computations were obtained from the regression equations reported earlier and the known thermal properties of the bricks. The f_h values in this way were then compared with experimental results for the same test conditions.

Results and Discussion

Limiting h values. Some representative values of the limiting surface heat transfer coefficient for various package dimensions and

he corresponding f_h values for a range of thermal diffusivities common
o foods at a thermal conductivity value of 0·5 W/m °C, are given in
Table V. The f_h values for infinite surface heat transfer can be
obtained either by using Eq. (1) or by dividing the values in Table V
by 1·05. Approximate minimal surface heat transfer coefficient values,
h'', at conductivities, k'', can be obtained from any value of h' at k' in
Table V, using the relationship, $h'' = h'(k''/k')$. Note that the value of
k' employed in Table V is 0·5 W/m °C.

For food materials with a representative conductivity value of
0·5 W/m °C, at the commonly used pouch thickness of 1·9 cm
(0·75 in), the minimum surface heat transfer coefficient could be
about 2000 W/m² °C. From the previous section dealing with surface
heat transfer as a function of fractional steam content in the pilot scale
positive flow and Lagarde retorts, steam contents of 0·6 and 0·5,
respectively, are the lower limits for providing an h value of about
2000 W/m² °C. When the surface heat transfer coefficients exceed that
value (at higher steam contents) the thermal diffusivity of the food
governs the rate of heat transfer into the center of the package. Since
the packaging method and the volume of entrapped air within the
pouch can significantly influence heat transfer into the product center,
the above analysis must be viewed with some caution. Furthermore,
without adequate turbulent flow in a steam/air mixture of a given
composition, the surface heat transfer coefficients shown in the earlier
section may not be achieved, and this could lead to a surface limiting

TABLE V

Limiting surface heat transfer coefficients[a] and associated f_h values for various rectangular
bricks and product thermal properties

Dimensions[b] (cm)				f_h value (min)		
			Limiting h	Thermal diffusivity ($\times 10^7 \, m^2/s$)		
T	W	L	(W/m² °C)	1·0	1·5	2·0
0·5	12·0	18·0	8 030	1·02	0·68	0·51
1·0	12·0	18·0	3 990	4·04	2·70	2·02
2·0	12·0	18·0	1 940	15·71	10·47	7·85
3·0	12·0	18·0	1 250	33·72	22·48	16·86
4·0	12·0	18·0	900	56·33	37·55	28·17
5·0	12·0	18·0	700	81·65	54·43	40·82
6·0	12·0	18·0	570	108·03	72·02	54·02

[a] Calculated for a thermal conductivity of 0·5 W/m °C.
[b] T, W and L are the thickness, width and length of the rectangular bricks.

heat transfer situation. In any case, the above analysis should provide a useful approach to assessing the efficacy of steam/air mixtures for retort pouch processing.

Comparison of heat rates. The concept of limiting surface heat transfer and its potential influence on heating rates was evaluated by comparison of experimentally measured f_h values with those calculated knowing the thermal properties and dimensions of silicone rubber and nylon bricks, and the heat transfer coefficients achieved under a range of processing conditions. The results are shown in Table VI for selected conditions in the positive flow and Lagarde retorts. At thermal conductivity values of 0·21 and 0·23 W/m °C for silicone rubber and nylon bricks, the limiting heat transfer coefficient would be about 700 W/m² °C, thus, the heating media can be assumed to be adequate for all tests in these experiments.

In comparison with the predicted values for f_h in the positive flow

TABLE VI

Comparison of predicted and experimental heating rates for silicone rubber[a] and nylon bricks[b] in the positive flow and Lagarde retorts

| Fractional steam content | $(W/m^2h\,°C)$ | Positive flow retort[b] f_h value (min) | | | |
| | | Rubber | | Nylon, thick | |
		Predicted	Experiment	Predicted	Experiment
0·50	1 260	10·62	11·65	22·47	23·71
0·65	2 360	10·45	11·37	22·17	23·65
0·85	5 480	10·34	10·75	21·98	23·41
1·00	10 310	10·31	10·50	21·91	22·64

| | | Lagarde retort[c] f_h value (min) | | | |
| | | Rubber | | Nylon, thin | |
		Predicted	Experiment	Predicted	Experiment
0·50	3 290	10·40	10·53	13·31	12·70
0·65	4 010	10·37	10·49	13·28	12·72
0·85	5 220	10·35	10·44	13·24	12·59
1·00	6 360	10·33	10·53	13·23	13·12

[a] Silicone rubber bricks measured 1·9 × 12·1 × 17·8 cm; nylon (thick) measured 2·4 × 12·1 × 17·8 cm; nylon (thin) measured 2·1 × 12·1 × 17·8 cm.
[b] Brick orientation: vertical.
[c] Brick orientation: horizontal.

retort, the experimental f_h values were on the average 6·1 and 5·5% higher for silicone rubber and nylon bricks. For the Lagarde retort studies, the experimental values were 1·3% higher and 3·6% lower for silicone rubber and nylon bricks respectively. These results are roughly within the ±5% limits on which this analysis was based.

From these studies, it appears that food-simulating test objects can be used for assessing the efficacy of heating media used in thermal processing applications. Test objects of appropriate configurations and thermal properties may be placed within a retort load of food containers and the thermal response (f_h value) measured to compare with values obtained in heating conditions known to be optimal. In this way, it may be possible to assess 'heat transfer distribution' under practical processing conditions which, up the present time, has not been demonstrated.

ACKNOWLEDGEMENTS

The authors wish to acknowledge the assistance of Ian Britt, Trudi Smith, Sara Weintraub, Edwin Kwong, Kirsten Young and Agnes Papke in various parts of this project. The cooperation and assistance of Robert Stark and his technical staff during the research periods at the Agriculture Canada Research Station in Kentville, and the management and staff at Magic Pantry Foods Inc., Hamilton are appreciated.

Support for this research and development project by the Agriculture Canada PDR Program, the Natural Sciences and Engineering Research Council of Canada Strategic Grants Program and the Canadian Commonwealth Scholarship and Fellowship Plan is also appreciated.

REFERENCES

1. Ball, C. O. and Olson, F. C. W. *Sterilization in Food Technology*. McGraw-Hill, New York, 1957.
2. Othmer, D. J. The condensation of steam. *Ind. Eng. Chem.* **21**(6): 576, 1929.
3. Lampi, R. A. Flexible packaging for thermoprocessed foods. *Adv. Food Res.* **23**: 305, 1977.
4. Mermelstein, N. H. An overview of the retort pouch in the U.S. *Food Technol.* **30**(2): 28, 1976.
5. Mermelstein, N. H. Retort pouch earns 1978 IFT Food Technology Industrial Achievement Award. *Food Technol.* **32**(6): 22, 1978.

6. Ball, C. O. Thermal process time for canned food. Bull. 37. National Research Council, Washington, DC, 1923.
7. Martens, T. Mathematical model of heat processing in flat containers. Ph.D. thesis, Catholic University, Louvain, Belgium, 1980.
8. Berry, R., Jr. The sterilization of food in pouches—critical parameters for still processing. Proc. of the Conference, held in Indianapolis, IN. Using Retort Pouches Worldwide—Focus on the Present with a Look to the Future. Sponsored by Food Sciences Inst., Purdue Univ., March 14–15, p.7, 1979.
9. Blaisdell, J. L. Natural convection heating of liquids in unagitated food containers. Ph.D. thesis, Michigan State University, East Lansing, MI, 1963.
10. Pflug, I. J., Bock, J. H. and Long, F. E. Sterilization of food in flexible packages. *Food Technol.* **17**(9):87, 1963.
11. Pflug, I. J. Evaluation of heating media for producing shelf stable food in flexible packages. Phase I. Final Rep., Contract DA19-AMC-145 (N). U.S. Army Natick Laboratories, Natic, MA, 1964.
12. Yamano, Y. Studies on thermal processing of flexible food packages by steam-and-air retort. Ph.D. thesis, Kyoto University, Kyoto, Japan, 1976.
13. Abdul-Hadi, M. I. An analytical investigation into dropwise condensation of different steam/air mixtures on substrates of various materials. *Can. J. Chem. Eng.* **57**(4):459, 1979.
14. Coulson, J. M. and Richardson, J. F. *Chemical Engineering,* Vol. 1, 3rd ed. Pergamon Press, Oxford, 1977.
15. Kisaalita, W. S. A study of heat transfer from steam/air mixtures to a retort pouch substrate. M.A.Sc. thesis, University of British Columbia, Vancouver, B.C. 1981.
16. Kusak, L. J. The condensation of vapors from noncondensing gases. Ph.D. thesis, Cornell University, Ithaca, New York, 1958.
17. Ramaswamy, H. S., Tung, M. A. and Stark, R. A method to measure surface heat transfer from steam/air mixtures in batch retorts. *J. Food Sci.* **48**(3): 900, 1983.
18. Adams, J. P. and Peterson, W. R. Processing of seafood in institutionalized retort pouches. *Food Technol.* **37**(7): 123, 1983.
19. Pflug, I. J. and Borrero, C. Heating media for processing food in flexible packages. Phase II. Tech. Rep. 67-47-GP. U.S. Army Natick Laboratories, Natick, MA, 1967.
20. Taguchi, G. *Experimental Designs.* Maruzen Publishing Co., Tokyo, Japan, 1957.
21. Snedecor, G. W. *Statistical Methods,* 5th ed. The Iowa State University Press, Ames, IA, 1965.
22. Merrill, D. G. Heating rates of glass containers. *Ind. Eng. Chem.* **40**: 2263, 1948.
23. Tung, M. A., Ramaswamy, H. S., Smith, T. and Stark, R. Surface heat transfer coefficients for steam/air mixtures in two pilot scale retorts. *J. Food Sci.* **49**: 939, 1983.
24. Tung, M. A., Ramaswamy, H. S. and Papke, A. M. Thermophysical studies for improved food processes. Final Report. Agriculture Canada DSS File No. 35SZ.01804-9-0001, 74 pp., 1984.
25. Ramaswamy, H. S. Heat transfer studies of steam/air mixtures for food processing in retort pouches. Ph.D. thesis. University of British Columbia. Vancouver, B.C., 1983.
26. Tung, M. A. Temperature distribution in a steam/air retort for thermally processed foods in flexible pouches. University of British Columbia, Vancouver, B.C., 9pp., 1974.
27. Shappee, J. and Werkowski, S. J. Study of a nondestructive test for determining the volume of air in flexible food packages. Tech. Rep. 73-4-GP. U.S. Army Natick Laboratories, Natick, M.A., 1972.
28. Tung, M. A. and Garland, T. D. Computer calculation of thermal processes. *J. Food Sci.* **43**(2): 365, 1978.

48

COMPUTERIZED DATA ACQUISITION AND CONTROL IN THERMAL PROCESSING

T. A. GILL, J. W. THOMPSON and B. LEBLANC

Canadian Institute of Fisheries Technology, Technical University of Nova Scotia, P.O. Box 1000, Halifax, Nova Scotia, Canada B3J 2X4

ABSTRACT

Two retorts were retrofitted with computerized data acquisition and control systems. Process control was carried out on the basis of up to ten test cans equipped with thermocouples. Three methods of process control were compared with the Ball formula method for both safety and accuracy. The system provided excellent on-line feed-forward control for conductively heated products, with anticipatory correction for cool-down lethality. A separate algorithm was used for convectively heated products with ρ values exceeding 0·9.

INTRODUCTION

Thermal processing of low acid foods in hermetically-sealed containers is designed to protect the consumer from microorganisms of public health significance while providing a convenient shelf-stable product which does not require refrigeration. Thermal processing conditions (temperature, process time) are traditionally determined by one of two methods:

(a) Improved General Method.[1,2]
(b) Ball Equation.[3]

Although the general method is applicable to convective, conductive and even some complex heating regimes, the original Ball equation was designed to fit only linear heat penetration curves. Both approaches require the establishment of a heat penetration curve for each product formulation and can size. Once a process has been established by one of the traditional methods, it is imperative that initial product temperature, processing temperature, product formulation and can size remain constant, since deviation from any of these parameters could result in under-processing.

Other approaches have also been described in the literature. The use of modern high speed computers has made it possible to simulate the heat penetration characteristics of conductively heated foods, knowing only the retort temperature, initial product temperature and thermal diffusivity of the product.[4-7] Although retort temperature deviation may be corrected by Teixeira's finite difference approach to computerized retort control, the method is applicable only to conductivity heated foods in cylindrical containers and the heat penetration characteristics of the product must be known in advance. Thus, any changes in formulation or container geometry would require more heat penetration work to be carried out. The object of the present study was to construct a computerized control system with the following features:

—feed-forward process control to cook to a desired F_0 value or cook time;
—automatic record keeping for the purpose of quality/safety assurance;
—a retrofit system which could be applied to modern conventional retort control situations;
—the retrofit computer control system should not in any way alter the function of the existing control system so that either control system could be used;
—a computerized control system which could be used for batch, semi-continuous and continuous retorts would be preferable but not essential.

The advantages of a computerized system are many. On-line correction for retort temperature deviations and automatic record-keeping are perhaps most important with regard to product safety. Since a computerized feed-forward process controller could conceivably deliver process lethality with greater precision and accuracy, re-processing could be reduced thereby reducing energy costs. The present report describes the design, construction, and initial testing of a computerized retort control system.

MATERIALS AND METHODS

Hardware

Since the system was to control processes for both conductively and convectively heated products, the concept of computer simulation of can temperatures was rejected in favor of temperature monitoring of a real product in real containers on a real time basis. Standard 'T' type thermocouple equipment was selected although telemetry was considered at the beginning of the project. Temperatures were monitored in up to 10 test cans fitted with CNL needle type thermocouple probes (O. F. Ecklund, Cape Coral Fla.). Teflon extruded thermocouple wire was used to conduct temperature readings to a Hewlett Packard Model 3054 DL data acquisition and control system equipped to monitor 19 input channels and control 16 output channels. The HP computer (HP-85) was equipped with 32K RAM, a printer/plotter ROM, an input/output ROM and matrix ROM.

Two retorts were retrofitted with computerized control. A WSF (WSF Industries, Tonawanda N.Y.) thermal process simulator (Fig. 1) was purchased, already equipped with a Taylor Fulscope Controller and Taylor electronic DSP programmer. This system allows a step-by-step progression through a pre-set processing sequence, allowing the dwell time on each step to be programmed from a keyboard. Controls of the retort functions (steam, water, air, sequencing and timing) are mediated by pneumatic, electrical, or electrical/pneumatic means. Computer control was gained over the Taylor equipment by the inclusion of 6 external relays (Potter and Brumfield) and 7 normally open quick exhaust solenoid valves (Ascoelectric, Brantford, Ont.). Temperature and pressure controls were modified by the installation of two DC stepping motors (Superior Electric, Bristol, Connecticut) to the Taylor Fulscope Controller. Functions were derived relating control knob cycle of rotation to temperature or pressure. Thus, temperature or pressure setting could be achieved by a series of pulses generated by the computer.

The second retrofit system was installed on a Lagarde (Autoclaves J. Lagarde, Montelimar, France) retort with internal dimensions 1 m × 1·2 m (Fig. 2). This retort system is normally controlled by a series of electrical relays which are activated and deactivated by eight photo-sensors. An aluminum card which is cut out to reflect all of the processing conditions at each step of the process is used to either interrupt (turn off) or permit (turn on) passage of light which in turn

A, solenoid valves (3-way quick exhaust N.O.); B, low voltage relays (DPDT, N.O.); C, HP85 computer; D, 3497 Data logger and controller; E, DC stepping motors; F, temperature and pressure controls; G, stepping motor controls; H, Taylor pneumatic and electric controls.

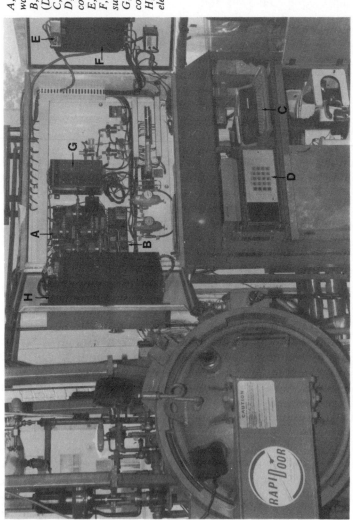

Fig. 1. A WSF thermal process simulator equipped with standard Taylor controls but retrofitted with computerized data acquisition and control capability.

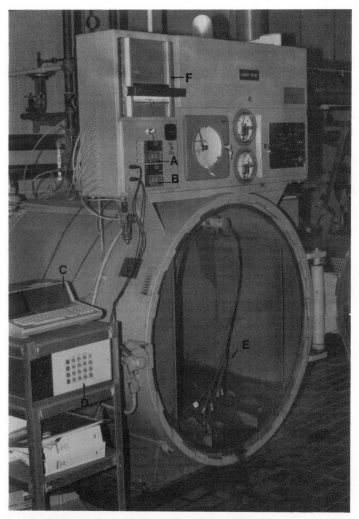

Fig. 2. A Lagarde retort system equipped with standard controls but retrofitted with computerized data acquisition and control capability. A, Shimaden temperature controller; B, Shimaden pressure controller; C, HP85 computer; D, 3497 Datalogger and controller; E, thermocouple wires for cans; F, Lagarde program card holder/controller.

activates or deactivates the sensor relays which control the retort function (air, steam, water, etc.). A different aluminum card is therefore required for each different process.

This system was modified such that all relays could be controlled by the data acquisition and control system. Two time-proportional controllers (Shimaden Controls, Tokyo, Japan) were installed to replace the standard temperature and pressure controls supplied by Lagarde. As a result, the retort pressure and temperature could not be adjusted up or down, however other model controllers would be able to perform this function.

Software

Figure 3 illustrates the simplified logic of the control program. The first program was developed for a steam cook and water cool using the lethal rate equation:

$$LR = 10^{(T-250)/z}$$

where LR is lethal rate (F_0 units per min), T is product temperature (°C), and $z = 10$ °C for *Cl. botulinum*.

The lethal effect of a process was then calculated as the sum of products $LR \times \Delta t$ for all time intervals (Δt) between temperature

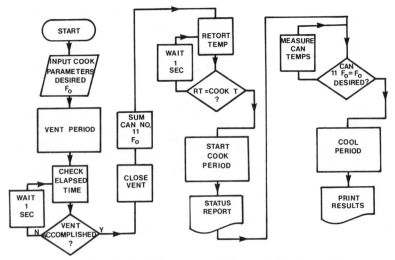

Fig. 3. Simplified logic for computerized control of a steam retort.

readings in test cans. For runs using ten test cans, the average duration between successive readings in any particular can was $16\cdot8$ s. Upon achieving the desired cumulative lethality (F_0-value), the computer shuts off the fan and steam and opens the cooling water inlet valve. This program (FC) was a prototype and worked well for convectively heated products.

Two approaches to feed-forward control logic were then developed in order to account for lethality contribution of the cool portion of the cycle. The first approach (BC) utilized the polynomial approximation of the ρ versus g tables.[8].

$$\rho = -(0\cdot002\ 307)\ \log g^5 - (0\cdot007\ 145\ 6)\ \log g^4$$
$$-(0\cdot026\ 104)\ \log g^3 - (0\cdot055\ 490)\ \log g^2$$
$$-(0\cdot080\ 565)\ \log g + 0\cdot900\ 85$$

where ρ is the fraction of lethality contributed by the heating portion of the process, expressed as a decimal, i.e. $1 - \rho$ is the fraction of lethality contributed during the cool; g is the difference between retort temperature and product temperature.

Thus feed forward control was gained by comparison of a computed F_{cum}/ρ with the desired F_0 value, where F_{cum} and ρ are the cumulative total lethality and lethality due to heating, at any point in time. The computer terminates heating and initializes cooling when $F_{\text{cum}}/\rho =$ desired F_0.

Another feed-forward program (NC) was based on the work of Naveh *et al.*[9–11] These authors used a finite element analysis to predict the relationship between ρ and g which they found useful in eliminating the problem of overcooking conduction-heating products in large containers. Two equations were derived by least squares to fit the published curve.[11]

$$\text{if } g > 0\cdot35\ \rho = 0\cdot843 \times e^{-0\cdot113 \times g}$$
$$g < 0\cdot35\ \rho = 0\cdot917 - (0\cdot28 \times g)$$

Again, feed-forward control was gained by comparison of F_{cum}/ρ with the desired F_0 entered by the retort operator at the beginning of each cook. All three approaches to computer control were compared to the Ball formula method (BF)[3] for accuracy and safety.

Testing was carried out using a 5% bentonite suspension in order to simulate a purely conductively-heated product. Five 307×115 cans were monitored for temperature during a series of cooks. Each of the four algorithms FC, BC, NC and BF were compared for their ability to deliver F_0 values of 4, 6, 8, 10, 12 and 14 at 121·1 °C. Plots of delivered F_0 versus desired F_0 were constructed for each of the four processing approaches.

RESULTS AND DISCUSSION

The computerized retort systems depicted in Figs. 1 and 2 can deliver either a desired cook time (B) or lethality (F_0). The latter is based upon real time and product temperature measurements in up to 10 cans.

After each iteration of temperature scan for all cans, the computer selects the lowest temperature reading to calculate lethality for that particular time interval. This value is then added to a file called 'can

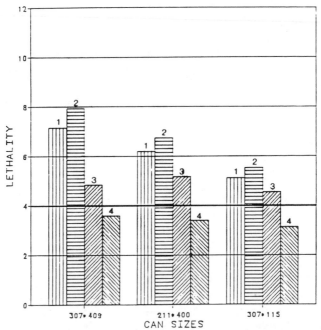

Fig. 4. *Histogram of average F_0 values delivered to test cans (sample size $n = 5$) filled with 5% bentonite suspension. Retort temperature was 121·1 °C and target F_0 was 4·0. Control algorithms were: 1, formula method (BF); 2, general method, no cool effect prediction (FC); 3, general method, Ball cool (BC); 4, general method, Naveh cool (NC).*

no. 11'. Thus, the F_{cum} value for the theoretical can no. 11 at the end of the cook represents the sum of the lowest lethalities, each determined at a 16·8 s time interval. As might be expected, the four control strategies delivered quite different results.

Figure 4 illustrates the relative safety and accuracy of the four methods using four different can sizes. In all cases, product consisted of 5% bentonite suspensions while cook temperature and target F_0 were 121·1 °C and 4·0, respectively. These data represent average lethalities for five test cans equipped with thermocouples. The FC procedure which did not correct for cool lethality was the safest but least accurate method of process control. The BC feed-forward control procedure was judged relatively safe with no individual test cans receiving less than the desired F_0 value of 4·0. Although the NC

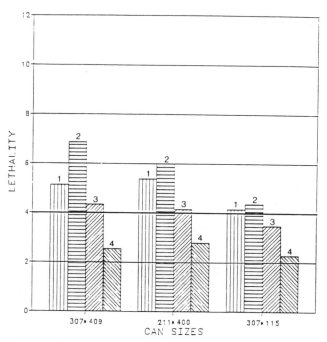

Fig. 5. Histogram of can no. 11 F_0 values delivered to test cans (sample size $n = 5$) filled with 5% bentonite suspensions. Retort temperature was 121·1 °C and target F_0 was 4·0. Control algorithms were: 1, formula method (BF); 2, general method, no cool effect prediction (FC); 3, general method, Ball cool (BC); 4, general method, Naveh cool (NC).

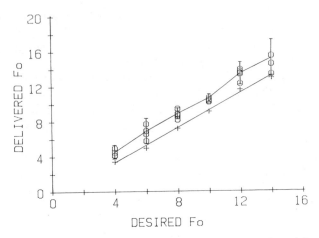

Fig. 6. Graph indicating relationship between F_0 desired and F_0 delivered for 307 × 115 cans filled with 5% bentonite (BC approach). Upper curve shows average F_0 for 5 test cans. Error bars show 95% probabilities. Lower curve shows best-fitting straight line through can no. 11 data: slope = 0·995; intercept = −0·657; $r^2 = 0·995$.

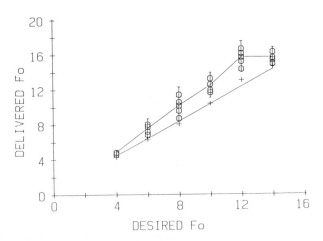

Fig. 7. Graph indicating relationship between F_0 desired and F_0 delivered for 307 × 409 cans filled with 5% bentonite (BC approach). Upper curve shows average F_0 for 5 test cans. Error bars show 95% probabilities. Lower curve shows best fitting straight line through can no. 11 data: slope = 0·992; intercept = 0·442; $r^2 = 0·984$.

approach apparently produces best results with large can sizes (Naveh *et al.*[9–11]), this procedure consistently delivered lethalities which were lower than desired. The accuracy of all methods except BC appeared to decrease but their safety increased as can size increased. The FC procedure delivered nearly a 100% overcook to the average 307 × 409 can size. The BC procedure delivered more than the target lethality to each of the individual test cans of all three sizes but less than the desired lethality to can no. 11 for the smallest can size (Fig. 5). The BC method delivered best results, using the can no. 11 criterion, to intermediate (211 × 400) and large (307 × 409) can sizes.

Figures 6 and 7 illustrate the relationship between desired and delivered lethalities for the computerized retort system using the BC software. The slopes, intercepts and r^2 values were 0·995, −0·657 and 0·995, for the best fit straight line for can no. 11 data in Fig. 6. The slope, intercept and r^2 for Fig. 7 was 0·992, 0·442, and 0·984, respectively. The error bars on both figures represent the 95% probability levels for the individual can data (open circles).

CONCLUSIONS

The computerized feed-forward control systems are capable of delivering F_0 values desired by the operator and are applicable to conductively and convectively-heated product types. Preliminary testing performed with test cans filled with 5% bentonite suspensions illustrate that the BC approach delivered best cool correction for conductively-heated product.

ACKNOWLEDGEMENT

This work was funded under DSS contract #OSC83-00561 by the request of Agriculture Canada as part of the ERDAF program.

REFERENCES

1. Ball, C. O. Mathematical solution of problems on thermal processing of canned food. Univ. Calif. Publ. Public Health 1, 230 pp., 1928.
2. Schultz, O. T. and Olson, F. C. W. Thermal processing of foods in tin containers III. Recent improvements in the general method of thermal process calculations—a

special coordinate paper and methods of converting initial and retort temperatures. *Food Res.* **5:** 399, 1940.

3. Ball, C. O. Thermal process time for canned foods. Bull. Nat. Res. Council 7, Part 1, No. 37, 1923.

4. Teixeira, A. A., Dixon, J. R., Zahradnik, J. W. and Zinsmeister, G. E. Computer determination of spore survival distributions in thermally-processed conduction-heated foods. *Food Technol.* **23:** 353, 1969.

5. Teixeira, A. A., Dixon, J. R., Zahradnik, J. W. and Zinsmeister, G. E. Computer optimization of nutrient retention in thermal processing of conduction-heated foods. *Food Technol.* **23:** 845, 1969.

6. Teixeira, A. A., Zinsmeister, G. E. and Zahradnik, J. W. Computer simulation of variable retort control and container geometry as a possible means of improving thiamine retention in thermally processed foods. *J. Food Sci.* **40:** 656, 1975.

7. Teixeira, A. A. and Manson, J. E. Computer control of batch retort operations with on-line correction of process deviations. *Food Technol.* **36**(4): 85, 1982.

8. Ball, C. O. and Olson, F. C. W. *Sterilization in Food Technology.* McGraw–Hill, New York, 1957.

9. Naveh, D., Kopelman, I. J. and Pflug, I. J. The finite element method in thermal processing of foods. *J. Food Sci.* **48:** 1086, 1983.

10. Naveh, D., Kopelman, I. J., Zechman, L. and Pflug, I. J. Transient cooling of conduction heating products during sterilization: temperature histories. *J. Food Proc. Pres.* **7:** 259, 1983.

11. Naveh, D., Pflug, I. J. and Kopelman, I. J. Transient cooling of conductive heating products during sterilization: sterilization values. *J. Food Proc. Pres.* **7:** 275, 1983.

49

OPTIMIZATION OF THE THERMAL PROCESSING OF FOOD

ROBERT KOK

Department of Agricultural Engineering, Macdonald College of McGill University, 21,111 Lakeshore Blvd, Ste Anne de Bellevue, Quebec, Canada H9X 1C0

ABSTRACT

Although the overriding concern in thermal processing of food is public safety, many other factors may be taken into account in process design. These may include the destruction of secondary organisms of non-public health concern, but also the destruction and creation of nutrients, antinutritionals and other attributes. The various process requirements may be either made into process constraints (conditions that must be met); included in the objective function (wherein conditions can be traded off against one another), or used for both the above functions. An optimal process may then be calculated so that the objective function is maximized while all the constraints imposed are satisfied.

Two computer packages were written, one to optimize batch processes, the other for aseptic process optimization. Both are extremely user-friendly and allow user access to all intermediate data such as temperatures, velocities, viscosities, flows, or concentrations.

INTRODUCTION

Two major types of systems are available to thermally process food: batch and aseptic. The major difference between the two is that in the former the food is first packaged and then processed, whereas in the latter this order of events is reversed. The term 'batch' refers in this instance to the method of treatment of the food, not the operation of the equipment. Batch containers of food (cans, pouches) may be processed batchwise, e.g. in the classical retort, or continuously, e.g.

559

in a hydrostatic retort. Aseptic processes are invariably continuous in operation. In both types of systems, the objective is to produce food that is shelf-stable and microbiologically safe, while only minimally degrading the nutrients and sensory properties. Frequently, a minimal level of texture, flavor or color determination must also be attained. Process designers and operating staffs have available to them a wide variety of options to meet the microbiological safety criteria for any given product. The objective of process optimization is to determine which option is the most favorable. Several user-friendly computer program packages were created to make optimization techniques available to designers and operation managers of batch and aseptic processes. These packages were written to be accessible and useful to persons being only minimally familiar with computers.

OPTIMIZATION

For a batch process a variety of temperature–time combinations applied to the outside of the container will cause adequate lethality within it.[1] If the equipment is operated batchwise the temperature–time history (i.e. the 'input function' to the heat transfer system) may for example consist of a fairly slow rise (the retort 'come-up' time) followed by a stable period (the cooking time) and a relatively fast decrease (retort emptying). For continuously operating batch processing equipment the initial temperature increase rate and the final temperature decrease rate on the outside of the container may be somewhat higher, but in either case the food inside the batch container undergoes heating and cooling. The pattern of food temperature change may be described by means of a distribution of temperature–time histories, the heat transfer system 'output function'. This output function is the convolution of the input function and the heat transfer function[2,3] which depends on the heat transfer mechanism. The contaminant destruction attained within the container is the convolution of the distribution of temperature–time histories and the contaminant temperature–death function. Thus, many different input functions may satisfy the overall lethality requirement. Similarly, the destruction of nutrients or antinutritional factors, the texture changes or development of off-flavor, and the lethalities of various secondary contaminating organisms may be found by convoluting the heat transfer output function with the various component temperature–

destruction or temperature–creation functions.[4,5] The heat sensitive components in food are all different in their responses so that any thermal process input function results in a vector of component destruction/creation output values. To choose a 'best' input function requires the combination of the significant vector elements in some rational fashion to obtain a scalar.[6,17] This scalar is called the 'objective function'. Input functions may be compared in terms of the magnitudes of their associated objective function values.

For an aseptic process the situation is very similar to that of the batch arrangement. However, the food moves through the equipment continuously and, unless perfect plug flow conditions are maintained throughout, it will exhibit a residence time distribution. (In contrast, in batch processing, all the food has exactly the same residence time.) The residence time distribution will be determined by the conditions of flow in the equipment and the rheological behaviour of the food.[7] The temperature–time history distribution is determined by both the heat transfer mechanism (e.g. convection, turbulence, diffusion) and the residence time distribution. In this case, the output function is more complex than for the batch process because of the extra degree of freedom. Again, a component creation/destruction vector can be calculated for each input function and various input functions can be compared in terms of their resulting objective function values.

For practical reasons, it may be difficult to propose an almost infinite number of possible input functions, calculate their associated objective function values and then choose the most appropriate one accordingly. In 'true' optimization the process is reversed; rather than following the 'trial-and-error' method, optimization mathematics directly yields the input function which maximizes the objective function.[6,8,18] For a batch process the result might be the required temperature–time history which must be applied at the outside of the container.[9,10] For an aseptic process it might be the heat flux required as a function of distance along the food flow path. A characteristic of 'dynamic' optimization[17] is that the solution is not a scalar but instead, a continuous function (or set of functions) in one or more dimensions, or the discrete equivalent—a vector or a matrix. For food processing applications, the situation becomes more complex. The solution must be constrained to occur within physically realizable limits. For example, the retort temperature and its first derivative with respect to time can vary only within certain limits. Moreover, a number of other constraints are normally imposed on the process. The most common of these is the lethality requirement but minimal levels of texture development and antinutritional factor destruction are also often required. These constraints confine the range of allowable solution input functions and make the solution finding procedure mathematically arduous. The complexity of the problem may however be greatly reduced by further limiting the solution. First, the solution can be forced to be a one-dimensional function (i.e. one independent variable) and secondly, the first derivative of the solution can be forced to zero. In essence, the problem is then reduced to finding a scalar value of one independent variable at which all the process constraints are satisfied and the objective function is maximized. This is a minimization/maximization or 'static' optimization problem.[17]

Throughout the literature the term 'optimization' is used to refer to a wide variety of problems and methods of searching for solutions. Although optimization provides a formal and structured approach to finding a 'best' process, a great deal of subjective judgement is required in its implementation. It is ironic that the constitution of the 'objective function' is totally subjective; the destruction or creation of a component may arbitrarily be assigned any significance—this may be based on cost, nutritional value, social demand, etc. The constraints imposed are also largely subjectively determined and are often based on long-term operating experience (e.g. the lethality requirement) and market demand (e.g. the color of green peas). The constraints on the input function are determined by the capabilities of the equipment and the cost of its operation. It is physically possible to build a retort which can execute practically any temperature–time history but it may not be cost effective to do so.[12] Mostly, retort temperatures are not variable with time and aseptically processed food is held at a constant temperature in a holding tube so that severe constraints on the input function are applicable in practice, but there is no reason *a priori* why this should be so.

The optimization process depends totally on mathematical descriptions or models of the heat transfer mechanism, fluid flow behaviour, and the various temperature-related effects.[13] These models describe reality to only a limited extent so that the results from their use must be treated with a certain caution.[14–16] In short, optimization procedures provide a structured approach combining subjectively established criteria with limited descriptions of reality. As such, they can considerably reduce the amount of physical experimentation needed to find an optimal process. In the limit, if the mathematical models used are sufficiently accurate, physical experimentation can practically be eliminated. The two computer packages written allow for the optimization of batch and aseptic processes, based on various models of heat transfer, fluid flow and component destruction/creation.

THE BATCH PROCESS PROGRAM PACKAGE

The batch process package was designed to simulate and optimize thermal processing in a variety of container types and sizes. Many of its methods and routines were adaptations of those described by Finnegan.[19] The package consists of a set of hierarchically arranged modules: system startup programs, menu displays, user-friendly interfaces and work routines. This modular approach facilitates package expansion. If the necessary work routines are already in place, addition of a new application may only require the writing of an interface. During operation, control is transferred between the various program levels but the user communicates exclusively with intelligent, interactive interfaces while the work routines remain invisible. The interfaces ask the user for appropriate information and check the validity and allow correction of unreasonable data. Because of the user-friendliness of the package, minimal learning time is required. All the programs are written in compilable BASIC; the system is set up to run on an IBM PC with 640 kilobytes of memory and two double-sided disk drives or a hard disk.

Five work routines and five application interfaces are presently incorporated in the package. These are called MAINA to MAINE and SUB1 to SUB5 respectively. SUB1 calculates the centre temperature of a cylindrical can according to Ball and Olson's[1] method—several *j*-factor options are available. SUB2 and SUB3 calculate the temperature at any location in a retort pouch modelled as a brick—for SUB3 a convective heat transfer coefficient must be supplied. SUB4 and SUB5 calculate the temperature at any location in a cylindrical can—for SUB5 a convective container surface heat transfer coefficient must again be specified. The MAINA application interface is used to simulate and display the spatial temperature distribution in a container for any of the models incorporated in SUB1 to SUB5. MAINB calculates the lethality and nutrient retention in a cylindrical container based on Ball and Olson's[1] methods incorporated in SUB1. MAINC and MAIND calculate temporal and spatial temperature, lethality and nutrient retention distributions in pouches and cans respectively with the aid of SUB2 to SUB5. Container surface heat transfer coefficients may be specified. MAINE finds the batch process temperature at which maximal nutrient retention will result. Its conclusions are based upon the centre temperature found by means of SUB1. In this case, 'optimization' is accomplished by calculating the objective function value at a number of temperatures and choosing the temperature at which the maximum value is obtained, while satisfying the lethality constraint. The results can be displayed graphically on the computer screen or may be printed. A typical objective function curve is shown in Fig. 1. Independent variable values were: food initial temperature = 50 °C; cooling water temperature = 25 °C; heating curve slope = 2500 s; cooling curve slope = 2300 s; heating curve lag factor = 1·41; cooling curve lag factor = 1·41; total processing time = 7000 s; organism $F_0 = 2·45$ min, $z = 10$ °C; nutrient no. 1 $F_0 = 700$ min, $z = 27$ °C, relative weight = 1·0; nutrient no. 2 $F_0 = 1000$ min, $z = 17$ °C,

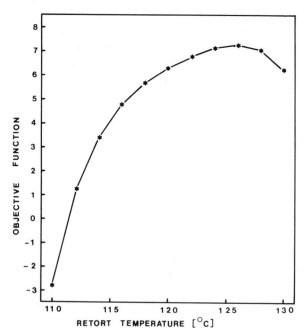

Fig. 1. Typical objective function curve from the batch program package.

relative weight $= -0.75$ (antinutritional). The maximum objective function value occurred at 125 °C.

THE ASEPTIC PROCESS PACKAGE

In the design of this package a number of features described by Sidaway[20] were adopted. The aseptic process model was based on a number of assumptions: (1) the process consists of three separate stages: heating, holding (in a 'holding tube') and cooling, (2) the food being processed is a liquid whose rheological behavior can be described by one of five models (ideal Newtonian, pseudo plastic, dilatant, Bingham plastic or Herschel–Bulkley), (3) the process is operating at steady state, (4) the holding tube cross section is circular, (5) flow in the tube is laminar and fully developed, (6) the tube is perfectly insulated so that holding is isothermal, (7) heating and cooling of the liquid before and after holding have negligible effects on the lethality and the destruction or development of nutrients, (8) contaminants, attributes and nutrients are uniformly distributed throughout the fluid, (9) nutrient, attribute and contaminant destruction and creation proceed according to the first order reaction kinetics model, (10) the temperature dependence of the contaminant death rate can be described by the classical approach using F and z values, and (11) the nutrient and attribute destruction and creation depend on temperature according to the Arrhenius model. In this package a number of optimization constraints may simultaneously be specified. Thus, process optimization may take place while the program ensures that up to five different organisms are deactivated (lethality constraints), up to five factors are minimally destroyed (destruction constraints, e.g. antinutritional factors) and up to five factors are minimally created (creation constraints, e.g. cooked flavour development). The objective function is composed of four types of factors: positive and negative attributes destroyed and positive and negative attributes created. Up to five attributes of each type can be included in the objective function. With this approach the destruction of an antinutritional factor can be traded off versus the development of a desirable color versus the destruction of a vitamin while two target organisms are deactivated. The weights accorded to the various attributes as well as all the kinetic parameters must be supplied by the user. This is done via an extremely friendly interface. The process independent variables that must also be specified are: (1) holding tube diameter, (2) mass flow, (3) fluid density and density temperature coefficient, (4) temperature search range and number of temperatures searched, (5) rheological parameters and (6) the number of radial elements into which the tube cross section is to be divided for the calculations.

The package runs on an IBM PC with 640 kilobytes of memory and two double-sided disk drives. Again, optimization is accomplished by calculation of the objective function at a number of temperatures and comparing the values. An objective function curve is shown in Fig. 2. Independent variable values were: tube diameter = 2 cm; mass flow = 1 kg/s; fluid density = 1000 kg/m^3, temperature coefficient = −1 kg/ m^3 °C; temperature search range 120–140 °C; fluid viscosity = 1.0 Pa s; activation energy of viscosity–temperature function = −30 kJ/mole; number of radial elements = 10; organism $F = 2.45$ min, $z = 10$ °C; nutrient no. 1 $D_0 = 3000$ s, $z = 32$ °C, relative weight = 0.8; nutrient

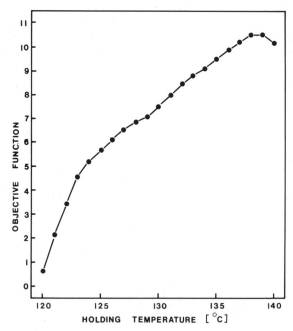

Fig. 2. Objective function curve from the aseptic processing program.

no. 2 $D_0 = 5000$ sec, $z = 22\,°C$, relative weight $= -0\cdot8$ (antinutritional). The maximum objective function occurred at $138\,°C$.

CONCLUSIONS

The two program packages can be used to investigate alternate processes or to find optimal ones. Both packages allow the user access to all intermediate calculated results such as temperature and survival distributions, velocity profiles, etc. The process designer can therefore quickly gain a thorough understanding of the details of his process and how variations in independent variables affect the dependent ones. Many process design methods were previously based on short-cut mathematical procedures to reduce the calculation effort. By means of detailed models contained in user-friendly computer programs, better designs can be generated. For example, in many cases the aseptic process package will specify holding tube lengths substantially different (i.e. by a factor of 2 or more) from those based on the average fluid velocity. This is because in the program the calculations are based on the velocity profile. It is, however, preferable to shield the user from such calculations. A user-friendly program makes the results of sophisticated calculations available with very little effort.

ACKNOWLEDGEMENTS

The author gratefully acknowledges the generous financial support of the Conseil des Recherches et Services Agricoles du Quebec in support of this work.

REFERENCES

1. Ball, C. O. and Olson, F. C. W. *Sterilization in Food Technology*. McGraw-Hill, New York, 1957.
2. Carslaw, H. S. and Jaeger, J. C. *Conduction of Heat in Solids,* 2nd edn. Oxford University Press, Oxford, 1959.
3. Luikov, A. V. *Analytical Heat Diffusion Theory*. Academic Press, New York, 1968.
4. Lund, D. B. Quantifying reactions influencing quality of foods: texture, flavor and appearance. *J. Food Proc. Preserv.* 6(3): 133–53, 1982.
5. Manson, J. E., Zahradnik, J. W. and Stumbo, C. R. Evaluation of lethality and nutrient retentions of conduction heating foods in rectangular containers. *Food Technol.* 24(11): 109–12, 1970.

6. Beveridge, G. S. G. and Schechter, R. S. *Optimization: Theory and Practice.* McGraw-Hill, New York, 773 pp., 1970.
7. Teixeira, A. A. and Manson, J. E. Thermal process control for aseptic processing systems. *Food Technol.* **37**(4): 128–33, 1983.
8. Bender, F. E., Kramer, A. and Kahan, G. Linear programming and its applications in the food industry. *Food Technol.* **36**(7): 94–6, 1982.
9. Saguy, I. and Karel, M. Optimal retort temperature profile in optimizing thiamin retention in conduction type heating of canned foods. *J. Food Sci.* **44**(5): 1485–90, 1979.
10. Teixeira, A. A., Zinsmeister, G. E. and Zharadnik, J. W. Computer simulation of variable retort control and container geometry as a possible means of improving thiamine retention in thermally processed food. *J. Food Sci.* **40**(4): 656–9, 1975.
11. Lund, D. B. Applications of optimization in heat processing. *Food Technol.* **36**(7): 97–100, 1982.
12. Teixeira, A. A., Dixon, J. R., Zahradnik, J. W. and Zinsmeister, G. E. Computer optimization of nutrient retention in the thermal processing of conduction heated foods. *Food Technol.* **23**(3): 137–42, 1969.
13. Saguy, I. Optimization theory, techniques, and their implementation in the food industry: introduction. *Food Technol.* **36**(7): 88–93, 1982.
14. Lund, D. B. Considerations in modeling food processes. *Food Technol.* **37**(1): 92–4, 1983.
15. Lenz, M. K. and Lund, D. B. Experimental procedures for determining destruction kinetics of food components. *Food Technol.* **34**(2): 51–5, 1980.
16. Saguy, I. and Karel, M. Modeling of quality deterioration during food processing and storage. *Food Technol.* **34**(2): 78–85, 1980.
17. Saguy, I. Optimization methods and applications. In *Computer-Aided Techniques in Food Technology* (I. Saguy Ed.). Marcel Dekker, New York, 494 pp., 1983.
18. Saguy, I. Optimization of dynamic systems utilizing the maximum principle. In *Computer-Aided Techniques in Food Technology* (I. Saguy Ed.). Marcel Dekker, New York, 494 pp., 1983.
19. Finnegan, N. Development of an interactive microcomputer software package for the optimization of batch sterilization processes. M.Sc. thesis, McGill University, 431 pp., 1984.
20. Sidaway, D. M. Optimization of continuous sterilization of fluid foods by means of an interactive computer package. M.Sc. thesis, McGill University, 201 pp., 1984.

50

ESTIMATION OF PROCESS CONDITIONS FOR BULK STERILIZATION OF PARTICULATE FOODS IN WATER-FLUIDIZED BEDS

HIROSHI SAWADA and R. L. MERSON

Department of Food Science and Technology, University of California, Davis, California 95616, U.S.A.

ABSTRACT

A water-fluidized bed system was designed for sterilizing particulate foods for aseptic filling. A mathematical model describing heat transfer in a fluidized bed of spheres was used to optimize thermal process conditions in terms of volume-averaged quality F_0. Simulated optimum conditions for sterilizing 500 kg of beef or potato spherical particulates (1·27–2·54 cm diameter) in a 1 m diameter fluidization column should be achievable in practice. The quality F_0 values calculated for these conditions indicate that high levels of quality retention could be expected in the finished product.

NOMENCLATURE

$A(\lambda_k)$ = constant defined by Eq. (9)
Ar   = Archimedes number $= g D_p^3 (\rho_s - \rho_f) \rho_f / \mu^2$
$B(\lambda_k)$ = constant defined by Eq. (10)
Bi   = Biot number $= hR / K_s$
C_1 = $3h(1 - \varepsilon)R / (\alpha \rho_f C_{pf} \varepsilon)$
C_2 = $QR^2 / (\alpha V_b \varepsilon)$
C_{pf} = heat capacity of fluid (J/kg K)
C_{ps} = heat capacity of solid (J/kg K)
D_{121} = decimal reduction time at 121·1 °C (min)
D_p = diameter of spherical particle (m)
F_{0P} = process $F_0 = \int_0^{t_p} 10^{(T - 121 \cdot 1/z)} \, dt$ (min)
F_{0Q} = quality $F_0 = \int_0^{t_p} 10^{(T - 121 \cdot 1/z_0)} \, dt$ (min)

g = acceleration due to gravity (m/s^2)

h = surface heat transfer coefficient at particle/fluid interface $(W/m^2\,K)$

j_h = Colburn j factor for heat transfer $= (h/C_{pf}\rho_f u)\,(Pr)^{2/3}$

K_f = thermal conductivity of fluid $(W/m\,K)$

K_s = thermal conductivity of solid $(W/m\,K)$

Pr = Prandtl number $= C_{pf}\mu/K_f$

Q = volumetric flow rate (m^3/s)

r = radial position within sphere (m)

R = radius of sphere (m)

Re_p = modified particle Reynolds number $= \rho_f u D_p/\mu(1-\varepsilon)$

t = time (s)

t_h = heating time (s)

t_p = combined time of heating and cooling (s)

T_0 = initial temperature (°C)

$T_{fl}(t)$ = fluid temperature (°C)

T_{hm} = heating medium temperature (°C)

$T_{sp}(r, t)$ = sphere temperature (°C)

u = superficial fluid velocity $= Q/$column cross section (m/s)

u_t = terminal free falling velocity of isolated particle (m/s)

V_b = total volume of bed (m^3)

z = z-value for thermal death of spores, taken as 10 °C

z_Q = z-value for thermal degradation of quality attributes of foods, taken as 27·8 °C

α = thermal diffusivity of particulate $= K_s/\rho_s C_{ps}$ (m^2/s)

ε = void fraction, fluid volume/V_b

θ = Fourier number $= \alpha t/R^2$

θ_h = Fourier number for heating time, $= \alpha t_h/R^2$

λ_k = roots of the Eigen equations

μ = viscosity of fluid (Pa s)

ρ_f = density of fluid (kg/m^3)

ρ_s = density of solid (kg/m^3)

INTRODUCTION

Despite many attempts to process low acid products containing discrete particulates aseptically, commercial success has been limited because of difficulties in both sterilization and packaging.[1] Continuous sterilization of particulate-containing products has been investigated by several researchers.[2-5] However, because the heating rate for the solid is slow, the faster heating liquid is often overprocessed. The advantage of the high temperature–short time process decreases as particle size increases.[2] Moreover, there are design difficulties in assessing the heat transfer rate to suspended particles[3,6] and in determining the residence time distribution;[5,7] in fact, the long holding time required to sterilize particulates increases the dispersion of residence times encountered.

Accordingly, Lund[8] suggested thermally processing the particulates batchwise, separately from the liquid, to precisely control process time. This technique has been successfully developed[9] using a large rotating vessel to sterilize the particulates; however, equipment construction was rather complex.

This work describes an alternative batch method, a water-fluidized bed of particulates in which heat transfer would be rapid and uniform, process control could be accomplished easily, and equipment would be simple.[10] Conceptually (Fig. 1), food particulates are fluidized with hot water for sterilization and cold sterile water for cooling. The auxiliary

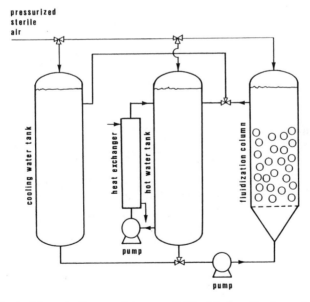

Fig. 1. Schematic diagram of the water-fluidized bed sterilization system.

heater maintains the temperature in the hot water tank. Recycling the hot water minimizes energy usage. Heat regeneration may also be readily incorporated into the system, because only water is used as the heat transfer medium. The whole system is pressurized with sterile air to achieve temperatures above 100 °C. Pump requirements are minimal since both sides of the pump are equally pressurized.

The objective of this study was to use a mathematical model for heat transfer in such a fluidized bed system to predict optimal process conditions for bulk sterilization of spherical particulate foods.

PREDICTION OF TIME–TEMPERATURE PROFILES

Derivation and experimental verification of the heat transfer model are reported elsewhere.[11] The analysis considered a bed of identical spheres fluidized by water flowing at constant volumetric flow rate Q. At zero time the influx fluid temperature changed stepwise from temperature T_0 to heating medium temperature T_{hm}. Assuming perfect mixing in the bed, the fluid temperature T_{fl} is uniform and increases with time from initial T_0. Accounting for convective heat transfer to the spheres but neglecting heat flow across the column wall, the macroscopic energy balance on the fluid is:

$$Q\rho_f C_{pf}(T_{hm} - T_{fl}) = \varepsilon V_b \rho_f C_{pf} \frac{dT_{fl}}{dt} + h\frac{3(1-\varepsilon)V_b}{R}(T_{fl} - T_{sp}|_{r=R}) \quad (1)$$

with initial condition

$$T_{fl}(0) = T_0 \quad (2)$$

The temperature $T_{sp}(r, t)$ in the individual spheres is described[12] by:

$$\frac{\partial^2(rT_{sp})}{\partial r^2} = \frac{1}{\alpha}\frac{\partial(rT_{sp})}{\partial t} \quad (3)$$

with the spheres initially at uniform temperature T_0:

$$T_{sp}(r, 0) = T_0 \quad (4)$$

and boundary conditions at the center ($r = 0$) and surface ($r = R$):

$$T_{sp}(0, t) = \text{finite} \quad (5)$$

$$-K_s \frac{\partial T_{sp}}{\partial r}\bigg|_{r=R} = h(T_{sp}|_{r=R} - T_{fl}) \quad (6)$$

Laplace transform solution[11,13] of Eqs. (1)–(6) yields the temperature of the fluid as a function of time during heating:

$$\frac{T_{fl} - T_0}{T_{hm} - T_0} = 1 - 2C_1 C_2 \text{Bi} \sum_{k=1}^{\infty} \frac{e^{-\lambda_k^2 \theta}}{B(\lambda_k)} \tag{7}$$

and the temperature of the spheres as a function of time and radial position

$$\frac{T_{sp} - T_0}{T_{hm} - T_0} = 1 - \frac{2C_2 \text{Bi}}{r/R} \sum_{k=1}^{\infty} \frac{A(\lambda_k)}{(C_1 + C_2 - \lambda_k^2) B(\lambda_k)} \frac{\sin(\lambda_k)}{\lambda_k^2} \sin(\lambda_k r/R) e^{-\lambda_k \theta} \tag{8}$$

where

$$A(\lambda_k) = (C_1 + C_2 - \lambda_k^2)^2 \lambda_k^2 + [(C_2 - \lambda_k^2)\text{Bi} - (C_1 + C_2 - \lambda_k^2)]^2 \tag{9}$$

$$B(\lambda_k) = 2\lambda_k^2 C_1 \text{Bi} + (C_1 + C_2 - \lambda_k^2)^2 \lambda_k^2$$
$$+ (C_2 - \lambda_k^2)\text{Bi}[(C_2 - \lambda_k^2)\text{Bi} - (C_1 + C_2 \lambda_k^2)] \tag{10}$$

and λ_k is the kth root of Eq. (11).

$$(C_1 + C_2 - \lambda^2)\lambda \cos \lambda + [(C_2 - \lambda^2)\text{Bi} - (C_1 + C_2 - \lambda^2)] \sin \lambda = 0 \tag{11}$$

To cool the particles after heating for time t_h (Fourier number θ_h), the influx temperature is changed stepwise from T_{hm} to T_0:[11] The fluid temperature cools according to:

$$\frac{T_{fl} - T_0}{T_{hm} - T_0} = 2C_1 C_2 \text{Bi} \sum_{k=1}^{\infty} \frac{e^{-\lambda_k^2(\theta - \theta_h)} - e^{-\lambda_k^2 \theta}}{B(\lambda_k)} \tag{12}$$

and the spheres according to:

$$\frac{T_{sp} - T_0}{T_{hm} - T_0} = \frac{2C_2 \text{Bi}}{r/R} \sum_{k=1}^{\infty} \frac{A(\lambda_k)}{(C_1 + C_2 - \lambda_k^2) B(\lambda_k)} \frac{\sin(\lambda_k)}{\lambda_k^2} \sin(\lambda_k r/R).$$
$$\cdot (e^{-\lambda_k^2(\theta - \theta_h)} - e^{-\lambda_k^2 \theta}) \tag{13}$$

Using Eqs. (7), (8), (12) and (13) a FORTRAN program was written to generate dimensionless particle and fluid time–temperature profiles. At the particle center, L'Hospital's rule yields

$$\lim_{r/R \to 0} \frac{\sin(\lambda_k r/R)}{r/R} = \lambda_k \tag{14}$$

Eigen values (λ_k) were determined to the 25th root by the Regula Falsi method.[16] Calculations were terminated when the last term of the center temperature series became less than 10^{-6}, which always occurred within the 25th term.

In fluidized bed systems, the void fraction, the particle-fluid heat transfer coefficient, and the fluid flow rate are interrelated and cannot be set independently. Values of ε and h needed to predict time–temperature profiles using the mathematical model were obtained from correlations. Void fraction was calculated from

$$u/u_t = 0.825\varepsilon^{2.38} \tag{15}$$

determined experimentally,[11] where, according to Ref. 14

$$u_t = 1.74[gD_p(\rho_s - \rho_f)/\rho_f]^{1/2} \tag{16}$$

With the high Biot numbers encountered in the fluidized bed, exact h values were not critical in the time–temperature predictions. Values were calculated[15] from

$$j_h = 0.097 Re_p^{-0.502} Ar^{0.198} \tag{17}$$

ESTIMATION OF STERILIZATION CONDITIONS

Process conditions were predicted by calculating the minimum heating medium temperature for a given heating time which would give a final process $F_0(F_{0P})$ of no less than 6.0 min at the particulate center. Since more than one time–temperature combination would yield the given lethality value, the quality F_0

$$F_{0Q} = \int_0^{t_p} 10^{(T - 121 \cdot 1/z_Q)} \, dt \tag{18}$$

was used as the optimization parameter. The z_Q value, which represents the temperature dependence of the quality deterioration kinetics, was chosen to be $27.8\,°C$, a median of literature z-values[17] for vitamins (25–$31\,°C$), color, texture, flavor (25–$47\,°C$) and enzymes (7–$56\,°C$). The z used in F_{0P} calculations was $10\,°C$. Among the three operating parameters (ε, u and h), void fraction was chosen to be the input parameter, corresponding superficial fluid velocity and surface heat transfer coefficient were calculated from Eqs. (15) and (17), respectively. Dimensionless fluid temperature and particle temperatures at $0.1R$ spacing were calculated at $10\,s$ intervals. Using these temperatures, the heating medium temperature required for $F_{0P} >$

TABLE I
Thermal and physical properties used for process simulations

	Density (kg/m^3)	Specific heat $(J/kg\,K)$	Thermal conductivity $(W/m\,K)$	Thermal diffusivity $(\times 10^{-7}\,m^2/s)$	Viscosity $(\times 10^{-4}\,Pa\,s)$
Beef[a]	1 150	3 520	0·450	1·112	—
Potato[b]	1 070	3 270	0·556	1·589	—
Water[c] (80 °C)	971·8	4 196·4	0·670 1	—	3·547

[a] For round, canner and cutter grade.[21–23]
[b] For Danshaku.[24]
[c] Ref. 25.

6·0 min at the particulate center was sought by an iteration method in which the heating medium temperature was varied successively between 110 °C and 160 °C by 5·0 °C (rough adjustment) and by 0·2 °C (fine adjustment). Initial product and cooling water temperatures were set at 25 °C. For all F_0 calculations, integrations were performed numerically for temperatures above 90 °C. Volume-averaged F_{0P} and F_{0Q} were also calculated from the temperatures at each $0·1R$. The heating time was varied (30 s intervals) and the whole procedure repeated to find the minimum volume-averaged F_{0Q}.

Several sample processes were simulated, sterilizing 500 kg of beef and potato particles in a 1 m diameter fluidization column. Table I lists thermal and physical properties used in the program.

RESULTS AND DISCUSSION

The profiles in Fig. 2 illustrate two processes with different heating times (180 s and 360 s) but equal lethalities at the particle center. Plotting heating medium temperatures required to reach particle center $F_{0P} = 6.0$ min against heating time (Fig. 3) yields equal-lethality curves[18] for particulates of 1·27, 1·91 and 2·54 cm diameter and void fractions of 0·5 and 0·7. The volume-averaged F_{0Q} for each equal-lethality process is plotted against heating time in Fig. 4.

To estimate process conditions, either critical-point analysis or mass-average analysis can be used.[7] In this study, critical-point analysis was adopted to estimate equal-lethality process conditions, since it is more conservative than mass-average analysis. However, to evaluate

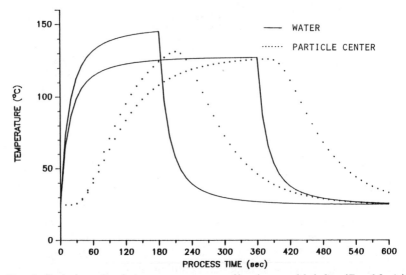

Fig. 2. *Typical predicted time–temperature profiles for equal-lethality* ($F_0 = 6·0$ min) *sterilization conditions with two heating times* (*500 kg of 1·91 cm diameter potato particles in 1 m diameter fluidization column*).

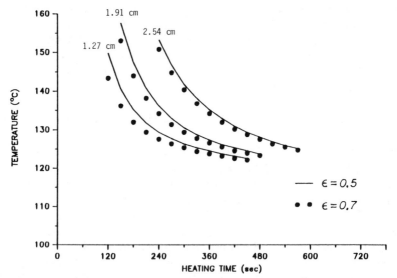

Fig. 3. *Predicted heating time–temperature requirements for critical* $F_0 = 6·0$ min *in potato particles of different diameter. Results are based on 500 kg of particles in a 1 m diameter fluidization column; ε is void fraction in column.*

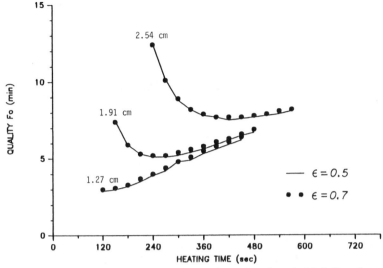

Fig. 4. Process optimization. Mass average quality values for equal lethality of potato particles (Process $F_0 = 6\cdot0\,min$). Quality F_0 is based on $z = 27\cdot8\,°C$; ε is void fraction in column.

quality retention, the volume-averaged F_{0Q} was considered appropriate, although the surface value would also be important, particularly for color and texture attributes.

Optimal process conditions (i.e. minimum F_{0Q}) can be found from Fig. 4 for 1·91 and 2·54 cm diameter potato particles. For 1·27 cm diameter particles, optimal conditions were not clearly seen, as F_{0Q} decreased with shorter heating time. However, heating times shorter than 120 s gave very high heating medium temperatures which were considered to be impractical. In addition, destruction of heat resistant enzymes may become the limiting factor[17] in evaluating optimal process conditions for 1·27 cm particulates.

Table II summarizes optimal sterilization conditions and corresponding F_{0P} and F_{0Q} values. Also included are total process times, defined as the time required to sterilize then cool the particle center to less than 30 °C.

For all simulations, predicted heating medium temperature and process time were well within practical ranges. Moreover, the volume averaged quality retention ranged from 82% (2·54 cm beef) to 94%

Hiroshi Sawada and R. L. Merson

TABLE II
Optimal process conditions for sterilization of 500 kg particulate foods in 1 m diameter fluidization column

Particulate diameter (cm)	Void fraction	Heating conditions			Processes and quality F_0^b (min)						Total process time (s)
		time (s)	θ_h^a (—)	temp. (°C)	F_{0Pc}	F_{0Ps}	F_{0Pa}	F_{0Qc}	F_{0Qs}	F_{0Qa}	
Potato											
1·27	0·5	120	0·47	149·8	6·0	58·4	23·4	1·9	4·4	2·9	310
	0·7	120	0·47	143·4	6·2	46·1	20·2	2·0	4·4	3·0	280
1·91	0·5	240	0·42	136·2	6·1	43·6	19·5	3·2	7·9	5·1	520
	0·7	240	0·42	134·2	6·1	40·6	18·3	3·2	8·1	5·2	500
2·54	0·5	420	0·41	131·0	6·1	39·0	17·7	4·7	11·9	7·5	860
	0·7	420	0·41	130·2	6·1	39·3	17·5	4·7	12·2	7·7	840
Beef											
1·27	0·5	150	0·41	142·2	6·0	60·1	24·5	2·3	6·1	3·8	350
	0·7	150	0·41	138·6	6·1	50·6	21·6	2·3	6·1	3·8	330
1·91	0·5	360	0·44	130·8	6·2	32·2	15·6	4·3	10·1	6·6	720
	0·7	330	0·40	131·8	6·1	43·5	18·8	4·0	10·8	6·7	670
2·54	0·5	630	0·43	127·4	6·2	32·8	15·5	6·2	15·2	9·8	1220
	0·7	600	0·41	128·0	6·1	39·6	17·3	6·0	15·9	9·8	1170

[a] Fourier number for heating time.
[b] c, s and a represent the center, surface and volume averaged values, respectively.

TABLE III
Water flow rates and bed height calculated for fluidization of
500 kg products in 1 m diameter fluidization column

Void fraction	Product	Bed height (m)	Particle diameter (cm)	Volumetric flow rate (m³/h)
0·5	Potato	1·19	1·27	87·5
			1·91	107
			2·54	124
	Beef	1·11	1·27	118
			1·91	144
			2·54	167
0·7	Potato	1·98	1·27	195
			1·91	239
			2·54	275
	Beef	1·85	1·27	262
			1·91	321
			2·54	371

(1·27 cm potato) when calculated from the quality F_0's and sample D_{121} value of 115 min for thiamine.[19] If the particle surface quality F_0 had been used, the lowest retention would be 73% (2·54 cm beef).

It is interesting to note that the Fourier numbers corresponding to optimal heating time (approximately 0·4–0·5) were very close to 0·5 suggested for conduction-heating packaged products.[20]

Optimal sterilization conditions and the resulting quality retention were practically independent of the levels of bed expansion (i.e. void fractions), although heat transfer rate did increase with increased void fraction. In contrast, Table III indicates that increasing void fraction from 0·5 to 0·7 roughly doubles the water flow rate and the bed height, thus requiring a larger pump and column. Even at low ε, the predicted water flow rate was very high. Further economic optimization of the product load and column size could result in a more economic operation size than the single case studied here.

CONCLUSIONS

Through mathematical simulation, bulk sterilization of particulate foods in a batch water-fluidized bed system was found to be practical in terms of sterilization conditions and resulting quality retention.

However, economic optimization of operation size is desirable before the process is commercialized. Further work is also needed to: (1) estimate quality losses due to leaching, (2) assess the influence of gases in the food tissue on fluidization characteristics and heat transfer rate, (3) determine axial temperature distribution and uniformity of heat treatment in large scale fluidized beds, and (4) design equipment which maintains asepsis of the particulates after sterilization in the column and during transfer to filling equipment. Despite these potential obstacles, the present findings indicate that water-fluidized beds should be considered as bulk sterilization systems for aseptic processing of particulate foods.

REFERENCES

1. Nelson, P. E. Outlook for aseptic bag-in-box packaging of products for remanufacture. *Food Technol.* **38**(3): 72–3, 1984.
2. de Ruyter, P. W. and Brunet, R. Estimation of process conditions for continuous sterilization of foods containing particulates. *Food Technol.* **27**(7): 44–51, 1973.
3. Hunter, G. M. Continuous sterilization of liquid media containing suspended particles. *Food Technol. in Australia.* **24**(4): 158–9, 162, 164–5, 1972.
4. Jacobs, R. A., Kempe, L. L. and Milone, N. A. High temperature–short time (HTST) processing of suspensions containing bacterial spores. *J. Food Sci.* **38**: 168–72, 1973.
5. Manson, J. E. and Cullen, J. F. Thermal process simulation of aseptic processing of foods containing discrete particulate matter. *J. Food Sci.* **39**: 1084–9, 1974.
6. Merson, R. L. and Paramo, G. Heat transfer in bulk food during heat sterilization. In *Heat Sterilization of Food* (T. Motohiro and K. Hayakawa Eds). Koseisha-Koseikaku Co., Ltd. Tokyo. pp. 98–108, 1983.
7. Merson, R. L. Mathematical procedures for estimating heat sterilization processes of bulk food in continuous heat exchangers. In *Heat Sterilization of Food* (T. Motohiro, and K. Hayakawa Eds). Koseisha-Koseikaku Co., Ltd., Tokyo, pp. 148–54, 1983.
8. Lund, D. B. Aseptic processing: Overview of commercial product sterilization process. *Proceedings, Conference on Aseptic Processing and the Bulk Storage and Distribution of Food.* Food Sciences Institute, Purdue University, March 15–18, 1978.
9. Hersom, A. C. and Shore, D. T. Aseptic processing of foods comprising sauce and solids. *Food Technol.* **35**(5): 53–62, 1981.
10. Davidson, J. F. and Harrison, D. *Fluidised Particles.* Cambridge University Press, London, pp. 1–3, 84–7, 1963.
11. Sawada, H. Estimation of process conditions for bulk sterilization of particulate foods in water fluidized beds. M.S. thesis, University of California, Davis, CA, 1984.
12. Carslaw, H. S. and Jaeger, J. C. *Conduction of Heat in Solids,* 2nd edn, Oxford University Press, London, p. 230, 1959.
13. Thomson, W. T. *Laplace Transformation: Theory and Engineering Applications.* Prentice-Hall, New York, 1950.

14. Boucher, D. F. and Alves, G. E. In *Chemical Engineering Handbook,* 5th edn, Section 5, Fluid and particle mechanics (R. H. Perry and C. H. Chilton Eds). McGraw-Hill, New York, p. 61, 1963.
15. Chang, T. M. and Wen, C. Y. Fluid-to-particle heat transfer in air-fluidized beds. Chem. Eng. Prog. Symp. Ser. No. 67, Vol. 62, pp. 111–17, 1966.
16. Abramowitz, M. Elementary analytical methods. In *Handbook of Mathematical Functions with Formulas, Graphs and Mathematical Tables* (M. Abramowitz and I. A. Stegun Eds). U.S. Government Printing Office, Washington, D.C., p. 18, 1964.
17. Lund, D. B. Design of thermal process for maximizing nutrient retention. *Food Technol.* **31**(2): 71–8, 1977.
18. Teixeira, A. A., Dixon, J. R., Zahradnik, J. W. and Zinsmeister, G. E. Computer optimization of nutrient retention in the thermal processing of conduction-heated foods. *Food Technol.* **23**: 845–50, 1969.
19. Feliciotti, E. and Esselen, W. B. Thermal destruction rates of thiamine in pureed meats and vegetables. *Food Technol.* **11**: 77–84, 1957.
20. Thijssen, H. A. C., Kerkhof, P. J. A. M. and Liefkens, A. A. A. Short-cut method for the calculation of sterilization conditions yielding optimum quality retention for conduction-type heating of packaged foods. *J. Food Sci.* **43**: 1096–101, 1978.
21. Hill, J. E. Thermal conductivity of beef. M.S. thesis, Georgia Institute of Technology, Atlanta, GA, 1966 (as cited in Dickerson[23]).
22. Riedel, L. Calorimetric investigations of the meat freezing process (in German). *Kaltetechnik* **9**(2): 38–40, 1957 (as cited in Dickerson[23]).
23. Dickerson, R. W. Jr. Thermal properties of foods. In *The Freezing Preservation of Foods,* 4th edn, Vol. 2, Chapt. 2 (D. K. Tressler, W. B. Arsdel and M. J. Copley Eds). AVI Publishing Co., Westport, CT, p. 39, 1968.
24. Yamada, T. The thermal properties of potato (in Japanese). *J. Agr. Chem. Soc. Japan* **44**: 587–90, 1970.
25. Weast, R. C. and Astle, M. J. (Eds). *CRC Handbook of Chemistry and Physics,* 62nd edn. CRC Press, Inc., Boca Raton, FL, pp. D-149, E-10, F-11, F-42, 1981.

51

A COMPARATIVE STUDY ON THE THERMAL INACTIVATION OF *B. STEAROTHERMOPHILUS* SPORES IN MICROWAVE AND CONVENTIONAL HEATING

H. KHALIL and R. VILLOTA

Department of Food Science, University of Illinois, Urbana, Illinois 61801, U.S.A.

ABSTRACT

The objective of this investigation was to compare microwave energy with traditional thermal inactivation techniques in commercial sterilization. Due to the dependence of microwave heating on food composition, the influence of various media on the heat inactivation of spores of Bacillus stearothermophilus *was monitored. Results obtained in microwave irradiated systems were compared with those obtained under similar conditions in conventionally heated samples.*

A temperature controlled water bath and a modified 600 W, 2450 MHz microwave cavity were utilized for the conventional and electromagnetic heating respectively. Survival curves and calculated D_{212} values showed consistently higher lethality for the microwave heated samples. The inhibitory effect of pH and sodium chloride also seemed to be enhanced in electromagnetic heating.

Based on information collected for sodium chloride and sucrose, trends indicate that solutes that have the ability to become ionized in solution would provide a more suitable environment for microbial inactivation when exposed to microwave irradiation.

INTRODUCTION

Commercial sterilization as a means of heat preservation gives a satisfactory shelf-life to many products. However, depending upon the food material, major possible drawbacks of commercial sterilization processes are scorching, development of cooked flavors and nutrient degradation. These undesirable changes are caused by exposure to high temperatures for relatively long periods of time to ensure proper enzyme inactivation and destruction of spores of pathogens and spoilage microorganisms. Because of the unique characteristics of dielectric heating by microwaves their utilization for the sterilization of food products offers an attractive alternative. The speed by which microwaves generate heat will most likely result in a minimum of thermal degradation of flavors and nutrients. In addition, there are possible energy savings due to the direct selective sorption of microwaves by the food resulting in short processing times. When discussing the subject of microwaves and its effect on microorganisms, the nature of lethality becomes of prime interest. While heat is the main lethal agent to microbes irradiated with microwaves, many investigators have suggested that athermal effects do exist. Early reports by Suskind and Vogelhut[12] and van Ummerson[13] initiated this hypothesis for both procaryotic and eucaryotic organisms.

Since food systems are nonconducting materials, the amount of power which can be generated in them when placed in an electromagnetic field is given by:

$$P = E^2 \times v \times \varepsilon_r'' \times 55 \cdot 61 \times 10^{-14}$$

where P is the power dissipated in watts/cm, E is the electric field strength (volts/cm), v is the frequency (c/s), and ε_r'', the dielectric loss factor.

From the above equation it can be seen that for a given frequency and field strength, the amount of heat generated in a food is related to its dielectric properties. The greater the 'lossiness' of material, the greater the absorption of the microwave energy and the greater the production of heat.

Dielectric properties are characteristic of each food component and depend on its chemical composition and physical structure. They also vary significantly with frequency and temperature. At the molecular level, microwave heating is caused by the disruption of weak hydrogen bonds resulting from dipole rotation of free water molecules and by electrophoretic migration of dissolved ions (i.e. free salts) in an electrical field of rapidly changing polarity (2·45 billion c/s at 2450 MHz). Therefore, volumetric displacement of fluid and ionic binding of water and ions by colloidal solids depress dielectric constants and loss levels of liquid and solid food products as compared with pure aqueous ionic solutions of the same activity and volume.

The aim of the present investigation was to determine how microwave thermal inactivation compares with that of conventional heating and to isolate the effect of food composition on sterilizing efficiency at isothermal conditions monitored through the destruction of *Bacillus stearothermophilus* spores using both heating modes.

MATERIALS AND METHODS

Temperature Control

For the microwave heating part of this study, a Sharp carousel microwave oven, Model SKR-7805 (Sharp Electronics Corporation, 10 Keystone Place, Parmus, New Jersey 07652) was utilized. Six test tubes, each containing a 10 ml sample, were placed on the inside periphery of a cylindrical pyrex container (18 cm I.D. and 9 cm in depth) filled with water. Sample tubes were closed with rubber stoppers. A removable temperature probe (a resistance thermocouple) provided with the microwave unit was inserted in the center of a representative sample tube through the rubber stopper. The probe jack was connected to a digital panel meter PH-349 (NON-linear Systems, Inc., 533 Stevens Ave., Solana Beach, CA 92075) modified to display millivolts which varied with the temperature of the sample monitored by the probe. A calibration curve was established in the temperature range of the experiment for easy conversion from millivolts to degrees Celsius. To avoid thermal runaway, the cylindrical container was filled with boiling distilled water immediately before irradiation. The boiling water served to stabilize sample temperature at 100 °C, which was the chosen isothermal condition, and also served as an underload protector. The turntable was rotated during heating for even wave distribution.

For the conventional heating part of this study, a Fisher immersion circulator heating Model 73 (Fisher Scientific Company, Pittsburgh, PA, sensitivity ±0·01 °C) was utilized to stabilize a distilled water bath at 100 °C.

Microbiological Procedures

Spores of *Bacillus stearothermophilus* (971-1 BC-SC, Ohio State University) were activated in tryptic soy broth (DIFCO) plus 0·5% dextrose. After three days of incubation at 55 °C, nutrient agar (DIFCO) slants were streaked, incubated, and the actively growing slants were kept refrigerated. The remaining vegetative cells were separated by centrifugal force from the broth, washed with phosphate buffer at pH 7 and stored in the same buffer solution at 4 °C. To prepare the spores, 500 ml nutrient agar (DIFCO) were inoculated with a loopful from the slants. After 48 h of incubation at 55 °C with frequent shaking, 1 ml of the cell suspension was spread over the entire surface of the sporulating medium. The medium was nutrient agar (DIFCO) supplemented with 0·03% manganese sulfate to stimulate sporulation and divided into 100 ml portions poured in 16 oz. prescription bottles. Bottles were then autoclaved and permitted to cool and solidify lying on their side. The spores grew on the surface for 3 days at 55 °C. The growth was gently scraped with sterilized glass rods with the aid of 10 ml of distilled water and centrifuged. The clean spores were treated with 0·1 ml/ml lysozyme, 3x crystalline (Sigma Chemical Co., St. Louis, MO) and washed again with sterile distilled 0·2 M phosphate buffer. The spore slurry was divided into 10 ml portions and stored at 4 °C for six weeks to increase thermal resistance. To activate the spores, they were heated at 100 °C for 5 min; this also served to kill any vegetative cells present. A series of dilutions was carried out to adjust the spore suspension to 10^6 cells/ml. A 9 ml sample was inoculated with 1 ml of the spore suspension to yield 10 ml of sample with a spore load of 10^5 cells/ml to be thermally treated. Tryptic soy agar (DIFCO) was the recovery medium used to monitor the extent of spore destruction following conventional or microwave heat treatments.

RESULTS AND DISCUSSION

When a spore suspension of *Bacillus stearothermophilus* (BGSC, 9A1) was inactivated by microwave or conventional heating in various media, higher lethalities resulted from microwave irradiation. This observation was found to be true in all the suspending media studied. Judging by survival curves, the magnitude of the spores' death phase varied with the medium composition, particularly in the case of microwave inactivated spores. Our survival curves varied slightly from those typical of *Bacillus stearothermophilus* spores as reported by Shull and Ernst.[11] Since spores were preactivated before inoculation, an initial rise in spore count was not observed (Fig. 1). The rest of the curve in most cases followed general trends observed by Shull and

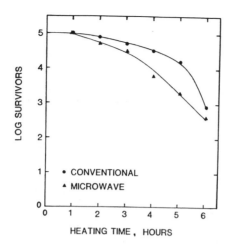

Fig. 1. *Survival curves for B. stearothermophilus in distilled water.*

Ernst.[11] Discrepancies may be attributed to heating temperature, type of spores, and suspending medium.

In an attempt to isolate the effect of individual food constituents on spore destruction, various simple model systems were formulated. Initial spore load, heating time and temperature were kept constant; the suspending medium and heating mode varied. Table I shows the D values at 100 °C calculated from survival curves. With the exception of the 6% sucrose solution, D values were significantly lower in the microwave heating mode at the 95% level of significance according to the T-test distribution (seven degrees of freedom).

Minor differences in come-up time from the initial temperature (5 °C) up to the holding temperature (100 °C) between both heating modes may account in part for the differences in D values. Come-up times were shown to be in the range of 58–83 s for microwave heating samples and 100–135 s in those conventionally heated.

Microwave added lethality may also be explained by the somewhat controversial theory of nonthermal lethality of microwaves. Grecz *et al.*[4] reported that microwave irradiation at 2450 MHz was consistently more lethal to *Cl. sporogenes* spores than with conventional heating. Chipley[2] pointed out the interdependence of heat and microwave effects as demonstrated by inactivation rates obtained for microwave irradiation versus conventional heating of spores. Results suggested a

TABLE I

D values for B. stearothermophilus in various suspending media when exposed to conventional and microwave heating

Suspending medium	D_{212} (min)	
	Microwave	Conventional
Distilled water	157	171
1% NaCl solution	133	144
2% NaCl solution	120	138
4% NaCl solution	109	129
6% NaCl solution	90	113
1% Sucrose solution	189	225
2% Sucrose solution	180	212
4% Sucrose solution	157	164
6% Sucrose solution	144	133
Phthalate buffer (pH 5)	106	138
Phthalate buffer (pH 5.5)	126	150
Phosphate buffer (pH 6.5)	144	157
Phosphate buffer (pH 6·75)	144	189
Phosphate buffer (pH 7)	190	240
Phosphate buffer (pH 8)	159	225
Phosphate buffer (pH 9)	150	212

nonthermal effect and a strong interdependence between thermal and electromagnetic effects. Barnes and Hu[1] investigated the nonthermal effect of microwave energy per se and theorized that it could result from ion shifts across membranes and reorientation of long-chain molecules.

Another electromagnetic related effect is that proteinaceous foods exhibit different textural changes when cooked with microwave energy as compared to traditional cooking methods. Kroger and Kalafat[6] reported that the reason for these changes is that the amount of heat energy applied to the proteins in these foods is directly related to the formation of amino acid bonds. In other words, microwaves may have enough energy to interfere with intermolecular binding.

The results from this investigation seem to be in agreement with the above findings. Our unpublished data also indicate higher lethality of microwaves for vegetative cells of Bacillus stearothermophilus. Since the spores' water content is much lower than that of the vegetative counterpart, electromagnetic heating efficiency in inactivation cannot be based solely on dielectric properties of the cell itself. The added lethality of microwaves may result from interference with the spores' heat stability mechanisms. Heat resistance of thermophilic spores has been attributed to the calcium salt of dipicolinic acid (DPA). Microwaves may interfere with the mechanism of bonding of DPA to calcium. Another characteristic of thermophilic spores is their high content DNA thermostable proteins, which may resist denaturation by heat but may be prone to microwave reorientation.

Weibb[14] studied microwave effects on DNA, RNA and protein synthesis and on metabolic rates of *E. coli* and found that certain frequencies had specific effects on those subcellular events, and that the effects were not due to temperature changes.

Effect of Sodium Chloride

The adverse effect of NaCl on microorganisms has been known and utilized for a long time as a preservative for a multitude of foods as well as for other functions. This adverse effect is clear from the increased kill of spores with increased concentrations of salt in conventionally heated samples. Alteration of the osmotic environment and denaturation of the ribosomal polypeptides may cause microorganisms to become less thermostable when salt concentration increases in the environment. The effect of NaCl has an added dimension in electronic heating. The dissociation of the salt causes an increase in the electrical heating and an increase in the electrical activity of the

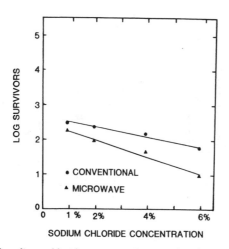

Fig. 2. *Effect of sodium chloride concentration on the thermal inactivation of B. stearothermophilus spores.*

medium through its ionic conductivity. Ohlsson and Bengtsson[9] showed the dielectric constant and loss factor of water to be 56·7 and 2·4 respectively at 100 °C and 2800 MHz, while for 0·1 M NaCl solutions, these values changed to 59·2 and 15·6. The loss factor governs the amount of energy converted into heat.[7] This could probably explain the higher slope of the inactivation curve for the microwave heated samples (Fig. 2) when plotted against salt concentration after a total heating time of 6 h.

It is clear that the salt content of the food will influence microwave sterilization due to its effect on the dielectric properties of the system. It must be stressed that the above analysis has only been shown for liquid systems. Solid foods undergoing electronic heating may exhibit a different behavior as a function of salt concentration with penetration depth being a more critical factor.

Effect of Sucrose
Sucrose as a solute may cause osmotic pressure changes that enhance the inactivation of spores. Comparing survivors versus sucrose concentration curves (Fig. 3), it appears that there is no significant difference between conventional and microwave inactivation on the rate of magnitude of spore destruction. Sucrose does not dissociate into ions and thus will not increase the amount of electrical energy converted into heat. In other words, sugar does not improve the

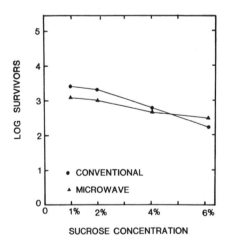

Fig. 3. Effect of sucrose concentration on the thermal inactivation of B. stearo thermophilus spores.

dielectric properties of the solution. On the contrary, it may hinder the electric activity of the water by binding portions of the water. Bound water is less free to move in an electric field than unbound water. This may explain the smaller D value for conventionally heated spores at the 6% sucrose concentration compared to those heated with microwaves. Increasing sugar concentration would result in more bound water and, as a result, less electrical activity.

Sucrose solution as a heating menstruum decreased the sensitivity of the spores to conventional and microwave heating, judging by the relatively higher D values as compared with other suspending media. This is characteristic of carbohydrates in general and sucrose in particular. Cory[3] compared five different carbohydrates (sucrose, glucose, sorbitol, fructose and glycerol) for effects on the thermal resistance of *Salmonella senftenberg* and found sucrose to be the most influential in increasing heat resistance. It is speculated that a similar effect might have taken place for the microorganism under investigation.

Comparing D values from salt solutions with those of sugar solutions, it is clear that for the same concentration, salt gave lower D values than did sucrose. Food preservation by plasmolysis generally requires six times more sucrose than NaCl to give the same degree of microbial inhibition. This shows an added lethality of the NaCl over sucrose and partially explains the higher D values obtained when spores were suspended in sucrose solutions.

Effect of pH

It it well established that bacteria are more heat resistant when suspended in media close to their optimum pH which for the specific case of *B. stearothermophilus* is around neutrality. This phenomenon was observed in our investigation and can be seen in Fig. 4 with the maximum number of survivors being around pH 7. As pH deviated from neutrality in either direction of the pH scale, the number of spores which survived heat treatment decreased consistently. Microwave heated samples showed added lethality in the whole pH range studied. It was also noticeable that acidic pH resulted in more inactivation of spores than did basic pH. Similar trends were observed by Headlee[5] working with *Cl. tetani* spores. Since most foods are neutral or slightly acidic and not many reach pH 9, with some exceptions such as egg whites, there is not much information available on the heat destruction of thermophilic spores in this alkaline range. Shafi *et al.*[10] found surviving thermophilic bacteria in commercial egg

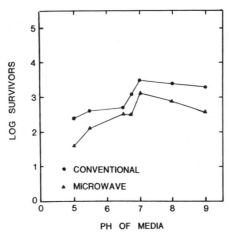

Fig. 4. Effect of pH on the thermal inactivation of B. stearothermophilus spores.

products which have been pasteurized and frozen. Murray[8] indicated that *B. anthracis* spores showed greatest resistance at pH 8. Other microorganisms such as *Cl. perfringens* tolerate acid more than alkali and are most resistant at pH 5. Since foods with pH below 5 do not normally require harsh commercial sterilization, the low end of the pH scale was not investigated.

The pH could influence the type of ion absorbed on the spore surface, particularly at the acidic pH levels, altering its heat stability. Conjugated-pair solution, as the name implies, consists of an acid–base conjugated pair. Acids and bases are electrolytes and they dissociate to various extents into ions to display their buffering capacity. The presence of ions is believed to cause the added lethality of the microwaves, in this case enhancing the electromagnetic properties. Opposite-charged ions will try to orient themselves with the rapidly alternating electric field, which will improve the dielectric heating lethality.

Composition of the buffer must be taken into account when discussing the pH effect. It is common to have a different number of survivors for two different buffer compositions at a given pH.

CONCLUSIONS

Microwave heating is effective for thermophilic spore destruction. However, due to the dependency of electronic heating on the dielectric properties of the suspending medium and the microorganism, varying degrees of inactivation may result for each system. The nonthermal effect of microwaves has been very controversial among researchers in the field. Our results seem to indicate that this may occur to some extent. It is also possible that temperature differences in the microenvironment of the cell or within the cell may contribute to lethality differences of the two heating modes. It is speculated that microwaves' added lethality on spores may result from interference with the spores' heat stability mechanisms. Microwaves could interfere with the mechanism of bonding of dipicolinic acid to calcium and/or cause reorientation in the thermostable protein content of the spores' DNA. Any solute that ionizes in water enhances microwave heating through improved conductivity.

Microwave energy has a potential in food processing. Although quite different from traditional thermal processing techniques, it is effective in destroying one of the most heat-resistant spores. A process design requires, however, taking into account the physical and chemical nature of the food being processed, the mechanism of heat induction, the make-up of the microbial cell itself and factors influencing energy coupling to the food and the magnitude of its penetration into the food system.

REFERENCES

1. Barnes, F. S. and Hu, C. L. J. Model for some nonthermal effects of radio and microwave fields on biological membranes. *I.E.E.E. Trans. Microwave Theory Tech.*, **25:** 42, 1977.
2. Chipley, J. F. Effect of microwave irradiation on microorganisms. *Adv. Appl. Microbiol.*, **26:** 129, 145, 1980.
3. Cory, J. E. L. The effect of sugars and polyols on the heat resistance of salmonella. *J. Appl. Bacteriol.*, **37:** 31, 1974.
4. Grecz, N., Walker, A. A. and Anellis, A. Effect of radio frequency energy (2480 MHz) on bacterial spores. *Bacteriol. Proc.*, 145, 1964.
5. Headlee, M. R. Thermal death point—spores of *Clostridium tetani*. *J. Infect. Dis.*, **48:** 4, 436, 1931.
6. Kroger, M. and Kalafat, S. R. Microwave heating of foods—use and safety consideration. *Critical Reviews in Food and Technology*, **4**(2): 141, 1973.
7. Metaxas, A. C. Properties of materials at microwave frequencies. *Trans. I.M.P.I.*, **2:** 19, 1976.
8. Murray, T. J. Thermal death point—spores of *Bacillus anthracis*. *J. Infect Dis.*, **48:** 4, 457, 1931.
9. Ohlsson, T. H. and Bengtsson, N. E. Dielectric food data for microwave sterilization processing. *J. Microwave Power*, **10**(1): 93, 1975.
10. Shafi, R., Cotterill, O. J. and Nichols, M. L. Microbial flora of commercially pasteurized egg products. *Poultry Sci.*, **49**(2): 578, 1970.

11. Shull, J. J. and Ernst, R. R. Graphical procedure for comparing thermal death of *Bacillus stearothermophilus* spores in saturated and superheated steam. *Appl. Microbiol,* **10:** 452, 1962.
12. Susskind, C. and Vogelhut, P. O. Longevity and cellular studies with microwaves. In *Proceedings of the Third Annual Tri-Service Conference on Biological Effects of Microwave Radiation,* Vol. 1, U.S. Department of Commerce, Springfield, Virginia, p. 135, 1959.
13. Van Ummerson, C. In *Biological Effects of Microwave Radiation* (M. F. Peyton Ed.) Vol. 1, Plenum, New York, p. 201, 1961.
14. Weibb, S. J. Genetic continuity and metabolic regulation as seen by the black light frequencies on these phenomena. *Acad. Sci. Ann. Rep.,* **247:** 327, 1975.

52

AN OVERVIEW OF NEW INFRARED RADIATION PROCESSES FOR VARIOUS AGRICULTURAL PRODUCTS

D. J. VAN ZUILICHEM, K. VAN'T RIET and W. STOLP

Food Process and Bio Engineering Group, Department of Food Technology, Agricultural University, De Dreyer 12, 6703 BC Wageningen, The Netherlands

ABSTRACT

Several infrared (IR-) radiation processes have been developed for the heat treatment of agricultural products and crops in food and feed processing. The purpose of the heating step is to inactivate hazardous enzyme activity (e.g. trypsin inhibitor in soy), to stop enzyme activity responsible for the development of off-flavors (e.g. lipoxygenase and FFA's), to take out undesirable proteins (e.g. phasine in flageolet beans) or for applications such as dry-blanching of horticulture goods, seed dehulling, decontamination of microbial germs, moulds and yeasts.

The procedures involve exposure to IR radiation for a short time period (15–65 s), depending on the purpose and the size of the crops, possibly followed by a period of holding in a well insulated vessel for 0–20 min for temperature equilibration. Calculations have been made which show that the heat penetration time is short compared with the holding time.

The advantage, compared with conventional low steam pressure heating is in the HTST-effects of these processes, as demonstrated with unchanged available lysine-numbers for soy, which means protection of valuable amino acids as well as savings in process costs.

Whereas the investigations described concerned the selective inactivation of enzymes, the problem in the canning of horticulture products also concerns physical properties such as the loss of the consistency and colour after the conventional process of water- and steam-blanching, followed by sterilization. The IR radiation process appears suitable for dry-blanching of products like carrots, peas, brown beans, dun-peas or red cabbage in order to improve their physical properties.

INTRODUCTION

Although infrared heating as a means of heat transfer has always been popular for mechanical process technologists, the application in the food industry has been restricted to drying and thawing applications. In the late 1960s the availability of natural gas in Holland became so wide-spread that 70% of the direct fired furnaces and boilers in the energy supply sector were re-designed and operated by natural gas from the Slochteren gas recovery field. The food industry could benefit from this type of heating as well.

Since 1975 the Food Science Group of the Agricultural University has been studying various applications of direct heating of crops by combustion of natural gas. Cocoa beans, soy beans, broad beans, wheat and rape seed have been used as model material for food and feed purposes.

The research objectives have been to make the crops suitable for consumption by inactivation of hazardous enzymes, to stop enzyme activity responsible for the development of by-products and off-flavours, or to benefit from using this high temperature-short time (HTST) heating procedure for suppressing the total microbial contamination, moulds or yeasts present on the crops. Other research goals are the application of IR equipment for dehulling of seeds, the dry-blanching of horticulture goods, on thawing and drying applications. Roughly, the developed IR-radiation processing of seeds can be divided into three groups; (a) processes where the treatment of the kernel outer layers is essential, (b) processes imparting a certain change in the kernel internal structure or composition, and (c) processes where internal and external changes are required simultaneously. Examples of the three types of processes developed until now with their advantages and disadvantages will be given.

KERNEL OUTER LAYER TREATMENT

Decontamination

In our tests the IR equipment proved to be suitable for dehulling and at the same time capable of removing moulds and yeasts and reducing microbial contamination to a certain extent. When crops such as seeds are contaminated by microorganisms mostly fast chemical methods are chosen for treatment. Examples include exposure for a certain time to toxic gases such as ethylene oxide, propylene oxide and mixtures of ethylene oxide and methyl bromide, in general known as the ETO processes.

The use of these toxic materials poses potential problems and this has been recognized by the American Environmental Protection

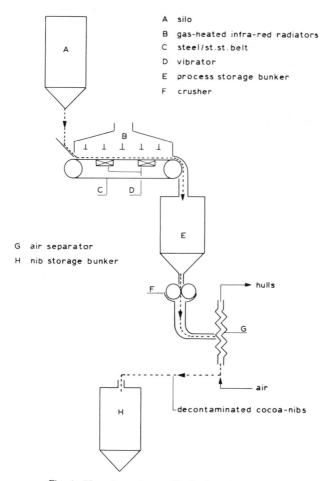

A silo
B gas-heated infra-red radiators
C steel/st.st.belt
D vibrator
E process storage bunker
F crusher

G air separator
H nib storage bunker

hulls

decontaminated cocoa-nibs

air

Fig. 1. Flow sheet of a modified infrared process.

Agency who in 1975, issued strict rules for the use of the ETO processes.[1] Another disadvantage of ETO processes is their increasing costs. In order to find a suitable substitution the possibility was studied of applying an infrared radiation process for this purpose. In Fig. 1 a schematic flow sheet of this process is given. Food products are conveyed lying on an endless metal belt under a bed of gas-heated infrared radiators. A process similar to this was used in the feed industry in the early 1970s with the objective of improving the digestibility of whole grains such as maize. After the heat treatment in question, the maize kernels are crushed or flaked in a roll-mill.[2] Those products were called micronized flakes.[3]

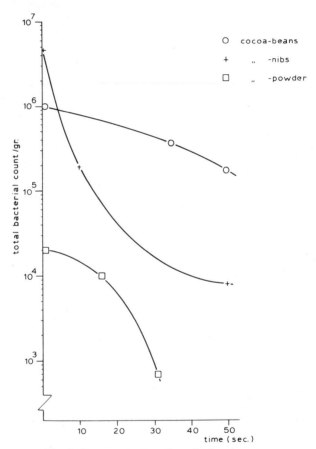

Fig. 2. *Decontamination effect of infrared process.*

TABLE I
Effect of Infrared Treatment of cocoa nibs on microbial counts

	Before infrared treatment (count/g.)	*After infrared treatment (count/g.)*
Total count	5×10^6	2×10^5
Enterobact.	10^4	$\leqslant 10$
Yeasts	8×10^4	$< 10^2$
Moulds	6×10^4	$< 10^2$

In the Wageningen system, however, a shorter belt (in comparison with the micronizing process) was operated as a piece of HTST equipment. Ceramic plates were heated up to 970 °C and a residence time of 10–50 s was then used for the products on the belt as a IR-radiation time. For a model material like cocoa beans, cocoa nibs and defatted cocoa powder the resulting decrease in total microbial count is given in Fig. 2. Table I gives the breakdown of the results for pathogenic organisms, moulds and yeasts. It can be seen that the IR treatment effectively removed the pathogenic germs, moulds and yeasts whilst the remaining total count consisted of less heat sensitive groups such as spore-formers. This is better demonstrated by the plate count of a model material (curcuma powder) in Table II that was processed on the belt. After the IR treatment there was a slight reduction in the count of spore-formers. This has led to the idea of

TABLE II
Plate count of infrared heated curcuma powder

Count	*cFu/g*
Total count	$2 \cdot 1 \times 10^7$
Coliforms	10^5
E. coli	23
Staph. aureus	$< 10^2$
Yeasts	$< 10^2$
Moulds	$1 \cdot 4 \times 10^3$
Enterococci	4 800
Aerobe spore f. (*Bacillus subtilus*)	$1 \cdot 9 \times 10^7$

considering a process consisting of a pretreatment of the spices, such as curcuma and paprika, by a γ-ray plant with an extremely low dose of γ-radiation of the order of 2 kGy (200 krads), followed by IR radiation based on a supposed synergetic effect making the spores more sensitive to heat after the γ-ray pretreatment.[4] The results are

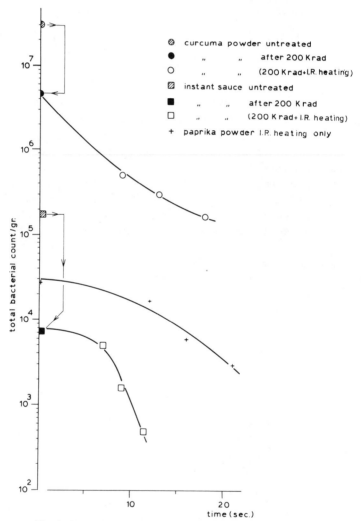

Fig. 3. Decontamination by γ-radiation and IR heat treatment.

given in Fig. 3 showing how the total count of spore-formers will be reduced to acceptable values.

A series of IR equipment was built for the health-food industry (e.g. muesli, breakfast cereals) recently, based on the described effects.

Dehulling

The IR equipment also proved to be suitable as a dehuller. For cocoa beans, depending on the place or origin, an increase in nib-percentage of 0·1–1·6% can be realized when applying the IR equipment in a cocoa-bean line. This is caused by a more effective separation between bean material and hulls compared with the conventional hot air dehullers.

The cocoa companies appear interested in this IR treatment, based on the Wageningen results, because of the decontamination effect and the better simultaneous dehulling. In practice such an infrared unit will handle up to 4 t cocoa beans hourly.

KERNEL INNER BODY TREATMENT

New Soybean Process

With the HTST gas-heated IR pilot plant a procedure was developed using the residual heat within the heat-treated material leaving the conveyor belt for a continued enzyme inactivation. After being subjected to IR radiation for a specific heating period the products are held for a predetermined period in a well insulated container. There the residual heat equilibrates and further acts to achieve the process objectives, as described by Van Zuilichem *et al.*[5]

This procedure offers a possibility for reducing the energy consumption. In addition, the problem of lysine losses associated with the application of the Micronizer-feed process (e.g. soy beans) was minimized by this new procedure. Full fat soy flour can be produced at lower temperatures (110–130 °C) with the gas consumption reduced by 50% as compared with the micronizer-method (180 °C). At the same time, the heat labile components of oil seeds and cereals (e.g. lysine) will be kept at their original level. This is demonstrated by the results of test runs on soybeans shown in Table III. A design of such a soybean process on an industrial scale is given in Fig. 4. The capacity of such a process is ≈7 t/h. The gas consumption per 7 t is about 80 m^3, depending on the temperature of the stocked soy beans at the

TABLE III
Process indicators and process variables in the infrared treatment of soy

Sample	Urease[a]	tui[b]	nsi[c]	pdi[d]	Available lysine[e]	Moisture (%)	Residence time (s)[f]	Temp. (°C)[g]	Holding time (min)[h]
Raw	2·20	72·0	83	91	2·3	8·5	—	—	—
1	0·40	18·8	25	30	2·2	7·8	80	133	0
2	0·05	6·8	10	18	2·1	7·3	80	133	15
3	0·00	5·9	10	15	1·9	7·0	80	133	25
4	0·50	26·1	31	42	2·4	8·0	60	124	0
5	0·05	8·2	13	20	2·3	7·6	60	124	15
6	0·05	7·1	10	18	2·2	7·7	60	124	25

[a] Units of pH rise.
[b] Trypsin units inhibited per mg sample.
[c] Nitrogen solubility index (%).
[d] Protein dispersibility index (%).
[e] % of full-fat soy flour (dry matter).
[f] Residence time (s) (exposure to IR radiation).
[g] Bulk temperature of soy beans immediately after IR.
[h] Holding time (min) of sample immediately after IR.

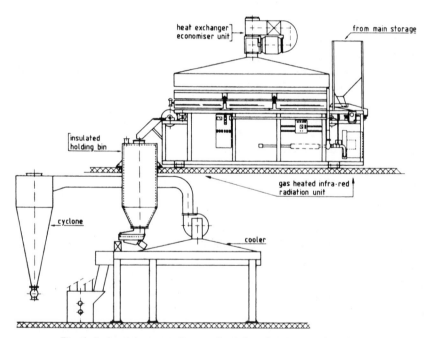

Fig. 4. Industrial process diagram for infrared treatment of soy beans.

LIPOXYGENASE

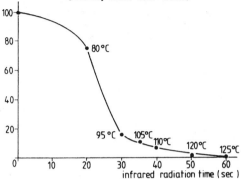

Polarographic assay of the enzyme in full fat soy flours produced according to the laboratory process without holding.

Fig. 5. Polarographic assay of the enzyme in full fat soy flours produced according to the laboratory process without holding.

belt entry side. The beans are exposed to IR heating for ±45 s, which raises the bean temperature to 125–133 °C. The following additional holding time should be 15–25 min prior to the cracking, dehulling and grinding to full fat flour. The effectiveness of the process was investigated by determining the indicators commonly used in soybean heat processing, namely urease, trypsin inhibitor activity (TUI), nitrogen solubility index (NSI) and protein dispersibility index (PDI). The lysine measurement was used as an indicator for overheating. In the case of trypsin inhibitor activity the enzyme is present in the whole seed, as is the case with lipoxygenase, the enzyme responsible for the short-time-rancidity development in full fat flour. Figure 5 shows the relation between decrease of the lipoxygenase activity and IR radiation time. To investigate the oxidative stability and shelf-life of full fat flours, samples were kept for more than one year. Peroxide values (PV) were determined on the extracted oil before and after storage. Rancidity was investigated in a sensory test. An optimum procedure was found to be 60 s IR radiation (125 °C) and 15 min holding.[7,8]

Treatment of Peas
Based on the same principles, new processes were developed and used for fresh green peas. Here the objective is to inactivate the lipoxyge-

nase activity prior to the freezing step. This IR dry heating process can replace the conventional steam or hot water-blanching step, thus eliminating the need for use of water or steam. The retention of ascorbic acid in peas with the IR process proved to be comparable with the hot water-blanching method. Taste and flavour of the IR process peas showed a somewhat better score in the taste panel test. Some work remains to be done regarding the loss of water and the color of the peas.

Broad Beans—Animal Feed

A new IR process for the enzyme inactivation of phasine, known as a growth inhibitor in beans, causing hemagglutination, has been developed. Broad beans, horse beans or field beans have been subjected to IR radiation and a substantial inactivation proved to be possible.

Wheat Flours for Pie-baking

A new IR process was developed to treat wheat kernels in such a way that a flour, obtained after the roll milling process, is comparable to the chlorinated flours that are widely used for pie-baking.

Here the target is to produce a flour with a certain water absorption index and water solubility index. Baking tests with IR treated flours gave a very high score in volume of the batter as well as the structure of the pies. Compared with the chlorinated flours the mouthfeel of pies and cakes baked with the 'IR-treated' flour was preferred due to a better moist-taste, which is important for Dutch cakes. Some results are shown in Fig. 6 and Table IV. The Brabender diagram in Fig. 6 is given for French wheat that is IR treated for 22 s prior to roll milling.

Rapeseed Treatment

A new IR process was developed for the treatment of rapeseed. The varieties that are most often used are the so-called 'single zero' types, which means low in eruca-acid (1–5%) and the 'double-zero' types, which means low in glucosinolates as well (10–20 μmol/g defatted). Glucosinolates can be broken down by the endogenous enzyme myrosinase to harmful chemical combinations like isothiocyanates, nitriles and oxazolidine-thiones.[9] Most of this matter will remain in the presscake and can limit the applications as cattle and pig feed, due to toxic evidence and antinutritional properties. All of these sulfur containing products will poison the nickel catalyst in the oil hydroge-

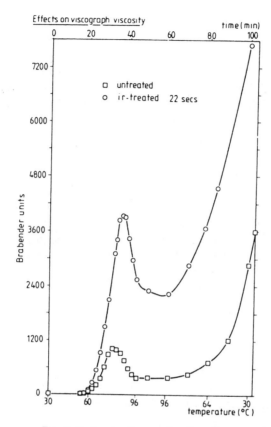

Fig. 6. Brabender diagram for wheat flour.

TABLE IV
Layer cake-baking test—comparison of flows from untreated and infrared radiation treated wheat

	'Conventional' method		'All-in' method	
	Untreated	*IR-treated 22 s*	*Untreated*	*IR-treated 22 s*
Specific volume Batter (ml/g)	3·41	3·51	3·03	3·09
Specific volume Cake (ml/g)	4·91	5·13	4·28	4·61

nation process.[10] Thus, it is necessary to avoid the development of these sulfur compounds resulting from the myrosinase enzyme activity, by inactivation of the enzyme.

Now an IR process is available where the myrosinase activity is reduced by 95%. A very short IR process time ($\approx 3 \cdot 2$ s) proved to be adequate which means that a production capacity of many tons per hour can be realized by a reasonably small production unit. In comparison with the soybean equipment a throughput of 20 t/h is realistic.

Combined Internal/External Changes

An example where the combined effects are desirable, (i.e. a change in the plant tissue protecting the agricultural crop and at the same time a change in the internal structure), is the IR process developed for fresh and dried pulses in the canning industry. The process is a variant of the green pea IR dry-blanching process. It proved to be possible to accelerate the soaking process of dried pulses (brown and white flageolet) considerably using an IR treatment, reducing the soaking time from 8 h to 80 min.

PROCESS CALCULATIONS

Heat Penetration in the Seeds

The heating of the seeds can be assumed to be a nonstationary heat penetration, described by the differential equation:

$$\frac{\partial T}{\partial t} = a \left\{ \frac{\partial^2 T}{\partial r^2} + \frac{1}{r} \frac{2\partial T}{\partial r} \right\}$$

in which

a = thermal diffusivity coefficient ($m^2 s^{-1}$)
T = temperature (K)
t = time (s)
r = radius (seed) (m)

Carslaw and Jaeger[11] applied Fourier integrals and Fourier series and found the expression for the temperature T at the location r as:

$$T - T_e = \frac{2h(T_0 - T_e)}{T} \sum_{h=1}^{\infty} \exp(-a\alpha_n^2 t)$$
$$\times \frac{A^2 \alpha_n^2 + (Ah - 1)^2}{\alpha_n^2 [A^2 \alpha_n^2 + Ah(Ah - 1)]} \sin A\alpha_n \sin r\alpha_n \quad (1)$$

in which

T_e = ambient temperature (K)
h = radiation constant (m^{-1})
T = starting temperature (K)
r = sphere radius (m)
a = thermal diffusivity coefficient (m^2 s^{-1})
t = residence time heating (s)
A = max. radius (product) (m)

α_n (n = 1, 2, 3, . . .) are the roots of the equation

$$A\alpha_n \, \text{Cotg}\,(A\alpha_n) + (Ah - 1) = 0 \qquad (2)$$

The temperature of the product leaving the endless belt of the IR equipment can be calculated using the energy balance:
ϕ = radiation influx = heating losses, written as:

$$\phi = \sigma T_b^4 = \rho c_p \, \text{d} \frac{\partial T}{\partial t}$$

neglecting the losses in belt temperature, convection heat of the ambient air, radiation and free convection on the burner topside (T_b), it follows after integration:

$$\sigma T_b^4 t = \rho c_p dT + C_1$$

When $t = 0 \rightarrow T = T_0$, thus

$$T_b^4 t = \rho c_p d(T - T_0),$$

or

$$T = T_0 + [\sigma T_b^4 (\rho c_p d)^{-1}]t \qquad (3)$$

where

ϕ = heat flux (W m^{-2})
σ = radiation constant (5.76 $\times$ 10^{-8}) (J^{s-1} m^{-2} K^{-4})
T_b = burner temperature (K)
ρ = solid density (kg m^{-3})
C_p = heat capacity (J kg^{-1} K^{-1})
d = product diameter (m)
$\dfrac{\partial T}{\partial t}$ = (temp.-time) gradient

Temperature profile Determination

Equations (1) and (3) will give the temperature profile in the product. Many physical properties are known from handbooks[12] and some have to be measured. The thermal diffusivity coefficient $a = (\lambda/\rho c)$ is determined using the method of Dickerson under transient heat transfer conditions.[13] The radiation constant h can be calculated from the relation

$$h = \frac{H}{\lambda} = \frac{\text{surface heat transfer coefficient}}{\text{heat conductivity factor}}$$

The surface heat coefficient H is calculated from

$$H = \phi(T_b - T_{surface})^{-1},$$

in which $T_{surface}$ is the surface temperature of the product, leaving the belt.

The influx $\phi = \sigma F(T_b^4 - \bar{T}^4)$,
where

   T_b = burner temperature
   $\bar{T}$ = average product temperature
   F = configuration factor
and the radiation constant

$$h = \sigma F(T_b^4 - \bar{T}^4)/(T_b - T_{surface})\lambda \qquad (4)$$

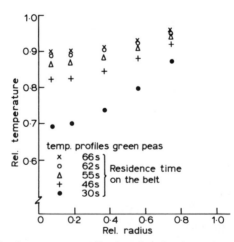

Fig. 7. *Calculated temperature profiles for infrared radiation heating of green peas.*

From these data the temperature profiles can be calculated, for example, the temperature profiles for green peas in Fig. 7.

CONCLUSIONS

It has been proven that crops can be treated at stock-moist conditions (e.g. soy) in order to inactivate hazardous enzymes or to improve the oil quality taken from the seeds.

It is possible to operate an IR–HTST equipment as a dry-blanching process line, avoiding the use of process water, protecting the ascorbic acid level and improving the product texture after the sterilization step.

The IR treatment also proved to be successful for dehulling purposes and/or for microbial decontamination.

ACKNOWLEDGEMENTS

The cooperation with ALMEX company, the manufacturer of the IR equipment, and their support of this research, is gratefully acknowledged. The cooperation with the group of Food Chemistry and Food Hygiene was much appreciated.

REFERENCES

1. Federal Register, July 1975, Vol. 40, number 29, Part. II, pp. 28242–36571.
2. Livingstone, H. G. *The Manual of Heat Processing of Cereals.* Framhingham, Woodbridge, Suffolk, England, 1977.
3. Lawrence, T. L. J. *Optimising the Utilisation of Cereal Energy by Cattle and Pigs,* U.S. Feed Grains Council, London, 1976.
4. van Zuilichem, D. J., Beumer, R. R. and Stolp, W. Decontamination methods in instant food preservation. *Proc. Symp. Instantisieren III,* Solingen, Gräfrath, W. Germany, 1978.
5. van Zuilichem, D. J., Beumer, R. R. and Stolp, W. Preservation of food materials with infrared radiation. *Proc. Symp. Instantisieren IV,* Solingen, Gräfrath, W. Germany, 1980.
6. Kouzeh Kanani, M., van Zuilichem, D. J., Roozen, J. P. and Pilnik, W. *Lebensm. Wiss. u. Technol.* **14:** 242, 1981.
7. Kouzeh Kanani, M., van Zuilichem, D. J., Roozen, J. P. and Pilnik, W. *Qual. Plant, Plant Foods Hum. Nutr.* **33:** 139, 1983.
8. Kouzeh Kanani, M., van Zuilichem, D. J., Roozen, J. P. and Pilnik, W. *Lebensm. Wiss. u. Technol.* **15:** 139–42, 1982.

9. Wilkinson, A. P., Rhodes, M. J. C. and Fenwick, R. G. Myrosinase activity of cruciferous vegetables. *J. Sci. Food Agric.* **35:** 543–552, 1984.
10. Babuchowski, K. and Rutkowski, A. Sulphur and phosphorus compounds as inhibitors in rapeseed oil hydrogenation. *Seife-Öle-Fette-Wachse* **95:** 27–30,   .
11. Carslaw, H. S. and Jaeger, J. C. *Conduction of Heat in Solids.* Oxford University Press, Oxford, 1959.
12. Productgegevens groente en fruit, Wageningen, Sprenger Instituut, Comm. no. 30, 1977.
13. Roger, W. and Dickerson, R. W. Jr. An apparatus for the measurement of thermal diffusivity of foods. *Food Technol.,* May, 198–204. 1965.

53

A WATER SOURCE HEAT PUMP IN THE VEGETABLE CANNING INDUSTRY—SYSTEMS ANALYSIS

WILLIAM D. KEITH and GAURI S. MITTAL*

Ontario Centre for Farm Machinery and Food Processing Technology, Chatham, Ontario, Canada

School of Engineering, University of Guelph, Guelph, Ontario, Canada N1G 2W1

ABSTRACT

A water source heat pump based system was designed to recover energy from the processing effluent of a pea canning process. The most attractive layout was optimized using Transient System Simulation (TRNSYS). A total processing energy load of 65% was supplied by the optimized retrofitting of a heat pump installation to an existing oil-fired heating system. The effect of a ±20% change in system operating parameters on total heat energy delivered, system performance and evaporator outlet temperature was also analyzed.

NOMENCLATURE

COP	= coefficient of performance
HP	= heat pump
M	= mass flow rate (kg/h)
QL	= energy transferred to liquid (GJ/h)
QR	= rate of energy delivered to the process load by heat pump (GJ/h)
SUMQR	= total energy delivered to the process load by heat pump (GJ)
SUMWAH	= total power input into the heat pump (GJ)
T	= temperature (°C)
THP10CO	= temperature at the outlet of heat pump no. 10 condenser (°C)

W   = energy required (kW)
WAH   = Power input into the heat pump (GJ/h)

Suffixes

10	= heat pump no. 10
11	= heat pump no. 11
C	= condenser
E	= evaporator
I, i	= inlet
O	= outlet
R	= condenser outlet

INTRODUCTION

Heat pump technology is being applied to an increasing variety of domestic, commercial, and industrial applications in attempts to reduce the energy costs. The ability of the heat pump to combine with a wide variety of energy sources makes it an attractive consideration in industrial processing operations. The food processing industry is a major energy consumer with most of its energy used as hot water or stream for washing, heating, grading, sterilizing and packaging of food products. Heat recovery techniques have been employed with limited success in industrial processes to reduce energy use. However, rising energy costs have forced looking beyond the traditional heat exchanger equipment. Unlike heat exchangers, heat pumps facilitate the upgrading of energy from low temperature sources to higher temperature sinks with some energy input.

As early as 1954, successful industrial heat pump applications were described[1] in the U.S. for concentrating fruit juices and milk. In Canada, experiments were conducted[2] near Elie, Manitoba and reported a payback of four years on a heat pump installation utilizing condenser heat from a bulk milk cooler for heating of hot water on a dairy farm.

The feasibility of applying heat pumps to the vegetable canning industry to improve upon current heat generation and recovery techniques was investigated.[3] This paper describes the simulation of the system and optimization of system performance using a Transient System Simulation (TRNSYS) program.[4] Sensitivity of the system to changes in the system parameters was also analyzed.

SYSTEM DESIGN

The energy load data from a vegetable processing plant located in the midwest United States was selected for this study.[5,6] The plant produced canned and frozen peas and corn. The flow-chart in Fig. 1 displays the pea processing operations following a wash after receipt of the product from the field trucks. The details regarding process conditions and description, heat pump selection (Carrier −30 HM model), and heat pump layout and comparison are described in detail elsewhere.[3] (The use of firm names or trade products does not imply

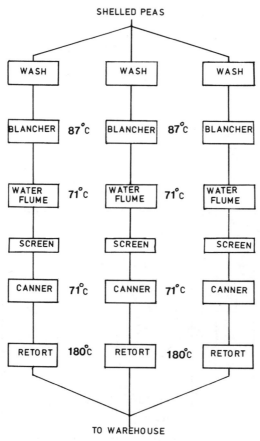

Fig. 1. Process flow chart for pea canning.

endorsement or recommendation over other firms or similar products not mentioned.)

Four layout configurations of in-line and parallel in-line heat pump layouts with varying multiples of units were analyzed by calculations for contribution to the total process energy load. Several operating conditions determined the size of the heat pumps including condenser temperature rise, flow rate, and condenser outlet temperature.

Design no. 100 (Fig. 2) required only two heat pumps to supply approximately 47·4% of the total load. Comparison of capacity revealed an advantage over other designs. This design has the highest reserve capacity and uses more of the process effluent water flow for heat recovery. Table I describes the performance data of this design.

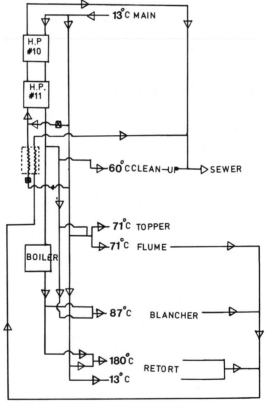

Fig. 2. Design no. 100.

TABLE I
Design no. 100 heat pump performance data. (Cycle A, 0500–0800 hours; Cycle B, 0800–2400 hours)

| Heat pump no. | 10 | 11 | 10 | 11 |
Cycle	A	A	B	B
Evaporator inlet temp. (THPEI)(°C)	12·8	12·8	26·7	43·3
Evaporator outlet temp. (THPEO)(°C)	4·4	4·4	10·0	26·7
Condenser inlet temp. (THPCI)(°C)	12·8	37·8	12·8	37·8
Condenser outlet temp. (THCO)(°C)	37·8	60·0	37·8	71·1
Class	I	III	I	III
Pass type[a]	6P	6S	6P	6S
Unit	100	160	100	160
MC (kg/h)	11 360	11 360	12 003	12 003
QL (GJ/h)	1·189	1·057	1·257	1·676
QC (GJ/h)	1·432	1·210	1·734	2·364
QA (GJ/h)	1·383	1·021	1·720	2·157
W (kW)	85·7	110·0	92·0	173·1
COP	4·64	3·06	5·23	3·79
ME (Req'd kg/h)	39 647	29 270	24 649	30 915[b]

[a] Parallel (P); Series (S).
[b] 31321 kg/h available during B cycle.

Class 1 provides 40 °C, class 2 60 °C, and class 3 71 °C maximum condenser outlet temperature. Units from 015 to 160 are available based on 3 or 6 parallel and series passes through the heat pumps.

SIMULATION

In a transient system simulation (TRNSYS) program, a system is a group of inter-connected component modules which perform a specific function. By collectively simulating the performance of individual inter-connected components, the entire system performance is simulated. This modular simulation technique greatly reduces the complexity of one large system problem into a group of smaller problem components which are more easily solved independently. Each module's description is based on fixed parameters, inputs, outputs, and time dependent forcing functions.[4]

The following time dependent forcing functions were used in the simulation. The details are given elsewhere.[7]

(1) Evaporator inlet temperature (0–8 h : 13 °C, and 8–24 h : 43 °C).
(2) Evaporator flow rate (0–5 h : 0 kg/h, 5–8 h : 40 000 kg/h, and 8–24 h : 31 000 kg/h).

(3) Heat pump operating load for heat pump nos. 10 and 11 as selected.[3]

(4) Heat pump on/off function (canning: 0–8 h—OFF, and 8–24 h—ON; clean up: 0–5 h—OFF, 5–8 h—ON, and 8–24 h—OFF).

The simulation was set up such that only one evaporator flow rate could be processed for the heat pump's second parameter. To accommodate a transient flow rate of two values, a second set of heat pumps was used. Each set of two heat pumps was controlled by a time dependent forcing function to be on or off as appropriate. This effectively caused the program to simulate the time dependent nature of the evaporator flow rate even though it was not originally intended for it. Thus, the clean-up cycle and canning cycle represented the resultant two sets of heat pump components.

The information flow diagram was constructed by connecting various components for each design.[7] Specific blocks were assigned type numbers and each component was assigned an individual unit number. The order of parameters, inputs, and outputs was specific for each component type. The starting and stopping times of the simulation were set at 0 h and 24 h representing one operating day. The time segment at which integrations were to take place was set at 0·1 h.

OPTIMIZATION

The simulated optimization of the system involved minimizing/maximizing the performance variables (dependent) relative to optimum values of system parameters (independent). While optimization for unit COP and least energy input (WAH) per energy output (QR) is desired, this may not occur at the greatest cumulative output of the units when auxiliary fuel costs and capital amortization costs are the lowest.

One performance variable to be optimized is SUMQR/SUMWAH, which reflects the optimum combined system COP and is affected by TR and QL. This is maximized for optimum operating efficiency. Another dependent variable optimized is evaporator flow rate, ME, which will be the lowest when TE010 is the closest to the minimum allowable temperature of 4·5 °C during the clean-up cycle.

The system parameters are sometimes dependent on a ratio of the heat pump unit inputs or outputs. A change in THP10CO affects a corresponding change in QL10 (portion of load assigned to first heat pump in series) and QL11 (portion of load assigned to second heat pump in series) due to the series connection of the heat pumps in supplying the load at a constant condenser outlet temperature for each load cycle (A = clean-up, B = canning).

The change in cumulative COP (SUMQR/SUMWAH) with the change in THP10CO was small, however, the optimization technique improved optimum system performance at the maximum THP10CO allowable of 40·6 °C. This indicates a better intermediate temperature level and load proportion between the series connected heat pumps as influenced by individual unit characteristics.

The simulation runs at various ME10 flow rates, shown in Fig. 3, reveal optimum (minimum) flow rates of 31 000 kg/h for HP no. 10

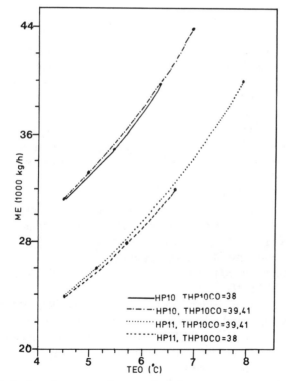

Fig. 3. Optimization of evaporator flow rate dependent on evaporator outlet temperature.

and 23 950 kg/h for HP no. 11. The maximum use of the main water flow is made by absorbing energy in the evaporator, reducing the discharge temperature to 4·5 °C (minimum allowed) and minimizing consumption charges for municipal water use.

With these optimized system parameters, 65% of the process energy load is supplied by the design.

SENSITIVITY ANALYSIS

Changes of ±10% and ±20% in evaporator flow rate, evaporator inlet temperature and condenser flow rate and ±20% in plant processing capacity (load) were simulated to observe the sensitivity of the system to possible future plant modifications or fluctuations in water supply. This also provides an indication of system performance if applied to other similar sized processing plants at alternate locations.

Evaporator Flow Rate (ME)

The effect of an increased ME on SUMQR is seen in Table II. At a 20% ME increase, only a 2·4% SUMQR increase resulted. However, a 20% negative change in ME causes a 3·5% corresponding decrease in SUMQR. A direct relationship to ME increase was noted for SUMQR/SUMWAH while only slight changes (1·5%) occurred when ME was decreased.

Slight (less than 3 °C) changes in TEO occurred but the drop of TEO below 4·5 °C would result in evaporator freeze-up and shutdown of the system so no evaporator flow rate decreases can be allowed.

Evaporator Inlet Temperature (TEI)

Similar effects on SUMQR resulted from an increase in TEI as in the case of an increase in ME. However, almost 20% decrease in SUMQR resulted from a 2·6 °C decrease in temperature. Freeze-up of the evaporator and unit shutdown resulting from TEO less than 4·5 °C would prevent any consideration of a decrease in TEI without system alterations (Table II).

Minimal effect on system performance (SUMQR/SUMWAH) was noted from increased TEI of 1·3 °C, and the rate of increase rapidly diminished past the first TEI increase point. This indicated that no significant improvement in system performance (SUMQR/ SUMWAH) could be expected from further TEI increase, unless direct heat exchangers are applied in place of heat pumps.

TABLE II
Sensitivity of system to changes in evaporator flow rate, evaporator inlet temperature, condenser flow rate, and plant load

% changes in variable from optimum value	SUMQR	SUMQR/SUMWAH	TEO
ME			
−20	6·95	4·01	2·4
−10	7·01	4·07	3·6
0	7·20	4·12	4·5
10	7·30	4·17	5·3
20	7·38	4·20	5·9
MCO			
−20	7·06	4·13	4·5
−10	7·06	4·13	4·5
0	7·20	4·12	4·5
10	7·06	4·13	4·5
20	7·06	4·13	4·5
Plant load			
−20	7·06	4·13	4·5
0	7·20	4·12	4·5
20	7·25	4·12	4·5
TEI (°C)			
−2·6	5·89	3·75	1·9
−1·3	6·46	3·95	3·2
0	7·20	4·12	4·5
1·3	7·39	4·29	5·3
2·6	7·43	4·31	6·1

Condenser Flow Rate

As shown in Table II, a slight decrease in SUMQR resulted from a change in condenser flow rate, and no significant change in evaporator outlet temperature resulted, since the heat pump would deliver the same heat output at a lower TCO with increased MCO. Minimal effects on system performance resulted from a change in MCO.

Plant Load

As displayed in Table II, negligible (<2%) changes in SUMQR, TEO and system performance (SUMQR/SUMWAH) resulted from a 20% change in load. This occurred because the heat pump system was already operating at near capacity with only a slight change (2%) in heat energy delivered resulting from a 20% system load decrease.

It is noted, however, that the system performance SUMQR/SUMWAH did increase only when the system load was decreased, indicating the heat pumps unit COP may be higher at reduced capacity.

CONCLUSIONS

The transient thermal processing energy load for a canning plant was simulated using computer simulation techniques. Supply of 65% of the simulated total transient thermal processing energy load was achieved using an optimized heat pump based system (design no. 100) with an intermediate temperature of 40·6 °C (THP10CO). Computer simulation facilitated optimization of the dependent system variables, SUMQR/SUMWAH and ME.

A reduced payback period for the heat pump assisted system would be realized by the use of the chilled evaporator water for pre-cooling vegetables on a freezing line while supplying hot water to the canning line.

REFERENCES

1. Stoecker, W. F. *Refrigeration and Air-conditioning.* McGraw-Hill, New York, pp. 233–4, 1954.
2. Boris, R. E. Utilization of condenser heat from bulk milk cooler for water heating in a dairy operation. Paper No. 81–207, American Society of Agricultural Engineers, St. Joseph, MI, 1981.
3. Keith, W. D. and Mittal, G. S. Technical and economic feasibility of a water source heat pump in the vegetable canning industry. Paper No. 84–218, Canadian Society of Agricultural Engineers, Ottawa, 1984.
4. Klein, S. A. (Ed.) TRNSYS—A transient system simulation program, EES report 38–10. Solar Energy Laboratory, University of Wisconsin, Madison, 1979.
5. Levonowich, P. F. Determination of feasibility of using solar energy in a food processing plant. M.Sc. thesis, University of Wisconsin, Madison, 1978.
6. Lund, D. B. Compatibility of solar energy supply, collection and storage with food processing energy demands. Project report, University of Wisconsin, Madison, 1978.
7. Keith, W. D. Technical and economic feasibility of a water source heat pump in the Canadian food industry. M.Sc. thesis, University of Guelph, Guelph, Ontario, 1984.

Part VII
Irradiation Processing of Food

54

LOW DOSE IRRADIATION OF FOODS—
PROSPECTS AND PROBLEMS*

J. H. MOY

*Department of Food Science and Human Nutrition, University of Hawaii at
Manoa, Honolulu, Hawaii 96822, U.S.A.*

ABSTRACT

*Radiation preservation of food is an effective, emerging technology that
should have worldwide applications in the coming years either by itself
or as part of a combined treatment. For example, ionizing radiation can
substitute for fumigation as an efficacious quarantine treatment method
because of the controversy and recent ban of ethylene dibromide (EDB)
and other fumigants. Results of more than three decades of research on
food irradiation around the world have indicated several technically,
and quite possibly economically, feasible applications: radiation deinfestation and shelf-life extension of fruits and vegetables; pasteurization
of seafoods, poultry and meats combined with refrigeration; and control
of parasites in pork products.*

*The prospect of low dose (less than 10 kGy) irradiation of selected
foods is good because the problems previously existing as barriers to
early commercialization of the radiation process are beginning to be
resolved. In a number of countries, government regulations either exist
or are being proposed to allow commercial irradiation of selected foods
at 1·0–10 kGy. As more chemicals are banned and more studies
demonstrating economic feasibility become available, industry interest
in irradiation will increase. Few trade agreements exist for irradiated
foods in international trade, but they could be established bilaterally.
Results of consumer acceptance surveys vary, but an increasing desire
to use nonchemical means to treat foods plus the launching of a*

* Journal Series No. 2972 of the Hawaii Institute of Tropical Agriculture and Human
Resources, University of Hawaii at Manoa, Honolulu, Hawaii 96822, U.S.A.

consumer education program on irradiated foods will help to adapt radiation technology for industrial food processing.

INTRODUCTION

Never before in the history of food preservation have so much effort and money been expended in the research and development of a food preservation method as radiation processing of foods.[11] After more than three decades of study, the effectiveness and feasibility of using ionizing radiation to preserve foods for six different purposes have been adequately proved. Yet, commercial applications of this preservation technique have been rather limited when compared to the more traditional methods of preservation such as drying, low temperature preservation, thermal processing, and chemical and biochemical preservation.

Recent events and controversies over chemicals and pesticides in our foods suggest that radiation preservation of foods may emerge as an effective, alternative technology that should have worldwide applications in the coming years either by itself or as part of a combined process. Results of research in food irradiation around the world have indicated that irradiation of certain foods at low dose, defined as 10 kGy (kilogray) and below, may be the most technically and economically feasible application. This would include radiation deinfestation and shelf-life extension of fruits and vegetables, radiation pasteurization of seafoods and meats followed by refrigeration, and radiation control of parasites in pork and pork products.

In spite of these prospective uses, several problems still exist as barriers to early commercialization of the radiation process: (a) government regulations; (b) industry interest including economic feasibility; (c) international trade agreements; and (d) consumer acceptance of irradiated foods. The objectives of this paper are to summarize those promising applications of radiation processing, to indicate the current status of some of the problems, and to suggest the prospects of overcoming them.

METHODOLOGY

Gamma-radiation for Deinfestation

Almost all of the earlier work on radiation deinfestation was carried out on tropical fruits such as papaya and mango.[6,7] The purpose of deinfestation was to meet quarantine requirements by using a minimum absorbed dose on infested fruits to prevent the emergence of three species of adult fruit flies (Mediterranean, Oriental and melon flies) prevalent in the Hawaiian islands and other tropical and subtropical areas so that these insects could not reproduce and invade fruits in noninfested areas such as California. For example, during 1975–6 and 1980–1, there were two medfly outbreaks in central and South California which caused great concern to the $14 billion a year fruit industry there.

The radiation source used for deinfestation study has been mainly Cobalt-60, a gamma source. The process is simple. Fruit samples such as papayas, oranges, peaches, nectarines and plums are irradiated either in a batch-type irradiator or in a conveyorized pilot-scale irradiator with cartons being transported to and from the source. Concurrent with determining the dose requirement for deinfestation, tolerance dose is also studied. Tolerance dose for a fresh commodity is defined as the highest dose at which there are no external and internal visible and/or measurable product injury symptoms, and the radiation treatment imparts no adverse effects to the biochemistry and sensory qualities of the edible pulp.

For fruit fly deinfestation, the radiation doses applied to a fruit may correspond to three concepts on which scientists have not fully agreed: (a) sufficiently high dose to result in nonhatchability of the eggs, usually 0·40–0·60 kGy; (b) moderate dose to cause the insect not to develop normally into the adult stage, resulting in negligible pest risk, also known as probit 9 security (99·9968% nonemergence), usually 0·25–0·35 kGy; and (c) low dose to affect the genes of the insects to the point of causing them to lose the ability to produce viable offsprings, usually 0·05–0·10 kGy.

In addition to laboratory studies, shipping studies are also being conducted to demonstrate that the various quality attributes of the irradiated fruit will be retained when shipped to distant markets either by sea, rail or air.[10]

Shelf-life Extension

Extending the postharvest shelf-life of various commodities by irradiation takes two forms: (a) sprout inhibition of tubers and bulbs such as potatoes and onions; and (b) delayed ripening of fresh fruits such as papayas. Again, the shelf-life extension doses must be below the tolerance dose, and they are often above the deinfestation dose.

Experimental methods of determining shelf-life extension of fruits by gamma-radiation have been described.[1,2,9,15] As an addition to the radiation process, a hot water immersion treatment (49 °C, 20 min) is applied to minimize fungal decay of the fruit.

The mechanism of shelf-life extension by irradiation is by delaying the ripening or the senescence of the fruit. Some of the fruits that have been studied by various researchers[3] include pears, peaches, nectarines, strawberries, apples, apricots, pineapples, bananas, papayas, mangoes, oranges and tomatoes. The doses applied varied from 0·10 to 5 kGy.

For sprout inhibition of potatoes and onions, doses less than 0·20 kGy are applied. The effectiveness of extending the shelf-life of these tubers and bulbs up to six months by irradiation is influenced by the timing of irradiation regarding (whether the tubers are dormant), radiation dose, dose rate, variety, and pre- and post-irradiation storage conditions.

Pasteurization

Radiation pasteurization of seafoods, poultry, and meats can reduce the microbial population on these products thus minimizing food poisoning and spoilage incidence. For reasons of product quality and microbiological safety, the radiation process must be combined with refrigeration. The doses applied are usually 1·0 to 2·0 kGy with refrigeration at 0–5 °C.

The advantages of this combined process are: stabilization of quality, expansion of market, stabilization of supply and demand, and greater use of the product. The disadvantages include: possible relaxation and abuse in handling and some uncertainty in marketing because of the term 'irradiated'.

Control of Parasites

Trichinella spiralis, a parasite in pork and pork products has been studied as a target of radiation deinfestation with an applied dose of 0·15–0·30 kGy.[16]

EXPERIMENTAL FINDINGS

Table I gives examples of gamma-radiation of various foods at low doses for different purposes and effects. On fresh fruits, the desirable

TABLE I
Gamma-radiation of various foods at low doses

Purpose/Effect	Dose, kGy	Food
Insect deinfestation	0·15–0·35	Papayas, Mangoes, Oranges, Peaches, Nectarines, Apples
Sprout inhibition	0·02–0·15	Potatoes, Onions, Carrots
Delayed ripening	0·12–0·75	Bananas, Papayas, Mangoes
Delayed senescence	0·75–3·0	Papayas, Apricots, Sweet Cherries
Pasteurization	1·0–2·0	Seafoods, Poultry, Beef
Parasite control	0·15–0·30	Pork

effect is to control insect infestation such as tropical fruit flies on papayas, oranges and peaches, mango seed weevils in the mangoes, and codling moths in apples and cherries. The applied dose of 0·15–0·35 kGy retains the quality of the fruit completely.[12]

For shelf-life extension, applying doses of 0·02–0·15 kGy will inhibit sprouting of potatoes and onions for up to 6 months, while doses of 0·12–0·75 kGy will delay the ripening of several tropical fruits. While results of studies have also shown some delay in senescence in papayas, apricots and sweet cherries at doses varying from 0·75 to 2·0 or 3·0 kGy, it is believed that the higher doses of 2·0–3·0 kGy would exceed the tolerance dose of apricots and sweet cherries which cancels the benefits. Thus, among all 27 fruits that have been studied worldwide, papaya appears to be the fruit most tolerant and receptive to gamma-radiation up to 1 kGy and would benefit from the treatment for fruit fly deinfestation (0·26 kGy) and delayed ripening and senescence (0·75 kGy).

For pasteurization, applying doses of 1·0–2·0 kGy will extend the marketable life of raw unshelled shrimps and cooked lobster meat and king crabs by 1–2 weeks, and that of beef, veal, pork, lamb and chickens by 2–3 weeks.[14,17]

For controlling *Trichinella* in pork, results suggest that a dose of 0·15–0·30 kGy might be adequate. However, since one usually has to handle carcasses of pork, the variation of absorbed dose and the max/min dose rate of a commercial irradiator may raise the required dose to the range of 3–5 kGy.

CURRENT STATUS AND NEAR-TERM PROSPECTS

Government Regulations

Worldwide situation. In October, 1980, the Joint Expert Committee on Food Irradiation (JECFI) of the Food and Agriculture Organization/International Atomic Energy Agency/World Health Organization (FAO/IAEA/WHO) reviewed all available toxicological and radiation chemistry data in relation to the wholesomeness of irradiated foods and declared that the 'irradiation of any food commodity up to an overall average dose of 10 kGy (1 Mrad) presents no toxicological hazard and no nutritional or microbiological problems'. It urged that 'the technological and economic feasibility of food irradiation on an industrial scale be established'.[4]

As of November, 1984, 28 countries have had clearances on 42 irradiated food items or food groups. The Netherlands has cleared 21 foods. USSR has cleared 9 products and as early as 1958 irradiation was permitted on potatoes and 1959 on grains. South Africa has also[9] cleared items including mango, strawberry, papaya and dried banana since 1977–8. Japan has been irradiating 150 000 metric tons of potatoes per season since 1973.[8]

Regulations in the USA. Food irradiation in the United States has been classified as a food additive under the 1958 Food Additive Amendment of the Federal Food, Drug and Cosmetic Act. For every irradiated food to be marketed commercially, its safety, technical efficacy and benefit/cost to the consumer must be demonstrated through a series of extensive testing. The test data must support a petition to the U.S. Food and Drug Administration (FDA) which has the authority to clear or disapprove the request.

Two clearances were granted by the FDA in 1962–3, one on irradiated potato for shelf-life extension through sprout inhibition and another on irradiated wheat and wheat products for insect control. Research on irradiated food continued since that time, but no additional petition was cleared by FDA.

Having established in the latter half of 1979 its task force to 'review, evaluate and recommend criteria for safety evaluation of irradiated food', FDA concluded in November 1980 that 'food irradiated to doses up to 1 kGy (100 krad) is wholesome and safe for human consumption and needs no safety tests to market the irradiated food'.[5]

On February 14, 1984, the Food and Drug Administration published in the *Federal Register* a notice of proposed rulemaking for using ionizing radiation for treating food. The proposal was designed to insure that: (a) irradiated foods are safe; (b) foods are irradiated only at the dose reasonably required and under conditions that would accomplish the intended technical effect; and (c) current good manufacturing practice will be followed.

The proposed regulations would permit food to be irradiated: (a) to inhibit the growth and maturation of fresh fruits and vegetables; (b) to deinfest food of insects at doses below 1·0 kGy (100 krad); (c) to deinfect spices of microbes at levels up to 30 kGy (3 Mrad). The unique nature of individual spices and their relatively low consumption leads FDA to conclude that this higher dose poses no safety risk.

After reviewing the scientific evidence, FDA believes that the sources of radiation that would be allowed under this proposal will not produce radioactivity in any food, and thus cannot expose the consumer to radiation. FDA also believes that the chemical differences between irradiated foods processed at the above doses and nonirradiated foods are too small to affect the safety of the foods. Finally, the Agency believes that foods irradiated up to 1 kGy will have the same nutritional values as similar foods that have not been irradiated.

Industry Interest
Interest in using the radiation process for whatever purpose and application must be shown by the food industry because it is the beneficiary of all the research. There may be two scenarios to this factor, however. Food industries in the developed countries have not been too quick to participate in and consider this technology because there are other competitive, established food preservation technologies available such as canning and freezing. They are also aware of the sizable capital investment a food irradiator will require. Food industries in the developing countries, on the other hand, might see the larger benefits of food irradiation because the need to minimize food spoilage is more urgent and other forms of processing and energy to preserve foods are not as readily available. However, economic factors still play a role because a commercial irradiator of any size still requires a major investment.

Banning of some of the chemicals on foods and the economic feasibility of the radiation process are two factors the food industry is observing closely to help decide whether or not to use the process. The papaya industry in recent months was faced with the problem of the banning of ethylene dibromide (EDB) as a fumigant. They opted for the double dip hot water treatment which resulted in the fruit not being able to ripen normally. When they recognized that the cost of an irradiator facility would be of the order of US $0·055 per kg with the option to buy shares into the facility, some of them began to show interest because the cost of irradiation seems very reasonable.

A recent economic feasibility study on irradiation of Mexican fruits sponsored by IAEA and conducted at the National Institute of Nuclear Research, Salazar, Mexico[13] shows that with a projected throughput of 50 000 and 100 000 metric tons of mangoes irradiated per year, and 100 000 and 150 000 metric tons of oranges and tangerines irradiated per year, the irradiation costs will be US $0·026–0·041 per kg of mangoes, and US $0·022–0·026 per kg of citrus fruits, respectively, at an assumed absorbed dose of 0·30 kGy for controlling the emergence of Mexican fruit flies. The cost is realistic and is certainly very competitive with chemical fumigation ($0·050 per kg papaya in Hawaii). Still lower cost can be realized if the cost of the irradiator facility is less than that indicated in the study (ca. US $2·1–3·3 million per irradiator plant).

Trade Agreements
If food irradiation is to be used worldwide, there must be agreements between countries on the import and export of irradiated foods, much like for other established, well known processed foods. At present, every country studying the feasibility and potential of food irradiation and contemplating its commercialization seems to be mainly concerned with using irradiation to help solve some of the domestic food spoilage or contamination problems. Regulations being developed by national health and agriculture authorities are aiming at applications to foods which will be transported between states or provinces.

Examples of potential bilateral or international marketing of irradiated foods are easy to find. For example, Canada and the United States may find it desirable to irradiate grains for deinfestation purpose before shipping to importing countries. Each of the recipient countries must then be informed and be willing to accept irradiated grains for their quality and safety. Many tropical fruits grown in Mexico, the Caribbean, South America, or Southeast Asia could undergo radiation deinfestation before being exported to the United States or other noninfested markets. The US must then be willing to accept imported fruits irradiated in each of the fruit-growing countries.

At present, international trade agreements on irradiated foods do not exist, but they do not seem too difficult to develop especially in the interest of promoting bilateral trade and having insect- and contaminant-free foods. Mutual recognition of the safety and quality of irradiated foods, willingness in accepting radiation treatments as a process, interest in improving bilateral trade, and assistance by international organizations are needed to develop international agreements to promote trade of irradiated foods.

Consumer Acceptance

In recent years, because of negative publicity about nuclear reactors and nuclear weapons, the idea of using ionizing radiation to preserve food invokes suspicion about the safety of irradiated foods. It is unfortunate that during the past several decades when food irradiation research was conducted around the world, there had been very few programs to inform the consumers of the safety and quality of irradiated foods. From the standpoint of the food industry, the uncertainty of the market share of irradiated foods is probably one of the most important factors in commercial application of food irradiation. Fortunately, many scientific, medical, government and trade organizations have recognized the safety and benefits of food irradiation, and are endorsing it. In the United States, these include the Institute of Food Technologists, the American Medical Association, the Department of Agriculture of the State of Washington, the Washington State Apple Commission, the National Pork Council, and the American Spice Association.

By recognizing an increasing desire to use nonchemical means to treat foods and by launching a consumer education program on irradiated foods, the industry is steering toward the selective adaptation of radiation technology, and expects to complement, not necessarily compete with, the variety of foods offered to the consumers.

OUTLOOK AND CONCLUSION

Radiation preservation and processing of food at low dose is a technically and economically feasible technology whose time has come. Based on a large volume of research data and with the selection of a proper source, foods irradiated for various purposes do not become radioactive. The radiolytic products formed in very minute amounts with low dose irradiation are either similar to some of the natural food components or their concentrations are too low to become any health hazard. The sensory and nutrient qualities of low dose irradiated foods are preserved. Thus, irradiated foods are wholesome and safe for human consumption.

The most technically and economically feasible applications are for deinfestation of insects on fruits and vegetables as a quarantine treatment, shelf-life extension of fruits through delayed ripening, of tubers through sprout inhibition, and of seafoods and meat products through controlling the microbial population in combination with refrigeration, and control of *Trichinella* parasites on pork.

The next step in acceptance of the irradiation technology would be to conduct an effective consumer education program on the safety and benefits of irradiated foods, a joint effort by the food industry, government agencies and researchers. Concurrently, certain segments of the food industry should seriously consider and prepare for the processing and marketing of irradiated foods.

Commercializing food irradiation has worldwide implications. Economic experts view it as a means of increasing the world's food supply. It could also mean expanding exports of many agricultural products. The process could help save some of the estimated 25–30% of the world's food supply which is lost each year because of pests and spoilage.

REFERENCES

1. Akamine, E. K. and Goo, T. Respiration, ethylene production, and shelf life extension in irradiated papaya fruit after storage under simulated shipping conditions. Haw. Agric. Exp. Stn. Tech. Bull., Vol. 93, p. 1, 1977.
2. Akamine, E. K. and Goo, T. Effects of gamma irradiation on shelf life extension of fresh papayas (*Carica papaya* L. var. Solo), Haw. Agri. Exp. Stn. Res. Bull., Vol. 1 165, p. 1, 1977.
3. Akamine, E. K. and Moy, J. H. Delay in postharvest ripening and senescence of fruits. In *Preservation of Food by Ionizing Radiation*, Vol. III (E. S. Josephson and M. Peterson Eds). CRC Press, Boca Raton, FL, p. 129, 1983.
4. Anon. Wholesomeness of irradiated food. A joint FAO/IAEA/WHO Expert Committee Report on the wholesomeness of irradiated food. Rpt. Series No. 659. Geneva, 1981.
5. Anon. Policy for irradiation: Advance notices of preparing procedures for the regulation of irradiated foods for human consumption. *Fed. Register* **46**(59): 18922, 1981.
6. Balock, J. W., Burditt, A. K. Jr. and Christenson, L. D. Effects of gamma-radiation on various stages of three fruit fly species. *J. Econ. Entomol.* **56**(1): 42, 1963.

7. Balock, J. W., Burditt, A. K. Jr., Seo, S. T. and Akamine, E. K. Gamma radiation as a quarantine treatment for Hawaiian fruit flies. *J. Econ. Entomol.* **59**(1): 202, 1966.

8. Loaharanu, P. Radiation disinfestation—a viable technology for developing countries. *Proc. Int. Conf. on Rad. Disinfestation of Food & Agri. Prod.*, Nov. 1983, Honolulu, 1985 (in press).

9. Massey, L. M. Jr. Food irradiation. U.S. Dept. Agri. Sci. Rev., Vol. 5, p. 29, 1967.

10. Moy, J. H. Dosimetry, tolerance and shelf life extension related to disinfestation of fruit and vegetable by gamma irradiation. Final Summary Rpt. to USAEC, UH-235P 5-X, 1964-71. Radioisot. Rad. Appl. TID-4500, 41 pp., 1972.

11. Moy, J. H. Problems and prospects of radiation disinfestation and shelf-life extension of tropical fruits and vegetables. *Proc. Int. Panel on Aspects of the Introduction of Food Irradiation in Developing Countries.* IAEA STI/PUB/362, 13, 1973.

12. Moy, J. H., Kaneshiro, K. Y., Ohta, A. T. and Nagai, N. Radiation disinfestation of California stone fruits infested by Medfly—effectiveness and fruit quality. *J. Food Sci.* **48**(3): 928, 1983.

13. Moy, J. H., Reye L. J., Ramirez G. T. and Bustos R. E. Economic feasibility studies: Irradiation of Mexican fruits. IAEA Proj. Rpt. MEX/5/011–01, 42 pp., 1984.

14. Nickerson, J. T. R., Licciardello, J. J. and Ronsivalli, L. J. Radurization and radicidation: fish and shellfish. In *Preservation of Food by Ionizing Radiation,* Vol. III (E. S. Josephson, and M. S. Peterson Eds). CRC Press, Boca Raton, FL, p. 18, 1983.

15. Pablo, I. S., Akamine, E. K. and Chachin, K. Irradiation. In *Postharvest Physiology, Handling and Utilization of Tropical and Subtropical Fruits and Vegetables* (E. G. Pantastico Ed.), Chap. 11, AVI Pub. Co., Westport, Conn., 1975.

16. Switzer, R. K. and Sivinski, J. S. Low-dose irradiation: A promising option for Trichina-safe pork certification. *Proc. Int. Conf. on Rad. Disinfestation of Food & Agri. Prod.,* Nov. 1983, Honolulu, 1985 (in press).

17. Urbain, W. M. Radurization and radicidation: meat and poultry. In *Preservation of Food by Ionizing Radiation,* Vol. III (E. S. Josephson and M. S. Peterson Eds). CRC Press, Boca Raton, FL, p. 2, 1983.

55

SOME DESIGN TRADE-OFFS IN A FIRST GENERATION PRODUCTION FOOD IRRADIATOR

E. T. O'SULLIVAN and A. L. GUNBY

International Nutronics, Inc., 1000 Elwell Court, Suite 232, Palo Alto, California 94303, U.S.A.

ABSTRACT

Work at the University of Hawaii established that papayas are an excellent candidate fruit for the use of low-dose gamma radiation treatment. The announcement by the US Environmental Protection Agency in 1983 that ethylene dibromide could no longer be used for post-harvest treatment of papaya, effective in September, 1984, seemed to provide incentive for the use of gamma radiation technology of food crops. Those companies which provide radiation facilities, such as International Nutronics, Inc., began the process of evaluating basic design concepts and reviewing the criteria with the growers, packers, brokers and marketing specialists involved.

This paper follows the path of one such design and examines the trade-off questions to be considered. It is presented as a case study, to be of value in the dialogue which must precede any decision of 'what to build' and 'how to operate a gamma treatment facility'.

INTRODUCTION

The Papaya Administrative Committee (PAC) of Hawaii did not welcome the prospect of gamma irradiation treatment with open arms. There were concerns about public acceptance of treated papaya in the market, as well as the reluctance toward being a pioneer. The industry was also concerned about giving up some of the competitive individuality by having to rely on a single independent processor, but the PAC did begin by commissioning an independent consultant to do a feasibility study. This study was of value, not just because it did show that low-dose gamma processing was feasible, but because it set up an agreed upon hypothetical plant with established production volumes and a plan for growth.

A target processing capacity of 90 million lbs/y (nearly 41 000 metric tons/y) was established. Papaya has the advantage of being a year-round crop in Hawaii with a small peak in volume in the spring and another peak in late fall. To allow for the peak throughput periods and to coincide with operations in the fields and packing houses, a 3 shift–5 days/week operation was selected. This calculates to 180 tons/day or 6818 kg/h (15 000 lb/h). This volume is certainly significant from an economic standpoint, yet for gamma irradiation it would be a small plant when compared to the multi-megacurie medical products processing plants operating throughout the world.

METHODOLOGY

The question of plant location was addressed first. The two papaya production areas in the State of Hawaii are on the islands at the opposite ends of the island chain. The island of Hawaii, the Big Island, at the eastern end of the chain, produced about 80% of the papaya and had a sufficient volume to support a gamma processing plant. The island of Kauai, at the western end, with only 20% of the crop could not support an economical plant, but had the capability of rapidly expanding production if the market would support it.

The question of where to locate the gamma processing step is not an isolated one but is generic to situations where independent growers and packing plants exist, most of which do not have sufficient volume to justify a gamma facility.

A possible solution came to light by examining the field-to-market sequence for papaya. At that time approximately 80% of the crop was shipped to the mainland US by air on wide body aircraft, out of Honolulu. When the papaya were received at Honolulu the cartons were restacked into the LD-3 cargo containers. Since so much hand labor was involved at Honolulu, it seemed like a good place to insert the gamma processing step. This was particularly important because the irradiator designer could now control the target size and process conditions.

Two of the principal areas of design trade-off had to be examined, namely, (1) target depth (1 row or 2) versus conveyor cost, and (2) target overlap versus source overlay.

To do this we had to keep in mind the other factors which could impact on the decisions. It was found helpful to begin with the product and work toward the process. The sequence was as follows:

(1) Establish allowable max:min ratio, where
   (a) min is the absorbed dose required to achieve the intended technical effect;
   (b) the max allowable is normally set by the onset, or some limiting value, of a phytotoxic effect.
(2) The allowable max:min ratio established the combination of target depth and distance from the source.
(3) The depth–distance selection combined with the choice of source or target overlap determined cobalt efficiency.
(4) The cobalt efficiency (gamma utilization efficiency) established the number of curies required for a given throughput and thus impacts on unit cost.

First, the max:min ratio was established as the minimum dose—that is the dose at the minimum point in the target—required to achieve the intended technical effect. Moy[1] established that 26 krad (0·26 kGy) is required to achieve the quarantine release treatment to meet the US Dept. of Agriculture Probit 9 requirement. For papaya, which is a very radiation tolerant fruit, the maximum (before unacceptable damage occurs) is nearly 10 times this amount. For other fruits, such as citrus, preliminary studies indicate the phytotoxicity may impose a max:min ratio of 2·0. In our current case the max allowable may be determined not by the fruit but by an arbitrary Regulatory Maximum of 100 krad or 1 kGy. For 'quarantine release only' this is not a problem, but according to Moy[1], an extension of shelf-life can be obtained at a minimum dose of 75 krad (0·75 kGy). With a 100 krad max, we would have a max:min ratio of 1·33. Should the plant design include this tight max:min as a design objective? Before this question can be answered attention must be paid to the target depth and source–target distance problem.

Figure 1 shows the effect on surface:center ratio of 1 large target versus 2 smaller targets. The large target (lower boxes), representing a 1·2 m (48″) pallet at 0·3 m (12″) from the source has a surface:center ratio of 2·45. The curve represents the fall-off in dose with increased distance through the target. The box to the right is the cumulative

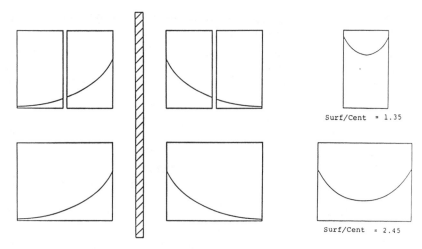

Surf/Cent = 1.35

Surf/Cent = 2.45

Fig. 1. Target depth effect on surface: center ratio.

effect of one pass for each of the opposite faces, i.e. a two pass system. Figure 1 illustrates only the depth effect, not the vertical distribution. The upper set shows targets of approximately $\frac{1}{2}$ the thickness which now make 4 passes of the source. This technique is routine for low-density medical products irradiators. The shape of the curve, the logarithmic fall-off, is basic to the geometry of the source–target relationship, but the magnitude is affected by density. This curve represents measured values for citrus with density of $0.4\,\mathrm{g/cm^3}$. Medical products would have a much smaller density effect. However, since the higher density food items are more efficient gamma absorbers than medical products the question is raised—is it worth the added cost of an outer loop to pick up this marginal effect? The four pass target gives us a surface:center ratio of 1·35—very close to our 1·3 objective. Actually, papaya with a lower average bulk density than citrus will meet 1·33 comfortably. For citrus we would simply increase the spacing if we have a fixed target thickness.

The density–spacing relationship can be illustrated with some actual cases. It is known that the process efficiency will be based on the minimum absorbed dose within the target and that the max:min ratio should approach 1·0 within the constraints of other parameters (cost, throughput, etc.) We have also seen that increasing target thickness for a given density increases the max:min ratio. Increasing target density for a given thickness also increases the max:min ratio.

Increasing source to target distance for a given thickness and/or density will act in the opposite manner, that is, reduce (or improve) the max:min ratio. Tables I and II give specific examples of the magnitude of this effect. Since we are presenting only the depth (thickness) dimension we use surface:center ratio (max:min generally denotes those quantities within a three-dimensional target).

The question of the value of the outer passes can now be resolved. Table III gives the results of INI's HA-3A computer code. The throughput increase of 20% was sufficient to justify the added conveyor cost. For more densely-packed foods or thicker targets, however, the outer pass becomes less desirable. For this package width (tote depth of target) the design sacrificed the future use of the 1·33 max:min which could be recovered by thinner target tote loading when required.

The final problem to be resolved concerns the target overlap versus source overlap.

To get maximum utilization of the gamma photons the source should be surrounded with target, so the target overlaps the source. However the end effects of the source profile give a greatly reduced

TABLE I

(a) Effect of package thickness at constant density (for density of $0·3 \, g/cm^3$) on the surface:center ratio

Thickness		Surface:center ratio[a]
in	cm	
20	50·8	1·41
25	63·5	1·61
30	76·2	1·83
35	88·9	2·09

[a] Build-up included.

(b) Effect of variable density at constant thickness on the surface:center ratio

Density (g/cm^3)	surface:center ratio[a]
0·2	1·39
0·3	1·61
0·5	2·26
0·7	3·15

[a] Build-up included.
Source–target gap = 30·5 cm (12″).

TABLE II
Effect of spacing on surface : center dose
ratio for 55 cm (22″) thick target

Source–target gap		Surface : center ratio
in	cm	
4	10	1·465
7	18	1·365
10	25	1·277
13	33	1·222
19	48	1·153
25	64	1·112

Density—0·3 gm/cc
Target—rectangular array–40 position (2
tier × 4 rows/tier × 5 pos/row).

dose at the top and bottom of the target stack. Therefore another pass is needed with the positions reversed. In this manner, the absorbed dose in the target can be made quite uniform vertically. This interchange can be accomplished in a number of ways, but generally involves exiting the chamber for re-positioning and then re-entering. The technique must be extremely reliable so that a given package cannot be only partly processed. This applies to medical products for sterilization as well as food products for quarantine treatment.

If the package is sufficiently tall or heavy so that multiple vertical stacking is not practical, it might be advantageous to use the source overlap. Here the source flux pattern is shaped by placing more source

TABLE III
Calculated papaya irradiator results

	Inner pass	Inner plus outer pass	% improvement
Throughput (tons/day)	172	207·1	20·4
Efficiency (%)	30·5	36·7	20·4
Surf : center ratio	1·687	1·609	4·8

Conditions:
Density = 0·3 g/cm^3.
Tote dimensions = 73·7 cm × 63·5 cm × 102·9 cm.
Source target gap = 30·5 cm.
Source : 100 kCi, uniform loading
Target–overlap—2 tier × 6 pos/row.

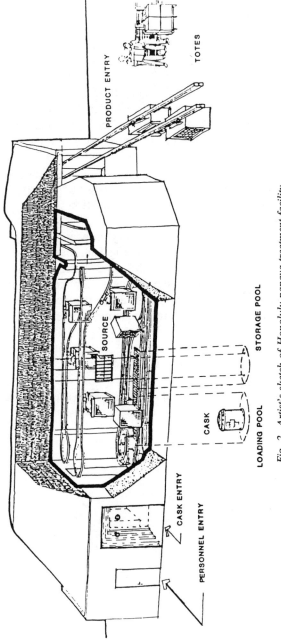

Fig. 2. Artist's sketch of Honolulu papaya treatment facility.

at the ends and actually overlapping the target. Good vertical flux distribution can still be obtained but the source at the ends is not being used very efficiently. When all these considerations were examined simultaneously, a reference design for Honolulu was obtained as shown in the artist's concept (Fig. 2).

Here the product totes carry twenty four 10-lb cartons or 109 kg (240 lb) in a $0.36 m^3$ ($12.8 ft^3$) cage. They make two passes by the source, proceeding through a reversing switch to maintain face balance and on to two more passes still on the upper level. They transfer to the lower level at a transfer station and then reverse their patch on the bottom loop, a total of 8 passes. Once the system is filled, totes come off at the rate of one a minute. This is a target overlap design, a 1.3 max:min ratio over 36% cobalt utilization efficiency, with a loading slightly more than 100 kCi.

At the present time, the papaya industry on Kauai is in an economic depression. If only the industry on the Big Island would be served by an irradiation plant, this would alter the basic assumptions and probably favor a different design concept. By keeping the design assumptions clearly in view and delineating the resultant trade-offs, the task of evaluating major changes becomes clearer.

REFERENCES

1. Moy, James H. Low dose irradiation of foods—prospects and problems, this volume, pp. 623–33.

INDEX

Note: The volume number is indicated by the figure in parentheses following the entry.